Praise for *Nonprofit Management 101*

"In these troubled times, the work of nonprofits is more important than ever. But sorting through all the available support resources can be daunting. This book does an impressive job of highlighting only the most valuable lessons, tactics, and go-to resources, and is sure to benefit anyone looking to succeed in the nonprofit world."

—Arianna Huffington, Cofounder and Editor in Chief,
The Huffington Post (now owned by AOL)

"To all those who want to change their world, you now have a how-to operator's manual for the nonprofit sector. This invaluable tool is sure to help you advance your cause and develop your organization—it's a must-read."

—Jody Williams, Nobel Peace Prize Laureate (1997);
Chair, Nobel Women's Initiative

"*Nonprofit Management 101* is a big deal for nonprofit professionals who want to get the job done. If you're new to the nonprofit world, or doing something new, this will really help out."

—Craig Newmark, Customer Service
Representative and Founder, craigslist.org

"If you do one thing to support someone who dreams of building a better world, buy them this book."

—Van Jones, Cofounder of Green For All, Color of Change,
and Ella Baker Center for Human Rights

Nonprofit Management 101

Nonprofit Management 101

A Complete and Practical Guide for Leaders and Professionals

Essential Resources, Tools, and Hard-Earned
Wisdom from Fifty Leading Experts

Edited by

DARIAN RODRIGUEZ HEYMAN

JOSSEY-BASS
A Wiley Imprint
www.josseybass.com

Published by Jossey-Bass
A Wiley Imprint
989 Market Street, San Francisco, CA 94103-1741—www.josseybass.com

Readers should be aware that Internet Web sites offered as citations and/or sources for further information may have changed or disappeared between the time this was written and when it is read.

Jossey-Bass books and products are available through most bookstores. To contact Jossey-Bass directly call our Customer Care Department within the U.S. at 800-956-7739, outside the U.S. at 317-572-3986, or fax 317-572-4002.

Jossey-Bass also publishes its books in a variety of electronic formats. Some content that appears in print may not be available in electronic books.

Library of Congress Cataloging-in-Publication Data

Nonprofit management 101 : a complete and practical guide for leaders and professionals / edited by Darian Rodriguez Heyman. – 1st ed.
     p. cm.
   Includes bibliographical references and indexes.
   ISBN 978-0-470-28596-1 (pbk); 978-1-118-01792-0 (ebk); ISBN 978-1-118-01793-7 (ebk); ISBN 978-1-118-01794-4 (ebk)
   1. Nonprofit organizations. 2. Leadership. I. Heyman, Darian Rodriguez, 1974- II. Title: Nonprofit management one hundred one. III. Title: Nonprofit management one hundred and one.
   HD62.6.N657 2011
   658'.048–dc22

                                                   2010053638

Printed in the United States of America
FIRST EDITION
Printing   10   9   8   7   6   5   4

CONTENTS

Foreword   xv
Ami Dar, Idealist.org/Action Without Borders

About the Book   xix
Darian Rodriguez Heyman

Acknowledgments   xxvii
Darian Rodriguez Heyman

PART ONE

The Big Picture—What the Field Is All About and Where You Fit In   1
Darian Rodriguez Heyman

Chapter 1   **The Role of Nonprofits in American Life**   5
             Robert Glavin, MNA, Robert Glavin, Inc. and
             University of San Francisco

Chapter 2   **Welcome to the Movement**   21
             Paul Hawken, Author

Chapter 3   **On Leadership in the Nonprofit Sector**   29
             Emmett D. Carson, PhD, Silicon Valley
             Community Foundation

Chapter 4   **Taking Charge of Your Nonprofit Sector Career**   41
             Kim Hendler, iMentor, and Shelly Cryer, Consultant

PART TWO

Managing Organizations and People 57

Darian Rodriguez Heyman

Chapter 5 **Strategy and Planning: Turning a Dream into Reality** 63
Jeanne Bell, MNA, CompassPoint Nonprofit Services

Chapter 6 **Strategic Restructuring: Collaboration, Alliances, and Mergers** 77
David La Piana and Bob Harington, La Piana Consulting

Chapter 7 **Risk Management and Insurance** 93
Pamela Davis, Nonprofits Insurance Alliance Group

Chapter 8 **Making Human Resources Work for You: Best Practices in
Nonprofit Human Capital Management** 107
James Weinberg and Cassie Scarano,
Commongood Careers

Chapter 9 **The Importance of Diversity** 127
Michael Watson, Girl Scouts of the USA

Chapter 10 **Bridging the Generation Gap** 149
Peter Brinckerhoff, Corporate Alternatives, Inc.,
and Vincent Hyman, Vincent Hyman Editorial Services

PART THREE

Nonprofit Law and Finance 161

Darian Rodriguez Heyman

Chapter 11 **Nonprofit Law** 165
Bruce Hopkins and Virginia Gross, Polsinelli Shughart

Chapter 12 **Nonprofit Advocacy and Lobbying** 181
Nayantara Mehta, Alliance for Justice, Nancy Chen,
Neighborhood Legal Services of Los Angeles, and Marcia
Avner and Jeannie Fox, Minnesota Council of Nonprofits

Chapter 13 **Nonprofit Financial Management** 197
David Greco, Nonprofit Finance Fund

PART FOUR

Nonprofit Technology and IT   217

Darian Rodriguez Heyman

Chapter 14 **The Technology Foundation: Hardware and Software**   221
Holly Ross, NTEN: The Nonprofit Technology Network

Chapter 15 **A Cooperative Approach to Web Design**   239
Elliot Harmon, TechSoup Global

Chapter 16 **Online Community Building: How to Wire a Network
to Support Your Nonprofit's Mission**   257
Jon Warnow and Joe Solomon, 350.org

Chapter 17 **Constituent Relationship Management**   273
Steve Wright, Grameen Foundation

PART FIVE

Fundraising   287

Darian Rodriguez Heyman

Chapter 18 **Fundraising: Knowing When to Do What**   291
Andrea McManus, CFRE, The Development Group
and The Association of Fundraising Professionals

Chapter 19 **Individual Donor and Major Gift Strategies: The
83% Solution to Fundraising**   309
Kay Sprinkel Grace, CFRE, Transforming Philanthropy, LLC

Chapter 20 **How to Seek a Grant**   325
Tori O'Neal-McElrath, Center for Community Change

Chapter 21 **Online Fundraising**   341
Katya Andresen and Rebecca Ruby Higman, Network for
Good

Chapter 22 **Online Peer-to-Peer Fundraising**   357
Nicci Noble, CFRE, Noble Services, and Sean Sullivan,
Center for Environmental Health

Chapter 23 **Cause-Related Marketing**   373
            Jay Aldous, Social Capital Partnerships

Chapter 24 **Social Enterprise 101: An Overview of the Basic Principles**   389
            Rick Aubry, PhD, New Foundry Ventures and
            Stanford University Graduate School of Business

PART SIX

Marketing and Communications   405
            Darian Rodriguez Heyman

Chapter 25 **Nonprofit Marketing**   409
            Jennie Winton and Zach Hochstadt, Mission Minded

Chapter 26 **Using Web 2.0 Tools to Tell Your Organization's Story:**
            Blogs, Flickr, and YouTube   429
            Beth Kanter, Zoetica

Chapter 27 **Crafting an Effective Newsletter Strategy**   445
            Kivi Leroux Miller, NonprofitMarketingGuide.com

Chapter 28 **Painless and Effective Event Planning:**
            Let's Get This Party Started!   459
            Marika Holmgren, Organic Events

Chapter 29 **Public Relations for Nonprofits: Getting Ink for Your Cause** 479
            David Fenton and Lisa Chen, Fenton

PART SEVEN

Boards and Volunteers   495
            Darian Rodriguez Heyman

Chapter 30 **Board Governance**   501
            Vernetta Walker and Emily Heard, BoardSource

Chapter 31 **Getting Your Board to Fundraise**   519
            Bob Zimmerman, Zimmerman Lehman

Chapter 32 **Volunteer Recruitment**   533
            Greg Baldwin, VolunteerMatch

Chapter 33 **Volunteer Engagement and Management**   551
            Michelle Nunn, HandsOn Network

            Closing Thoughts   569
            Darian Rodriguez Heyman

            Afterword   573
            Lynne Twist, Soul of Money Institute and
            The Pachamama Alliance

Book Partners   579

            About the Editor   599

            Endnotes   601

            Name Index   613

            Subject Index   619

Dedication

To my grandfather, Harry Heyman, the soft-spoken patriarch of my family, and to Bob Zimmerman, for his contribution to this book and to the sector he cared so very much about. Rest in peace.

FOREWORD

By Ami Dar,
Founder and Executive Director,
Idealist.org/Action Without Borders

When Darian told me about this book and asked me to write a Foreword, two thoughts immediately came to mind. The first was, "Really? Another introduction to the sector? Do we really need this?" But then I saw the list of authors that Darian had assembled—many of whom I've known for years— and it was clear that he couldn't have found a better group of people to write this.

The second thought was more of a wish: the wish that when I started Idealist.org in 1995 I could have had this amazing group of people whispering in my ear, and stopping me from making some of the bigger mistakes I've made over the years.

So in thinking about this Foreword I decided that the most useful thing I could do was share some of those mistakes with you, and then encourage you to read this book in the hope that you can avoid repeating them.

Here then are my Top Ten Lessons from the past fifteen years.

1. Focus. Focus! Mission creep is Enemy #1. Once you know what you want to do, do *that* and nothing else. Resist temptations, especially from funders who have their own agendas and who can blow you off-course with a sweet-sounding grant. If the grant is not for something you *want* to do, the money is not worth it.

2. Build a good board, but first decide what "good" means for you. More or less engaged? More or less supportive? More or less meddlesome? The key here is that serious people who take on a task usually also want the

authority to do it well. And so you need to decide: Do you want a board that *does* a lot but then also wants a say in how the work is done? Or do you want a board that is more hands-off, but gives you and your staff more freedom? What you should avoid at all costs is the worst of both worlds: a board that meddles but doesn't help.

3. Hire good people. Skilled and smart, of course, but what I really mean is people you *like*. You'll spend long days with this group, so hire kind and interesting people who make you laugh.

4. When you make a hiring mistake, and you probably will, try to fix it as soon as possible. There is one test that usually works well. Think about your entire team once in a while, and ask yourself, "If that person resigned, would I be upset or would I be relieved?" If the answer is that you'd be relieved, you should probably not wait for them to resign.

5. Learn some accounting. Money is the fuel on which your organization will run, and you should *always* know your numbers. Some people start nonprofit organizations as a way of avoiding what they see as the money-centeredness of the corporate world. But the truth is that money is at least as important in our sector as in any other, and you should know enough accounting to always know how your organization is doing.

6. Use free stuff; there is so much of it now. Blogs, Google Apps, Facebook Pages, Twitter accounts, Salesforce licenses, and much, much more. We run our whole organization on Google Apps, for example, which means that all our email and office software is free, and there is no reason why you should pay for it, either.

7. Build your network. And I don't mean by "networking," going to conferences, and exchanging business cards or Facebook connections. What I really mean is to try, wherever possible, to treat people the way you like to be treated. If you do this, over time you'll have a real network of people who will be there when you need them most.

8. Collaborations, coalitions, alliances, mergers . . . Before jumping in, can you imagine a way out? Working closely with other organizations can be both good and necessary, but exactly at the point when the collaboration seems most tempting, stop for a moment and see if you can imagine a

way out in case things go wrong. If you can't, and the thought makes you queasy, it might be worth looking at the whole thing again.

9. Be careful with your time. Fight hyperbolic discounting! "Hyperbolic discounting" is a fancy term for the tendency that many of us have to make choices today that our future self would prefer not to make. For example, someone invites you to attend a conference across the country five months from now. It sounds good, and it's easy to say "yes" at that moment, but when the day arrives and you have to take the trip, you deeply regret that quick "yes." Most of us do this with all kinds of commitments, but these days, having regretted a "yes" once too often, I make a conscious effort not to commit to doing anything in the future without trying to imagine myself <u>then</u>.

10. Think big! Having said all this, what's the worst thing that could happen if you fail? Think big, and go for it! Some days will be challenging and frustrating, but if you are doing what you want, they will never be boring. What more can we ask for?

Good luck!

Ami Dar

Ami Dar is the founder and executive director of Idealist.org. Built in 1996 with $3,500, Idealist has become one of the most popular nonprofit resources on the Web, with information provided by 100,000 organizations around the world and 70,000 visitors every day. Ami is an Ashoka Fellow and currently serves on the boards of the Nonprofit Finance Fund and Allforgood.org. He was born in Jerusalem, grew up in Peru and Mexico, and lives in New York.

ABOUT THE BOOK

> You don't have to know all the answers, you just need to know where to find them.
>
> —Albert Einstein

Here in one volume are the collected insights and strategies for success from some of the nonprofit sector's most accomplished leaders, many of whom I met during my tenure as executive director of Craigslist Foundation. What follows are tales from the trenches and practical, tactical dos and don'ts; think of <u>Nonprofit Management 101</u> as boot camp in a book. I asked all 50 contributors to write from the perspective of "if I knew then what I know now," with an eye toward offering real-world advice to people in the early stages of their careers and positions in the social benefit sector.

The cast of experts here assembled will guide you through the entire nonprofit management landscape, and they'll point you in the right direction for more information at every turn.

Book Overview and Purpose

Perhaps the clearest way to describe this book is to explain what it's *not*. It is not a textbook, written by and for academics. *This book is not a how-to or a do-it-yourself manual designed to help you start a new organization*, nor is it a career guide for people looking to enter the sector. Finally, it is not a book that zeros in on only one nonprofit management discipline, e.g., fundraising, marketing, board governance, and so forth. All of these kinds of books exist many times over, and my intention is to make a truly unique contribution to the sector.

So what *is* this book, then?

This book is *a reference guide for professionals taking on new responsibilities*, even though they aren't completely prepared . . . what, you thought you were alone?

Actually, the majority of us, especially at small, grassroots organizations, are just little kids wearing our dads' suits, building the plane while flying it. *This book will make the orientation process quicker and less painful, allowing you to benefit from the experience of those who came before you.* Also, by covering such a broad spectrum of management issues, my hope is that the reader will gain a clear sense of the implicit interconnectedness of all the topics addressed herein; it is not through the mastery of any *one* of these disciplines that you will lead your cause to success, but rather by cohesively weaving them all together. So let's talk about how to connect these important dots a bit.

How to Read This Book—In Search of Nuggets

Whenever I advise anyone looking to get the most out of an educational experience, I always start by reviewing the ideal outcome. After all, when we fail to ask ourselves *"What does success look like?"* at the beginning of any endeavor, we curtail the power of mindfulness and intention, leading us to react, instead of create.

So what does success look like for the reader of this book, and moreover for anyone participating in an educational experience? To me, the answer lies in an analogy to the forty-niners, those intrepid souls who went West, seeking their fortunes in the United States during the gold rush. As we all know, most of them didn't strike it rich, but the ones that did all possessed three things: maps, picks and shovels, and nuggets. So how do these apply to the content that follows, not to mention all other opportunities for learning? In educational environments, you should always be on the lookout for:

• *Maps*, which are the *strategic frameworks* you use to plan your approach to your goal. Think of these as the philosophies and paradigms that guide your efforts.

- *Picks and shovels*, which represent the *tools* you will use on a day-to-day basis to go about your work. These are the resources that make your job and life easier.

- *Nuggets*, which are the object of your pursuit; the actionable insights or *kernels of wisdom* that allow you to distill a complex idea into its simplest form.

Most educational forums focus on relaying maps; lecturers frequently stand at the front of a hall, telling their audience how to *think* about a concept or field. Although strategy cannot be discounted, my experience has taught me that emerging leaders benefit most from the actual tools and resources that help facilitate their daily work. Along these lines, be on the lookout for books, websites, conferences, and other tools and tactics highlighted throughout the entire handbook, especially in the Resource Reviews that cap each chapter (all resources listed also appear on my website at www.Nonprofits.101.org, along with a tip of the week). Doing the heavy lifting to launch an organization, event, or initiative takes a tremendous amount of effort, and to the extent we can work smarter and not harder, the cause and the community are better served. At the same time, nuggets like Kay Sprinkel Grace's "people don't give to you, they give *through* you" have helped reframe how I look at my work, and therefore made it easier and more exciting; may they have the same impact on you.

The Story Behind the Story

Some of you may be wondering how this field guide came to be. This handbook is a direct result of the knowledge, people, and organizations I gained while serving as executive director of Craigslist Foundation from 2004 to 2008. The organization's focus on "helping people help" guided our work connecting emerging nonprofit leaders and social entrepreneurs to the resources they need to build a better world. Our flagship program was *Nonprofit Boot Camp*, also known as "Woodstock for Nonprofits." We launched the program and educated, empowered, and connected over 10,000 leaders in the San Francisco Bay Area and New York City to rave reviews under my direction. In the process, we partnered with hundreds of "capacity builders," or groups that provide valuable support services and training to community-based organizations.

It seemed there was a huge, untapped need to connect emerging leaders to established resources, and to introduce them to road-tested best practices and techniques in the process. In order to address this gap, I worked with Jesse Wiley from Jossey-Bass, an imprint of John Wiley & Sons, to craft the structure and vision for this project—which was designed to capture and convey the energy and wisdom of *Nonprofit Boot Camp* in a book. After spending almost two years refining the concept and recruiting the most insightful, dynamic experts we could find, here we are.

Chapter Structure

My objective for this project is to provide the reader with easy-to-implement, high-value practices across seven major nonprofit management disciplines: strategy and leadership; operations; law and finance; technology; fundraising; marketing; and board and volunteer management.

Accordingly, the book is divided into seven sections, or parts. These do not exactly map to the headings listed above, as there is some natural crossover between them. Each part is arranged into several chapters, which represent important elements of that discipline, and I recruited leading practitioners to write each chapter with a focus on practical, tactical takeaways and tips for emerging nonprofit leaders and social entrepreneurs.

Anytime you bring 50 leading minds together and you attempt to cover so much ground, a lot of thought needs to be put into ensuring the content is somehow connected. I have done everything possible to allow the contributors to speak in their own voice, but at the same time I've integrated an overarching structure and common chapter format to increase readability and usefulness.

Each chapter found in this handbook includes the following:

- Introduction to the Topic: No-nonsense background and context, including basic concepts in the field and possibly statistics, facts, and trends

- <u>Critical Skills and Competencies</u>: The key things you must know to succeed in the given area, including the concepts, resources, and tactics the authors wish they would have known early on in their careers, with an emphasis on how-to's and practical guidance—key insights are *italicized* in order to ensure they get the attention they deserve

- <u>Short Case Study (or Studies)</u>: Success and horror stories from the field, highlighting major pitfalls and tips for success

- <u>Dos and Don'ts</u>: A synopsis of key points and practical, tactical tips and takeaways from the Critical Skills and Competencies portion of each chapter

- <u>Conclusion</u>: Brief wrap-up and inspiration

- <u>Resource Review</u>: A list of some of the most helpful resources on the topic, including websites, support organizations, books, conferences, newsletters, blogs, reports, FAQs, and more, along with a short description of the value of each

Flow of the Book

Now that you have a sense of how the book is structured, I'd like to talk you through a brief outline of the content. We begin Part One by talking about the big picture. What is the role, history, and significance of our mission-based sector, and how do you step up within it, not just as a manager but as a *leader*? What career opportunities exist now that you've already taken the plunge?

From there, Part Two gets into some of the most important strategic considerations and factors that are integral to the success of any community effort. How do you get started, how do you plan, and why is it important to seek out opportunities to collaborate? Part Two also covers some of the core operational issues that face nonprofits, including insurance, HR, and tips on how to recruit and lead a diverse, competent staff. Parts Three and Four deal with some of the more specialized areas of nonprofit operations: legal considerations, lobbying and advocacy, finance, and then technology. This completes the operational picture. By addressing all of these issues successfully, you can be assured that you've created a solid organization, but always remember that this is not an "if you build it they will come" sector; *you have to get out in the world and let people know about the good work you're doing if you want to maximize impact.*

To this end, Parts Five and Six cover fundraising and marketing, respectively. These sections are squarely focused on spreading the good world, and securing the resources and attention needed to make change. Finally, a linchpin of any organization, especially one in its early stages, is the strength of its board and its volunteers, which are addressed in Part Seven. The contributors provide tangible insights and strategies for identifying, recruiting, maintaining, and engaging the best quality talent.

Be on the lookout for *important themes throughout all these sections.* These include the need to *focus on impact*—to tell your story in a personal way and focusing on the change you make possible, versus the resources you need. It's all about what's in it for them, not you. You'll also note an emphasis on not only recruiting support, in the form of donations, volunteers, and so on, but on *stewarding people and resources* over time. After all, it's much harder to get them in the door than to keep them engaged. Speaking of engagement, we'll address the significance of *pursuing and honoring diversity* in all its forms, another key to the success of any cause. Finally, you'll read about the importance of *establishing a clear strategy before moving to implementation.* When thinking about the power of intention, remember to "be careful where you point that thing," because life is indeed a self-fulfilling prophecy. Look, and think, before you leap.

Another important note about the book: *feel free to skip around.* I've laid out the content in what I consider to be the most logical progression, and I strongly believe that *it behooves any nonprofit professional to have at least a cursory, working knowledge of all these areas.* With that said, if what you really care about is fundraising from foundations, then by all means, just flip directly to Chapter Twenty. If you're fixing to redesign your website, then knock yourself out with Chapter Fifteen. This book can serve you as an encyclopedia or a cookbook, just as it can be read as a novel that takes you on a linear journey to a finale. Ultimately, *this book is a tool to help you change the world,* so use it as it best suits you. That said, I implore you to make the time to *explore the resource reviews at the end of the chapters most relevant to your work;*

I'd wager that you'll look back on these "yellow pages" as a huge chunk of the value you received from this book.

In the end, I had to make some hard decisions. Beyond the content and contributors featured, there is no shortage of other topics I could have addressed, nor is there a lack of additional brilliant minds with a lot to share. My filter for deciding what and who made the cut revolved squarely around what I felt would be most useful to emerging leaders. These "101" techniques and resources will get you on the path to success and cover the basic building blocks of great nonprofit management. When combined with strong leadership and a bold vision, *eureka*, you will strike gold!

ACKNOWLEDGMENTS

This publication is the result of the hard work of a large community of dedicated experts, leaders, and organizations, all committed to developing the next generation of nonprofit sector leaders. Their participation proves that "many hands make light work," for this book would have taken me years to write on my own, as if that would even be possible. Accordingly, many thanks to the 50 authors who helped create this field guide and to the scores of promotional partners that let the world know about it.

I offer special thanks to Jesse Wiley from John Wiley & Sons and Jossey-Bass. His vision, support, and flexibility were the greatest contributing factors in making this book possible. Vincent Hyman, my development editor, played an invaluable role in ensuring that the content herein fulfilled the overarching vision I had for this project. Thanks to Steven Bauer from Nonprofit Leadership Alliance (formerly American Humanics), our core marketing partner, who also helped secure some of our esteemed writers, to the dozens of volunteer proofreaders that reviewed the final drafts of the manuscript, and to Sam Richard, who served tirelessly as my partner and contributor liaison. Sam is one of the most passionate young leaders I've come across and I know the community will be better off for his leadership.

This book is based on the knowledge, relationships, and experience I gained at Craigslist Foundation, the producer of *Nonprofit Boot Camp* and the place I called home for almost five years. I'm grateful to Laila Brenner for continuing to support my efforts to this day as marketing director for this book and the associated website and blog, www.Nonprofits101.org. Also, I thank the board for allowing me to take on this project, and especially Bill Ryan for his unwavering friendship and vision. Also, let us not forget craigslist.org Founder and Customer Service Rep Craig Newmark and CEO Jim Buckmaster for their bold attachment to always putting the community first.

Special thanks to Ritu Sharma for her incredible support during the final stages of the preparation of this manuscript—our time together in the Russian River Valley is something I'll always cherish.

I'd also like to thank my family. To my Dad and to his family in Argentina, thank you for teaching me that philanthropy starts in the home. To my Mom, my brother, and the rest of the Heyman family, please know the love, support, and understanding that you showered me with since birth have given me the confidence to pursue the life I lead.

Last but not least, I want to thank *you*, the reader. Thank you for the good work that you do in our beloved community, for your tireless efforts to build the world we all know is possible. Together we can—no, together we *will* build a better tomorrow.

Part One

The Big Picture—What the Field Is All About and Where You Fit In

What would you do if you knew you could not fail?

—Robert H. Schuller

So you want to change the world, huh? Well, welcome to the movement . . . to the "Movement" with a capital "M," actually. The Movement for peace, for social justice, for sustainability, for the world we all know is possible. There is an infinite amount of work to be done, so we can use all the help we can get, and we need all of you on board giving it your best. All of this beckons the question, *how can you most effectively channel your passion, your vision, and your time toward a cause that you care about?*

Welcome to <u>Nonprofit Management 101: A Complete and Practical Guide for Leaders and Professionals</u>. You've already decided to work in the nonprofit sector, whether you started an organization or joined one. I don't know what kind of organization, how large, how fast it's growing, or how long it's been around, but I do know this: *there are a common set of management needs that*

1

face all nonprofits. And those are the issues that addressed in this manual, this handbook.

Before we get into it, let me offer a reality check for those of you talking and thinking about "my cause" or "my community." You may be in for a rough ride. You see, it's important to realize that *all nonprofits, at least in the United States, have the same owner.* "Who is that?" you ask. "The board?" "The staff?" "The founder?" "Me?" Well, not quite. Every one of the over 1.5 million registered 501(c)(3)s in this country is owned by . . . the public. Point being, it's not about "my cause," it's about *the* cause. A board of directors is merely a group of people entrusted to represent the public interest—that's why they're called "trustees."

So please, *please* remember who you work for.

I bring this point up at this early juncture because all too often people run out and start a nonprofit or launch a program without taking the time to see who else is out there working on similar issues. The fact is, you *owe* it to the cause and to the community to do your homework and survey the landscape before you pitch your tent. In fact, I would take it one step further and say that *you are obliged to reach out proactively to potential collaborators and competitors and seek out opportunities to support their efforts before starting something anew.* In the end, if you still decide to go it alone, at least you'll have a sense of other efforts in the field and how your contribution is unique.

President Bill Clinton said it best: *"Seek first to collaborate, and only then to lead."*

The problem is, we are taught from the time that we are children that it's a "dog-eat-dog" world, a zero-sum game ruled only by the natural law of survival of the fittest. Well, brothers and sisters, I am here today to tell you that we've been duped, hoodwinked, fooled, and misled. Yes, that's right: we've been lied to. You see, if you take a look at the natural world, you'll note, as my good friend Dr. Kevin Danaher is fond of pointing out, that *dogs don't eat dogs.* Moreover, if you read through all of Charles Darwin's writings, never will you see the phrase "survival of the fittest." In fact, it's an incorrect paraphrase developed years after his death. Darwin's real assertion was more along the lines of "survival of the collaborative"—see for yourself.

All of this to say *collaborate, collaborate, collaborate*; "your" community, "your" cause, and the people you serve will thank you for it—this much I can promise. And along these lines, if you have done your homework and are still committed to starting a new organization, please consider getting a "fiscal sponsor." A fiscal sponsor is an established nonprofit that allows you to come under their umbrella, thereby enabling you to accept tax-deductible donations and receive most of the benefits of being a standalone organization. Some groups like Tides Foundation specialize in this work, but any nonprofit that is so inclined can offer to house you. Especially during the early days, this can be a great way to avoid the cost and administrative headache of starting and maintaining a nonprofit, enabling you to focus on the actual work instead.

My friend Arun Nemani once said, *"A good leader inspires, a good manager motivates."* The nonprofit sector has been accused of being overled and undermanaged. Personally, I've often heard of the difficulties facing organizations started by a charismatic founder who is able to deftly craft a compelling vision, mobilize the support needed to make it real, and launch an ongoing effort to sustain it. The problems all too often come later, when the heavy lifting is complete and the infrastructure and maintenance take priority; when values on paper need to be lived in everyday life, and when the need for personal balance and sustainability make it evident that *this work is a marathon, not a sprint.* May this handbook serve as a useful tool for both leaders and managers looking to bridge the gap and expand their capabilities.

One final word as long as I have the stage, or the page, as it were. Often I wonder what the world would be like if we had a different Golden Rule. I believe we should all live our lives striving to *be the kind of person the world needs more of.* If we internalized such a bold yet elegantly simple maxim, what would the impact be on philanthropy, community engagement, and collaboration, both domestically and around the globe? Thankfully, we have chosen to work in a sector where many people have already taken the most significant step possible toward this way of life, which is *living one's daily life in service to others.* We should rest easy knowing that we are in good company, surrounded by people with the best intentions who are willing to put in the work needed to build a better world. Let us proceed with the confidence needed to persevere through the difficult times. For when we stumble, or our colleagues stumble into us, we are reminded that *unwavering tenacity is one of the most crucial elements to success for anyone in a leadership position.*

Ah, leadership. That fine act of mobilizing support around a vision—of blazing a trail for others to follow. As we begin our journey through this guide, we will begin with the big picture, for any effective leader must have a clear grasp of the field on and in which she operates. How did this huge and vibrant sector get started in the United States, and just how big is it, anyway? Are we all in this together, as some claim, or are our efforts disjointed and disparate? Am I a leader or a manager, neither or both, and what is the difference, *really*? More important, what are some tips and techniques for maximizing my effectiveness as an emerging leader dedicated to a cause? Finally, what career pathways does the social sector offer to an ambitious and committed leader, and how do I most gracefully scale that ladder? All of these issues and more will be covered in Part One.

CHAPTER 1

The Role of Nonprofits in American Life

By Robert Glavin, MNA, President, Robert Glavin, Inc., and Faculty Member, University of San Francisco

Today, what nonprofits do is vast, diverse, and invaluable to American life. Nonprofits are the primary drivers of social change and the providers of a wide array of goods and services; are essential to public policy and advocacy; hold critical responsibility for meeting broad social needs; share responsibility for education with government and, to a lesser degree, with the private sector; hold a declining but still large responsibility for providing health care; are the home of most fine arts and culture; and they include all religious organizations. This chapter will provide essential facts about what nonprofit organizations are, what values they serve, and their numbers and types. A brief history of American nonprofit activity will show how they have developed and expressed American ideals and beliefs. The final section presents some key trends and their implications for the future roles of nonprofit organizations in their service to society.

What Is a Nonprofit Organization?

A nonprofit organization is, most simply, a means for voluntary group action for mutual benefit or the benefit of others. Nonprofits form a third sector of society apart from both the government (the public sector) and for-profit businesses (the private sector). Unlike the government, which undertakes public action for public good, or business, which undertakes private action for private gain (the shareholders), nonprofit organizations are an expression of private action for public good. They "lie beyond family, market, and state."[1]

Public benefit nonprofit organizations have six defining characteristics:[2]

- They are organized, though not necessarily incorporated.

- They are private, not governmental.

- They operate under the nondistribution constraint, that is, profits may only be applied to the mission.

- They are self-governing.

- They are voluntary.

- They seek to provide a societal benefit.

What Values Does the Nonprofit Sector Serve?

By joining the sector, you are contributing to a great legacy of social change. Standing apart from business and government, *nonprofit organizations are where social reform efforts have most often arisen.* Made possible by American freedoms of association, speech, and religion, the nonprofit sector is a highly effective expression of American pluralism, providing a stabilizing means for voluntary community building and public benefit. It makes possible evolutionary rather than revolutionary social change. Today's nonprofits are the successors to barn-raising and other community-building efforts of colonial America. Although their specific roles have changed throughout American history, the larger, societal functions that nonprofits fill are more stable. They are a reflection of and a mechanism for the expression of several important social values, such as:

- Nonprofits identify societal problems and advocate for change.

- Nonprofits provide a structure for the investment of private capital to cause social change.

- Nonprofits relieve government burden.

- Nonprofits preserve and promote knowledge, cultures, values, and traditions.

- Nonprofits offer opportunities for personal fulfillment and self-realization.

- The nonprofit sector is the place of spiritual expression in America.

Nonprofits in America Today

The American nonprofit sector is made up of the approximately 1.5 million organizations that have been granted tax-exempt status by the Internal Revenue Service (see Table 1.1). These nonprofits include public charities, private foundations, religious congregations, and membership associations. Of these, roughly 1 million are organized to provide a social good and are classified by the Internal Revenue Code as 501(c)(3) public charities, or "public benefit organizations." This classification qualifies them to receive gifts

Table 1.1: Nonprofit Numbers

Numbers (2009)	
TAX-EXEMPT ORGANIZATIONS	1,569,572
PUBLIC CHARITIES	997,579
PRIVATE FOUNDATIONS	118,423
OTHER NONPROFITS	453,570
REVENUES (2007)	$1.4 trillion
ASSETS (2007)	$2.6 trillion

Source: National Center for Charitable Statistics, "NCCS Quick Facts About Nonprofits" (Urban Institute, Oct. 2009), www.nccs.urban.org/statistics/quickfacts.cfm (retrieved Feb. 2, 2010).

that donors may deduct from their income taxes, with certain limits.[3] In addition to the registered nonprofits, there are many uncounted efforts (especially those with less than $5,000 in annual revenues) that may have formed to meet the specific needs of a community, a neighborhood, a school, or their own members. If these very small nonprofits were counted, the numbers of nonprofits would certainly be much higher.[4]

Diverse Needs, Responsive Nonprofits

Although U.S. tax laws allow 27 types of exempt organizations, including organizations such as fraternal groups, professional associations, and political parties, when using the term "nonprofit" most people are thinking of incorporated 501(c)(3) public charities. These organizations serve such a wide variety of purposes that the National Taxonomy of Exempt Entities (NTEE) system used by the Internal Revenue Service classifies nonprofit organizations into over 400 categories of activity.[5] Among the major categories (see Table 1.2), Human Services, which includes organizations engaged in job training, inmate support, and abuse prevention, as well as those providing food, housing, and shelter, has the most organizations—more than 115,000 as of 2009. The Health category, which includes hospitals and primary care facilities, as well as mental health services and medical research, has the highest revenues, expenses, and assets. The Health category also employs the greatest number of people, accounting for over 41% of nonprofit employment.[6] Education is a major category that includes elementary and secondary schools, charter schools, universities, adult education, and libraries. Public and Societal Benefit includes over 40,000 organizations that work for civil rights, community improvement, scientific research, and changes in public policy. Although having the least number of organizations, the International, Foreign Affairs, & National Security category and the Environment and Animals categories have shown the fastest growth in recent years.[7]

The majority of nonprofit funding comes from earned revenue. Earned revenue may come from fees for services or products, ticket sales, dues and membership fees, and tuition, and *accounts for 50% of nonprofit revenue.* Government at all levels accounts for 29.4% of nonprofit revenue, provided as grants and contracts. Charitable contributions from individuals, foundations, and

Table 1.2: Nonprofit Categories: 501(C)(3) Public Charities

Nonprofit Category	# of Orgs	Revenues	Expenses	Assets
Arts, Culture & Humanities	38,772	32,316,336,324	28,298,338,340	98,828,363,709
Education	64,362	266,655,237,172	221,693,681,689	845,019,216,480
Environment and Animal-Related	15,293	13,858,004,996	11,943,284,580	33,105,099,438
Health Care	43,592	816,974,665,642	788,364,602,947	1,013,249,929,736
Human Services	118,416	181,386,508,441	175,497,790,668	275,195,500,873
International, Foreign Affairs & National Security	6,793	31,894,220,842	30,938,307,141	31,591,030,972
Public, Societal Benefit	42,261	83,715,978,124	72,090,092,580	284,176,332,828
Religion-Related	22,398	12,263,526,139	11,501,896,473	26,711,870,566
Mutual & Membership Benefit	883	2,444,863,589	2,045,362,530	15,033,504,714
Unknown	927	391,946,810	379,532,910	696,401,174
Total	353,697	1,441,901,288,079	1,342,752,889,858	2,623,607,250,490

Source: Adapted from National Center for Charitable Statistics, "Number of 501(c)(3) Public Charities by NTEE Activity/Purpose—Annual Filers Only, static version of NTEEs released Apr. 2010" (Urban Institute), www.nccsdataweb.urban.org/PubApps/nonprofit-overview-sumRpt.php?v=nteeFilers&t=pc&f=0 (retrieved Dec. 2, 2010).

corporations account for 12.3%, and 8.3% of revenues come from other sources including investment income.[8] More detail on the makeup of charitable contributions is included in the fundraising chapters of this book.

Economic Impact

Beyond the variety and scope of their activities and services, nonprofits are a significant part of the U.S. economy, both in terms of income and employment. The Urban Institute, a leading contributor to our knowledge of the sector, estimates that in 2006 nonprofits contributed $666 billion to the U.S. economy. The Government Accounting Office testified, "During the period 1998 through 2002, spending reported by tax-exempt entities was *roughly 11 to 12 percent of the nation's gross domestic product."*[9]

Nonprofits also contribute significant wages and salaries to the economy: In 2005, *nonprofits employed 12.9 million people, approximately 9.7% of the U.S. economy,* and they employed more people than the construction (7.3 million), finance and insurance (5.8 million), and real estate (2.0 million) sectors.[10] In 2006, nonprofit wages and salaries totaled $489.4 billion—*8.11% of all salaries and wages paid in the United States.*[11] If the American nonprofit sector were a country, in 2006 it would have been the *sixteenth largest economy in the world,* based on wages paid.[12]

Social Impact

Nonprofits are a major organizing force in society. They encourage people to volunteer for their communities, act in response to need, and pursue personal goals and opportunities. In 2005, 61.2 million people volunteered their time with a nonprofit organization. In 2006, 26.7% of American adults said they volunteered a total of 12.9 billion hours, the equivalent of 7.6 million full-time employees. The estimated value of volunteer time was $215.6 billion.[13]

How We Got Here

Philanthropy has always been a force in American life. In Native American communities as in colonial and frontier communities, mutual support was essential to the survival of the group. Caring for others in need was prescribed by the religious beliefs of the colonial settlers. Forms of caring for those in need, whether expressed through tithing, helping others, or giving alms, can be found in the cultures and religions of all of the people who came to make up the United States. Out of these traditions, the United States has evolved a particular nongovernmental, organizational, and egalitarian structure for providing aid and addressing social needs. Initially, most care delivered outside the family was delivered by religious congregations and organizations. As notions of democracy and freedom evolved, religious organizations were joined by secular ones, motivated by civic purpose.

The need for group effort to aid society grew as the United States experienced social needs arising from wars, immigration, and industrialization. At each stage, voluntary associations provided charitable assistance and care to individuals in need. As America matured, nonprofit organizations and foundations sought to go beyond simple charity and to improve society through philanthropy, in the effort to address the underlying causes of social needs.

From Colonies to a Nation

The lack of a nobility or an autocratic state made self-governing group action a principal means of building our society. After the Revolutionary War, chartered corporations, voluntary associations, fraternal societies, and political parties were founded to help build the new nation. In the first half of the nineteenth century in New England, wealthy merchants funded universities, asylums, hospitals, professional schools, scholarship funds, lecture series, and reform societies. Religious and evangelical movements, primarily originating in Europe, led to greater voluntary activity and, by the middle of the nineteenth century, to broad social action for temperance, prison reform, and the abolition of slavery.

In response to the Civil War, individuals created many voluntary groups to raise funds, gather supplies, and marshal volunteers. In 1861, Clara Barton formed a group to distribute aid to the wounded that led, in 1881, to the American Red Cross. The U.S. Sanitary Commission was established in 1861 as a privately funded national federation to provide health care and relief to the military. The U.S. Christian Commission was a religiously motivated effort to raise funds and provide care for the armed forces.[14] Each established roles and models for other voluntary groups[15] and what would become an organized and critical sector of society.

After the War, devastation resulted in enormous social needs, and the end of slavery resulted in a new class of citizens in need. Voluntary groups played key roles in assisting the government, particularly in educating and training newly freed men and women. Philanthropic funds that resemble today's foundations, such as the Peabody Fund founded in 1868, were created to support and educate former slaves and to develop public health policy. Voluntary efforts created educational institutions such as Fisk University

(1866) and Howard University (1867) to serve newly educated former slaves. The Salvation Army, a major provider of religiously motivated charity, was founded in the United States in 1880.[16,17,18]

Progressives and Philanthropists

Industrialization, urbanization, immigration, and economic crises created new and increased social hardships that voluntary groups could not meet with traditional charity. During the Progressive Era, which began in the latter part of the nineteenth century, there arose a pervasive movement of organized associations of all kinds, some for mutual benefit and others devoted to organized citizen efforts to address workplace conditions, housing, child labor, and women's suffrage. Churches, too, undertook greater action for social relief and reform.[19]

In the same period, industrialists, whom many progressives blamed for urban welfare conditions, began to seek social change through philanthropy rather than charity. Andrew Carnegie initiated a national dialogue on the power of philanthropy in his 1889 essay "Wealth," in which he urged the wealthy to address the root causes of social problems as opposed to providing simple relief of hunger or need, charity that he believed only contributed to the continuation of poverty and slothfulness. He advocated and undertook the creation of institutions designed to offer knowledge and opportunity to the masses. These included libraries, museums, parks, concert halls, and educational institutions. He and other wealthy industrialists began to set aside significant sums for systemic reform. The Russell Sage Foundation was founded by Margaret Olivia Slocum Sage in 1907 with nationwide activities in child welfare, industrial relations, housing, and city planning. This was followed by the Carnegie Corporation of New York in 1911 and the Rockefeller Foundation in 1913. Their work led to the creation of numerous institutions and to the professionalization and expansion of fields including medicine, engineering, and social work.[20]

Nonprofit Professionals Arise

Social benefit activity itself became more professional. As the creators of foundations undertook social change, they increasingly hired well-educated, skilled managers. Reliance on professionals increased with foundation assets, and with the death or retirement of founding donors. Fundraising, too, became professionalized, as communities undertook organized, staffed efforts to fund universities, hospitals, YMCAs, and other organizations.

More democratic efforts to encourage and professionalize philanthropy arose, with two important community-based models arising at the same place and time. The Community Chest, founded in Cleveland in 1913, was the first major effort to collect money from a broad community for a variety of causes. Its successor, the United Way, is today joined by many other such efforts collectively known as workplace and community giving campaigns. In 1914, the Cleveland Foundation was created as the first community foundation. Like private foundations, community foundations make grants, but they differ in that they are funded by contributions from many sources and governed by a board that represents those they serve, generally a specific group or geographic area. Both of these new types of organization were, from the start, run by informed, paid, professional managers. As philanthropic institutions funded and governed by the community, rather than by the wealthy, community giving campaigns and community foundations enabled social action by and for the people.[21]

The Government Joins In

Before the Great Depression of the 1930s, the federal government's role in addressing social needs was limited and expressed mostly through the provision of legal privileges and tax exemptions. The massive crisis of the Depression was far beyond the capacity of voluntary organizations and led to the assumption by the government, for the first time, of certain social needs, including aid to the poor and unemployed and the creation of the Social Security system in 1935.[22] Thus began the shared role of both the nonprofit and the government sectors in caring for the good of the people.

Thereafter, social action by the government and the nonprofit sector grew, aided by the establishment of more private foundations (from 203 in 1929 to 2,058 by 1959). Foundations, corporations, and government programs funded the creation and growth of many nonprofits, particularly in health care, the performing arts, and international affairs. A larger government role prompted the emergence of new organizations that advocated for changes in public policy in civil rights, the environment, and international causes.[23]

This continued during the 1960s with the Great Society, an effort of the U.S. government to increase its involvement in providing health care, education, welfare, and other social services. New programs included Medicare, Medicaid, the National Endowments for the Arts and Humanities, Head Start, Legal Services, and more. The government, at all levels, began to work with nonprofits, contracting extensively with them to carry out large parts of these programs.[24]

Government Cuts, New Responses

Government's role in providing a variety of services grew until the Reagan administration, when an emphasis on decreased government responsibility and privatization dominated public policy. The administration's conservative theorists believed that reduced support for social welfare, health, education, environment, and culture would stimulate private responses that would be flexible, competitive, and effective.[25]

During the 1980s and 1990s, the government greatly reduced its support and services for the needy. The reduction in government funding affected millions and placed burdens on nonprofit organizations far beyond their capacity. Nonprofits responded with greater activity and, ultimately, with increased professionalization, improved models, and greater impact, although many social needs remained unmet. And when government contracting mechanisms put nonprofit organizations in competition with the private sector, particularly in health care, health insurance, and education, nonprofits responded by becoming more skillful, commercial, and entrepreneurial.[26]

The 10-year period from 1998 to 2008 saw an impressive rise in the total numbers, revenues, and assets of nonprofits. Between 1998 and 2008, the number of nonprofits registered with the IRS increased 60%, total revenues for reporting nonprofits increased 91%, and total assets for reporting nonprofits increased 106%.[27] A varied and vibrant sector began to emerge.

During this period, nonprofits also found new partners in people who had acquired recent and great business wealth, often in technology, and who brought with them for-profit perspectives and practices. The field of "venture philanthropy" arose, where donors began to look at themselves as investors, seeking to help nonprofit organizations to create earned-income programs, test solutions, apply technologies, or otherwise accomplish social change through the employment of entrepreneurial strategies. These projects generally involve high engagement by the investors and have preestablished measures for accountability, efficiency, and overall performance. This phenomenon of business attention to and investment in the operations of the nonprofit sector has continued to increase focus on quantifying and measuring accomplishment throughout the nonprofit sector.[28]

In addition, a number of foundations now employ methods to leverage capital to strengthen organizations and cause social change in new ways. Significant examples include "socially responsible investing," which is the practice of aligning investment policies with an organization's mission by investing in causes that are in line with its goals; and "program-related investments," which are loans, loan guarantees, purchases of stock, or other kinds of financial support or investment made by a foundation from its asset base rather than its grant-making budget[29]—see Chapter Twenty, "How to Seek a Grant," for more information on this topic.

What's Next: Trends and Implications

Though unforeseeable challenges and opportunities for nonprofits will arise, key trends that are most likely to affect the nonprofit sector in the immediate future include:

- Economic pressures. Social needs will continue to exceed the capacity of nonprofit organizations to meet them. The recession of 2008–2009 increased demand, particularly for housing, food, employment, and social services, and its consequences will be felt for some years to come.[30] Estimates are that as many as 100,000 nonprofit organizations may close as a result of the financial downturn.[31] Even in stronger economies, the pressures of demand and competition for resources will challenge nonprofits economically. Innovative and entrepreneurial solutions to social problems and organizational difficulties will be crucial for success in the sector.

- Cultural and racial composition. America is becoming a minority-majority society made up of a group of individuals of various and mixed races and backgrounds.[32] The growth in Hispanic and other minority groups in the United States will call for cross-cultural communication and cooperation skills, and inclusive behaviors that leverage diverse ideas and skills will become more important to those providing social benefit.[33,34] Organizations will need to be culturally fluent and competent to meet their missions in the future.

- Age. Predicted changes in the age of the population include the approaching retirement of an entire generation of experienced nonprofit leaders.[35,36] At the same time, a growing number of able retirees from all sectors will offer the potential for highly valuable service to causes, and the volunteer rate of youth (16 to 24) nearly doubled between 1989 and 2005 and has since held steady.[37,38,39] The increased presence of these two generations as volunteers and employees will create a need for strong intergenerational communication and cooperation, and will lead to new models of "skills-based" volunteerism, which is addressed in detail in the chapters on volunteer management. Finally, the generational transfer of funds that will occur with the death of the Baby Boomer generation will provide the largest transfer of wealth in the history of the nation and holds great potential for gifts to nonprofits in the form of bequests.[40] Successful nonprofits will need to be effective in communicating with and engaging supporters and employees of all ages to remain competitive in the coming decades.

- Global concerns. The population served by nonprofits has been expanding, even as the world appears to be shrinking. In addition to addressing domestic needs, American nonprofit organizations today are attempting to alleviate and solve social needs all over the world. There has been a dramatic growth in concern and effort toward global humanitarian needs. Such issues as climate change, AIDS, poverty, and natural disasters have attracted billions of dollars in funding from American donors and a growing group of international philanthropists.[41] In an increasingly interconnected world, it is imperative that nonprofits understand how their efforts fit into a larger context.

- Communication technologies. Exciting and revolutionary developments in technology offer new and fast-changing opportunities to nonprofits, especially in their efforts to communicate, raise funds, engage volunteers, and increase impact. Technology is enabling new ways to build, share, and use data and knowledge about social needs, while at the same time providing new means to interact, support, network, and collaborate. Nonprofits now have fast, viral, democratic, and ever-improving tools for building community, prompting action, and seeking support from people with shared values, regardless of distance or boundaries. Technology has provided a means for anyone to support disaster relief or other efforts instantly anywhere in the world and has greatly accelerated people's willingness to donate online. To be successful and competitive, nonprofits must learn the power and potential of technology to help an organization achieve its mission. At the same time, today's electronic communication tools allow the formation of loose, temporary networks organized around ideas and initiatives, rather than around existing nonprofit organizations, which means that successful nonprofits will focus on the cause and the audience more than their own needs and agenda.[42,43]

- Cross-sector partnerships. Nonprofit organizations are increasingly working in close relation to other nonprofits, government agencies, for-profits, and networks to accomplish change. Collaborative financing, contracts, commercial arrangements, and other partnerships involving two or more organizations and even sectors are occurring nationwide and globally, often in research, community development, and health care, effectively blurring many traditional boundaries.[44,45] To have the greatest possible impact, nonprofits may need to step outside their organizations and explore opportunities for partnership and alliance.

- Social entrepreneurship. The movement toward social enterprise by nonprofits has been funded largely by business leaders who have sought to adapt business skills to a nonprofit environment. Initially, they wanted to experiment with ways in which nonprofit organizations could both earn income and achieve their missions. This concern with social benefit has now been embraced by some in the for-profit sector as well. Some corporations have embraced "corporate social responsibility" as a way to benefit the community and shareholders alike. In addition, new corporate structures such as the low-profit limited liability corporation (L3C) and the B corporation ("benevolent" corporation) offer innovative ways for the private sector to cause social change.[46] These corporations can receive program-related investments from foundations and other socially minded investors to create businesses that earn a profit but have social benefit as a primary purpose. As individuals, investors, and foundations become more "sector agnostic," nonprofits will find themselves competing with these efforts for funding and employees as they seek ways to work together toward social change.[47,48,49]

- Scrutiny and transparency. High-profile scandals and public questioning of nonprofit effectiveness have led to a decline in public confidence in nonprofits. A 2008 poll found that only 25% of Americans thought that nonprofit groups do a "very good" job, down from 34% in 2003.[50] Several states are challenging the property tax exemptions of hospitals and other nonprofit institutions that compete with and closely resemble for-profits.[51] To respond, nonprofits need to present information and communicate their distinctions and benefits to society more powerfully and proactively. Nonprofit boards of directors will be held to higher and more clearly defined standards of governance and responsibility for progress toward mission.

- Focus on results. Efforts to quantify impact and to identify and replicate successful models will continue to be dominant forces as traditional and venture philanthropists increasingly demand more accountability and clearer measures of nonprofit success.[52] The White House Social Innovation Fund is also seeking to assess nonprofit effectiveness and select good models to multiply.[53] Yet each organization is different and there is little agreement about what gauges are appropriate or useful as measures of organizational potential, mission adherence and fulfillment, and the accomplishment of social change.[54] It is essential that nonprofits find persuasive ways to quantify their goals, progress, and results to those who would support them. Pressure from funders, a harsh financial landscape, and a continuing focus on effectiveness will encourage collaboration within the sector and prompt merger considerations by many nonprofits.[55]

- Earned income. Attention to earned revenue sources as a means to diversify revenue and ensure sustainability will continue, both through conventional means and through the efforts of social entrepreneurs to create new and more effective income-generating mechanisms. The successful pursuit of greater earned revenue while honoring a mission will call for careful decision making and will demand professionalism, efficiency, and competitive expertise.

- Contributed income. Raising funds from individuals, the source of the great majority of donations, has never been more complicated—or more possible. The environment is filled with challenges (donor skepticism, competition to be heard and noticed) and promises (exciting new ways to engage people and to identify, cultivate, solicit, and steward gifts). Nonprofits must commit to steady and constant effort to create, build, and maintain relationships with those who care about and can fund the change they seek to cause through their annual, capital, and planned gifts.

Conclusion

The nonprofit sector in America was born of various traditions and religions and is today a reflection of the evolution of American values and beliefs about duty, community, and social good. Shaped by political, economic, social, religious, environmental, and global forces, the nonprofit sector continues to grow in size and responsibility. As the needs that nonprofits address grow in scale, scope, and complexity, and as their work occurs more in the public eye and in relation to the for-profit and government sectors, demand for skill and impact will grow. If nonprofit leaders are to prompt others to embrace and support their missions and efforts, they will need clear and practical guidance. In the following chapters, experts will inform, share their experience, offer practical advice, and provide direction for further learning and engagement. Our shared goal is to inspire you and equip you for the great work of group action for the common good.

Robert Glavin is a consultant, teacher, public speaker, writer, and volunteer. As president of Robert Glavin, Inc., he counsels nonprofits nationwide in fundraising, governance, and management. He helps clients to plan, increase capacity, raise funds, and execute lasting change. Previously, he was executive director of the San Francisco Shakespeare Festival, director of development and marketing at the California Academy of Sciences, director of development at the University of San Francisco and Georgetown University Medical Center, and legislative representative for the American Hospital Association. He has a bachelor's degree in government from Georgetown and a master's in nonprofit administration from the University of San Francisco, where he teaches graduate courses in fundraising, strategic planning, and governance.

CHAPTER 2

Welcome to the Movement

By Paul Hawken, Author

While so much is going wrong, so much is going right. Over the years the ingenuity of organizations, engineers, designers, social entrepreneurs, and individuals has created a powerful arsenal of alternatives. The financial and technical means are in place to address and restore the needs of the biosphere and society. Poverty, hunger, and preventable childhood diseases can be eliminated in a single generation. Energy use can be reduced 80 percent in developed countries within thirty years with an improvement in the quality of life, and the remaining 20 percent can be replaced by renewable sources. Living-wage jobs can be created for every man and woman who wants one. The toxins and poisons that permeate our daily lives can be completely eliminated through green chemistry. Biological agriculture can increase yields and reduce petroleum-based pollution into soil and water. Green, safe, livable cities are at the fingertips of architects and designers. Inexpensive

This chapter is an excerpt from the author's book *Blessed Unrest: How the Largest Movement in the World Came into Being and Why No One Saw It Coming* (New York: Viking, 2007).

technologies can decrease usage and improve purity so that every person on earth has clean drinking water. So what is stopping us from accomplishing these tasks?

It has been said that we cannot save our planet unless humankind undergoes a widespread spiritual and religious awakening. In other words, fixes won't fix unless we fix our souls as well. So let's ask ourselves this question: Would we recognize a worldwide spiritual awakening if we saw one? Or let me put the question another way: What if there is already in place a large-scale spiritual awakening and we are simply not recognizing it?

In a seminal work, <u>The Great Transformation</u>, Karen Armstrong details the origins of our religious traditions during what is called the Axial Age, a seven-hundred-year period dating from 900 to 200 BCE, during which much of the world turned away from violence, cruelty, and barbarity. The upwelling of philosophy, insight, and intellect from that era lives today in the works of Socrates, Plato, Lao-tzu, Confucius, Mencius, Buddha, Jeremiah, Rabbi Hillel, and others. Rather than establishing doctrinaire religious institutions, these teachers created social movements that addressed human suffering. These movements were later called Buddhism, Hinduism, Confucianism, monotheistic Judaism, democracy, and philosophical rationalism; the second flowering of the Axial Age brought forth Christianity, Islam, and Rabbinical Judaism. The point Armstrong strongly emphasizes is that the early expressions of religiosity during the Axial Age were not theocratic systems requiring belief, but instructional practices requiring action. The arthritic catechisms and rituals that we now accept as religion had no place in the precepts of these sages, prophets, and mystics. Their goal was to foster a compassionate society, and the question of whether there was an omnipotent G-d was irrelevant to how one might lead a moral life. They asked their students to question and challenge and, as opposed to modern religion, to take nothing on faith. They did not proselytize, sell, urge people to succeed, give motivational sermons, or harangue sinners. They urged their followers to change how they behaved in the world. All relied on a common principle, the Golden Rule: Never do to anyone what you would not have done to yourself.[1]

> The Axial sages were not interested in providing their disciples with a little edifying uplift, after which they could return with renewed vigor to their

ordinary self-centered lives. Their objective was to create an entirely different kind of human being. All the sages preached a spirituality of empathy and compassion; they insisted that people must abandon their egotism and greed, their violence and unkindness. Not only was it wrong to kill another human being; you must not even speak a hostile word or make an irritable gesture. Further, nearly all of the Axial sages realized that you could not confine your benevolence to your own people; your concern must somehow extend to the entire world. . . . If people behaved with kindness and generosity to their fellows, they could save the world.[2]

No one in the Axial Age imagined that he was living in an age of spiritual awakening. It was a difficult time, riddled with betrayals, misunderstandings, and petty jealousies. But the philosophy and spirituality of these centuries constituted a movement nevertheless, a movement we can recognize in hindsight. Just as today, the Axial sages lived in a time of war. Their aim was to understand the source of violence, not to combat it. All roads led to self, psyche, thought, and mind. The spiritual practices that evolved were varied, but all concentrated on focusing and guiding the mind with simple precepts and practices whose repetition in daily life would gradually and truly change the heart. Enlightenment was not an end—equanimity, kindness, and compassion were.

These teachings were the original source of charities in the ancient world, and they are the true source of NGOs, volunteerism, trusts, foundations, and faith-based charities in the modern world. I suggest that the contemporary movement is unknowingly returning the favor to the Axial Age, and is collectively forming the basis of an awakening. But it is a very different awakening, because it encompasses a refined understanding of biology, ecology, physiology, quantum physics, and cosmology. Unlike the massive failing of the Axial Age, it sees the feminine as sacred and holy, and it recognizes the wisdom of indigenous peoples all over the world, from Africa to Nunavut.

I have friends who would vigorously protest this assertion, pointing out the small-mindedness, competition, and selfishness of a number of NGOs and the people who lead them. But I am not questioning whether the human condition permeates the movement. It does so, most surely. Clay feet march in all protests. My question is whether the underlying values of the movement are beginning to permeate global society. And there is even a larger issue, the matter of intent. What is the intention of the movement? If you examine its values, missions, goals, and principles, and I urge you to do so, you will see that at the core of all organizations are two principles, albeit unstated: first is the Golden Rule; second is the sacredness of all life, whether it be a creature, child, or culture. The prophets we now enshrine were ridiculed in their day. Amos was constantly in trouble with the authorities. Jeremiah became the root of the word *jeremiad*, which means a recitation of woes, but like Cassandra, he was right. David Suzuki has been prescient for forty years. Donella Meadows was prophetic about biological limits to growth and was scorned by fellow scientists. Bill McKibben has been unwavering and unerring in his cautions about climate change. Martin Luther King was killed one year after he delivered his "Beyond Vietnam" address opposing the Vietnam War and berating the American military for "taking the young black men who have been crippled by our society and sending them 8,000 miles away to guarantee liberties in Southeast Asia which they had not found in southwest Georgia and East Harlem."[3] Jane Goodall travels three hundred days a year on behalf of the earth, speaking, teaching, supporting, and urging others to act. Wangari Maathai was denounced in Parliament, publicly mocked for divorcing her husband, and beaten unconscious for her work on behalf of women and the African environment. It matters not how these six and other leaders will be seen in the future; for now, they are teachers who try or have tried to address the suffering they witness on earth.

I once watched a large demonstration while waiting to meet a friend. Tens of thousands of people carrying a variety of handmade placards strolled down a wide boulevard accompanied by chants, slogans, and song. The signs referred to politicians, different species, prisoners of conscience, corporate campaigns, wars, agriculture, water, workers' rights, dissidents, and more. Standing near me a policeman was trying to understand what appeared to be a political Tower of Babel. The broad-shouldered Irishman shook his head and asked rhetorically, "What do these people want?" Fair question.

There are two kinds of games—games that end, and games that don't. In the first game the rules are fixed and rigid. In the second, the rules change whenever necessary to keep the game going. James Carse called these, respectively, finite and infinite games.[4] We play finite games to compete and win. They always have losers and are called business, banking, war, NBA, Wall Street, and politics. We play infinite games to play: they have no losers because the object of the game is to keep playing. Infinite games pay it forward and fill future coffers. They are called potlatch, family, samba, prayer, culture, tree planting, storytelling, and gospel singing. Sustainability, ensuring the future of life on earth, is an infinite game, the endless expression of generosity on behalf of all. Any action that threatens sustainability can end the game, which is why groups dedicated to keeping the game going assiduously address *any* harmful policy, law, or endeavor. With no invitation, they invade and take charge of the finite games of the world, not to win but to transform finite games into infinite ones. They want to keep the fish game going, so they go after polluters of rivers. They want to keep the culture game going, so they confront oil exploration in Ecuador. They want to keep the hope game alive in the world, so they go after the roots of poverty. They want to keep the species game happening, so they buy swaths of habitat and undeveloped land. They want to keep the child game going; consequently, when the United States violated the Geneva Conventions and bombed the 1,400 Iraqi water and sewage treatment plants in the first Gulf War, creating sewage-, cholera-, and typhus-laden water, they condemned it as morally repugnant. When the same country that dropped the bombs persuaded the United Nations to prevent shipments of chlorine and medicine to treat the resulting diseases, the infinite-game players thought it hideous and traveled to the heart of that darkness to start NGOs to serve the abandoned. People trying to keep the game going are activists, conservationists, biophiles, nuns, immigrants, outsiders, puppeteers, protesters, Christians, biologists, permaculturists, refugees, green architects, doctors without borders, engineers without borders, reformers, healers, poets, environmental educators, organic farmers, Buddhists, rainwater harvesters, meddlers, meditators, mediators, agitators, schoolchildren, ecofeminists, biomimics, Muslims, and social entrepreneurs.[5]

David James Duncan penned a response to the hostile takeover of Christianity by fundamentalists, with advice that applies to all fundamentalisms: the people of the world do not need religious fanatics to save them any more than they need oleaginous free-trade hucksters to do so; they need *us* for their salvation, and *us* stands for the crazy-quilt assemblage of global humanity that is willing to stand up to the raw, cancerous insults that come from the mouths, guns, checkbooks, and policies of ideologues, because the movement is not merely trying to prevent wrongs but actively seeks to love this world. Compassion and love of others are at the heart of all religions, and at the heart of this movement. "When small things are done with love it's not a flawed you or me who does them: it's love. I have no faith in any political party, left, right, or centrist. I have boundless faith in love. In keeping with this faith, the only spiritually responsible way I know to be a citizen, artist, or activist in these strange times is by giving little or no thought to 'great things' such as saving the planet, achieving world peace, or stopping neocon greed. Great things tend to be undoable things. Whereas small things, lovingly done, are always within our reach."[6] Some people think the movement is defined primarily by what it is against, but the language of the movement is first and foremost about keeping the conversation going, because ideas that inform it never end: growth without inequality, wealth without plunder, work without exploitation, a future without fear.[7] To answer the policeman's question, "these people" are reimagining the world.

To salve the world's wounds demands a response from the heart. There is a world of hurt out there, and to heal the past requires apologies, reconciliation, reparation, and forgiveness. A viable future isn't possible until the past is faced objectively and communion is made with our errant history. I suspect that just about everyone owes an apology and merits one, but there are races, cultures, and people that are particularly deserving. The idea that we cannot apologize to former enslaved and first peoples for past iniquities because we are not the ones who perpetuated the evil misses the point. By receiving sorrow, hearing admissions, allowing reparation, and participating in reconciliation, people and tribes whose ancestors were abused give new life to all of us in the world we share. Making amends is the beginning of the healing of the world. These spiritual deeds and acts of moral imagination lay the groundwork for the great work ahead.[8]

The movement is not coercive, but it is relentless and unafraid. It cannot be mollified, pacified, or suppressed. There can be no Berlin Wall moment, no treaty to sign, no morning to awaken to when the superpowers agree to stand down. This is a movement away from the maximization of anything that is not conducive to life. It will continue to take myriad forms. It will not rest. There will be no Marx, Alexander, or Kennedy to lead it. No book can explain it, no person can represent it, no group can stand at its forefront, no words can encompass it, because the movement is the breathing, sentient testament of the living world. The movement is an outgrowth of apostasies and it is now self-generating. The first cells that assembled and metabolized under the most difficult of circumstances deep in the ocean nearly 40 million centuries ago are in our bodies now, and we are, in Mary Oliver's words, determined, as they were then, to save the only life we can.[9] Life can occur only in a cell, and a cell is where all disease starts, as well. In Franklin Harold's book *The Way of the Cell*, he points out that for all its hard-bitten rationalism, molecular science asks us to accept a "real humdinger . . . that all organisms have descended . . . from a single ancestral cell."[10] This quivering, gelatinous sensate mote is the core of everything we cherish, and places us in direct relation to every other form of life. That primordial connection, so incomprehensible to some yet so manifest and sacred and incontestable to others, links us inseparably to our common fate. The first gene was the password to all subsequent forms of life, and the word *gene* has the same etymological root as the words *kin, kind, genus, generous,* and *nature.* It is our nature to cultivate life, and this movement is a collective kindness produced over the course of 4 million millennia.

I believe this movement will prevail. I don't mean it will defeat, conquer, or create harm to someone else. Quite the opposite. I don't tender the claim in an oracular sense. I mean that the thinking that informs the movement's goals will reign. It will soon suffuse most institutions, but before then, it will change a sufficient number of people so as to begin the reversal of centuries of frenzied self-destructive behavior. Some say it is too late, but people never change when they are comfortable. Helen Keller threw aside the gnawing fears of chronic bad news when she declared, "I rejoice to live in such a splendidly disturbing time!" In such a time, history is suspended and thus unfinished. It will be the stroke of midnight for the rest of our lives.

My hopefulness about the resilience of human nature is matched by the gravity of our environmental and social condition. If we squander all our attention on what is wrong, we will miss the prize: In the chaos engulfing the world, a hopeful future resides because the past is disintegrating before us. If that is difficult to believe, take a winter off and calculate what it requires to create a single springtime. It's not too late for the world's largest institutions and corporations to join in saving the planet, but cooperation must be on the planet's terms. The "Help Wanted" signs are everywhere. All people and institutions, including commerce, governments, schools, churches, and cities, need to learn from life and reimagine the world from the bottom up, based on first principles of justice and ecology. Ecological restoration is extraordinarily simple: You remove whatever prevents the system from healing itself. Social restoration is no different. We have the heart, knowledge, money, and sense to optimize our social and ecological fabric. It is time for all that is harmful to leave. One million escorts are here to transform the nightmares of empire and the disgrace of war on people and place. We are the transgressors and we are the forgivers. "We" means all of us, everyone. There can be no green movement unless there is also a black, brown, and copper movement. What is most harmful resides within us, the accumulated wounds of the past, the sorrow, shame, deceit, and ignominy shared by every culture, passed down to every person, as surely as DNA, a history of violence, and greed. There is no question that the environmental movement is critical to our survival. Our house is literally burning, and it is only logical that environmentalists expect the social justice movement to get on the environmental bus. But it is the other way around; the only way we are going to put out the fire is to get on the social justice bus and heal our wounds, because in the end, there is only one bus. Armed with that growing realization, we can address all that is harmful externally. What will guide us is a living intelligence that creates miracles every second, carried forth by a movement with no name.

Paul Hawken has written seven books, including four national bestsellers: The Next Economy, Growing a Business, The Ecology of Commerce, and Blessed Unrest. He coauthored Natural Capitalism: Creating the Next Industrial Revolution with Amory Lovins. His books have been published in over 50 countries in 27 languages. He is currently CEO of OneSun Solar and cofounder of Highwater Global Fund. He has served on the board of several environmental organizations, including Point Foundation (publisher of the Whole Earth Catalogs), Center for Plant Conservation, Trust for Public Land, and the National Audubon Society.

On Leadership in the Nonprofit Sector

By Emmett D. Carson, PhD, CEO and President,
Silicon Valley Community Foundation

Introduction

Leadership matters. Sooner or later most nonprofit leaders learn to accept this uncomfortable truth. I say uncomfortable because before I became a CEO, I underestimated the importance of executive leadership and believed that strong staff members could still be successful even when led by weak leaders. Though such staff may persevere, and on occasion can meet with success, they cannot achieve their best work on a consistent basis without strong leadership at the chief executive level. Since becoming a CEO, and having served on numerous boards, I have come to realize that *executive leadership is perhaps the single most important component for understanding why nonprofits, corporations, and governments succeed or fail in achieving their goals.*

Although leaders at every level of an institution do matter, higher-level leaders—managers, department heads, vice presidents—generally have a disproportionate impact on organizations relative to other staff, and CEOs, presidents, and executive directors in particular play the crucial role of providing vision, determining the culture, helping to set the strategy, and inspiring both internal and external constituents to believe in the vision, mission, and values of the organization. Great leaders can make the impossible happen under the most challenging situations, whereas poor leaders have the uncanny ability to make the easiest things harder, more time-consuming, and infinitely more frustrating for all involved.

Every leadership or "followership" experience can teach you something if you are open to learning from the experience. For individuals to lead, someone must follow. I have had the benefit of serving in a variety of followership roles and have learned equally valuable lessons from both exceptional and mediocre leaders. I have derived leadership lessons throughout my life, whether at church, the Boy Scouts, student council, sports, or professional settings. Over time, seeing what works and what doesn't, whether leading or following, has shaped my views about leadership.

Most of my formal leadership experiences have been in the nonprofit sector, hence my comments will come from that perspective. More than anything, what I have learned is that *success in the nonprofit sector requires unique leadership skills.* Specifically, the nonprofit sector's reliance on board and staff volunteers, the need to raise charitable contributions to fund operations, and a heavy dependence on "knowledge workers" who think for a living, make leadership in this area especially challenging.

Critical Skills and Competencies

What follows are seven lessons about leadership that I have learned and relearned over many years. These lessons are not static and will likely continue to be refined and supplemented as I continue my own leadership journey.

1. Leadership Style Must Match the Circumstances

A lot has been written about leadership style, ranging from charismatic to servant leadership. I have found such notions of leadership to be unduly narrow and limiting. I believe that an effective leader has to examine the situation, context, and audience and select the leadership style that is most appropriate for the situation. Rather than a one-size-fits-all approach, leaders need a toolkit of different skills and abilities to bring to their jobs.

Some situations require the charismatic leader in the face of seemingly insurmountable challenges, whereas other situations require the reflective leader, and still others require the collaborative leader. For example, *when confronted with an unanticipated financial challenge, a leader is best served by expressing unwavering confidence that the organization will weather the storm.* To do otherwise only serves to undermine the confidence of both internal and external stakeholders, to the detriment of the institution.

Knowing when to lead, when to follow, and when to speak first, last, or not at all should be determined by the circumstances and a keen assessment of the people involved and what they need from the leader at a specific point and time.

2. Values Guide Your Leadership

A leader without moral values is the captain of a ship adrift without a rudder. Values are about right and wrong—what you will do and will *not* do. Values are those things that you believe so strongly in that you will resign from the job rather than compromise. Values are about ethics, morals, and core beliefs, which too many leaders of all sectors seem to have either never learned or forgotten. Values inspire staff to do their best and enable external partners to put their trust in the ethics and integrity of the organization. *Values shape the culture of the organization.*

For example, I am aware of a nonprofit organization that held that one of its core values was diversity and inclusiveness as it related to people of color and gays and lesbians. A member of the organization's management team was heard on several occasions making disparaging comments about gays and lesbians. The issue was brought to the CEO's attention several times over the course of a year, and the CEO told the offending staff member to "tone it down." Though this action may have been sufficient to avoid legal repercussions, it was wholly insufficient given the stated organizational culture, values, and norms. *A good leader establishes, follows, and enforces the organization's values and ensures that every employee adheres to them in word and deed.*

By the time the issue reached the attention of the board, morale had reached an all-time low, and the organization required significant time and training to convince staff that this was indeed an important organizational core value, which was affirmed when the offending manager was dismissed.

Another example has to do with a well-known national nonprofit organization that promotes early childhood literacy. The nonprofit promotes reading to children by circulating books through a distinctive, eye-catching book bag. The book bags were purchased from a vendor in China and had to meet very specific manufacturing requirements. Following a rash of reports about lead contamination in children's toys made in China, a concerned staff member asked the executive director (ED) to have the book bags checked. The ED, wanting to ensure the safety of the kids in the program, undertook the expense of having the bags checked and found that the coating used did not meet the quality control standards for lead content.

The board was faced with what, if any, action to take. Not all of the bags failed the test and children could only be harmed if part of the bag was ingested, a highly unlikely occurrence. Moreover, collecting the bags and properly disposing of them would be very expensive and it would take months before new bags could be manufactured and delivered, greatly disrupting the program's operation. After deliberating on the issue, the board unanimously voted to recall *every* book bag. They concluded that the organization should not take the risk that even one child might be harmed. The board's action galvanized support by the local affiliates across the country, who worked diligently to recover and properly dispose of literally thousands of book bags and created workarounds to keep the program operational. The board's courageous decision reaffirmed the organization's core value of enhancing children's lives for all of its internal and external stakeholders.

Eventually, the organization was successful in recouping much of its expenses from the Chinese manufacturer, although this was considered improbable when the board made its decision.

3. Understanding Racism, Sexism, and Ageism

These three "isms" can confront leaders in various ways. I was 33 years old when I was appointed CEO of The Minneapolis Foundation. In many ways, my age was as much and as often a challenge as my race—African American. We don't like to admit it, but people often determine their own self-worth by comparing themselves to others. Working for someone younger can raise questions about an employee's own drive and talent or conversely lead people to question the talent and skills of the leader. Add two of the "isms" together and you really set the stage for problems. In the eyes of an older person, a young person of color or a young woman may not be perceived as qualified for the job and so must have succeeded due to reverse racism or the need to be politically correct.

Even when employees who may have such "isms" accept the qualifications of a leader, it is critically important that the leader remember that this could well be the first time in his employees' careers that they have had to hear "no" in the workplace from a person of color, a woman, or someone younger. Similarly, board members, donors, clients or customers, and institutional partners may have similar reactions that may need to be understood and addressed. Without a doubt, these can be jarring experiences for all involved.

My advice is for the leader to *be self-aware of these issues, assess the extent to which they may be affecting the work and, if so, confront the issues directly and with delicacy.* Once an "ism" starts to affect the leader's role or the workplace dynamic it can no longer be ignored. However, any discussion of racism, sexism, or ageism must be handled with extreme care and sensitivity. These are all issues that can go to the center of what people believe and how they were raised. Moreover, the individual staff member may be completely unaware of how his subconscious attitudes are influencing his behavior. Of course, *any discussion on these topics should focus on observable behavior and actions and not on feelings and perceptions.*

4. Passion Motivates People

People respond positively to passion. When the leader is genuinely excited, believes in the work, and shows his or her excitement, it is infectious. Similarly, when the leader is disinterested in the work, fails to respond in a timely manner or not at all to new ideas or requests for decisions, staff find it hard to keep their own passion for the work. When CEOs lose their passion, it is time for them to either voluntarily move on or for their boards to ask them to leave.

5. Leaders Delegate; Managers Manage

Although delegating and managing are related, I find it useful to think of them in very distinct ways. *Delegating* is giving someone the authority and the resources to make a set of independent decisions to reach an established goal. *Good leaders delegate responsibility and then hold people accountable for the results.* They remain available to help the staff evaluate options and overcome obstacles, but unless they see that staff are about to fall off the mountain, they largely let staff climb the mountain their way.

Managing occurs when someone is tasked with completing an assignment and regular checkpoints and meetings are established, at which the work to date is reviewed and new follow-up tasks and checkpoints are set. In effect, the staff member is responsible for discrete tasks and not the overall outcome. In all but the smallest organizations, *when leaders find themselves managing more than delegating, then either the leader needs a different staff or the staff needs a different leader.*

6. The CEO-Board Relationship Makes or Breaks Your Success

The most critical determinant of a CEO's success is her relationship with the board of directors and the board chair. Because the principle responsibility of the board is to hire and fire the CEO, the leader has a self-interest in preserving and maintaining this relationship. Even if this was not the case, the board and the CEO together are responsible for the vision and direction of the nonprofit organization. Typically, the board's role is to set the vision, hire and fire the CEO, and ensure that proper financial resources are available. The CEO's role is to manage the staff, programs, and operations. To the extent that they have clearly defined their roles and expectations, great things can happen. To the extent that they are not in full agreement on the mission, vision, and approach, both staff and community mission suffer.

Although the titles of chief executive officer (CEO) and executive director (ED) are often used interchangeably, they convey important differences. The CEO title conveys that the individual has *full* authority for the day-to-day operations of the organization, including the hiring and dismissal of staff. CEOs largely interact with the board to get strategic directions and then are responsible for implementing them. Typically, larger nonprofits use the title CEO because their operations require a day-to-day decision maker. In contrast, executive directors do not have the full operational authority for day-to-day decision-making. Depending on the size and/or the age of the nonprofit, the board may retain significant authority over the organization's daily operation in addition to setting the strategic direction. In my opinion, this is *not* a semantic decision or a difference between corporate norms and nonprofit norms. It is important shorthand for explaining how an organization has determined whether daily operational leadership is shared or delegated and it defines roles and responsibilities between the board and management.

The relationship between the CEO and the board chair is especially important. The board chair's role is to serve as spokesperson for the full board. Board chairs must also see their role as reminding the full board of prior discussions and agreements. This ensures continuity, providing accountability and responsibility for the things that go right, as well as for the things that go wrong, which are equally shared by the board and staff leadership. When board chairs change, it is critically important for the CEO to understand that he or she may need to communicate in different ways and with different information to accommodate the learning style and interests of a new board chair.

One way to avoid misunderstanding and miscommunication is for the CEO to *insist on an annual personal and organizational evaluation against stated goals and objectives.* Such a process ensures that the board and the CEO have similar expectations about priorities and goals and that the CEO is provided with feedback against those goals. This is critical to ensuring that the CEO and the board are aligned about the organization's direction and progress.

In a perfect world, the evaluation process begins at the start of the fiscal year with the CEO outlining his or her performance goals for the year. These goals typically include metrics related to each department of the organization, e.g., program, development or fundraising, finance, and so on. In addition, the evaluation should also address special projects, as well as organizational culture and professional development for the CEO and key leaders. These metrics should be reviewed with the board chair and the appropriate board committee, ideally the executive committee if there is one. At the end of the year, the CEO should prepare a candid self-assessment of progress against these goals and others that may have been added during the year. The self-assessment provides important context for the board members and helps highlight any gaps between the CEO's and the board's perception of progress. Once the self-assessment is completed, it should be sent to the full board along with the annual goals. By involving the full board, the organization helps to ensure that board members are engaged in one of their primary duties—evaluating the CEO—and that there is alignment between the CEO and the board about what went well during the year and what went awry. The board chair's role is to summarize the board's feedback and share it with the CEO, and then with the full board along with the CEO's reactions. Afterward, the board chair should discuss any changes to the CEO's compensation with the relevant board committee and bring a recommendation forward to be approved by the full board.

7. Good Leaders Are Good Listeners

While I was growing up, my mother used to say that people were born with two ears and one mouth so that they could listen twice as much as they talk. It is especially important for CEOs to cultivate their listening skills. The nonprofit sector is more likely to have knowledge workers, board members, donors, and volunteers who are essential to achieving successful outcomes and who need to know that their ideas and suggestions have been heard and acknowledged by the leader. Yes, this is the dreaded p-word: process. Listening is especially important for CEOs who are confident, strong willed, or exceptionally smart.

Under the best of circumstances it is difficult for staff or others to express a contrary opinion once the CEO has staked out a position or a point of view.

Encouraging debate and discussion only works when people believe that the CEO will hear them out and honestly consider their ideas. The reality is that *the best CEOs often think through multiple options and scenarios before ever raising an issue for discussion.* Regardless, the CEO must allow others the opportunity and time to collect their ideas and voice their concerns and aspirations.

Finally, do not pretend you are open to input if you are not. When there are lines in the sand that the CEO feels must be drawn around a certain issue, the CEO is obligated to disclose his or her point of view at the outset of the discussion. The worst thing in the world is for staff to spend time and energy thinking that the CEO is open to other points of view, only to be later shut down because the CEO never really was open to the process.

Dos and Don'ts

Nonprofit Leadership Dos and Don'ts

- DO lead consistently with passion and explicitly stated organizational values to inspire those around you.

- DO insist on a comprehensive annual evaluation.

- DO learn equally from outstanding and mediocre leaders.

- DO cultivate the art of active listening.

- DON'T ever surprise your board.

- DON'T avoid confronting the -isms of racism, sexism, and ageism in your organization.

- DON'T confuse delegating with managing.

- DON'T rely on a one-size-fits-all leadership style.

Conclusion

I believe that most leaders are taught by watching others and are made by their own successes and mistakes. Although some leaders are surely born into the role, we can all benefit by seeing leadership as a broad set of skills that can be refined and improved upon. Leadership does matter, perhaps more so today than ever before, as nonprofit organizations confront challenging budgets and increasing competition. Leadership is the edge that will set nonprofit organizations apart and define the winners and losers in fulfilling their dreams for making their communities, our nation, and the world better places.

Emmett D. Carson, PhD is founding CEO and president of Silicon Valley Community Foundation, one of the largest community foundations in the United States. During two decades as a nonprofit leader, Emmett has participated in national and international efforts to develop best practices within the field of philanthropy, and has authored more than a hundred works on philanthropy and social justice. His seminal research on African American giving and volunteering helped to spark broad public interest in ethnic philanthropic studies.

Nonprofit Leadership Resource Review

Frances Hesselbein, Marshall Goldsmith, and Richard Bechard. <u>The Leader of the Future</u>. New York: The Peter F. Drucker Foundation for Nonprofit Management, 1996.

A thought-provoking collection of essays that gets readers up to speed on the most important trends facing today's leaders. It's a one-stop shopping guide that shows how leaders can be successful. Thirty-seven notables, such as Peter Senge, Charles Handy, Rosabeth Kanter, and Stephen Covey, offer their views on leadership, examining what the organization of the future will be like and how leaders might be developed.

Patrick Lencioni. <u>The Five Temptations of a CEO</u>. San Francisco: Jossey-Bass, 1998.

This is the story of Andrew, a CEO with five issues blocking his leadership from its fullest vision of success: putting self first, wanting to be liked rather than to lead, making decisions reluctantly, elevating harmony above productive argument, and not trusting subordinates.

Pat Kaufman and Cindy Wetmore. <u>Brass Tacks Manager</u>. New York: Doubleday, 1994.

Provides a practical pocket guide to success that pares business advice to the essential core—a bulleted list of salient points for more than seventy alphabetized topics, from "Assertiveness" to "Performance Appraisals" to "Unions."

Brian O'Connell. The Board Member's Book. New York: The Foundation Center, 1985.

Dennis R. Young, Robert M. Hollister, Virginia A. Hodgkinson, and Associates. Governing, Leading and Managing Nonprofit Organizations. San Francisco: Jossey-Bass, 1993.

William G. Bowen. Inside the Boardroom: Governance by Directors and Trustees. New York: Wiley, 1994.

Based on a five-year study, this book goes behind the scenes to reveal the inner workings of boards of directors, candid interviews with directors, and a comprehensive investigation into boardroom processes. It challenges the status quo thinking on corporate governance and provides ground-breaking prescriptions for building better boards.

James M. Kouzes and Barry Z. Posner. The Leadership Challenge. San Francisco: Jossey-Bass, 2007.

Drawing on interviews and a questionnaire survey of more than 3,000 leaders, the authors identify five fundamental practices of exemplary leadership: challenge the status quo; inspire a shared vision; enable others to act; model the way forward by setting an example; tap individuals' inner drives by linking rewards and performance. Kouzes, chairman and CEO of TPG/Learning Systems, and Posner, managing partner of Santa Clara University's Executive Development Center in California, write insightful, down-to-earth, jargon-free prose. This new edition has been substantially updated to reflect the challenges of shrinking work forces, rising cynicism and expanded telecommunications.

Ronald A Heifitz and Marty Linsky. Leadership on the Line. Boston: Harvard Business Press, 2002.

Recognizing that it can be both lonely and difficult at the top, the faculty members of Harvard University's Kennedy School of Government set out to lend emotional and practical support. Whether leaders represent a local planning board or a Fortune 500 company, they "live dangerously," say the authors, "because when leadership counts, when you lead people through difficult change, you challenge what people hold dear their daily habits, tools, loyalties, and ways of thinking with nothing more to offer perhaps than a possibility."

Seth Godin. Tribes. New York: Penguin Group, 2008.

Smart innovators find or assemble a movement of similarly minded individuals and get the tribe excited by a new product, service or message, often via the Internet (consider, for example, the popularity of the Obama campaign, Facebook, or Twitter). Tribes can be within or outside a corporation, and almost everyone can be a leader; most are kept from realizing their potential by fear of criticism and fear of being wrong.

o o o

All these resources, plus nonprofit management tips of the week and more, can be found at Nonprofits101.org.

CHAPTER 4

Taking Charge of Your Nonprofit Sector Career

By Kimberly Hendler, Managing Director of Talent, iMentor, and Shelly Cryer, Communications Consultant to Nonprofits

Introduction

You may already be working in the nonprofit sector and know that it's where you want to spend your career. Or, you might have turned—or returned—to the nonprofit sector after developing skills and experiences in government or business. Regardless, you are committed to having work with meaning. You aspire to or already enjoy a senior leadership position at a nonprofit organization. And you want a career that gives you the fulfillment, sustenance, and financial security you need. You can find this in the nonprofit sector, but it requires direction and determination to get there.

In this chapter, we discuss the diversity of opportunities within the sector and the implications that this has for you and your career. We present why and how to build skills, experiences, and networks in order to become an effective nonprofit leader. We address the nuts-and-bolts of job hunting and strategies to land a position that is right for you. And we provide a few examples of good resources for the nonprofit career builder. Throughout the chapter, we discuss how to ensure that the decisions you make lead to a fulfilling and sustainable career.

Your commitment to the nonprofit sector demonstrates that you have heard the "call to serve." Today's nonprofit leaders—hungry for talented and committed individuals to whom they can entrust their organizations—are glad you have heeded that call. We hope that this chapter will help you become one of tomorrow's most effective leaders.

Leadership Development in a Diverse Sector

The 1.6 million organizations that comprise this country's nonprofit sector[1] vary widely in their mission and approach, size, and culture.

There are as many different organizational missions as there are human needs in our society. Nonprofits engage in everything from running local libraries to providing food during a natural disaster. Organizations also vary in the way they approach their work—the strategies they use to advance their goals.

Another difference is the size of an organization. This affects how jobs are organized and the responsibilities that staff members have. It also informs both what the organization expects of its leaders and what employees can expect of leadership opportunities. In the smallest nonprofits, a single person handles all responsibilities (probably with help from volunteers, and while working closely with board members). In larger organizations, job functions can be organized in countless ways. Leadership responsibilities are apt to be spread out among numerous senior staff members concentrating on specific areas. And interaction with the board may be limited to only the very top-tier staffers.

The variety of nonprofit organizations and diversity of roles have exciting implications for your career. Just as there are no cookie-cutter jobs or organizations in the nonprofit sector, there is no single career path. How you approach your career—and the path you follow to achieve your leadership goals—is up to you.

But the freedom this diversity offers also brings with it great complexity. Because there are no clear "sign posts" to navigate your career path, you have to do more research, have better direction, and make deeper connections than your peers in government or business. Two of the best ways to tackle the diversity of organizations and opportunities in the nonprofit sector are, first, to truly know who you are and what you want; and, second, to network.

Critical Skills and Competencies

Let's dive into some of the most useful skills, tactics, and techniques for getting to know yourself and what drives you. We'll also explore the power of networks, explain nonprofit career paths, and help you position yourself for success. Finally, we'll offer a few comments on universal skills in the sector and some tips for building a sustainable career.

Part I: Know Who You Are

The first (and ongoing) step in advancing your nonprofit career and becoming an effective leader is to *know yourself, your interests, and your skills as well as possible.* You can't achieve your goals if you don't know what they are. Even if you contemplated these when first making your entry into the sector, *it's imperative to reflect continuously on what "makes your heart sing."* Ask yourself a few key questions about who you are, what you need, and what you want.

What Issues Do You Care About?

- What policies and practices are you most passionate about?

- What are the news items you are drawn to?

- What programs and which leaders inspire you most?

What Skills Do You Possess?

- What type of work and roles do you most enjoy?

- What tasks do you relish in doing on a daily basis?

- What have others said you are particularly good at?

Where Do You Want to Live and How Do You Want to Work?

- Is the work you want to do specific to a geographic region?

- In what kind of organization—approach, size, and culture—do you thrive?

- What kind of people do you want to work alongside?

- What are your salary requirements? What other benefits are critical for you?

Take the time to *establish which aspects of your work life should have priority.* Some people might prioritize the cause they work on; others might rank the skills they use as key. You might only want to live in a given city or only be able to accept a certain minimum salary. Remember, *you do not have to have every answer; you just need to know your current priorities and then refine them throughout your career.*

Next, *test your interests against reality.* Figure out where the situation you are looking for exists and what it takes to get there. Use research and networking to learn more about prospective organizations and positions.

Note which organizations are working on the issues that most interest you. Establish what positions tap your skills, experiences, and career goals. Make sure these job functions reflect the actual day-to-day work you want to do (consider, for example, whether you really want all of the responsibilities associated with being an executive director).

Search for organizations with missions and programs that interest you and leverage your network to learn more about them. Participate in conferences and events sponsored by your local nonprofit support center. Even though you're already working in the sector, you also may want to browse job sites to identify positions that speak to you and note the experience and skills they require. Again, *the process of self-discovery is not a destination, but an ongoing journey.*

Keep in mind that rarely does one job have it all. You're looking for your next best position, with an eye toward your longer-term leadership goals. And while your goals may shift over time, you need direction.

Determining what you want to do is a lifelong and often difficult quest for many people. But at a certain point, you need to make decisions, concentrate on a specific career objective, and act. The bottom line? Knowledge is power.

The more you know about issues, organizations, and jobs—through research, networking, and volunteer and paid work—the better equipped you will be to build a meaningful career.

Part II: Know Others (AKA "The Power of Networks")

Yes, knowing yourself is important, but so is knowing others. Networks play a vital role in navigating the array of possible organizations, roles, and paths available to a nonprofit professional. Networking also keeps you up to date on developments in your field. The best networks provide connections to leaders in your field who care about your success, and can help you achieve it. They offer feedback on your work, advice on career paths, and connections to organizations and jobs. As you advance, your networks will also connect you to key decision makers in hiring new leaders.

Networking is vital for nonprofit professionals, especially as you reach more senior positions. Sector leaders, especially those at organizations with no human resources department, want candidates who come recommended by someone they trust. They consider their staff a "family" and weigh whether a candidate will fit into their culture. Someone making calls on your behalf gives your application—and career—a tremendous boost.

Networking is essential in every phase of your career, and you'll see it as a component of every aspect of this chapter. At the end of the chapter, you will find some practical networking dos and don'ts.

To network successfully, you need to be willing to ask for an expert's time and believe you're worthy of it. Nonprofit professionals are passionate about their work. They're busy, but most enjoy reflecting on their careers and organizations. They get recharged if they determine they're in the presence of a future leader. If you're a savvy and professional networker, you'll make your contacts feel good about time they spend with you.

Nonprofit Career Paths: Ladders, Monkey Bars, and Lattices

The nonprofit sector offers few established career paths. This means *you have to be your own career strategist*, and think carefully and act intentionally as you advance your career.

Will you move up a career "ladder," staying in the same field and type of work, but gaining more responsibility? For example, will you move from program coordinator to program manager, staying within the same organization and assuming new management responsibilities? This is often easier at larger organizations with many staff members and more frequent vacancies. If you are seeking a more senior role as quickly as possible, this is your best bet.

Will you move across "monkey bars," maintaining similar responsibilities and level but at a different organization? For example, will you move from a grant-writing position at one nonprofit to a general fundraising associate position at another? This is often necessary in the nonprofit sector, which is comprised mostly of small and mid-sized organizations with small staffs and low turnover. This is a great strategy if you are trying to move from an organization with no opportunities for upward mobility to one with more senior positions.

Will you move as if on a "lattice," moving up, down, and across organizations in order to gain knowledge in a new issue area or skills in a new job function? For example, will you go from serving as an advocacy director at a larger organization, to an executive director at a smaller organization, and then to an associate director at a mid-sized group? Although it might seem untraditional, it might be the appropriate path for the skills and experiences you want to develop. This approach might work best if you are interested in trying out a variety of roles and organizations and is often your only choice when you prioritize other life factors such as location, salary, or flexibility.

Whatever path you decide to take to build the career you want, you must be intentional about your choices. Once you have determined your interests, the kind of work you like, and the types of organizations you want to work for, it's time to evaluate whether your current position is helping you become the leader you envision.

When is it time to make a change? Ask yourself:

- Are you learning and do you still have opportunities for professional growth in your current role?

- Do you feel supported by your manager, energized by your colleagues, and proud of your organization?

- Are you being compensated appropriately, given the size of the organization, its financial health, where it is based, and the work you are doing? Review job boards, IRS Form 990s, and salary surveys to determine if your pay is competitive. If necessary, use these resources to demonstrate why a salary increase is right for your organization.

- Do you still find the mission, vision, and approach of the organization you work for compelling?

- Is there another position or added responsibilities you could take on or create at your current employer?

- Have you made a contribution you are proud of? Have you demonstrated reasonable commitment to your current employer and built a record of stability to future employers?

- Do you have a good quality of life?

Sometimes it makes sense to try to get more from your current job and employer. If you're a respected member of the team, you may be surprised by your ability to negotiate for more responsibility, a higher salary, or a different position. Other times, you may have exhausted the opportunities available at your organization and know you are ready for a move. Ideally you will have built a network and developed yourself so you are perfectly positioned to climb up the ladder or across the monkey bars or lattice.

Developing Yourself Personally and Professionally

Regardless of where you are in your career—whether you have a position you are happy with, are job seeking, or are ready to make a move—you should always be developing yourself. Gaining experience and building knowledge is a lifelong undertaking. Use your research skills, your network, and what you know about yourself and your career goals to identify opportunities that help you fill holes in your résumé, develop needed skills, and advance your career. Be proactive in building and leveraging your network to access these opportunities.

Four ways to develop yourself personally and professionally are to (1) assume additional responsibilities in your current role; (2) learn by reading and research; (3) pursue volunteer and freelance opportunities; and (4) apply for leadership and professional development programs, work with a professional coach, or join a peer support group.

1. Assume additional responsibilities in your current role

   ○ Share your interests with your supervisor and colleagues and ask for guidance.

   ○ Suggest how you might support current and new projects.

   ○ Ask to shadow a colleague who has skills you want to learn.

   ○ Find a mentor or be a mentor. Learn from someone more experienced and from teaching someone.

   ○ Become a spokesperson on your issues. Prepare a speaker's bio, submit conference session ideas, teach classes at your local college, start a blog, or write opinion pieces and letters to the editor.

2. Learn more by reading and research

   ○ Follow the experts in your field on blogs and Twitter, at conferences, and through research. Monitor the news and information posted on relevant websites.

   ○ Stay apprised of developments in your area of interest by reading current books and journal articles. Share what you learn with others and thereby establish yourself as an expert.

   ○ Participate actively and pursue leadership appointments in relevant trade associations and coalitions.

3. Pursue volunteer and freelance opportunities

   ○ Join a nonprofit board to help direct an organization while honing your leadership, strategic planning, and finance skills.

   ○ Volunteer to apply existing skills and develop new ones, and to meet other organizations, board members, and nonprofit professionals.

   ○ If appropriate, take on consulting or part-time work that leverages your skills and keeps you visible in the field.

4. Apply for leadership and professional development programs, work with a professional coach, or join a peer support group

   ○ Learn about leadership programs available in your community and within your discipline, especially those pursued by leaders in your field.

   ○ Enroll in trainings and continuing education classes to fill gaps in your skills or knowledge. Attend relevant workshops, conferences, and webinars.

   ○ Consider graduate school or certificate programs. Carefully review prospective programs and make sure they offer credentials appropriate for you and your goals.

   ○ Explore the services of a professional coach to help you achieve your career objectives.

   ○ Ask your employer for professional development funds to offset the costs of these programs.

   ○ Find groups that can offer professional support and networking opportunities.

Opportunities for personal and professional development are endless, but hours in your day are not. Prioritize activities that will bring you pleasure *and* help you professionally. Make strategic use of your free time and be sure you don't overschedule or diminish your quality of life.

A Note on "Universal" Nonprofit Sector Skills

Certain skills and experiences are critical for every nonprofit leader, regardless of their specific work. Some "universal" nonprofit sector leadership skills include:

- Fundraising. Being able to raise funds and build a financially sound organization is increasingly vital as competition for resources mounts.

- Communications. Strong written and verbal communications are critical, but remember that the best communicators are also great listeners.

- Financial management. "Nonprofit" is a misnomer, and the sector's leaders must know how to budget, manage, and account for funds.

- <u>Strategic planning</u>. Great leaders are both visionary and practical. You must know and be able to articulate what you want your organization to achieve, and provide a plan to get there.

- <u>Identifying talent</u>. Great leaders surround themselves with strength. Learn how to hire great people, cultivate them, and effectively delegate responsibilities.

- <u>Political savvy and confidence</u>. Nonprofit leaders understand their environment and the field's key partners. You must know when to toe the party line, when to be assertive, when to collaborate, and when to stand alone.

- <u>Blending personal humility with professional will</u>. As Jim Collins notes, nonprofit leaders put their issue, organization, and the work first . . . not themselves.[2]

If you don't have these skills well developed, gain them. And pay special attention to fundraising. Even the strongest nonprofits want staff members who can think strategically about how their work intersects with fundraising, as every organization has to raise resources to do its work. Volunteer to work on a foundation or government grant proposal. Add a fundraising course or certificate to your résumé (check out AFP, The Foundation Center, or your local nonprofit support center). And secure a board position to learn volumes about fiscal oversight.

Building a Sustainable Career

Nonprofits are known for doing more in less time and with fewer resources than any other type of organization. The sector relies on the often Herculean efforts and passionate dedication of those who work in it. Nonprofit professionals tend to go beyond the 9-to-5 work day and the stated parameters of their job descriptions. They may also accept lower pay than business or government counterparts. Regardless of how you're paid or how hard you work, it's important that you build a career that is fulfilling and sustainable. You need to *figure out the combination of mission, workload, salary, pace, culture, and stress that works for you.*

The organization you work for must be a good fit in terms of mission, strategies, and culture. If you decide to engage once again in job hunting, always *remember that the organization isn't just interviewing you; you are interviewing it, too.* By asking questions in interviews, observing the environment, and speaking with people familiar with the organization, you can learn about its culture, the stated and unstated expectations of staff, its pace, its stressors (for example, financial challenges or recent program cuts), and the investment it makes in its employees. What you learn will help you determine if you'll be happy working there.

In addition to working at an organization that's right for you, another way to make your career sustainable is ongoing learning. Take time outside of your daily responsibilities to keep up on news, attend conferences, and network with your peers. Make space for reflection in your professional and personal life.

Finally, *if you start feelings the "pangs" of burnout, pause and reflect.* What can you do to mitigate the stress involved with working on issues you care passionately about? Some tips on combating burnout include:

- Work for organizations committed to sustainable schedules and workloads.

- Talk with your manager at the first signs of burnout and strategize solutions.

- Set boundaries that help you to preserve your personal time. Recognize that, in the end, you control your life, how you work, and the environment you create for yourself.

- Pursue hobbies and relationships outside of work. Schedule classes or dates that force you to leave work by a reasonable hour.

- Keep honing your time-management skills and take responsibility for working efficiently and effectively.

- Build a network of people who will look out for you professionally, provide perspective, and offer a hand if you get overwhelmed.

- Use your vacation, preserve weekends, and take time off between jobs. At the appropriate time, plan a sabbatical. If you are sick, take sick days.

The best organizations will respect and honor staff members who take care of themselves. They recognize that a happy worker is an effective worker. *Be good to yourself and your career will thank you, as will the people you serve.*

Dos and Don'ts

Networking Dos and Don'ts

- DO cast a wide net and create as large a network as possible. Who do you know? How can they help you connect to people and organizations you want to know?

- DO articulate what you care about with passion and clarity. Be able to articulate a compelling story about what you've done and what you want to do. Show commitment to mission.

- DO your research. Learn about individuals and organizations before a meeting. Prepare appropriate questions and comments.

- DO follow up promptly on every lead. If someone makes a connection for you, act on it immediately. Continue to update the person who gave you the lead on your efforts. Prompt follow-up displays professionalism, diligence, and other traits needed for leadership success.

- DO thank people for their help. Send out professional, personalized thank you letters after any phone call or meeting. Find reasons to stay in touch with people who have helped you, since you want them to always have you in mind when they hear about new opportunities, even if you're not in the process of searching for a job.

- DON'T use email to ask for advice. Use email to set up calls or meetings and ask specific follow-up questions. Ask for advice during in-person meetings or scheduled telephone calls.

- DON'T expect your contact to guide the conversation or relationship. Be the "host," ask questions, and lead the conversation.

- DON'T be overly modest. Informational meetings and interviews are the time to articulate your strengths and experiences. Sell yourself (but still ask questions and make it a dialogue).

- DON'T ask for a job in an informational interview. Focus on learning about the organization and any suggestions for other people and resources to leverage. (Of course, if someone mentions an open position during a conversation, explore it as fully as appropriate.)

Conclusion

Developing a meaningful career in the nonprofit sector takes perseverance and dedication. We hope this chapter provides valuable advice, resources, and career-building strategies to help you become the nonprofit leader you want to be. But only you can apply the information so that it benefits your life and advances your career goals.

Pay attention to your career. Focus on activities that will help you become the nonprofit professional you dream of being. Be deliberate but flexible in your actions. Solicit advice and heed the best of it. Set yourself up so that you have the time to make good decisions. Visualize success.

Be true to your own personality and style, but if you are reserved, push yourself to be as extroverted as possible in your career-building efforts, even if it doesn't come naturally to you. Humility is a virtue, but false modesty serves no one, and certainly not your career aspirations.

Be discriminating in your job search and committed to finding stellar jobs. When job hunting, end the search process being able to tell yourself you did everything possible to land the best job for you. And then go on to do everything in your power to make your new career step as interesting and rewarding as possible.

And above all, have fun. Build a career where you find joy in your work, feel good about the organization and mission you are contributing to, and are inspired by your colleagues.

Kim Hendler is the managing director of talent at iMentor, an organization dedicated to improving the lives of young people from underserved communities through technology-based approaches to mentoring. Prior to working at iMentor, Kim was executive director of Princeton Project 55 where she oversaw initiatives to engage university alumni and recent graduates in public interest work. Kim also worked at El Pomar Foundation where she participated in a nonprofit leadership development fellowship program while supporting grant making and operating programs. Kim was a member of the Young Nonprofit Professionals Network's national board from 2007 to 2010 and served as vice chair from 2008 to 2010.

Shelly Cryer is the author of <u>The Nonprofit Career Guide: How to Land a Job</u>
<u>That Makes a Difference</u> *(Turner Publishing; www.nonprofitcareerguide.org/)*
and founder of the Initiative for Nonprofit Sector Careers and Nonprofit Sector
Workforce Coalition (housed at Nonprofit Leadership Alliance). Shelly works as a
communications consultant to nonprofits. She has taught courses on the media and
nonprofits at Columbia University and The City University. She received an MIA
from Columbia University's School of International and Public Affairs (SIPA) and a
BA from Duke. She and her husband, Michael Stern, a conductor, have two
daughters and live in Connecticut.

Key Career-Building Resources

Everyone's career-building journey requires personalized, targeted research
and knowledge. The resources listed below are just ten examples of many
that might prove useful to an emerging nonprofit sector leader.

○ ○ ○

Alliance for Nonprofit Management (www.allianceonline.org)

The Alliance provides nonprofit-related learning opportunities through its
network of individuals and organizations, and offers connections to local
nonprofit support centers (also known as management support
organizations, or MSOs) which host and promote many nonprofit
professional development opportunities.

Bridgestar (www.bridgestar.org)

Bridgestar provides a nonprofit management job board, content, and tools
designed to help nonprofit organizations build strong leadership teams and
individuals pursue career paths as nonprofit leaders. It's focused on the
more senior nonprofit professional and leaders transitioning into the
nonprofit sector.

The Chronicle of Philanthropy (www.philanthropy.com)

The Chronicle is a must-read publication for leaders in the nonprofit sector,
but be sure to stay up-to-date with your daily newspaper and key news
outlets for your issue area.

GuideStar (www.guidestar.org)

GuideStar gathers and publicizes information about nonprofit
organizations. A nonprofit's IRS Form 990 (which you can access here)
provides useful information about an organization's budget, programs,
and salaries.

Idealist/Action Without Borders (www.idealist.org)

Idealist is the most widely known nonprofit job board and also a hub for
career resources, including *The Idealist Guide to Nonprofit Careers*. It's geared
towards entry- and mid-level positions. There are many other nonprofit job
sites worth checking out, such as CommonGood Careers
(www.cgcareers.org) and Jobs for Change (www.jobs.change.org).

James P. Shannon Leadership Institute (www.wilder.org/shannon.0.html)

The Shannon Institute offers a leadership development programs targeted to
nonprofit sector professionals. Be sure to explore professional development
and other continuing education opportunities at your local college,
including cross-sector programs that might be housed at a business school,
for example.

National Council of Nonprofits (www.councilofnonprofits.org)

The Council is a resource for nonprofit sector information, as well as a
network of state and regional nonprofit associations that provide programs
and resources in a given area. Be sure to check out other nonprofit umbrella
organizations such as Independent Sector (www.independentsector.org).

The Nonprofit Career Guide: How to Land a Job That Makes a Difference
(www.nonprofitcareerguide.org)

Written by one of the authors of this chapter, this career guide is one
resource for the nonprofit career builder.

List of nonprofit management education programs (www.academic.shu.edu/
npo/)

Roseanne Mirabella of Seton Hall University created an online master
listing—both alphabetical and by state—of all colleges and universities with
nonprofit management courses. She provides links to the summary pages

for all colleges and universities that detail information about their programs, including a listing of all nonprofit management courses offered.

Young Nonprofit Professionals Network (www.ynpn.org)

YNPN is a nonprofit-focused professional development network geared toward younger emerging leaders. Another one is Emerging Practitioners in Philanthropy (ePIP).

∘ ∘ ∘

All these resources, plus nonprofit management tips of the week and more, can be found at Nonprofits101.org.

Part Two

Managing Organizations and People

Be bold, and mighty forces will come to your aid.

—Goethe

Now that we've covered the historical and modern-day context for the role of the nonprofit sector in society, sector leadership, and tips on advancing your career, let's get down to brass tacks. The next part of the book speaks directly to overcoming the challenges and opportunities associated with managing organizations and people. We'll look at some strategies that prove useful when starting *anything*, and dive deeper into strategic planning and collaboration. We will then transition into the core operational needs of an organization, starting with insurance and risk management, and then moving on to human resources and special considerations around diversity.

Before we get started, I wanted to highlight a few concepts that have proven useful to me as a nonprofit leader. First off, although strategy and vision are integral to the success of any effort, let us remember that the *operational and infrastructural supports serve as the ball bearings that make success and growth possible.* You simply can't have one without the other if you are looking to be effective, but there's a fine line between systems and bureaucracy. That said, a bold vision that speaks to a pressing need or opportunity is absolutely the starting point of any worthy initiative. A compelling vision inspires, generating funds and attracting partners and other support in the process. Unfortunately, nonprofit leaders frequently don't take the time to map out what achieving the vision would actually look like, to "dream your dreams with open eyes, and make them come true," as T. E. Lawrence once said. In the business sector, they talk about "key performance indicators," or KPIs. We would do well to follow suit and put quantifiable benchmarks in place to monitor our performance as we go about our work—see Chapter Five authored by Jeanne Bell for more information.

B to the Y

As we talk about the power of a bold vision and of an inspiring visionary, let us consider: *what is the difference between a dreamer and a visionary?* I believe visionaries are dreamers, but with a substantial, added edge. Both can see A to Z, where A is the world as it stands today, rife with its problems and injustices, and Z is the utopian dream of tomorrow, the sustainable, prosperous Brotherhood of Man that we all long for. But the difference, the difference is that *the visionary can see the B to the Y.* These represent the steps between A and Z—the processes, people, and partnerships that serve as stepping-stones on our path toward achieving the dream. It is the ability to proactively plan for and strategize around the B to the Y that differentiate the visionary, and that makes systemic change possible.

Paint the Picture

Speaking of possibility, I think it's important to mention that one of the most important components of a compelling vision is *what it is*, not what it's not. I know, this sounds confusing, but let me put it this way: what did Dr. Martin Luther King Jr. *not* say? He didn't say, "I have a nightmare." He did not say, "I have a complaint." The man said he had a *dream*, and he painted a picture so beautifully, clearly, and compellingly that everyone could see herself in it. After all, who *doesn't* want to live in a world where their children are "not judged by the color of their skin, but by the content of their character"; a world where "injustice anywhere is perceived as a threat to justice everywhere"?

This is what I mean by *paint the picture.* Let me also speak briefly on the importance of *strike the root, do less, and it starts with staff.*

Strike the Root

Henry David Thoreau once observed, *"thousands hack at the branches of evil for each one that strikes at the root."* As we move forward in a life dedicated to service, we must all consider how we can *maximize leverage to optimize impact.* Are we hacking at the branches, or striking at the root of the problem we seek to solve? Are we approaching our work from a symptomatic or a systemic perspective, giving the man a fish to feed him for the day, or teaching him to fish so he can provide his own livelihood? By all means, I appreciate the value and necessity of soup kitchens and homeless shelters, but let us always remember Dr. King's insight, "True compassion is more than flinging a coin to a beggar; it comes to see that *an edifice which produces beggars needs restructuring."*

As we consider how to channel our efforts to maximize change, I find myself often playing with the imagery of tipping over dominoes, setting wheels in motion, and pushing a little snowball off the top of a white-capped peak. At some point, though, you can go so far upstream that you lose your sense of connection to the community that you serve, and holding onto that connection is the source of our passion—the fuel that allows us to carry on. *Never allow yourself to get so caught up in "doing the most good"[1] possible that you find yourself disconnected from your service.* Find your own sweet spot, and pursue it with zeal. Don't worry, there are other do-gooders out there who will fill in the gaps.

Do Less

Ah, the gaps. There are oh so many of those in the community, aren't there? That brings me to my final insight on the nature of a compelling vision and its pursuit: *do less.* The problem is that we're all compassionate people—the fact that we are in this line of work testifies to that. At the same time, there's no shortage of problems in the world. But *when we run around chasing every opportunity to make things better, we dilute our efforts and ultimately undermine our impact.* That is exactly why having a razor-sharp focus and being able to speak concretely about why your organization needs to exist, how the world will look once you achieve your objective, *and* what you're doing to move things forward (your mission, vision, and programs, respectively) is so crucial to the success of your work. In design, they say "less is more," and so, too, is this true in the wonderful world of service.

It Starts with Staff

Finally, let me say a quick word about people. *The staff of an organization is the linchpin of its work.* Although you may have great partners and an engaged board, the people conducting your day-to-day activities represent how your organization lives in the real, everyday world. If they're not the right people, or they're not properly inspired and motivated, then you're sunk, and so is your cause. That is why although human resource issues tend to fall into that "important, but not urgent" Franklin Covey quadrant, they need to be at the top of the agenda of any nonprofit professional. *Interviews for staff additions at all levels merit direct participation by top brass,* and ensuring that your staff and board reflect the diversity of the community you serve is key in establishing your legitimacy and relevance. At the same time, with 78 million Baby Boomers retiring and only 38 million Gen Xers to replace them, looking at ways to engage Boomers while developing younger leaders also deserves a prime-time spot in the lineup of any organization.

B to the Y, paint the picture, strike the root, do less, and start with staff. To the extent you are able to put these concepts to work in crafting and pursuing a compelling vision, and you have a strategy mapped out to achieve your goals, all supported by a strong team to drive your efforts, you are already well along the way to making a huge impact in the community, and on the cause.

CHAPTER 5

Strategy and Planning: Turning a Dream into Reality

By Jeanne Bell, MNA, CEO, CompassPoint Nonprofit Services

Introduction

Nonprofits develop strategic plans to clarify or update their reason for being—or mission—and to commit to a set of coordinated activities that will best accomplish that mission. In his book <u>The Nonprofit Strategy Revolution</u>, planning consultant David La Piana defines a strategy as "an organized pattern of behavior toward an end" (p. 4). *In creating strategic plans, nonprofit leaders are determining which set of strategies are key to the impact they want to achieve in their communities.* The benefits of strategic planning, when done well, include providing direction and focus to staff and board efforts; developing language to describe the organization's current community goals and impact, which is essential to effective marketing and fundraising; and making key adjustments to the financial assumptions and plans that will make implementation of the chosen strategies financially viable. Yet many strategic plans sit on a shelf collecting dust after months of hard work is invested in them; *the most useful plans guide both strategy and execution*, providing coordinated vision and bolstering a nonprofit's ability to achieve impact.

For instance, the founders of an education nonprofit have a vision of a United States where every child, regardless of family socioeconomic status, graduates from high school. The organization's leadership acknowledged that they cannot achieve that vision alone; indeed, a myriad of public and private efforts are needed for that outcome to be achieved. Thus, they determined their organization's mission as a critical piece of realizing that vision: "To increase the high school readiness of low-income junior high students through rigorous summer school programming." The "program strategy," or a specific means of achieving that stated objective, that the organization selected to achieve that mission was to: "Develop and maintain strong partnerships with inner city junior high school counselors to identify target students for program enrollment." Their plan then went on to detail how *exactly* the organization was to go about achieving this, providing a time line, communication templates, and an outreach and relationship management strategy. The documentation of this vision, mission, and these strategies is typically called the organization's *strategic plan*.

What Strategic Planning Looks Like

Strategic planning is traditionally done and redone at regular interludes, every three or five years, for instance. The assumption is that each change in the operating environment—be it a new client population, new public policies, or shifts in funding availability—requires a reexamination of current strategies and the potential for new ones. *Strategic planning processes generally take 3–9 months*, depending on the complexity of the organization and the amount of analysis undertaken, and include both staff and board members. They are also often facilitated by a planning consultant, though they do not need to be. The board is involved both as key representatives of the community and its needs, and also as a means to fulfill the primary board responsibility of setting strategic direction. It is standard practice for the board to officially adopt the strategic plan once it is complete. Consultants may be used to organize the various phases of the process, to interview outside stakeholders with objectivity, to allow staff and board to fully participate in rather than manage the process, and to add value based on their planning experience with other nonprofits. Once complete, strategic plans are theoretically used internally to guide decision making throughout the years of the plan's identified shelf life. *These plans are also frequently used externally—with funders who want to understand a nonprofit's strategic direction before they invest, as well as in the recruitment of new staff, board members, and organizational partners.*

There are many guides to and models for strategic planning. Most are variations on the aforementioned standard of setting vision, committing to a mission, and determining the nonprofit's priority strategies and their financing. In <u>Strategic Planning for Nonprofit Organizations</u>, planning consultants Mike Allison and Jude Kaye identify seven phases in the process:

- Phase one, *Get Ready*: Identify the reasons for planning and establish a work plan for the process.

- Phase two, *Articulate Mission, Vision, and Values*: Create a mission statement a vision statement, and an articulation of organizational values.

- Phase three, *Assess Your Situation*: Conduct a deep review of accomplishments and strategies to date, and review evaluation and other feedback data from key stakeholders.

- Phase four, *Agree on Priorities*: Assess current activities—both in terms of impact and financial return—and determine which strategies can best grow or strengthen the organization going forward.

- Phase five, *Write the Plan*: Delineate specific goals and objectives, each accompanied by long-range financial projections (in this phase, the plan is documented and adopted by the board).

- Phase six, *Implement the Plan*: Make the necessary organizational changes to implement new strategies, as well as build good annual plans and budgets that align to the strategic plan.

- Phase seven, *Evaluate and Monitor the Plan*: Continuously improve the discipline of planning and regularly monitor progress on the plan's goals and objectives.

Core Skills and Competencies

Make the Numbers Work

First and foremost, strategic planning without disciplined financial planning is naive at best and dangerous at worst. It's simply not feasible for nonprofits to focus only on mission and objectives—or even only on what their constituents say they most need and want—without also evaluating the specific financial requirements and funding prospects. *Any and all strategies adopted must factor in current or potential financing.* Looking again at our hypothetical educational nonprofit, if leadership wants to hire a grant writer to pursue foundation funding—a fairly typical nonprofit strategy—what makes it so sure it has a chance to attract those dollars? What is the specific case for support? What evidence have they collected to date that a grant writer would in fact pay for him or herself by raising more than their salary costs within a specified time period? What would be the foundation dollars-raised targets for the coming two years? In short, what is the *financial* analysis of this strategy? The truth is that there are many brilliant strategies for which there is no current or potential funding, and without money, there is no execution. Competency number one is therefore:

Every strategy identified in a strategic plan should have an accompanying financial analysis that details the cost to implement the strategy and the sources of financing for it.

Planning in Real Time

Second, strategic thinking should not be limited to official periods of strategic planning. The tools and frameworks of sophisticated strategic planning—from environmental scans to financial projections—can and should be deployed in real time as new opportunities and threats emerge for an organization. Staff should develop these habits and skill sets so that outside support is not required every time a significant planning question emerges; instead, *leaders must feel comfortable doing intentional strategic thinking on an as-needed basis.* This includes working with staff and board teams in meetings as short as one hour, full-day or weekend-long retreats, and everything in between. For example, in evaluating whether to add a third language to their curriculum, the effective education nonprofit ED assigned her program director the task of compiling the number of requests received for the third language to date, the demographic trends of their student participants for the past two years, and the cost of three possible consultants who would do the initial translation. She also tasked her grant writer with researching possible foundation funders of these up-front translation and curriculum testing costs. Then the three of them had a two-hour strategic thinking meeting to determine if and when to invest in adding the third language. And so competency number two is:

Good leaders are always developing and revising strategy using the best data they can collect readily to make good decisions in real time.

Staff-Run, Board-Directed

A third important competency in strategic planning is clarity of roles among staff and board. The idea that boards set strategic direction and staffs implement it—a nonprofit sector cliché—is rarely in fact the case. Except for the case of all-volunteer organizations, paid staff typically have their ears closer to the ground than board members do and inevitably begin identifying and even pursuing new strategies as opportunities arise. More commonly, as new strategies emerge, leaders bring them to their boards for further discussion and vetting. Indeed, one of the challenges of the executive director role is knowing which opportunities to bring to the board, and when to do so. What rises to the level of "setting organizational direction"? How much latitude do the executive or other senior staff have to be entrepreneurial and opportunistic? It's important to clarify these expectations in the context of each specific organization, as these norms will vary across nonprofit cultures and leaders.

In our education nonprofit, the executive director and board chair agreed that the executive director is ultimately responsible for the success of the strategic planning process; she was charged with leading its design with the consultant, doing most of the actual writing of the plan, and so forth. They agreed that the board chair is responsible for the board's active engagement in the process. Together, they established a board-staff planning task force that existed only while the plan was being developed. Its participants were chosen for their knowledge and enthusiasm about the key strategic questions facing the organization at the time. The task force members did the heavy lifting in the planning process—from co-designing it, to stakeholder engagement, to drafting goals and objectives for feedback from the full staff and board.

This raises the issue of a "democratic" or consensus-based culture, treasured in many nonprofits. In these organizations, there is an expectation that all staff—from entry level to the executive director—will be involved in formal strategic planning processes. These groups generally assume that this inclusiveness will establish a level of buy-in for new strategies organization-wide. This rationale gets at an important cultural norm in many community nonprofits: the notion that leaders need "buy-in" *before* they can implement a new strategy. Though this sounds great, it's simply not true. In fact, leaders *only* need the best available data and the key staff and board members with direct insight to the strategic question in order to set strategy. Too many cooks tend to spoil the broth. Once a good strategy has been set, however, a clear communication plan to the rest of the staff and key supporters is critical. *Too often the strategic planning process is designed to generate buy-in up front, instead of focusing on how best to make a rigorous decision about strategy.* "Buy-in" to new strategies, however, can be accomplished through transparent communication about how and why a new strategy is being adopted, as well as consistent supervision to help each staff person understand how his or her role changes within the new strategy. So the third critical competency is:

Clarify board and staff roles in planning—putting realistic assignments on the right people for maximum productivity and quality strategy development.

Think: What Questions Are We Trying to Answer?

Before beginning a strategic planning process, an effective leader or manager always clarifies, *"What are the most relevant and timely questions that this process must answer?"* This is as true for a real-time one-day process or a six-month one supported by a consultant. Traditionally, strategic planning starts with revisiting your vision and mission, but if those fundamental points are not in question, why revisit them? Dedicating time to a generic rather than focused planning effort is not a good use of invaluable board and staff time. Instead, an organization should *choose to focus on two or three key questions.* Our educational nonprofit wisely narrowed its planning focus to the following:

1. How do we grow to serve three new counties within two years?

2. How do we provide services in a third language to meet the needs of a changing student demographic in our region?

3. How do we diversify our income to include more donations from foundations and individual donors?

A thoughtfully facilitated meeting of board and staff can identify these questions in advance. With clear questions from the outset, staff and board can set about collecting the right data, engaging the right constituents, and ensuring that planning time is used effectively and efficiently to drive towards the best possible decisions and ultimately, results. So, our fourth competency is

Identify specific questions for the planning process to answer, rather than embarking on generic, organization-wide planning.

Rigorously Consider the Environment and External Input

Weaker strategic plans fail to take into account important shifts in the operating environment, or they don't elicit sufficient critical feedback from stakeholders, or both. Planning processes that are too insular protect leaders from important input that must be accounted for in the formation of successful strategy. SWOT analysis, a central tool in the planning process, is geared towards tackling this potential downfall. SWOT is an acronym for a review of Strengths, Weaknesses, Opportunities, and Threats. Many books are written on this technique, but suffice to say in this phase of the planning process, the organization scans internally and externally to determine where its greatest strengths lie, where the greatest opportunities are in the marketplace, what its most pressing weaknesses are, and what external threats must be navigated. Revisiting the education nonprofit, they identified their bilingual teachers and well-developed curriculum as core strengths; new federal education innovation funding as an opportunity; low brand recognition among foundations as a weakness, and the growth of for-profit educational companies as a threat. A good planning process does more than merely state these findings and must provide insight on how to capitalize on the good news and address the bad. In this case, it laid out specific strategies for overcoming low brand recognition, cutting off threats from for-profit players, and developing specific and realistic goals and objectives to address them.

The meaningful engagement of people other than board and staff is another critical component of effective strategy formation. It is easy—and dangerous—to make assumptions about how clients, constituents, funders, and community partners perceive your organization and initiatives. With the aforementioned driving questions in sharp focus, *surveys and interviews of stakeholders generate not only useful data, but also community goodwill and future support.* For instance, given its strategic question about expansion to additional counties, the educational nonprofit elected to interview the executive directors of five community-based organizations in the new counties who provide complementary services. By proactively asking the EDs about unfulfilled needs in the counties and requesting their input and direction for the program's expansion, leadership received both invaluable guidance and the opportunity to build relationships and trust with future colleagues and partners. Here's one very effective tactic: *engage board members as interviewers of external stakeholders during strategic planning processes.* The upside here is great: board members get more engaged as they learn more about how the organization is positioned in the community, while community stakeholders are typically flattered and impressed that volunteer board leaders are so deeply engaged in planning and community listening. So, our fifth competency is:

Develop strategies only __after__ rigorously considering the external environment and the feedback of clients, funders, collaborators, and other stakeholders.

Set Milestones and Benchmarks for Success

Finally, a critical skill in developing and delivering on good strategy is setting measurable targets to gauge successful execution. When setting strategy, *you must be very disciplined, defining and even quantifying what success will look like.* This forces a deeper discussion of success requirements, realistic time frames, necessary financing, and other reality-based considerations. In short, defining success makes for better articulation of strategy in the first place. Once strategies are articulated, staff and board must consistently and regularly monitor progress based on these benchmarks, thereby providing an important performance motivator. Indeed, the adage "what gets measured gets done" has considerable truth to it. So, our final competency is:

Develop measures of success and use them to determine whether your strategic decisions are being effectively implemented.

The Nonprofit Dashboard

"Organizational dashboards" are an incredibly effective tool for monitoring progress against established metrics (see Table 5.1). Just like the dashboard in your car, an organizational dashboard is a holistic, though not comprehensive, visual representation of an nonprofit's key success indicators in a variety of important management arenas, i.e., program, finance, development and fundraising, human resources, and governance. Three to five indicators are chosen in each arena along with what results constitute Green (Celebrate), Yellow (Monitor), and Red (Act Now) flags. The dashboard is then populated with current results and a restatement of results from the two most recent reports to highlight trends—I recommend doing this quarterly. Once complete, the reader gets a quick and colorful scan of what's going as planned and where refinements or serious rethinking may be in order, thereby providing a powerful yet simple management tool to guide decision making.

Dashboards are most powerful when they include success indicators that are linked directly to key strategies identified in a strategic plan. In its effort to increase foundation grant funding with its new grant writer, the educational nonprofit identified a development success indicator of two new grant proposals submitted per quarter. In its effort to reach additional student participants in new counties, they established the program success indicator of initiating relationships with two new junior high school principals and guidance counselors per quarter. Thus, the dashboard becomes a powerful complement to the strategic plan—increasing the likelihood that staff and board will pay serious attention to execution. Several indicators from the education nonprofit are included in the example.

Table 5.1: The Components of a Dashboard

Key: Act Now / Monitor / Celebrate

Education Nonprofit Performance Indicators	Target	Trend/Result			Cumulative Status	Comment
Indicators		Q1	Q2	Current		
Program						
School counselor relationships established	2 per qtr.	1	3	2		We are on pace with 6 relationships at 75% through the year.
Indicator 2						
Indicator 3						
Fundraising						
Foundation grants submitted	2 per qtr.	3	0	0		After initial success, we have been unable to identify additional foundation prospects.
Indicator 2						
Indicator 3						
Category 3						
Indicator 1						
Indicator 2						
Indicator 3						

Strategic Planning Dos and Don'ts

Dos and Don'ts

- DON'T develop strategies without a corresponding financial analysis of how much the strategies will cost to implement over time *and* a breakdown of where those resources will come from.

- DON'T undertake generic planning processes simply because the last strategic plan has expired. Instead, define clear planning questions and pursue their answers rigorously.

- DON'T overemphasize staff buy-in when designing planning processes. Staff will be most pleased when good decisions are made and then thoughtfully communicated and implemented.

- DO engage the board of directors in planning in substantive ways, not by pretending that they are the lone direction setters and staff the lone implementers. Instead, use their knowledge and talents as individuals and as a collective body to make more informed decisions together.

- DO listen deeply to the community as you are developing strategies. This includes clients, constituents, funders, and current and potential partners.

- DO define success for each strategy and consider implementing an organizational dashboard to support board and staff in monitoring progress.

Conclusion

The setting and continuous refinement of organizational strategy is essential to nonprofit impact and sustainability. Without a clear, compelling vision and mission, supported by solid strategies, nonprofits lose relevance and financial strength over time. It is critical to regard the investment of staff and board time in strategic planning—not to mention organizational dollars—as an *investment* that must show great return. A positive and inclusive planning process is not enough; ultimately, the most effective strategy formation is about making good decisions based on the best available data and then *executing*. These decisions always include a realistic financial analysis and the input of community stakeholders. Though there are many process options for arriving there, staff and board share in the responsibility to frame and answer the organization's most pressing questions together. Ultimately, by investing the appropriate time, resources, and perspectives into strategic planning, a nonprofit stands to better engage and serve its community, improve upon its communications and fundraising efforts, and provide staff and board a valuable touch point for ongoing decision making.

Jeanne Bell, MNA, is CEO of CompassPoint Nonprofit Services, a leading training and consulting firm for community-based organizations. She coauthored Financial Leadership for Nonprofit Executives: Guiding Your Organization to Long Term Success *(Wilder) and conducted a series of research projects, including* Daring to Lead 2006: A National Study of Nonprofit Executive Leadership. *Jeanne is chair of the board of the Alliance for Nonprofit Management and a board member with the Nonprofits' Insurance Alliance of California and with Intersection for the Arts. She serves as a contributing editor to* The Nonprofit Quarterly.

Strategic Planning Resource Review

Jeanne Bell, Jan Masaoka, and Steve Zimmerman. Nonprofit Sustainability: Making Strategic Decisions for Financial Viability. San Francisco: Wiley, 2010.

This book focuses on strategic decision making and employing a dual bottom-line approach wherein both programmatic impact and financial return are evaluated to refine organizational direction.

Michael Allison and Jude Kaye. CompassPoint Nonprofit Services. Strategic Planning for Nonprofit Organizations: A Practical Guide and Workbook (2nd ed.). New York: Wiley, 2005.

Now in its second version, this book details an updated approach to strategic planning and includes numerous worksheets on an accompanying CD.

David La Piana. The Nonprofit Strategy Revolution: Real-Time Strategic Planning in a Rapid-Response World. Saint Paul, MN: Fieldstone Press, 2008.

After a cogent critique of traditional strategic planning, this book details an approach to planning that is focused issue-wise and contained time-wise.

Lawrence Butler. The Nonprofit Dashboard: A Tool for Tracking Progress. San Francisco: BoardSource, 2007.

This clear, 50-page guide with accompanying CD walks though the why and how of building an organizational dashboard.

The Nonprofit Quarterly (www.nonprofitquarterly.org)

This exceptional nonprofit-specific management journal has frequent articles on strategy and finance targeted to progressive, community-based nonprofits.

Stanford Social Innovation Review (www.ssireview.com)

This management journal affiliated with Stanford University Graduate School of Business focuses on social innovation and has frequent articles on nonprofit strategy and impact measurement.

Bridgespan (www.bridgespan.org)

This website of the nonprofit Bridgespan has numerous downloadable articles and case studies about strategy development, decision making, and financing your mission.

TCC Group (www.tccgrp.com)

This website of the consulting firm, TCC Group has numerous downloadable articles, including "Ten Keys to Successful Strategic Planning for Nonprofit and Foundation Leaders."

∘ ∘ ∘

All these resources, plus nonprofit management tips of the week and more, can be found at Nonprofits101.org.

CHAPTER 6

Strategic Restructuring: Collaboration, Alliances, and Mergers

By David La Piana, President, and Bob Harrington, Director, Strategic Restructuring Practice, La Piana Consulting

Introduction

Nonprofits are founded and grow out of the deepest longings of the people who create, lead, and work in them. These longings are generally related to a desire for greater social, political, or environmental justice. When grappling with these types of challenges, the old adage "there is strength in numbers" definitely holds true. Often, the best way to advance an organization's cause is by working closely with similarly motivated partners. But the path to successful partnerships is not an easy one. It requires an honest assessment of what your organization and its potential partner(s) each bring to the table, clarity about what you seek to achieve together, and a significant investment

Figure 6.1: The Partnership Matrix[1]

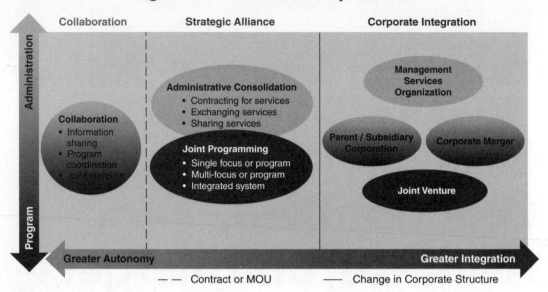

of time and energy. We call the process by which two or more nonprofits combine their efforts in a partnership "strategic restructuring." This general term includes collaborations, strategic alliances, and corporate integrations, such as mergers. Figure 6.1, The Partnership Matrix, portrays the different forms of partnership available to nonprofits, ranging along a continuum of different levels of commitment and permanence.

The Partnership Matrix

Collaboration rests on the left, or low-integration, end of the Partnership Matrix. Collaboration is as old as the nonprofit sector itself. It occurs when different nonprofits perceive a fairly limited need to work together to achieve a common goal. This may be as simple as standing up together during the annual local government budget battle, opposing reductions that may have an impact on them or on other organizations. Another collaborative arrangement may involve a nonprofit assigning some of its staff to provide services at another nonprofit's site. For example, a nurse from a health center may be stationed at a homeless shelter to provide health screenings to residents there.

The key to collaboration is that it is simple, easy to arrange, and often episodic, in that it usually does not involve any formal long-term commitments.

When a collaboration moves toward more extended and detailed commitments, it becomes a *strategic alliance*, found in the center of the Partnership Matrix. This form of partnership is usually characterized by a written agreement in the form of a memorandum of understanding or contract among the parties. The focus of the alliance could be programmatic, as when one organization receives a foundation grant and then subcontracts pieces of the work to other organizations; or administrative, as when a larger nonprofit provides accounting and other "back office" services for smaller groups. The key to strategic alliances is that they commit the partners to specific arrangements within a certain set of parameters—e.g., in the area of a shared grant—but they otherwise leave the organizations free to function entirely independently. For example, a group of nonprofits might share the administrative back office of one partner for accounting, information technology, and human resources functions, but still maintain separate programming, boards of directors, and executive directors.

When nonprofits decide that an even closer partnership is required to advance their missions, they can choose from various forms of *corporate integration*. These occupy the far right, or most integrative, section of the Partnership Matrix and include options such as a management services organization (MSO). In this example, the shared back office functions described earlier are moved into an entirely separate organizational home, which is usually owned and controlled by the partners (MSOs typically have more than two partners). Another form of corporate integration is a parent-subsidiary arrangement wherein one nonprofit comes under the control of another, while maintaining a separate organizational identity. Finally, a full merger allows two or more organizations to become one. Corporate integrations involve much closer partnerships than do strategic alliances. Upon execution of a merger, for example, there remains only one organization, one board, and one staff leader. These can be the most powerful forms of partnership, but are also the most challenging, because so much is at stake.

Are You Ready for a Partnership?

We are often asked to help a nonprofit find a suitable partner, for a merger, for example. We always respond that *the nonprofits your organization is most likely to partner with are among those groups you already know.* Before asking which organizations to consider partnering with, it is important to be clear both about why your organization wants to partner in the first place and what it is looking to gain from the arrangement.

An organization considering a partnership will need to assess the potential of such an alliance before trying to negotiate the details. This process includes a self-assessment as well as a potential partner assessment. Sometimes a self-assessment will be performed prior to approaching a potential partner, while at other times both potential partners conduct their self- and partner assessments simultaneously. *A self-assessment should address the following questions:*

1. What are the key challenges or critical issues (strategic, operational, and programmatic) facing your organization? What gaps or needs make it difficult for you to fully succeed (i.e., to develop and execute strategies related to programs or services, staffing, operations, management, and so on)? How might a partnership help your organization to address these challenges more successfully than it can on its own?

2. How will a partnership help your organization accomplish its mission or better serve its clients, customers, or audiences?

   A partnership, first and foremost, must enhance your ability to deliver on your organizational mission.

3. What experience do you have in working with other groups?

   Organizations that have been collaborative in nature and philosophy are better prepared to enter into a strategic restructuring process. Conversely, organizations that have been more internally focused or have not worked as extensively with others may have difficulty making the cultural adaptations required of a successful partnership.

4. What is the potential reaction of funders and other significant stakeholders (donors, contracting organizations, and so on) to a partnership? Is there

general support for developing closer working relationships within your community or field?

For the past ten years, there has been a growing interest in and support for partnerships among nonprofits. However, you need to assess your community's and your most significant organizational stakeholders' receptivity before proceeding. Otherwise, you risk alienating essential supporters.

5. Do you have any specific organizational "red flags" to which a potential partner may react? These could be reputational (e.g., a scandal that played out in the news), financial (e.g., a significant funding stream is at risk or a balloon payment is due on a property loan), or programmatic (e.g., a program is known to be performing poorly and needs retooling).

   Identifying and understanding issues that may be of concern to a potential partner will prepare you for the inevitable conversation that will take place, during any negotiation, on how to mitigate these red flag issues.

6. What is your organization's current financial condition? How strong, predictable, and diverse are its funding sources? What has been its funding history? Will a potential partnership enhance the funding potential of the combined organizations?

7. What are your competitive advantages, if any, in the marketplace? *A competitive advantage is a unique asset, outstanding execution, or both that differentiates your organization from others doing similar work.*

   You should identify any competitive advantages and strive to understand how a potential partnership will enhance, weaken, or change them.

8. What parameters or screens should you use to determine whether to engage in a potential partnership? These may include:
   a. Will the partnership advance your mission and strategies?
   b. Will the potential benefits justify the costs (both financial and board or staff time)?
   c. What is the potential for funding to support the negotiations and implementation of a potential partnership?
   d. Will the potential partnership position your organization for sustainability or growth?

Once your organization is clear about its readiness to enter into a potential partnership, and understands the assets and liabilities (both financial and organizational) that it brings to the table, it should move on to identifying and considering potential partners through a partner assessment. *A partner assessment should address the following questions:*

1. Are the missions, visions, and programs of the organizations compatible or complementary?

   An ideal partnership does not require that the organizations do the same work, in the same geographic area, for the same constituents. Indeed, the best partnerships often enhance each partner's contribution with new programs, skill sets, or locations for service delivery. An ideal partner is compatible and complementary in mission, *and* brings new things to the table. If program growth is the goal of the partnership, perhaps a partner that does the same work as your organization is the right fit. But if diversification and innovation are the goals, a complementary partner may be a better choice.

2. Do the organizations have a history of working together or of competing? What is the level of trust between them?

   Organizations with experience working together and a history that has led to the development of trust will find the partnership development process easier. An awareness of any lack of trust between the boards or staff—and especially between the executive directors and senior management—is critical. If trust is lacking or weak this does not mean a partnership is impossible, but it does mean that more time and attention will be needed to build trust between the organizations during the negotiation process and afterward.

3. Are the organizations' cultures compatible?

   This assessment can be difficult because of the subtle, nuanced nature of organizational culture. Some questions to examine include different approaches to consensus as opposed to hierarchical decision making, formality or informality of systems and processes, and the basic values of the staff members who will need to work together in a partnership. Keep in mind that compatibility of cultures is, obviously, a less important question in a low-integration collaborative relationship than it is in a merger, where the organizations will become one. Similar to the issue of trust, cultural differences do not mean a partnership cannot work. They do mean, however, that (depending on the level of integration involved) the parties will need to address this issue during the negotiations and especially during the implementation of a partnership.

4. What are the strengths and weakness of a potential partner? What usable skills and assets do they bring to the table? What competitive advantages, if any, does a potential partner possess?

   Learning how a potential partner will strengthen your organization's work is a critical task of the assessment process. Consider the potential partner's programmatic assets, reputational issues, administrative capability, and staff skills. How will these either enhance or detract from your work?

5. What is the financial condition of a potential partner?

   You can begin to assess the financial condition of a potential partner prior to engaging in formal discussions. The organization's website may contain annual reports; www.GuideStar.org provides access to IRS Form 990 (an informational tax return required of all nonprofits with at least $25,000 in annual expenditures); and an internet search may reveal recent grants awarded to it. Once more formal discussions begin (and, again, depending upon the depth of the partnership sought), budgets, audits, and other financial information will be exchanged, providing an overview of the financial condition of a potential partner.

The assessment process (both self-assessment and partner assessment) can be accomplished in a variety of ways and at differing levels of intensity, depending on the needs of the organizations. Least formally, the executive directors and some senior staff can meet to ask and answer questions in order to determine whether there is reason to recommend a more formal negotiation process. Usually, if the process moves forward, all but the smallest nonprofits and simplest partnerships will engage consultants to provide a more intensive and objective assessment of the potential partnership's pros and cons, as well as to facilitate the negotiations. One last note on assessment: remember that all the questions you have for a potential partner are likely to be the same questions they will have for you!

Critical Skills and Competencies

In order to partner effectively with another organization, a nonprofit needs certain skills and competencies, which, because they are not otherwise required of the organization, may be in short supply. For example, an organization that normally stands alone to fight injustice may not have much experience working collaboratively with others. More generally, executive directors of nonprofits tend to be entrepreneurial, hard-driving, and accustomed to a great deal of independence. After all, these are essential skills for survival in the role, let alone success. Still, when it comes time to partner with another nonprofit these very same abilities can become liabilities. "The ship may be leaky, but at least I am its captain" seems to be the mantra of many nonprofit leaders.

We have been in the same boat (so to speak). Both authors were formerly longtime nonprofit executive directors for whom working collaboratively with other organizations was an acquired skill, not a natural outgrowth of our day-to-day work. Here, we offer some lessons learned from our experience.

Five Things We Wish We Had Known About Partnering Earlier in Our Careers

1. Be open to viewing the cultures and processes of groups you wish to partner with as they see themselves. Other organizations do things differently—not necessarily better or worse, but differently. The tendency to see another organization's different ways of doing things as "wrong" is not helpful to your partnership.

2. You must build trust. The major variable in a partnership isn't money, or time, or even mission—it is trust. If the groups trust one another, anything is possible; if they do not, very little can be accomplished. Your early efforts in a partnering process should focus on building trust. If that proves difficult, perhaps the partnership is not meant to be.

3. Be clear about leadership. As nonhierarchical and inclusive as any partnership is, there can still only be one leader. Groups undertaking

collaboration should name a single staff person to take the lead. At the other end of the continuum, a merger must result in the selection of a single executive director. *Don't opt for a coleader arrangement; they almost always fail within the first year.*

4. Partnerships take time. They are not a quick fix and nonprofit leaders tend to underestimate the amount of time they will take to put together, to implement, and to produce positive results. *We usually estimate about four months to negotiate a merger*, for example. The concept of "opportunity cost" is important: What else could you be doing with the time you will devote to building and nurturing your partnership? Would some other set of activities be more likely to produce good outcomes for your mission? If so, perhaps you should pursue these other activities rather than a partnership.

5. Don't let the three most common roadblocks derail your partnership. These include:

   ○ The drive for autonomy within each organization. Nonprofit leaders prize their independence. The more intense the partnership the more that independence is threatened. Name your own and your partners' autonomy concerns so you can work together to address them in the context of your growing relationship.

   ○ The interest of each person (board or staff) in keeping his or her position and role after the partnership is executed. It is only natural to want to protect your role, so be aware of the resistance any necessary changes will engender. *Transparency, treating one another with respect, and avoiding power plays will build trust and lessen concerns* about "what will happen to me?"

   ○ Staff's ability to adjust to new roles, build new relationships, and work in new ways. *Be sure to engage staff and volunteers in open discussions about cultural differences and the reasons behind the partnership.* If they feel the change they are undergoing is in service of something worthwhile they will be more supportive of the effort.

Pay attention to these issues, and to building trust, and your partnership will be far more likely to succeed.

Strategic Restructuring Case Study: The importance of Cultural Integration in A Merger Between Affordable Housing Nonprofits

On July 1, 2008, following six months of negotiations, the Urban Affordable Housing Group and North County Housing Coalition[2] merged. The process in which the two housing development nonprofits engaged was facilitated by a board member, which is not typically recommended, but did result in the successful consolidation of the two organizations. At least it was *structurally* successful, in that a merger did actually occur. In fact, the consolidation resulted in significant and unusually high[3] savings of well over $600,000, the majority of which came from the reduction of duplicative staff positions (salary and benefits), but the merged organization also realized savings in direct mail costs, rent, annual reports, fundraising materials, software licenses, and letterhead. Integration costs for the merger totaled $100,000, resulting in a positive net of more than $500,000 in the first year's combined budget. This level of savings in a merger is actually quite unusual. Most mergers are undertaken not for cost savings, but in order to combine complementary skills, strengthen the organization's public profile, or expand services, which was the case here. Cost savings, when they happen, are a plus but not a primary motivation.

However, the merger of Urban and North County also brought significant challenges. Unrecognized during the negotiations process was the level of difference between the cultures of the two organizations. Urban was quite hierarchical. Nearly all significant decisions were made by the CEO, who expected that management and staff would simply carry out her directives. This produced a streamlined decision-making process, as projects were carried out without question or debate. Urban was an efficient housing development machine. North County, on the other hand, was a more consensus-oriented organization. The CEO would gather the majority of staff members together for long meetings where they would thoroughly discuss and consider the strategic options facing the organization. The staff worked hard to reach consensus on all major decisions. Like Urban, North County was quite successful in achieving its affordable housing development goals, but did so with a very different culture.

After due consideration by the merging boards, North County's CEO was deemed to possess the best mix of skills and style and so was chosen to lead the merged entity, whereas Urban's CEO was given a small severance package and left the organization. As a result of cultural differences, the merged organization found itself with a dysfunctionally merged culture. Staff did not know how to communicate or work together to make or carry out joint decisions. Staff from Urban expected decisions to be made by their new CEO, and waited for directives for carrying out these decisions, whereas North County staff could not understand why their new colleagues from Urban seemed so uncomfortable with the freewheeling discussions that had long characterized their culture. This clash of cultures resulted in significant infighting, continual misunderstandings, and a decline in both morale and productivity. Two previously successful organizations now struggled to accomplish their work.

Fortunately, the managers appointed to lead the integration process (one from Urban and one from North County) recognized that they needed help to understand the nature of the dysfunction within their new merged culture. They brought in a consultant experienced in merger integration to assess the situation and design a process to develop and implement a new decision-making culture. This process included gathering information from interviews, surveys, and focus groups in order to inform an understanding of the previous organizations' cultures. This led to a series of facilitated retreats to help staff get to know each other, to talk through their common goals, and to develop a shared commitment to their merged mission. The process not only gave the CEO an opportunity to recognize and explain her preferred decision-making style (which was, as already noted, far more inclusive than that of Urban's previous CEO), but allowed a safe space for staff from Urban to share their difficulties with this unfamiliar style. As a result, the CEO was motivated to develop a new decision-making culture that is consultative rather than consensus-driven. The merged organization now includes a strong management team that leads the decision-making process, but asks for staff input during consideration of a major issue and later delegates portions of implementation back to staff groups.

Strategic Restructuring Dos and Don'ts

- DO take the time to assess your own and your partner's motivations, assets, and challenges going into a partnership.

- DO work to build trust. It is the essential ingredient to a successful partnership.

- DO name a single staff person to take the lead. In a merger name a single chief executive.

- DON'T opt for a coleadership arrangement; they almost always fail within the first year.

- DON'T rush it, but keep the process moving forward. Estimate about four months to negotiate a merger, longer if the partnership is more complex.

- DON'T let the partners' concerns about autonomy derail the partnership.

- DO treat one another with respect; avoiding power plays will build trust.

- DO engage staff and volunteers in open discussions about cultural differences and the reasons behind the partnership.

Conclusion

Strategic restructuring offers an array of options for nonprofits looking to share resources, leverage strengths, and achieve a greater scale and impact through partnering with other, like-minded organizations. The process is not easy, often requiring difficult discussions about the structure of the organization, the future roles of current leaders, and the differences in approach that the partnering organizations may have developed. Navigating this process requires a thorough self-assessment, a keen assessment of any potential partners, and a well-structured negotiations process. It also requires lots of time and energy, but when it succeeds it can supercharge an organization's work. Nonprofit leaders considering strategic restructuring should first ask themselves what motivates them to do so, what they hope to gain from a partnership, and how much time and other resources they are willing to invest to achieve these ends. If they and their boards agree that the potential reward is worth the effort and risk then they should move forward, with their top priority being the establishment of trust with the potential partner. As a trusting relationship develops between the entities, greater flexibility and willingness to change will emerge. Building on this trust, the partnering organizations can realize substantial benefits of scale and efficiency, leading to an enhanced ability to pursue their shared mission.

David La Piana founded La Piana Consulting in 1998. Recognized as a leading expert on nonprofit management and governance, David has worked extensively with funders and nonprofits across subsectors. A popular author, speaker, and teacher, David is a regular contributor to the national dialogue on nonprofit and foundation effectiveness. Prior to founding La Piana Consulting, David held senior management positions with the YMCA, The International Institute, and the East Bay Agency for Children, a multifaceted human services agency that grew tenfold under his leadership. A Fellow of the Salzburg Seminar, David currently serves as board chair of the Craigslist Foundation.

With more than ten years of nonprofit consulting experience, Bob Harrington leads La Piana Consulting's Strategic Restructuring Practice. As director, Bob draws on his extensive nonprofit management experience to assist today's leaders in exploring the spectrum of nonprofit partnerships, such as mergers, joint ventures, and administrative consolidations. Prior to consulting, Bob worked in the nonprofit social services field for close to 30 years, leading organizations ranging from small community-based groups to statewide organizations. He received his bachelor's degree in psychology from the University of California, Davis, and his masters of social work degree from the University of Wisconsin at Milwaukee.

Strategic Restructuring Resource Review

David La Piana and Robert Harrington. <u>The Nonprofit Mergers Workbook, Part I: The Leader's Guide to Considering, Negotiating, and Executing a Merger</u>. Saint Paul, MN: Fieldstone Alliance (July 2000—Revised 2008).

This leading practical publication in the field has been helping nonprofit leaders to succeed at mergers for more than a decade. A newly revised version updates this classic with lessons from the authors' additional decade of experience.

La Piana Associates. <u>The Nonprofit Mergers Workbook, Part II: Unifying the Organization after a Merger</u>. Saint Paul, MN: Fieldstone Alliance (June 2004).

Written for the nonprofit leader, this companion volume to the popular *Nonprofit Mergers Workbook Part I* helps organizations create a comprehensive plan to achieve post-merger integration—bringing together people, programs, processes, and systems from different organizations into a single, unified whole.

David La Piana. "Merging Wisely." <u>Stanford Social Innovation Review</u>, Spring 2010. (www.ssireview.org/articles/entry/merging_wisely/)

This article discusses the increasing pressure from grant makers for nonprofits to merge in the face of economic turmoil. Yet mergers are not always the right path for nonprofits in financial distress. David describes why funders should consider a wide variety of partnership options.

Other La Piana Consulting Resource Publications (www.lapiana.org/research-publications/publications)

Drawing from over a decade of experience in strategic restructuring for nonprofits, La Piana Consulting has developed a range of resources, from research-based publications, to monographs for funders, to case studies illustrating various forms of nonprofit partnerships. (Many resources are downloadable.)

Thomas A. McLaughlin. <u>Nonprofit Mergers and Alliances: A Strategic Planning Guide</u>. New York: Wiley, 2010.

This book is a practical, step-by-step guide to the process of mergers, alliances, and affiliations—from design and preliminary considerations to actual implementation.

The Collaboration Prize—Nonprofit Collaboration Database, The Lodestar Foundation, 2009. (www.thecollaborationprize.org/search/index.php)

Drawing from more than 700 nominations for the first annual Collaboration Prize in 2008, this database provides searchable access to information about nonprofit partnerships from all across the country.

The Lodestar Foundation (www.lodestarfoundation.org/collaboration_resources.html)

A leader among funders in encouraging the use of collaborative strategies among nonprofits, the Lodestar Foundation provides access to resources on nonprofit partnerships of various kinds.

NonprofitExpert.com (in strategic partnership with Diversified Nonprofit Services) (www.nonprofitexpert.com/merger.htm)

This site offers a collection of resources and information related to the IRS compliance aspects of nonprofit merger, as well as other helpful links.

Alexander Cortez, William Foster, and Katie Smith Milway. "Nonprofit M&A: More Than a Tool for Tough Times." Bridgespan Group, 2009. (www. bridgespan.org/uploadedFiles/Homepage/Articles/Mergers_and_Acquisitions/091702-Nonprofit%20Mergers%20and%20Acquisitions.pdf)

This report, based on a study of nonprofit merger activity in four states, offers valuable insight into the frequency of such alliances while highlighting the need for a more thoughtful approach among nonprofit leaders in order to leverage the full potential of merger as a strategic choice.

Mandel Center for Nonprofit Organizations at Case Western Reserve University (www.case.edu/mandelcenter/publications/casestudies/)

This site provides access to research and case studies on the topic of nonprofit mergers and strategic alliances, including: "Merging Nonprofit Organizations: The Art and Science of the Deal," "Nonprofit Strategic

Alliances Case Studies: Lessons from the Trenches," and "Nonprofit Strategic Alliances Case Studies: The Role of Trust."

Denise L. Gammal. "The Merger Proposal: Before You Say 'I Do'." Stanford Social Innovation Review, Summer 2007. (www.ssireview.org/images/ articles/2007SU_feature_mergerproposal_gammal.pdf)

This article provides a thoughtful look at some of the challenges and potential pitfalls of nonprofit merger, while acknowledging that there are times when a merger may be the right strategy.

∘ ∘ ∘

All these resources, plus nonprofit management tips of the week and more, can be found at Nonprofits101.org.

CHAPTER 7

Risk Management and Insurance

By Pamela Davis, Founder, President, and CEO,
Nonprofits Insurance Alliance Group

Introduction

Insurance is not often seen as a core part of an organization's work toward meeting its mission. But it is actually an important factor in running and maintaining a strong organization. It has an impact on your ability to provide services to your clients, especially after a loss, and on your organization's sustainability. Insurance enables you to quickly and successfully get back to business after a fire, theft, accident, or lawsuit. It is true, insurance policies can be hard to understand, the decisions about what coverage is needed often seem capricious, and it is often not clear how to prevent risks, accidents, and claims. Don't let this deter you from seeing how insurance is a building block of great mission performance.

In this chapter, you will find the key risks that nonprofits face and some key strategies to mitigate those risks. I will review the types of insurance you want to have in case your best efforts to prevent accidents fail. I will try to demystify the process of purchasing insurance and working with a broker and give you tips and recommendations, so that when you are finished reading you have clear ideas on how to implement the best insurance and risk prevention techniques in your organization.

Critical Skills and Competencies

Let's take a look at some of the most important risks faced by nonprofits, tips on how to avoid them, and the various kinds of insurance you may want to consider for your organization.

Risks Your Organization May Face and How to Prevent Them

The majority of claims reported by nonprofit organizations are accidents and injuries related to automobiles, or slips, trips, and falls at offices, other facilities, and special events. Fewer claims result from allegations of improper employment practices, professional errors and omissions, and sexual abuse. Though less frequent, these claims tend to be the ones that are litigated and more difficult, time-consuming, and expensive to resolve. In Table 7.1 you will find some common categories of claims seen in nonprofits and the types of insurance policies that best cover these claims. This is by no means an exhaustive list, and more information on each type of coverage and recommended limits can be found below, but these examples are meant to help you think about the risks your organization may face. More information on all these topics and types of insurance for nonprofits can be found on our website at www.insurancefornonprofits.org.

Table 7.1: Representative Nonprofit Insurance Claims and Relevant Insurance Coverage, Plus Other Useful Solutions

Risks	Examples	Insurance Coverage	Other Solutions and Recommendations
Injuries (to Volunteers, Clients, and the Public)	Slips, trips, falls, food poisoning	General Liability	Create a Safety Program designed specifically for the risks your organization faces; ensure that your facilities (and any venues you use) are well lit, handrails and guardrails are installed, and general physical safety precautions are in place.
Injuries (to Employees)	Slips, trips, falls, lifting injuries, violence in the workplace, ergonomic injuries	Worker's Compensation	Employees should follow safety program guidelines, and be sure to offer training in proper lifting and transferring techniques. Use precautionary measures when handling any toxic or flammable substances. Have a plan to deal with violence in the workplace. Ensure that workspaces are ergonomically correct.
Auto Accidents	Accidents in vehicles owned by the nonprofit, or vehicles driven on behalf of the nonprofit by employees or volunteers	Commercial Auto Liability; Auto Physical Damage; Non-Owned and Hired Auto	Ask your broker or insurer about driver training programs for volunteers and employees who regularly drive on behalf of an organization.
Damage to Your Property	Fire, wind, or hail	Property	Install smoke alarms, fire extinguishers, and sprinklers to protect your property from extensive damage.
Theft of Your Property	Theft of computer or other equipment	Property	Make sure property is secured when not occupied and institute controlled key access. Get a police report if property is stolen, as *there must be proof of illegal entry in order for the loss to be covered.*

(Continued)

Table 7.1: Continued

Risks	Examples	Insurance Coverage	Other Solutions and Recommendations
Damage to Others' Property	Damage to another's property during an event, or a pick-up of donated goods	General Liability	Train employees or volunteers about the risks of damage when they enter others' property.
Employment-Related Wrongful Acts	Discrimination, harassment (including sexual), and wrongful termination	Directors and Officers	*Have a personnel handbook* that has been read and signed by every employee that includes policies prohibiting sexual harassment and discrimination. Consult with an attorney before taking a significant employment action, such as layoffs, demotions, or firing.
Theft of Client or Donor Data	Theft of a computer with donor or client data on it	General Liability	*Require password protection* on your network, computers, and databases.
Sexual Abuse	An employee molests a client of your afterschool program	Sexual Abuse Coverage	Anyone working with children, seniors, or the disabled should be required to submit background checks and go through extensive interviews and reference checks. Consider requiring fingerprint checks depending upon the law in your state.
Professional Errors and Omissions	A teen in your counseling program commits suicide	Social Services Professional	Ensure that your staff has the necessary qualifications for the work they are doing and that they understand and follow proper policies and procedures. Documentation, at every step of the way, is essential.

The Importance of D&O Coverage

Although a minority of claims are professional errors and omissions (typically covered by your Directors and Officers or "D&O" policy), 95% of these are employment related, including harassment, discrimination, and wrongful termination. According to data at the Nonprofits' Insurance Alliance Group (www.insurancefornonprofits.org), in any given year approximately one in fifty nonprofits will have a D&O claim against them, nearly all of them employment related. The average D&O claim will cost $35,000 to resolve—a combination of legal defense costs and, in a few cases, settlement payments. However, one out of ten claims will cost more than $100,000 to resolve. Especially, if you have employees, *don't take the risk of going without this important coverage* or you may put your organization in financial peril, and board members personally at risk, if you are sued for an employment-related claim.

Insurance Coverages and Limits

All nonprofit organizations should carry general liability insurance; other types of insurance you should carry depend upon the specific activities of the organization, the size of your assets, and the number and type of staff you have (volunteer or paid professionals). The list below is not an exhaustive list, but addresses the key insurance coverages that are applicable to nonprofit organizations. As always, *consult a trusted insurance broker for advice* about what is best for your nonprofit.

General Liability: Also known as "casualty" insurance, this is the minimum an organization should have, as it covers "bodily injury" caused by "accidents" that may have resulted from the "negligence" of your operations.

Directors and Officers: This is intended to cover claims related to decisions made by your organization. This includes damages that are not covered under the General Liability policy, such as employment-related actions, allegations by employees of wrongful termination, harassment, discrimination, and failure to hire.

<u>Business Auto (or Business Auto Liability and Auto Physical Damage)</u>: This is necessary for vehicles the nonprofit owns or leases.

<u>Non-Owned/Hired Auto Liability</u>: This protects your nonprofit if your employees or volunteers are involved in accidents when using their own vehicles on company business.

Auto Insurance

Many people don't understand that *an employee's or volunteer's own auto insurance always applies first if they are driving their own vehicle.* But if the amount of that insurance is not enough, the plaintiff will generally look for more money from the nonprofit—that's where Non-Owned/Hired Auto Liability insurance comes in handy.

<u>Property</u>: This coverage protects the physical assets you own or lease, such as buildings, office equipment, furniture, and fixtures.

<u>Improper Sexual Conduct</u>: This coverage is intended to provide defense and pay for damages from sexual abuse of a client under your care, for which the nonprofit is alleged to be responsible.

<u>Social Service Professional</u>: This typically provides coverage for errors or omissions as a result of professional activities. Note, however, that it typically does not cover physicians and the prescribing of medication, which requires medical malpractice coverage.

<u>Accident Insurance</u>: Unlike General Liability, which is intended to cover damages caused by the negligence of a nonprofit, accident insurance provides a limited amount of coverage without regard to whose negligence resulted in an accident causing bodily harm to a student, volunteer, or participant. For example, if a volunteer trips over his own feet and injures himself, accident insurance would pay for medical expenses of the injury, even though your nonprofit was not at fault for the volunteer's injury.

<u>Umbrella</u>: This typically provides higher liability limits for a variety of other coverages you have purchased in the event that the limits on your other policy are exhausted, or for damages that are not covered by the other policies you have purchased.

Here are two less common policies that can also be important, especially if your organization has staff:

<u>Employee Benefits Liability</u>: This coverage is intended to cover specified damages from your organization's negligent handling of the administration of your employee benefits program.

<u>Fidelity or Employee Dishonesty</u>: This is intended to provide a source for recovery of funds embezzled by employees or volunteers.

Coverage Limits

Most small to mid-sized nonprofits will find annual limits of $1 million per policy quite sufficient for their insurance needs; however, organizations should consider their level of assets and activities when determining whether to purchase higher limits. *If you want to purchase more than $1 million in coverage, we recommend securing an umbrella policy* that provides extra limits over many different coverages at the same time.

Worker's Comp and Health Insurance

Worker's Compensation coverage is required if you have any employees. This coverage provides benefits, prescribed by state law, by an employer to an employee due to a job-related injury (including death) resulting from an accident or occupational disease.

Health insurance coverage is presently in considerable flux. Organizations of a certain size may be required to provide coverage or pay a fine. Your current broker may be able to provide health insurance options for you and, if so, can provide quotes for your needs.

Purchasing Insurance

Your first step toward purchasing insurance is to find a good broker. Someone with prior experience providing similar services to nonprofits is ideal. Ask your peers about their insurance broker; they may be able to give you good advice.

Definition: "Broker"

Professional advisers or consultants who are intermediaries between clients and insurance companies are called brokers. Insurance companies pay the broker a commission based on a percentage of the cost of coverage (or "premium"), typically 15% on liability business.

How to Work with Your Broker

Your broker will have you fill out informational applications. As you complete the applications for insurance, treat this process as carefully as you would a grant application. Include all activities and events, however minor they seem, and *don't forget to list your assets and property addresses for property insurance.*

Once your applications have been completed, your broker will typically seek out quotes from various insurance companies. They may go to all-purpose commercial insurance companies, such as Aetna or Hartford, or to insurance companies that specialize in nonprofits, such as Nonprofits' Insurance Alliance of California (NIAC) and the Alliance of Nonprofits for Insurance, Risk Retention Group (ANI), both of which are 501(c)(3) nonprofits themselves and only insure other nonprofits. The insurance companies determine the premium at which they will offer you coverage and present quotes to the broker, who reviews them with you.

Keep in mind, *the cheapest price won't always offer you the best service*—whether in claims processing or in risk management support. In addition, it is important *to look for a policy that is an "occurrence" or "event trigger" policy.* This means that your organization will be covered in the event of late reporting of a claim, and covers an incident occurring while the policy is in force regardless of when the claim is filed, whether in the effective period or years later. This is particularly important in the case of improper sexual conduct claims, which often take years to surface. You should also *find out what risk management and risk control services are offered* by each company. Some companies offer driver training, reduced cost background checks, webinars, and other support and resources. Finally, *ask the broker for her recommendation* and why she is making that recommendation, and whether there are any financial incentives for the broker to recommend one carrier over the other.

Read Your Policy!

Ask your broker to explain things you don't understand. Make sure your name, location(s), and other organization information are accurate and complete. Check to see if the limits are as you discussed and that you are aware of any deductible that applies. Also *consider whether there are conditions in your policy that affect coverage,* such as a requirement to have smoke alarms. Are there any conditions with which you need to comply in order for coverage to be in effect? Very small organizations are often encouraged to purchase a "BOP" policy, also known as Business Owners Policy, but beware that this type of policy only covers your activities at your stated location. If you have fundraisers or special events, a BOP policy usually won't cover incidents outside of your stated location. Your broker should work with you so that you understand the legal contract into which you are entering.

Every three or four years you should review your relationship with your broker. Review the coverages that are being purchased, at what rates, from which insurance companies, and whether your organization is getting the services (such as prompt payment of claims) it deserves. Evaluate your relationships with your broker and your insurance company like you would any other important business relationship. Ultimately, insurance is a piece of paper that is a contract to pay damages when something goes wrong. But there are a lot of different types of insurance contracts and different practices in how willingly and quickly insurers pay claims. Don't change your insurance relationship if you are satisfied, but also don't allow your organization to stay in an unsatisfactory situation because of inertia or personal connections or friendships. Remember, it is about doing what is best for the organization and your mission.

Your Board's Role in Risk Management

It is important for your board to realize that there are risks to operating any nonprofit, and that these risks can be managed through appropriate policies and procedures and staff training. Insurance is there to cover those things that happen when risk control techniques are not completely successful. Following are some ways that the board can be involved in risk management.

Monitor Suits, Threats of Suits, and Accidents

The board (or a risk management committee of the board) should be informed of any claims made against the nonprofit and when threats of lawsuits arise. If you are a small nonprofit, you may not have any sort of claim for many, many years. Or something could go wrong the first day you open for business. In larger organizations, it's appropriate for the board to set goals and monitor progress on safety and risk reduction, such as reports on the number and type of injuries and accidents. They should also monitor allegations of wrongful employment actions and consider what might have been done to prevent them. Whether you represent a large or small organization, it is crucial that the board of directors recognizes that risk management is good management, and it is one of their responsibilities to see that the organization has the resources it needs to prevent avoidable accidents and injuries, and that it has the appropriate insurance coverage in place in case something goes wrong. Good risk management means having policies in place to provide information to the board about risks the organization faces, as well as making sure that there are procedures in place to train staff and monitor activities so that accidents are kept to a minimum. When accidents or near accidents happen, the organization needs to have a process to learn from these and incorporate more effective practices in the future. Small organizations should have a member of the board of directors responsible for this function, and in any organization the board chair should make it clear that the organization is meant to do its work without injuring clients, volunteers, members of the public, or damaging property.

Periodically Review Risks, Risk Control Techniques, and Insurance Coverages

Depending on the size of the organization, the board, a board committee, a board-staff task force, or another group should *develop a list of the key risks faced by the nonprofit* and have a process to periodically review incidents or claims. Obvious areas of concern are driver selection and training, policies to protect vulnerable clients, and potential for fraud and damage to property. Even if you are a very small nonprofit with only one or two employees, there is a risk of employment practices litigation. It is essential that your employment policies are in compliance with the law and that they be followed rigorously and consistently. It goes without saying that employees should be treated with respect and courtesy at all times, particularly when unpopular employment actions are necessary. A less obvious but real risk is the damage to reputation and staff morale from poor management or decision making.

Insurance and Risk Management Dos and Don'ts: Final Tips and Recommendations

- DO use a professional, licensed broker to help assess your risks and recommend coverages.

- DO use risk management resources made available from your insurer or broker.

- DO discuss your organization's risks and recommended coverages and limits with your board of directors.

- DO remind your board of directors that it is their responsibility to oversee risk management.

- DO establish written policies and procedures, train your volunteers and employees about these policies, and consistently make sure they are followed.

- DON'T forget to add and delete assets from your policy (new equipment, buildings, vehicles, and so on) when you purchase or dispose of them.

- DON'T forget to ask for a certificate of insurance from contractors or anyone providing professional services to you.

- DON'T assume claims are inevitable; many of the most common claims (slips and falls) can be avoided if the appropriate safety precautions are taken.

- DON'T be afraid to ask questions of your insurance broker—insurance is a complex topic and it is her job to help you understand the risks you face and to make sure they are properly addressed through risk mitigation and insurance.

Conclusion

Small or large, nonprofit organizations are in positions of trust in our communities. Nonprofits are created by people who want to make a positive difference in their communities—not to harm them. Because of the wide variety of services that nonprofits provide, it is impossible in this short chapter to provide an exhaustive list of the risks you may face. But frankly, good risk management isn't a list; it's a state of mind. It is a keen awareness of the workings of your organization and how you interact with your clients, your staff, your volunteers, and members of the public. Successful nonprofit managers and leaders put policies and procedures in place to anticipate what may go wrong with these interactions and train staff and volunteers on how to conduct themselves, so that problems will be avoided whenever possible and so that they are properly handled if and when they occur. High-performing boards of directors recognize that risk management is not something you have to do to keep your insurance company happy; it is discipline exercised to help you achieve your mission. When working in unison, these passionate and informed leaders can help protect an organization's downside and ensure that you have the peace of mind and support needed to do your best work in the community.

Pamela Davis is the founder, president, and CEO of an affiliated group of charitable risk pools known as the Nonprofits Insurance Alliance Group. Together, Nonprofits' Insurance Alliance of California (NIAC) and Alliance of Nonprofits of Insurance, Risk Retention Group (ANI) insure more than 10,000 nonprofits in 26 states for all types of liability insurance. One of the very early social entrepreneurs, Ms. Davis has grown these companies from a loan of $1 million from a group of foundations to organizations with nearly $300 million in assets. All companies in the group are 501(c)(3) nonprofits, like the organizations that they insure.

Risk Management Resources

Nonprofits' Insurance Alliance Group (www.insurancefornonprofits.org)

Information about the Nonprofits' Insurance Alliance Group companies, 501(c)(3) nonprofit insurance companies providing insurance coverage to nonprofits in 25 states, with specialty coverages and risk management resources specifically designed for nonprofit needs.

NIAC Guest—Member Resources (https://www.niac.org/Nonprofit-Insurance-Member-Resources.cfm)

ANI Guest—Member Resources: https://www.ani-rrg.org/Nonprofit-Insurance-Member-Resources.cfm)

Blue Avocado (www.blueavocado.org)

A nonprofit online magazine for community nonprofits, with practical and usable information about nonprofit organizations and the people who work in them, offering columns on HR, board management, personal finance, and life-and-work balance.

Nonprofit Risk Management Center (www.nonprofitrisk.org)

The Nonprofit Risk Management Center was established in 1990 to provide assistance and resources for community-serving nonprofit organizations. They offer a wide range of services on a vast array of risk management topics.

National Safety Council (www.nsc.org)

Local Safety Councils are also a good resource; a master listing of all local councils is available at the NSC site.

Occupational Safety & Health Administration OSHA (www.osha.gov/SLTC/index.html)

OSHA NET, Gateway for Safety & Health Information Resources (www.osh.net/)

Advocates for Highway & Auto Safety, Safety Related Links (www.saferoads.org/sec_links_safety.htm)

○ ○ ○

All these resources, plus nonprofit management tips of the week and more, can be found at Nonprofits101.org.

CHAPTER 8

Making Human Resources Work for You: Best Practices in Nonprofit Human Capital Management

By James Weinberg, Founder and CEO, and Cassie Scarano, President and Cofounder, Commongood Careers

Introduction

The war for talent is more competitive than ever and the opportunities facing organizations that successfully attract, manage, and develop talent are huge. Successful companies have known for decades that getting the most out of your people, or your "human capital," is the most important lever to drive organizational success. Being strategic and integrating best practices in the area of human capital management will make your organization stronger, and stronger organizations have greater impact.

Although human capital management refers to a broad array of systems, processes, and philosophies that need to align in order to ensure organizational success, one critical component is effective recruiting and hiring. This chapter will describe some best practices in this area and provide tips for integrating these into your work.

Critical Skills and Competencies

Investment in human capital management requires a recognition that *people are your organization's most valuable resource* and the first step is ensuring that the right people are brought on board in the right roles at the right time. Recruiting and hiring isn't rocket science, but there are definitely some important best practices to integrate as you build your organization. In this chapter, we will share some of the most actionable ideas in three key areas:

1. Planning to hire

2. Attracting and selecting great people to work at your organization

3. Compensating new staff appropriately

Let's get started!

Planning to Hire: Building a Competency Model

Do any of these situations sound familiar?

- A grant comes through and you have to start running a new program in three weeks, but you have no staff for it.

- One of your strongest employees just announced that she is relocating across the country, leaving in four weeks.

- Your organization has ten positions open, but no one is managing the hiring process, so résumés are piling up.

Our best advice: *slow down*. Making a bad hire is much more costly than operating without a hire for a few more weeks. In fact, it has been estimated that *a bad hire can cost an organization between two and five times that position's annual salary*. For example, one organization was so anxious to fill a program assistant position that they hired one of the first candidates they met, without utilizing a thorough hiring process. Six months later, the position was vacant again, the supervisor was frustrated and had lost countless hours trying to "make it work," the program had suffered from lack of attention, and the organization had to go through another hiring process. Developing a strategic hiring plan that incorporates adequate preparation will minimize the possibility that your organization will incur the financial and emotional costs of making a bad hire.

Get started by underlining conducting an assessment of your organization. What are the major needs of the organization, what functional roles are required to meet those, what expertise do you already have on staff, and which needs are not being met? Most people have a natural tendency to hire for the exact same position that is being vacated—this can be a mistake. As organizations change and grow over time, other staff members develop additional competencies, and what was needed in the past is most likely not what is needed for the future.

As you are scoping roles, make sure that they are realistic, appealing, and strategic. Avoid lumping too many different types of responsibilities into one position—what we call the "kitchen-sink" position because (a) it will be hard to find strong candidates who are competent in that combination of skills; (b) the job will be too much for one person; and (c) most likely, the person will not be successful in at least one of their roles. Instead, think creatively about how to get your needs met. One organization realized that their needs didn't require a full-time, senior level finance position—and their budget couldn't support such a position—so they outsourced bookkeeping to one firm and brought on a part-time consultant to act as chief financial officer. This solution elevated the level of expertise in that functional area significantly while saving them a considerable amount every year.

The most effective hiring processes are built around a competency model. This is a predetermined set of experiences, hard and soft skills, and competencies that will make a candidate successful in a particular role. Building a competency model will focus your entire hiring process on the requirements of the position and will help to avoid common mistakes like hiring too quickly, hiring someone you like, hiring someone just like the last person in the role, or getting part way through a hiring process only to realize that what you need in the role is different from what you are looking for.

In order to determine the competencies required, ask the people who know the position best—managers, direct reports, others in similar positions—what three to five competencies are most important to ensure success in the role, then compile and prioritize their responses.

Table 8.1: Sample Competency Models

Position	Competencies
Executive Director	Leadership
	Strategic thinking
	Staff management
	Quantitative analysis
	Relationship-building/management
Program Director	Staff management
	Project management
	Interpersonal skills
	Cross-cultural sensitivity
	Collaboration
Executive Assistant	Detail orientation
	Multitasking
	Project management
	Flexibility

o o o

Planning the Hiring Process

Now that you know what you are looking for, it's time to plan the process you are going to use to evaluate candidates against required competencies. Remember that *the best predictor of future success is past accomplishment, so any hiring process should allow candidates multiple opportunities to provide evidence of how they have successfully demonstrated the required competencies in past situations.* As you narrow down your pool of candidates and proceed through the stages of the hiring process, you will delve deeper and deeper into the backgrounds of fewer and fewer candidates, until you find the right fit. For most positions, the following process is recommended (a detailed description of each stage follows later in this chapter):

1. Application review

2. Phone screen

3. Initial in-person interview

4. Follow-up interview(s)

5. Reference and background checking

6. Offer negotiation and hiring

Each of these stages should integrate the four tenets of an effective hiring process:

Clarity = everyone involved knows exactly what you want

Consistency = every candidate participates in the same process

Equity = every candidate is treated equally

Legality = the process is nondiscriminatory (see Ensuring Legal Compliance sidebar)

Now that you have your process designed, it's time to *think about how you are going to assess candidates at every stage.* Any assessment tool (see Exhibit 8.1) should clearly reflect the components of the competency model and should be kept as simple as possible while focusing attention squarely on the required competencies.

Exhibit 8.1 Sample Candidate Assessment Form: Program Director

Competency	Evidence	Areas of Concern	Comments
Staff management			
Project management			
Interpersonal skills			
Cross-cultural sensitivity			
Collaboration			
Overall Comments and Recommendations			

extract

Ensuring Legal Compliance

Many of the tools and processes we outline in this chapter are not only best practices, but they will ensure that your hiring process is legal. Hiring can be a very complex process from a legal standpoint. In general, *all hiring practices must be based on Bona Fide Occupational Qualifications* (BFOQ)—those qualifications required to perform a job safely and efficiently and that are reasonably necessary to the operation of your business. Federal law states that hiring decisions can <u>only</u> be based on these qualifications and cannot be discriminatory.

That means that when interviewing, you should remember this simple rule: *if you don't need to know it to evaluate whether or not this person can effectively do their job, don't ask it.* Do you need to know if they are married or have kids? No. So don't ask it. Instead say, "This position requires some overnight travel. Would that be a problem for you?"

These guidelines will help ensure the legality of your hiring practices:

extract

Stage	Considerations
Planning	Identify the core competencies and requirements of the position. Develop a job description that clearly details the position requirements. Outline and stick to a process that is standardized across *all* candidates and focuses *only* on BFOQs.
Screening and Interviewing	Ask only questions that directly relate to position requirements. *Unless it is clearly a BFOQ,* avoid asking any questions that relate to: marital status, age, religion, race, sexual orientation, national origin, citizenship, disability, education, or arrests and convictions. *If you are unsure about the legality of a question, err on the side of caution and do not ask it.*
Documentation	Make sure that all notes taken or comments made about candidates are directly job-related; they can be subpoenaed as evidence. Remember, any one party can sue any other at any time for any reason—your preparation and documentation may determine the outcome of such a suit.

Visit the U.S. Equal Employment Opportunity Commission's website to learn more about preventing discriminatory hiring practices: www.eeoc. gov/abouteeo/overview_laws.html. Visit www.shrm.org/hrresources/ stresources to learn about the laws governing your state.

Visit www.legalrecords.findlaw.com/ss/search_index.jsp to find local employment lawyers and firms.

Attracting and Selecting Great People

Now that you have clear competencies and a consistent, equitable, and legal process in place to screen candidates, it is time to start working on attracting quality candidates. *To attract great talent, you will need a compelling job description.* A job description is, at heart, a marketing tool: it must engage potential candidates by communicating the opportunities available through the position, as well as outline the requirements so job seekers can determine their fit.

<u>A strong job description generally consists of the following components</u>:

1. <u>Title</u>: Keep it short, concise, descriptive of the position, and widely recognizable.

2. <u>Organizational Overview</u>: Introduce your organization through a succinct and enthusiastic paragraph that outlines the organization's mission and programs, success to date, growth plans and future opportunities, and culture. Remember to include your organization's website.

3. <u>Position Overview</u>: Use one well-written paragraph to describe the overall function of the position and highlight the opportunities for impact and leadership.

4. <u>Responsibilities</u>: Use five to seven bullets to provide detail about the responsibilities of the position. To effectively describe the opportunities of the position, *use engaging and active language* and avoid jargon.

5. <u>Qualifications</u>: This section should outline the experience and competencies required for success in the position and your organization, without being overly prescriptive.

6. <u>Compensation Range</u>: *Disclosing specific compensation information is not required* and in fact, is not recommended, as it limits the candidates you will see.

7. <u>Application Instructions</u>: *Be very specific about how you want candidates to apply for the position.* Generally, organizations request a cover letter and résumé, addressed to the hiring manager and emailed to a specific address. *Keep the application process simple*, as you do not want strong candidates to self-select out of the process.

8. <u>Equal Opportunity Statement</u>: It is good practice to have an equal opportunity employer policy and to include that on your job descriptions. In most cases, a simple "XYZ is an equal opportunity employer" should suffice. If you have a more detailed or descriptive policy, it is a good idea to talk to an employment lawyer to ensure it is legally compliant.

Generating a Candidate Pool

Now that the job description is crafted, you need to make sure the right people see it, so that you will have a pool of great candidates to choose from. *When it comes to hiring for a specific position, it should be all-hands-on-deck.* Most people think "I don't know anyone who would be good for that job, so I won't distribute it to my network," but in truth, *nearly half of all nonprofit positions are filled through the organization's own network.* For example, one nonprofit recently hired the daughter of a candidate who had been a finalist a year earlier for another role at that same organization.

Start by mapping your network—board members, community partners, funders, and organizational "friends"—and sending the job description, with a personalized and engaging email, to the people in your network. Encourage them to forward it to as many other people as possible—people who may be candidates themselves or who may know candidates. *Offering a referral bonus for strong candidates is a great way to encourage participation in the recruitment process.*

Next, make sure to post the position widely on all available online job boards, listservs, and partner sites (some examples are listed in the Resource Review at the end of the chapter). Don't forget to post it on your organization's website as well! Remember to budget for paid posting— advertising for an entry to mid-level position will likely run between $500 and $1,000; for a more senior level position, the cost will likely run about $1,500. Make sure to utilize social networking sites like LinkedIn, Facebook, and Twitter to let your contacts know about the available position.

Screening for Quality

Now that you have a pool of candidates, it is time to put the evaluation process that you developed initially into practice. Remember to ensure clarity, consistency, equity, and legality at every step!

During the <u>application review</u> stage, consider each candidate's cover letter and résumé and evaluate the candidate against your predetermined set of criteria. Don't expect too much from these initial documents, as they are only meant to provide an overview of the candidate so you can determine whether he or she may have enough of the required competencies to warrant moving to the next step.

A phone screen is a very efficient way to narrow down your pool. *Develop a list of open-ended and pointed questions specific to the role* (see sidebar for examples) and use your assessment tool to evaluate responses. The phone screen should hit on the whole range of required competencies and experience so that you can develop a baseline knowledge of the candidate and determine whether he or she represents a potential fit for the role.

Sample Phone Interview Questions: Director of Development Position

- Please tell me about why you are interested in the director of development position with our organization.

- In what type of organizational culture do you thrive? In what kind of culture do you feel less successful?

- Why are you leaving your current position?

- What skills and experience do you have that make you particularly qualified for this position?

- Tell me about the successes you have had raising money for nonprofit organizations. Specifically, how much money did you raise on an annual basis? What were the proportions of money raised from different sources (foundations, corporations, individuals, and government)?

- Can you give me some examples of partnerships you created that led to increased revenue or opportunity for your organization? How did you create them? What were the results?

- Have you ever done a successful major "ask"? If so, please tell me about it. Please describe an example of a donor relationship that you initiated; how did you identify, cultivate, solicit, and steward the donor?

- Please describe your experience working in partnership with a board of directors. What strategies did you implement to ensure an effective and productive partnership?

- To what extent have you been a part of a start-up organization, new initiative or high-growth environment? What was the situation and what roles did you play?

- What is your salary history? What are your current salary requirements?

- How soon would you be able to start a new position?

The <u>initial in-person interview</u> provides an opportunity to go into more depth with a smaller group of candidates. *The interview should be approximately 45-minutes* and include the hiring manager and perhaps one other organizational representative. Remember that you are still in the early stages of the process, so you don't want to invest too many resources in an initial interview process. *Be careful not to make snap judgments;* some candidates take a few minutes to warm up, for they may not be practiced at interviewing or may not be comfortable talking about themselves. *Make sure to give candidates at least three opportunities to demonstrate their fit with the requirements of the position before deciding they are not a good match.* At that point, it is generally acceptable to end an interview a few minutes early—in a respectful, courteous, and professional manner.

<u>Follow-up interview(s)</u> provide an opportunity for a small group of final candidates to learn more about the opportunity and meet additional representatives of the organization, while the organization develops a deeper understanding of the candidate's potential for success. The type and seniority of the position will dictate the number and structure of follow-up interviews, as will organizational structure. While only one additional interview may be needed for a more junior role, it is not unusual for a senior candidate to have two to three follow-up interviews. Exhibit 8.2 gives us a look at how the numbers typically break down:

Exhibit 8.2 Numbers to Expect: Typical Search in a Metropolitan Area

Applications Received	150–200
Applicants Invited for Phone Interviews	15–20 (~10% of total pool)
Applicants Invited for In-Person Interviews	8–10 (~50% of those phone interviewed)
Finalists with References Checked	2–3

Regardless of the interview process you develop, *we recommend utilizing "behaviorally based" interviewing techniques.* Recalling our premise that the best predictor of future success is past accomplishment, behaviorally-based interviewing asks candidates to give specific examples of times when they successfully demonstrated particular competencies in the past. Instead of asking a candidate to hypothetically describe how he would tell your organization's story in a grant proposal, for example, ask him to describe how he developed a compelling story for his previous organization. Table 8.2 offers a list of some of the most important qualities for your interview questions to have, with corresponding examples:

The <u>reference and background checking</u> stage is often overlooked, since organizations are anxious to get someone on board and their energy for the hiring process wanes. However, *we strongly recommend that every organization speak with at least three professional references before making an employment offer to any candidate.* In addition to helping you make the best hiring decision possible, reference checking also provides insight on how to best manage the individual, if hired. For example, one organization recently decided not to hire a candidate everyone had been really excited about because they learned from her references that she needs a significant amount of managerial support in order to be successful and the organization didn't feel that it could provide that.

Table 8.2: Characteristics of Effective Interview Questions

Effective interview questions are:	Examples
<u>Behaviorally based</u>: asking candidates to describe past experiences when they were able to demonstrate specific competencies	*Please describe a time when you identified the need for a new program based on the requirements of a community partner and then developed that program.* *Tell me about an instance in which you created systems to increase operational efficiency and how you approached the development of measurable outcomes.*
<u>Relevant</u>: focusing on core competencies identified in the planning stage	*Talk about a time when you worked in an "all-hands-on-deck" environment and, specifically, what you appreciated and found challenging about that.* *Tell me about how you approached a past experience when you were asked to manage a project with limited access to resources and guidance.*
<u>Open-ended</u>: providing insight into thought processes and competencies	*Describe how you handled a difficult past experience that centered around issues of diversity, as well as how you might handle that situation differently today.* *What do you consider to be your most innovative or creative idea, and through what process did you come up with and develop that concept?*
<u>Initiating</u>: allowing for a variety of follow-up and clarifying questions, such as:	*How did you gain buy-in for that idea? What were the results of that improvement? What did you learn from that situation?*

Finally, it is time for <u>offer negotiation and hiring!</u> This is both the most exciting and most nerve-wracking part of the process because there is always the fear that your top candidate won't accept your offer and that you'll be back at square one. One organization recently fell in love with a candidate for a director of development position and was heartbroken to get to the offer stage and realize that the candidate required $30,000 more in salary than the organization could offer. When discussing the situation internally, the organization realized that salary had not been discussed in any of the candidate's interviews!

The three keys to ensuring that your offer will be accepted are understanding what the candidate wants and needs in an offer, being open and honest throughout the process about what you can provide, and not trying to "get a deal." Make sure that your offer lays out, in detail, the responsibilities and expectations of the position, reporting structure, terms of employment, compensation and benefits (medical, dental, retirement, insurance and disability, paid time off, and so on), and any privacy, non-compete, or confidentiality policies. See www.smallbusiness.findlaw.com/business-forms-contracts/business-forms-contracts-a-to-z/form1-33.html_for a sample offer letter.

Compensating Staff Appropriately

It used to be that mission-driven professionals had no choice but to take a low-paying position within a nonprofit if they wanted to live their values on a daily basis. With the advent of corporate social responsibility, green businesses, and socially driven for-profit enterprises, there are now many more options. So, nonprofits need to consider how they can compete with other industries to attract and retain the best talent.

First, *remember that salary is just one aspect of total compensation.* A full compensation package could include any or all of the following: a performance-based bonus, medical and dental benefits, access to retirement savings accounts (preferably with a matching policy), disability and life insurance policies, paid leave policies, tuition reimbursement, and flexible work schedules. *Make sure that you highlight all elements of the package when negotiating with potential hires* and concentrate on the aspects that are most important to individual candidates.

When determining salary levels for a particular position, do as much research as possible but recognize that there is only a limited amount of current salary data publicly available to nonprofits, and most of that data is more applicable to larger organizations. Try to find benchmark organizations that are comparable to yours in terms of geography, size, staff levels, and mission area.

Furthermore, when "selling" your organization to a strong candidate, think about what makes working at your organization better than working for higher pay at a different organization. Do your employees have greater decision-making power or the ability to work on a wider range of projects? Is your culture more laid-back? Identify and highlight the unique benefits to working at your organization.

Having a compensation philosophy and structure can be helpful when setting salaries and communicating expectations to candidates. "Compensation philosophy" refers to the goals and intent of your approach to compensation. For example, one organization is committed to being as competitive as possible with corporate consulting firms and pays very competitively. Another organization purposefully sets their salary ranges fairly low because they believe that the prestige of working at that organization provides an additional benefit to their employees.

"Compensation structure" refers to how the system is set up—for example, whether there is only a base salary, or a combination of base plus bonus. If there is a bonus, what is the amount of the bonus and in what situations is it distributed? Structure also refers to a stated intention of annual salary adjustments. A general rule of thumb in terms of salary adjustments is shown in Table 8.3:

Table 8.3: Standard Annual Salary Adjustments

Employee Performance Level	Annual Salary Adjustments
Exceeding Expectations	4–5%
Meeting Expectations	2–3%
Needs Improvement	N/A
Unsatisfactory	N/A

Human Capital Management Dos and Don'ts

- DO slow down and plan your hiring process thoughtfully before getting started.

- DO utilize a hiring process that incorporates the four tenets: clarity, consistency, equity, legality.

- DO develop a competency model to inform all stages of the hiring process.

- DO develop a deep and wide candidate pool through multiple, strategic, and targeted sources, including job boards, listservs, organizational and personal networks, social media sites, and professional associations.

- DO use behaviorally based interview questions; the best predictor of future success is past accomplishment, so any hiring process should allow candidates multiple opportunities to provide evidence of how they have demonstrated the needed competencies in the past.

- DO provide the most competitive compensation package possible.

- DON'T make snap judgments in an in-person interview; give the candidate at least three chances to prove their qualifications for the position.

- DON'T ask interview questions that you do not need to know in order to evaluate whether or not this person can effectively do their job.

Conclusion

There is no doubt that talent is an organization's greatest asset. On the one hand, if you took away all of an organization's resources—money, technology, facilities—but kept its people, they would find a way to make things happen. On the other hand, if you took away an organization's people but left their other resources, nothing would happen. That is why it is critical to ensure that you are attracting and hiring the best people as the first step in ensuring that your organization builds and develops the best team. Of course, the orientation, development, management, and retention of talent are of utmost importance, but integrating a few simple processes and best practices like those outlined in this chapter will enable your organization to significantly improve its hiring practices and be better positioned to maximize impact.

James Weinberg is the founder and CEO of Commongood Careers, a retained search firm that enables innovative nonprofits across the country to recruit and hire outstanding talent at every organizational level. Concurrently, James also serves as the founder & CEO of Talent Initiative, a nonprofit consulting firm dedicated to enhancing human capital management in the social sector. Previously, James served as national development director at BELL and as executive director at Homeless Children's Education Fund. He was a Coro Fellow, has a master's in management and public policy from Carnegie Mellon, and a BA in psychology from Tufts University.

As president and cofounder of Commongood Careers, Cassie Scarano provides strategic vision and daily management for the organization. Cassie has over 15 years of experience in the nonprofit sector, having served as the dean of admissions at The Steppingstone Foundation, director of Operations for The New Teacher Project, and director of Summerbridge Cambridge. She holds a BA in sociology from Northwestern University, an MA in education from Boston University, and an MBA in nonprofit management from Boston University. Currently an active board member of Breakthrough Cambridge, Cassie lives outside of Boston with her husband and son and enjoys spending time on her boat on Cape Cod.

Human Capital Management Resource Review

Commongood Careers Knowledge Center (www.cgcareers.org/
knowledge-center/)

A collection of articles focused on best practices and how-to's on a variety of topics related to nonprofit recruitment and hiring.

Commongood Careers Group on LinkedIn (www.linkedin.com/e/gis/2708)

A community of nonprofit hiring managers and other social sector professionals. Members post questions, discussion topics, and other information related to human capital management.

Guidestar (www.guidestar.org)

Free searchable database of over 1.5 million nonprofit organizations, including Form 990 tax return data that documents salary information for the highest paid positions at each organization.

HR.com (www.hr.com)

Portal site for human resources information, including a section on public sector and nonprofit human resources.

Idealist.org (www.idealist.org)

The go-to job board for nonprofit positions, which also includes a searchable, international database of nonprofit organizations, volunteer positions, and other information about the sector. Go to www.idealist.org/if/i/en/faq/901–37/48–68 for answers to frequently asked questions and links to discussions about nonprofit human resources.

Mission-Based Management Blog (www.missionbased.blogspot.com/)

Musings on nonprofit management, funding, fundraising, technology, and policy from Peter Brinckerhoff.

Professionals for Nonprofits (www.nonprofitstaffing.com)

Staffing firm for nonprofits in New York and Washington, DC that publishes an annual salary survey for New York City and Washington positions in management, finance, fundraising, marketing, programs, and IT.

Society for Human Resources Management (www.shrm.com)

An association for human resources professionals that provides a significant number of resources, tools, and templates for all areas of HR.

U.S. Equal Employment Opportunity Commission (www.eeoc.gov/)

Website published by the federal government with resources and information related to employment discrimination laws.

∘ ∘ ∘

All these resources, plus nonprofit management tips of the week and more, can be found at Nonprofits101.org.

CHAPTER 9

The Importance of Diversity

By Michael Watson, Senior Vice President, Human Resources and Diversity, Girl Scouts of the USA

Introduction

The historic roots of diversity reach back into the early 1800s, when a burgeoning women's suffrage movement focused on attaining the right of women to hold citizenship, vote, and own property. Then in 1868, the ratification of the 14th Amendment to the United States Constitution stated that those born or naturalized in the United States were American citizens, including those born as slaves—this gave African Americans citizenship and the rights that accompany it. The underlying and passionate spirit of this long fight to provide equality, the right to vote, and access to a wide range of jobs was based on this simple principle: it was the right thing to do. Among the early nonprofits, the settlement house movement and other immigrant services organizations met the needs of underserved and overlooked groups, like the poor and the disabled—also working off the same conviction.

Legislative action continued in the twentieth century, providing the legal basis of major shifts in hiring and employment practices. In 1964 Title VII of the Civil Rights Act was enacted. This had a major impact on workplace practices, prohibiting discrimination on the basis of race, color, national origin, religion, and sex.

Today, diversity combines elements of compliance and doing the right thing, but it has acquired new urgency due to sweeping changes in the nation's demographics. These include a larger presence of people of color, increases in longevity leading to a four-generation workforce, and a much greater proportion of women working than ever before. Finally, we also have widespread concern that the large proportion of Baby Boomers leaving the workforce over the next decade will create a huge need to grow and sustain our talent pipeline.

If nonprofits are to effectively serve their clients, maintain their impact and ongoing relevance, they must demonstrate continued leadership in all aspects of managing diversity.

The premise of this chapter is this: *when you effectively integrate diversity into your nonprofit's service delivery strategy, more individuals will benefit from the services you offer.* The diversity-enabled nonprofit will promote greater opportunity for a broader swath of clients, employees, and volunteers. The end result is that your nonprofit will achieve far greater organizational impact and potential for growth.

Before we dive in, let's get our definition straight. *Diversity* refers to all the differences—from racial and ethnic to gender, age, disability, economic status, and beyond. Diversity itself is diverse!

Because diversity represents many differences among people and groups, this chapter focuses on three major areas—race and ethnicity, generations, and disabilities. We can apply many of the approaches and considerations in these three areas to other diversity categories, including gender, age, geography, and so forth.

Critical Skills and Competencies

As nonprofits seek to embrace diversity within their organizations, there are a few important considerations to keep in mind, as well as some strongly recommended best practices. Let's take a look.

Integrating Diversity into Your Organization

Successfully achieving diversity within your organization will require your commitment to making it a key aspect of your nonprofit's strategy, culture, and relationships. In particular, you must *pay close attention to achieving diversity at four major levels of your organization*: staff, volunteer, population served, and board of directors.

Start out by taking inventory of the diversity of these various groups. I recommend using a matrix like that shown in Table 9.1, customized based on desired populations and priorities:

Now let's dive into these audiences and explore crucial competencies for integrating diversity within each of them.

Who Are Your Employees?

Reviewing your employee demographics helps determine whether your organization is diverse enough to provide the range of perspectives needed to serve your clients effectively. After you've completed the matrix above, here are four key questions to ask and discuss with your leadership team about your current staff:

1. Do our employees reflect the pool of talent available in our community?

2. Do we have a mix of employees with the perspectives and backgrounds needed to effectively communicate with our constituency, thereby enabling us to best serve them?

3. To what extent can our employees relate to the life experiences and issues of those we serve and of our volunteers?

Table 9.1: Sample Nonprofit Diversity Analysis Matrix

Categories	Men	Women	African American	Latino/ Hispanic	Native American	Low Income	People with Disabilities	Age 18–34	Age 35–54	Age 55+
Board Officers										
Board of Directors										
Direct Reports to CEO										
Staff										
Volunteers										
Population Served										

4. Have we created an organizational environment that leverages the talents and skills of our employees, regardless of age, ethnic/racial category, gender, educational attainment, or other relevant differences?

After you review of your employee demographics and answers to the questions above, you may determine that you need greater diversity within your staff to better represent the community you serve. In this case, *be sure to leverage targeted and relevant media outlets, associations, and networks.* For example, if you are looking to fill an accounting position and you want to ensure that you attract candidates from a variety of ethnic and racial groups, you could take the following ten steps:

1. *Contact local leaders of relevant professional organizations,* such as the National Association of Black Accountants, National Black MBA Association, the Association of Latino Professionals in Finance and Accounting, the Society of Hispanic MBAs, and Pan-Asian Leaders in Finance and Accounting. Professional associations like these can easily be found through online searches, and if there isn't a local chapter, contact the national organization.

2. *Contact individuals from underrepresented communities* who are in the accounting field, or who have broad networks, and ask for referrals.

3. *Talk to religious leaders* whose congregations are attended by diverse professionals.

4. *Advertise positions in newspapers and on websites* read by diverse candidates. The Riley guide (www.rileyguide.com/diverse.html) offers a directory of websites that can be used to attract diverse talent.

5. Speak with leaders of nonprofit organizations that tailor to a diverse clientele (i.e., Urban League, National Council de La Raza, NAACP, and so on).

6. Attend diversity recruiting fairs.

7. *Contact the Career Services offices at nearby colleges and universities* and ask how you can reach out to diverse students or alumni. Search online to see if there are any Historically Black Colleges and Universities or Hispanic

Serving Institutions in your area, and also reach out to local sororities and fraternities that focus on diverse membership.

8. Post job descriptions on websites frequented by diverse professionals, including www.diversityinc.com.

9. *Put your network to work.* Ask your employees, board members, and volunteers for their recommendations and contact individuals you know with networks in diverse communities.

10. If you work with a search firm, select them based on their track record of recruiting and placing diverse talent.

Also, remember that achieving diversity is not a one-time goal. It's crucial to regularly review the diversity of your staff and the success of your efforts to attract and recruit diverse employees. *Reinforce those practices that work best and develop new approaches to replace those are least effective.*

Who Are Your Volunteers?

Although paid staff drive the work of many nonprofits, volunteers make up a key component of most nonprofits' ability to serve. Any nonprofit making substantial use of volunteers should assess whether or not its volunteer pool has a demographic gap and if it's missing volunteers who would help the organization better serve its constituents. This is a worthwhile time investment that provides high payoff, and *a volunteer assessment and action plan involves four simple steps*:

1. Assess whether you have an adequate number of volunteers to meet your needs and goals.

2. Based on the completed diversity matrix, determine whether your volunteer population reflects the diversity of the population you serve. *If there is a demographic gap, find out why.* Is it the lack of diversity at the beginning of the recruitment process, or is turnover higher among volunteers from specific diverse backgrounds?

3. If turnover is a problem, determine the primary causes and implement an action plan to address it.

Table 9.2: Neighborhood Nonprofit Volunteer Analysis by Age

Age Categories	Volunteer Demographics (%)	Client Demographics (%)	Gap (%)
18–29	15	15	0
30–40	5	25	–20
41–50	40	40	0
51+	40	20	+20

4. If you need to recruit more diverse volunteers, consider adding new recruitment sources (see staffing section above for ideas) and customizing your orientation process for key populations.

As you can tell from the Neighborhood Nonprofit volunteer analysis in Table 9.2, 25% of the organization's population served is between ages 30–40. Only 5% of their volunteers fall into the 30–40 age category. Similarly, there is a surplus of volunteers ages 51+. If these gaps are relevant and have a negative impact on the individuals served, they should expand recruitment of volunteers in this/these age groups.

o o o

To recruit diverse volunteers, your strategy would be to approach the same types of organizations you would for recruiting diverse staff, as listed in the section above.

Are You Serving Everyone?

Based on readily available U.S. Census data, comparing the population you serve to local demographics will quickly tell you whether you are serving a representative sample of local residents. Of course, you will want to drill down a bit, because, for example, low-income populations tend to have their own demographic makeup. Your analysis can be based upon education, income, race, age, or a variety of other dimensions relevant to your local area and to the services you provide. When unexpected gaps are found, conduct surveys, focus groups, and other outreach strategies to understand what prevents utilization of services by those who are underserved. The insights you gain will assist you in improving the services you provide and extending the reach and relevance of your services.

Who Is on Your Board?

Last but certainly not least, the composition of your board is an important factor in your organization's success. Membership needs to be diverse enough to discuss governance issues from a variety of perspectives and to understand the needs of the various communities you serve. *Effective boards need diverse membership*, including race, ethnicity, gender, as well as a range of skill sets, networks, perspectives, and styles. Embracing diversity in all its forms at the board level will enhance your relevance in the community and expand your ability to serve.

To increase the diversity of your board, consider the following actions:

1. Lead a discussion with board members to obtain agreement on the benefits and importance of greater board diversity.

2. Based on how the board defines greater diversity, determine whether a current board committee can take on the recruiting task or whether additional help will be needed.

3. Obtain clear agreement by board members on metrics that will be used to assess diversity progress and determine the frequency of reviews for progress.

4. Determine appropriate candidate sources. Several sources are similar to those for recruiting staff, but given the unique nature and role of a board, it's also recommended to contact:

   - Board members of other nonprofits who represent the diversity you seek—they may be able to refer individuals who have similar skills and professional backgrounds

   - Corporations with strong reputations for diversity, which can offer access to highly skilled and networked employees

   - Vendors and suppliers (i.e., your accounting firm, telecommunications provider, and so forth), which can introduce you to their human resource departments for recommendations of individuals or organizations

See the Chapter Thirty for additional tips on how to attract great talent at this level, and as mentioned there, be sure to have a board member agreement in place to help convey clear expectations and needs.

What I Wish I Knew

When I began my human resources career, I gained a number of diversity insights that I did not anticipate. They include:

1. Diversity within populations

   Groups that appear to be the same on the outside are more different than we think. As an example, Hispanics may be considered one ethnic category, but there are cultural, economic, educational, and other differences between Cubans, Mexicans, and other Latinos. For maximum effectiveness, you cannot approach all Hispanics, African Americans, Asians, Baby Boomers, disabled people, or any other group the same way. Your approach to service and outreach has to be tailored to the specific characteristics of the groups and subgroups you are targeting.

2. People want things their way

   If you approach everyone in the same manner, you will fail to connect with a significant proportion of the individuals you serve. For example, if your nonprofit is in an area where a large percentage of people speak a primary language other than English, consider hiring staff that speak the language. For areas where literacy levels are low, alternative strategies should be implemented to provide assistance with completing forms and paperwork. Instead of a "lowest common denominator" approach, invest in understanding the unique characteristics of the populations you serve and their particular wants and needs—this will enable you to implement relevant strategies and improve the services you provide.

3. Diversity is a source of strength

   Studies show that *diverse groups perform better than homogeneous ones.* They perform best when leaders and managers *take the time to ensure that newly added members from diverse groups are fully oriented, welcomed, included, supported, and encouraged* to make a significant contribution to your organization. New employees and volunteers who do not feel included will either be underutilized, or they will turn over at a higher rate. However, it is important to remember that when diverse groups are not managed well, they are likely to underperform compared with homogeneous counterparts.

4. A case still needs to be made for diversity

Diversity as an organizational priority has come a long way over the past decade. That said, you still can't assume that people are on the same page on this issue, or that they sufficiently understand the business case for diversity. So count on having to explain the benefits of diversity, demonstrate how it is important to the service you deliver, and how an effective strategy will strengthen your organization's ability to achieve its mission. *Making a diversity business case tailored to your organization and culture is crucial if you are to move this important agenda forward.* Bearing in mind the approaches and tactics outlined above, *utilize these eight common elements to research and present as part of your case*:

1. Analysis of the diversity of

   a. Your staff

   b. Your volunteers

   c. The clients you serve

   d. Your board

2. Identification of areas of concern

   a. Numerical gaps

   b. Gaps in perspective

   c. Potential concerns from constituents—those served, funders

3. Implications

   a. How greater diversity will improve service to clients

   b. How attention to diversity will expand the number of those served

   c. Can attention to diversity increase the pool of volunteers or board members?

    d. If changing demographics are ignored, what is the future of your organization? Will it shrink, or become less relevant?

    e. Will attention to diversity increase access to funding?

4. Call for action

    a. Define the impact diversity will have on the future of your organization

    b. Review implications of a failure to act

    c. Present case for change to senior management and board

5. Create an action plan

    a. Identify gaps and present an operational plan to address each of them

    b. Estimate resources needed—people, money, expertise

    c. Assess return on investment and specify what the targeted result of the investments will be

    d. Identify real and potential barriers and plan to address each

    e. Define and vet metrics for success

    f. Develop time lines and milestones

    g. Identify individuals with major accountability for results

6. Clearly communicate strategy and vision to major constituencies

7. Develop process for reviewing progress

8. Get feedback and make adjustments as needed

A Guide to Making Your Diversity Plan Succeed

Many organizations make commitments to achieving diversity, only to fail in their quest because they overlook the factors essential to making their plan sustainable. *These ten factors should be incorporated into your action plan from the beginning to ensure diversity's success in your organization:*

1. Ensure that top management demonstrates genuine commitment to diversity. Lack of commitment from the CEO or senior managers creates significant barriers that can sink your plans, including demotivating other levels of management and employees.

2. Develop and communicate a well-articulated, customized business case for diversity. Use multiple communications platforms—memos, meetings, and new employee and volunteer orientations to ensure people at every level of the organization fully understand and can state the importance of diversity.

3. Integrate diversity policies across all work activities—outreach, volunteer and staff recruitment, individuals served, and other relevant areas to maximize your plan's effectiveness and sustainability.

4. Obtain ongoing input from those you want to serve about the needs of diverse populations. Extend your outreach and keep in touch with the populations you serve.

5. Implement metrics to assess progress toward your diversity goals. Measuring changes in the diversity of the population you serve, your employees, volunteers, and board provides you with feedback regarding the effectiveness of your strategies. Survey the satisfaction of those served to ensure that approval is relatively equal across the diverse populations you serve and to spot issues that need to be addressed.

6. Pay attention to emerging trends. A changing economy, movement of new individuals into or out of your community, policy and legislative changes, and other factors can change your community and those whom you should be prepared to serve.

7. Learn from others. Make this an organizational priority. No one has all the answers and you can learn effective diversity strategies from other nonprofits, politicians, corporations, or the government. This is a two-way street, so be open to exchanging best practices.

8. Learn from your mistakes. You have to be willing to try new approaches to achieve progress in diversity. At the same time, recognize that some of these approaches will not work. Examine what has worked and what has not, then decide whether to abandon or modify specific tactics and approaches.

9. Providing recognition for successes in diversity encourages staff and volunteers to keep diversity top of mind and to try new approaches.

10. Realize that success at diversity is an ongoing process. The needs of your community, your volunteers, and employees continually evolve. Continually monitor the needs and changes of your constituents, volunteers, and staff.

extracts

Actions CEOs Can Take

Present diversity to board as part of organizational service strategy.

Ensure that candidates for open positions are diverse.

Talk to direct reports and staff about why diversity is important to accomplishment of organization's mission.

extracts

Actions Emerging Leaders Can Take to Support Diversity

Develop and present the business case to your CEO and senior management.

Identify and build relationships with organizations and partnerships that may serve as sources of diverse candidates for staff, volunteer, and board openings.

Take Charge of Your Education

The following actions will help you keep up with diversity trends:

1. Read books, magazines, articles, and blogs that focus on the needs of diverse populations. See resources at end of chapter for examples of great places to learn best practices.

2. Prioritize meeting people from different groups who can provide you with a new perspective on the needs of diverse populations.

3. Attend local meetings of professional associations and other groups where you can develop relationships with members of diverse groups.

4. Track diversity trends. Business and marketing magazines, as well as major newspapers, will help you track and understand societal changes that may affect your work.

Definitions and Background

Race and Ethnicity

Racial and ethnic demographic change in the United States is charting a new future for America. Figure 9.1 shows the remarkable changes predicted within the next generation: by 2050, we will be a majority minority nation.

Generational Diversity

Diversity in the United States takes many forms. Beyond ethnicity, we now are experiencing four generations working alongside one another for the first time

Figure 9.1: Percent Minority of the U.S. Population by Selected Age Groups—All Ages

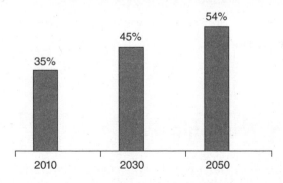

Source: Population Division, U.S. Census Bureau, released August 14, 2008.

in U.S. history. Chapter Ten focuses specifically on working across generations, but here is a brief overview of three key characteristics that have differentiated Gen@ members (a term coined by Peter Brinckerhoff, one of the authors of Chapter Ten, for people born between 1978 and 1996—also known as Millennials or GenY) and Baby Boomers (born between 1946 and 1964) from their older counterparts.

1. Approach Toward Work. Work/life balance has been growing in importance across generations. However, Gen@ members both expect and demand that balance now. Your nonprofit's ability to attract and engage both Gen@ members and Baby Boomers depends upon how well you provide flexibility and honor the need for balance. This must be conveyed clearly in the workplace and in your recruiting process.

2. Feedback. Receiving feedback for work performed is important to all—in varying degrees. Frequent feedback is important for and expected by Gen@, but this is not as central a need for Baby Boomers. Failure to adjust your feedback frequency and style to the various generations' styles and to individuals within each generation is likely to have a negative impact on their productivity and retention.

3. Communication Preferences. Gen@ members are sometimes referred to as "digital natives," given their high utilization of technology and social media. This is a stark contrast to older populations—a 2010 FCC study (Broadband Adoption and Use in America by John B. Horrigan, PhD) showed that only 21% of African Americans over 65 have adopted broadband and 22% of American adults are not Internet users. Nonprofits that place all their materials and information online may inadvertently overlook large groups of their constituents and volunteers.

Disabilities

Numbering approximately 54 million, *people with disabilities are the largest minority in the United States* and the only minority anyone can become a part of at any time. Disability crosses all racial, ethnic, religious, and socioeconomic boundaries. Efforts to ensure that individuals with disabilities have access to information, services, and the workforce have increased substantially since The Americans with Disabilities Act was passed in 1990, which prevents employment discrimination and seeks to include people with disabilities fully into the mainstream of American life. Legally, an individual with a disability is any person who:

- Has a physical or mental impairment that substantially limits one or more major life activities;

- Has a record of such an impairment; or

- Is regarded (based on the perception of others) as having such impairment.

Solutions to improve access may include labeling in Braille, providing optical aids, and physical changes to structures, including ramps and other changes that enable access via wheelchairs or other devices. Some of these, especially regarding larger facilitates, may be legally required regardless of the makeup of your staff.

Because disabilities tend to increase with age, we can expect the number of disabled to grow substantially given our aging population. *Nonprofits that consider the needs of the disabled will serve more of those in need and have access to more volunteers and employees.* Figure 9.2 gives us a quick view of the numbers:

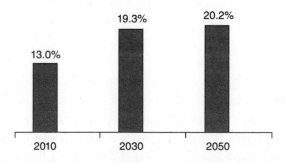

Figure 9.2: Project Percent of the U.S. Population Aged 65 and Older

Source: Population Division, U.S. Census Bureau, released August 14, 2008.

case study

Case Studies of How Diversity Can Be Integrated into Nonprofit Strategy

The Girl Scouts: Outreach Based on Religion and Ethnicity

Several years ago, the Girl Scout council in Minneapolis developed membership outreach coordinators for a variety of minority groups, including the Muslim community. To overcome resistance from parents, Girl Scouts troop leaders included Muslim traditions in their activities. Some simple adaptations included ensuring that Islamic law dietary requirements were adhered to, including, at troop events, only serving hot dogs that were made of beef instead of pork. The leaders also sought out opportunities to highlight Muslim culture. The Khadija Club was developed, named for the first wife of Prophet Muhammad, geared towards exposing girls to the history of prominent Muslim women.

The outreach in Minneapolis resulted in 280 girls joining Girl Scouts, including many who may have not considered it before. In addition to Muslim girls learning American traditions, the opposite was also true, resulting in an increased understanding of Muslim culture and religion (Neil MacFarquhar, <u>New York Times</u>, November 28, 2007).

Similarly, in 2005 Girl Scouts was given a grant to expand Hispanic membership in Georgia. Part of the strategy included recruiting, training, and sustaining a strong base of Hispanic volunteers, and bilingual staff were increased from five to 30. These staff members began working in partnership with other Girl Scout employees to implement highly effective, customized outreach strategies. Between 2005 and 2008, Girl Scouts increased Hispanic membership by 40%, volunteers by 20%, and a whopping 76% increase in community partnerships with Hispanic organizations. *The bottom line is that with diverse population, a little sensitivity and effort can go a very long way.*

Diversity Dos and Don'ts

Dos and Don'ts

- DO pay close attention to achieving diversity at four major levels of your organization: staff, volunteer, population served, and board of directors.

- DO create a diversity business case tailored to your organization and culture, wherein you explain the benefits of diversity, demonstrate how it is important to the service you deliver, and how an effective strategy will strengthen your organization's ability to achieve its mission.

- DO create staff, volunteer, and board assessment and action plans to guide your efforts.

- DO leverage targeted and relevant media outlets, associations, and networks in your efforts to recruit diverse candidates.

- DO ask your employees, board members, and volunteers for their recommendations of diverse candidates, and tap people you know with networks in diverse communities.

- DON'T assume you know why demographic gaps exist—take the time to research what the real problem is.

- DON'T forget that studies have shown that diverse groups perform better than homogeneous ones, and that they perform best when leaders and managers take the time to ensure that newly added members from diverse groups are fully oriented, welcomed, included, supported, and encouraged.

- DO implement metrics to assess progress toward your diversity goals.

Conclusion

Know this: the population of the United States will become increasing diverse, even in ways that we cannot anticipate today. Embracing this diversity can be a source of continued innovation, success, and competitive advantage. Nonprofits are uniquely positioned to use their understanding of diversity, especially among those most in need, to create a better society for all. Failure to consider diversity in a nonprofit's strategy will result in a decline in your organization's relevance and even possible extinction. Successfully integrating diversity into your operations requires a commitment to sustained research, effort, and open-mindedness, all of which lead to better-managed nonprofits that serve their clients more effectively.

As a professional, your ability to work with diverse employees and volunteers and develop effective strategies to ensure that all are included will strengthen your personal impact and contribute to your career success.

Perhaps most importantly, I believe that nonprofit organizations' collective embrace of diversity will help create a society where everyone enjoys greater opportunity to reach their full potential and determine America's future. Join the adventure.

Michael Watson directs development of human resources strategy for Girl Scouts of the USA. Prior to Girl Scouts, Watson held positions at IBM Global Services, Time Warner Inc., and GE Capital. He is a GE Human Resources Management Program graduate and recipient of GE Capital's Pinnacle Club and IBM's Golden Circle awards. Watson serves as the National Human Services Assembly's Human Resources Council chair and was former board treasurer for the Nonprofit Workforce Coalition. Watson has a BA in economics from Yale University and MS in organizational management and human resource development from Manhattanville College.

Diversity Resource Review

Nonprofit Workforce Coalition (www.humanics.org/site/c.omL2KiN4LvH/ b.1537159/k.3F31/Nonprofit_Workforce_Coalition.htm)

Works on workforce and diversity challenges faced by the nonprofit sector.

Practices for Good (www.npgoodpractice.org/Topics/ diversityculturalcompetency/Default.aspx)

Frances Kunreuther, Helen Kim, and Robby Rodriguez. <u>Working Across Generations: Defining the Future of Nonprofit Leadership</u>. San Francisco: Jossey Bass, 2008.

Highlights best practices in advocacy, evaluation, fundraising, governance, human resources, information management, legal policies, marketing, and organizational development.

Working Mother Magazine (www.workingmother.com)

Provides annual rankings of best places for working mothers, along with recommendations for achieving work-life balance.

Diversity Inc. Magazine (www.diversityinc.com)

A monthly publication dedicated to chronicling diversity best practices and trends.

Lynne C. Lancaster and David Stillman. When Generations Collide: Who They Are, Why They Clash, How to Solve the Generational Puzzle at Work. New York: HarperBusiness, 2002.

This book describes how generational differences at work may be resolved.

Ron Zemke, Claire Raines, and Bob Filipczak. Generations at Work: Managing the Clash of Veterans, Boomers, Xers, and Nexters in Your Workplace. New York: AMACOM, 2000.

This book helps the reader understand generational differences that may exist at work.

American Institute for Managing Diversity (www.aimd.org)

This organization partners with academic institutions, businesses, corporations, civic and community organizations, government leaders, and their agencies to advance the study of diversity.

Diversity Executive Magazine (www.diversity-executive.com/)

Contains information and insights that help leaders committed to diversity move from awareness to action.

Disability Statistics (www.ilr.cornell.edu/edi/DisabilityStatistics/)

This site provides detailed disability statistics, including employment and household income.

<u>Ability Magazine</u> (www.abilitymagazine.com/)

Regular publication focused on disability issues, including new technologies, civil rights, employment opportunities, and medical developments.

○ ○ ○

All these resources, plus nonprofit management tips of the week and more, can be found at Nonprofits101.org.

CHAPTER 10

Bridging the Generation Gap

By Peter Brinckerhoff, Founder,
Corporate Alternatives, Inc. and Vincent Hyman,
President, Vincent Hyman Editorial Services

Introduction

Generational differences are like humidity: right in front of you, but invisible. These differences are good for you (and your organization) most days, but when there's too much difference, just as with humidity, it's oppressive for everyone, and no one can hide. In this chapter we'll cover the topic of leading across generations, a task that has always vexed managers, but never more so than right now. We'll look at what motivates each generation, the traps that managers fall into, and give you some tips on how to manage and work with generations different from your own, as well as how to motivate and lead your own generation to reduce intergenerational conflict.

A few facts to get us started. The different generations in our nonprofits (the Greatest Generation, Silent Generation, Baby Boomers, Generation X, and Gen@) are more differentiated than any set of generations in history. We'll talk about why in a bit, but the key for you to understand here is that these *generations* meet all the criteria of different *cultures*. You probably work hard at your organization to stay diverse in your staff, your board, your volunteers. And, when you consider the word "diverse," you probably first think of people of different racial or ethnic backgrounds, gender or sexual orientation. No question that having that kind diversity is essential to better mission performance in a lot of ways. *But so is generational diversity.* The key here is to remember that every culture has its own uniqueness, its own history, its own touchstones, and that you need to work hard to learn about another culture; it doesn't just happen. Let's get started by taking a look at some of the unique characteristics of each of these generational cultures.

A Five-Generation Mashup

Our cultural sensitivity training begins with a look at each generation and what motivates them. One word of caution: when you group people arbitrarily, you necessarily stereotype. Obviously, there will be members of each of the generations below who do not fit the stereotypes described here, just as there are millions of teenagers who aren't difficult to raise, men who actually ask for directions, and people over 70 who love to be online. With that caveat, let's take a look.

"Greatest Generation": Born 1901–1924

The 20 million members of this generation, named by Tom Brokaw's terrific book, grew up in the Great Depression, fought and won World War II, and built the American economy into the international Goliath it still is today. Though members of this generation are fewer every day, many still are active as volunteers and donors in nonprofits.

The key to motivation for these people is being part of a large-scale, valuable change. Thus, you can say to them, "Come work with us. We're a local organization, but part of a national network of nonprofits committed to our mission." The shorthand here: These people are very comfortable being a small cog in a big machine.

"Silent Generation": Born 1925–1945

The 30 million members of the Silent Generation grew up in the shadow of their older peers, much the way that GenX members grew up in the shadow of the Baby Boomers. Most of the men in this generation served in the military, but a smaller percentage served in combat than the generation that preceded them, or followed them.

Silent Generation members are all around nonprofits. They are staff members, board members, nongoverning volunteers, and donors. When working with these people, make sure to find out what their "thing" is. Silent Generation members are very focused on one or two things that have affected them specifically. So, if a member of their family has a disability—that's where they'll spend their nonprofit time, talent, and treasure. If cancer has affected their circle of family and friends, they'll move in that direction. If they are fascinated by art, expect them to focus on visual arts organizations. This means that for this group you have to ask and listen to what they are passionate about.

"Boomer Generation" (Baby Boomers): Born 1946–1962

At *last* we get to talk about the Boomers! We Boomers (yes, the authors are) love to talk about ourselves because it really is all about us. Or at least that's the opinion of many GenXers—that Boomers can't see beyond their own generational issues, and to a certain extent, that's true. There were so many of us (78 million) that we have always dominated society as we've grown up, reached adulthood and gone into the workforce. More than that, though, is our memory of what happened collectively in our youth. Not only were we the first generation to openly rebel against the government since the Revolution, but in our collective memory, we were all at Woodstock! (It was *very* crowded there.)

Which leads to a key point about Boomers. We did carve out significant social change in our youth, and many, many Boomers are seeking in our older years to get back to "saving the world." We can't emphasize it enough: if you want to attract Boomer staff, donors, or volunteers, *your mission is your competitive advantage.* And, you will connect with Boomers if you tell them that they can come with you and save the world . . . again.

"Generation X": Born 1963–1980

One of the main issues for the 38 million GenXers is waiting for the Boomers to get out of the way. The vast majority of nonprofit board and senior managers are still Boomers, and with most nonprofits being small organizations offering a limited ability to move up the career ladder, many GenX members see Boomers as an impediment to their success.

Though GenXers have always worked in the shadow of the Boomers, they are confident and very focused on their career path. They value independence, self-reliance, stability, informality, and fun.

When you work with GenX members, make sure to emphasize their value to the mission of the organization. In addition, you have to lead in a way that allows people to think independently and have at least some level of work-life balance. More on this huge challenge in a bit.

"Gen@" (GenY, Millenials): Born 1981–2002

To put it directly: these people were born digital. Gen@ members (also called GenY and Millenials) cannot remember a time when there wasn't personal technology. They are connected and integrated with their friends and peers in ways that Boomers cannot truly comprehend. One Gen@ member described how he promoted himself for a job: "I told the company that they wouldn't just get me; I'm a node on a network, I come with all my friends as well." That's a perfect description of the connectedness that this generation feels and acts with.

When you motivate Gen@ members, you want to emphasize the good that they *and their friends* can do through your mission. These are group animals—not herd animals, as they think very independently—but they are comfortable in groups, whether it be dating or donating, so accommodate that need.

Gen@ members also have a deeply ingrained need to be heard, which often vexes Boomer managers. Think about it: when they were in school, from elementary school through college, they did much of their work in groups. They learned to collaborate, speak up, accommodate different skills, and participate in decision making at all levels. Boomers, and some GenX members, didn't have these experiences. So when a Gen@ person expects to have his or her idea listened to, it's natural, not an inflated ego. *It's what they were taught to do.*

With that thumbnail of the different generations, let's get to some specific ideas on how to lead across generations.

Critical Skills and Competencies: Leading Across Generations

Now that we've looked at the differences between the generations, let's dive into some concrete tips and tactics for working with these different groups.

1. Remember That Different Generations Are Different Cultures

As different groups have permeated the workforce, managers have had to adapt their leadership styles to accommodate the new diversity in outlooks, backgrounds, attitudes, and insights; in short, the new culture. Those readers whose mission is in human services know full well that reaching a parent born in, say, Southeast Asia regarding a child with a disability, or an addiction, or a mental health problem, is a much different task than reaching a parent from, say, Western Europe. Not easier, not harder, just different. If the disabilities or mental health or addiction professional is not sensitive to those differences, she can't do her job as well.

Same thing for managers. We need to celebrate all the diverse outlooks of the people we work with, and that means diversity of age as well. A Silent Generation member is not "old . . . out of touch"; rather, she has a viewpoint, experience, and advice that can help focus us on mission. Same thing for the 21-year-old Gen@ worker. Are they just "young whippersnappers" (to use a phrase from four generations ago)? Or do they bring a different cultural outlook that can help us better achieve our mission? As a steward of your nonprofit, your job is to get the most mission out the door every day with the resources you have. One of those resources is generational perspective. Don't dis those perspectives, and *never assume that your generation is the "right" one.*

Remember, if you are a supervisor, your job is not to dictate, control, or be single minded. It's to support the people you supervise, who are almost certainly closer to the mission provision of your organization every day than you are. If management is a support function (and it is), if managers are best when they act like coaches and use the particular talents of each of their "players" (and they are), then why wouldn't you do this?

But how do you do it? It's easy to say you'll be generationally sensitive, but what do you do, exactly?

There are six actions that can help the leader be sensitive to generational issues, as Peter noted in his book, <u>Generations: The Challenge of a Lifetime for Your Nonprofit</u>.

First, you should be sure to include generational issues in all your planning activities. This means gathering the data you need about each generation and including representatives or representative opinions of each group.

Second, you need to create an environment of open discussion and mentoring among generations. This does not mean "old teaches young." Quite the opposite. It means that members of one generation should seek to learn from the key strengths of other generations. Discussion and mentoring arrangement may be both formal and informal.

Third, rethink your marketing efforts along generational lines. This means adapting your approaches to fit the interests of the generation you are trying to reach. For example, don't try to reach Gen@ people through a quarterly newsletter; they'll expect Facebook, Twitter, or whatever is the newest personal contact. And don't target members of the Greatest Generation using email. Most won't see it.

Fourth, age down. This means you should be seeking to reduce the mean age of your board, management, volunteers, and donors. This is especially important among those nonprofits that were founded and still run by the Boomers, who helped bring the nonprofit sector to its maturity and who still dominate its leadership.

Fifth, meet the technology expectations of the generation you are communicating with (we'll call them *techspectations*). Use tech to bridge the divide between generations, but also to fit the disparate needs of different generations. Boomers need big type fonts. GenX and Gen@ want short bursts of information.

Sixth, always start by asking, observing, engaging in conversation and, above all, listening. As Boomer Caucasian males (or as Peter's Korean-born daughter loves to tell him, "pale, male, and stale, Dad"), the authors would never dream of telling our African American friends how they should see the world—we ask them how they see it so we can understand them better. Same here. *Ask, and ask a lot.* This is the way you can learn to work with the culture of other generations.

2. Remember the Rules of Work-Life Balance

Think of this scenario: A Boomer manager is approached by a Gen@ staff who wants to do more work from home so that she can cut her commute time and spend the time saved on her second passion: working with homeless youth. The Boomer manager often thinks (and sometimes says) "What's *wrong* with her? Doesn't she care enough about *our* mission to be here? Why would she not want to be here 60 hours a week working on *our* mission? Ugh. Uncommitted youth these days."

And if the manager voices those thoughts to the Gen@ staff person, she thinks, "What's wrong with my boss? Can't he get a life? Why would he need to be here 60 hours a week just to prove his mission chops? And, why can't he see I can care about two things at once? Ugh. . . ."

Both desires (work 60 hours, have a work-life balance) are right, from a generational perspective.

We Boomers define ourselves through our work, for better or worse. During the early 2000s boom, as many Boomers began to reach their fifties and sixties, papers and magazines were full of advice for them about what to do next. Most of these articles and books were not titled "Tips for Retirement" or "Plan to Relax," but rather "How to Pick a Second Career," "Work from Home," and the like. When the Annie E. Casey Foundation made a bold prediction in 2003 that 40% of nonprofit CEOs would retire in the following ten years, they really just ran the numbers. A huge number of nonprofit execs were, in fact, approaching traditional retirement age, and Casey figured they would follow suit with their parents. We haven't, to say the least.

So, Boomers like to work and, having started our careers in a pre-work-from-home world, we equate dedication to the job (and our mission) with the number of hours put in *at the office.*

Contrast that to the GenX/Gen@ worker, whose parent was often a workaholic Boomer. They don't want to be like their parents, working day and night. They struggle to find the right mix of friends, family, and work, but a core value of both of these generations is that they "Work to Live!" which is a stark contrast to Boomers' mentality of "Live to Work!"

Add to this the Gen@ ease with high productivity through technology, and you have younger people wondering why they have to be on site to be seen as working. See the set up for conflict?

How to solve this? Live by two work-life balance rules.

Rule #1: All work-life balance decisions are right.

If someone comes to you in your nonprofit and wants to change her work life in some way, ask why and then tell her, "Good for you!" *Never, ever, ever criticize a work-life balance choice*, or wonder aloud if she's thought her decision through enough, or suggest they wait until a particular project is done. *Assume she is a thinking adult and support her decision.* This is harder than it looks, particularly when it puts you in a tough position as a manager, but never criticize. Ever—because to do so is to dump on something that your worker cares deeply about.

Rule #2: Not all work-life balance decisions are right *for your nonprofit*.

There will be cases when such a decision by a staff person requires you to say "Good for you . . ." and then this: "I respect that choice, but we can't accommodate the hours, (or the availability, and so on) here, so we're going to have to reassign you, or change your compensation. . . ." In some cases, the person may have to completely leave. You should try to be as flexible as you can, but always remember that the people your organization serves are the most important ones, and that your employees are enablers of mission—not the mission themselves.

These two rules will go a long way to help you beating back the work-life balance beast. If you don't, it can consume nearly any team that is generationally diverse.

3. Lead Your Team Across the Generational Divide

Lead from the front. Walk the talk. And this is never more important than with values. Thus, if you are a manager, supervisor, or executive, the value of respect for the diversity of generational perspective has to start with you, and you have to enforce that value by not tolerating behaviors that violate it. We know you would never tolerate sexual harassment, or racially tinged jokes, or demeaning behavior based on backgrounds, and this is no different.

John Maxwell, the gifted leadership author, notes that the values of a team start with their leader. He writes, "If you look at the people you hire and supervise and don't like their behavior, look to yourself first." We have certainly seen that to be true throughout our management and consulting work. A leader winds up leading people who model the leader's behavior. And, *if you set a high bar on behavior, people will meet that bar.* Set a low bar, they'll meet that bar, too.

What might this mean in practice? If you're a Boomer, maybe you should seek a mentor from among your youngest staff to learn about Twitter, or the latest tech. If you are a young graduate of a nonprofit leadership program in charge of a number of older professionals, take the time to ask and listen. If you are recruiting new board members, tend to the mean age of your board and look to the kind of board you will need to meet the demands of a new population.

Generational Leadership Dos and Don'ts

- DON'T assume that blanket statements about a generation apply to an individual member of that generation. Ask, and listen to what people tell you.

- DO tailor your work style, benefits, and retention policies to provide the flexibility needed across generations.

- DON'T communicate in a one-size-fits-all mode. Adapt communications and technology choices to fit the generations you are appealing to.

- DO know how each generation is represented on your board, staff, volunteers, and constituents.

- DON'T avoid the issue of generational differences. Lead by example, holding discussions about the ways different generations think about the issues that matter to your organization.

- DO prepare for the financial, human resources, and program ramifications of increased retirement.

- DO examine every planning process to ensure its consequences are calculated across generations.

Conclusion

Generational leadership is a crucial skill in your nonprofit, because you deal with so many generations both inside and outside your organization. Leading across generations requires that you:

1. Remember that different generations are different cultures;

2. Remember the rules of work-life balance; and

3. Lead your team across the generational divide.

Follow these three core ideas, and you'll be able to be a leader for your own generation, and for all the others you touch. Good luck!

Peter Brinckerhoff is an internationally renowned trainer, author, and consultant to not-for-profit organizations. He brings years of experience in the field to his work, as he is a former board member of local, state, and national organizations, and has worked as both staff and ED. Since founding his consulting firm Corporate Alternatives in 1982, Brinckerhoff has helped thousands of organizations become more mission-capable. Peter is the award-winning author of <u>Mission-Based Management</u>, <u>Financial Empowerment</u>, <u>Mission-Based Marketing</u>, <u>Faith-Based Management</u>, <u>Social Entrepreneurship</u>, <u>Nonprofit Stewardship</u>, and most recently, <u>Generations: The Challenge of a Lifetime for Your Nonprofit</u>.

Vincent L. Hyman is an award-winning writer, editor, and publisher with three decades of experience in writing, editing, and organizational communications. After leading the nonprofit publishing centers at Amherst H. Wilder Foundation and Fieldstone Alliance, Inc., he founded Vincent Hyman Editorial Services (www.VinceHyman.com), with diverse content expertise in nonprofit management, foundation effectiveness, policy, marketing, business, mental health, addictions, health promotion, corrections, and music. He is editor of scores of books, author of the forthcoming <u>Nonprofit Risk Management Guidebook</u>, coauthor of <u>Coping with Cutbacks: The Nonprofit Guide to Success When Times Are Tight</u>, series editor for <u>Ten Things Every Board Member Should Know . . .</u>, and author of numerous web and print articles.

Generational Leadership Resource Review

Rick and Kathy Hicks. <u>Boomers, Xers, and Other Strangers: Understanding the Generational Differences That Divide Us</u>. Carol Stream, IL: Tyndale House, 1999.

Explains how the current cultural events we experience in youth shape our perspective—and the perspective of our generation.

Carolyn Martin and Bruce Tulgan. <u>Managing the Generation Mix: From Collision to Collaboration</u>. Amherst, MA: HRD Press, 2002.

Helps build teams across generations for more effective collaborative work.

Frances Kunreuther. <u>Up Next: Generation Change and the Leadership of Nonprofit Organizations</u>. Baltimore: Annie E. Casey Foundation, 2005.

Recommendations for handing-off leadership from the Boomers to GenX and Gen@. www.aecf.org/upload/publicationfiles/ld2928k643.pdf.

Manda Salls and Susan Moses. "The Nonprofit Boon from the Boomers." <u>Harvard Business School Working Knowledge for Business Leader</u>. October 18, 2004.

Explains the roles Boomers can play as volunteers for the nonprofit sector—and how to recruit them (www.hbswk.hbs.edu/archive/4416.html).

American Demographics (www.adage.com/americandemographics/)

This is a great website for looking at trends by age group.

U.S. Census main page (www.census.gov)

This site is a terrific resource for gathering information about population groups.

o o o

All these resources, plus nonprofit management tips of the week and more, can be found at Nonprofits101.org.

Part Three

Nonprofit Law and Finance

I slept and dreamt that life was joy. I awoke and saw that life was service. I acted and beheld that service was joy.

—Rabindranath Tagore

By now, things should be starting to come into focus. Ideally, you've already gained a good sense of the strategic considerations that are crucial to the successful launch of an organization or initiative, and that enable you to personally excel at your role.

Now we're going to delve deeper into the operational issues, in particular on the legal and financial fronts. In addition to primers on these two topics, we'll also hear from lobbying and advocacy experts, with their tips on how to achieve policy reform within the limits of the law.

I already mentioned that operational issues like this can be the ball bearings that make an organization glide forward, or, if ignored, they can be the Achilles' heel that prove to be its downfall. Trust me, I've seen it happen up close and personal. Those of you with some exposure to the ancient practice of *Feng Shui* or traditional Chinese medicine may equate this with the concept of *chi*, or energy, stagnation. Simply put, if you have clutter in your office, your organization, or your mind and body, then things get "stuck" there, inhibiting your ability to get actual work done. In other words, no matter how great a vision you have, if your printer doesn't work and your phone lines are down, you're going to have a rough go of it. On the other side, if you have a keen sense of your financials, and if your legal counsel advises you properly on how to structure an agreement, it makes both strategic and tactical decisions a million times easier.

Think of operational issues like finance and the law not as burdens to be borne, but as management systems that give you a better understanding of, and more control over, your efforts—thereby advancing your mission. They can also make things possible that you may have previously discounted. For example, many nonprofit leaders think that they are unable to do lobbying and advocacy work at all, thereby impeding their ability to seek policy reform and promote worthy pieces of legislation. Not true, but there are absolutely some important caveats here, all of which will be covered in Chapter Twelve.

It's also important to note that *financial and legal best practices in the social sector differ from those in the corporate world.* Nonprofit finance includes special rules around restricted versus unrestricted funds, endowments, unrelated business income tax, mandatory audits for organizations of a certain size, and more. Compliance with these requirements is a prerequisite for operating a nonprofit, and only after they're addressed can an organization set its sights even higher, and look to integrate useful management reports and the key performance indicators I spoke of earlier. Which programs are generating revenue, and which ones can't cover costs? What does it cost us to serve each client? Questions like these can lead to a host of useful revelations.

Employment or HR law varies from state to state, and as such we will not attempt to cover it in this book. That said, hopefully some of the insights from Chapters Eight and Eleven will prove helpful by providing useful basic considerations regardless of where you're operating. On another legal note, I strongly recommend that *every nonprofit seek pro bono legal counsel*, whether through recruiting someone to the board, or by retaining a firm at no cost. Lawyers at big firms are usually *required* to donate some of their time, and many are so busy that they find it difficult to identify a worthy cause. It's amazing what you can accomplish with a few calls and meetings. That said, remember nonprofit law varies from its for-profit counterpart, so look to recruit someone who has experience in the field. For the purposes of Chapter Eleven in this guide, we'll focus mainly on the requirements to maintain tax-exempt status, as well as accepted ethical practices and accountability standards.

Andy Stern, former president of the Service Employees International Union (SEIU), once said, *"Change is inevitable, but progress is optional, and leadership makes all the difference."* Legal and financial tools can often provide nonprofit executives with the resources they need to let their leadership shine, so pay attention, enjoy, and good luck.

CHAPTER 11

Nonprofit Law

By Bruce R. Hopkins, Senior Partner, and Virginia C. Gross,
Shareholder in the Nonprofit Organizations Group,
Polsinelli Shughart PC

Introduction

Nonprofit law can be a bit daunting and even scary for some, but having an understanding of the law applicable to the field is important to the success of any nonprofit leader. Our goal in this chapter is to provide you with this basic understanding, and to offer a resource guide in case issues pop up for you down the road.

The law governing our sector is derived from many sources—principally federal tax, state corporation, trust, and fundraising law. At the federal level, nonprofit organizations need to be concerned with additional bodies of nonprofit law in the antitrust, consumer protection, health, labor, postal, securities, and other fields. That may sound intimidating, especially if you don't have "Esquire" at the end of your name. Our intention here is to provide a broad overview, along with some salient insights and practical tips. As such, this chapter focuses principally on federal tax and corporate

165

governance laws, and in particular on the issues that emerging leaders are more likely to face, including:

- The definition and forms of nonprofit organizations

- What it takes to maintain tax-exempt status

- Types of public charities and private foundations

- Intermediate sanctions rules

- Filing of information returns

- Nonprofit governance

Defining Nonprofit Organizations

The term *nonprofit organization* does not mean an organization that is prohibited by law from earning a profit (that is, an excess of gross earnings over expenses). Rather, the definition of a nonprofit organization essentially relates to requirements as to what must be done with the profit earned or otherwise received.

A fundamental distinction between nonprofit and for-profit entities is that the for-profit organization has owners that hold the equity in the enterprise, such as stockholders of a corporation, and the organization operates for the economic benefit of these owners. By contrast, a nonprofit organization is *not* permitted to distribute its profits (net earnings) to those who control it, such as its directors and officers.

Not all nonprofits are created equal. As you already read in Chapter One, there are different types of tax-exempt status available to nonprofits, depending on their purposes and activities. Not all nonprofits are fully tax-exempt, although *all charitable organizations must file an application with the IRS to obtain recognition of their exempt status.* Most noncharitable tax-exempt organizations do not have to file an application with the IRS.

A nonprofit organization can take many forms, most prominently a corporation, an unincorporated association, or a trust. In brief, a nonprofit corporation is an entity that is formed by filing incorporation documents with a state, an unincorporated association is an entity formed by means of a constitution, and a trust is an entity that has been formed pursuant to a trust agreement or declaration. Most states have laws governing nonprofit corporations and trusts, which address their formation, governance, purposes, operations, and dissolution. Corporations provide liability protection to their directors, which is not the case with unincorporated associations and trusts.

The IRS can revoke tax exemption based on changes in the law, but generally *once an organization has been recognized as exempt by the IRS, it can rely on that determination as long as there are no substantial changes in its character, purposes, or methods of operation.* If material changes occur, the organization should notify the IRS; it may have to undergo a re-evaluation of its exempt status.

Critical Skills and Competencies

Now that we're clear on the basics, in terms of what defines a nonprofit organization, let's focus on the required standards and considerations you'll need to navigate in order to maintain tax-exempt status.

Maintenance of Tax-Exempt Status

Of utmost importance to tax-exempt organizations is an understanding of what it takes to maintain exempt status. Readers who have questions regarding setting up new organizations can visit www.irs.gov and the websites of the various Secretaries of State for more information, as this book is geared towards existing organizations, and as such this chapter focuses on maintaining rather than securing exempt status.

Organizational Test

All charitable organizations—that is, Section 501(c)(3)s—must pass an organizational test. This test focuses on the content of an organization's "statement of purposes" and the "dissolution clause" in its organizing document. The former describes the mission of the entity, although there may also be a mission statement. The latter preserves the assets and net income of an organization for charitable purposes, should it dissolve or liquidate. *Charitable organizations must meet the organizational test throughout their existence.*

Operational Test

Charitable organizations must also pass an operational test. The basic requirements are advancement of one or more exempt purposes, and avoidance of private inurement, unwarranted private benefit, substantial legislative activity, political campaign activity, and excessive unrelated business activities. Heady terms, we know, so let's look at each of these, as failure to comply with the operational test can result in loss of exempt status.

Private Inurement Doctrine

The doctrine of private inurement basically says that *a nonprofit can't be set up to benefit a person instead of a cause.* Specifically, this means that none of the income or assets of a tax-exempt organization may be permitted to directly or indirectly benefit an individual or other person who has a close relationship with the organization, particularly when that person is in a position to exercise a significant degree of control over the entity.

These people, typically referred to as "insiders," may include the organization's founders, trustees, directors, officers, members of their families, entities controlled by these individuals, or anybody else having a significant personal and private interest in the activities of the organization. The doctrine requires that these transactions or arrangements be tested against a standard of *reasonableness*, meaning that all transactions with insiders must be in line with industry norms.

If your organization is found in violation of the private inurement doctrine, its tax-exempt status can be revoked or denied, so be sure to keep an eye out when entering into business deals with "insiders."

Private Benefit Doctrine

Beyond proving they don't exist to benefit individuals, tax-exempt, *charitable organizations must establish that they are not organized or operated for the benefit of other private interests.* The IRS has found private benefit, for example, where a husband and wife formed a private school and entered into a management agreement to operate nearly all aspects of the school and thus were using the school's exemption for their own private benefit. Another common example occurs when a public charity enters into a joint venture with a for-profit corporation and lacks control of the venture; the idea here is that the for-profit is really just looking to benefit from the tax-exempt partner in the partnership. "Incidental" private benefit is permitted, meaning a small amount of private benefit will be tolerated.

If your organization is found in violation of the private benefit doctrine, its tax-exempt status can be revoked or denied, so once again, be extra careful when entering into transactions or other arrangements.

Legislative Activities and Political Campaign Activities Law

Please read Chapter Twelve if you're interested in conducting advocacy or lobbying work through your nonprofit. Given that this is covered elsewhere, we will skip this important topic here, but we will take this opportunity to remind you to remember of the three basics of this field:

- Noncharitable, tax-exempt organizations such as 501(c)(4)s and 501(c)(6)s generally may engage in lobbying.

- Tax-exempt public charities—501(c)(3)s that are not private foundations— may engage in legislative activities to the extent that lobbying is not a *substantial* part of their overall functions (generally considered to be about 5–15% of its revenue).

- A tax-exempt charitable organization (a public charity or a private foundation) may not participate or intervene in a political campaign on behalf of or in opposition to a candidate for public office.

Unrelated Business Income Tax (UBIT)

Nowadays, many nonprofits are looking to diversify and increase their income streams through earned-income strategies. This is covered in some detail in Chapter Twenty-Four, but from a legal standpoint there are a few things to keep in mind. *Tax-exempt organizations must pay income tax, called the "unrelated business income tax" or UBIT, on their net income from unrelated business activities.* Most importantly, too much unrelated business can imperil an organization's exempt status. There is no clear definition of the maximum threshold of allowable unrelated business income or activity, and the IRS is mainly looking to make sure that your focus remains on the mission rather than the side businesses. Taxable unrelated business income is reported to the IRS on Form 990-T.

A *business* of a tax-exempt organization is "an activity that is carried on for the production of income from the sale of goods or the performance of services." *A business is considered unrelated if it is a business that is regularly carried on and is not substantially related to the accomplishment of your mission.* Before conceding that an activity is unrelated and therefore that its net income is taxable, you should determine if you can cause the activity to be related to your exempt purposes, and specifically establish a "causal" link between the business and your mission. For example, a group that does training and rehabilitation work could consider a retail grocery business related if its purpose is to further the emotional rehabilitation of its adolescent staff, *and* if the business is conducted on a scale no larger than is reasonably necessary for this purpose. Also, *there are exceptions from the imposition of UBIT for activities that are substantially conducted by volunteers, the sale of donated items, activities meeting a convenience exception, and qualified convention and trade show activities.* Passive income, such as dividends and interest, is also not subject to UBIT.

Subsidiaries

It is common for tax-exempt organizations to have one or more subsidiaries, which can be nonprofits or for-profits. Most commonly, this is done to shield the parent organization from liability, or because the subsidiary's activity is not related to the nonprofit entity's exempt purpose. Subsidiaries can be quite complicated and merit thorough consideration from a legal, business, and mission standpoint. If you are interested in reading more about this topic, please refer to our list of resources at the end of this chapter.

Joint Ventures

As referenced in Chapter Six, nonprofit, tax-exempt organizations may participate in partnerships and other forms of joint ventures. These can be arranged with one or more other nonprofit or for-profit entities. More information on this complex topic can be found in the material in our resource list, but for now we should at least mention that *nearly all joint ventures take place within an LLC* (limited liability company) framework, and that a participating nonprofit can enter into a joint venture and not endanger its exempt status when (1) the participation of the exempt organization furthers its exempt purpose, (2) the exempt organization does not maintain day-to-day responsibilities of the venture, and (3) private inurement and private benefit concerns are adequately addressed.

Other Tax-Exempt Legal Basics

Now that we've covered some of the nonprofit legal basics, let's look at the difference between public charities and private foundations, how penalties work for people who unfairly benefit from their relationship with a nonprofit, and at the Form 990, which most nonprofits must file annually with the IRS.

Public Charities and Private Foundations

The realm of charitable organizations is divided into two categories: public charities (e.g., the Humane Society) and private foundations (e.g., the Bill & Melinda Gates Foundation). *Every tax-exempt charitable organization is presumed to be a private foundation unless it demonstrates otherwise* and a charitable organization that loses its public charity status automatically becomes a private foundation.

A private foundation is funded from one or just a few sources, including ongoing support, and typically makes grants, usually to public charities. Private foundations frequently have an "endowment" that they draw upon, meaning a sum of money where the principal remains invested, but where the income is used for grants or other charitable purposes. Even in lean years, these charitable institutions are required to give away an amount equal to at least 5% of the value of their endowments. In general, private foundations are subject to many more restrictions than public charities and must pay a tax on their net investment income, meaning whatever money is earned from their endowment. Also, donations to a private foundation can be limited or more difficult for a donor to deduct.

There are three basic types of charitable organizations that are *not* private foundations: publicly supported charities, charitable institutions, and supporting organizations.

Publicly supported charities are divided into two basic categories: *donative* publicly supported charities and *service provider* publicly supported charities. The donative type of publicly supported charity normally receives a substantial part of its support (other than revenue from carrying out its exempt activities) in the form of contributions from the public or grants from one or more governmental agencies. The term "substantial" in this context generally means at least one-third, although *a charity's public support can be as low as 10% of its total support* if the organization meets other criteria for public charity status. The amount of a gift that may be counted towards this public support test is only the amount that does not exceed 2% of the total amount of support the organization received during its most recent five years (including its current year). Under certain circumstances, *a large one-time gift can be excluded from the public support calculation.*

The *service provider* type of publicly supported charity (such as a museum) normally receives more than one-third of its support in the form of contributions, grants, membership fees, and fee-for-service revenue from *permitted sources*, and normally does not receive more than one-third of its support in the form of gross investment income and net unrelated business income. Permitted sources do not include disqualified persons (see the following "Intermediate Sanctions" section for more information on this) with respect to the organization. Public support for these organizations is determined over the same measuring period of the entity's most recent five years (including its current year).

Certain tax-exempt *institutions* are classified as public charities regardless of the source of their financial support. These institutions include churches, certain other religious organizations, formal educational institutions (such as colleges, universities, and other schools), hospitals, medical research organizations, and governmental units.

Typical functions of a *supporting organization* are fundraising and maintaining an endowment fund. A supporting organization is a public charity organized and operated exclusively for the benefit of, to perform the functions of, or to carry out the purposes of one or more supported organizations, with which it has a relationship. More information on this topic is provided in the resources listed later, but for now we'll simply say that there are four types of supporting organizations: Type I, Type II, Type III functionally integrated, and Type III nonfunctionally integrated. Stringent law provisions are directed at Type III supporting organizations, particularly those that are not functionally integrated with a supported organization. These organizations must satisfy a notification requirement, a responsiveness test, and an integral part test. Certain Type III supporting organizations must comply with a distribution requirement, similar to that imposed on private foundations. Again, if you are working with or considering starting such an organization, we strongly recommend reviewing the resources listed at the end of this chapter ahead of time.

Intermediate Sanctions

The intermediate sanctions rules are used to tax "disqualified persons" who impermissibly engage in transactions with public charities, social welfare organizations, and certain health insurance issuers, wherein they enjoy "excess benefit" in the transaction. They're designed to punish the person, not the entity. Taxes are applied to the amount of the excess benefit derived from the transaction, and consist of an *initial* tax and an *additional* tax.

A person who has a close relationship with a tax-exempt organization is a *disqualified person*. A disqualified person generally is a person who has, or is in a position to have, some type or degree of control over the operations of the tax-exempt organization involved. The term *disqualified person* is defined in this context as: (1) any person who was, at any time during the five-year period ending on the date of the transaction involved, in a position to exercise substantial influence over the affairs of the organization (whether by virtue of being an organizational manager, such as an officer or director, or otherwise); (2) a member of the family of an individual described in the preceding category; and (3) an entity (such as a corporation) in which individuals described in the preceding two categories own more than a 35% interest.

For the intermediate sanctions to apply, as mentioned before there must be an *excess benefit transaction*, which is a transaction in which an economic benefit is provided by a tax-exempt organization, to or for the use of a disqualified person, that exceeds the value of the consideration (including the performance of services) received by the person for providing the benefit. One of the most common forms of an excess benefit transaction is excessive compensation.

A key component of the intermediate sanctions rules is the *rebuttable presumption of reasonableness*, which shifts the burden to the IRS to prove that an element of a transaction or arrangement was unreasonable. (The IRS can rebut this presumption with relevant facts of its own.) This presumption comes into play where the decision to engage in the transaction was made by an independent board or board committee, the board considered appropriate data as to comparability, and the decision was properly and timely documented (including in minutes). When possible, *organizations should seek to invoke the rebuttable presumption of reasonableness for its transactions with insiders.*

The intermediate sanctions rules consist of an initial tax, which is 25% of the excess benefit, payable by the disqualified person or persons involved. In addition, the transaction must be undone, by placing the parties in the same economic position they were in before the transaction was entered into; this is "correction" of the transaction. *If the initial tax is not paid in a timely manner and the transaction is not quickly and properly corrected, an additional tax may have to be paid;* this tax is 200% of the excess benefit. *Board members are subject to a tax of 10% of the amount involved if they knowingly participated in the excess benefit transaction,* unless the participation was not willful and was due to reasonable cause. The board members subject to the 10% excise tax are jointly and severally liable for this tax, which is capped at $20,000 per transaction.

Filing and Disclosure Requirements

Nearly all tax-exempt organizations must file *information returns* with the IRS, on which they report their income, expenses, information regarding their governance and structure, and information on their activities, and, in the case of publicly supported charities, demonstrate that they comply with one of more of the public support tests. Most tax-exempt organizations file a Form 990. Private foundations must file a Form 990-PF. Small organizations other than private foundations, supporting organizations, and certain credit counseling entities, may file a Form 990-EZ. With limited exceptions, very small organizations may file a Form 990-N. *If a tax-exempt organization that is otherwise required to file a Form 990 fails to do so for three consecutive years, it automatically loses its tax-exempt status.* Certain organizations, such as churches and their affiliates and governmental entities, are not required to file information returns.

Tax-exempt organizations must make available their Forms 990 for a period of three years from the later of when the return was due to be filed or was actually filed. They must also publish their application for recognition of tax exemption (if it filed one with the IRS) for public inspection, without charge. In addition, organizations must provide a copy without charge, other than a reasonable fee for copying and postage, to anyone who requests a copy of one of these documents, unless the organization makes the documents *widely available*, such as publishing the documents on the Internet.

Nonprofit Governance and the Law

Generally, the body of law applicable to the governance of a tax-exempt organization is state, not federal, law. The nature of the governance of a nonprofit, exempt organization depends mainly on the form of the entity. The state act governing the creation and operation of a nonprofit entity addresses matters relating to the organization's governance.

Tax-exempt organizations that are corporations are typically governed by either a board of directors or a board of trustees. If the exempt organization is a trust, it may have a board of trustees or be governed by a single, sometimes corporate, trustee. How the nonprofit organization is organized determines how its directors are selected. Some nonprofit organizations are established with a self-perpetuating board of directors, meaning that the directors elect their successors. In the case of a nonprofit organization formed as a membership entity, the members of the nonprofit organization typically elect the directors. In the rare instance of a nonprofit corporation organized as a stock corporation, which is allowable only in a few states, the stockholders elect the directors. With trusts, the trust document often appoints the trustees. Certain director positions may be "ex officio," meaning that an individual serves as a director because of a position held in an entity. For example, the president of a corporation may be an ex officio director of the corporation's private foundation, or the executive director of a nonprofit may enjoy a seat on the board so long as they serve in that capacity. However selected, *the governing board of a nonprofit organization is responsible for overseeing its affairs.* A nonprofit organization's officers are usually elected by the governing body or by the organization's members, with the election process typically governed by the organization's bylaws.

There is no general requirement that a nonprofit organization have a certain number of independent board members. However, *the inclusion of independent directors on the board of a nonprofit entity is considered a good governance practice.* An independent board member is generally one with no financial or family connections with the organization, other than serving as a board member. IRS agents, when reviewing initial applications of exempt organizations, often try to impose their own views on board compositions, such as requiring the addition of independent directors; such views are not correct assertions of the law. One IRS representative stated publicly that "outside of the very smallest organizations, or possibly family foundations," *an active, independent, and engaged board of directors is the "gold standard" of board composition.*

Congress, the IRS, and other groups are exercising more influence and control over the governance of tax-exempt organizations, particularly public charities. Many organizations have published best practice governance standards for charitable organizations. At this time, however, there is little federal law applicable to the governance of tax-exempt organizations. The IRS, principally by means of the annual information return filed by most tax-exempt organizations, is working assiduously to influence the governance practices of charitable organizations.

Tax-exempt organizations implement policies that are relevant to their organization as a matter of good governance and to demonstrate that they are effectively governed in the event of an audit or investigation. These policies include a conflicts-of-interest policy, a whistleblower policy, a document retention and destruction policy, a code of ethics, an investment policy, a travel and reimbursement policy, and a fundraising policy. *Organizations must determine the appropriate policies that are applicable and relevant and support them with an effective governance structure.*

Nonprofit Law Dos and Don'ts

Dos and Don'ts

- DO understand the type of tax-exempt organization with which you are working and what it takes to maintain its exempt status.

- DO, when entering into transactions, keep in mind the private inurement and private benefit rules.

- DO know the legal restrictions (such as the unrelated business income rules, lobbying restrictions, and intermediate sanctions rules) to which your organization is subject.

- DO know whether the 501(c)(3) organization you're working with is a public charity or a private foundation.

- DON'T ignore the organization's filing requirements (such as IRS returns and state annual reports), which should be made on a timely basis.

- DO consider the legal consequences of new or expanded activities for your organization and consult a lawyer if you are unsure if the activities create issues for the continuing tax exemption of your organization.

- DO have a governing board that exercises its oversight responsibilities in an effective, diligent manner.

Conclusion

Tax exemption is a privilege, not a right, and tax-exempt organizations and those that manage them must understand the legal requirements for maintaining exemption. Reviewing the topics contained in this chapter will be helpful in staying on course for continuing exemption and effectively managing an exempt entity.

Bruce Hopkins's practice focuses on the representation of tax-exempt organizations. He authored or coauthored The Law of Tax-Exempt Organizations; The New Form 990: Law, Policy, and Preparation; The Tax Law of Charitable Giving; Starting and Managing a Nonprofit Organization: A Legal Guide; IRS Audits of Tax-Exempt

Organizations: Policies, Practices, and Procedures; Private Foundations: Tax Law and Compliance; and Nonprofit Governance: Law, Practices & Trends. He writes an award-winning monthly newsletter, _Bruce R. Hopkins' Nonprofit Counsel_ and received the Nonprofit Lawyers Award (2007) from the American Bar Association. He is presently on the faculty of the University of Kansas Law School.

Virginia Gross concentrates her practice in the fields of tax and nonprofit law. She represents a variety of nonprofit clients on tax-exempt matters, including charitable and educational organizations, private foundations, associations, supporting organizations, medical research and other healthcare organizations, social welfare organizations, and social clubs. Virginia is a frequent speaker on nonprofit issues and has coauthored two books on nonprofit law. She was listed in The Best Lawyers in America, Nonprofit Organizations/Charities Law, for 2008–2011. She has served on the governing board of several charities. Ms. Gross earned her JD from the University of Texas and her BS from Texas A&M University.

Nonprofit Law Resource Review

www.irs.gov/charities

> The official website of the Internal Revenue Service; This page contains publications and other information relating to tax-exempt organizations.

Bruce R. Hopkins. <u>Starting and Managing a Nonprofit Organization</u> (5th ed.). New York: Wiley, 2009.

> This book offers a detailed analysis of the legal issues facing nonprofits.

www.nonprofitlawcenter.com

> An updated website providing information on the law, including current developments, as applicable to nonprofit and tax-exempt organizations.

Bruce R. Hopkins and Virginia C. Gross. <u>Nonprofit Governance: Law, Practices, & Trends</u>. New York: Wiley, 2009.

> A guide to current trends and best practices for the governance of nonprofit organizations.

www.boardsource.org

A website dedicated to increasing the effectiveness of nonprofit boards of directors and the organizations they serve.

Bruce R. Hopkins' Nonprofit Counsel

This subscriber-based monthly newsletter providing updates on nonprofit law is published by John Wiley & Sons; available through www.wileyonlinelibrary.com

www.nasconet.org

A website maintained by the National Association of State Charity Officials to provide information to charitable organizations regarding the state regulation of fundraising.

Bruce R. Hopkins, Douglas A. Anning, Virginia C. Gross, and Thomas J. Schenkelberg. The New Form 990: Law, Policy and Preparation. New York: Wiley, 2009.

A book dedicated to the preparation of the Form 990 and the law relating to the issues presented by the form.

www.pesilaw.com

Website of PESI Law and Accounting, a leading provider of tax and accounting continuing education conferences.

www.nonprofitpanel.org

The Panel on the Nonprofit Sector's website providing downloadable copies of the Panel's "Principles for Good Governance and Ethical Practice" and other resources for nonprofit organizations.

∘ ∘ ∘

All these resources, plus nonprofit management tips of the week and more, can be found at Nonprofits101.org.

CHAPTER 12

Nonprofit Advocacy and Lobbying

*By Nayantara Mehta, Senior Counsel, Alliance for Justice;
Nancy Chen, Staff Attorney, Medical Legal Community
Partnership Program, Neighborhood Legal Services of Los
Angeles; Marcia Avner, Senior Fellow, and Jeannie Fox,
Deputy Director of Public Policy, Minnesota Council of
Nonprofits*

Introduction

Nonprofit, community-based organizations provide unique opportunities for individuals to combine their energy, talents, and values for community improvement and enrichment. But with power comes responsibility. Nonprofits are obligated to understand their role as entities that engage and inspire individuals and communities for public benefit.

We recognize that the nonprofit role in society differs from the roles of government and business. Nonprofits have a special ability to organize the energy and ideas of a community to achieve together what individuals cannot accomplish alone. By tapping into the values, interests, and relationships of individuals, nonprofits can mobilize their supporters and the larger community to realize their vision. Unlike government entities, nonprofits can focus on very local, specific, or new matters. Nonprofit organizations emerge from expressed community needs and are not restricted to the marketplace priorities and constraints that define success for the for-profit sector.

Indeed, nonprofits have been at the forefront of most major social movements in American history. Many advances in civil rights, workers' rights, voting reforms, housing and health services, and campaigns for clean air and water were rooted in the organizing and persuading ability of on-the-ground nonprofits. The public dialogue is not complete without the expertise of organizations who serve on the front lines of battles against inequality, injustice, and increasing gaps in achievement and opportunity for all people.

You can do this! *Nonprofit advocacy and lobbying is legal, and furthermore, it's part of meeting mission.* This chapter will cover the basic rules of nonprofit advocacy and provide you simple tips and tactics for building relationships with key decision makers, strategies for grassroots organizing to build support for your cause, and suggestions for effective use of the media to increase public awareness of your issues.

Let's begin!

What Do You Need to Do This Work?

You have expertise. Decisions that affect nonprofits and the people nonprofits serve are made at all levels of government, with or without you. *It is imperative that nonprofit organizations bring information to the public debate.* You have research and data, personal stories, and time-tested strategies for building communities and enhancing individuals' quality of life. Plus, your trusted relationships as community organizations will allow you to encourage and support community members to engage in the civic activities that build leadership and result in healthier, safer communities. By acting as organizational agents of change, you can also bring people who are most often left out of democratic processes to the political arena, building individual and community power.

Once you have determined to use your clout and credibility to advance social change, it is important to organize your goals and strategies around a simple framework for advocacy. It may be helpful to envision your work based on the following triangle diagram:

Figure 12.1:

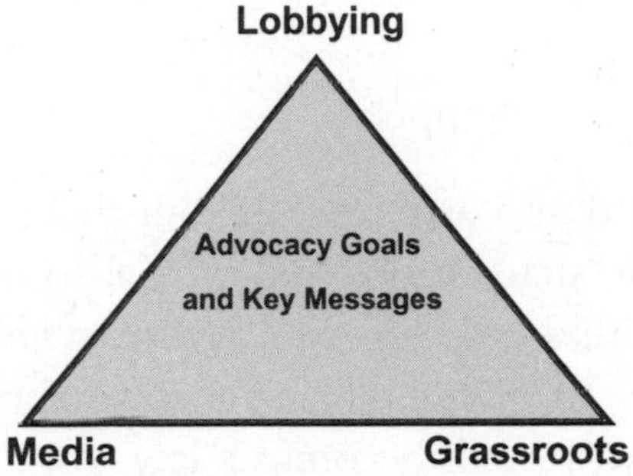

Lobbying

Advocacy Goals
and Key Messages

Media   Grassroots

Critical Skills and Competencies

Having identified your key goals and messages, you can begin to advance your work by utilizing the three strategies of direct lobbying, grassroots organizing, and media advocacy. To begin to develop your advocacy plan you need to be able to answer the following four questions with a fair amount of specificity:

1. What is the problem or opportunity?

2. What do you want to have happen?

3. Who decides?

4. How do you influence them?

Whether your objective is to pass legislation, build a community coalition, or increase public awareness of an issue, identifying clear responses to these simple questions will help you target your limited resources for highest impact. Being systematic and strategic will ensure precious resources of time, talent, and money are effectively and efficiently employed.

Before we dive into the ins and outs of the lobbying and advocacy rules and regulations, let's take a look at these key questions one by one:

1. What is the problem or opportunity?

   First of all, based on your nonprofit and community-building experience, you know what works. Which means you also know what doesn't work. This will help you identify policy situations (current laws, rules for eligibility, or standard practices) that can be improved. Just think about something you've complained about recently where you said, "If only we could . . ."

2. What do you want to have happen?

   It's nice to be "for good and against evil," but that's not particularly helpful when attempting to persuade an elected official to take action. *One key to building better communities is using your expertise to help craft solid, specific policies that will achieve your mission.* Don't worry about not understanding "legalese" or exactly how a bill becomes a law. Your champion legislator or county elected official can help you through that process. Your job is to bring them your good ideas.

3. Who decides?

   Not all things are decided at the state capitol or assembly. It is important to discern who has jurisdiction and authority over your issues. Is it primarily a federal matter, like immigration or Medical Assistance services? Would a standardized state law be helpful, perhaps to ensure equal access to services for all citizens? Or, could it be very local . . . perhaps state-mandated, but county-administered mental health services? Looking at who has the regulatory responsibility for various arenas will help you target your lobbying directives appropriately.

4. How do you influence them?

   You've probably heard this saying before in other settings, but the advocacy world is no exception, *it's really all about the relationships.* This is long-term work. It should never be about any one legislative session or election. *Getting to know decision makers and opinion shapers long before you have any "ask" is crucial.* A few important tips to build and maintain those relationships:

- Assume good intentions. Most officials are inspired to run for public office because of a belief in wanting to contribute to their communities. You may at times disagree about how to pursue positive change, but start from a place of a shared common value.

- Become a resource to public leaders. Invite them to your organization for a "kitchen-table" style conversation so they can learn about your role in enhancing the communities they represent.

- Make public policy real to them. *Include personal stories to give the issues a human face.* Elected officials and their staff members often have to pore through spreadsheet after spreadsheet of budget figures; remind them that their decisions have an impact on real people and real communities.

- Be 100% accurate and forthcoming. Never make up facts or overstate your case. Integrity is critical to this process; *if you lose your credibility it is very hard to get it back.* If you don't have an answer to one of their questions, say, "I don't know, but I will find out and get back to you." And then, do! Follow-up is key.

- Never burn bridges. The person who's against you on one issue may very well be a champion on something else you care about. Again, whether it's an elected official, program administrator, or local reporter, the goal is to build long-term relationships that are mutually beneficial. They have access to the political process and public sentiment, but you have information, relationships, and expertise that they need.

You Don't Have to Do It Alone!

A word about coalitions. A hallmark of advocacy in the public interest is coming together around a common goal. *Nonprofits gain strength when they unite across their varied interests in numbers*, forming powerful networks and coalitions. As Benjamin Franklin once said, "We must hang together, or we shall surely hang separately."

Coalitions are alliances formed for specific purposes, which are often quickly able to mobilize large groups to influence outcomes that can be key in advancing advocacy goals. Collaboration of this sort involves determining common goals, creating structures for planning and execution (including clear definitions of responsibilities and roles), and being willing to share risks and rewards. Coalitions build power and influence by achieving greater scale and reach, increased resources, and the ability to propel momentum. Like many other relationships, coalitions are built upon mutual trust, a shared understanding of the needs, and an ability to compromise for the greater good.

Where Does the Media Fit In?

Creating a media communications plan is an essential ingredient to building advocacy campaigns. Not unlike your efforts to move messages in your lobbying and organizing work, building relationships with media outlets can help meet numerous policy objectives:

- Positive media coverage can move your message to the general public, who may not know much about your issue or organization.

- News that features stories on your issue, framed in a favorable way, can shore up your position and increase your influence.

- Elected officials are watching! In striving to represent their own constituents, community leaders keep careful track of what is being said in all forms of media (print, radio, TV) in order to gauge public will on an issue.

More information on putting together a communications plan to develop and support your efforts is included in Chapter Twenty-Five.

And Yes, It Is Legal!

This is not rocket science. There are a few basic rules governing 501(c)(3) tax-exempt, charitable organizations, which we will discuss below. But the list of what you *can* do is far longer than the list of what you cannot do. The IRS has long made clear the legal and appropriate role of nonprofits to engage in lobbying and election-related activities.

As mentioned in Chapter One, most of the organizations that we think of as "nonprofits" are 501(c)(3) public charities, and they must comply with the tax code and the IRS regulations that dictate what kind of activities they may engage in.

Most forms of advocacy for 501(c)(3) nonprofits are unrestricted and unlimited by the IRS, but there are two important exceptions: lobbying and election-related activity. 501(c)(3) public charities are permitted to lobby a certain amount each year (see below for details), while 501(c)(3) private foundations pay a significant tax on any lobbying expenditures. *All 501(c)(3)s can engage in nonpartisan election-year activities, such as registering people to vote, but they are not allowed to support or oppose any candidate for public office.*

For organizations that want to spend more of their resources on lobbying and on getting candidates elected, there are other tax-exempt structures that are more appropriate to accomplish these activities. For more information about this or other laws governing nonprofit advocacy, please see Chapter Eleven or visit Alliance for Justice's website at www.afj.org, or call or email for free technical assistance (advocacy@afj.org or 866-NP-LOBBY).

Lobbying or Advocacy?

It is important to be clear from the beginning that *the terms "lobbying" and "advocacy" are not exactly the same.* Lobbying is just one type of advocacy that an organization may engage in to achieve its goals, and only occurs when an organization specifically works to advance legislation at the local, state, or federal level. *The IRS only limits lobbying that attempts to influence legislation*, not your communications to government entities on administrative regulations or appeals for executive orders.

Other forms of non-lobbying advocacy may include educating the public or policymakers about the issues you work on, helping voters get information about the candidates in an upcoming election, and bringing the residents of a community together to stand up for their rights.

Limits on Lobbying

In order for a 501(c)(3) public charity to know how much it can spend on lobbying in a year, it must first choose how it will measure its lobbying limits. There are two options for public charities to calculate their annual lobbying limits: the "insubstantial part test" and the 501(h) expenditure test.

The insubstantial part test is the default test that automatically applies to 501(c)(3) charities unless they choose the alternate option. Under this test, lobbying may not be a "substantial" part of an organization's overall activity. However, the IRS has not provided guidance on what it considers to be an appropriately insubstantial amount of lobbying, nor has it provided a definition of what exactly it considers to be lobbying under this test. Most lawyers who advise 501(c)(3) charities believe that *if a public charity keeps its lobbying activity to less than 5% of its overall activities, that entails an insubstantial amount of lobbying.*

Not surprisingly, charities were not pleased that they were told by the IRS that they could lobby, but not told how much or what exactly counted as lobbying. In response, Congress introduced the 501(h) expenditure test in 1976 to provide charities with clarity on how much lobbying they can legally conduct. 501(c)(3) charities opting to be bound by the 501(h) expenditure test submit the IRS form 5768 and then use a simple formula to calculate how much money it can spend on lobbying in a year. A charity with $500,000 or less in annual expenditures can spend 20% of its annual expenditures on lobbying. Charities with expenditures greater than $500,000 can calculate their lobbying limit by using a formula: 20% of its first $500,000 in expenditures, + 15% of the next $500,000, + 10% of the next $500,000, + 5% of the remaining expenditures, with a cap of $1,000,000 on the lobbying any charity is permitted to do in a year.

The 501(h) expenditure test also provides clear definitions of what constitutes lobbying, so a charity can know what activities to count toward its annual lobbying limit. Under this test, lobbying is separated into direct lobbying and grassroots lobbying. For more information on how these terms are defined, and for additional details on the benefits of choosing to come under the 501(h) expenditure test, please visit Alliance for Justice's website—in particular, be sure to review the in-depth publication *Worry Free Lobbying for Nonprofits.* This is a relatively involved topic and our focus here is on relaying the skills and tactics needed to actually do lobbying and advocacy work.

If you are interested in doing substantially more lobbying than is permitted under 501(c)(3) status, another option is to establish your nonprofit as a 501(c)(4), 501(c)(5) or 501(c)(6).

In addition to staying within the IRS's lobbying limit, all types of nonprofits should also be aware of other laws that may apply. Federal, state, and municipal lobbying disclosure laws may impose additional reporting requirements on both nonprofit and for-profit organizations that are substantially involved in lobbying activities.

For more information about these lobbying disclosure laws or the pros and cons of establishing a nonprofit as a non-501(c)(3), please visit www.afj.org or call for technical assistance.

No Partisan Political Activities

One final note on the regulations concerning nonprofits' advocacy activities. While lobbying by 501(c)(3) public charities is perfectly legal within limits, federal tax law imposes an absolute prohibition on engaging in partisan political activities. *A 501(c)(3) may not support or oppose any candidate for public office, at the federal, state, or local level.* The prohibition means that a 501(c)(3) organization should not be making candidate endorsements or contributions to candidate, and it also means that 501(c)(3)s may not even indirectly support or oppose candidates. Indirect support may be seen in a slanted candidate questionnaire, in which the 501(c)(3) asked questions in a way that was designed to make one candidate look good (or bad), or other communications that suggest that there is a better or worse candidate. But again, all 501(c)(3) organizations may engage in <u>nonpartisan</u> election-related activities. They can continue to engage with current legislators and other policymakers in an election year; they can encourage the public to register to vote and engage in get-out-the-vote activities; they can educate voters about where the candidates stand on the issues important to the electorate through candidate forums and debates; and they can and should help the candidates better understand the issues they work on. Finally, although charities are prohibited from supporting or opposing candidates for elected public office, they may still influence the appointment process of government officials, such as agency heads or federal judges. Urging the Senate confirmation of a U.S. Supreme Court nominee, for example, is permitted and will count as a lobbying activity, because that confirmation has to go through the legislative process.

Planning for Advocacy

As we introduced in the triangle framework for advocacy, it is important to be deliberate in this work. To gain effectiveness and impact, *advocacy should play a central role in all the work your organization does.* Various planning tools and assessments exist to help you build your organizational capacity for advocacy, but a few key considerations include:

- Are the organization's board and staff in agreement on policy goals?

- Do you have established criteria for deciding on issues?

- Does advocacy appear in your organization's strategic plan and job descriptions?

- Are you obtaining the necessary skills and training needed to perform this work effectively and legally?

- Have you secured and designated the appropriate resources (people, time, and money) to carry out this work?

You may have experienced resistance or barriers to engaging in advocacy in your organization. Many times misinformation about the rules related to advocacy can be enough to scare off board members or accounting staff. Funders can express hesitation about your organization taking a visible role on an issue. These are obstacles that can be overcome with factual presentation of the rules, along with expressing the need to strive toward social, systemic change in order to meet mission. Great historical advances have not been made by thinking small or defining ourselves too narrowly.

Integrating advocacy into your work can enhance all of the other ways your organization seeks to achieve its goals. Taking public stands on issues or being a vocal advocate can increase your organization's visibility and clout, resulting in increased donations and funding, interest in volunteering, and other public support for your mission. *If you are not engaged in advocacy you are certain to be missing opportunities and, more important, your stakeholders and constituents are probably not experiencing the full potential of your efforts.*

So what does this work really look like? We'll close this chapter with a case study description of nonprofit advocacy in action.

case study

Advocacy Case Study: The Hmong Health Collaborative (HHC)

When it began in 2004, the Hmong Health Collaborative (HHC) was a response to an immediate need: a new wave of 6,000 Hmong refugees were to arrive shortly in California's Central Valley from a refugee camp in Thailand, where they had been raising their families since assisting the United States during the war in Vietnam. It was expected that many of these refugees would need treatment for chronic diseases and mental health issues. The HHC is a coalition made up of community organizations and health service providers throughout California that work with the Hmong community. The HHC partners realized that by working together to implement lessons learned from previous waves of resettlement, they could help ease the transition for the newly arrived refugees and help them more quickly access needed health services. The HHC's coordinated effort allowed them to effectively respond to the concerns of these newcomers, who were overwhelmed by the amount of paperwork and complexity of the tiers of care available within the U.S. health system.

Serving as bridges between their local health system and the Hmong community, the HHC partners combined their successful service models with community organizing, research, and advocacy systems change efforts, and introduced strategies for engaging voices from within the Hmong community. Although the staff members of each of the partner organizations were familiar with the issues facing the new refugee population, the collaborative benefited from having clients voice their concerns directly. This strategy enabled the members of the Hmong community to identify their own policy priorities and agenda, rather than allowing service providers and policymakers to define an agenda "on behalf of" the Hmong community. Given that the clan system and leadership network are deeply embedded in Hmong culture, HHC partners recognized that only by tapping into these preexisting social networks could their agendas take root, flourish, and be sustainable across the community.

HHC's advocacy for increased mental health services for the Hmong community resulted in beneficial statewide policy changes. HHC partners participated in budget hearings and legislative briefings, and met with local elected officials to discuss concerns about cuts to public programs

case study

that led to reduced mental health services and staff. In addition, HHC partners monitored mental health services in the Central Valley to ensure that programs established by a statewide ballot initiative were culturally and linguistically appropriate for the Hmong community. The partners created a Mental Health Advocacy workgroup and the members attended local Mental Health Board and Board of Supervisors meetings to voice concerns and needs of the Hmong community. HHC member organizations were able to provide this needed information and guidance to policymakers as a result of their monitoring of mental health services in the state and their awareness of the needs of the Hmong community, including the cultural and linguistic barriers faced. As a result of these efforts, several HHC partners were awarded funds to specifically engage in outreach around mental health issues and treatment to this otherwise underserved community. HHC partners also engaged in a day of action at the state capitol to educate state legislatures on the impact of Medi-Cal budget cuts on families across the state. HHC members collected stories of families impacted and organized the participation of 150 community members.

Building on these successes, the members of the HHC are continuing to champion systems change in California's health care system to benefit the Hmong community as a whole. The partners continue to advocate for policy changes to increase culturally competent health care provisions and empower the Hmong community through their involvement this process.

Conclusion

Nonprofits provide a vital channel of communication for the communities they serve in policy discussions that affect us all. Advocacy enables nonprofits and their constituents to participate in systems change to create long-term benefits to our communities, while giving a voice to those historically marginalized in policy development. Before engaging in policy advocacy, nonprofits must be aware of the laws that affect their advocacy activities, as well as the strategies, planning, and media tactics that have been successful for organizations actively engaged in this work. We hope this chapter and its related resources helps your organization better understand relevant legal guidelines and gets you started on the path of positive policy change and civic engagement.

Nayantara Mehta is senior counsel with Alliance for Justice in Oakland, California. She works through AFJ's Advocacy Program to help strengthen the capacity of the public interest community to influence public policy. She conducts trainings on the rules governing advocacy and lobbying by public charities and private foundations. Nayantara holds a JD from the University of California, Berkeley School of Law (Boalt Hall), an MA from the University of Chicago, and a BA from the College of William and Mary in Virginia. Nayantara also serves on the board of the Youth Justice Institute and the American Constitution Society's Bay Area lawyer chapter.

Nancy Chen holds a JD from the University of California, Berkeley School of Law (Boalt Hall), and a BSFS from Georgetown University. She previously worked through Alliance for Justice's Nonprofit Advocacy Project and Foundation Advocacy Initiative to help strengthen the capacity of the public interest community to influence public policy. Among other roles, she supported the Immigrant Advocacy Initiative of the Nonprofit Advocacy Project, through which AFJ supports the ability of immigrant rights groups to engage in nonprofit advocacy work

Marcia Avner is a senior fellow at the Minnesota Council of Nonprofits, where she served as public policy director from 1996 to 2010. Avner also teaches at the Center on Advocacy and Political Leadership at the University of Minnesota-Duluth. Her practice, Avner Consulting, works with nonprofits and foundations on advocacy-related issues. Avner authored <u>The Lobbying and Advocacy Handbook for Nonprofit Organizations: Shaping Public Policy at the State and Local Level</u>, <u>The Board Member's Guide to Lobbying and Advocacy</u>, and advocacy manuals for several national organizations. She does national advocacy training and serves on the boards of Wellstone Action!, The Nonprofit Quarterly, and United Family Medicine.

In her current role at MCN, Jeannie Fox is responsible for direct and grassroots lobbying and advocacy efforts on behalf of the nonprofit sector in Minnesota, and is a frequent speaker and trainer to various nonprofits increasing their capacity to do advocacy and civic engagement work. Jeannie is also a Training Fellow for the Center for Lobbying in the Public Interest and is adjunct faculty for the University of Minnesota-Duluth Master's program in advocacy and political leadership and at the Hubert H. Humphrey Institute of Public Affairs. She serves on numerous nonprofit steering committees, public policy advisory councils, and boards of directors.

Lobbying and Advocacy Resources Review

Alliance for Justice (AFJ)

AFJ provides plain-language publications on the legal rules governing advocacy for nonprofits and foundations. AFJ offers an online advocacy capacity assessment tool for nonprofits to determine how ready they are to undertake an advocacy campaign, as well as resources for evaluating community organizing.

www.afj.org/for-nonprofits-foundations/

www.advocacyevaluation.org/

www.afj.org/for-nonprofits-foundations/reco/

Marcia Avner. The Lobbying and Advocacy Handbook for Nonprofit Organizations: Shaping Public Policy at the State and Local Level. Saint Paul, MN: Wilder Foundation, 2002.

This book provides detailed, step-by-step instructions for developing an effective plan to shape public policy at the state and local level, and guidance on how to put that plan into action. Available for purchase from the Fieldstone Alliance website (www.fieldstonealliance.org/).

David Arons (Ed.). Power in Policy: A Funder's Guide to Advocacy and Civic Participation. Saint Paul, MN: Fieldstone Alliance, 2007.

This book was written primarily by foundation practitioners for foundations, and argues that engagement in public policy and advocacy is an important role for foundations. Available for purchase from the Fieldstone Alliance website (www.fieldstonealliance.org/).

Bob Smucker. The Nonprofit Lobbying Guide (2nd edition). Washington, DC: Independent Sector, 1999.

This publication is no longer in print, but can be downloaded from the website of Independent Sector (www.independentsector.org/lobby_guide). The guide demonstrates the many ways in which charitable organizations can use lobbying to advance their causes in federal, state, and local legislatures.

National Committee on Responsive Philanthropy (NCRP) (www.ncrp.org/publications)

NCRP has published a series of reports on the impact of advocacy, organizing, and civic engagement, which show the high rate of return on foundation investments due to advocacy by their grantees. These reports can be downloaded for free and hard copies are available for a fee.

Spitfire Strategies Smart Chart 3.0 (www.smartchart.org/)

The interactive Smart Chart 3.0 is an online tool that can help you make and assess strategic communications decisions if you are just starting the communications planning process, evaluating a communications effort already in progress, or reviewing a communications effort you've already completed. Access to the Smart Chart 3.0 is free, but requires registration.

Center for Lobbying in the Public Interest (CLPI)

CLPI provides a range of legal and "how to" resources for charities and foundations on nonprofit advocacy. Specific materials include a legislative advocacy resource guide; online advocacy handbook; ethical lobbying principles and benchmarking chart; lobbying tactics; and advocacy and civic engagement toolkits for private and community foundations. CLPI Fellows—experienced state-based advocates and educators—provide customized training and coaching.

www.clpi.org/the-law

www.clpi.org/press-publications/clpi-publications

www.clpi.org/press-publications/publications-saleww2.wkkf.org/advocacyhandbook/index.html

www.clpi.org/nuts-a-bolts/lobbying-tactics

Praxis Project (www.thepraxisproject.org/irc/tools.html)

The Praxis Project provides online tools and publications for organizers, researchers, and program managers working to develop policies and coalitions at the state and local level.

Nancy Amidei. <u>So You Want to Make A Difference: Advocacy Is the Key</u>. Washington, DC: OMB Watch, 1991.

This is an advocacy manual that encourages citizens to get involved in policy advocacy and equips local leaders with the tools to teach others about policy advocacy. The report is out of print, but is available in digital format through OMB Watch (www.ombwatch.org/node/169).

Asian Communities for Reproductive Justice (ACRJ) (www.reproductivejustice.org/download.html)

ACRJ's Movement Building Indicators were developed for reproductive justice advocates and provide effective ways to assess leadership development, policy advocacy, communications, and relationship building with easy-to-use worksheets to guide your work.

○ ○ ○

All these resources, plus nonprofit management tips of the week and more, can be found at Nonprofits101.org.

CHAPTER 13

Nonprofit Financial Management

By David Greco, Vice President, Nonprofit Finance Fund

Introduction

At the core of financial management is the fact that money and mission are inseparably linked. Nonprofit organizations exist to provide services that the commercial sector is unable or unwilling to provide, and *financial data should serve the mission, not drive it.* Leaders have an obligation to understand the nature of their business model, to know the fully loaded cost of delivering programs and services, and to communicate to funders, supporters, and other stakeholders the organization's programmatic story in financial terms.

When a nonprofit organization has to close its doors, it is usually not for lack of talented and smart people. It's not because they do not understand how to deliver excellent programs. And in general, it is not because they can not raise money. More often than not, it is because there has been a series of decisions that have put the organization into a financially unsustainable position. They are undercapitalized, have illiquid assets, and lack unrestricted revenue to cover operating costs. We'll address these three major pitfalls within this chapter, and provide clear tips on how to avoid them.

In the nonprofit sector, finance is too often thought of as something unrelated to, or even interfering with, program delivery. Many managers dread dealing with finance and do the bare minimum to comply with policies, regulations, and legal requirements.

In order to remain focused on mission, nonprofits must understand how their organization is managed financially and what its lines of business are. These issues are directly and inextricably linked to your organization's ability to respond to the needs of your community and a changing economic landscape. They are questions of leadership.

concept

Is It a Nonprofit or a *Business*?

You will see that throughout this chapter we use the term "nonprofit business." Does that mean nonprofits should act more like businesses? No. *Nonprofits shouldn't act like businesses; they are businesses.* Being a 501(c)(3) is a tax status, not a business model. Like any business, most nonprofits earn most of their revenue from one or two sources; they require profits (surpluses) to operate effectively (AKA "in the black" versus "in the red"); and they need to cover overhead, train and pay employees, and refresh service offerings in the regular course of business.

Critical Skills and Competencies

Given those introductory comments and considerations, we're now ready to tackle some of the core skills you'll need when running your nonprofit "business."

Five Steps to Mastering Nonprofit Finances

To make good decisions, nonprofit managers need good information. This is especially true when it comes to financial information. The goal of this chapter is to help nonprofit leaders find and use financial information to make better decisions by gaining a deeper understanding of their financial situation. I will also provide tips and techniques that will help you more effectively communicate your financial needs to supporters, funders, and your board.

Unfortunately, it's not always easy for nonprofits to know where they stand. Nonprofit financial statements, audits, and the IRS Form 990 all provide a good deal of data. However, these sources of financial information were all create exclusively for tax and legal compliance reasons, not as management tools. Consequently, executives and boards must do some additional work to develop an accurate understanding of their organizations' financial dynamics.

There are a number of financial statements the executive needs to learn to read and interpret—more than can be covered here. Several excellent resources for this are included at the end of this chapter. Here, we will provide five steps to help you read, understand, and interpret the most important financial statements, so that you know your organization's overall financial health. Your accountant, auditor, or financial adviser should be able to guide you through reading and understanding other statements and point you to the numbers that matter for tax and legal compliance.

Let's examine how to find the financial data that matters most to you as a manager.

Introduction to the Statement of Activities (AKA Income Statement, Profit & Loss, P&L)

To help identify valuable financial information on your Statement of Activities, we are going to use a real example (Table 13.1) from an actual but anonymous social services agency, ABC Center.

The Statement of Activities tallies up all of the financial events during a particular period of time (usually a quarter or fiscal year). It shows how much revenue the organization generated (1) and the operating expenses for the given time period (6). Change in Net Assets (9)—also called Surplus/(Deficit) or Profit/ (Loss)—reveals if the organization made or lost money within the period. The Statement of Activities is not that different from a personal income statement, in which your salary and other sources of revenue (investments, gifts, etc.) are compared against your living expenses.

Table 13.1: ABC Center Statement of Activities

Year Ended December 31, 2011 ($ in thousands)

Operating Activity	Unrestricted	Temporarily Restricted	Permanently Restricted	Total
Revenues, Gains, and Other Support[1]	—	—	—	—
Support[2]	—	—	—	—
Foundations	113	58	—	171
Government	57	—	—	57
Corporations	49	—	—	49
Individuals	248	—	—	248
Total Support	467	58	—	525
Investment Income[3]	7	—	—	7
Earned Income (Fees, Dues, Other)[4]	484	—	—	484
Net Assets Released from Restriction[5]	749	–749	—	—
Total Revenues, Gains, and Other Support	1,707	–691	—	1,016
Operating Expenses[6]	—	—		
Program Services[7]	1,004	—	—	1,004
Supporting Services[8]	—	—		
Administrative	209	—	—	209
Development	49	—	—	49
Total Supporting Services	258	—	—	258
Total Expenses	1,262	—	—	1,262
Change in Net Assets[9]	[10]445	[11]–691	—	[12]–246

Source: Nonprofit Finance Fund, 2011 ©.

Restrictions on Use of Funds

Before we analyze our Statement of Activities, it's essential to discuss the restrictions on the use of money in the nonprofit sector.

In the for-profit world, most revenue is considered a "liquid" asset that can be used to fund the business as needed. But in the nonprofit sector, which relies heavily on contributed revenue, cash often comes with strings attached, as overviewed in the "Classifications of Revenue" sidebar. *Restricted contributions are funds that organizations must use <u>only</u> to pay for specific business costs, or they must be spent before or after a specified timeframe.* These are generally geared towards program expenses, as opposed to indirect or overhead costs such as rent, which are not directly related to a nonprofit's programs, but which are necessary for the nonprofit to operate. These costs also include management and general administration, fundraising and membership-development activities. Some donors, especially foundations and government funders, may place a cap on how much of their grants can be used for overhead or indirect expenses, if any. You can have all the cash in the world, but if it's restricted to a specific program or time, we can't use it to cover payroll—even in an emergency.

Classifications of Revenue

Unrestricted Revenue

As in the for-profit world, this cash comes with no restrictions and is considered "liquid." Often it is generated by earned income (selling products, services, and memberships) or from unrestricted contributions from funders or donors. This revenue, which the organization can use at its discretion, often covers general operating and other costs that aren't supported by restricted revenue.

Temporarily Restricted Revenue

With this cash, funders restrict the use of their donations either to specific programs (purpose restrictions) or provide donations that are spread over a certain amount of time (time restrictions). Although this can ensure money is there for specific programs or future use, an organization can't use it to pay for immediate or urgent expenses that fall outside the specific parameters of the contribution. If the donor's restrictions are somehow met and funds are left over, the remainder of this revenue transitions into unrestricted funds.

Permanently Restricted Revenue

Most often this cash is for an organization's endowment. Organizations can often use the interest generated from investing these funds however they like, but they are restricted from touching the principal.

Figure 13.1 is an Illustration of the different classifications of revenue and how they relate to one another.

Figure 13.1: Classification of Revenue

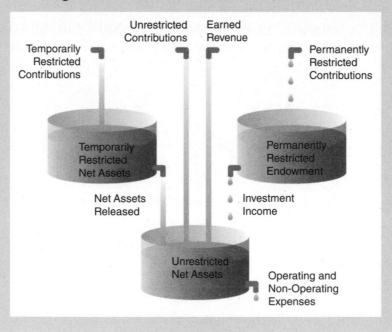

IMPORTANT: All operating expenses (salaries, utilities, rent, and so forth) can only be paid out of unrestricted funds. So as restrictions are met (i.e., the new fiscal year begins or you start work on a specific program), funds are "released" from the temporarily restricted bucket, reclassified as unrestricted revenue, and can then pay for operating expenses. For permanently restricted funds, often the interest income flows into the unrestricted bucket and then is available for use. This may appear overly complicated, but it's simply the way money moves in the nonprofit sector.

Step 1: Understanding Revenue Dynamics

When analyzed carefully, the Statement of Activities reveals key pieces of an organization's financial story, such as patterns in revenue streams and how diversified they are. By looking at multiple years of data, *consecutive statements also show how consistent and reliable revenue is over time.* Below are some key assessment questions to help you make better programmatic decisions and plan for the future in a thoughtful, planned manner.

Where Does the Organization's Money Come from?

Revisiting the previous sample, the "Support" section (2) of the Statement of Activities reveals the sources of revenue from foundations, government sources, corporations, and individuals. Other items shown in this category are investment income, earned revenue (ticket or product sales, membership dues, and the like), and funds released from restrictions given the conditions mentioned above.

Is Revenue Reasonably Diversified or at Risk?

If an organization's revenue is heavily concentrated in one area (such as government funding), this highlights the risk of changes in the funder's priorities. In our example, we see a fairly well-diversified funding stream with earned income and contributions being the major sources of revenue (not unexpected for a social services agency).

Step 2: Understanding Cost Dynamics

In the Operating Expenses section of the Statement of Activities, you can see the two main subsections of costs: Program Services and Supporting Services. Program Services (7) are costs for services directly related to fulfilling the nonprofit's mission. Supporting Services (8) are activities not directly related to the purpose or mission for which the nonprofit organization exists, but which are necessary for the organization to operate. Supporting services generally include management and general expenses, fundraising, and membership-development activities.

The expense line items that most people are familiar with (such as personnel, rent, travel, and utilities) are listed on a separate financial statement called the Statement of Functional Expenses, which is not covered in this discussion.

Here are some key questions to ask in examining cost dynamics:

What Does the Organization Spend on Operating Activities?

Recognizing that expenses are grouped in broad categories, the *Program and Support classifications provide management with a high-level look at exactly where funding is going.* Board members also look at these to get a top-level assessment of how well the organization is performing.

IMPORTANT: Many nonprofit watchdog organizations and donor websites use a ratio of program expenses to administrative or fundraising expenses as a way to measure an organization's efficiency. Though a common "rule of thumb," these ratios are not an accurate representation of an organization's financial health or effectiveness, and fail to take into account the individual needs of different nonprofits. For example, some organizations, such as health services agencies, have high regulatory burdens that require additional administrative support, whereas other organizations require safe, well-maintained facilities resulting in higher occupancy costs.

Are Fluctuations in Expenses in Line with Changes in Revenue?

When looking at financial information from year to year, you can see if expenses map to revenue changes. For example, if an organization lost a major grant or contract from one year to the next, did it keep spending at a constant level, or did it reduce expenses accordingly?

Step 3: Analyze Profitability and Savings

The first thing most people want to know when reviewing a Statement of Activities is "Did the organization generate a surplus or deficit?" This "bottom line" or Surplus/Deficit is called "Change in Net Assets" (9), and reveals the organization's overall profitability. However, there are actually a number of bottom lines we can look at, each presenting a different picture.

Most people look at *Total* Change in Net Assets (12) but *it's crucial for managers to know whether the nonprofit brought in more than it spent on an unrestricted basis* (10). Remember because temporarily or permanently restricted funds are off limits, the only money available to pay for operating expenses is from the unrestricted column (6). An organization might have an operating deficit but a positive Change in Net Assets because it receives a large amount of temporarily restricted funds.

Are Surpluses Sufficient to Meet Other Obligations?

Just as in the for-profit world, the cost of doing business for a nonprofit includes more than just the direct operational expenses. In addition to an organization's operating expenses—salaries, rent, electricity, and so on—there are other costs that must be factored in to calculate the "full cost" of doing business. These items include:

- Depreciation allocation: setting aside money to cover the cost of future repairs to facilities and related building systems

- Program or capital investments: investments in technology upgrades, facilities improvements, or retraining staff

- Debt payments: money to cover interest on loans, lines of credit, or mortgages

- Savings: setting aside reserves for future needs, which can be anything from facility repair to managing unforeseen change, such as funding losses

The amounts for each of these items vary by organization, but every nonprofit needs to generate enough of a surplus to set aside savings and invest in infrastructure.

And If the Agency Is Saving, Is It Enough?

Organizations must save to protect themselves from both expected and unexpected change. As we'll discuss when looking at the Balance Sheet, the appropriate amount an organization should be setting aside for a reserve is based on many factors, such as risk tolerance and exposure, reliability of funding, future plans, and cash flow. As a general guideline, *most nonprofits strive to set aside "rainy day" funds that amount to at least 90 days of operating expenses.*

For the last two steps in analyzing our financial statements, we need to move from the Statement of Activities to the Balance Sheet.

Introduction to the Balance Sheet

The Balance Sheet, known formally as the Statement of Financial Position, shows the assets, financial resources, debts, and other liabilities at any given moment, typically the last day of a fiscal year. Think of it as a snapshot that reveals the net assets—particularly the unrestricted net assets—available to support the organization.

The three basic elements of a Balance Sheet are:

• Assets: everything the organization has or owns

• Liabilities: everything an organization owes

• Net Assets: what the organization has or owns, free and clear of any liabilities. Although for-profit businesses have something called Owners' Equity, nonprofits aren't "owned" by anyone, hence they have Net Assets (i.e., Total Assets less Liabilities). For individuals, this is called "Net Worth."

Step 4: Identify Patterns in the Balance Sheet

Below are some questions that will reveal the organization's financial decisions, how much risk it can now tolerate, and how financially stable it is.

Is the Distribution of Assets (1) Appropriate, Given the Core Business?

For organizations that require a facility to deliver their programs—such as a theater, a homeless shelter, or health care clinic—expect to see large fixed assets (their building and equipment). But for a people-intensive business—such as a visiting nurses association—that generates revenue through fee-for-service contracts, expect large receivables (money owed to the organization),

Table 13.2: ABC Center Statement of Financial Position

($ in thousands)

	Dec 31, 2011		Dec 31, 2011
Assets[1]		**Liabilities[6]**	
Current		**Current**	
Cash and Equivalents[2]	191	Accounts Payable	57
Grants & Pledges Receivable[3]	55	Accrued Salaries & Benefits	—
Accounts Receivable	—	Other Current Liabilities	—
Inventory	—	Total Deferred Revenue	—
Prepaid Expenses	41	Short-Term Debt	—
Other Current Assets	—	**Total Current Liabilities**	57
Total Current Assets	287	**Long-Term**	
Long-Term		Long-Term Liabilities	—
Long-Term Investments	—	Long-Term Debt[7]	114
Deposits and Prepaid Rent	—	Other Long-Term Liabilities	—
Grants & Pledges Receivable	—	**Total Long-Term Liabilities**	114
Net Fixed Assets (P&E)[4]	760	**Total Liabilities[8]**	171
Other Long-Term Assets	—	**Net Assets[9]**	
Total Long-Term Assets	760	Unrestricted	
Total Assets[5]	1,047	Undesignated[10]	11
		Unrestr.—Board Designated[11]	—
		Unrestr.—P&E[12]	760
		Total Unrestr. Net Assets[13]	771
		Temp. Restricted Net Assets[14]	105
		Perm. Restricted Net Assets	—
		Total Net Assets[15]	876
		Total Liab. & Net Assets[16]	1,047

as they submit reimbursements after delivering their service. *The distribution of assets should follow the logic and direct needs of the business model;* if it doesn't, then it should be further examined.

How "Leveraged" Is the Organization?

Has the organization used significant debt (loans) to fund its business? If so, are there steady income streams designed to cover the associated payments? In the case of ABC Center, you see they have some debt (7) in the amount of $114,000, but given the overall assets of the organization, this level of debt would not be considered excessive.

What Is the Composition of Net Assets?

Again, Net Assets (9) are the assets an organization owns free of any liabilities. These are what the nonprofit manager really has available to support her programs and mission. They are divided into Unrestricted Net Assets, Temporarily Restricted Net Assets (timing or purpose restrictions), and Permanently Restricted Net Assets (Endowment). In our example, most of the organization's net assets are unrestricted ($771,000 out of Total Assets of $1,047,000) and can be used for any purposes.

Step 5: Understand Your Liquidity

In our final step, we'll look at the organization's liquidity. "Liquidity" refers to how quickly and cheaply an asset can be converted into cash. Assets like real estate that generally can only be sold after a long exhaustive search for a buyer are known as illiquid. You can determine liquidity with information from the two statements we've studied.

How Many Months of Cash Do We Have?

"Months of Cash," one of the most common measurements of an organization's liquidity, represents the number of months an organization could operate if no additional funds were received and is calculated with this simple formula:

$$\frac{\text{Cash and Equivalents (2)}}{\text{Average Monthly Expenses}}$$

You will often see the term "Cash and Equivalents" or "Cash and Near-Cash" on the Balance Sheet. This simply means that you add both actual cash on hand plus bonds, money market mutual funds, T-bills, and other short-term investments that can be readily converted into cash. This is usually the first line on the Assets side of the Balance Sheet. In our case this totals $191,000 (2).

You can calculate Average Monthly Expenses by taking the annual operating expenses on the Statement of Activities and dividing by 12 months. ABC Center's annual operating expenses were $1,262,000, which when divided by 12 equals $105,166 in average monthly expenses.

$$\frac{\text{Cash and Equivalents (\$191,000)}}{\text{Average Monthly Expenses (\$105,166)}} = 1.8 \text{ months of cash}$$

Most organizations should aim for three months through a combination of cash (and near-cash) on hand and access to cash through a line of credit. Organizations may need more or less liquidity depending on stage of development, cash flow cycles, capital needs, and reliability of funding sources.

IMPORTANT: This is a quick measurement to determine liquidity. But remember, some cash is spoken for, because there are restrictions on its use as discussed above.

Is There a More Accurate Way to Measure Nonprofit Liquidity?

Yes, there is a much more accurate measure, but it requires a little more math. If this is important to you, you'll need to calculate your Unrestricted Liquid Net Assets (ULNA), which articulates a nonprofit's ability to meet its obligations while recognizing that cash is not always readily available for operational use.

What Are Unrestricted "Liquid" Net Assets?

Most Balance Sheets will simply list Unrestricted, Temporarily Restricted, and Permanently Restricted Net Assets. The challenge for the nonprofit manager is that this does not reveal how much of those Unrestricted Assets are "liquid"— that is, readily available to pay operating expenses today. For example, while Property & Equipment (P&E) is unrestricted, it is not considered liquid, in that a building is very difficult to convert into cash to pay bills. To get this

Table 13.3: Calculating Liquid Net Assets

	ABC Center
Total Unrestricted Net Assets (13)	$771,000
– Unrestricted—Board Designated (11)	$0
– Unrestricted—P&E (12)	$760,000
= Unrestricted Liquid Net Assets	$11,000

information, you will need to break down the Unrestricted Net Assets (13) further into Undesignated (10), Board Designated (11), and Property & Equipment (12)– your accountant should easily be able to do this for you as we have done above.

The basic calculation for liquid net assets is shown in Table 13.3.

o o o

Remember that ABC Center has average monthly expenses of approximately $105,166—and they only have $11,000 available to use as a reserve or cash cushion. If you were to calculate months of unrestricted liquid net assets for ABC Center (Liquid Net Assets of $11,000 divided by average monthly expenses of $105,166), you would have .1 months (or about 3 days) of unrestricted "liquid" net assets. That is a very different picture from 1.8 months of cash on hand. Would you be making different decisions if you had 3 days of cash available versus 2 months' worth? Probably, which is why it is so important to understand the different measures of liquidity.

If an organization has limited or no unrestricted liquid net assets, it has very little ability to responsibly invest in new programs or infrastructure, respond to changes, or take advantage of opportunities. ULNA is a powerful tool to highlight the assets available for use by the nonprofit manager, and provides a good indication of overall financial health.

Communicating Your Financial Story

The nonprofit executive who understands revenue and expense dynamics, and has a clear grasp of the organization's balance sheet and liquidity position, is better able to tell the organization's financial story to staff, board members, donors, and the community. For ABC Center, what is their financial story?

The Good Part

ABC Center has a diversified revenue stream and did generate an unrestricted operating surplus. They do not have a significant amount of debt or loans for an organization of their size. The large majority of their Net Assets— what they own free and clear of any liabilities—is unrestricted and available for use by the organization. And they have almost two months of cash on hand.

The Not-So-Good Part

ABC Center relied heavily on funds being released from restrictions to cover operating expenses this year. That left only $105,000 in temporarily restricted net assets that were available to fund future program activities. The vast majority of their unrestricted net assets is tied up in their building and not liquid. And almost all of the cash on hand is spoken for. So in reality, they only have about 3 days worth of unrestricted "liquid" net assets, which for a $1.2 million organization presents a high degree of risk.

Should this organization experience government payment delays, a decline in contributed revenue, or need to make some major repairs to their building, do they have the resources available to cushion their organization? Not really. ABC Center is not immediately in danger of closing as these things might not happen, but it does mean there is a high degree of risk if any of these things should happen—and the management team and board members need to be aware of these risks.

In communicating your nonprofit's financial story to staff, board members, and donors, you need to know how much it really costs the organization to do what it does, and why. *You need to understand that what may look good on paper can hide risk*—such as most of your net assets being unrestricted. Though board members may be looking at months of cash, you need to be able to explain your *real* liquidity position. Most important, you need to be able to articulate *why* it is necessary to generate surpluses, and how these surpluses help sustain an organization through good times and bad.

Nonprofit Finance Dos and Don'ts:

- DON'T forget that financial data should serve the mission, not drive it.

- DO remember that nonprofits are businesses, too, and must meet a financial bottom line to continue operations. Being a 501(c)(3) is a tax status, not a business model.

- DO review your Statement of Activities at least quarterly to assess your finances over a particular period of time, and to establish the consistency and reliability of your revenue.

- DON'T ever use restricted contributions for *any* purpose other than the one they were intended for, as conveyed by the donor or funder (i.e. specific programs, or before or after a specified timeframe).

- DO pay all operating expenses (salaries, utilities, rent, and so forth) out of unrestricted funds and pay attention to whether your nonprofit brought in more than it spent on an unrestricted basis.

- DO understand your cost dynamics, especially the ratio of your program expenses to administrative and fundraising expenses. If these ratios are relatively high, be prepared to explain why.

- DO set aside a "rainy day" fund with at least 90 days of operating expenses.

- DO regularly review your Statement of Financial Position (Balance Sheet) to reveal the net assets available to support your organization at a specific moment in time.

- DO monitor "Months of Cash" in order to protect against your worst case scenario; calculate Unrestricted Liquid Net Assets (ULNA) if a more accurate measurement is needed.

[Sidebar: Dos and Don'ts]

Conclusion: Tips for Effective Nonprofit Financial Leadership

Effective leaders must . . .

. . . Understand that nonprofit finance operates under different rules from the for-profit world

Many for-profit rules and conventions on are reversed in the nonprofit environment: growth almost always increases the need for fundraising; cash is not always available for use; "surpluses" are often prohibited; expenditures on overhead are seen as wasteful . . . and more. Leaders from the for-profit world must understand these and other nonprofit management issues to be able to make better decisions.

. . . Realize that "nonprofit" is a tax status, not a business plan

Nonprofits exist for a reason. They enter the market when the for-profit and governmental sectors can't, won't, or shouldn't, generally due to a gap or failure in the market economy. This commercial flaw is why nonprofit (501(c)(3)'s are provided two powerful tools to reliably subsidize operations: tax exemption and access to tax-advantaged charitable contributions.

. . . Nonprofits need profits

Nonprofits operate in a changing, uncertain environment and a cash cushion (surplus) can help manage this risk. Nonprofits need to be able to generate surpluses sufficient to:

○ Pay for the annual "wear-and-tear" of Property & Equipment ("P&E")

○ Finance investments in new fixed assets (such as P&E) or improvements that may not be fully financed through a capital campaign

○ Cover any debt payments

○ Contribute to growth and savings

. . . Insist on having clear, reliable, routine, management-friendly financial information

Effective leaders share their financial data with their board, funders, and internal and external stakeholders, and use it as a tool to effectively communicate their organization's financial story. *You should have monthly or quarterly financial statements* that:

○ Compare year-to-date actuals to budget, and to actual results from the previous year

○ Project year-end results to reflect material changes to budget

- Focus on unrestricted revenue (including revenue released from restriction) available to support operations

- Monitor balance sheet areas, such as liquidity, payments of debt principal, investments in fixed assets, and so on.

. . . Own your nonprofit's numbers

Making sound business choices requires reliable, accurate, and timely financial data. Nonprofit executives need to understand this data and use it to tell their financial story transparently. Nonprofit managers and board members need to fluidly connect money and mission, based on the needs and perspectives of who they're talking to and what they're talking about.

David Greco is the vice president of the Nonprofit Finance Fund, bringing more than 20 years of experience in building nonprofit programs and earned income ventures.

Previously, David served as vice president of the Youth Leadership Institute, bringing youth and adults together to create more just and sustainable communities. He also served as the corporate and foundation relations manager for the National Wildlife Federation, and director of programs for the Horatio Alger Association, where he worked with economically disadvantaged youth. He earned his MA in political science from Villanova University and BS in history and politics from Drexel University.

Nonprofit Finance Resource Review

Nonprofit Finance Fund (www.nonprofitfinancefund.org)

An excellent source of tools, tips, and resources for organizations looking to strengthen financial health, as well as articles and research on effectively managing nonprofits.

Thomas A. McLaughlin. Streetsmart Financial Basics for Nonprofit Managers (3rd ed.). New York: Wiley, 2009.

A very practical guide to understanding and managing the finances of a nonprofit organization. It is a superb introduction for new nonprofit executives, board members, and students.

Murray Dropkin. The Cash Flow Management Book for Nonprofits: A Step-by-Step Guide for Managers and Boards. San Francisco, Jossey-Bass, 2001.

This guide offers you nuts-and-bolts suggestions for using a cash flow analysis to develop successful strategies for the day-to-day and long-term financial planning of any nonprofit organization. Filled with practical to-do lists, sample forms, worksheets, schedules, policies and procedures, and checklists.

John Carver and Miriam Carver. The Governance of Financial Management, Revised and Updated. A Carver Policy Governance Guide. San Francisco: Jossey-Bass, 2009.

Reveals how a board can effectively govern an organization's financial planning by controlling budget values rather than budget numbers. The guide addresses the issue of actual fiscal conditions by creating policies that safeguard an organization's fiscal health.

Dan Pallotta. Uncharitable: How Restraints on Nonprofits Undermine Their Potential. Medford: Tufts University, 2000.

An excellent—if provocative—look at how the rules governing nonprofit finance, especially restrictions, actually undermine nonprofits' abilities to achieve their mission.

Clara Miller. "The Looking Glass World of Nonprofit Money." The Nonprofit Quarterly, Spring 2005.

Step into the nonprofit sector and you enter a new and irrational world, where the financial rules, when they apply at all, are reversed, and the science turns topsy-turvy. This article examines seven time-honored business rules and explores how they fit (or don't) in the nonprofit world.

Clara Miller. "Risk Minus Cash Equals Crisis." State of Philanthropy 2004, National Committee For Responsive Philanthropy, January 2005.

Debate rages over the pros and cons, the wisdom and effectiveness, of providing general operating support to nonprofit organizations. This article illustrates three counterintuitive business realities, which, if understood and acted upon, might lead us to different kinds of conversations with grantees and, ultimately, higher impact grants.

Clara Miller. "Hidden in Plain Sight: Understanding Nonprofit Capital Structure." <u>The Nonprofit Quarterly</u>, Spring 2003.

This article highlights capital structure as a critical driver of mission and programs, as well as organizational capacity. It also illustrates how funders often inadvertently contribute to the undercapitalization of nonprofits and suggests ways of reversing poor funding practices.

o o o

All these resources, plus nonprofit management tips of the week and more, can be found at Nonprofits101.org.

Part Four

Nonprofit Technology and IT

Technology does not drive change—it enables change.

—Anonymous

The world we live in is changing rapidly, and the speed of that change is only increasing. When I think about the fact that my parents grew up without the Internet, computers, microwave ovens, DVD and even VHS players, and that as children they had to wait for the TV to warm up before watching a show, it makes me wonder how things ever got done. Can you even *imagine* a workplace without email? No doubt, the children growing up today, texting in class and glued to their PlayStations®, will wonder the same about my generation. Today, we find ourselves in a world where Facebook boasts 500 million *active* users, making it the equivalent of the third most populous nation in the world, and growing at a rate of 700,000 daily—the size of the <u>Los Angeles Times</u>' entire subscription base.

So what are the implications of the information revolution and, more important, what opportunities does this new digital age present? First and foremost, *technology is the greatest empowering force of the masses in history.* It

217

gives voice to the voiceless, names to the nameless. It flattens hierarchy and allows information to flow freely. You may have heard the term "Web 2.0" thrown around a lot lately, but what does that mean, exactly? The short answer is that it means whatever you want it to, as there's no established definition. Some consider it to be a term used to describe state-of-the-art websites that integrate video and other dynamic, multimedia content pulled from other sources, but to me that misses the crucial component that makes it such a powerful force.

I believe that Web 2.0 can only be understood in the context of its predecessor. Web 1.0, representing the early days of the Internet and the World Wide Web, was all about *content*. Suddenly, a new medium exploded on the scene, allowing anyone to cheaply publish information about their business, nonprofit, or personal interests to the entire world. The word "brochureware" was used a lot to convey the notion that people were really just taking their existing marketing materials and posting them online. But the new environment brought with it new rules: power to the people versus the publisher; pull versus push-based content; direct, immediate, and complete accountability versus relying on focus groups of representative samples; and a medium that was both a direct marketing *and* a branding vehicle. Everything marketers thought they knew went out the window.

It was a fascinating time, working in the dot-com sector in the late nineties. Rules were being rewritten every day, including some by us, a group of kids right out of college that had started the fastest growing digital ad agency in the sector. After a while, though, industry caught up and really started putting the technology to use. Enter Web 2.0, with the charge led by players such as MySpace, Facebook, YouTube, and (at least based on my definition) craigslist.org.

If Web 1.0 is about content, says my colleague Bill Ryan, *Web 2.0 is about community*. They used to say "content is king," but nowadays, *context* is the new game in town. To me, the defining principle of Web 2.0 is that it integrates *user-generated content*. Web 2.0 websites are merely platforms, empty shells or frameworks that rely on the community for their content. Do you really think YouTube's staff is out there finding over 24 hours of content every *minute*, posting them online, and rating them? Do you think that Wikipedia's small but mighty staff personally created something that is now several times more robust (and accurate, I should add) than the *Encyclopedia Britannica*, and that's just counting their English version? Nope, not quite.

You see, in this *"everyone is smarter than anyone"* world, these innovative companies have figured out how to get the community to work for them, leveraging the wisdom of the masses—AKA "crowdsourcing." So what does that make possible? A prime example is craigslist.org, which until recently was the only top-ten website with under 10,000 employees; at my last count, they had 30. *That* is the power of Web 2.0.

Now let's relate all of that to the nonprofit sector. In a world where resources are stretched thin, where everyone is working at or over capacity, the real question is *how can you leverage technology to put the community to work for you, and for the cause?* The chapters contained herein, combined with some related contributions in the marketing and fundraising sections, are designed to provide you with exactly these kinds of insights. In addition, they will help you harness the power of IT to make your organization run more smoothly. But remember the words of the world's richest man and biggest philanthropist, Bill Gates:

> The first rule of any technology . . . is that automation applied to an efficient operation will magnify the efficiency. The second is that automation applied to an inefficient operation will magnify the inefficiency.

Technology is unique in that it is both an internally and an externally facing tool. Within a nonprofit, it can play a crucial role with helping manage information, whether that be for operational issues, intra-staff communication via email, board correspondence, and so forth. Externally, technology can support marketing and engagement efforts, enabling you to raise funds, alert the community to your efforts, keep tabs on partners, and more. Either way, technology is the lifeblood of a successful nonprofit, even if you're not fully in with the 2.0 crowd.

In this portion of the book, we'll look at both of the inward- and outward-facing roles of technology as they relate to your nonprofit. We'll start with a broad overview of all things tech, then dive into website design, community building, and how to maximize IT's role in building and maintaining a database of your constituents. I've asked our writers to make sure that they explain their topics, no matter how involved, in simple, easy to understand language. So it's okay if you have not heard about Moore's Law, which says that the speed of computer processors is doubling every 18 months. Instead, you'll hear us talk about the increasing speed of change, the opportunities that surface as a result, and how to seize them. In general, *the focus of this book is not on the "what" but rather on the "so what,"* meaning how these concepts and strategies relate and can be useful to you and the cause you serve.

CHAPTER 14

The Technology Foundation: Hardware and Software

By Holly Ross, Executive Director, NTEN: The Nonprofit Technology Network

Introduction

Let's get the obvious out of the way first. Managing technology can be one of the scariest aspects of your work as a nonprofit leader. It changes all the time, most of us don't have any formal tech training, and when we make mistakes with technology, they can be expensive.

But here's the funny thing about technology: you don't actually need any technical skills to manage it effectively for your organization. In fact, the skills that have you on the path to a successful nonprofit career are the same ones that will help you manage technology successfully. *Creating a vision, understanding your needs, and solid planning are key skills identified in a multitude of articles*[1] *and papers as the key to making technology work for your organization.*

221

It's also not the case that you need a lot of money to use technology effectively. Especially today, as hardware costs drop and software moves to the Internet, even the smallest organizations can do big things with tiny tech budgets. In a 2009 report, the Nonprofit Technology Network asked nonprofits how satisfied they were with technology in their organizations. The research found that there was no relationship between "satisfaction and the size of the capital budget for technology, or the size of the salary expenditures for maintaining and supporting technology."[2]

So technology is less like science fiction, and more like accounting. You don't need to be a CPA to manage your organization's finances, but you do need to grasp a few key concepts so that you can make the right decisions. Technology is much the same. In this chapter, we'll explore some basic technology concepts, as well as the big-picture management skills you'll need.

Critical Skills and Competencies

If you're going to be successful in the wonderful world of nonprofit technology, there are a few crucial concepts and strategies to master. It all starts with putting your mission first and building a strong foundation for your efforts. I'll review these two key considerations, and then provide some practical tips around hardware, safety, and software, and finally discuss importance of solid technology planning.

Remember Who Brought You to the Party

If you can remember just one thing from this chapter, remember this: *your mission is the only thing that matters when it comes to technology.* When your board wants you to get that fancy database, your staff wants new phones, or you are thinking of getting mobile broadband cards for your field staff, you only really need to ask one question to make a decent decision: "Will this help us better meet our mission?"

Your mission is the reason you're here. It's what inspires you to go to the office every morning. It's the reason you're in this sector to begin with. Your mission is what brought you to this party. Even though it's tough to see what a server or a laptop has to do with your mission, you must make those connections to manage technology effectively.

Let's take a classic example: donated computers. Many nonprofits use technology hand-me-downs generously donated by volunteers and other supporters. And many nonprofit staffers spend 10% of their day (or more!) rebooting, defragging, troubleshooting, and begging the technology gods as they try to make these computers work.

As opposed to focusing on the few hundred dollars that a donated computer can save your organization, freeing funds up to go straight to programs, *you must view technology as an investment in meeting your mission*. Technology that actually works increases staff productivity over several years, allowing them to spend more time with your clients, delivering on your mission. A 2007 study reported that "information technology and telecommunications hardware, software, and services turns out to be a powerful driver of growth, having an impact on worker productivity three to five times that of non-IT capital (e.g., buildings and machines)."[3]

Tim Wilson, executive director of Western Arts Alliance (WAA) recognized the connection between mission and technology clearly when he initiated the search for a new membership database. "A big part of our strategic plan is creating connections between the people in our community," said Wilson. "The new database had to be a key component of meeting this goal by helping us facilitate and track connections between our members."

Although the price tag was high for a new database and a consultant to help them with their search, Tim knew that it was about much more than the money. "It's easy to say that it's too expensive," he shared. "But the investment means that we will be better able to serve our community, and that our staff will spend less time trying to use a system that just doesn't work for us anymore. It costs a lot up front, but it saves us in the long term."

Whether it's a new mobile phone, a computer, a database, or a website, you can use the mission filter to help you decide what to implement. If the staff, board member, or consultant can clearly articulate how the investment will further your mission, you've got something you can consider. If they can't, it's probably not worth your time.

Build a Strong Foundation

When you look to buy a house, you have a list of things you want: four bedrooms, two bathrooms, and so on. Anyone who has ever bought a house can tell you that there are lots of properties that meet your needs on paper. When you get there though, you may very find that the "4br/2ba cutie!" may *technically* meet your needs, but has a leaking roof, shag carpet older than your mother, and a serious termite problem.

The technology in your organization is very similar. When we ask ourselves what we want out of our technology, we often rattle off a list that includes lots of important things, like a good database, slick website, and so on. Many nonprofit leaders pursue those important pieces. Like many home-buyers though, they neglect the stuff that's most important—the foundation.

The WAA staff felt this pain point very clearly. The old database made it incredibly cumbersome to keep member records up-to-date. Several times a week (daily during their annual conference season), data had to be manually synced across systems, which was time consuming and resulted in costly mistakes.

Every nonprofit will have different software and hardware needs, but we can agree that there are a few key elements every organization should set in place, and then reinforce regularly. Without these elements, it's more likely that your printers won't print, your computers will run slowly, and you'll spend more time responding to emergencies rather than focusing on your mission. You can have the fanciest website in the world, but if the fundraising department can't print mailing labels . . .

Of course, I'd love to tell you exactly which hardware and software to buy, but I can't. Your exact needs vary greatly from those of other organizations, and anything I'd list here would be out of date by the time you read it. But I can tell you the hardware and software basics you'll need to have in place.

Computers

There are hundreds of computers to choose from; determining what's best for your organization is no easy task. But, there are a few questions you can ask yourself (or a tech-savvy friend) to put you on the right path.

- **Question 1:** How powerful and fast does the computer need to be?

  There are some really powerful computers out there, but the data-entry clerk probably doesn't need one. Know what kinds of software will be run on each machine, and make sure you buy a computer with enough memory and processor speed to accommodate that. Look at the minimum systems requirements for software to be used on the machine to find out what ballpark you need to be in. One word of advice—buy computers like you do kids' clothes and leave yourself some room to grow. Get a little more memory and processor speed than you need so that you can accommodate software upgrades and other growing pains.

- **Question 2:** How much hard drive space do I need?

  This question stumps a lot of people. As computers become more powerful, software has become bigger, taking up a lot more space. Add to that the preponderance of digital media (photos, songs, videos) that are being downloaded and stored, and you've got a serious real estate issue. Generally speaking, *50GB (gigabytes) will be enough storage space for your average office worker.* Staff that are creating and editing graphics, videos, and photos will require two to three times that amount of space.

- **Question 3:** Do I need a laptop?

  Laptops are more expensive, and usually suffer from increased maintenance issues. (How many laptops have you seen dropped at airports?) So, be sure that staff will travel or work in the field enough to require a laptop. If travel is moderate or infrequent, it may make more sense to purchase one or two laptops for staff to share.

- **Question 4:** How many computers should I buy?

  That may seem like a silly question, but it bears asking. It's easier to support and maintain five of the same machine than it is to support and maintain five different machines. Budget permitting, purchase several of the same machine at once, with the same operating system, to save headaches later on.

Other Hardware

In addition to computers for your staff, you'll need to consider a few other pieces of hardware for your office. These pieces of equipment are merely supporting players in your technology infrastructure. They are, however, also the things that tend to cause the most frustration when they don't work correctly. *It's worth an investment of time to get it right.*

Following are some kinds of equipment to consider for your organization:

- Printers: There are a few key considerations in selecting the office printer. The first is volume. You need to know approximately how many pages you need to produce every year. For example, *laser printers are much better at producing larger volumes of print jobs throughout the year than an inkjet printer.* If you only occasionally need to run a large print job, it may make more sense for you to purchase an inkjet printer and outsource large jobs. The second consideration is your network. Unless you're purchasing a printer to be used by only one staff member, *you'll need a printer that can be shared by any computer that's connected to your network.* Additionally, consider if your printer will be connecting to a wired or a wireless network.

- Fax machine: It's true, people still send faxes. Again, volume will dictate the kind of machine you should purchase. *A dedicated, stand-alone fax machine best serves heavy volume usage.* If you're not planning on sending faxes very often, however, you may find that an all-in-one printer, copier, scanner, and fax machine works just fine. Alternately, you can sign up for an e-fax service that will convert your Word, PDF, and other documents into faxes via email, allowing you to skip the machine altogether (and save some trees!).

Safety

Safety first! If you had one of those factory posters touting "It's been 39 days since our last accident" for the technology in your office, what would it read? Here are some of the things you'll need to think about to keep that number ticking up:

- Firewall. A firewall is simply a gate between the outside world and your network of computers. It's essential that you have a firewall set up to keep spammers, hackers, and other malicious people from infiltrating your network to use it for nefarious purposes. A firewall can be either software or hardware. You should work with a consultant to find the right option for you, set it up, and test it regularly.

- Antivirus protection. Antivirus software should be installed on each of the PC computers on your network (Macs have not yet been the target of viruses and other malware). Worms and viruses continue to be written every day, so it's essential that you purchase the regular update package for antivirus software to make sure that you're protected against the most recent dangers. In 2003, it's estimated that the "Slammer Worm" cost $1.2 billion in lost productivity worldwide.[4] Can you really afford to pull your staff away from your mission to deal with something that could have easily been avoided?

- Backup. Most people view backing up as insurance for extreme situations like natural disasters, but the backup is most important in many day-to-day situations. A 2008 survey of London cab companies found that more than 60,000 electronic devices, including laptops, were left in cabs during a six-month period.[5] What would you do if you left your laptop in the back of a cab? You can back up your data and files via hardware in your own office using CDs, DVDs, tapes, and so on. Another option is to choose an online backup service that will store your files in a space online for you. Whichever option you choose, it's essential that you set each computer in your network to back up automatically and that you test regularly to ensure that files are easily accessible.

- Passwords. You can have the greatest security technology employed at your organization and still put your information in grave danger. The best technology in the world can't protect us from ourselves. Most individuals use the same password for the many applications they need to access throughout the day, including key systems like accounting software or databases. This makes it incredibly easy for a hacker, a disgruntled employee, or other malicious people to access not just one, but every application that individual uses. The simplest thing you can do to protect your organization's data and files is to put in place a strong password policy. Ensure that staff are both using different passwords for logins and changing their passwords frequently.

- <u>Physical security</u>. Again, it's the human foibles that will most often fail us when it comes to security. Having strong passwords is no defense against someone coming into your office, picking up a laptop, and walking out. There are many simple things you can do to ensure the physical security of the technology in your organization. Equipment like laptops, printers, and desktop computers should be secured to desks with cable locks so they can't be removed. Servers and other pieces of equipment with very sensitive data should be kept in locked areas, accessible only to those who need them.

Software

Selecting software is one of the most challenging tasks for any nonprofit, requiring a balancing act between budget, features, training, and staff requests. You will find an ocean of feedback, features, and opinions on every type of software you evaluate. *The key to selecting the right software for your organization is understanding and documenting your needs.* That said, for most software decisions, you won't need to go through a lengthy process—it doesn't make sense to spend 50 hours evaluating software in order to save a few hundred dollars. In most cases you can use a simple process outlined by our colleagues at <u>idealware.org</u>[6]:

1. Identify your top needs.

   Think through the need you're trying to address by acquiring new software. For example, if you are looking for graphics software, will you be making graphics primarily for the Web or for print? Will you perform basic graphics manipulations or high-end original illustrations? Be sure to include feedback from all the individuals who will be using the software. Prioritize the features you consider to be "must-haves."

2. Can your existing software already do it?

   Before you head out into the software selection process, be sure to evaluate your existing software to see if it can get the job done. Let staff, colleagues, and friends know what you're trying to accomplish and what tools you already have available. Many times, you'll find the job can be done with your current software, saving you the time, money, and hassle of finding and learning new applications.

3. Find out what your peers are using.

Referrals can often be the best way to find the right piece of software for your organization. Make friends with staff at organizations like yours with similar needs. Check out the communities at idealware.org, nten.org, and techsoup.org. Be sure to get several perspectives. It's worth the extra time to make sure that one person's experience isn't outside the norm.

4. Identify some scenarios and test.

Most software packages and vendors allow you access to a demo or trial version. Select the tool or two that seem most promising to you and try them out. To make this most efficient, come up with a few scenarios for how you would actually use the software. Then, run through those scenarios with several different staff members to see if the software meets your needs. If you can't get access to a trial version, at least be sure to have a sales representative run through those demos for you. Asking if a database can store multiple addresses and seeing how it's actually done are two different things entirely.

5. Decide whether this software will meet your needs.

This is the scary part. Remember that *no piece of software will meet every one of your needs.* Instead, you should look for software that will best meet your most critical needs.

You will find that at times you need to select software for the mission-critical tasks of your organization. Software to meet these needs—databases, content management systems to manage your websites (see Chapter Seventeen), and so on—require a more formal and lengthy investigative process. Because these tools can transform how you do your work, it's worth the time and effort to get it right. To select these types of software tools, you'll follow much the same process. Identify your needs, find some common options, review with your peers, and test, test, test.

When assessing mission-critical software, you will need to be much more rigorous about documenting your needs and common business processes. It's worth your time to document exactly *how* you do your work so that you can find a tool that best matches your existing processes. Understanding how to document these "business processes" will be critical to your software selection success.

Figure 14.1: Sample Online Gift Processing Map

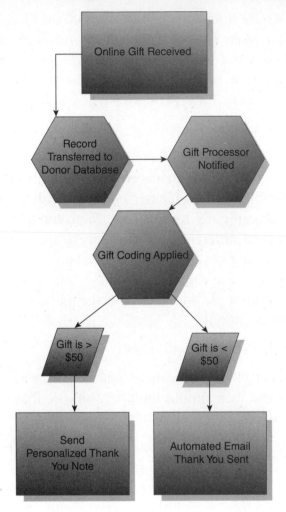

In <u>Managing Technology to Meet Your Mission: A Strategic Guide for Nonprofit Leaders</u>, Peter Campbell provides us with an excellent example of a business process map (see Figure 14.1) for a situation common to many nonprofits—receiving an online gift.

Mapping business processes turned out to be the key to Western Arts Alliance's success in selecting a new database. Though time-consuming, specifying each of WAA's key processes and sharing those with potential vendors meant that they could more easily compare their proposals. "It allowed us to compare apples to apples in a process that would have been very confusing otherwise," Tim Wilson shared. "Additionally, we actually identified a few things that weren't working well for us or our community, and were able to map the process we wanted to see in the new system so that we wouldn't be repeating our mistakes."

Plan for Today, Tomorrow, and Five Years from Now

Creating a technology plan can sometimes feel like looking into crystal ball. Even if you have a clear understanding of where your organization is going to be in three years, it's unclear where the technology will be after that same amount of time. Nonetheless, we have to plan for technology or we'll always be stuck in crisis mode, putting out techno-fires.

Don't Plan in a Silo

Although a technology plan is just that—a plan—that doesn't mean you can create the plan in a silo. A good plan not only addresses the key infrastructure needs of the organization, such as printer replacement and software upgrades, it also accounts for the strategy and mission of the organization. For example, if you plan to open a new telephone hotline, your technology plan should include an assessment of your current telephone systems. You may also need to look at call center software or a database for documenting call interactions. The key is to *tie each plan item to the organizational strategy*. If it doesn't relate, it's probably not essential.

You must also *include more than your technology team in your plan*. The staff that will use the systems and software should have a say in what is implemented. This will help you tremendously when it comes to user adoption—staff are much more supportive when they help create the plan.

In his role as executive director, Tim makes most of the technology decisions at WAA. Still, when it came time to select the new database, he made sure all staff were involved. Everyone was interviewed to get a sense of what he wanted and needed in a new database, and what he hated about the old one. All staff members attended the product demos of the four finalists, and each had the chance to give his input on what he liked and didn't for each of the systems presented. Now Tim has a staff that is excited about the new database and is invested in making it work.

Long-Term Thinking

Planning effectively requires that you think about technology in both the short and long term. Your long-term plan will look at the next three to five years and address the large system acquisitions and upgrades you will need to make, such as new databases or website redesigns. These projects require a lot of resources, including time and money. Planning for the long term allows you to assign the resources and spread out the costs over several years, instead of trying to make it all happen at once.

Remember that *your long-term plan is about where you're headed, not the details of how you're going to get there.* You won't always be able to identify the exact software or hardware you will purchase in three years, but you can plan for a general hardware refresh every three years, or a database upgrade two years from now. You can fill in the details as you get closer.

At WAA, an estimate for the anticipated costs of the database and the database selection process was included in the budget before the project launched. To make the up-front costs more bearable, the process was spread across two fiscal years. Planning ahead can facilitate creative thinking when funding your technology initiatives.

Effective planning helps you identify where you want to be in the future, while offering the flexibility to change how exactly you get there.

Short-Term Action: Annual Technology Plans

Each year, refer to your strategic plan and technology plan to create an annual technology plan. Your short-term plan should include four key areas:

- Strategy

- Objectives

- Measures

- Targets

Strategy relates to the goals or mission of the organization. Objectives are the tactics you will use to support the strategy. Measures identify how you will know you are meeting your objectives. Finally, the targets assign quantitative outcomes to the measures. Peter Campbell shares an example (see Table 14.1) from <u>Managing Technology to Meet Your Mission: A Strategic Guide for Nonprofit Leaders</u>. Your short-term technology plan might include pieces that look something like this:

Table 14.1: Sample Annual Technology Plan Excerpt

Strategy	Objectives	Measures	Targets
Increase constituent awareness of our accomplishments by distributing a monthly email newsletter	Increase mission awareness Increase donations Improve communication	ECRM statistics Donations increase	5% increase in new prospects 7% increase in donations

Your annual technology plan is a little like the classic board game Risk. In Risk, players vie for total world domination by deploying their resources (armies) strategically on the board, hoping that they win battles (via dice rolls). If you're doing it right, *strategy will overcome luck in every game.* Your plan helps deploy resources throughout the organization to meet your technology goals, in service of the mission. A thoughtful plan and good strategy will help you win, no matter what luck the proverbial roll of the dice may bring your way.

Evaluate Continuously

Evaluation has long been seen as that thing that you do when a project is over. In our sector, we tend to plan a project for a year and a half, implement it for nine months, evaluate it for a month, and then walk away. Though it may seem like overkill, *evaluation works best when it happens before, during, and after project implementation.* Making this investment in time will help you choose projects with a higher likelihood of success, steer projects towards better outcomes, and learn valuable lessons for the future.

WAA will be tracking two different kinds of outcomes for their new database—increased staff efficiency and community connections. The first is relatively easy to track. Are staff spending less time trying to get their database to work? In the second area, WAA will track metrics like more member profiles in the system and other related metrics.

Return on Investment (ROI) Before and After

Return on investment, or ROI, is a process used to assess the costs and benefits of any particular investment, including technology. At its most basic level, ROI is a simple mathematical equation:

$$ROI = Benefits - Costs$$

We usually want our ROI to be a positive number, indicating that the benefits have outweighed the costs. Typically we associate ROI with a financial calculation, but benefits and costs can be nonfinancial, too. In fact, a good ROI process will go far beyond the simple question "How much does it cost?" and look towards many other benefits and costs. Factors such as productivity, morale, and client satisfaction can all be benefits when thinking about ROI. Programming time, strain on employees, and training are all examples of costs.

ROI analysis is a helpful decision-making tool before you take on a project. For small decisions you can use a "back of the envelope" approach. For larger decisions, you should go through a more rigorous process to outline your thinking and provide a narrative for the decision makers in your organization. You'll also want to use the ROI process at the conclusion of a project so that you can learn if your assumptions were right or wrong and apply lessons learned to the next go around.

Dashboards

Jeanne Bell addresses the importance of organizational Dashboards in Chapter Five, but I wanted to share one quick note on their relevance to tracking success as it relates to your technology plan. Just as a dashboard does for the driver of a car, you'll want to constantly evaluate your progress in an ongoing way to make sure you're actually getting towards your goals. Let's take a target from the previous example: a 7% increase in donations. You could run a newsletter for a year, then stop and check in on the rate of donations. But if you track the number of donations on a weekly or even a monthly basis, you can tweak your tactics along the way to help you arrive at your ideal outcome.

Dos and Don'ts

Nonprofit Technology Dos and Don'ts

- DO let your mission and strategy be your guides when making technology decisions.

- DO establish strong systems. Your staff can't get much mission-critical work done if they have to reboot the computers every hour.

- DO plan! You don't have to get out your crystal ball to plan effectively for your technology needs.

- DO evaluate continuously. You can't learn from your experiences if you never stop to reflect.

- DON'T make technology decisions based solely on cost. *Cost is only one factor in determining the value and expense of technology.*

- DON'T forget to include staff in your technology decisions. You'll need allies as you implement new systems.

- DON'T select mission-critical software like a donor database without first documenting your key business processes.

Conclusion

There. That wasn't so painful, was it? We hardly uttered a word about RAM, CPUs, server arrays, or anything else that might make you break out in hives. It's true: everything you need to know about managing technology has very little to do with technology itself. Instead you just need to keep four principles in mind:

- Mission first

- Keep your foundation strong

- Tie your technology planning to organizational strategy

- Evaluate continuously

Use these principles in your work and you will soon find that you are making technology decisions with confidence and ease. We're pretty sure you'll find something to do with all that extra time.

Holly has spent more than seven years at NTEN, working with community members to identify the technology trends that will reshape the nonprofit sector. From ubiquitous access to technology leadership to social media, Holly brings the wisdom of the NTEN crowd to the nonprofit sector. Holly has been recognized as one of the Nonprofit Times Power and Influence Top 50 twice, in 2009 and 2010. Holly is also editor of <u>Managing Technology to Meet Your Mission: A Strategic Guide for Nonprofit Leaders</u>.

Nonprofit Tech Resource Review

Nten.org (www.nten.org)

A community transforming technology into social change. NTEN is a membership organization for anyone using technology to create the change they want to see in their communities.

Idealware.org (www.idealware.org)

This 501(c)(3) nonprofit provides thoroughly researched, impartial, and accessible resources to help nonprofits make smart software decisions.

Techsoup Global (www.techsoup.org)

Offers nonprofits a one-stop resource for technology needs by providing free information, resources, and support. In addition to online information and resources, they offer access to seriously discounted software through TechSoup Stock.

AspirationTech.org (www.aspirationtech.org/)

Helps nonprofits and foundations use software tools more effectively and sustainably. They serve as ally, coach, strategist, mentor, and facilitator to those trying to make more impactful use of technology in social change.

TechRepublic.com (www.techrepublic.com/)

A technology site devoted to small business that covers tech and management issues. Many of the discussions and articles are very applicable to the nonprofit sector.

Holly Ross, Katrin Verclas, and Allison Levine (Eds.). Managing Technology to Meet your Mission: A Strategic Guide for Nonprofit Leaders. San Francisco: Jossey-Bass, 2009.

This practical resource helps nonprofit professionals make smart, strategic decisions about technology. The book shows how to effectively manage technology and offers practical advice for decision makers and staff with little or no tech experience.

Nonprofit Technology Conference (www.nten.org/ntc)

The annual gathering for people using technology to change the world. More than 1,500 people gather each year to share and learn about how technology is used in nonprofits, from social media to fundraising.

Ted Hart, James M. Greenfield, Steve MacLaughlin, and Philip H. Geier, Jr. Internet Management for Nonprofits: Strategies, Tools, and Trade Secrets. San Francisco: Jossey-Bass, 2010.

Reveals how current technologies can be utilized most effectively by nonprofits and addresses how to manage various applications for internal operations and community service.

Ouellette and Associates Consulting, Inc. Leading IT Transformation: The Roadmap to Success. Dubuque: Kendall Hunt, 2008.

Guides IT leaders in transforming their workforce and culture to meet the challenges of today's increasingly complex, ever changing business environment.

Joni Podolsky. <u>Wired for Good: Strategic Technology Planning for Nonprofits</u>. San Francisco: Jossey-Bass, 2003.

A nuts-and-bolts guide to strategic technology planning for nonprofit organizations of all sizes.

o o o

All these resources, plus nonprofit management tips of the week and more, can be found at Nonprofits101.org.

CHAPTER 15

A Cooperative Approach to Web Design

By Elliot Harmon, Staff Writer, TechSoup Global

Introduction

You've probably heard that creating a website doesn't have to be hard. Actually, it can be *very* hard, but with a few tips and techniques the process can be fairly straightforward and, in fact, enlightening. You can build a nice-looking, professional website for your nonprofit without breaking the bank or being an expert, but only if you take the time to consider a few key questions.

What's your nonprofit's story? In less than fifty words, what's your message? What are you asking your website's visitors to *do*? For some organizations, building a website may present the first time you answer these questions, and it may require intense discussions about your audience and goals. If your site lacks a clear call to action, then it doesn't matter how pretty it is: it brands your organization as confused and disarrayed; on the other hand, if your website's message is clear, direct, and actionable, then even the most technically crude site can engage with visitors in a meaningful way.

If you're thinking of creating a new website for your nonprofit, you're probably asking who can help you design it and what it will cost. Those are great questions to ask, but the answers will vary depending on the website's purpose. Let's start, then, not with the *how* of building a website, but with the *why*.

Critical Skills and Competencies

Before hiring a designer, spend a month or two assembling key stakeholders from inside and outside your organization, discussing the needs of the website with them, putting together a loose outline of the website, and establishing measurable goals. This will inform your request for proposal (RFP) and guide your initial discussions with a designer. Depending on the complexity of the site, actual site development might range from a few weeks to several months. Upon completion, it's key to *budget time for training your staff in using and updating the site.* Finally, you'll need to schedule updates on at least a quarterly basis. In this chapter, we'll go over each of these steps in more detail.

What's Your Website's Purpose?

In the 1990s and early 2000s, a friend of mine who was working as a web design consultant used to joke that her job was the world's easiest con. All you have to do, she told me, is type up the organization's contact info and pick a background color to match the letterhead. Those days are long gone. Today, your nonprofit's website must increasingly be more than a token presence; the most successful nonprofits are those whose websites are closely aligned with their goals, missions, programs, and metrics.

Why are you designing or redesigning your nonprofit's site? Who is the intended audience? Potential donors? Current donors? Volunteers or evangelists for your organization's cause? People who could benefit from your services? It's tempting to answer, "Everyone," but is that accurate? As most nonprofit websites barely appeal to *anyone*, one that appeals to everyone is a tall order. Even if the answer *is* everyone, the way that different segments of everyone interact with your website will vary a lot, and *identifying the most important audiences of your website must drive your efforts.* The more specific your understanding of how users will interact with your site, the better.

In talking about how nonprofits' websites can shape their relationships with their constituents, I often find myself referring to two corporate websites: Apple and Mighty Putty (see Figure 15.1).

Both sites were designed with the same purpose—to sell a product—and they're both very successful. The difference is not in the desired action, *but in the time investment put toward that action.* One site tries to sell you a product the moment you visit; the other presents you with dozens of ways to get involved, learn more, and develop brand loyalty—all eventually pointing to a sale. The funny thing is that at least in the nonprofit world, it's a lot harder to be a Mighty Putty than an Apple.

Some nonprofits try to be Mighty Putties, but most of them fail at it. Political strategy architect Anne Keenan describes her experience with a political advocacy site. Presented with a large donate button moments after signing up for a mailing list, "All of a sudden we'd skipped from flirting to something a little more intimate, and I felt icky and strangely violated."[1]

George Weiner of DoSomething.org encourages nonprofits to think of their websites as relationship-building vehicles, not fundraising ones: "Most non-Vegas marriages don't happen on the first date, it starts with a reasonable ask and comes after a relationship has been developed. Having a donate button is fine, but *donating as your primary or only call-to-action is not a reasonable ask to the vast majority of your traffic.*" Weiner goes on to suggest ways to court your website's visitors before popping the question: *put an inspiring story on your homepage, ask for newsletter signups, and recruit people to volunteer or spread your message.*[2]

Can your website spread awareness of your cause directly? If your nonprofit educates people, can your website help you educate more people? If you advocate for changes in the community, can your website strengthen that advocacy? Can your website empower people to evangelize for your cause more effectively? Of course, none of this is to say that your website shouldn't

Figure 15.1: Website Examples—Mighty Putty and Apple

Both www.buymightyputtynow.com and www.apple.com were designed with the primary goal of selling a product. The difference between the radically different designs is the time investment they expect of the customer.

accept online donations. It's only to say that for most nonprofits, donations shouldn't be the primary venue for visitors to interact with your site. *Your website should have a donate button, but your website shouldn't be a donate button.*

Setting and Measuring Goals

Don't set vague goals for your website. *You must be able to clearly articulate the site's objectives in order to put good metrics in place for evaluating its success.* If the goal is to increase awareness of your nonprofit, ask yourself among whom you want to raise awareness. Ask what that audience will do when its awareness of your nonprofit has risen, and what metrics you can use to measure those actions. Ask what time frame you'd like to see this change happen in. Ask whether the website will have a different goal in two years from what it has now.

Web designers usually start with the desired outcome of a visit and work backward from there (in web analytics terminology, these desired actions are referred to as "conversions"). Donations may be one of the conversions that you measure, but they shouldn't be the only one. You should also *measure newsletter signups, visitors signing up for a service that you provide, and people finding important information on your site.*

Many designers work under the premise that *users should never be more than one click away from the desired outcome*; in other words, no matter what page a visitor is looking at, there should be a prominent link that the user can click in order to perform the desired response. That's because user tests show that each time users are asked to click to another page, a portion of them will leave the site out of boredom or confusion.

The goals for your website should be tied to the goals for the rest of your organization. A good web designer can show you how to measure the percentage of people who click on a link in your email newsletter, for example, or the number of people who seek out more information on your site because of a direct-mail campaign.

Identifying the Stakeholders

Later in the chapter, we'll review tips for working with a designer—be it someone on your staff, a volunteer, or a consultant. Regardless of whether your designer is on staff or not, you'll need someone to act as project manager. If that's you, you'll need a beginner's understanding of web design and development (there are some resources at the end of this chapter to help you get up to speed). If you're delegating someone to be the point person, it should be someone who has some knowledge of the field, as well as the ability to collate the needs of various stakeholders, internal and external.

Well before bringing a designer into the mix, identify the key stakeholders for the project and establish regular communications with them. Which members of your staff should be consulted? That depends a lot on the goals for your site, which we'll discuss in a minute, but it's good to cast a wide net, particularly in the planning stages.

Outside of your primary team, there's a broader group of core users. Remember that your employees aren't the only stakeholders; that's why the core user group should also include key volunteers, evangelists, and allies in the sector. These people feel strongly about your organization and its image: you'll likely be surprised by their perspective when they talk about your organization and what they need from your website.

How do you maintain communication with this group? Answer: With whatever tools the group is comfortable using. There are numerous online collaboration tools on the market—many of them free to nonprofits—but it doesn't matter how cool your tool is if no one uses it. If some of the stakeholders won't use Basecamp no matter how many times you explain it to them, use email.

Throughout the web design process, conduct meetings once or twice a month to keep your primary team informed, make sure that outstanding issues are being addressed, and discuss any questions that are arising. The larger core users group won't need that many face-to-face meetings, but if possible, there should be one early in the process for generating user stories (see the next section) and another to familiarize them with the site before it goes public.

Different types of stakeholders might have wildly different ideas about the website's purposes and audiences, but with some creative brainstorming, you should be able to identify the recurring themes and the most important user stories.

Conceptualizing Your Website

The bridge between the goals you've established for your site and the site design itself comes in the form of *user stories*, sketches of how and why users will interact with the website and the appropriate results of those interactions.

If your organization already has a website, many of your user stories may come from how users currently interact with your site and whether they're getting the information they need. Questions that your organization frequently gets are another source, as well as discussions you have with your stakeholders.

User stories don't need to be complicated; they're just short, specific examples of how people should get the information or services they need from your site. Here are some examples:

> Adam learns about our nonprofit by word-of-mouth and finds our site through a Google search. He reads the story of our nonprofit, watches a testimonial video, and signs up for our mailing list.
>
> Bonnie visits our site to respond to a fundraising letter. She chooses from three donation levels and donates with a credit card.
>
> Carl notices an interruption in services provided by the organization. He visits the site and immediately finds an updated service schedule and contact information.

With your goals and user stories in hand, you can start to draft the *information architecture*, a simple outline of what content will appear on the website and how it will be arranged. Here's a minimal example, though your own may not be much more complicated than this:

Homepage

About Us

   Our Story

   Mission

   Programs

   Board

Events and Services

   Calendar

News

   Board Meeting Minutes

   Blog

Contact Us

Donate

Assemble your core team and engage them in the process of answering these key questions:

- Does the information architecture reflect the most important user stories?

- Will new content or sections need to be added in the future?

- Who will create the content for each section?

Referring back to your user stories and information architecture, *put together a wireframe, a visual representation of the elements of your website.* The wireframe can be a Microsoft Word document, an Illustrator graphic, or even a pencil drawing. The wireframe isn't really a literal instruction for the designer; it's more of a visual aid to use in your discussions with both designers and stakeholders (see Figure 15.2). It's a way to think about key user stories and how site design will guide users to appropriate actions.

Figure 15.2: Sample Website Wireframe

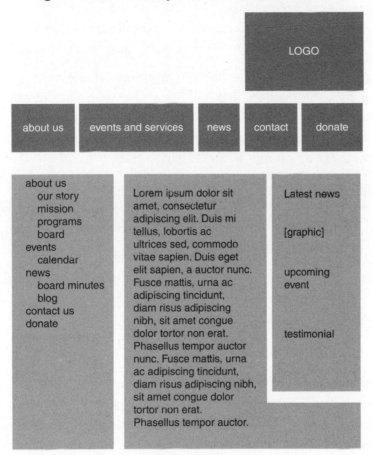

The wireframe presents the same components as the information architecture, but arranged visually. The wireframe will become the skeleton of your nonprofit's website.

Web Content Management Systems

Web Jargon

Here are some terms you'll probably come across. At the end of the chapter, we'll point to some resources with more information.

HTML: The language in which most websites are written. Compared to other programming languages, HTML is relatively easy for non-geeks to learn and understand.

Web Browser: The program you use to access the Internet, such as Mozilla Firefox, Microsoft Internet Explorer, or Apple Safari. Web browsers interpret HTML code and turn it into colors, fonts, links, and layouts.

Cascading Style Sheets: CSS is like a web design shortcut. Instead of including style information on every page of a website, designers create "style sheets" that impose a consistent design on every page in a website. Good CSS can make your website more attractive, easier to update, and more accessible to people with disabilities.

Web Server: The web server is the computer where your website is stored. Most organizations opt to rent space on a web server from a web hosting provider. At the end of this chapter, we'll offer some resources to help you find a provider.

Web Content Management System: A CMS is a program installed on a web server that manages your site. Many CMSes are designed to let nontechnical staff make updates to the website.

A web content management system (Web CMS, or just CMS) is a piece of software installed on a web server that delivers many types of information in a consistent design. CMSes are designed to integrate disparate features like blogs, forums, and wikis into a seamless user experience and enable easy site updates.

Most CMSes have browser interfaces, which means there's no need to install web editing software on every computer you'll use to update the site; you can add or edit content directly from any web browser. Most modern CMSes include a WYSIWYG (what you see is what you get) editor, meaning that you can format text and add links without getting your hands dirty in HTML code. When you enter content into your CMS interface, the CMS translates that content into code to be interpreted by the end user's web browser. As such, *CMSes enable you to keep your site up to date without employing a professional designer on an ongoing basis.* A CMS uses instructions received via an online editing interface to automatically create HTML and CSS code, which is then interpreted by a visitor's web browser as viewable content (see Figure 15.3).

Figure 15.3: Visual Representation of How a CMS Works

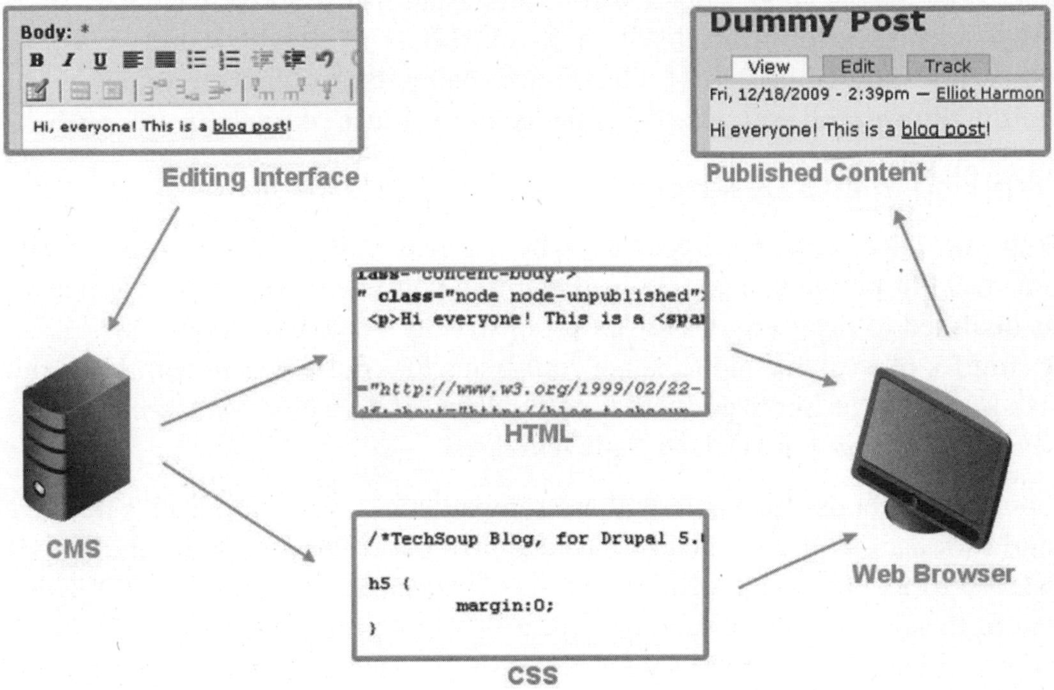

Most experts would recommend that you use a CMS for all but the very simplest of websites. There are numerous "open source" and proprietary CMSes on the market. Open source CMSes are usually free, and maintained by a community of users rather than a single software company. Proprietary CMSes usually cost money, but that price may include support or other perks.

Open source CMSes are more flexible than their proprietary counterparts and less reliant on the livelihood of software companies and service providers. Also, it's generally easier to migrate content from one open source CMS to another than between proprietary systems. There are a few open source CMSes to choose from that are thoroughly used and well-supported in the nonprofit community. Idealware.org has put together an authoritative guide to the big four open source CMSes: Drupal, Joomla, Plone, and WordPress. You can find the URL for downloading the guide at the end of this chapter.

Of course, no one solution is right for every organization. Putting my personal preference aside, I'd encourage you to understand what you're paying for when you use a commercial system. If you choose to go with a proprietary CMS, it should be because it offers functionality that you need or vital compatibility with your existing systems, not because of a sales pitch.

Working with a Designer

You may have access to a volunteer who can help you build your new website for free, but before you go too far down that path, make sure that that person is qualified to design a serious nonprofit website. Have him show you examples of work he's done, share your plans for your new site with him, and ask him what technologies he'd use. *If you're working with a volunteer, that doesn't mean that you shouldn't check references.*

Some consultants—particularly those sympathetic to your nonprofit's mission and message—will offer a clean, professional, basic website for around $1,500 to $2,500; many will quote prices between $2,000 and $10,000. This is not to say that you shouldn't pay outside of that range, but if you do, be sure you know what you're paying for. If you're paying for custom coding or integration with existing systems, you can expect a higher price; otherwise, you may be paying more for a designer's reputation and ego than for the service provided.

Your first and most effective source for finding potential designers to work with is referrals from nonprofit colleagues. Ask your contacts who designed their website, especially if it's in line with what you're looking for. Ask for referrals on NTEN's online community. Be sure to *solicit proposals from at least two or three vendors before you make a commitment.*

There's a wealth of great information on the Internet about putting together a request for proposal (RFP) for a web design project; I've compiled some good places to start at the end of this chapter.

Regardless of who you're working with, be sure that training is included in your plans (*if a consultant's proposal doesn't include training, that's a bad sign*). The designer should educate you and your staff on updating content and customizing the site's design; in fact, *the people who'll be updating content regularly should add the initial content to the site.* It's good practice, plus it'll save you on consulting fees.

Collaboration or Paint-by-Number?

Some nonprofits think of web design as a paint-by-number process, in which the ED or another decision maker creates a list of needs for the website, hands the list to a designer, and approves the final site eight weeks later. The problem with that mentality is that *if you don't play an active role in site development, there's no way to be sure the finished website will work the way you imagined it;* conversely, even if what you're imagining *is* possible, an experienced designer may be able to help you find a more elegant alternative that achieves the same goal.

That's why I suggest what I call a cooperative approach. Work with a designer with whom you're comfortable collaborating and sharing ideas back and forth. *Think of conceptualizing the site and designing it not as two distinct steps in a web design project, but as intertwined processes that can learn from and inform each other.* You may be working with a communications department, a consultant, or a volunteer; perhaps you'll design the site yourself. Whatever the case, a cooperative approach will ensure that the website's design and content work together toward serving your greater goals. Through iterative improvements and regular check-ins, you can work with the designer to build a site that reflects the best of *all* of your skills.

Bring your user stories, information architecture, and wireframes to your first meeting with the designer. Talk about your goals for the site and what you've identified as the key user actions. Remember that nothing is set in stone; be open to the designer's ideas. Combining your knowledge of your audience and mission with her design experience, you should be able to work together on a great website.

Case Study: When Impressive Doesn't Work

My friend Molly is the manager of marketing and communications for the East Bay Music Collective[3] (EBMC), a small nonprofit opera company in the San Francisco Bay Area. EBMC has been struggling with its website for years, and it's all because seven years ago, the organization was wowed by a nice-looking design.

In early 2003, EBMC's executive director was looking to build a website to advertise the company's 2003–04 season, and she wanted to help brand EBMC as a slick, sexy company with a site as shiny and impressive

case study

as those of major movie studios or clothing companies. Using the site craiglist.org, she managed to find a young designer in art school willing to build the site for free.

And sure enough, the website was gorgeous. The volunteer had built the entire site in Adobe Flash, complete with rolling menu items and animations. The site offered music samples from each opera in the season and videos of rehearsals. It was easy to buy tickets, easy to make a donation, and easy to invite your friends.

I sensed all was not well when it came time to advertise for auditions for the 2004–05 season. Rather than incorporate the announcement into the fancy site, someone at EBMC had just moved all of the old content down a few lines to make room for a plain-text announcement. "We don't even own Flash," Molly told me. "We have had no idea how to add something to our page."

Emails were exchanged with the old volunteer, but he never quite followed through with making any updates. He was out of school and trying to make it as a professional Flash developer; EBMC was low on his list of priorities. Over the next four years, I watched with bemusement as the Flash site—still stuck in 2003—moved further and further down the page to make way for more and more announcements.

Finally, the executive director accepted that there was no way to revive the old site. She put Molly in charge of the redesign project, and Molly found a Drupal developer in the Bay Area who, being an opera fan, was willing to create a simple site for about a thousand dollars; more importantly, he trained Molly and a few other staff members on how to update the site.

The new site's not only more functional than the old one, it's actually more attractive, too. As staff begin to post new updates and blog entries, the number of visits and conversions is slowly going up. Visitors recognize the new EBMC site as reflective of an actual small organization they can engage with, not the entertainment empire its old site pretended to represent.

Web Design Dos and Don'ts

- DON'T hire a colleague's kid to design your site because he helped you download "Battlestar Galactica."

- DO check references (even for volunteers), especially previous non-profit clients.

- DON'T clutter your homepage with too many links and choices.

- DO present a clear message with clear calls to action, not a watered-down compromise among several different messages.

- DON'T spend extra money on proprietary systems and custom code if it's not crucial to your site's needs.

- DO include training in your design contract, and make sure you've allocated appropriate staff time to maintain the site.

- DON'T create a website that conceals your organization's size, staff, or personality.

- DO publish a staff list, *real* contact information, board meeting minutes, and your IRS Form 990s.

- DON'T forget about your website once it's up—schedule regular updates.

- DO plan to revisit and update at least once a quarter. Measure your website's performance against its goals and make adjustments as necessary.

Dos and Don'ts

Conclusion

Your nonprofit's website is your first line of interaction with many people; as such, *its primary job is to be an inviting place that draws people in and connects them to your cause and organization.* The best way to ensure that's the case when designing a website is to define clear goals for your site, conceptualize a site based on how real users will interact with it, and measure your site's performance.

At every step of the way, there are temptations to stray from your goals—to make a site that's pretty but not functional, to make a site that your staff can't update, to buy custom code that you won't be able to maintain. Keep your focus on the user: your site is an opportunity to engage, not an opportunity to advertise.

As a staff writer at TechSoup Global, Elliot Harmon writes content to educate nonprofits and public libraries on effective use of technology. He has degrees from the University of South Dakota and the California College of the Arts.

Web Design Resources

Links to all of these resources are available at www.techsoup.org/go/webdesign

What Should a Website Cost? (www.techsoup.org/go/websitecost)

In this excellent webinar recording, Allen Gunn walks viewers through scoping and planning a website, writing an RFP, identifying key needs and stakeholders, working with consultants, and ongoing maintenance.

How to Write a Website RFP (www.bit.ly/websiterfp)

In this recorded session from the Nonprofit Technology Conference, Community IT Innovators staff members walk you through the process of writing an RFP, finding designers, and negotiating a contract.

Comparing Open Source Content Management Systems (www.idealware.org/comparing_os_cms/)

This free Idealware guide offers best practices for using a CMS; compares the key features of WordPress, Joomla, Drupal, and Plone; and lists consultants and firms working with each system (access requires an email signup).

OpenSourceCMS (www.php.opensourcecms.com/)

This site lets you play with pre-installed CMSes to see what they look like from an administrator's perspective.

Will You Marry Me? What Not-for-Profits Get Wrong on the Web
(www.huffingtonpost.com/george-weiner/will-you-marry-me-what-
no_b_383216.html)

> DoSomething.org Chief Technical Officer George Weiner explains what he
> thinks is wrong with most nonprofit websites.

Tips for Designing (or Redesigning) a Nonprofit Website (www.techsoup.org/
go/redesigning)

> This article outlines key questions to ask and key stakeholders to involve
> when designing a website.

A Nonprofit's Guide to Building Simple, Low-Cost Websites
(www.techsoup.org/go/lowcost)

> In this chapter, I've focused primarily on CMS-based sites; this article offers
> great tips and resources for developing non-CMS sites.

A Few Good Web Analytics Tools (www.techsoup.org/go/webanalytics)

> Learn what tools to use for measuring your website's performance and what
> to measure.

W3Schools (www.w3schools.com)

> An essential bookmark, this site offers dozens of HTML and CSS tutorials.

Tom Watson. CauseWired. New York: Wiley, 2008.

> One-third how-to manual and two-thirds pep talk, Tom Watson's book will
> get you excited about how nonprofits can use the Internet to connect and
> empower their audiences.

o o o

All these resources, plus nonprofit management tips of the week and more,
can be found at Nonprofits101.org.

CHAPTER 16

Online Community Building: How to Wire a Network to Support Your Nonprofit's Mission

By Jon Warnow, Cofounder, and Joe Solomon,
Social Media Coordinator, 350.org

Introduction

Regardless of how deep you choose to dive, online community building can be a great asset to almost every nonprofit—global or local, large or small. The hype about so-called "social networks" like Facebook and Twitter can sometimes be over the top, but an online community truly does offer the potential to network people in ways unimaginable just a decade ago.

257

Networks of people have always driven meaningful change forward—and now social networking offers new tools to empower your organization's supporters to create the change you want to see in the world.

Critical Skills and Competencies

Before we plunge into the nitty-gritty of community building, we suggest taking a step back to define your goals, identify where your community hangs out on the Web, and choose the right tools for the job.

Putting the Why Before the How: Creating Goals for an Online Community

Most of us don't get involved with online community building for the sole sake of building community—we have specific objectives, and we think our networks can help us accomplish them. Setting specific goals early on will ensure that you have a compass for your social media work.

Before setting these goals, it's good to ask yourself two questions. First, "What are the changes you want to see in the world?" Then, the second, most crucial question: "How can a networked community of supporters help create those changes?"

Asking yourself these questions early on can lead to inspiring, creative goals for your online community—and ensure that you ground your virtual engagement strategy in real world impact.

Meet Them Where They're At: Locating Your Community Online

The Web connects an unfathomably large and growing global community. Figuring out where your supporters and potential supporters plug in will be key in determining how you will engage with them. It may be that your community isn't that engaged on online networks—or maybe they just use email. You need to map this out before setting up shop with your online communities.

As of this writing, there's a tendency for most nonprofits to focus on www.facebook.com and www.twitter.com. While both Facebook and Twitter have reached a certain degree of mainstream standing (case in point: Oprah is active on both), that doesn't necessarily mean that's where your organization's online network is most active.

We suggest spending more time researching local and niche networks and seeing where potential supporters are most active—for a comprehensive list of social networks alongside their corresponding themes, visit: http://en.wikipedia.org/wiki/List_of_social_networking_websites. You should also look for niche networks by doing a web search for "social network" + [your cause].

More important, check in with your current supporters to see what websites they use. Sending a survey via email, phone-based polling, or hosting a local focus group with a diverse spectrum of constituents are all great ways to get your finger on their digital pulse.

Function Over Form: Choosing Tools to Fit Your Mission

Choosing the technology platforms for your community can be one of the more overwhelming steps as you get started in this process. New tools are being developed nearly every day and tech pundits are apt to tout a new network as the next incredible fad. Remember: your job isn't to be a technology innovator, it's a community builder—so don't sweat the technobuzz too much.

As you browse the latest technology platforms, it's important to consider three crucial questions:

- Is a good chunk of your community already active on the network?

- Does the network allow you to reach users via email? (Email is still the most effective way to reach people online.)

- Is the network customizable and flexible enough to allow your community to connect and express itself fully?

To be honest, it's unlikely you'll find a network that provides affirmative answers to all three questions listed above. Yet if you prioritize based on your goals and are willing to compromise (and repurpose), you'll probably find some good matches.

Table 16.1: Sample Social Network Analysis

Social Network	Member Already	Email Communication	Customizable	Cost
Facebook	X	~	~	Free
Twitter	X			Free
Google Group, Listserv		X		Free
Ning		X	X	$
Build Your Own Network		X	X	$$$

Table 16.1 shows an example of how you might study network options as you figure out the ones that best meet your goals.

○ ○ ○

Let's take a closer look at various popular social networking platforms, so you can get a sense of when each is most useful.

Facebook

Among social networks, Facebook (for now, anyway) is likely the one where a considerable amount of your wired network is already engaged—its audience is already larger than the entire population of North America, and growing by millions a month. You don't need to invite your supporters to "sign up" for a new network—a virtual hurdle that can turn people away. If you find that your community is active on Facebook, there are a few choices to set up a beacon there.

For Facebook, we usually suggest creating a "Page" for your nonprofit. A Page is similar to a personal profile. It allows members to become a "friend" of your nonprofit, allowing them to subscribe to your updates, and engage in dialogue with you and other supporters. However, Facebook Pages fall short in one crucial arena: you can't communicate with your Facebook community en masse via email. Your updates, however, generally appear on your supporters' "News Feed"—a regularly updated stream of news that many people check as often as email. To set up your Facebook Page, visit: www.facebook.com/pages/create.php (but keep reading this chapter to ensure it takes off!).

If reaching your supporters' inboxes is a top priority, or if privacy is important to you, create a Facebook "Group." With a Group, your updates will not show in your supporters' News Feeds, but as long your group stays below 5,000 members, you can send an update to most of your members' inboxes. See www.facebook.com/groups/create.php.

Finally, "Causes" is a tool built for Facebook that allows you to fundraise within the Facebook network. While it's difficult to build a community within Causes, it's worth exploring as a fundraising supplement to your Page or Group. Get a better feel for this tool at www.causes.com.

Twitter

Twitter.com is a social network that allows anyone to post very short updates (up to 140 characters each) and "follow" other people doing the same thing. Welcome to the short-attention-span society.

There's a lot of hype around this network, and with good reason: its growth has been meteoric, and it is spawning brand new ways to build a following, spread ideas, and engage supporters in real time. Though dramatically smaller in population than Facebook or MySpace, it still has more users than Mexico has citizens, so check to see if your current stakeholders and potential influencers are already active on this network.

A Quick Note on Global Social Networks

If you're looking to reach an international audience, here's some good news: as of this writing, Twitter reports that over 60% of their users are from outside the United States, while Facebook reports their global reach at around 70%.

But if your campaign is specifically focused on an area of the world outside the United States, there are a number of international networks with audiences you may not want to ignore (i.e., Orkut in India, Hi5 in Latin

America, QQ in China, and so on). The key to success is to focus your social network efforts on a select few platforms where you can most effectively engage your community—if you try to do them all, you'll spread yourself thin and won't be able to engage deeply within any of them.

Listservs (Google Groups, Yahoo! Groups, and Others)

Setting up a listserv is one of the simplest yet most effective tools in a wired community builder's toolbox, plus it's generally free. A listserv essentially makes it easier for a bunch of people to easily communicate with a like-minded group via email—for any kind of project. For many smaller communities, allowing people to connect with each other via email is all that's needed.

Build Your Own Social Network—Ning

Do your visions of community building grandeur transcend the features offered by the bigger social networks like Facebook and Twitter? If so, check out Ning. com. It's not perfect, but Ning basically lets you build, personalize, and invite supporters to your own social network. You determine the features (such as profiles, forums, blogs, photo sharing, and so forth) as well as the design.

It's worth noting that Ning networks require members to register and create a profile, which will naturally turn some people off, but that may be a good thing if you're looking to recruit more committed individuals.

As with any social network, in order for the community to thrive, you'll want folks to return on a regular basis—which requires a lot of nurturing and upkeep.

Building Your Own Network from Scratch

If you find that a platform like Ning doesn't meet your needs, there are other options out there, too (see BuddyPress.com, and WiserEarth.org). But, if after careful review, you can't find anything to meet your needs, then you can always hire a team to build a custom-made community infrastructure. This is the priciest, riskiest, and most labor-intensive option—and one we wouldn't recommend for most organizations. Before you take the plunge, do a thorough assessment of available tools, get feedback on your social networking ideas, and make sure you have the money and capacity to make your project fly.

How to Avoid a Digital Ghost Town: Building an Online Community

Too often, nonprofits will naively jump into the social networking space with a "build it and they will come" approach. We *wish* this were the case. Alas, it's quite the opposite—the Web is littered with digital ghost towns, online communities that have been essentially abandoned, usually due to lack of upkeep and investment. Whipping together a Facebook Group or spending a bunch of money on a fancy new website is the relative easy part. The real challenge is in recruiting, fostering, and ultimately empowering an engaged community. Outlined below are the seven most important things we've learned from our work with 350.org and from watching sister communities sprout and flourish.

1. Realize What's Required

A vibrant online hub of sharing, support, and action doesn't just emerge out of the ether—it takes a bit of legwork. Just starting an online community and seeing what happens is a recipe for disaster, so it's critical to properly allocate resources in advance.

The upfront and ongoing time and money your online community will require will vary wildly depending on your organization's size, goals, and areas of focus. Although some organizations devote several full-time staff to online community building and social media, most won't need that kind of investment—especially not in the beginning. For a small organization just ramping up, creating a social media game plan that demands about five hours a week is a good place to start.

2. Empower a Community Builder

Behind almost every amazing online community is an equally inspiring and dedicated community builder. Imagine your favorite party host—someone who has a passion for sparking conversations, connecting people, and ensuring that everyone feels special and welcome. That's who you're looking for in a community builder; only yours should also have a passion for navigating the digital world. Finding and empowering someone who fits this description may be the most influential step you take in fostering a successful online community.

3. Lift Up Your Wired Champions

Every thriving community has a small handful of committed community members who define the tone for a group and model behavior for the group as a whole. In general, the 80/20 rule applies to online communities—20% of the network will drive 80% of the content. People in this 20% are your wired champions—and *after your community builder, they're the secret to success.*

This 20% will stand out—they'll be commenting most frequently on posts, or tweeting most fervently. Reach out to these folks to express your gratitude and get to know them a bit better. As you determine the passions and interests of your wired champions, offer them special responsibilities and projects to help you grow your community. Examples of unique tasks might include welcoming new members or reaching out to other communities.

4. Prioritize Stories—Both Yours and Your Community's

People intuitively relate to stories. Sharing the story of your organization and the people it touches is the best way to build relationships and draw people in.

Stories are happening all around you, every moment of the day—capturing them and giving them wings through your social networks will give your supporters a glimpse of your behind-the-scenes work, and inspire people to get more involved and build the narrative with you.

To help draw these stories out, think in questions: "Whose life did your organization change today?" "What first drew you to your nonprofit's mission?" "What keeps you going?" Answer these and you'll have plenty of fodder for your own stories—and you'll inspire people in your online community to share their own too.

5. Be a Conversation Starter

To transform your online community into conversation hub, figure out a way to ask a question with your update, and start a dialogue. We get involved with campaigns through conversations, and you can spark some very unexpected and exciting comments just by putting out the call for them.

A classic way to turn a static update into dynamic dialogue is to end it with "What do you think?" Then in private ask a few of your champions to add their thoughts in order to seed the conversation.

6. Share Thanks in Spades

Gratitude is the chief currency of an online community, so express your thanks for member contributions generously and frequently. A powerful way to give thanks is to do it publicly—public recognition helps spread camaraderie and reinforces the kind of actions you're seeking. Consider regularly focusing a spotlight on your supporters in a newsletter, special interview, homepage profile highlight, and so on.

If you find yourself thanking a few certain supporters consistently, consider taking your thanks to the next level: empowerment. Offer your key members extra responsibilities or unique roles in projects as you grow your community.

7. Invite Everybody Outside: Face-to-Face Meet-Ups Are Where the Magic Happens

Online networks can express, deepen, and sustain real-world connections. So, as you build your wired community, think about ways to bring your supporters together to meet you and each other in the real world.

Going Viral: Best Approaches for Growing Your Community

The desire to go "viral" (i.e., wanting to reach 1,000,000 fans on Facebook within a week) is often strong among beginner community builders. It's an understandable impulse—more people equals more power, right? Not necessarily.

Reaching big benchmarks for popularity can be impressive, but when it comes to actually creating change a small group of 100 powerfully engaged supporters is vastly more effective than a million inactive fans. Rather than getting big quick, we hope you'll focus on growing a committed and engaged network, that spreads ever-outward at a confident clip. Here are some simple tips we've found helpful for growing your numbers strategically and organically:

1. Promote your social networks and online presence in real world communications. Headed to conferences with brochures, doing a presentation, or posting fliers around town? Add your web addresses and your social network profiles so people can stay in touch.

2. Feature links on your website. Your website is your virtual headquarters—so make sure to add a prominent button to your Facebook Page, Twitter Profile, YouTube channel, etc.

3. Already communicating via email? Add a P.S. to your email signature. Make invitations to join your networks a staple of your newsletters.

4. Just ask. Issue a request to your current network to invite their friends to join as a way to celebrate campaign moments, or get the word out during a crisis. Include specific goals: "Can you pass on this video of our victory celebration to five people?"

5. Take advantage of your address book. Most social networks allow you to access the address books of major email services like Gmail and Yahoo! and "friend" everyone in your black book. You can browse your contacts to see who is on the social network and invite them to connect with you, too.

6. Create compelling content that links back to you, which people can forward on. This is the Web's best-kept secret among professional web traffic builders. Put time and energy into creating powerful, well-worded updates and encourage your supporters to repost them. A simple way to boost an update's chance of going viral is to start or end it with two words: "Please Share."

7. Set up a laptop at your next rally, volunteer event, film screening, etc. As members mill about, urge them to jump on the computer and join your network on the spot. You can even take it a step further and ask them to fire off a few invites to their friends.

When It's Go Time: Mobilizing Your Community for Action

Every organization's journey will include some critical moments—times when an extra push can make all the difference for your cause. Whether it's more calls made to Congress, more volunteer hours pledged, more meetings organized, or more money donated, these are precisely the times when the potential of a passionate online network can be fully realized. Just as important, it's also when potential is highest to grow and strengthen your online community.

You'll be the best judge of when these moments come along for your organization—and how to best spread your message given the nature of your community. That said, here are a five basic guidelines that will help steer your community towards an effective mobilization:

1. Communicate the "crisitunity." Originally coined by Homer Simpson, a "crisitunity" is the moment when crisis meets opportunity—and it has a slightly better ring than "opporisis." Regardless of the word choice, the principle is straightforward: by communicating a time-sensitive problem your organization faces, along with how your online community can help solve the problem, people will be motivated to act.

2. Articulate your theory of change. Time is the most precious commodity of the modern age—and nobody wants to waste it on something they don't think will make a difference. That's why it's crucial that you communicate exactly how the action you're mobilizing around will effect tangible change. Don't underestimate the intelligence of your online community, and definitely don't ask people to do something if you can't explain precisely how their action will genuinely help to tip the balance.

3. Get specific. Vagueness can weaken your case, and make your appeals seem wishy-washy. Your case for mobilization will be more credible if you provide hard facts. Specify a particular milestone that will mark victory, a goal that you're aiming for to make a difference.

4. Use peer pressure. It might seem juvenile, but no one wants to go out on a limb by herself. Let your network know they won't be alone—in fact, make the case that that they'll be going it alone if they don't participate.

5. Make it human. People tend to initially engage in causes because they truly care on a deep level, not because they are told to. So do your best to tap into what makes us human—our emotional core—and weave a human story into your call to action.

Getting Real: Case Studies in Online Community Building

TuDiabetes.org

TuDiabetes is an explosive social network, with over 18,000 members and tons of rich conversation happening every hour. It helps those touched by diabetes exchange and share ideas, and support each other. There are many secrets to this community's success, but a few have proven to be especially high impact and replicable. The first thing you'll notice when you join TuDiabetes is a warm onslaught of welcome messages from veteran community members. It's as close as you can get to a series of hugs online—helping you feel at home within a new group of relative strangers. The greetings are delivered by the TuDiabetes "Care Team", a group of volunteers, who offer support to new members as they get settled in. TuDiabetes' founder and lead community builder, Manny Hernandez, started the group in 2007 using the social-network creator Ning.com. Manny, like many great community builders, is extremely invested in his community, is active in threads, is a storyteller and conversation starter, and is always generous with thanks and props for his wired champions. When you visit the TuDiabetes website, you also can't help but notice the emphasis on personal photos. TuDiabetes members have uploaded over 35,000 different photos of themselves and their family and friends, which are showcased all over the site, and reflect a beautifully diverse, proud, and massive network. Who wouldn't want to join this community?

NetSquared.org

NetSquared helps nonprofits take advantage of social media tools. One of their main projects is equipping and supporting volunteer organizers all over the world, who convene their respective communities to learn about new technologies, share ideas, and make connections. The principal tool used by the NetSquared team to support and communicate with their organizers is a simple Google Group. Like TuDiabetes, NetSquared has a passionate and active community builder, Amy Sample Ward, who loves helping fellow organizers. NetSquared.org's homepage regularly features profiles of organizers: including photos and interviews (with an emphasis on stories) to demonstrate just how crucial they are to the organization. In many ways, NetSquared's online community is fueled by its offline network, which includes over 80 local affiliates from Seattle to South Africa. NetSquared's primary social networking tools are a Facebook Group (for email), Facebook Page (for occasional "news feed" updates), Twitter (for regular updates and conversations), and LinkedIn (a professional social network that NetSquared started a group on early, and partly as a result, has a large following). While we were hesitant to feature a case study of a technology-focused organization, this organization does a great job walking the "best practice" talk.

Online Community Building Dos and Don'ts

- DO set up a personal account on a social network and dabble before launching your organization there. It's better to experiment (and even fail) with a personal account first.

- DO collaborate. If you come across a networked community that's surprisingly close to what you imagined for yours, explore the benefits of partnering up, instead of attempting to build and recruit a competing community.

- DO use photos generously—they help enormously in storytelling. Document what you are working on, even if it seems mundane.

- DON'T assign an intern or volunteer to manage your community, if you can help it By encouraging a staff member to take on the community building role, you'll provide a deeper understanding of your mission, as well as develop a consistent presence and voice on your networks.

- DO invite and train your staff and volunteers to set up personal accounts and share their stories on your social networks. Then you can use your main organizational account to filter and amplify the most compelling stories and news.

- DON'T solely use your social networks to post links to your website and news articles about your issue—make sure to weave in personal stories, unique observations, as well as conversation-starters. People sign into social networks to connect and feel the pulse of humanity, not just be presented with blog posts to read and videos to watch.

- DO use the "ladder of engagement." When members are engaging with you frequently online, invite them to get more involved in building your network by assigning special tasks and status. If you find yourself thanking a few certain supporters consistently, consider taking your thanks to the next level: empowerment. Offer your key members extra responsibilities or unique roles in projects as you grow your community.

- DO dive deep into a few social networks, rather than spreading yourself thin on a wide array of networks. Your networks will trust you more, you'll develop richer relationships, and you'll ultimately make a bigger impact.

- DON'T measure your community building success by the size of your fan base. Instead, measure your success by the quality of relationships you build that will get you closer to your world-changing goals.

- DO set goals with (rather than for) your community, which builds a sense of ownership and creates plans that are more likely to succeed. Use surveys and similar tools to involve your community.

- DO keep the corner of your eye trained on new networks and major trends. Nonprofits that are the first to act and adopt often reap the most benefits.

Conclusion: "To the Internet and Beyond!"

For every techno-utopian who evangelizes about the Web's potential to bring people together and save the world, there is a curmudgeon who shakes an angry fist at how the Web isolates people and will be the downfall of civilized discourse—if not civilization itself. But in the humble view of these two authors, the Internet is just a tool. Whether it's used as a benevolent connector or an insidious divider is largely up to all of us.

This is precisely why the job of online community building is so important—it enables us to be architects, planners of an entirely new social space with enormous potential to connect people for change. But don't get caught in the hype—remember to stay focused on your organization's mission, and never forget that real change doesn't generally happen online, it happens on the ground.

It seems to us that the nonprofit sector has thus far barely scratched the surface of how to harness the Web to change the world, so we'll be listening up for what you're doing out there. We're all connected now, so we'll see you online and in the streets. Let's get to work.

Jonathan Warnow is a cofounder of 350.org, an innovative global campaign to stop the climate crisis. His work focuses on harnessing new media and social technology to catalyze large-scale change. In additional to developing the tools and outreach strategy that facilitated over 10,000 offline events, Warnow has worked to develop a model of "open-source activism"—a new framework for social change that creates deeper engagement, empowered constituencies, and lasting results.

Joe Solomon (@EngageJoe on Twitter) is a strategist, writer, and campaigner at the frontlines of wiring new movements, combining grassroots community organizing with the power of the Internet. His most recent work is as the Social Media Coordinator for 350.org.

Online Community Resources: Nine Websites to Launch You From Zero to Community Building Rock Star

Below are a few resources that were either pivotal in reaching our evolving understanding of online community building—or some we wish were around when we first got started:

www.bethkanter.org

> The blog of Beth Kanter, a fellow contributor to this book, who is a powerhouse educator and explorer at the intersection of nonprofits and social media.

www.WeareMedia.org

Community-created resource for nonprofits who are new to social media, with specific resources on online community building.

www.SocialbySocial.com

A practical guide to using new technologies to create social impact.

www.SocialBrite.org

A blog with rich resources on social media for social causes—including a national calendar of events and conferences.

www.Communityspark.com

Chock-full of resources on online community building for businesses, including many examples relevant to nonprofits.

www.Netsquared.org/share/meetup

Local "meetups" where nonprofiteers and technologists gather around the world on a regular basis.

www.AmySampleWard.org

Leading and highly insightful voice in the networking movements space.

www.Neworganizing.com

Organization committed to training wired organizers with regular webinars and real-world trainings; offers a focus on progressive campaigning.

www.Twitter.com/nptechblogs

A daily publishing house of the latest news and resources in nonprofit technology, many of which are relevant to social networking for change.

○ ○ ○

All these resources, plus nonprofit management tips of the week and more, can be found at Nonprofits101.org.

CHAPTER 17

Constituent Relationship Management

By Steve Wright, Director of Social Performance Management Center, Grameen Foundation

Introduction: What Is Constituent Relationship Management (CRM)?

Running a nonprofit is complex. An effective director is not only responsible for creating public good by advancing the mission of her organization; she must also manage multiple constituent groups (program beneficiaries, investors/donors, volunteers, board, and staff) each with their own needs and expectations. Directly managing all of this is impossible for one person and, while adding staff can alleviate a director's workload, it can also limit the ability to "see" across an organization. This is where Constituent Relationship Management (CRM), a powerful tool that's available for free to smaller organizations, comes in.

What Are the Benefits of CRM?

CRM can help you:

- Streamline your organization, making it more efficient

- Increase information sharing within the organization

- Deepen your relationships with supporters

- Make informed decisions about programmatic and organizational strategy

- Enforce process inside an organization

- Manage staff turnover and create "institutional memory"

Before we dive into how to use and select a CRM platform, let's dive a bit deeper into how it can help you meet your mission more efficiently and effectively.

What Does CRM Do?

CRM is generally considered to be "enterprise class," meaning it's designed to meet the needs of the entire organization, as opposed to a single department or program. *CRM is a database that provides both data storage and process facilitation.* Examples of data storage include lists of important contacts or repositories for shared documents. Process examples are "how to acknowledge a new donation" or "how to post new content to the website" or, for direct service organizations, "how to intake a new program participant."

In general, *the deeper the use of CRM, the more value received.* Using CRM exclusively for data storage (i.e., contacts and documents) is just scratching the surface of what's possible. Although it is valuable to store important information in easily accessible places, which CRM does very well, the secret sauce is really in facilitating your organization's processes. When properly used, this powerful tool facilitates process management or, better yet, process automation, meaning that your CRM actually does your work for you (at least the parts that a machine can do). Building off the earlier examples of processes, you can automate the process of sending donation acknowledgement letters by configuring your CRM to send a customized letter to the donor when recording a specific event, such as "check is received." In the direct service example, when a new program participant is entered into your CRM, such as a student, she can automatically be added to a class roster, or the system can immediately send an invoice to her parents or guardians.

CRM is primarily a tool for managing internal information and processes and is therefore mainly used by staff. That said, there are many reasons why you might want to expose your CRM to a public or external audience in limited ways. Maybe you want to create a contact form on your website, where visitors can enter information that is saved directly to your CRM, from which you can easily email them or mail them a letter. Or you can create a secure website where external VIPs (such as donors) can interact by donating, asking questions, commenting on your work, register dissatisfaction, fill out questionnaires, and so forth. CRM allows you to track that and view the history of those interactions. As you can tell by these examples, security and user access settings are critical components to ensuring that each user has access *only* to the data she needs.

Core Skills and Competencies: Using CRM

Now that we've reviewed some of the main reasons why nonprofit leaders choose to implement CRM platforms in their organizations, let's look at how to get the most out of a system.

Contacts and Communications

The core purpose of a CRM system is to help you manage your organization's relationship with three key constituencies: investors and donors, program beneficiaries, and employees. The central role of CRM is to record encounters (often referred to as "Touches") with these stakeholders. They are entered into CRM as "Contacts." You can easily send email directly through the CRM to an individual Contact, everyone in a certain constituency, or your entire database. You can even schedule an email to be sent out at a specific time or based on a specific condition (i.e., once your fundraising target is reached). In each case, all emails sent through the system are recorded on each Contact's file so anyone else looking up that record can see the history of your communication with a Contact. That's what we mean when using the phrase, "creating institutional memory"—even if the point person on a relationship moves on, you still have access to all that information. The same is true for phone calls or postal mail—by logging all your Touches with your various Contacts, your CRM helps you track and optimize relationships. Imagine being on a call with a prospective donor. You bring up the donor's record and notice his daughter recently participated in a volunteer event and his wife is an executive at a local nonprofit. This background information supports a more thoughtful and productive conversation, creating a stronger sense that you "know" the prospect better and increasing the likelihood of a contribution. Similarly, if you run a nonprofit that houses abandoned animals, when planning your annual fundraising campaign, you could easily identify anyone who previously adopted a dog or any veterinarians that provided medical services.

Outreach: Measuring Financial and Other Forms of Value

Classically, outreach campaigns are meant to generate a financial return on investment, meaning where money is spent to build awareness and attract donations. Obviously, you want to spend less money than you raise, unless your goals focus on education, advocacy, and so on. However, an outreach effort to increase awareness about a political or social issue will also have a return, just not a financial one. They key is to *first assess how important or valuable a particular return (money, voter registration, newsletter signups, and the like) is, then decide what it's worth to you.* How might this work?

With CRM, you set up a campaign and input your upfront costs, as well as set goals for your desired return. These goals could be to register volunteers, or to drive engagement via letters to the editor or house parties. *All CRM platforms contain mass communication features that can be used to initiate a campaign.* Let's assume that you are sending out a call to action asking your constituents to (1) donate, (2) contact their local representatives, or (3) hold a house party. Donations are easy to track, assuming you set up an e-commerce function on your website so any donation will be recorded in your CRM, or any checks received from the campaign will be properly logged in the system.

How about the other two? You can simply ask your constituents to tell you after they contact their local representative or, for a higher initial cost, you can create a form on your website that creates and even sends a letter, ensuring full accountability and streamlining the process by which people can take this action. Similarly, for the house party you can ask hosts to send an email with a report back from the event, or you can create a house party host website where supporters can access resources to support and promote the party. Again, this entails a higher initial investment, but it makes it easier for hosts, increasing the likelihood that they'll take the action, plus you enjoy enhanced accountability. Assuming you managed the entire campaign with your CRM, you will be able to assess your efficacy and use that information to inform future efforts.

case study

Online Advocacy and the No Tankers Campaign

Contributed by Charles Campbell of Dogwood Initiative and Sara Freedman of Groundwire

Background

Dogwood Initiative (DI) is a leading environmental organization working to protect British Columbia's diverse ecosystems and vast natural resources. One of their ongoing campaigns, the "No Tankers" campaign, engages community members as advocates to protect the coastline from possible oil spills. Oil companies are pushing to build a port for tankers on Canada's Pacific coast to ship crude to China and other parts of Asia, and Dogwood is intent on stopping the project.

List Building

The No Tankers online campaign focuses on generating and effectively using a list of people opposed to oil tankers on British Columbia's coast, thereby creating a large group of supporters that can be quickly mobilized. The primary means of generating this list is an online petition on Dogwood's website. Consultants worked with Dogwood to set up the online petition on Groundwire, which integrates with their Salesforce.com CRM. By promoting the effort in the local media and through grassroots organization, Dogwood has grown the No Tankers list to over 40,000 members, 15,000 of whom "opted in" to receive other emails from Dogwood Initiative.

case study

Targeting by Region and by Leadership Level

Petition signers are added to Dogwood's Salesforce.com database and receive regular communication: action alerts, email appeals, and a monthly e-newsletter. The list is segmented geographically, facilitating actions with a regional focus. Each online action is given a leadership level from 1 to 5, a measure of the level of effort and engagement it takes to complete that action. For example, signing a petition is a level 1 action, donating is level 3, and organizing a rally is level 5. Once people reach a certain number of "points" in their database, they are automatically asked to join the "No Tankers Action Team," and are invited to participate in actions that require a higher level of effort and engagement, such as writing personal letters and organizing activities for the campaign.

Successful Outcomes

In April 2009, Dogwood Initiative asked its constituents to send letters to the Canadian Environmental Assessment Agency (CEAA, the Canadian equivalent of the EPA) regarding the inadequacy of their review process for the oil tanker port and a related pipeline project. Dogwood supporters sent 646 letters to the CEAA, dwarfing the usual number of submissions for similar projects (typically under 100). As a direct result, the CEAA significantly expanded the scope of their review of the projects, taking into account many of the concerns of Dogwood's supporters.

Just a few months later, tanker proponent Enbridge Inc. was reportedly on the verge of signing agreements with a number of oil producers and buyers and submitting its official application for the port to the CEAA. Dogwood asked their supporters to send letters directly to oil company CEOs, as well as to the Chinese and Korean companies that were said to be interested in the project. 12,000 letters were sent to ten companies. Almost a year later, Enbridge had yet to submit its application to the regulator, largely due to its failure to secure firm commitments from suppliers and buyers.

case study

What's Next

Dogwood Initiative plans to use Salesforce.com to implement an educational campaign for new supporters of the No Tankers campaign to quickly bring them up to speed. They're also developing more regionally focused actions for the campaign, leveraging their CRM's ability to segment their mailing list and drive local actions. They are improving outcomes tracking and analysis to better identify leaders and refine communications, and of course, they're keeping a keen eye on the port, Enbridge, and the CEAA. Power to the people!

Just about all nonprofits plan at least some of their external communications; ideally, by now CRM's ability to support this is clear. Using your database to manage critical business processes is definitely more involved, but it also offers great rewards to those leaders willing to invest in their technology and information infrastructure. Let's look at another case study, this time highlighting how an established nonprofit makes use of CRM to support their programs, even in light of some very unique requirements. Even if you run a smaller organization, there are many lessons to be learned from FSA's experience.

case study

Program Management and the Family Service Agency

Challenge

Family Service Agency (FSA) of San Francisco, the city's oldest nonsectarian, nonprofit social services provider, wanted a better system to help program managers and clinicians manage data for their 12,000 clients. Management wanted staff to have easier and more reliable access to key client information. As a major nonprofit partner of the City and County of San Francisco, FSA needed a solution compliant with the requirements of HIPAA and SF's Department of Health & Human Services. At the time, the organization provided over 30 programs to needy individuals and families of all ages in 11 languages. They were looking to grow even further, but were saddled with a decades-old system of paper records for client tracking and reporting. Managers did not have easy access to data on key agency metrics. FSA wanted to increase the amount of time that clinicians could spend with clients—they were averaging 60 minutes of paperwork for every 60 minutes of face time. FSA also needed to address the requirements of 66 funders, including the state of California's Proposition 63, which provides financial support to develop new services for people with serious mental illness, and requires increased documentation. FSA sought to make it easier to bill government agencies and eliminate the loss of funding that sometimes occurred when documentation was lost. Most importantly, they needed to ensure that their records met the auditing requirements of their many funding sources in a timely and accurate manner.

Solution

Using licenses donated by the Salesforce.com Foundation, FSA worked with a consultant (Exponent Partners) to customize their CRM and create San Francisco's first automated client and case management system. Using the Salesforce.com platform, FSA built a custom human services case management application. Initial deployments addressed the need for client progress notes and documentation; subsequent phases included development of tools for client diagnosis and assessment, and tools for care planning. Further iterations included expert systems diagnosis support, and integration with accounting and fundraising. The solution was deployed to 215 users across all organizational functions, including 120 caseworkers spread across four locations. All employees were made to attend training and certification programs, ensuring their familiarity with the new system, and use of the CRM was mandated. Their platform now automates key functions, including prepopulating forms to save administrative time. *All* documentation is stored within the CRM, eliminating the need for paper forms and making it easy to share information. Clinicians and support personnel can easily share diagnoses, client objectives, progress notes, and plans of care.

Results

The new streamlined reporting process enables clinicians to spend less time on paperwork and documentation—time spent with clients has increased by 50%. Clients benefit substantially from this improved care, which translates to donors seeing more impact from their contributions, thereby fueling fundraising efforts. Information collection is more consistent and aligned with the Department of Public Health standards, creating easier reporting; time spent reconciling billing problems with the city of San Francisco has been significantly reduced. FSA has not lost funding once due to chart error or lost documentation since implementing the new system. Dashboards, as addressed in Chapter Five, provide easy access to operational and client data; managers can track individual client outcomes, plus program and clinician productivity. Reports can easily be generated for billing and reporting purposes. Productivity reports, which used to take two months to compile, can now be compiled on the fly. What a difference a database makes.

User Adoption

What good is software, a database, or a computer if nobody uses it? In this case, "adoption" refers to how deeply and effectively your employees use your CRM. *Any CRM enables effective data input and access*, but it's useless without data. While you can create automated ways to get data in to your system, employees must enter most information. If your staff doesn't find the tool to be intuitive and effective, or perceive the value it can provide, they won't use it. *There are two ways to increase user adoption—the carrot and the stick.* Carrots entice, sticks compel. Sticks without carrots are counterproductive and carrots without sticks are insufficient. A classic example of a CRM stick is, "If it's not in the database, it doesn't exist," AKA without evidence of an employee's work in the CRM, that employee didn't do his work. A more positive way to talk about this is to say that all employees must "live in the CRM." While this sort of performance management is a critical aspect of user adoption, the carrot side of the equation is just as important. If employees "live" inside a well-implemented CRM, then everyone in your organization will be able to do their jobs more effectively and with more autonomy. As discussed, fundraising employees will benefit from CRM by learning more about how donors interact with your organization, increasing results. Similarly, we looked at how process automation can enhance service delivery. *CRM helps employees by providing them all of the information they need, along with the context in which they need it.*

Business Intelligence: Reporting and Analytics

Business intelligence is the process of examining organizational data to guide strategic decisions. Once you have a CRM full of information, you can use that data to gain greater insight in to your successes and failures, enabling more informed decisions about your future. Reporting is a basic feature of any CRM (i.e., how many $10,000+ donations have we received in the last five years?). Analytics is the process of gaining insight from that data—akin to the difference between information and wisdom. Analytics can be applied to understand what types of donors are most likely to give again, or which kinds of people are most likely to benefit from your services. *Analytics help you understand trends and identify where your efforts are best spent moving forward.* There is arguably nothing more important to your organization, so it is key to get as much data into the system as possible—garbage in, garbage out. Money or financial returns are reasonably easy to count. However, counting program-generated returns are equally, if not more, important. Just think back to how the Family Service Agency was able to generate reports and analyze the data to improve their services.

Dos and Don'ts

CRM Dos and Don'ts

- DO dedicate appropriate resources. CRM is "enterprise class" and is most useful when it is used to manage your entire organization. Investing resources in choosing, designing, and implementing CRM is critical.

- DON'T think that donors are your only constituents. Relationships with program beneficiaries, staff, vendors, board members, and employees should also be managed by your database.

- DO focus on the relationships. Managing relationships is a long-term process, requiring ongoing investment. Good relationships fuel a healthy organization.

Dos and Don'ts

- DON'T use your CRM as a data bucket. Managing process is more important that collecting data, and always remember that CRM is simply a tool to help you meet mission. Process automation features in CRM will create new efficiencies and allow your staff to focus on what is most important.

- DO focus on user adoption. *All staff should use the CRM to manage their work* and "live in the database," but be sure to provide the appropriate training and to build the system to meet the needs of your employees.

- DON'T ever think you are done. Your CRM is a reflection of the processes that are critical to your organization. If your CRM is static, so is your organization.

- DO focus on reporting. You built an organization to solve a problem. *Imagine what the world would look like if you were successful, then imagine what report you would need to prove you had done it.* That report will drive what data you need and what processes you need to manage.

Conclusion

A well-used and well-designed CRM will help you run your organization efficiently and effectively. CRM provides an easily accessible home for *all* of your data. Users will be able to see who has been contacted and with what message. Constituents will receive more targeted and more relevant communications, leading to better response rates to all forms of appeals. Through process automation, CRM will help you "manage what matters," providing even better services with greater speed and accuracy. And finally, the data that you collect in the process of using your CRM can be analyzed to provide real time insight in to the efficacy of your organization. All in all, CRM presents a tremendous opportunity for any organization looking to enhance its ability to fulfill its mission.

Steve Wright strives to serve as a catalyst for a better world, aggressively pursuing avenues for global collaboration on social outcomes. He is an educator and social technologist who introduces visionary people with complementary goals. Prior to his role at Grameen Foundation, he served as director of innovation at the Salesforce. com Foundation, the nonprofit arm of one of the leading CRM providers.

CRM Resource Review

www.nten.org/learn/bytopic/crm

> Several CRM resources from the Nonprofit Technology Network.

www.nten.org/ecosystem_report

> NTEN 2009 Study of data management tools in use by nonprofit organizations.

www.nten.org/events/webinar/2008/12/11/
crm-101-manage-your-constituent-information-with-ease

> NTEN CRM 101: Manage Your Constituent Information with Ease.

www.nten.org/events/webinar/2010/02/22/free-kittens-civicrm-and-salesforce

> A great webinar giving overviews of two great CRM platforms, CiviCRM and Salesforce.com—the former is free and open source and the later is available for free for smaller nonprofits (up to 10 licenses) at www.salesforce.com/ foundation.

www.idealware.org/CRM

> Great list of reviews from Idealware.

www.idealware.org/articles/crm_constituents_processes.php

> "In search of CRM: Understanding Constituents and Processes"
> A helpful article when thinking through how to get the most out of your CRM.

www.idealware.org/articles/relationship_centric_org.php

Creating the Relationship Centric Organization—A great article on how to structure your organization when integrating CRM.

www.techsoup.org/learningcenter/databases/page5961.cfm?cg=searchterms&sg =comparison

A very useful donor management software comparison.

socialsourcecommons.org/toolbox/show/1661

Social Source Commons list of free, open source CRM software and services.

www.slideshare.net/deangraham/spreadsheets-to-crm-graham

From Spreadsheets to CRM—A great presentation featuring many how-to's regarding CRM.

o o o

All these resources, plus nonprofit management tips of the week and more, can be found at Nonprofits101.org.

Part Five

Fundraising

Fundraising is the gentle art of teaching the joy of giving.

—Hank Rosso

Whenever I talk about fundraising, I like to share two of my favorite stories. The first is about Bill Cosby, during his college days at Temple University. Bill was pursuing a master's degree and enrolled in a philosophy class, full of 100 other master's and doctorate students. One day, they spent the entire class debating the age-old quagmire, "Is the glass half full, or half empty?" As you might imagine, it was a bit of a circular debate and, after an hour-and-a-half, Bill walked home, frustrated and none the wiser. After winding his way through the Philadelphia streets for a mile or two, he got to his house where, as always, his grandmother was waiting for him.

"How was class today, Bill?" his grandma asked. "I don't want to talk about it," he replied, not wanting to revisit what he considered a complete waste of time. "No really, I want to know. How was class today, Bill?" she pressed.

Then he let it out. "Well, if you must know, it was incredibly frustrating, Grandma. 100 master's and PhD students sat around for 90 minutes debating if a glass was half full or half empty," he huffed.

Without missing a beat, his grandmother, with all of a third grade education, hit him with a zinger he'd never forget: "Well, that's easy. *It depends on whether you're pouring or drinking.*"

They say that perception defines reality. I share this story with current and would-be fundraisers because I think all too often in the nonprofit work, we think of ourselves as the drinkers, begging for alms so that we can go on about our work. When in fact, we are the pourers, the nurturers of society—*we do our supporters a great favor by providing them with a worthy philanthropic outlet for their positive intentions.* In short, we're selling impact, which—when properly presented—people are honored and excited to buy. The actual organization you're fundraising for *isn't* the beneficiary of the gift, and certainly neither are you personally. Rather, *a donor's gift is to the community, and to the impact you have within it.* So go forth and be bold, and remember Hank's other famous adage about the number one reason why people don't give, "because they're not asked."

So how do we transcend this issue with perspective, with self-image? Personally, I see this as one of the biggest problems holding back the nonprofit sector. Just the name, "nonprofit," is telling; they say *we are the only sector to define ourselves by what we're not.* As it relates to fundraising, perhaps the solution is to set our sights a bit higher, instead of focusing on simple sustenance.

This brings me to my other favorite story, which echoes a message frequently heard on the mountain, "go big, or go home." It seems that Cindy, the executive director of a nonprofit-operated hospital, was reading the *Chronicle of Philanthropy* one day. While flipping through the industry trade rag, she noted that St. Luke's, which is the other main hospital in town, had received a $6,000,000 donation. Her attention quickly fixed, she read on, only to find out that the contribution had come from *one of her board members.* Now, this board member had never made a donation even close to that size to their hospital, so of course she was a bit upset. She took a walk to get some fresh air, calmed herself down, and then called the board member and set up a lunch date. A few days later, they got together.

Their lunch started with small talk about the wife and kids, the weather, the hospital . . . the usual prattle. Eventually, though, the time came for Cindy to ask the question she was *really* there to ask.

"Bob, I was reading the paper the other day and I noticed that you made a very generous contribution to St. Luke's hospital," she began. "I have to ask, why didn't *we* get that $6,000,000 gift?"

"That's easy," Bob responded, "nobody ever brought me a $6,000,000 idea."

Let this story be a lesson to us all—*never discount the philanthropic potential of those you meet, and especially those closest to you.* It was Leo Burnett, the famous advertising guru, who once said that "if you reach for the stars, you might not quite get one, but you won't end up with a handful of mud, either."

We have worked hard to assemble some of the sector's leading fundraising experts in the chapters that follow. These are people and organizations with decades of experience, combined with an uncanny ability to concisely convey the maps, the picks and shovels, and definitely the nuggets that fundraisers need to be successful.

We'll start this section with a broad overview of many of the various fundraising (or "development") strategies available to your nonprofit, including the pros and cons of each, and when each is most appropriate. Then we'll move into individual donors, which is where the lion's share of philanthropic dollars originate. Most leaders new to the sector fail to realize that *over 80% of nongovernmental support of nonprofits comes from individuals*, compared to roughly 13% from foundations and 5% from companies.[1] From there, we'll offer some solid tips for approaching foundations, and then we will look at online fundraising, both to a wide audience and to a tighter network of your peers and supporters. We'll then look at best practices for securing corporate support without compromising your ideals. Finally, we will cover earned income business strategies for nonprofits, which are increasingly important as we look for ways to become self-sustained.

Ultimately, no *one* strategy can float a publicly supported nonprofit by itself; *diversification is key, especially during difficult economic times.* The key is to take the best of all worlds and weave together a strategy that works for you, the cause, and the community. This is not a static process with a fixed end—in fact, it constantly requires fine-tuning. Although I'm not one to say that nonprofits need to be more businesslike, I do think it's imperative that we realize that we are, in fact, running a business, or rather a "business plus." Just as all businesses, we have a financial bottom line we need to meet to keep the lights on. In addition to that consideration, however, social benefit organizations also have a mission to meet—a social bottom line. It is in the pursuit of this goal that we garner our most significant support.

Some of you may be familiar with Lynne Twist, author of *The Soul of Money*. She was kind enough to provide the Afterword to this handbook, and as you *consider bringing who you are to what you do*, and looking more at of the spiritual role of money as it relates to fundraising, I encourage you to review her comments.

A quick note on a topic that I wish we could have added to the mix here: in-kind donations (a brief mention appears in Chapter Twenty-Eight, as it relates to events). When I started Craigslist Foundation out of my bedroom with scant funds and no established programs or fundraising prospects, securing donations of goods and services proved to be much easier than scoring cash contributions. This included everything from hundreds of volunteers to offers of wine, beer, and food; free office space; donated advertising, legal counsel, and accounting services; and much more. It's crucial that you *look at where you're spending money (or planning to), and see if you can zero out some of the larger line items through in-kind support*; by the time we grew Craigslist Foundation to an annual budget of almost $2 million dollars, almost half of that was provided as donated goods and services.

As you move forward with your fundraising efforts, remember the importance of perspective, of going big, of not being afraid to ask, and of a diversified strategy which should include non-cash support. All these lessons will serve you well, and all of them will be fleshed out in greater detail in the chapters that follow.

CHAPTER 18

Fundraising: Knowing When to Do What

By Andrea McManus, CFRE, President,
The Development Group

Introduction

Fundraising is a scary word for many and the subject of much debate, many objections, lots of procrastination, and has been likened to the fear of flying, the fear of heights, and the fear of the unknown.

Where do we start? What kind of fundraising should we do? How do we make the best use of our available hard-earned and scarce dollars? How do we make our fundraising grow and be sustainable over the long term? Who are our donors and how do we identify and reach them? These are questions that nonprofit leaders wrestle with in an attempt to diversify and stabilize their revenue base.

According to Giving USA Foundation, during the recession of 2009 total charitable giving fell 3.6% (−3.2% adjusted for inflation) to an estimated

$303.75 billion. The report went on to say "Last year was also the worst year economically in America since the Great Depression. At least through mid-year, financial transactions of all kinds slowed while people considered and worried about the future. Nonetheless, Americans continued to give—less often perhaps, more quietly than in the past—to charity." However, in 2008, charitable giving in the United States exceeded $300 billion for the second year in a row, with donations reaching an estimated $307.65 billion, or 2.2% of GDP.[1] Clearly, fundraising is serious work that is not to be taken lightly—getting a piece of that pie can often make or break a nonprofit's ability to achieve its mission.

Like strategic planning, financial planning, or human resource planning, the fundraising direction you take is unique to your organization and its particular set of circumstances. *There is no one-size-fits-all solution when it comes to fundraising.* However, there are some basic principles, general fundraising methodologies and typical donor categories that have proven their value to all nonprofits across all fundraising approaches (i.e., individual donors, foundations, companies, and so on). This chapter gives you the framework you will need to address these questions for your organization and choose fundraising strategies that suit you and position you for success.

As a general background, it is important to understand the difference between "fundraising" and "fund development." According to the Association of Fundraising Professionals' (AFP) Fundraising Dictionary Online, fund development is "the planning and implementing of programs that are meant to increase contributed financial support for an organization" and fundraising is "the raising of assets and resources from various sources for the support of an organization or a specific project."[2]

So what's the difference? Fund development is a process, part art and part science, that moves in an orderly and logical sequence. It starts with preparation and planning; moves to execution; is subject to constant oversight, tracking, evaluation, and measuring; and then circles back to renewal of the original plan. No matter how large or small your organization, the cycle is neither haphazard nor reactive, but proactive and strategically planned. Fundraising, on the other hand, is the actual act of getting money in the door, of making "the ask." It is a small but very important piece of fund development.

Critical Skills and Competencies

As you'll learn in this chapter, I didn't know what fund development was when I got started. Though this chapter is about the tactical process of fundraising, I now operate under the assumption that *good fundraising flows out of the principles of strategic fund development.* In this chapter, you'll see those principles at work behind the scenes. But I want to start by talking about what I did wrong when I got started. Later, you'll see what I should have done.

Six Things I Wish I Had Known at the Beginning of My Career

I am one of those fundraisers who literally "fell into" this profession. I did not aspire to work in the nonprofit sector, nor did I even know what a professional fundraiser was. In fact, I was on a pretty dynamic career track in the for-profit marketing world that had most recently included a stint working for the 1988 Olympic Winter Organizing Committee with its top international corporate sponsors. Nevertheless, as I was enjoying my first maternity leave I found myself agreeing to do a corporate campaign for a local nonprofit. I wish I could say that it was a huge success, but that would be revisionist history! Basically, here is what I did and what happened:

- Agreed to the contract and immediately reported to work.

- Identified 70–80 top corporations and businesses in the City of Calgary.

- Made phone calls (this was before the Internet) to determine the correct person to receive the letter. If unable to identify a specific recipient, sent it to "Dear Sir/Madam."

- Wrote one letter to all organizations and customized only when I had an identified recipient; but the letter did contain a specific (but the same) ask in all letters.

- Mailed it on a Friday.

- Woke up on Tuesday morning to headlines in the major local newspaper that read "ABC Organization (mine of course!) Stockpiles $750,000 Surplus." Letters landed on desks the same day.

• Watched campaign momentum tank and spent lots of unanticipated time explaining.

I didn't do *everything* wrong my first time out, but if I had known what I now know, if I had understood the fundamentals of philanthropic giving and fund development, I would have saved myself and my nonprofit a lot of time and energy and had greater immediate and long-term results. If I had known and understood these *six key fundraising principles*, my first time out would likely have been very different indeed:

1. *People give to people.* People are motivated to give for a variety of reasons.

   ○ They or someone close to them has been touched by a specific cause, i.e., a family member has cancer, a child with a disability, graduated from a particular college. For fundraisers, this means that if you don't know *why* people give it is very difficult to understand what will interest a particular donor or group in your mission, or what will motivate them to make a gift. *Take the time to identify what interests particular donors in your organization specifically.*

   ○ People don't give to organizations, they give to the people your mission serves. For fundraisers, this means *don't talk about how great your organization is, talk about the change you make in people's lives and in the community.* Link them directly to your mission.

   ○ *People give because they are asked* and if you don't ask, the answer will always be "no."

   ○ For fundraisers, this means don't make the mistake of not asking because "you think they will know what you want." Make sure your staff, your board members, and your volunteers make *direct and specific* asks.

   ○ People give to help, to build, to change, to care for, or to invest. They don't make a decision to give because of a tax receipt; however, this can determine the size of some gifts.

2. *Much comes from few.* The Pareto Principle, or the 80/20 rule, can be applied to just about anything: 20% of the people in a business make 80 percent of the decisions; 20% of the work consumes 80% of your time;

and so on. *A successful fund development program will receive 80% of its donations from 20% of its donors.* This is true pretty much across the broad spectrum of any fund development program. Follow the 80/20 rule when making strategic decisions on how and where to spend your time and money. For example, don't send out a mass mailing to 70–80 potential corporate prospects! Take the time to identify the top 10 who have some alignment with your mission and organization and put 80% of your time there, leaving 20% for the other 60–70.

3. *Wealth is not always obvious nor is it necessarily interested in your cause.* Too many organizations spend too much time trying to secure donations from the "usual suspects," i.e., the high-profile community leaders who do good works for many organizations. The same ones every other organization in your community is pursuing. You need to *take a broader view that includes the many individuals with less, or less obvious, wealth* who still have the means and the interest to support your organization, and the businesses that may not be the corporate leaders but still have a strong sense of community. The challenge for you is to identify *your* potential donors and leaders and then find a way to approach them. Therefore, challenge your definition of "wealth" and the way others, particularly your board members, perceive it. A person doesn't have to have gazillions of dollars to be generous. Wealth is relative.

4. *It's not about the money—it's about building the relationship.* Donors are your friends and they play a large and vitally important role in your organization. They contribute to you because they believe in your mission. Getting to know and understand your donors, being "donor-centric," is important, not just to get that first gift, but to get the next one after that and the next one after that. Today's donors are smart and savvy and you should expect that they have checked you out. Thoroughly. You need to be smart and savvy as well. Get to know them, engage them, listen to them. Don't waste their time and they won't waste yours.

5. *Fundraising is not a stand-alone activity. One of the biggest mistakes you can make is to treat fundraising as if it operates in a silo,* separate and distinct from everything else that happens in your organization. In order to be successful in reaching your fundraising goals be sure to

○ Work in synergy and collaboration with strategic planning. Fundraising is very likely a key part of achieving your goals. Therefore, *include fundraising in the strategic planning process from the beginning* and use it to inform the environmental scanning process. And *before* your organization launches that new program, ask "Can we fund this?"

○ Recognize governance responsibility. One of the board's primary responsibilities is your organization's financial health. If fundraising is a revenue source, then it is part of your financial health and sustainability. *Engage the board in fundraising planning* (see Chapter Thirty-One for more on this topic).

○ Involve everyone in the many different aspects of raising money— prospect identification, information gathering, cultivating and building relationships, opening doors, thanking, and stewarding. Asking is just one small piece. There are lots of tasks for everyone to do. *Take a frontline worker or a board member on a call and let them speak passionately about why they do what they do and what difference their work makes.*

6. *Philanthropy is something to be proud of, and fundraising exists to enable philanthropy.* Philanthropy is often defined as "the gift of time, talent and resources" or in the dictionary as "love of humankind." People who give to your organization do so because they believe in *your* mission. They are proud of their act of giving and consider it a privilege to be able to help change conditions through the work of your organization. Be proud of the work you do to help philanthropists as they use their resources to help others.

Identifying Your Best Strategies

Nonprofit organizations come in all sizes and shapes, as do development programs. Clearly, what is necessary in terms of staff, resources, volunteers, planning, evaluation, and communication to reach the large financial goals of a major university is not going to be what is required, let alone even feasible, for a small, grassroots nonprofit that has much smaller goals and no staff.

In order to be successful and sustainable over the long term, to have renewal and growth, to develop mutually beneficial relationships with donors, and to be accountable to those donors, you want to have a diversified donor base (corporations, individuals, and foundations) with a number of fundraising vehicles (special events, direct mail, online, and face-to-face major gifts).

Identifying the development approach that offers the best return on investment and is suitable for a particular organization and campaign is the key to success. Although diversity is always important, each fundraising vehicle needs to be designed in a way that capitalizes on the organization's strengths and its financial and human (staff and volunteer) resources. Though not exhaustive, Exhibit 18.1 outlines the financial and human resources generally required for each type of fundraising and how they might apply to nonprofits of different sizes.

Exhibit 18.1 Identifying What Works

Annual Giving. An annual gift is one that is reasonably expected to be given year after year. Most annual gifts are small, but *the important thing for the annual giving program is that there are gift renewal mechanisms in place*. Like anything else, it costs more to get the gift in the first place than it does to renew that gift, so having a planned and proactive renewal program in place is a must. A successful annual fund can provide several benefits such as:

- A reliable base of annual funding

- A foundation for all other fundraising

- Support for annual operating and program needs not funded by other means

- A source for "undesignated" or unrestricted gifts that can be used by the organization where most needed

- An excellent way to attract new donors into the organization with the potential to move up the giving ladder toward the major gift status

- An increase in the profile of your organization in the community on a mass-market basis

(Continued)

Most annual giving occurs in non face-to-face activities, such as personalized mail, special events, door-to-door campaigns, telephone solicitation, online giving, or other mass promotional opportunities, such as organizational newsletters. Although *face-to-face fundraising is by far the most effective*, it can also be expensive, requiring more staff resources. Since annual gifts tend to be smaller, mass-market appeals often make sense from a cost versus benefit perspective.

Typical annual giving vehicles include:

Type of Fundraising and Donor Category	What It Is	Financial Resources	Human Resources	Most Suitable for
Direct Mail *Individuals, small business*	Personalized mailings remain one of the most commonly used fundraising vehicles for acquiring, renewing, and upgrading donors	Significant upfront investment of dollars over multiple years with no guarantee of ROI in early years.	Small, irregular mailings can be done by volunteers. Larger programs require staff to either run in-house or manage an out-sourced campaign; no volunteer involvement necessary.	All sizes of nonprofits, but it's difficult for all-volunteer organizations to conduct a program with regular mailings.
Telemarketing *Individuals*	Telephone solicitation, which is particularly effective for thanking, renewing, and upgrading donors	Significant investment in equipment, space, and administrative infrastructure. Hired callers add to costs.	Recruiting volunteers to make calls can be challenging. Staff to run in-house program or monitor outsourced one. Outsourcing requires no volunteers.	Volunteer phone solicitors are an effective way to thank and renew donors. All nonprofits can run an outsourced telephone solicitation if budget allows.

Type of Fundraising and Donor Category	What It Is	Financial Resources	Human Resources	Most Suitable for
Door-to-door Campaign *Individuals*	Canvassing door-to-door, typically to acquire new donors	Investment in materials and administrative infrastructure. Hired canvassers add to costs.	Recruitment of volunteers can be challenging. Safety is an issue. Require staff to plan program, recruit, and monitor, and do follow-up.	Small organizations typically depend on volunteers. Good for community groups, including sports organizations that draw from an invested group in a localized area. Larger nonprofits can handle volunteer or hired canvassers.
Special Events *Individuals, business, community groups*	Figure prominently in many organizations Are used for both friend raising and fundraising, but *you must have clear goals*	Can be expensive and labor intensive	Require significant volunteer and staff time (the latter even if the event is contracted out)	All sizes of organizations *Most successful events are typically mission-focused*

(Continued)

Type of Fundraising and Donor Category	What It Is	Financial Resources	Human Resources	Most Suitable for
E-philanthropy *Individuals*	Using the Internet to raise money online	Investment in website capability and administrative infrastructure.	Staff to monitor; minimal volunteer involvement.	All organizations, either through their own website or a giving portal. Widely used for ticket sales and disaster relief, *online giving is particularly favored by younger donors* and is becoming a staple of many development programs. Should be integrated with existing programs rather than as a standalone tool.

Major gifts (corporations, individuals, and foundations). There are a variety of financial needs that a nonprofit has that are most suitable to a major gift program. Current programs and services, special projects, seed money for new projects, research, and capital needs are examples. Characteristics of major gifts include:

- They are almost always the result of a face-to-face cultivation and solicitation.

- They are generally one-time gifts, as opposed to gifts that an organization can reasonably expect to receive annually.

- They are almost always restricted, i.e., one that the donor is making for a specific purpose, and the nonprofit is legally obligated to use the gift according to the donor's intent.

- They can be made from cash or assets (gifts of stock, real estate, art, and the like).

- They are generally the top 10–20% of gifts received.

Major gift programs are a critical component of nonprofit development programs of all sizes for two main reasons. First, they are the most effective way of building what could be long-term relationships with donors to an organization and, second, because major gift fundraising is an individual, face-to-face exercise.

What constitutes a major gift varies from organization to organization. In smaller organizations, they could start at $1,000 and in larger institutions at $50,000. Historically, *major gifts tended to come from donors who had made several smaller annual gifts to a nonprofit over time.* However, major gifts can come from current donors or first time donors. Current donors are still the best prospects for greater giving and individuals, corporations, and foundations are all potential prospects for major gifts.

There are a number of vehicles through which major gifts are solicited and received.

Type of Fundraising and Donor Category	What It Is	Financial Resources	Human Resources	Most Suitable for
Major Gift Programs and Campaigns *Individuals, business, foundations, and community groups*	A seamless, ongoing initiative that is specifically focused on identifying potential major gift prospects	Materials, research, cultivation activities.	Volunteers, staff, and board all play a key role in identifying, opening doors with, and cultivating prospects. Can be volunteer only or staff/volunteer mixed.	Suitable for all organizations, tailored to size.

(Continued)

Type of Fundraising and Donor Category	What It Is	Financial Resources	Human Resources	Most Suitable for
Capital and Comprehensive Campaigns *Individuals, business, foundations, and community groups*	A one-time, deadline-driven campaign to raise a targeted amount for a specific bricks and mortar (capital) or combination bricks and mortar and program (comprehensive) project	Can require significant costs in materials, training, campaign counsel, and recognition.	Staff and volunteers together. Difficult to do an all-volunteer campaign (will take longer and may flounder without staff direction).	Suitable for all organizations, tailored to size.
Endowment Giving *Individuals*	Giving to a fund that is kept in reserve, where the interest is used for current needs; an endowment is self-sustaining as the principal is not touched	Financial costs are generally associated with other vehicles.	Same as for major gifts.	Same as for major gifts.
Planned Giving *Individuals*	Gifts made from current assets (such as stocks and bonds, real estate, life insurance) that are designed to maximize tax and other financial benefits. This also includes bequests made from a will, annuities, and other types of legacy gifts.	Start-up costs in materials, information, and technical expertise. The more complex the offerings, the more costly the program	Same as for major gifts.	Same as for major gifts. *Being more proactive in encouraging planned gifts is a good starting point for smaller nonprofits.* More complex gifts are not generally suitable for smaller organizations.

Type of Fundraising and Donor Category	What It Is	Financial Resources	Human Resources	Most Suitable for
Sponsorships *Business/ Corporate*	Gifts from corporate and business donors that purchase benefits and exposure for the sponsor	Recognition, event planning. Costs are part of event budget.	Can be volunteers or staff or mixed. Sponsor support should usually be handled by staff.	All sizes. Sponsor/ nonprofit alignment and clear goals are key.

Revisiting My Past

So if I had known and understood the six principles, and if I had understood the breadth and complexity of fundraising, what would I have done differently? I like to think it would have looked more like this:

Step One

Before I agreed to the contract, I would have researched the organization and its fundraising history. I would have asked some key questions:

- What is its fundraising history?

- Why do they want to do a corporate campaign?

- What is their fundraising target for this campaign?

- To what extent is the board willing to be engaged?

- What do I need to know about fundraising in general?

Step Two

I would have tried to understand the reasons why people might want to give to this organization. I should have:

- Talked to some clients to understand the benefits of this particular service from their perspective

Doing It Right

- Talked to some frontline staff to get their perspective on the organization's mission and value in the community

- Talked to other donors to find out why they give or gave

- Dug into the need for community support (why did they need the money, what would they do with it, what was the financial picture really like)

- *Built a case for support that captured the heart and soul, and the facts, about the organization and its mission*

Step Three

Once my research was completed I would have then made a presentation to the board that included a plan and recommended fundraising strategies. My key recommendation would have been related to whether or not a corporate campaign was the best strategy for this organization at that time.

Step Four

Assuming a corporate campaign was the best strategy, I would still have researched top corporate prospects with the following differences:

- I would have prioritized my top 10–15 prospects and identified strategies that included board members in building relationships with those prospects.

- Each cultivation and request would have been customized and personalized.

- Each ask would be face-to-face and letters would have only been sent to secure a meeting, provide information, or to follow up.

Step Five

This would have included timely and personalized follow-up to underscore the urgency of need and the value of their potential support. For example,

Doing It Right

if there is no follow-up to see if the recipient has any particular questions or *if the follow-up comes weeks rather than days after the package has been received, then the need will seem less urgent to the prospective donor*. Once contact has been completed with all initial prospects I would then move on to other lower priority candidates on the list.

If I had done all of these things, I would not have been surprised by newspaper headlines because I would have known this information in advance and built a plan that was appropriate.

Here's the thing . . . *fundraising is not just about getting out there and asking*. Asking is not step one. You need to understand, to plan thoughtfully and strategically, and to assess your particular organizational strengths, weaknesses, and competitive position in the community. Your organization and your environment are unique and your development program must be, too.

Dos and Don'ts

Fundraising Dos and Don'ts

- DON'T be a tin-cup fundraiser. You are not begging, you are offering an opportunity to meet a donor's needs.

- DO understand and promote the relationship between fundraising and philanthropy: *philanthropists need you*. This may well be the most important factor in your success.

- DON'T talk about how great your organization is; talk about the change you make in people's lives and in the community. Link potential donors directly to your mission.

- DON'T make the mistake of not asking because you think they will know what you want. Make sure your staff, your board members, and your volunteers make *direct and specific* asks.

- DO find out why people give and what will interest a particular donor or donor group in your mission or what will motivate them to make a gift.

Dos and Don'ts

- DON'T underestimate today's smart and savvy donors. Expect that they will have checked you out, and honor their time.

- DO include fundraising in the strategic planning process from the beginning.

- DON'T rely on one type of fundraising (special events) or one type of donor (businesses). Recognize that there are different motivations and preferred vehicles for giving.

Conclusion: A Noble Calling

I recently heard Archbishop Desmond Tutu speak to an audience of 3,000 fundraisers, executive directors, and nonprofit leaders. He said we had "a noble calling." Why? Because fundraising is an enabler of philanthropy and it is through philanthropy and nonprofit work that millions of children around the world are fed, clothed, and given clean water. It is through philanthropy and nonprofit work that women around the world are given the opportunity to be independent and free to create change. It is through philanthropy and nonprofit work that the research to cure cancer continues, that youth are taken care of on and off the streets, and that our communities are rich with art and culture for all to enjoy. Fundraising is important and meaningful work . . . and it is work to be proud of because it helps to change the world by making it a better place. But simply "getting" this isn't enough. It's about working smarter, not harder, and by putting the practices outlined above into action, you can be assured that your nonprofit can help interested and willing philanthropists connect with a cause they truly care about.

Andrea McManus is president of The Development Group, a full-service strategic philanthropic consulting firm in Calgary, Alberta, Canada. A leader in the nonprofit sector locally, nationally, and internationally, Andrea is currently chair of the Association of Fundraising Professionals (AFP) Board and is the first international chair of that organization. Recognized by the Calgary Chapter as its Outstanding Fundraising Professional for 2007 she is also an AFP Master Teacher and speaks frequently at conferences and workshops in Canada.

Nonprofit Fundraising Resource Review

The Association of Fundraising Professionals (AFP) (www.afpnet.org)

> AFP is the largest professional fundraising association in the world and offers education, training, and resources for all levels of fundraisers and all types of organizations, as well as a wonderful annual conference and over 205 local chapters.

S. P. Joyaux. Strategic Fund Development: Building Profitable Relationships That Last, (2nd ed.). Gaithersburg, MD: Aspen, 2001.

> A staple resource that guides you through developing a fund development plan that is strategic and relevant.

P. Burk. Thanks: A Guide to Donor-Centered Fundraising. Toronto, Ontario: Burk & Associates, 2000.

> A helpful and practical overview for creating a donor-centric fundraising program that builds long-lasting relationships with your supporters.

The Fundraising Beat (www.thedevelopmentgroup.ca/blog)

> My blog on all things near and dear to a fundraiser's heart.

G. Perry. Fired-Up Fundraising: Turn Board Passion into Action. Hoboken, NJ: Wiley, 2007.

> A fabulous resource on working with your board and engaging them in fundraising leadership roles.

Idealist's Tools for Nonprofits (www.idealist.org/tools/fundraising.html)

One of the most robust lists of nonprofit fundraising resources on the Internet.

Foundation Center (www.fdncenter.org)

Great online resource for researching potential foundation funders; they also have several physical locations in major cities around the United States where you can get free advice and access their robust database.

The Chronicle of Philanthropy (www.philanthropy.com)

Wonderful industry rag that does a good job announcing major gifts and other big industry news.

Cause Effective Perspective (www.causeeffectiveperspective.net/)

Insightful blog that frequently covers fundraising topics.

About.com's Fundraising Essentials (www.nonprofit.about.com/od/fundraising/Fundraising_Tips_and_Tools.htm)

Extensive directory of a wide array of nonprofit fundraising content.

∘ ∘ ∘

All these resources, plus nonprofit management tips of the week and more, can be found at Nonprofits101.org.

CHAPTER 19

Individual Donor and Major Gift Strategies: The 83% Solution to Fundraising

By Kay Sprinkel Grace, CFRE, Founder, Transforming Philanthropy, LLC

Introduction: The Biggest Slice of the Pie

Year after year, the data are the same. In the United States, *individuals, through outright and estate gifts, provide 83% or more of all gifts to nonprofits*. Given this, an individual donor strategy is crucial to the success of most any nonprofit. In June, 2010, Giving USA released their 2009 annual report of philanthropic gifts to nonprofits; of the total $303.75 billion dollars given, individuals gave $227.41 in outright gifts and $23.8 through their estates, for a total of $256.21 billion. Foundations provided $38.44 billion (13%) and corporations

$14.1 (4%). Let's take a deeper dive into the biggest slice of the philanthropic pie.

Individuals fund the full array of community needs. In 2009 they directed their gifts to religion, education, their own family foundations, human services, health, public benefit, arts/culture/humanities, international aid, and environment/animals. Their gifts ranged in size from a dollar left in an envelope at a church to texted donations of $5 in response to international social and environmental crises to the millions of dollars committed by individuals of great wealth and passion. In 2010, the world's attention was riveted to the list of individuals who participated in The Giving Pledge launched by Bill and Melinda Gates and Warren Buffett. This exceptional group of billionaires committed to give half or more of their assets to philanthropic causes.

What motivates individuals to give? Increasingly, *individual donors view their gifts as dynamic investments in both their community and in the social sector, rather than passive donations or contributions.* They hold huge expectations for return on investment and for reporting on impact—whether the gift is $5 or $5 million. They view these gifts as *social* investments—their stake in bettering society and improving the human condition. They exemplify the "two portfolio" approach to philanthropic investment: *they transfer money from their financial investment portfolio into their social investment portfolio because they want a values-based return*: children cured of cancer, families protected from domestic abuse, accessible arts and culture in their communities, superior education for children or any of the myriad issues in which donors invest.

Participation in individual giving is not limited to the United States. As the rest of the world looks increasingly beyond government funding, and welcomes both the surge of border-spanning online giving from "citizen philanthropists" and very large gifts from a rising number of wealthy individuals in countries from India to Mexico to China to Ukraine, their percentages are starting to change. An organization formed under the auspices of the Australian government, artsupport [*sic*], not only mentors arts organizations about attracting individual giving: it also works with philanthropists and their individual trusts to encourage them to invest in the arts. And, as an increasing number of governments in Europe and elsewhere consider ways to encourage posthumous "legacy" giving through tax advantages to cultural and other institutions, estate gifts will grow globally and tip the balance even more significantly towards individual investment.

In spite of these data, a myth persists that corporate and foundation giving is the quick fix for struggling, new, or even mature organizations. Although we do not minimize the impact of corporate and foundation giving, recent economic volatility has eroded foundation portfolios and led many corporations to lessen or cease giving until their shareholders once again give the green light. Individual giving has been the first to rebound from the dip experienced by nonprofits in 2008 and 2009. And government giving, which is not included in the annual survey of philanthropic support in the United States, has diminished significantly over the last 40 years in the United States—a trend that is prevalent now in many countries, particularly within Western Europe. Although the U.S. government stimulus funds granted to many nonprofits in 2009 countered this trend briefly, that was clearly emergency relief and cannot be anticipated in subsequent years. All the more reason why it's key to any nonprofit's success to engage individual donors to support their efforts.

So What's the Holdup?

If the data are so clear, why do organizations fail to embrace individual giving until the other sources of philanthropic revenue have begun to shrink? One problem is that *a healthy individual giving program—one in which donors will be grown from initial donors to long-term investors, requires board member participation.* Corporate and foundation giving (and government contracts) are staff responsibilities for the most part, and boards have handed off the responsibility all too willingly. Another is the reluctance of organizations to invest in building their giving programs: *it takes money to raise money*, but many organizations remain averse, still looking for the one-off, quick fix event or campaign rather than the systematic build up of loyal investors.

Successful individual giving at all levels is based in the capacity and determination of organizations to build relationships. This requires volunteer and staff commitment to donors from the first gift they make. It is a process that usually does not begin until a donor has self-identified with a larger gift: with the changing landscape of donor behavior and giving, the process for engaging donors needs rethinking. One donor who had stopped giving to an organization was part of a market study to determine how these donors could be brought back into the organization. Her reply became the mantra for this organization as it rebooted its donor relations programs: "They would have to *show me that they know me.*"

The Dot-Com Opportunity

As noted in Chapters Twenty-One and Twenty-Two, we have an immense opportunity, in this decade, to build individual giving programs in our organizations. The growth of Internet giving has been exponential, with the conversion of "shoppers" to "buyers" increasing significantly each year. These individual donors, like most donors, are looking for issues in which they can invest. They seek the causes they want to fund, and are driven largely by their own dreams and ideas. They may not know your organization at all, but they care about a cause and shop for organizations that serve those causes and issues. Their gifts come without invitation, and they bring a new set of challenges and opportunities to our organizations.

As social media vehicles for giving increase—particularly giving via cell phone texting which benefited many organizations during the Haitian earthquake fundraising in 2010—we are unable to follow up, track, and steward many of these donors. For crisis giving, this may not seem like a problem: the goal is to raise money quickly. However, the Red Cross is an excellent example of the need for sustainable funding between crises. In recent decades, with a series of natural disasters that led to significant restricted investment in emergency relief, Red Cross found itself without unrestricted funds to maintain operations in some communities (lifesaving programs, safety education, and so forth).

If your organization is looking to create long-term capacity through the investment of caring individuals, you will need to find a way to engage Internet, cell phone, and other social media donors, as well as more traditional donors. We have a long way to go relative to managing this new and powerful source of giving in a way that builds relationships and long-term investment.

And, in individual giving, relationships are key. *Build the relationships and the money will come; ignore the relationships and the money will go away.* The opportunity to strengthen your organization and its impact largely relies on your willingness to engage long-term social investors at all levels. Their loyalty can help increase your capacity to serve.

Critical Skills and Competencies

Individual giving begins with a conversation (or with self-identification through an online or direct mail gift) that matures into a relationship. Then, as we get to know the donor and they us, *the relationship evolves into a partnership, in which we offer continuing opportunities to invest* in causes that embrace and advance their values and address issues they care about. With requests for individual giving, there are usually no committees, no lengthy proposals, no agonizing wait. Individuals make their own decisions. And, in most cases, if you get to the point with someone where you sense it is time to ask, you will receive a gift from them. People who do not want to give will not continue to engage with you.

Securing and Stewarding Recurring Gifts

Monthly or quarterly giving is an excellent way to attract and retain donors, and it provides a much-needed stable base of support. But it can also be the enemy of relationship development unless it is constantly monitored. Donors who receive an email notice that their monthly or quarterly gift is about to happen (through EFT) may not build deep engagement with the organization unless careful stewardship is offered. Giving becomes habitual, rather than thoughtful, and some organizations are remiss at returning to the donor with reports on impact or to ask them to increase their gifts. Acknowledgement and recognition are part of stewardship, but that is not the full story. We will end this chapter with a look at the structure and importance of stewardship.

The failure of organizations to invest adequately in building an individual giving program is the other huge stumbling block. Boards and staff decision makers have to agree that it takes money to raise money, and that front-end investment in the systems, staffing, and structure to support individual giving will yield not only immediate revenue but, more important, long-term investors. Though we must monitor and be mindful of the cost of fundraising, *there are times in the life of a nonprofit when the amount invested in fundraising is a larger percentage: new donors and new strategies are being tested, analyzed for impact, modified for increased success, and developed until they gain traction and measurable results.*

Traditional teaching about individual giving likened the structure of donor support in any organization to a pyramid, with a strong base of initial and renewed donors which you retained while growing some of them into higher levels of the pyramid: moving donors towards increased gifts, special gifts for projects or programs, major gifts both annual and capital, and finally, at the top, the big gift– both outright and planned (estate or legacy). The pyramid hardly exists today. Working with organizations as they prepare for major fundraising programs, analysis reveals more of an hourglass: a base of regular individual giving donors (with a high level of "churn"—*the loss of first-time donors is as high as 40–50% in some organizations*), an equally imposing upper part of the hourglass where the well-stewarded and engaged larger gift donors reside—and in the middle, the slender waist of the hourglass—the shrinking number of donors who move up from the base to the top through engagement with the organization. One participant in a workshop, when presented with the hourglass model, remarked that his organization wasn't like that. Thrilled, I asked if had a true donor pyramid. "No," he said, "we have two ovals. We have no donors in the middle."

The churn in the base often leads to a frenzied donor acquisition program that is not embedded in a strategic individual giving plan. Immediate revenue is generated through direct mail and special events—two time- and fund-consuming activities—often with little follow up except a feeling of relief for having squeaked by a financial crisis. It also leads to urgent email "blasts" with little follow up. An established theatre company in one city sent out emergency emails to all of its subscribers and single ticket buyers, letting them know that unless they raised $200,000 within the month, they would have to close. People responded, and they met their goal. The nonprofit was lucky—people don't usually like to give to a sinking ship, so it's important to focus on your accomplishments and impact rather than putting out a tin cup. Said another way, *people don't give to you because you have needs, but because you meet needs.* Either way, donor follow-up is crucial. Unfortunately, 60 days later, the theatre company's donors had received no acknowledgment and no report. A donor reported she did not know they had reached their goal until she read it in the newspaper. A subsequent annual appeal failed. It is almost certain they will face another crisis, but there is no certainty that people will respond. *Timely thanking, reports on progress and success, and ongoing communications are essential to building a sustainable individual giving program.*

Another organization, evaluating its year-end results, said they had received 80 gifts from more than 500 solicitations—most by email and most personalized by a board member or other volunteer. They thought their work was done; that the disappointing response was something they simply had to live with. When told that meant they had over 420 open solicitations out in the community, they viewed their results in a different way, and made plans for follow-up. *It reflects poorly on organizations—and on the authors of those emails or letters—when there is no follow-up.* It may say to the prospective donor that this was a half-hearted outreach and that their investment is not really important. They are now launching activities to follow up with those 420 open asks, many of which were to new potential donors. *Acquisition is tough in the kind of economy we have been experiencing, but it is more successful when there is a link with someone they know.* With renewals, people will stick with the organizations they know but they need follow up. They will give, perhaps not as much, but their loyalty drives them to give what they can with hopes of giving more. *We spend too much time on acquisition because we don't spend time on building relationships that will help retain our donors*—in the business world they say it's seven times as expensive to acquire a customer as to retain one, and this is no different in our sector. This tilt in resource allocation is disrupting our long-term sustainability and capacity to serve our communities.

This, then, is the challenge we face. The top of the hourglass will age out, ideally setting up estate gifts that are directed to nonprofits when they pass away; others at the top will move on to different organizations as their interests shift. We need to replenish the top constantly by moving people up from the base. This takes not only staff-developed systems for acknowledgment, recognition and stewardship—it requires involvement of board and non-board volunteers who will participate actively in donor retention and stewardship.

Getting People to Make the Ask

Most of the problem is attitudinal. *People give to people—that has been a basic cornerstone of individual giving for decades.* Yet most people, including some board members, say they will do anything for your organization—except ask for money. The origins of that reluctance are easily identified: people fear rejection (especially from their friends) and they do not understand what they are really doing when they ask: inviting social investment in an organization that is making an impact in the geographical, social, cultural, educational, or environmental areas that the prospective donor cares about. Help them understand that and they'll be more likely to fundraise for you.

Volunteers respond well to some key principles that help them reset the notion of what individual solicitation is all about. These are the three that I emphasize in my work. They form the basis of successful giving programs—particularly individual giving:

- As mentioned, people give to an organization because the organization meets needs, not because the organization has needs. *We need to talk about impact and results, not financial needs.* Our sector is not about "needy" organizations—it is about strong organizations that meet critical human, societal, educational, cultural and other needs.

- *A gift to an organization is really a gift through an organization into the community.* The organization is not the end user of the gift. When impact is conveyed it is not about how the organization has grown, but how the organization is working in the arena of shared values to alleviate human suffering or enhance human potential (Payton).

- *Fundraising is not about money, it is about relationships.* Build the relationships and the money will come; ignore the relationship and the money will go away. There are a variety of roles people can play in the fundraising process, and even if their best role is introducing prospects into the pipeline, that is still an integral component of the fundraising process—make this known to your board, staff and volunteers and watch them get involved.

These principles provide a solid frame for all philanthropic giving regardless of source. However, the actual skill set for corporate and foundation giving staff may be different from that required of someone who will develop, direct and sustain an individual giving program. Often, when hiring a person for corporate and foundation giving we are looking for a good proposal writer. When looking for an individual giving manager, we look for interpersonal and relationship management skills. Although some people are gifted with both writing and interpersonal skills, that combination is harder to find. In a small shop, where there is cross-training or even just one person in charge of all kinds of giving, a common model is to hire for the interpersonal and relationship management skills (which are also handy for long-term foundation and corporation relations) and hire a contract grant writer to write the proposals.

The donor management database is also critical for successful individual giving. When people ask me what tools I wish I had in my early years in fundraising, I am quick to respond, "technology." Although I managed a successful program with three-by-five-inch and then four-by-six-inch cards with donor information, and generated reports on an electric typewriter which I then mimeographed for distribution—I often think of how much more I could have done with the tools and software I have now. These tools not only save time, they leverage our knowledge, connections, and impact.

The Fundraising Toolkit

If you want to engage volunteers (board and non-board) who will engage their friends and others from the community in your organization as investors, you will need to provide both tools and training.

Give them a volunteer "toolkit" stocked with:

- Stories of your impact to add a personal touch to your role in the community

- The elevator speech (and the elevator question—what do you say after you've said the speech to ensure that the conversation is just the beginning?)

- Facts about the organization (i.e., number of people served, before and after statistics, and so on)

- Analysis of the organization's impact measured against the needs of the community

- Most commonly heard questions and objections to giving and the recommended response (volunteers don't like to look stupid—some confess that is why they don't talk to their friends about the organization: they feel they do not know enough and cannot handle questions well)

- Highlights from the strategic plan (if you have one) that may be relevant to some potential donors

- Annotated list of board and staff members (people are curious—"who's in charge of that program?")

- Full financial information, presented in an understandable format (in addition to numbers, use pie charts or bar graphs—many people glaze over when looking at numbers)

Volunteer and Board Fundraising: Training Makes All the Difference

Training is the greatest source of confidence building. *Provide training in cultivating, asking and stewardship to all board members*, even those who have told you they will never ask for a gift. They should still know what it entails. There are numerous training programs you can use—my own choice is one that begins with a walk through the steps in the full development process from identification through renewal of the gift, and then to focus on the big three: cultivation, solicitation and stewardship. Showing them the various options for cultivation—tours, performances, meetings with staff leaders, attendance at lectures, visits to the prospect's workplace—opens them to the idea that there is more to this process than cold-calling. *Taking them through the sequence of activities that are employed before an ask is made has turned reluctant board and non-board volunteers to ones willing to share names and get involved.*

Once into the conversation, the dialogue rolls forward. It is exhilarating even if the person says no. Why? Because every conversation, every intersection, plants the seed for some future action. If a person does not give to you now, it probably means they don't know enough, this is not a current priority, or they are a bit short of risk capital to try out a new organization. It is far better to build a donor relationship gradually and know it is really an investment in the organization than to twist arms or rely on calling in personal favors. Otherwise, when the board member or volunteer steps aside from active involvement, that gift will go away.

Individual giving programs need not be a burden to an organization. *Start small, with a few donor prospects that are already closely connected to your work and your team.* Assure your board members of the process: you will not solicit anyone without their knowledge or participation. I have found that *board members are reluctant to submit names because they don't know how that information will be used.* Build confidence in your board members by focusing on the successes of those who have participated. Not all successes will be solicitations: it is equally important for board members to bring potential investors to the organization and let the executive director be the point person for the ask.

How to Secure Larger Gifts from People Over Time: Donor Stewardship

The goal of an individual giving program is to build a relationship that results not only in continued investment, but increased investment. At the theatre company mentioned earlier, it is more than likely that those donors who responded and then were not informed about the results of their giving will be less likely to give, and probably will not feel inspired to give more.

Stewardship is the ongoing relationship with a donor after the gift has been made. We put such time and effort into getting the gift, that it is tempting to feel the process is over: we acknowledge the gift, perhaps recognize the donor (depending on the size of the gift), and then we allow the donor to languish in the donor data maintenance system (see Chapter Seventeen on CRM) until—you guessed it—the next time we want money. This is a crippling sequence for the long-term growth of a potentially loyal donor. What we fail to recognize is that the transaction, as described above, is all about us: what we will do to bring a donor into our database. We need to think instead of the process as a transformation (Grace and Wendroff, <u>High Impact Philanthropy</u>)—one in which the donor is regarded as an investor and is provided a "return on investment" based on the values that led to the investment. We must keep people involved with information and reports, especially when we're not asking them for money—and technology has made that so much easier for us. Quick emails about an accomplishment or news about the issue your organization addresses are read and remembered. Few people today pore over lengthy printed annual reports—they take their news in sound bites and expect our information to be delivered that way, too.

Stewardship is defined by what the donor wants. We need to ask our donors how and how often they want to be informed of our progress, and then follow up appropriately. We need to provide a calendar for board members of opportunities to bring donors to our organizations. One organization I work with is conducting "Breakfast Briefings"—hour-long breakfast meetings, on-site, showcasing success stories told by former clients who were helped by the program, and providing an opportunity for the very articulate executive director to talk about the opportunities for community investment. They have proven to be incredibly effective at driving fundraising; anytime you can connect your work to real people and life-changing stories, it helps donors connect the dots and see the impact. A calendar of these briefings—or other tours, talks, or gatherings—encourages board members to invite those they meet to attend. The board member does not have to invent or organize the opportunity—it already exists.

In 2008, the U.S. Trust/Bank of America study of the giving behavior of high net worth individuals provided an alarming statistic relative to our lax stewardship practices. The study revealed that 37% of donors had stopped giving to organizations they had previously supported. That news is bad enough. But the primary reason was even worse: 58% said they stopped giving because they felt they no longer had a personal connection with the organization. We can fix that. It is a wonderful way to engage board members who are not confident about asking: have them be stewards of donors—the payoff will be simply astounding.

Individual Donor Dos and Don'ts

- DO get your board engaged in fundraising by providing training, a toolkit, an event calendar, and enlisting their help with stewarding current donors. Assure them of the process and that you will not solicit their contacts without their knowledge or participation.

- DON'T take a tin-cup approach to fundraising—remember that people don't give to you because you *have* needs, but because you *meet* needs, so focus on your accomplishments and impact. A gift *to* your organization is really a gift *through* you to a cause and community the prospective or current donor cares about.

- DO ask your donors how they want to be informed of your progress, and how often, and then follow up appropriately—timely thanking, reports on progress and success, and ongoing communications are essential to building a sustainable individual giving program.

- DON'T pursue an hourglass of donors versus a pyramid—steward your donors towards larger gifts over time by keeping them informed and engaged, and communicating with them when you're *not* asking for money. Move them seamlessly up the giving ladder.

- DO keep it personal—focus on personal stories of your impact, and leverage personal relationships with donor prospects whenever possible. People give to people, and fundraising is not about money, it is about relationships.

- DON'T ever forget that it's much more expensive and difficult to acquire a new donor than to keep an existing one.

- DO realize it takes money to raise money; an investment in your fundraising infrastructure and planning is an investment in your future and growth.

Conclusion

Individual donors remain our most abundant, reliable and easy-to-engage investors. The movement to social investment in this century has been accelerating. And, as financial markets have stumbled and caused alarm, we can still point with pride to the impact of people's social investment. Everyone carries two investment portfolios: financial (even if only the checkbook) and social. We move money from one to enrich the other. We need to focus on the impact of those social investments: people helped, environmental improvement, cultural and artistic accomplishments, educational achievement. That is the news we need to convey—not our persistent need for money. *The only reason we need money for our organizations is because we are meeting needs.* It is not about us, it is about the donor and the dreams they have for their communities, their region or the world.

In individuals, we have our most loyal and long-term donors. They become partners in achieving the vision of your organization, and their involvement will heighten their commitment and their willingness to become "donor champions" and bring in others. Allocate your resources increasingly to individual giving: it is the most reliable, beneficial, and consistent source of support you can have.

Kay Sprinkel Grace (www.kaygrace.org) is passionate about philanthropy and has devoted the last thirty years to the nonprofit sector, providing seminal thought, habit-breaking strategies, challenges to board and staff, and reengineering the vocabulary of fundraising. Her six books and frequent speaking engagements across the globe reflect her restless quest for an ever-improved capacity of organizations to truly serve their communities. A Stanford graduate (BA, MA), she has built on a career in journalism and education to create a business practice and reputation that draw from the best of both.

Individual Donor Resource Review

Penelope Burke. <u>Donor-Centered Fund Raising</u>. U.S. Edition. Chicago: Cygnus Applied Research, 2003.

Cygnus conducts an annual survey of 15,000 donor families in North America. This book, written by Cygnus' founder and CEO, makes the strongest case for remembering that when it comes to giving, it is all about the donor.

J. Gregory Dees, Jed Emerson, and Peter Economy. <u>Strategic Tools for Social Entrepreneurs</u>. New Jersey: Wiley, 2002.

Pioneers in social entrepreneurship, the authors gathered chapters from a variety of social investment and philanthropic professionals and compiled them into this comprehensive resource book about the growing emphasis on social investment.

Kay Sprinkel Grace, and Alan Wendroff. <u>High Impact Philanthropy</u>. New Jersey: Wiley, 2001.

The authors develop the key concept of transformational giving, and how it differs from transactional giving, and provide practical strategies for development marketing and solicitation of major gifts.

Kay Sprinkel Grace. <u>Beyond Fundraising</u>. New Jersey: Wiley, 2005.

Used by volunteers, professionals, and in many university nonprofit degree/certificate programs, this is the comprehensive A–Z book on relationship-based donor development and fundraising, including extensive chapters on mission, vision, values, and board engagement.

Tom Ralser. <u>ROI for Nonprofits: The New Key to Sustainability</u>. New Jersey: Wiley, 2007.

The ROI described is not just return on donor values: this book goes further into the wider return on investment to communities that encourage philanthropic organizations and participation.

Henry A. Rosso and Associates. <u>Achieving Excellence in Fund Raising</u>. San Francisco: Jossey-Bass, 2003.

A comprehensive compendium of essays by leaders in the nonprofit field, covering a variety of topics consistent with the founding principles and current practices of The Fundraising School at the Center on Philanthropy at Indiana University.

Kay Sprinkel Grace. <u>The AAA Way to Fundraising Success: Maximum Involvement, Maximum Results</u>. Whit Press, Jackson Hole, 2009.

If you are a nonprofit board member—or a professional who works with nonprofit board members—here is a solution for getting ALL board members engaged in donor development and fundraising. That's right: ALL.

Mal Warwick. <u>Fundraising When Money Is Tight</u>. San Francisco: Jossey Bass, 2009.

This book is really about sustainability: although inspired by the deep issues that surfaced in the Recession, the principles and advice offered by this guru are timeless.

Tactical Philanthropy (www.tacticalphilanthropy.com)

Insightful blog that offers stories and essays addressing the trends and challenges facing philanthropists and nonprofits.

The Chronicle of Philanthropy (www.philanthropy.com)

Online version of a great industry publication—offers news updates on major gifts, job opportunities, and stories covering current events and issues in the social sector.

○ ○ ○

All these resources, plus nonprofit management tips of the week and more, can be found at Nonprofits101.org.

CHAPTER 20

How to Seek a Grant

By Tori O'Neal-McElrath, Director of Institutional Advancement, Center for Community Change

> The majority of funders are much more interested in a meaningful and engaged relationship that is beyond the simple grant transaction.
>
> —Gwen Walden, Walden Philanthropy Advisors

Introduction

Much has been written on the technical aspects of grant seeking—and there certainly is a technique to it. But my truth is this: rarely have I ever simply "sought a grant" and ended up successful. It does happen. But it is rare.

The strictly technical approach presents grant seeking as transactional. It implies that there is nothing more involved than responding to the grant guidelines, writing a strong and compelling proposal, followed by securing the funding. This "grant seeking as sales" way of thinking is generally not effective. Experience has proven over and over again that *seeking relationships with those who make or recommend grants is what leads to securing funds*. This approach is *relational* rather than *transactional*, and it is the key to success.

In my first couple of years in development (fundraising), I quickly realized that I had a "heart-and-gut" approach to the work. For me to think of fundraising as sales would reduce what I considered a noble calling down to a transaction. So I began to *view fundraising as a transfer of enthusiasm*—an opportunity to connect my organization and its mission with a person who shared its passion and who had the resources to support it. It is from this perspective that I developed a philosophy that would carry me through twenty years and counting: relationship building, transferring enthusiasm, and connecting of passions as the true tools of development. Not transactions. And yes; this philosophy absolutely applies to grant seeking.

Critical Skills and Competencies

There are many things you should know and implement when it comes to grant seeking, the vast majority of which has nothing to do with writing the grant. What most people fail to realize is that *by the time you are actually writing the grant, approximately 70% of the work towards securing it should already be completed.* Think of it as building a house. Before you get to the bricks and mortar, there are architectural drawings to be rendered and approved, permits to be secured, land to be prepared, supplies to be gathered, and the right crew to be assembled. So it goes with grant writing.

Mission Speaks to Mission

Complete your homework—prospect research—up front to identify foundations whose missions align with your organization. Making sure the identified prospects are indeed a match for your organization in general and your program in specific (if seeking programmatic funding) is a must. Start locally by indentifying the funding sources available in your community . . . your town . . . your county or parish . . . your state. There are numerous resources for grant seekers, most of which can be found on the Internet and in the Resource Review at the end of this chapter, as well as in the local library and nonprofit resource centers like local volunteer centers or community foundations across the country.

Be creative and take a good look around: Is there a major corporation located in your community? Are there active service organizations in your city? Who are some of the institutions funding similar organizations in your area, but who are not yet funding your organization? These are all leads to possible funding opportunities and good places to begin your prospect research.

The mission connection referred to in this chapter may happen with the foundation's overall stated mission. The connection may also occur within a specific programmatic area of the foundation. A program area is a specific focus by the foundation in a direct effort to fulfill its mission. For example, a foundation focused on eliminating health disparities as its mission might have specific program areas focused on access to health and on the reduction of infant mortality.

A foundation might also have a particular "Theory of Change," with which you might seek a common connection. A theory of change is an organization's definition of all the building blocks required to bring about their given long-term goal (i.e., recycling as a component of addressing climate change).

Ultimately, prospect research should unearth those foundations with which your organization connects before any additional time is invested. After preliminary research is completed and possible funding prospects are identified, reach out to each foundation on your list to establish contact and find out more about the following:

- How much does the program officer know about your organization or your programs? What else would they like to know at this time?

- What does a success look like at their foundation?

- How has their previous grant making informed their current efforts?

- What are the top three qualities they look for in a grantee organization that are not specifically stated in the grant guidelines?

- Should it be determined that there is a match between the foundation and your organization, would the program officer be willing to review your Letter of Intent (LOI) or proposal *prior* to submission to provide feedback? (An LOI is generally a short two- to three-page summary that provides a brief snapshot of your organization and the project to be funded. It is meant to entice the program officer to invite a full proposal for consideration.)

- Do they know of colleagues at other foundations who might be interested in learning more about your organization or program? This is a relationship-leveraging question that can open doors you don't even know exist relative to other possible funding sources.

This list is only a random sampling of the kinds of questions you might want to ask a potential funder. Do your homework to gain a much better sense of what questions make sense to be asked relative to your funding request. Also, the answers to many of the most obvious questions can typically be found in the grant guidelines and on the foundation's website—research is key.

The optimal situation is to *engage a staff person working within the program area from which you are seeking funding.* Typically these people are "program officers," and their job is to do one or more of the following: create the funding guidelines for program areas based on their board's stated priorities, review grant requests, manage the budget for their program area, and make funding recommendations to the foundation's board of directors or grants committee. *Many family foundations do not have staff*; the donor or a family member on the foundation board might be the person with whom you make contact.

Reach out via email to request a meeting with a program officer. There are but so many hours in a day; therefore, every organization requesting an in-person meeting will not get one. Should efforts to secure an in-person meeting prove unsuccessful, try to schedule a phone call, though the same time limitations apply to phone calls as they do to meetings. That being said, you don't know until you ask!

Should an in-person meeting or phone call with a program officer be secured, *be prepared.* These meetings are likely to happen within a tight window of time (average time: 30–45 minutes), so you want to use it well and *listen as actively as you talk.* If an in-person or phone meeting cannot be secured, consider engaging the program officer via email. This strategy is typically met with a positive response as it allows maximum flexibility for foundation staff in terms of response time.

Engaging the program officer via email, in lieu of an in-person meeting or phone call, can be useful to answer key questions and help determine whether or not to submit a proposal or LOI. Establishing a longer-term rapport with a program officer can absolutely begin with a two-way email exchange.

There are times when contact with the program officer does not happen at any level for whatever reason. When this occurs, seek to connect with someone else at the foundation such as the grants manager/administrator or administrative assistant, who can provide the basic information you need—as well as allow you to get the name of your organization in the mind of someone on the inside the foundation.

The point here is that *investing in relationships with foundation staff starts well before a proposal or LOI is ever submitted.*

Clearly State Your Case

Make sure your organization's mission, vision, purpose, and goals are clear and easy both to articulate and comprehend. Sounds basic—common sense, right? When an organization has pressing demands, compelling missions, and growing needs to meet, sometimes common sense steps get lost in the shuffle; that mad dash with which we are all too familiar. Staff leadership is not always paying attention to the critical necessity of externally communicating the answers to some key questions:

- What was it that created the demand for your organization? Who benefits when you fulfill your mission—and why is that important?

- Why should people care? What makes your organization different from others providing similar services? *Focus on your uniqueness as an organization, rather than any perceived deficits of other organizations providing similar services.* Keep it positive.

- How do you do what you do? Are you a direct service or technical assistance provider? Do you have specific expertise in an area, or are you working with people from the community who are passionate about addressing a community need and you recruit people with specific expertise as needed?

- How do you measure impact, and *how will that impact be advanced if you were to receive a grant from this foundation?*

The ability to succinctly answer these questions is all a part of effectively stating your case. It is also serves as the connective tissue between your organization and potential funders.

Evaluate Your Organization's Capacity to Deliver on Your Promises

Being able to clearly articulate an unmet need that an organization can, will, and should meet is another important aspect of grant seeking. The selection of the words <u>can</u>, <u>will</u>, and <u>should</u> are deliberate. Funders want to know if an organization <u>can</u> successfully meet the challenge of the unmet need. It is not enough to identify the unmet need; the organization needs to be able to address it. This includes a solid plan of action, trained staff, and organizational commitment from the top.

Funders also want to know if an organization <u>will</u> do as promised in its proposal. Many an organization has started out with the best of intentions when the proposal is developed, yet by the time the grant is awarded and the money arrives, the "will"—both literally and figuratively speaking—is questionable. If the commitment to the funded project is not clear, the funding can sometimes inadvertently "morph" into funding for other projects, or for general operating support. I cannot emphasize strongly enough how dangerous a situation this is—inadvertent or otherwise. Using restricted funding for any purpose other than as specifically outlined in the grant agreement is illegal, violates the public trust, and can destroy the relationship an organization has with its funder. Please refer to Chapter Thirteen for more information on restricted grants.

Finally, the question of <u>should</u> is a valid one. Here's an example: A homeless shelter provides a place to rest, food, and psychosocial counseling for its clients. Someone on staff identifies an unmet need for reproductive health services, so staff begins to craft a proposal for funding to expand services to include it. Staff has documented the need for such services with clear and compelling data, and is passionate about seeing that this need is met. The question is: Should this organization be the one to meet this clearly identified need? Is it a core part of its mission? Is expansion into this service area included in its strategic plan? Has staff explored other options to meet this need, such as partnering with a community clinic in the area? If the organization did receive a grant to meet this unmet need, how would the new services be sustained upon completion of the grant?

Following <u>can</u>, <u>will</u>, and <u>should</u> is an organization's ability to demonstrate through a step-by-step plan how the organization will meet the need identified. This, too, is an indicator of an organization's readiness to seek grant funding. Program planning precedes grant writing because without a clearly articulated program plan, securing funding is a long shot at best. A program plan outlines how an organization proposes to do what it says it will. Think about it this way: if the program officer of a local foundation receives three proposals from three different youth programs targeting the same demographic, what will make one proposal stand out from another?

If a proposal successfully walks the reader through a program plan in a way that is easily understandable, and it demonstrates that it is somehow in a uniquely better position to meet the need, that particular organization stands a much better chance of pulling ahead of the pack. This means putting forth your best effort to leave the industry jargon by the wayside (easier said than done!) and speaking in plain language so that the reader can comprehend, and ideally connect, to what is being conveyed.

Highlight Your Organization's Unique Background

Each organization's experience, abilities, and talents should be crystallized by way of a strong background statement, which is an essential part of any proposal or LOI, and is discussed later in the chapter. This is an organization's chance to brag a little by presenting the evidence that confirms your readiness and qualifications to successfully address the issue being proposed. This "brag section"—your organization's background statement—should be continually updated, as many times those of us working in nonprofits forget to celebrate all the little (and not so little) victories we achieve along the way. An organization's consistently refreshed background statement will also *keep your overall approach positive and asset-based,* which is essential when grant seeking.

Stick to the Basics

Another important part of seeking a grant is understanding the basics of grant writing itself. You've already done a fair amount of writing, as you have crafted your case statement, created your program plan, and produced (and continually refreshed) your organization's background statement. You are well on your way. But there is still some writing to be completed, as information needs to be shaped into the form requested by each potential funder. A key point to keep in mind: *each funder has its own grant guidelines. One size does not fit all—or even most!* So while there is a basic grant writing methodology, which is discussed in the following paragraph, you must stick closely to each foundation's individual grant guidelines when constructing your proposal or LOI.

The general rule is that grant proposals—and to a modified extent LOIs—will contain the following standard components:

1. Executive summary/proposal summary/summary

2. Need statement/statement of need/problem statement

3. Goals and objectives

4. Methods and strategies

5. Evaluation

6. Sustainability

7. Organization background and background statement

8. Budget

Some funding institutions will require a detailed proposal, whereas others will request a two- to three-page proposal letter. Some foundations require an LOI prior to submitting a full proposal; others offer an online submission process where defined and space-limited fields are established in place of a written LOI. In other words, a scattershot approach to grant seeking will lead to frustration, disappointment and, ultimately, a lack of funding.

Foundations go to great lengths to establish and articulate what they are interested in funding. *The job of grant seekers is to develop a plan for meeting each individual funder's needs as articulated in their grant guidelines.*

Other Areas of Importance

The importance of establishing relationships with funding institutions is a recurring theme throughout this chapter. Its importance cannot be overstated. Now let's take a look at a few other areas of importance on which managers should focus.

Who Writes the Grant?

The grant writer needs to be someone who has a strong understanding of your organizational mission in general, and of your programmatic focus in specific. *In many cases, the best person to write the grant is the person running the program.* In other cases it is better to hire a consultant, as they bring fresh eyes to the process and can help identify programmatic gaps needing to be addressed, effectively translate your vision into words, and add capacity to your staff.

Because this process is primarily about building relationships, *staff should always be the point of contact with foundations.* Never, ever contract out your relationship building with funders.

How to Find an Outside Grant Writer

If you determine that outside assistance is needed, there are a few paths to consider to ensure the right services are secured. *Seek referrals from other organizations that have successfully used grant writers.* Many times colleagues will share the names of consultants who have proven successful for them. Secure referrals from the Grant Professionals Association (previously the American Association of Grant Professionals [AAGP]) and the Association of Fundraising Professionals (AFP). Both organizations have searchable online databases where you can find consultants. Reach out to a former staff person who is now freelancing. They already know your organization from the inside, which will serve you well. Finally, consider asking the program officer or administrative assistant at the foundation. Some foundations—community foundations in particular—compile a list of consultants they trust as a referral source for organizations.

A few basics to finding a grant writing consultant: *look for someone with a proven track record of writing grants that have been funded*; who has a strong familiarity with the kind of work central to your organization, or who is familiar with the population you serve; who has an understanding of your service area; and whose consulting rates you consider reasonable for your organization.

What an Outside Grant Writer Will Need

An outside grant writer will need a few key things from the organization. She will need access to staff to answer questions, address potential inconsistencies in the information provided, and review draft documents in a timely manner. Thorough information is key and this should not be a problem, because the case statement should have already been created, capacity to deliver has already been evaluated, the program plan is crafted, and the background statement is being continually updated. Remember earlier in the chapter when the 70% rule of grant writing was mentioned? This is how it all comes together.

Most organizations make a big mistake in assuming that once they hire the grant writer, they no longer have to be engaged in the process of developing the grant. Nothing could be more incorrect. A grant writer is not a program planner, nor is she the finance person for your organization. She is the professional writer retained for the specific purpose of completing your grant. Therefore, the staff members who have any part of the program being proposed need to remain engaged in the grant writing process and focused on making certain it is completed accurately.

Costs of Grant Writing Services

Some consultants charge an hourly rate, generally ranging from $50 to $195. Others charge a flat rate depending on their assessment of how much work is required, or will perhaps charge a daily or weekly retainer. *The price of the service does not necessarily correlate with the quality of the service received.* This is applicable to those consultants charging both significantly higher and significantly lower rates than the majority of their colleagues. It is up to each organization to do its homework and make an informed decision.

Grant writers are to be paid for their work writing the grant proposal. The Association of Fundraising Professionals has adopted a Fundraising Code of Ethics, which was also adopted by the Grant Professionals Association (previously the American Association of Grant Professionals), which makes it unethical for a grant writer (or any kind of fundraising consultant for that matter) to take a percentage of foundation grants.

If I Knew Then

I wish someone would have sat me down when I started working in development back in the late 1980s and said, "It's about relationships!" It would have saved me countless hours fretting over the perfect prepositional phrases and coming up with creative ways to say "innovative" and "strategic" in my proposals. I would have focused much more of my attention back in those days on the people who worked in the foundation, in addition to the foundation itself. I would have taken the time to get to know key foundation staff and how they approach their work—what it means to them. And I would have shared with them what my organization's work is about, *and what it means to me*. Most importantly, I would have found common ground and plugged them into the core of our work.

Even if I determined that there was not a match between our work and what the foundation was funding at the time, I would have continued to nurture those relationships out of mutual respect and a belief that if they couldn't fund my organization or program, it was likely that I could refer other deserving organizations or colleagues that would be more of a match with the foundation's direction. Or perhaps they may have expanded their program areas to include something relevant to our work, or moved onto another foundation. More than anything, I would have moved much more quickly to shatter the image I held those first few years of foundations as the end-all; the "easier" money where good writing alone could earn big money for your organization. Bottom line: I would have spent much less time thinking in transactional ways and made the pivot to relational thinking earlier than I did.

case study

A Lesson in What Not to Do

Experience is the best teacher, so it is often said. I'd go further and add that *the best learning comes from failure and outright mistakes.* Such is the case for one of my former clients, a women's organization, who bombed an incredible opportunity for funding:

The executive director was approached at an event by a program officer of a local foundation because of her work partnering with another organization already receiving funding. The connection between the program officer and the ED was great, and a meeting was set up between the two so that the program officer could learn more about my client's organization and programs.

The meeting happened and again the connection between the program officer and the ED was strong. The program officer expressed a particular interest in one of my client's signature programs. After the initial thank-you follow-up, my client did a much better job of keeping the lines of communication open with the program officer; however, she did not invite the program officer to three separate programmatic events that occurred the following month, even though the program officer specifically asked about that program.

The foundation's spring grant guidelines were issued approximately three months after their first meeting. My client crafted a proposal and submitted it. The proposal was for a different program—not the one to which the program officer expressed interest—even though that particular program was in need of funding as well. My client did not discuss her submission with the program officer in advance of crafting the proposal, did not seek guidance from the program officer on the program she submitted, and did not use the few touch bases she had with the program officer to find out more about what their selection process entailed. Needless to say, her proposal was declined.

The executive director did not understand the power of the connection she had with the program officer and the dynamic of the relationship that was developing between the two of them. She approached the grant making process in a transactional manner, while discounting the relational opportunities clearly present. And she simply didn't listen.

Had she bothered to touch bases with the program officer, she would have found out up front that the program she planned to submit was very similar to two other programs already being funded by the foundation. Had she inquired about the foundation's selection process (how it works, who reviews the proposals, what have been successful strategies by other organizations), she would have known to spend more time paying attention to the details of the proposal itself to make sure she used the correct formatting—that this was actually a very big deal for this particular foundation. In general, had she reached out to the program officer to let her know that her organization was going to submit a proposal, it would have shown a level of respect for the budding professional relationship growing between them.

Grant Seeking Dos and Don'ts

- DO take the executive summary portion of any proposal seriously. In many instances, it is the first section of the proposal that gets read.

- DON'T make your problem statement so bleak that it creates the perception of no hope. All cannot be bleak and dreary, or what's the point? Hope is a powerful motivator and intoxicant that is many times extremely underplayed in the nonprofit community.

- DO get your facts straight. Make sure your data is up to date and as accurate as possible.

- DON'T let a grant writing consultant develop your program plan. She can write the grant, but staff needs to develop the program plan.

- DO follow the grant guidelines as specifically as they are articulated. Never use a "one size fits all" approach to seeking grants.

- DO contact the funding institution and speak or meet with someone about your organization and/or program before submitting a proposal. Regardless of the outcome, nurture those relationships moving forward.

- DO think of everyone—funding institutions included—who invests in your organization as partners. It will keep you from leaving them out when you should be including them.

- DON'T try to convince a funder to invest in your organization if you do not fit within their specific areas of focus.

Conclusion

Foundations—most of them, anyway—exist to support worthy organizations benefiting the communities in which we live. How incredible is that: to have organizations established with the specific intent of investing resources to make our communities, our schools, our environment, our health, and our world in general a better place?

Yet even with the incredible promise held within the walls of foundations large and small, there are limits. There are wonderfully written proposals that do not get funded. There are strong and compelling programs that do not get funded. There are vibrant and much-needed organizations that do not get funded. This is the reality we face; *there are more worthy organizations and programs than there is money to fund them.* It is better to be clear and know the truth going in.

That said, foundations across the country—private, family, community, public, corporate, operating, and donor advised—are funding organizations and programs every single day. So why shouldn't your organization be one of those that get funded? What is it that you can do to set your organization apart from the rest? The answer to this million-dollar question has been woven throughout this chapter: *relationships.* Move beyond the transactional nature of grant making and begin to see these institutions with all their layers, complexities, protocols, and rules—as more than dispensaries of cash. There is a wealth of knowledge, experience, passion, and non-monetary resources that lie within those walls. Then there are the people; people in positions to make decisions about which organizations receive funding. People who are, for the most part, looking for real connection and a shared understanding of the journey.

> Recognize that the relationship you make with foundation staff is one <u>based on mutual need</u> and be on a mission to educate foundation staff on what they need from your organization. Do your homework.
>
> —Sandi Brock Jibrell, Annie E. Casey Foundation, (retired)

Tori O'Neal-McElrath is currently the director of development for the Center for Community Change in Washington, DC. She has worked in the nonprofit sector for more than 21 years in various management and consulting roles for both organizations and foundations focused on women and girls, health and community clinics, and social justice. She is a member of the Greater Washington, DC Chapter of the Association of Fundraising Professionals, the Black Philanthropic Alliance, and has served on various nonprofit boards of directors. Tori is also the coauthor of Winning Grants Step by Step *(3rd edition), published by Jossey-Bass.*

Grant Seeking Resource Review

Big Online USA (www.bigdatabase.com)

> A comprehensive source of fundraising information, opportunities, and resources for charities and nonprofits.

Chronicle of Philanthropy (www.philanthropy.com)

> News source for charity leaders, fundraisers, grant makers, and others involved the nonprofit sector.

Council on Foundations (www.cof.org)

> A national nonprofit membership association of foundations that offers an annual conference.

Forum of Regional Associations of Grant Makers (www.givingforum.org)

> A network of regional associations of grant makers that supports philanthropy by strengthening the ability of all regional associations to fulfill their missions.

Foundation Center (www.foundationcenter.org)

> Provides an incredibly comprehensive database of foundations, complete with detailed funding information and grant guidelines, and also provides useful tools and resources. Physical locations in major cities around the country offer free access to classes and research.

FoundationSearch America (www.foundationsearch.com)

> A source for domestic and international foundation funding information for nonprofits.

Future Fundraising Now (www.futurefundraisingnow.com)

A fundraising blog full of interesting conversation, studies, tips, and social media advice.

Grant Professionals Association (www.grantprofessionals.org)

An international community of grant professionals with a useful website, newsletter, and annual conference. Previously known as the American Association of Grant Professionals.

Grassroots Fundraising Journal (www.grassrootsfundraising.org)

Provides basic "101" knowledge about all aspects of fundraising.

National Center for Charitable Statistics (www.nccs.urban.org)

The national clearinghouse of data on the nonprofit sector in the United States.

The Agitator (www.theagitator.net)

A blog featuring fundraising and advocacy strategies, trends and tips . . . with an edge.

The Grantsmanship Center (www.tgci.com)

An organization offering grant seeking training to nonprofit and government agencies.

Mim Carlson and Tori O'Neal-McElrath, <u>Winning Grants, Step by Step</u> (3rd ed.). San Francisco: Jossey-Bass, 2008.

A part of the Nonprofit Guidebook Series, this practical publication directs the novice grant seeker and offers a refresher course for experienced grant writers.

Women's Funding Network (www.wfnet.org)

A member organization of over a hundred women's foundations and donor funds committed to providing grants and support to organizations focused on women and girls.

o o o

All these resources, plus nonprofit management tips of the week and more, can be found at Nonprofits101.org.

CHAPTER 21

Online Fundraising

By Katya Andresen, Chief Operating Officer, and
Rebecca Ruby Higman, Senior Product Marketing Manager,
Network for Good

A Caveat: Online Outreach in Wonderland

There's a scene in <u>Through the Looking Glass</u> where Alice runs lightning fast alongside the Queen. When she stops to rest after a long while, Alice can hardly believe her eyes, for she is in the same place she started. The Queen asked why Alice thinks this is remarkable.

> Alice says, "Well, in our country, you'd generally get to somewhere else—if you ran very fast for a long time, as we've been doing."

> The Queen responds Alice must be from a very slow country. She says: "Now, here, you see it takes all the running you can do, to keep in the same place. If you want to get somewhere else, you must run at least twice as fast as that!"

Writing anything about the state of online outreach—especially in a format as permanent as a book—is like venturing down the rabbit hole and learning the status quo is already obsolete. Because we agree with the Queen when it comes to all things technology, we are going to focus here on universal, evergreen truths.

Why Online Fundraising Matters

If you are a nonprofit and you need resources, you need to include an online giving program as part of your plans. But maybe you don't believe that. Or maybe you have a board or colleagues who aren't so sure. If so, *here are key reasons that online giving matters.*

1. <u>It's a growing portion of giving</u>. It's easy to get dollar signs in your eyes when you think of corporations or foundations, but don't forget that each year, the Giving USA report shows that at least three-quarters of all charitable giving comes from individuals rather than big institutions. And an increasing number of those individuals choose to do their giving online. At the time of this writing, various studies including one from Giving USA/ Blackbaud put online giving at around 5–10% of overall giving, but *online donations have been growing about 50% each year.* A good indicator of just how important online giving will be in the years ahead is the tragic earthquake in Haiti in 2010. The vast majority of donations in response to the crisis were made online or by phone.

2. <u>Online givers are the donors you want</u>. Online donors can be summed up with a phrase that would make an excellent soap opera title: the young and the generous. They tend to be more youthful than offline donors (they are Boomers or younger) and their *gifts are around $100.* We want more donors like them; they account for most of donor acquisition, *and they are a leading source of new revenue for most nonprofits.*

3. <u>Online fundraising is great for small or start-up groups</u>. An eBenchmarks study in 2009 by M+R Strategies and NTEN found that *smaller groups do especially well online.* Their giving levels were up strongly in 2009 compared to larger groups, and they reported double the email response rates. In addition, *online fundraising is far less expensive than direct mail or telemarketing.* Think of it as a great way to level the fundraising playing

field if you're not a huge, well-established nonprofit. Network for Good's own studies find *nonprofits typically raise $25 for every $1 they spend on online fundraising services.*

4. <u>You need to master it now as an integrated part of your fundraising strategy</u>. As more and more giving shifts online, your online presence will become paramount. Develop it now, in concert with your other fundraising activities. Ensure that your website and organization's social media outposts are easy to find. Start building your email lists immediately. Then make sure you integrate those online activities with your offline ones. This will position you well for the future. As an emerging leader in the nonprofit world, you will find your online efforts extremely important, especially if you're at a smaller, grassroots organization. *The Internet—unlike traditional media, telemarketing, or direct mail—is where you can successfully fundraise right alongside the biggest organizations, even if you don't have their resources.*

5. <u>Your web presence affects overall giving</u>. According to a study put out by Kintera (part of Blackbaud), *more than 65% of donors visit an organization's website prior to making a donation.* Whether that donor chooses to click the donate button or to find her checkbook, the information and opportunities for engagement you offer online will have a profound impact on your both your brand and your bottom line.

Critical Skills and Competencies

Now that we've established why online fundraising is so important to your organization's success, let's look at some of the tricks of the trade so you can get up and running and maximize your effectiveness.

Essentials of Online Giving

Here's a checklist of what you need to get started in online giving. In this chapter, we will go in-depth on your messaging, your giving page, and your email campaign tools.

1. <u>A website, or at least a web page</u>. Make sure your site meets the following criteria:

   ○ Can a stranger identify what you do and why they should care within two seconds? *Having a very brief way to convey what you do is key to success online.*

   ○ Do you have a big, emotionally affecting image or statement on the home page that connects on a personal level?

   ○ Can you find your donate button in 1–2 seconds?

   ○ Is your donation button above the fold, big, and colorful?

   ○ Is your donate button framed in a compelling way? What personally relevant, tangible change will result if someone gives now?

   ○ Is it clear where the money goes? To exactly which activities or people?

   ○ Is there a sense of immediacy around your donate button? A reason to give *right now*?

   ○ Do you have links to events and other opportunities for engagement? Remember the comments on website design in Chapter Fifteen—*many users won't necessarily want to give right away, so be sure to offer other ways they can support your work* and make them feel like more than an ATM machine.

   ○ Do you have clear third-party endorsement on the page? (For example: ratings from GuideStar and Charity Navigator, or a testimonial from someone else regarding your nonprofit's services (a volunteer, a beneficiary, and so on).

   ○ Does your website *give you and your potential donor the opportunity to form a relationship* (for example, email signup)?

   ○ Do you make it easy to share? For example, do you have social network sharing links, widgets, and so forth? Do you list where else donors can find you online, such as Twitter and Facebook?

   ○ Are you sure you *don't try to say too much*? Is the page clean, simple, and easy to use? That means intuitive navigation that even Aunt Pearl can handle.

2. <u>Legal boxes checked</u>. Make sure you're registered to collect donations in the states where you will receive them, or use a service that handles this for you. We're not lawyers, so we recommend you talk to yours for advice.

3. <u>Donation processing service</u>. Be sure you *enable online donations* for people ready to give. DonateNow from Network for Good is a good tool for this.

4. <u>Email tool</u>. You need an email campaign tool so you can effectively reach out to a community without running afoul of SPAM filters (more on this in Chapter Twenty-Two).

5. <u>Analytics tool</u>. Be sure you *have basic tracking tools on your website*, so you know how people find you and what they're doing on your website (we recommend Google Analytics, which is free).

6. <u>Follow-up procedures</u>. You must *have key internal processes in place to provide instant receipts to donors and support effective follow up*. If you're going to ask for and receive donations, you need to also be able to thank and cultivate those who give. A top reason people stop donating is dissatisfaction with a charity's follow-up. Don't let that happen to you—see Chapter Seventeen for more information on CRM as one approach.

7. <u>Plan for integration</u>. Too often, nonprofits have a team responsible for online outreach that is separate from direct mail or communications staff. That's too bad, because many studies show *the best strategy for building relationships with donors is one that is multichannel: a combined online and offline approach.* You want to make sure that your whole team is organized around your donors and seamlessly combines outreach types. A donor who gives online may prefer to give at an event next time. An offline donor may want to switch to online giving. An online donor may appreciate a handwritten thank-you received via postal (or "snail") mail. That means you need to get all of your outreach efforts coordinated seamlessly.

8. <u>Social networking plans.</u> Once you have a suitable website and email campaign tool, add social networking to your activities. See Chapters Sixteen and Twenty-Two for more information on this topic.

9. <u>Feedback loop</u>. This is a learning process. Continually test, analyze, get feedback, learn, and improve all you do online.

10. <u>Strong messaging</u>. The long list of technology and legalities here means nothing if you don't have winning messaging.

In Focus: Messaging, Website Fundraising, and Email

OK. Now you should have the basics for your online presence in place, but how do you leverage these tools to spread your message and raise the big bucks?

Messaging

To compel donors to give online—or anywhere for that matter—you *always* need to answer four questions for them: Why me? Why now? What for? Who says?

- Why me? *Your audience needs to care about what you are doing.* Show them why what you're doing is personally relevant to them. They need to connect to you on a human level. Use pictures, tell stories, and do anything that can help your audience relate.

- Why now? Most people donate online on two occasions. The first is towards the end of the year; people are in charitable mind-sets and looking to make year-end tax contributions. The other is when there's a humanitarian crisis, such as the earthquake in Haiti. What do you do the rest of the year?

  ○ *Create a sense of urgency and immediacy in your appeals.* Explain why a donation is needed right now.

  ○ Break down what you are currently doing and *show any immediately understandable or visible results that will make people want to take action.*

  ○ Set a goal and a deadline. There is plenty of research to show that people are more likely to act if they feel a goal is within reach—and they can help you achieve it with their gift. *Matching or challenge grants can make a campaign goal feel even more urgent.*

  ○ Engage your most ardent supporters in a personal fundraising effort. It's hard to say no to people we love, so you can bring urgency to your cause by having your champions reach out to those in their circles of influence.

- What for? People know you're a nonprofit organization and you need donations to help your cause. But where exactly is a donor's money going? What will they get in return for their donation—personally and in terms of the impact of your programs?

  - Don't just focus on need; explain specifically the impact a donation will make.

  - Show them that you will take care of their money, so a potential donor knows it won't be wasted or inefficiently used.

  - Clearly show which programs are being helped by a donation, or what good works are going to result.

  - Share human interest stories and success stories. Share how other donors made an impact or how donors impacted other individuals in need.

- Who says? The messenger is often as important as the message. Use trustworthy messengers—people you've actually helped, or other donors instead of just you. *Friends and family are the most influential factor in determining where people give money*, so think about how you can get your supporters to speak for you among their own circles of influence.

Website Fundraising

Imagine you're Kevin Costner. OK, to clarify, imagine you're Kevin Costner from about 20 years ago playing Ray Kinsella in "Field of Dreams." A raspy voice from beyond promises, "If you build it, they will come." It sounds like a pretty sweet deal: you just do a bit of work on the front end and you'll be rewarded fairly automatically.

Unfortunately, that is not the way of the online world when it comes to fundraising. Unlike wise old baseball players, internet users—as marketing guru Seth Godin points out—are lazy and in a hurry (no offense). And though nonprofits and marketing idealists of all shapes and sizes would prefer to believe that supporters will take their time and digest every thoughtfully constructed word on the organization's website, it's simply not the case.

Instead, nonprofits must approach online fundraising as with any other type of fundraising: *cater to the prospect's or supporter's needs, interests, and preferences, rather than hoping they kowtow to mission statements* sitting front and center, strategic plans cluttering up a home page and donate buttons that resemble a pea's worth of space instead of a peach's.

There are three steps to successfully raising money through your website:

- Make your donate button shine

- Tell a story to entice giving

- Above all else: make it easy and quick

Make Your Donate Button Shine   Once you have established a relationship with a donation-processing partner (as we mentioned in the Essentials of Online Giving section), you'll need to make that donate button big, shiny, and unmistakably easy to locate:

- <u>Take the two-second test</u>. Again, *visitors to your website should be able to find your donate button in two seconds or less.* If it's a tiny text link at the footer of your site, on-the-fence (or even diehard) donors will have a difficult time finding it. And place the button "above the fold" (meaning your visitor doesn't need to scroll down to find it) to help blaze trails to your button.

- <u>Avoid muted, camouflaged buttons</u>. The color of your donate button is also crucial in drawing a visitor's eye to it. Network for Good performed a test on its own website and found that it had a 30% greater conversion (yes, 3–0) when it changed from a gray button to a red one.

- <u>Don't be afraid to think beyond "donate now."</u> The verbiage you choose for your button dictates whether someone clicks on it or not. Try to relate a gift to something tangible (i.e., "donate a bed net" or "save a litter of puppies").

- <u>Ask any ad exec: babies and puppies work</u>. Don't be afraid to incorporate an image on your button. Depending on your mission you might consider an animal, a baby's face, a clean wave of water, and so on.

Tell a Story to Entice Giving   Some nonprofits decide to include a "why give" page between their donate button and the donation form, but as mentioned in Chapter Fifteen (on website design), you lose people at every click. We recommend streamlining the process and simply customizing the text above your giving form and providing a link for more information if needed. Either way, be sure to pay close attention to the story you're sharing with your soon-to-be supporter.

In the final stage of the giving process (and throughout the process, honestly), your donor will be influenced to abandon the process or question whether she is making a good decision. It's your job as a fundraiser to reassure the prospect how her gift will be used and how much you appreciate her generosity. *Paint a clear picture with personal stories and tangible anticipated results*—while avoiding statistics and overwhelming numbers—to make the final sale and encourage making it through the whole process.

Above All Else: Make It Easy and Quick Now that you've made it easy to find your donate page and shared the final call to action with your supporter, it's paramount to ensure the donation form itself is user-friendly.

- Make the donation page match your website to convey a sense of trust and build your brand.

- Keep the number of questions you ask to a minimum—*the more fields to complete, the fewer people who make it through to actually donate.*

- Choose a one-page donation form instead of multiple pages—the greater number of clicks, the lower your conversion rate (remember the "in a hurry" part about your donors?).

- Be sure your system offers automatic email tax receipts.

- Give your donor options: Offer the ability to accept recurring donations, choose designations, and create dedications. *Here are a few tips for encouraging recurring donations*:

  ○ Highlight the value donors get from setting up a recurring gift: it takes the onus of remembering to give again off of them; it is convenient and becomes a part of their overall budget (sort of like a happier version of auto-billpay); and larger gifts can be divided up over time.

  ○ Try to equate these gifts to tangible, relatable outcomes—think about the sponsor-a-child model—to make donors feel more connected.

○ *Be sure that recurring giving is an option every time a donor enters a gift amount.*

• Test different giving levels and configurations of your page to determine your best combination of custom questions and other areas of your form.

• Let donors opt-in to hear from you again via email—which brings us to our next section: email marketing.

Email

As supporters become increasingly web-savvy—and decreasingly engaged with printed material—it's important for nonprofits to meet their base where they are: in their inboxes. Though social networks often snag headlines for big traffic, there is no doubt that email is ubiquitous. (Do you even *know* anyone without an email address anymore?)

Chapter Twenty-Seven speaks to email marketing strategy in greater detail, but what follows are a few key points geared towards emerging nonprofit leaders looking at newsletters and email marketing as a fundraising strategy.

Email Fundraising 101: Steps to Success   The best way to approach an email outreach fundraising program is to *think of your campaigns from the outside in:* plan an overall strategy, determine what goes on the "envelope" of your message, develop stellar content for inside your campaign, *design content to be easy to read* (being fancy is not important!) and determine how often you want to arrive in your subscribers' inboxes.

1. Plan an overall strategy. When you're first getting started, *consider how much time and effort you're willing to commit to your email outreach.* What will you try to accomplish? What sort of content will you be sharing? Who will be the point person to ensure that all of this happens as planned? And as exciting as it is to imagine sending frequent fundraising appeals as part of your mix, *be sure your strategy includes the 3:1 rule: For every appeal for action you send, be sure to send three campaigns that are chock full of thanks, updates, and information.*

2. Make your micro-content catchy. Micro-content refers to the little bit of content your readers see prior to opening you message. You can equate this

to an envelope when you receive a snail mail message. It contains the "from" name and email address, as well as the subject line. Be familiar (use a person's name that people will recognize), persuasive (leave some mystery in your subject line) and accessible (be sure you monitor the email address where all the replies are going—*never use a "donotreply@nonprofit.org" address!*).

3. <u>Develop stellar content</u>. Email is designed to open a two-way conversation. *Be sure to share stories, updates, and content of interest to your supporters.* Keep the content easy to relate to and full of hopeful messages (no one likes doom and gloom) and ways to get involved and contribute to impact (*when fundraising on or offline, always tie your ask to impact*).

4. <u>Don't get hung up on design</u>. The most important design advice you can take is that your messages must be readable. *Avoid giant fonts, too many columns, and too much text within your campaigns.* Use your emails as a place to *begin* an article, and link to your website or a blog, where you can provide the full story and a link for people to make donations.

5. <u>Figure out frequency</u>. In general, nonprofits rarely venture into the territory of sending too many emails (usually the opposite is true). It is important not to feel intimidated or required to send messages every day, week, or even every other week. *Set a goal of at least one email per month* to ensure your cause stays top-of-mind with supporters, and tweak as you see fit. It never hurts to ask your subscribers' their preferences too!

Enterprise Community Partners

A national leader in investment capital and development services for housing and community revitalization, Enterprise Community Partners (based in Columbia, Maryland) found untapped potential in using the Internet for communications and fundraising. Prior to 2008, they had no coordinated plan and only a few online donations trickled in on their own.

How did they get started? The Enterprise team asked themselves five revealing questions before diving into the online space:

1. Who is our audience?

2. Where are they online?

3. What do they want to do and what are they currently doing online?

4. What do we want them to do?

5. How will we measure success?

In response to these inquiries, Enterprise approached the Internet with a clear strategy:

1. Develop personas (or "user stories" as described in Chapter Fifteen) to describe our audience.

2. Research where our audience is spending time online.

3. Observe and participate in online discussions and social networks.

4. Build a "ladder of engagement" to map out the path through which we hope to lead our online donors.

5. Set and monitor quantifiable goals to be sure we're on track.

With a healthy dose of research and internal planning, Enterprise acted on *the following ideas, which led to a 400% increase in the number of online donors* and even greater growth in donation amount:

- Getting senior management buy-in

- Coordinating efforts between different areas and departments of the organization

- *Defining one communications calendar for the entire nonprofit*

- Developing user stories to understand the various users who would be visiting their website

- Promoting online giving more significantly on their website

- Revamping the Enterprise home page to increase engagement with calls to action, such as the abilities to donate, stay informed via their e-newsletter, get involved with a campaign initiative, and take action via an online advocacy action center

- Offering an opportunity for potential supporters to sign up for communications *without being required to donate*

- Growing their email list by offering multiple opportunities to sign up online and creating offline systems to collect email addresses

- Sending fundraising appeals multiple times throughout a campaign (versus sending once and hoping for action), which also included updates, client impact profiles, announcements, and calls to action that were *not* geared towards fundraising

Now that Enterprise has gotten their online program off the ground, they have developed goals for the next three to five years that incorporate the following metrics to gauge progress: number of donors giving less than $1,000, total money raised from this group, and the average donation amount per donor at this giving level.

Online Fundraising Dos and Don'ts

- DO partner with an online donation processing organization that meets the needs of you and your donors.

- DO make your donate button big, bold, above the fold, and easy to find.

- DO incorporate a website analytics tool (like Google Analytics) to understand what content's working, as well as how your visitors are acting and engaging.

- DON'T rely on email services like Outlook or Gmail to stay in touch with your supporters on a large scale; instead use an email marketing service that will ensure you comply with "CAN-SPAM" guidelines and not require HTML or graphic design knowledge.

- DO ensure smooth integration between online and offline efforts by keeping your messaging consistent, appealing to donors and potential supporters via multiple channels, and providing different options for giving (for example, including your URL on a direct mail donation form with language to highlight the online giving option).

- DON'T think of online fundraising as a silver bullet; instead, be sure to determine concrete goals and compile regular reporting so you can learn and correct as you go.

Conclusion

Though you may feel a bit like Alice chasing the white rabbit down the rabbit hole, take heart in the fact that the basic principles of online fundraising and communications will continue to apply. *Well-conceived strategies, compelling stories, and open communication—as in any other avenue of fundraising—yield the best results.*

Your organization only stands to gain from venturing into the online space. You'll have the opportunity to increase your bottom line and give supporters (and potential donors!) a great experience when they land on your website. By following the best practices we've outlined, you'll blaze trails to your donation page, form valuable relationships with donors, and be on your way to growing an engaged audience online.

Given all of the other projects you're undertaking, online fundraising may seem intimidating. Take heart: there are plenty of resources and tips you can put into practice right away to start off on the right foot. And there are partners willing to work with you to take the technical burden off your shoulders with regard to donation processing and email marketing. You're not alone and you can succeed!

Katya Andresen is COO of Network for Good and a speaker, author, and blogger about nonprofit marketing, online outreach, and social media. She teaches at American University and serves on the board of NTEN. Katya has trained thousands of causes in effective marketing and media relations, and her marketing materials for nonprofits have won national and international awards. Author of <u>Robin Hood Marketing: Stealing Corporate Savvy to Sell Just Causes</u>, her work is also featured in <u>People to People Fundraising—Social Networking and Web 2.0 for Charities</u>. Fundraising Success Magazine named her "Fundraising Professional of the Year" in 2007.

Rebecca Higman is Network for Good's senior product marketing manager, as well as a speaker and writer about online fundraising, email marketing, and social networking. She manages nonprofit marketing activities, including new product development, website management, e-newsletter development, event marketing, business development strategy, and marketing of Network for Good's fundraising, email marketing, and online events services. Rebecca has spoken to diverse audiences in the nonprofit sector, including VOLUNTEER Hampton Roads, the Foundation Center, Maryland Nonprofits, NA'AMAT USA, CanadaHelps and Capital Area Food Bank. Her articles have appeared in the Direct Marketing Association's blog, Fundraising Success, and Philanthropy Journal.

Online Fundraising Resource Review

The Online Fundraiser's Checklist (www.web.networkforgood.org/ 201001ebook)

A must-have for veteran and rookie online fundraisers alike, this group of six checklists will ensure that your home page, copywriting, and much more are all up to par, and it includes links to additional resources if you score low on any given quiz.

The Nonprofit Email Marketing Guide: 7 Steps to Better Email Fundraising & Communications from Network for Good and Kivi Leroux Miller (www.web.networkforgood.org/email-fundraising-guide)

From choosing an email service provider to developing successful subject line, this step-by-step manual will get your email marketing program off the ground.

Fundraising Campaign in a Box (www.web.networkforgood.org/fundraising)

This guide features a seven-step process that will quickly lead you through the planning of a successful fundraising campaign.

Steps to Fall & Holiday Fundraising Success (www.web.networkforgood.org/ 25steps)

These steps will help you prepare for the giving season by taking you through ideas and best practices in the following five areas: campaign planning, website, emails, messaging, and marketing.

The Procrastinator's Guide to Year-end Fundraising (www.fundraising123.org/ article/procrastinators-guide-year-end-fundraising-1)

No matter what time of year you kick off your online efforts, this guide will provide quick action items to make your online giving experience the best it can be.

Nonprofit Marketing Blog (www.nonprofitmarketingblog.com)

From chapter author Katya Andresen, this blog discusses Robin Hood Marketing—the concept of stealing corporate secrets to sell social causes—and also offers insightful stories of Katya's life as a marketer, from Washington DC to Madagascar to points in between.

Nonprofit Marketing Guide.com (www.nonprofitmarketinguide.com)

From author Kivi Leroux Miller, this website and companion blog and book include specific advice on producing both print and email newsletters.

Benchmark Data

Each year the following sources release updated information and data regarding the state of online giving and fundraising practices in the nonprofit sector:

- Convio: Nonprofit Online Benchmark Study (www.convio.com)

- Blackbaud/Target Analytics: Donor Centrics™ Internet Giving Benchmarking Analysis (www.blackbaud.com)

- M+R Strategies/NTEN: eNonprofit Benchmarks Study (www.mrss.com or www.nten.org)

о о о

All these resources, plus nonprofit management tips of the week and more, can be found at Nonprofits101.org.

CHAPTER 22

Online Peer-to-Peer Fundraising

By Nicci Noble, CFRE, President, Noble Services LLC, and Sean Sullivan, Development Director, Center for Environmental Health

Introduction

Wikipedia defines a "social network" as "a social structure made of individuals (or organizations) called 'nodes,' which are tied (connected) by one or more specific types of interdependency, such as friendship, kinship, financial exchange, dislike, sexual relationships, or relationships of beliefs, knowledge, or prestige."

You've heard it in several chapters throughout this book: people give to people. The Internet, and social networking in particular, presents a tremendous opportunity for nonprofits large and small to grow their network of contacts, supporters, and donors—never before has there been such a powerful tool for getting more people connect to your cause.

Social networks existed long before the Internet, but the Web has opened up numerous connections that were nonexistent, or at least invisible, in the past. The Web's facilitation of networks—specifically via free commercial social networks such as Facebook, Twitter, LinkedIn, and numerous older forms, such as forums and bulletin boards—opens many doors for nonprofit fundraisers. Many of these allow you to aggregate your social networks all from one place and share with them as much or as little information as desired.

The use of these media online to raise friends and funds is a new variation on the old model of peer-to-peer fundraising. In the traditional model of friend raising and fundraising, nonprofits look for influential community leaders and donors of high worth to introduce them to their friends, thereby expanding the nonprofit's influence and fundraising ability. The larger the pool of donors, the larger the possibility of returns. This is basic social networking. Online fundraising through peer-to-peer networks makes this process electronic, often saving time and resources in the process, and increasing the ability to "scale," or grow, rapidly. And just as in real-world networking, *wise online networkers seek to cultivate connections to other individuals with large social networks.*

However, nonprofits don't need just *any* person with lots of connections. They need people who share an interest in the nonprofit's cause and have the ability to contribute to their cause. It is these type of people that you want as Fans, Followers, and commenters on your Facebook Page, Twitter account, and blog posts. This chapter will help you understand how to use online social networks for fundraising from one of your people to potential supporters, AKA "peer-to-peer fundraising."

Critical Skills and Competencies

Your organization needs three key capacities before you can leverage your online networks. Let's look at those first, and then we'll look at some of the skills associated with peer network fundraising.

1. Establish Your Online Presence

In preparing to launch into social media, nonprofits need both digital and staff infrastructure. Minimally, in addition to setting up a Facebook and Twitter account (see Chapter Sixteen for more on online communities), *you need Facebook and Twitter icons right on your homepage.* This allows people to connect with your networks. It also indicates that you "get it"—that you are savvy enough to merit their attention and investment of energy, if not money. In a twenty-first-century world, your website may be the main interaction that people have with your organization.

Social networks require support. Facebook, Twitter, and blogs are all free. Once you have these in place, you're out of the gate. But *once you begin you must maintain, support, and expand your presence, otherwise you run the risk of undermining your efforts by opening the equivalent of an empty store,* which reflects poorly on your organization. Think of your online presence and social networks as gardens—if you do not tend to them, they won't grow and produce. Even as Facebook crested past 500 million users,[1] making it the equivalent of the world's third largest nation, some continue to advise that nonprofits just hire any 21-year-old out of college. This is similar to adults struggling with the Internet in the late 1990s saying, "If you don't understand how to get on, just ask your 4-year-old." Cute in concept, but not very practical. You need professional support.

Already, mid-size nonprofits are adding jobs such as "social media coordinators" to their development and communications staff. Both functions require regular upkeep and updating. In this rapidly moving world, even going 24 hours without refreshing your status update or Twitter communication can mean you are stale, but that means allocating staff time. However, these tools are so easy that *you can take a single line from a case statement, a grant proposal, a press release, or an acknowledgment letter, and simply drop it into a 140-word character "Tweet" that Twitter instantly shares with all of your Followers. Moreover, your Tweets can update your other social network identities, such as Facebook and LinkedIn, if you set your account up properly and use tags like @ and #.*

2. Create an *Organizational* Cause and Fan Bases

Chapter Sixteen also mentioned that nonprofits that use Facebook to create their own "Causes" and recruit "Fans." *It is far more effective for nonprofits to create an organizational presence* of which people can become Fans, rather than creating a Profile, or individual account. Once you have established critical mass, you can ask supporters in your various networks to raise your visibility through posting it to their social media platforms—that's when things can go "viral," spreading exponentially from person to person, engaging your community in helping you spread the word faster than you could on your own. This will help cultivate online support for your cause—people ready to step forward when you ask for donations or other support.

3. Leverage *Personal* Social Networks

Once you are on a commercial social media platform like Facebook or Twitter, you need to promote your presence. Your current social networks can help with this—but remember *the networks you have access to extend beyond those formally attached to your organization*. They may include your personal networks, those of the board, the staff, and your close supporters.

Begin with leveraging your own personal social networks, reach out to your board and staff, and then supporters of your organization. Ask them to spread the word for you by asking their friends to become Fans or Followers. Some organizations worry about crossing the line by asking people to spread the word, but they shouldn't. For one thing, asking the board should be a no-brainer—their duty includes the duty of leveraging their networks and representing the nonprofit to the community, as outlined in Chapter Thirty. As for staff, leadership needs to think through the acceptability of asking staff to share their commitment to the organization through their personal networks. It may seem unfair to request them to open up their lives in this way. However, the boundaries between work life and personal life are blurring as we work longer and harder—and this blurring is especially common among younger workers. One executive director refers to staff usage of social media during the work day as "the twenty-first-century cigarette break." This director makes an agreement with staff: the organization is lenient about their use of personal social media while at work. In exchange, the organization asks staff to promote the agency through personal status updates on Facebook, "Tweets" on Twitter about new organization blog posts, and otherwise telling friends and networks about the organization's events, news media appearances, and so forth.

If the organization has a blog (see Chapter Sixteen), the board and staff should be asked to sign up for an RSS feed or notification of the agency's new posts, so that they can then help promote it. RSS (Really Simple Syndication) is a family of web feed formats used to publish frequently updated content— such as blog entries, news headlines, audio, and video—in a standardized format, aggregating content and automatically sending it to your email, phone, or web browser in one consolidated feed.[2] This tool allows the organization to keep tabs on important news streams, and to publicize itself when relevant stories are identified and forwarded.

With these capacities in place, you can turn to the work of raising friends and money via peer-to-peer networks.

Raising Money: Online or In-Person, the Same Rules Apply

One of the principles of fundraising established by Hank Rosso, a founder of the Center on Philanthropy and founding director of The Fund Raising School, is that "people give to people." *Promoting your nonprofit's good work is perceived to be more authentic and genuine if it comes from one of our friends or colleagues*—this is one of the key factors in engaging people in your efforts and educating them about your cause. This is as true online as it is in person.

As you've already read, *fundraising is not just about the money; it's about relationships.* We know that when a board member accompanies a development officer to meet with a prospective or current donor, the odds of securing a gift are far greater than if the fundraiser goes alone. What our parents and teachers have taught us about peer pressure is true. Fortunately, the peer pressure we are talking about here is moral, ethical, and socially responsible, and *peer-to-peer fundraising via social networks is a powerful way to put technology to work for your cause.*

The Seven Golden Rules of Email Solicitation

As part of your peer-to-peer fundraising efforts, you will no doubt be using email campaigns. Chapter Twenty-Seven covers the effective use of newsletters via email, but as it relates to peer-to-peer fundraising, it's crucial to note that *nonprofit email campaigns must adhere to seven federal regulations*. According to the Federal Trade Commission, "each separate e-mail in violation of the CAN-SPAM Act is subject to penalties of up to $16,000," so noncompliance can be costly. Thankfully, following the law isn't complicated. Here's a rundown of CAN-SPAM's main requirements:[3]

1. <u>Don't use false or misleading header information</u>. Your "From," "To," "Reply-To," and routing information—including the originating domain name and email address—must be accurate and identify the person or organization who initiated the message.

2. <u>Don't use deceptive subject lines</u>. The subject line must accurately reflect the content of the message.

3. <u>Identify the message as an advertisement</u>. The law gives you a lot of leeway in how to do this, but you must disclose clearly and conspicuously that your message is an advertisement. If you are soliciting funds, your message is considered an advertisement, so identify it as such.

4. <u>Tell recipients where you're located</u>. *Your message must include your valid physical postal address*. This can be your current street address, a post office box you've registered with the U.S. Postal Service, or a private mailbox you've registered with a commercial mail receiving agency established under Postal Service regulations.

5. <u>Tell recipients how to opt out of receiving future email from you</u>. Your message must include a clear and conspicuous explanation of how the recipient can opt out of (or unsubscribe from) getting email from you in the future. Craft the notice in a way that's easy for an ordinary person to recognize, read, and understand. Give a return email address or a link for people to unsubscribe. You may create a menu to allow a recipient to opt out of certain types of messages, but *you must include the option to stop all messages from you*. Make sure your spam filter doesn't block these opt out

requests and note that you must be able to process opt out requests for at least 30 days after you send your message.

6. <u>Honor "opt-out" requests promptly</u>. *You must honor a recipient's opt-out request within 10 business days.* You can't charge a fee, require the recipient to give you any personally identifying information beyond an email address, or make the recipient take any step other than sending a reply email or visiting a single page on a website to opt out. Once people have told you they don't want to receive more messages from you, you can't sell or transfer their email addresses, even in the form of a mailing list. The only exception is that you may transfer the addresses to a company you've hired to help you comply with the CAN-SPAM Act.

7. <u>Monitor what others are doing on your behalf</u>. Federal regulations are clear: even if you hire another company to handle your email marketing, *you can't contract away your responsibility to comply with the law.* Both the company promoted in the message and the company that actually sends the message may be held legally responsible.

A charity's privacy standards should be permission based and transparent to the volunteer fundraiser as well as the donor. Also, make it clear to anyone sharing contacts that this information will only be used by the nonprofit for future communication or solicitation efforts. Opt-out is required legally but "double opt in" is the ideal scenario for the highest quality constituent file.

Double opt-in is where a user has subscribed for a newsletter or other email marketing messages by explicitly requesting it and confirming the email address to be their own. This is usually done by responding to a confirmation email. This eliminates the possibility of somebody submitting somebody else's email address without their knowledge and against their will.[4]

Converting Donors into Fundraisers

When you use online social networking to improve your online giving campaigns, you're simultaneously building your potential base of volunteer online fundraisers. Remember the "pyramid" model of fundraising mentioned in earlier chapters? In the past, we supplied volunteer fundraisers with pledge forms, and they would collect many more donors and dollars than a sole fundraiser could. These volunteers were using their own real world social connections to find donors. The math of these types of campaigns is easy to understand. The more people who ask for money for your cause, the more other people will be inspired to donate. With the Web, it's simply a matter of translating the method to online social media. Think of it as pledge-based fundraising after a double espresso.

We can now sit on our couch, watch our TiVo'd shows while skipping commercials, email 100 people we know (either next door or on the other side of the world), and ask them to support our fundraising efforts or, better still, join in and become a volunteer fundraiser themselves. When peer-to-peer fundraisers receive real-time feedback about who has supported their request, and event organizers recognize them as a "good" fundraiser or identify a lagging fundraiser and give them the help they need to be more successful, everyone involved is a winner.

Organizations that provide an online giving platform to their constituents facilitate viral online giving. For the past 126 years, The Salvation Army volunteer bell ringers have stood at store doors ringing bells during the holiday season, wishing people well, and hoping they'd put some money in the Red Kettle. The Salvation Army created the Online Red Kettle to bring this traditional offline fundraising campaign online.

This web-based version of ringing a bell from the comfort of your keyboard was a peer-to-peer campaign that empowered and supported people to raise money by emailing their family and friends. Online Red Kettle hosts could customize their fundraising pages, track their progress, monitor the status of their invitations, and welcome others to join them in becoming an Online Red Kettle host. One volunteer fundraiser sent messages with eye-catching and daring calls to action by asking their contacts to "give or G-d will get you— and if He doesn't, I will." This joking personal solicitation raised more than $10,000 through one supporter's personal fundraising page in her first year of "ringing online."

Friend Raising Online

Many organizations like The Salvation Army have leveraged peer-to-peer fundraising for both raising money and "raising friends." The same rules apply to all disciplines of fundraising: again, it's not all about the money, it's also about relationships. *By growing your network of engaged, informed constituents, via all media and channels, you will increase overall fundraising success*. It's just that simple.

In his article "Roadmap to Fundraising Success," Timothy Seiler writes, "Fundraising is about relationships built on mutual interests and concerns. One of the secrets of fundraising is that people give to people with causes. The next action step in the cycle is to activate a volunteer corps of solicitors."[5]

One of the many challenges that arise in this new world of Internet-enabled, peer-based fundraising is how to recognize and reward volunteer friend-raisers and fundraisers. In a simpler model, where we simply search for donors, it is relatively easy to offer rewards based on the amount each person gives (think about the bags and CDs offered during telethons). But what about the amount each person raises? Using our couch-potato example above, let's imagine that from the 100 emails we sent, we get a 35% response rate (which would be quite impressive, by the way), and that our average gift is $100. That means that in addition to catching up on the nightly news, we raised $3,500! Let's also assume that we pull out our own credit card and make a $300 gift, to bring our total to $3,800.

How will that charity steward us? If they pull our record from their database it will show, quite accurately, that we are a $300 donor. However, more and more charities are faced with the challenge of needing to raise more money with fewer resources. Development professionals are in search of volunteer fundraisers (not just donors). These volunteer fundraisers need be to treated with the same genuine gratitude due to a $3,800 donor. How your organization recognizes a volunteer fundraiser who gives or raises at this level depends on how the development department has defined giving levels. Many nonprofits would consider $3,800 a major gift. If your organization has a major gifts officer stewarding major donors who give via traditional means, then they should be stewarding online donors and volunteer fundraisers in the same way. Having an appropriate staff or board member personally thank someone who has given or raised what is considered a major gift via any channel is a good practice. Ultimately, *nonprofits using peer-to-peer fundraising should develop methods that recognize and reward people for the amount they help raise through their personal networks.*

Using Social Networks to Promote Events

Events are the most commonly used tool used in peer-to-peer fundraising. Bike-a-thons, walks, dances, and yes, even yoga-thons, have harnessed the power of peer-to-peer giving to raise millions online. But in order to launch and support such an effort, you have to make an investment. The key is to begin with the end in mind. If the following questions remind you of those you've seen in other chapters, that's because answering them clearly is crucial to the success of launching any type of campaign:

- What type of campaign do want to launch? Are you bringing an offline annual event online, or starting a new event like a race or dance-a-thon?

- How many people do you want to engage?

- How will you measure success?

- What type of personnel support can you allocate? (i.e., staff or volunteers to provide training or support in using your social networking tools)

- What are your financial goals, if any?

- If this becomes successful, will you have the capacity to dedicate more time or staff to it?

case study

Two Case Studies on the Power of Online Social Networking

The Salvation Army: Getting Supporters to "Do More Than Give"

Hurricane Katrina was among the strongest hurricanes ever to strike the United States, according to scientists at the National Climatic Data Center. The American public's response to the hurricanes and floods of 2005 was as unprecedented as the devastation caused along the Gulf Coast. More money was given online in response to hurricanes Katrina and Rita than any other natural disaster in history.

The Salvation Army was challenged with a relief and recovery effort unparalleled to any other in its history. The public overwhelmingly supported their disaster work by giving five times more money via the Web

case study

in the 18 days after Katrina made land than the Army raised in its first four years of online gifts combined. But the Army knew people wanted to help on an even deeper level.

The Salvation Army empowered these would-be volunteers by providing a platform inspiring people to *"Do More Than Give."* They had learned from previous peer-to-peer campaigns, like the Online Red Kettle, that many of their online donors were comfortable with peer-to-peer fundraising. In addition to securing donations, they successfully enlisted the help of volunteer fundraisers in raising much-needed funds for the relief effort via this giving campaign. Providing volunteer fundraisers the ability to reach their family, friends, colleagues, and customers and leveraging their social networks enabled The Salvation Army to secure the support of thousands who wanted to *"Do More Than Give."*

Approximately 11,000 donors from The Salvation Army's Western Territory[6] who had opted in to its email list received a message announcing the *Do More Than Give* campaign. The recipients were asked make a donation, become a volunteer fundraiser by hosting a personalized web page, or both, with the funds going towards the Gulf Coast disaster relief effort.

- 10,951 emails sent to a select group of Salvation Army donors
- 375 gifts received within 72 hours = $73,191
- 1,476 gifts over 2 weeks = $217,968

This campaign had no marketing or media budget and took less than two days to configure, design, and deploy. This incredible return on investment clearly illustrates the power of a peer ask to quickly generate much-needed funds and support.

Equality California: Raising Funds and Influencing Policy

Equality California (EQCA) utilized peer-to-peer fundraising to raise funds to change same-sex marriage policy in California. They were fighting Proposition 8, a California ballot proposition to limit marriage to opposite-sex couples. EQCA's strategy was to connect people to the importance of marriage equality as an issue, personalize the cause by associating real faces, couples, and stories to it, and to engage people previously not connected to the issue or even out of the state and get them to give to the campaign.

To accomplish this, EQCA created a same-sex wedding registry to support its "No on 8" campaign. The registry gave LGBT couples an opportunity to register for gifts just as any couple intending to marry would. The catch was that the wedding registry was on EQCA's website, and instead of place settings and a microwave, couples asked friends to give financially towards EQCA's "No on 8" effort. The site allowed couples to make the page unique by adding pictures, details about their courtship, their own messages, and acknowledgments. All told, the effort raised a whopping $1.1 million.

How did the relatively small nonprofit pull this off? The wedding registry was supported by existing development and administrative staff who were able to build off the existing templates, press releases, and messaging of Equality California and the No on 8 campaign. These items moved in lockstep with each other and were supported by their social media sites. Remember, however, that in summer and fall 2008 Twitter was not what it is as of this writing. Today, you could use Twitter to draw even more eyeballs to your campaign and messaging.

In addition to direct solicitations and campaign updates, EQCA used its email database to promote and remind its network about the wedding registry and encourage them to either set up sites themselves, look for people they knew through an easy search tool on the registry by last name, or give to profiled couples. Hence, there were multiple directions to different audiences from both the organization and its supporters.

Effectively leveraging the Web also helped Equality California acquire hundreds of thousands of new contacts for future advocacy and fundraising communications, and it established them as the leading LGBT marriage equality group in the state of California.

Online Peer-to-Peer Fundraising Dos & Don'ts

- DON'T roll out until you are ready: have *all* your technology, internal and external, and staffing in place prior to launch of peer-to-peer fundraising campaign.

- DO set up your website and basic social media (Facebook and Twitter, as of this writing) before directing people to your site.

- DO go all the way—once you establish your social media efforts, make sure they're maintained, updated, and promoted.

- DON'T ask your Followers and Fans to take on too much—give them easy, actionable tasks.

- DON'T penalize staff for using social media—offer people the "twenty-first-century cigarette break" and let them use sites at work in exchange for helping to spread your message to their networks.

- DON'T reinvent the wheel—build your online Tweets and Facebook status updates off existing communications, grant proposals, acknowledgments, and so on.

- DO obey the Seven Golden Rules of E-mail Solicitation spelled out in the CAN-SPAM Act.

Conclusion

Online fundraising is growing at a pace unrivaled by any other fund development approach, with peer-to-peer efforts leading the charge. A nonprofit's ability to carve out a strategy and get a piece of the pie can make or break its ability to achieve its mission in today's times. In order to do this, it is critical to have a year-round strategy and team in place to recruit, renew, and grow donors via web-based giving programs. When done properly, these efforts can cost effectively help build sustainable communities of interest that support your organization's fundraising online and off, as well as spreading the good word about your good work.

Nicci Noble, CFRE is president of Noble Services LLC, an online fundraising, communications, marketing, and technology consulting company. Noble enjoys teaching nonprofit professionals how to ethically and effectively leverage technology and the Internet in their communication and fundraising efforts at educational events across the world. Noble is best known for her work at The Salvation Army, where she implemented their first email, online giving, and peer-to-peer programs for Christmas and disaster campaigns. Noble is a past president of the Association of Fundraising Professionals Golden Gate Chapter, served on the AFP International Committee on Directorship, and is currently a member of the AFP International External Relations Committee, Member Services Division, Marketing & Communications Task Force, and Chair of the Social Media Policy Guidelines Task Force.

Before joining the Center for Environmental Health as development director, Sean Sullivan served Equality California in the same role, where he lead the organization's $14 million No on Proposition 8 fundraising effort. Prior to that role, he served as the director of development and community relations for Covenant House California in Oakland, California, where he led multi-million-dollar fundraising campaigns over 10 years. Sean is the immediate past president of the Association of Fundraising Professionals Golden Gate Chapter and sits on the boards of several other community-based organizations. Sean holds his BA in journalism/mass communication from St. Bonaventure University and his certificate in nonprofit management from Stanford University.

Online Peer-to-Peer Fundraising Resource Review

Brandraising (www.bigducknyc.com/how/brandraising)

Outlines a mission-driven approach to communications and marketing, specifically designed to boost fundraising efforts.

The Next Generation of American Giving (www.convio.com/files/next-gen-whitepaper.pdf)

A research study into the charitable giving behaviors and attitudes of GenY, GenX, Boomers, and mature donors.

Nonprofit Social Network Benchmark Report
(www.nonprofitsocialnetworksurvey.com)

This report provides nonprofits with social networking insights and trends
that can support its marketing, communications, fundraising, and program
efforts.

My Charity Connects Web 2.0 Glossary (www.mycharityconnects.org/
web2_0glossary)

Useful dictionary of social network terms and other web-based jargon.

Mobile Active: <u>Using Mobile Phones in Fundraising Campaigns</u>
(www.mobileactive.org/files/MobileActive3_0.pdf)

This strategy guide examines the effectiveness of nonprofits using mobile
phones to build their constituent lists, influence political causes, and raise
money.

Choosing Bulk Email Software to Match Your Communication Goals
(www.idealware.org/articles/bulk_email_software_communication_
goals.php)

Tips on how to select your organization's broadcast email tool.

NTEN 501 Tech Clubs (www.nten.org/techclub)

Informal local groups of nonprofit techies and online fundraisers that meet
regularly to get to know their colleagues, develop a professional support
network, and talk shop.

Beth's Blog: <u>How Nonprofits Can Use Social Media</u> (www.bethkanter.org)

A place to share learning about nonprofits and social media, ROI, culture
change, strategy, and more.

Robert Weiner. <u>Online Fundraising Tools Checklist</u> (www.rlweiner.com/clf/
online_donations_checklist.pdf)

Issues to consider when looking for online donation tools.

<u>Sea Change Strategies: The Wired Wealthy—Using the Internet to Connect with Your Middle and Major Donors</u> (my.convio.com/?elqPURLPage=104)

This compelling study suggests that an "internet communications gap" exists between higher dollar donors and charities.

∘ ∘ ∘

All these resources, plus nonprofit management tips of the week and more, can be found at Nonprofits101.org.

CHAPTER 23

Cause-Related Marketing

By Jay Aldous, Chief Strategist, Social Capital Partnerships

Introduction

Cause-related marketing is the term broadly used to describe *partnerships between corporations and nonprofits,* which advance both the mission-related work of the nonprofit and the marketing objectives of the company. This has become an important means for nonprofit organizations to fulfill their respective missions. Its benefits are numerous, including generating revenue, building visibility and awareness, and securing in-kind and other mission-critical services. Many nonprofits recognize that cause-related marketing is an important component of the overall development and fundraising mix, and if they are not already pursuing these important relationships, they seek to do so.

So what does cause-related marketing look like in the real world? When a company supports a nonprofit organization in exchange for promotional rights and marketing benefits, and promotes that relationship to its employees, customers, beneficiaries, or stakeholders, *that* is cause-related marketing.

There are three forms of this powerful marketing and fundraising approach:

- Traditional cause-related marketing: donation-with-purchase of a company's products or services (funds from company)

- Consumer fundraising: company promotes an opportunity for its customers to make a donation at their place of business (funds from consumer)

- Event, initiative, or program sponsorship: traditional sponsorship model where a financial commitment is made in exchange for defined benefits around the sponsored asset (funds from company)

When it was first used as a marketing tool more than twenty years ago, most cause-related marketing relationships were *transactional*. That is, for each product purchased, a contribution would be made to a designated charity. One of the first and best-known transactional marketing campaigns was American Express's efforts in the early 1980s to restore the Statue of Liberty. During the promotional period, every time a member used her card, one cent was donated to The Statue of Liberty-Ellis Island Foundation to restore the monument so it could be reopened to the public.

Over the years, cause-related marketing has evolved and broadened. It now viewed as *any type of cooperative effort between a business and a nonprofit organization to market an image, product, or service for mutual benefit.* A 2009 PRWeek/Barkley survey showed indicated that *58% of for-profit marketers engaged in cause-related marketing.* Of those who do, 97% believed it's a valid business strategy. There's a market out there, and if you're not forming corporate partnerships to advance your mission, someone else will.

It is important to note what cause-related marketing is *not*. It is not "corporate philanthropy," where a gift or grant is made with nominal or no expectations regarding a direct impact on business. It does not include funding received from corporate foundations. And, it is also not a marketing campaign designed to change a social behavior or norm (e.g., don't drink and drive).

With that background in mind, let's look at what your organization needs to consider as it explores the benefits and risks of cause-related marketing.

Critical Skills and Competencies

For nonprofit organizations, successful cause-related partnerships are both *profitable* and *sustainable*. Unfortunately, many cause-related marketing partnerships fail to provide these benefits. Let's explore.

Profitability

For a nonprofit, *a profitable partnership is one that generates mission impact*. Mission impact can be measured in many ways: revenue for mission-critical programs, awareness and visibility for an issue or organization, or actions on behalf of individuals to support your mission. The ways a nonprofit determines profitability will vary, but there is a constant: *it is always important to consider whether a cause-related marketing relationship is the most efficient way to achieve your objectives given the costs incurred*. These costs can be hard (e.g., cash), soft (e.g., staff time), and opportunity (e.g., what could have otherwise been done). In many instances, a cause-related marketing partnership will not be profitable when measured in this way, so don't just go diving into any opportunity that comes your way—*take the time to assess expected impact, cost, and alternatives*.

Consider this fictional example. Company Do-Good approaches a nonprofit partner regarding a cause-related marketing opportunity. The company proposes a promotion where ten cents per sale of select products over a three-month period will go to the nonprofit. The nonprofit is excited about this opportunity. In particular, the executive director is excited about the opportunity in that she feels it will provide some "easy" money and visibility for her organization.

Fast-forward a year later. . . . The staff that worked on the relationship are frustrated by how much time has gone into managing the relationship. The nonprofit's executive director has been quoted as saying, "Never again." And the board is questioning why this partnership seems to be consuming so much staff time and resources.

What happened?

Although the company had represented that the promotion had the potential to generate $50,000, it only generated $37,000. Over time, the nonprofit learned that the sales projections were overly optimistic, but unfortunately failed to dig into the numbers initially. The expected visibility turned out to be limited to a small logo on point-of-sale materials and inclusion on limited local print advertising. The proposed national advertising never occurred.

An astute staff member thought it would be a good exercise to determine how much time and resources had been expended developing and supporting this relationship. A quick analysis revealed that $14,000 in staff time had been utilized creating proposals, managing the relationship, answering questions, and attending meetings with the partner. Review and negotiation of the contract by outside legal counsel cost $1,500. Travel expenses associated with meetings with the company, staffing a trade show booth, and speaking at a company meeting were slightly north of $8,000. The cost to provide the company's sales force with information kits about the organization and to supply the company's booth at a trade show with brochures and collateral was almost $2,500. All this effort netted an $11,000 return—a cost of $.58 to raise one dollar.

Was it worth it? Not likely, especially when you *consider the opportunity cost of this relationship.* This cost would factor in the following questions: Could the hundreds of hours spent by staff on this project been better utilized? Could the resources expended for travel and servicing the relationship generated a better return if spent on cultivating major donors or foundation grants? Did the final measure (the cost to raise a dollar) have a negative impact on the organization's efficiency ratings?

Unfortunately, this fictional example is not far from the reality of many cause-related marketing partnerships. Although you can never hope to know exactly how things will work out in advance, *the key to success, and to defending against a waste of precious time and money, is doing your homework before you enter into any type of partnership.* Set and manage realistic expectations. But let's imagine for a moment that the measure of profitability was acceptable. There's another hoop the nonprofit's cause-related marketing effort needs to jump through if it's to be considered successful: sustainability.

Sustainability

A sustainable partnership is one that endures, if not grows over the course of a number of years. There are up-front costs in establishing cause-related marketing partnerships, but these can be offset against the value of the partnership to your organization over time. As both the company and the nonprofit get to know each other and work better together, both groups can begin to collaborate more closely, plus targeted consumers begin to get familiar with the effort. As a result, partnership tactics are refined. Models of sustainability include Children's Miracle Network's 22-year partnership with Wal-Mart, which has raised more than $460 million for children's hospitals; Share Our Strength's 18-year relationship with American Express has generated $30 million for hunger programs; and finally, let's not forget Susan G. Komen Race for the Cure's 16-year relationship with Ford, which has resulted in more than 50,000 Ford employees participating in Race for the Cure events and raising more than $100 million for the organization.

In these examples, long-term partnerships increasingly offset the initial cost of setting up a program, and over time these partnerships became more efficient, dropping the cost per dollar ratio and making the partnerships more profitable.

Clearly there's a lot of potential in cause-related marketing, but how can smaller organizations get successful, sustainable, profitable programs off the ground?

The Five Timeless Truths

Any nonprofit considering or engaging in a cause-related marketing partnership should assess potential and actual profitability and sustainability initially and on an ongoing basis in order to gauge success and cost versus benefit. More important, they should draw on five timeless truths, all of which have been proven by the examples above, and also through the countless experiences of organizations, both large and small.

1. Cause-Related Marketing Is About More Than Money

Many nonprofit organizations have a myopic view as to the importance and value of cause-related marketing partnerships. Unfortunately, corporate partners are often viewed solely as funders, and not as strategic partners that can bring expertise, influence, and noncash resources towards the achievement of a nonprofit's mission. The key is to *think long term, and to explore how to make the best use of all the tools in the company's toolbox, not just their bank account—cause-related marketing partnerships are not the answer for near-term cash needs.* Nor are they generally the most efficient way to generate cash resources. In addition to cash support, cause-related marketing partners can be a tremendous resource in helping to secure and generate other mission-critical assets, such as budget-relieving in-kind, media, and technical expertise.

In-Kind Support   *In addition to contributing revenue, corporate partnerships can also help reduce costs through valuable in-kind support.* Make-A-Wish Foundation of America has been particularly successful at developing cause-related marketing partnerships with a variety of airlines, hotels, and travel providers, where the organization receives travel services that can be used in granting wishes. These in-kind contributions save the organization money that would have otherwise been expended, and are critical to fulfilling its mission of granting wishes to children with life-threatening medical conditions. Separately, Feeding America secures 740 million pounds of food from its corporate partners each year, enough to provide almost 580 million meals annually. This donated food helps Feeding America achieve its mission of eliminating food insecurity within the United States. How can corporate in-kind support advance your efforts and take money off your bottom line?

Contributed Media   Getting the word out is key to just about every nonprofit's mission, so *consider approaching websites and local ad agencies, TV and radio stations, and newspapers to try and secure free advertising.* The U.S. Fund for UNICEF has developed an innovative partnership with top advertising agencies. These agencies approach the companies they purchase media from and ask them to donate time and ad space to support UNICEF's Believe in Zero call-to-action campaign. Each year UNICEF receives more than $10 million in donated media to raise awareness for mission-critical initiatives, and it delivers a call to action to targeted audiences. This relationship has been critical to the U.S. Fund for UNICEF and has allowed it to increase its base of supporters and reduce the number of daily preventable deaths of children in the developing world from 26,000 to 24,000. Two thousand lives saved everyday—that's direct mission impact.

One of the most effective and accessible types of donated media is provided by Google Grants (www.google.com/grants), where *any nonprofit can apply for $10,000 a month in free Google AdWords advertising.*

Technical Expertise   As we saw in the technology section of this book, tech can be a great enabler of meeting mission. As part of their relationship with United Way of King County, the Seattle office of a global accounting firm reviewed United Way's IT infrastructure and provided pro bono recommendations on how multiple databases could be integrated and streamlined to provide more timely and accurate information, thereby improving and expanding United Way's service delivery. United Way would have been unable to pay for this kind of support otherwise, while the accounting firm enjoyed engaging employees in community building.

2. Cause-Related Marketing Success Is Built on Establishing Clear Objectives

Unfortunately, many cause-related marketing partnerships fail to clearly establish mutually agreed-on, quantified objectives. Few partnerships have written documents that *clearly articulate, in measurable terms, how partnership success is defined.* It is difficult to be an effective and valuable partner, the key to sustainable and profitable relationships, if you don't know how you will be evaluated and measured! Setting clear, tangible goals for both the company and the nonprofit is key to any effort to effectively steward resources and evaluate the mission impact of a partnership, not to mention that it ensures everyone is on the same page from the beginning, and moving forward.

Some examples of what a business partner might expect the partnership to accomplish include:

- A consumer package goods manufacturer seeks a 10% increase in presales of a product to retail customers

- A car dealer seeks 500 qualified test drives

- A health care provider desires a 15% increase in consumers who think of their company as "caring about and committed to the communities where they operate," as defined by their annual community survey

- A grocery retailer wants 10% of its workforce to volunteer for a nonprofit, raise $500,000 for the cause via its customers, and be acknowledged as a top-tier sponsor in order to improve its image

Some examples of what a nonprofit might expect the partnership to accomplish include:

- Generate $100,000 of unrestricted revenue

- Secure a commitment from a leading corporate CEO to serve on its board of directors

- Inclusion of the nonprofit in a paid advertising campaign, increasing awareness of its efforts with 20,000 new supporters

- Access to 5,000 employees for the purpose of volunteer recruitment and fundraising

As Einstein said, "If you can't explain something simply, you don't understand it." Before embarking on a partnership, *capture on a single page the metrics that define success for each organization, the time line for achieving these outcomes, and the person responsible for key activities.* Share this document with your corporate partner and verify that you are on the same page. Most importantly, make sure you're in agreement regarding what will be evaluated: when, how, and by whom.

3. Cause-Related Marketing Takes Time

Successful cause-related marketing partnerships take time to mature and unleash their potential. Speed daters need not apply. Look at some of what are considered model cause-related marketing partnerships, and the time they took time to develop. UNICEF and Pampers—almost two years. Susan G. Komen for the Cure and Yoplait—18 months. Whirlpool and Habitat for Humanity—14 months.

Successful cause-related marketing partnerships that have clearly defined objectives and are structured to provide returns beyond cash take time to sell, develop, plan, and execute. As a good rule of thumb, *it takes 12–18 months from when a nonprofit begins talking to a prospective business partner until a partnership is manifest* in-market and a nonprofit begins to enjoy the desired benefits.

First off, the solicitation of cause-related marketing partners takes time. Important steps in the solicitation process include: research on a prospective partner to understand their business objectives and needs, identification of key decision-makers at the prospective partner, getting the meeting or call, development of a proposal that shows how your organization can address their needs, and of course actually and closing the deal. As a general rule, you should attempt to present your proposal to a senior executive—Sales 101 tells us to *always go after the decision maker*. Use your organizational and personal relationships to see who can facilitate an introduction. Share the names of senior executives at a prospective partner with staff, your board, key donors and volunteers, and other corporate partners. Ideally, someone will know one of these individuals and can help arrange an initial meeting.

Once a meeting is secured, a compelling initial presentation must be made, wherein you *emphasize how the partnership can help the company meet the objectives you've identified through your research and conversations*. Remember to be flexible and to listen, since rarely does a nonprofit perfectly understand all of the objectives before the first meeting. Creating solid partnerships cannot be rushed—as mentioned earlier, the courtship process usually takes some time. If you're successful in getting the company to express interest in partnering with your nonprofit, it will likely take a series of subsequent meetings, proposals, and hopefully contracts to clearly and measurably define partnership objectives, determine the tactics and activities that will achieve these objectives, agree on who is responsible for what within both organizations, and determine how partnership success will be monitored and evaluated. Once the partnership objectives, activities, and responsibilities have been defined, you should *memorialize these agreements in a partnership agreement*, including the one-page top line document outlined above, as well as a formal legal agreement. You should *always seek qualified legal counsel in creating this agreement* to ensure that the cause-related marketing partnership is in compliance with appropriate laws, Better Business Bureau guidelines, and IRS regulations, and in general to ensure your risk is minimized and that you have a legally defensible "memorandum of understanding" or contract. In order to maintain more control over this process, most nonprofits prefer to utilize partnership agreements that their legal council has drafted, rather than have the corporate partner prepare the partnership agreement.

4. Both the Business and the Nonprofit Must Benefit.

Never forget this. A company does not choose to partner with you solely because your organization is worthy. Your partner expects something in return. Remember the term "mutual benefit" and those agreed-on objectives? (Timeless Truth #2.) It is important to define which assets, activities, and actions your organization will need to deliver to make sure that those objectives are met. Try this useful exercise: *Before developing cause-related marketing partnerships, conduct an inventory of the "assets" that you can provide a partner.* Assets may include: use of the organization's name and logo to enhance image or generate credibility; category exclusivity, attendance or presence at events; access to your donor or member base; and presence on your website, annual report, and other print and electronic collateral. Never forget that *the most valuable assets from the perspective of a corporate partner are those that will help them achieve their desired objectives.* Remember, you are not receiving a philanthropic gift. This is a partnership, and by definition a partnership requires contributions from both parties.

Your organization will probably incur both hard and soft costs in order to deliver your end of the deal. When developing a partnership, and *before negotiation of terms, you should have an understanding of what the costs will be to support the partnership.* Often these costs are significant and, as mentioned, it's always important to know what you're getting into ahead of time.

A few words about the people who work for the company you are partnering with. Ultimately, these people are accountable for the performance of their organization, department, or budget, just like you are. Doing their job well means leveraging the relationship with your nonprofit to achieve their business objectives. Though they may like you, the organization that you work for, and the issue your nonprofit represents, at the end of the day their responsibility is to manage their relationship with you in a way that advances the aims of their company.

As you sell, structure, and manage a cause-related marketing partnership, continually ask yourself, *"How is this partnership helping achieve our partner's objectives?"* If you are not delivering real, tangible value—as directed by the mutually agreed-on objectives—then a partnership is not likely to be sustainable.

5. Cause-Related Marketing Partnerships Must Result in Measurable Mission Impact

Successful partnerships translate into mission outcome. Nonprofits with successful cause-related marketing programs must be able to report back to a partner and tell them what impact or change has occurred because of the partnership. This is key to generating a strong sense of connection and ownership by the corporate partner, which helps pave the way for the expansion and extension of the initial agreement. As you've read earlier, just as with any donor, the key is to *focus on the impact that their support makes possible*.

Going back to our examples, in the Pampers-UNICEF partnership, every time a consumer purchases a designated package of Pampers, they purchase a tetanus vaccine for a pregnant mother via UNICEF. UNICEF is able to clearly report direct, measurable impact to Pampers, its retailer customers, and consumers regarding exactly what has been accomplished through the partnership. To date, 200 million tetanus vaccines have been provided. Feeding America provides seven meals for every $1 generated by their corporate partnerships; what a simple and eloquent way to show the impact their partners are making. Finally, The Nature Conservancy is addressing global warming through reforestation. Their "Plant a Billion Trees" campaign allows supporters to measure their impact, literally, one tree at time.

Partners and donors don't want to fund your organization's work—they want to purchase impact. Your partner, their employees, and their customers want to know what difference they made with their support. It's imperative to quantify and share the impact that their partnership is making in achieving your mission, and do so on a regular basis. Tell them how many lives have been saved because of vaccines they have funded, meals provided because of their support, or trees planted because of their efforts. Help them share the results of your combined efforts with their customers, employees, and other target audiences.

o o o

The first place to put these five timeless truths into practice is when creating a proposal for a prospective cause-related marketing partner, but only after you've done your homework and had initial calls or meetings to ascertain exactly what the prospect's goals are. *A good proposal will show how a partnership can achieve a company's business objectives and result in mission impact.* As you write your proposal, lead with the mission impact you are proposing, then speak to the objectives that can be achieved through a partnership with your organization, and finally show how these objectives can be achieved in partnership with your organization. Try and keep your initial proposal to twenty PowerPoint slides or less (or, no more than five pages). Remember, this proposal should be about what you can do for the prospective company and the social change that will result. It should not be about the worthiness of your organization, the need, or the good work your organization is already doing, although all of that can add helpful context if overviewed in brief. Most important, your proposal should *position your nonprofit as a solution to a company's business needs, not as a recipient for a donation.*

Cause-Related Marketing Dos and Don'ts

- DO examine the partnership in terms of its cost to raise a dollar.

- DO leverage your network to identity inroads with key decision makers at a prospect, and do your homework to identify the prospect's business objectives before an initial call or meeting.

- DON'T assume you have a perfect grasp on the company's goals before an initial meeting; realize you're just starting a conversation and use it to gain a better understanding of their needs before submitting a proposal.

- DO establish clear objectives, time lines, metrics, and personnel support before entering into any partnership, and summarize these in a one-page memorandum of understanding or legal contract signed by both parties.

- DON'T take sales projections (and your potential income) at face value. Ask to see how the projections were generated and for worst-case and best-case projections. Require a minimum guarantee if possible.

- DO allow adequate time (12–18 months) for the partnership to develop before expecting measurable benefits.

- DO tie the expected end results to some clear, measurable mission impact.

Dos and Don'ts

Conclusion

If structured, negotiated, and managed with an eye toward profitability and sustainability, cause-related marketing partnerships can play an important role in achieving your nonprofit's mission. How can you best develop business partnerships for your nonprofit? Work your network, always look to establish win-win partnerships, and do your homework, but remain a good listener, agree on expectations and metrics ahead of time, and track and share your mission impact. Also, become a student of successful partnerships and deploy the best practices you discover within your organization—talk with peers who are developing and managing cause-related marketing partnerships and learn from them. Finally, follow the five timeless truths and you will be well on your way to helping your nonprofit achieve mission-critical results through cause-related marketing.

Jay Aldous is chief strategist for Social Capital Partnerships, a consultancy that advises top-tier nonprofits on developing sustainable revenue sources. Prior, he was the chief marketing and communications officer for the U.S. Fund for UNICEF. During his tenure he created UNICEF's call-to-action campaign, Believe in Zero, and UNICEF's award-winning clean water initiative, the Tap Project. Previous positions included senior partner of The Brighton Group, a consultancy providing marketing and development services to nonprofit organizations, and senior vice president of Marketing for Children's Miracle Network. Aldous was recognized as the 2008 Nonprofit Marketer of the Year by the American Marketing Association.

Cause-Related Marketing Resource Review

Cause Marketing Forum (www.causemarketingforum.com)

Great resource with a variety of articles, tips, and an annual conference on cause-related marketing.

Social Capital Partnerships (www.socialcapitalpartnerships.com)

Industry-specific research and annual conference on cause-related marketing.

The Foundation Center (www.foundationcenter.org/getstarted/faqs/html/cause_marketing.html)

Robust resource on philanthropy, including information on corporate giving and cause-related marketing.

OnPhilanthropy.com (www.onphilanthropy.com)

A resource for several outstanding e-newsletters, rich with information on corporate giving, nonprofit marketing, and related topics.

Business in the Community (UK) (www.bitc.org.uk/resources/index.html)

This site provides resources, case studies, and links that provide an international perspective to cause-related marketing.

Osocio (www.osocio.org)

Excellent blog dedicated to social advertising and nonprofit marketing campaigns.

Hamish Pringle and Marjorie Thompson. <u>Brand Spirit: How Cause Related Marketing Builds Brands</u>. New York: Wiley, 2001.

Explains how many corporate campaigns were developed to assist nonprofits and enhance corporate image.

Peleg Top and Jonathan Cleveland. <u>Designing for the Greater Good: The Best in Cause-Related Marketing and Nonprofit Design</u>. New York: CollinsDesign, 2010.

Features hundreds of illustrated examples of the best nonprofit and cause-related design worldwide, plus 24 inspiring case studies and insights into great nonprofit branding campaigns.

Sue Adkins. <u>Cause Related Marketing</u>. Oxford: Butterworth Heinemann, 1999.

Useful book that covers all aspects of this important field.

Richard Earle. <u>The Art of Cause Marketing: How to Use Advertising to Change Personal Behavior and Public Policy</u>. Chicago: McGraw-Hill, 2000.

This book examines how to strategize effectively and develop a public service advertising campaign that seeks to change strongly ingrained behavior or firmly held beliefs. Includes case studies and 75 storyboards from actual cause advertising and print ads.

○ ○ ○

All these resources, plus nonprofit management tips of the week and more, can be found at Nonprofits101.org.

CHAPTER 24

Social Enterprise 101: An Overview of the Basic Principles

By Rick Aubry, PhD, CEO and Founder, New Foundry Ventures, and Faculty Member, Stanford University Graduate School of Business

Introduction

"Hey gang, I've got a great idea; let's start a business to make some money so we can further our mission!"

Nonprofit leaders who are fans of the old Andy Hardy movies of the 1940s might recognize the sentiment that with a little pluck and the inherent good will of a nonprofit, they, too can start a business to make some money to support the organization. It's a story where everybody wins.

Well, as you might imagine, it's not that simple.

Understandably, nonprofits are always looking for new ways to increase the revenue needed to do their work. Nonprofits, particularly those that provide direct services to at-risk communities are often dependent on funding sources that are notorious for providing too little resources to do a very big job. As such, the idea of a steady stream of financial support from a "social enterprise" that supports the organization's good work often seems like a rational decision for a nonprofit to make.

This brief chapter highlights the things to consider before starting a social enterprise or developing an "earned-income strategy" for your nonprofit; that is, a business venture within a nonprofit organization that generates income from selling goods and services to supplement philanthropic and grant support. In the coming pages, I'll address:

- Earned-income strategies for nonprofits

- How to use entrepreneurial principles, earned-income strategies and businesses to create social change

- Succeeding as an emerging social entrepreneur: tips on making it work

A quick reminder of the relationship between nonprofit *strategy* and nonprofit *mission* is an important starting point. Jim Phills, professor at Stanford University's Graduate School of Business, has laid out a critical framework for understanding the role of strategy in nonprofits and, most importantly, its relationship with the organization's mission. Phills contends:

1. Mission is the most critical element of a nonprofit, because at its core it defines the purpose, primary goals, and vision of the organization; because the mission is the raison d'être of the organization, it rarely changes. For example, if the mission is to cure polio, the organization knows what it is aiming for, and when it has achieved its mission

2. A nonprofit's strategy defines the particular steps the organization takes to most effectively achieve the mission. Strategies, as opposed to mission, can change over time. The organization focused on curing polio might think that an education strategy focused on teaching people not to share food with people possibly infected is the most effective way to combat the disease. Following that strategy, the organization could invest in an advertising campaign designed to reduce the number of people undertaking

this activity. As medical science advances, a new strategy, for example developing a vaccine, might replace the earlier one. As a result the organization would then devote its resources to scientists and labs to help discover the vaccine. Because organizations always have limited resources, *what is most critical is finding the most effective strategy that directly advances your mission.*

Earned income may seem like simply a way to make money independently of the mission, but given the very limited resources of nonprofits, *when the strategy does not directly advance the mission it is often a distraction and not advantageous to the organization.* Therefore, before thinking of a business as simply a revenue stream with no connection to the organization's overall mission, I would argue that for virtually all nonprofits, *the only earned-income strategy that makes sense is the one that directly advances the mission of the organization.*

Further, for the business to ultimately succeed, it must find and take advantage of the inherent competitive advantage of the organization. Understanding competitive advantage is a critical and complex challenge for all social businesses. Although a deep understanding of Michael Porter's concept of competitive advantage is beyond the scope of this brief chapter, for the sake of this discussion, *"competitive advantage" for a nonprofit is understanding what the organization's abilities and competencies are that make it best positioned to solve the social problem it is created to address.* What sets you apart and makes you better than others in some way? Does your organization have a stronger relationship with the community you serve? Do you have a way of providing the service more effectively for a lower cost? Do you have locations that would make a business succeed? Has your nonprofit developed a unique way of addressing the problem that would be very hard for someone else to copy without significant time and resources? Do members of your team offer skills and talents other organizations don't have? Does your group have a reputation and brand that would translate well into a social business? *What matters is not what your organization thinks of itself, but what its customers think.* See Chapter Twenty-Five for more information on this important topic.

Certainly there are exceptions to the rule. For example, a museum with a great location for a restaurant can probably generate a lot of revenue from such a business. A maritime museum with a large pier can probably make a lot of money renting out some boat slips commercially. These are unusual sources of competitive advantage not based on the mission, but connection to unique locations. If your nonprofit is lucky enough to enjoy a geographic advantage, there may be an earned-income strategy worth undertaking. Again, these are uncommon situations and may generate revenue, but they will rarely be responsible for creating the social change your organization's mission calls for.

Critical Skills and Competencies

Success will require the right organizational environment, the right funding, the right attitude toward risk, the right leadership, a real competitive advantage, and the right investor or key customer. Let's look at each of these.

The Organizational Environment

Before embarking on a social business strategy, the organization must recognize the difference between a social business and a "regular" business and at the same time be realistic about the inherent risks and challenges of operating any venture. A social business strategy adds the additional complexity of a focus on both the financial and social returns to be created, often called a "double bottom line." *Social businesses in particular need to establish clear, quantifiable metrics to identify what measurable social impact they hope to achieve.* In addition, they need to benchmark social goals against alternative ways to achieve the social goal (see "opportunity cost" in Chapter Twenty-Three). For example, a social business that has a goal of helping people find work must evaluate the cost of job creation when considering investing $500,000 in a business which would only create three jobs— probably not the best use of their precious resources.

For any business, whether social or traditional for-profit, success with a start-up is extremely difficult. *Social ventures run by nonprofits are almost always small businesses, and most studies agree that over 60% of small businesses fail within the first four years.* If the goal is simply to increase income for the organization, most investors, individuals, and organizations are probably best advised to place their resources in a savings account or other passive investment vehicle, rather than starting a business. That said, if you decide to press ahead, here are some tips and strategies that should prove helpful, as well as some advice for how to decide whether starting a business is the right decision for your nonprofit.

For a business to succeed in the nonprofit world, the same virtues and rules of the road that apply to traditional business hold true. The organizational environment must contain some key ingredients. *There must be a zealous and empowered entrepreneur for whom the business is an all-encompassing job for the first several years of the venture.* As investors in startup companies will tell you, the credibility and dedication of the management team is even more important than the business model.

In addition to impassioned leadership within the business, *the organization must have an environment in which the core leadership is fully committed to the business.* They must agree that the planned business is a core asset of the organization. Most nonprofits are resource constrained, with numerous competing needs for limited funds, time, and so on. Always remember that *your governing board signed on to advance the social mission, not run a business.* It is inevitable that a social business will use more resources for several years than it provides back to the organization. At least initially, resources must be raised and given to the business, rather than other parts of the organization. *Without a very clear and complete commitment of your staff leadership and board, the venture will suffer greatly* during the inevitable downturns, headaches, and the like.

Even with the right leadership and internal support in place, *finding and securing sufficient capital is both critical and difficult—social businesses often suffer from the mistake of undercapitalizing the business at the beginning.* Financial and other resources will always be needed in greater amounts than originally anticipated. A few rules of thumb usually apply. *Expect it to take twice as long to achieve the financial goals you optimistically project,* so make sure you have start-up capital, or the ability to deficit spend for such a contingency. Unexpected "miscellaneous costs of up to 25%" should be included in your budgets for all those things you cannot anticipate. It is almost always best to prepare your funders and your boards in advance for higher costs than to go back again and again hat in hand.

In addition, *building the board's and management's tolerance for a long-term start-up horizon is critical*, though often challenging within nonprofit organization. In virtually all cases, things will proceed much more slowly than planned. Do the board, funders, other members of the organization, and the management team really support the long, hard challenges of the business struggling? Make sure that everyone involved is in it for the long haul, and *plan for the likely contingency that those rosy numbers in your projections may take longer to achieve than you think*, if ever.

Your organization must develop a thoughtful and comprehensive business plan, which at the very least includes strategy, competitive analysis, market survey, financial projections, and a team of strong mentors and advisors. Good intentions and hope are not a plan, and although that's all many nonprofits have in place when they start out, this simply doesn't cut it in the business world. Suggestions for developing these key pieces to your business plan are beyond the scope of this chapter, but can be found in several nonprofit business planning books. Personally, I recommend <u>Generating and Sustaining Nonprofit Earned Income: A Guide to Successful Enterprise Strategies</u> by Yale School of Management–The Goldman Sachs Foundation Partnership on Nonprofit Ventures, Sharon M. Oster (Editor).

Finally, *your organization must have effective internal communication about the new business*. Staff who are focused on the "mission" activities of the organization often feel like second-class citizens when leadership time, resources, and focus flow towards the social business. Proactive, clear communication, effective leadership persuasion, and constant reminders of how the business advances the mission are critical to maintain the organization's esprit de corps and maintain organizational support for the business. This is one more reason why the business will be more successful if the activities are aligned with advancing the social mission.

The Funding Environment

Nonprofits need money to start their businesses, but they often can't go to the same sources as would a traditional small business operator. The nonprofit "social capital market" is a very different world, with different rules.

Social capital market is a term widely used to describe loans, program related investments, and other financing tools to support nonprofit ventures that are made available by foundations, government agencies, corporations, and individuals. This so-called market, however, is not well coordinated and the various actors operate independently of one another. In a real marketplace, the most effective organizations and ventures that have the potential to grow sizably have more ready access to start-up funds. This ensures good innovations are supported from the beginning stages through their development, growth, and scale phases. The social capital market is much smaller than traditional capital markets, which include bank loans, venture capital, and private equity. These are usually unavailable to nonprofits since they cannot issue equity (ownership) in their businesses without spinning them off, which creates a series of other considerations and challenges. *The social market focuses on social impact before financial return*, which is inherently much harder to gauge and monitor. As such it does not have the innate efficiency or discipline of the traditional market. The investors in the polio vaccine may have saved countless lives and billions of dollars, but the foundations that paid for it got less of a financial return than the investors in Pet Rocks.

If you are going to start a social business, be prepared to spend an inordinate amount of time raising money. By most estimates, traditional businesses invest 3–5% of leadership time raising funds for a venture, with the rest devoted to making the business work. Many nonprofits spend 20–50% of their leadership time raising money, a significant distraction from the actual work of the organization. "The disorderliness and complexity of the philanthropic funding environment," according to Allen Grossman of the Harvard Business School, "distracts nonprofit management, shifting focus away from organizational performance."

One last note on the need for true dedication when launching a social business. The capital challenge lies not just in the external problems in the social capital markets, but also in nonprofit organizations' internal issues around the use of capital. *For the business venture to grow, a significant amount of a nonprofit's overall resources must be devoted to the effort.* In addition to important management time and attention as outlined above, this includes other internal investments that deter resources away from activities otherwise devoted to the mission through established programs. For example, fund development efforts, or fundraising, may be focused more on the business and less on programs. Such efforts can add significant debt, which can affect the entire organization. Social businesses can generate substantial revenue and advance your mission as well, but be sure to know exactly what you're getting into, and set expectations realistically.

Risk Tolerance

Nonprofit ventures entail innately higher risks than typical mission-based programs. Nonprofit managers are used to raising grant and government funds, building a budget to spend those funds, and then managing to that budget. If a grant is cut, reductions of staff or services can keep the organization on budget. A social business, particularly at the startup and growth stages, has only projections of revenues, costs, labor needed to deliver the services or goods, etc. If it costs more to make a biscuit than the budget projected, you cannot simply cut out the butter to keep on budget. In addition the essential business-focused cost accounting, *production management and sales forecasting presents a completely different accounting challenge and risk profile for organizations more accustomed to nonprofit management.*

Further, the risk tolerance among managers of a nonprofit's core activities is not generally as high for running a business as it is for running the organization's programs, because *putting the programs at risk for a venture that might not succeed may prove unacceptable to staff and board*; yet another reason why mission-based businesses are key. Organizations that take an annual budget approach to business operations will be challenged to maintain a business. In good years, the excess revenues of the business will be used to staunch other organizational needs. But in bad years the businesses will be seen as "the problem"—the reason why the organization is short on funds. *It takes tremendous organizational discipline and commitment to a long-term strategy to incorporate the business cycle within a nonprofit's budget and focus.*

Leadership Skills

As noted, the first thing that smart venture capitalists look for in a start-up is a great management team. Once a nonprofit has the support of the board and executive team and a business strategy aligned with its mission, it needs to find the right leadership. The first step is to identify the critical skills for what Jed Emerson, an early pioneer in the field of social enterprise, has called "the mutant manager" of the social enterprise. *The most essential skills are a deep experience base in the specific business the nonprofit has chosen, a clear commitment to the social mission of the organization, and the ability to work well with the leadership teams of the organization and the business.*

There are several key factors when considering who should lead the business. Most important: under almost all circumstances, *don't promote the best nonprofit manager at your nonprofit to run a business not related to their experience.* Nonprofits generally promote people to departments or roles offering them new challenges as a career path. But the requirements for success in businesses are fundamentally different; it is simply a recipe for disaster to promote the smartest, most hard working nonprofit manager to run a business in an industry they don't know. Instead, *find people from the industry who are ready to devote the next phase of their professional life to advancing your social mission, along with the business.* Mid-career professionals are often eager to apply their skills and industry knowledge to a business that offers meaning beyond simple profit. The best managers in social businesses are often people eager for such a change.

Accordingly, *salaries for your social business venture must be in line with salaries in comparable for-profit businesses.* Business managers may join a nonprofit social venture at some discount of their salary potential, but that's entirely different from expecting them to be compensated in line with your nonprofit employees. Though there is no clear rule dictating what size salary adjustment a great manager might take, if any, in this author's experience *a 10–30% "discount" from traditional salaries is the best you can hope for from a committed, qualified manager—you must be ready and willing to pay competitive salaries to find the right person, even if this means addressing internal equity issues.*

Given the need for industry experience, it is likely that your new manager will come from the for-profit sector. She will need support "crossing over"— adjusting to nonprofit culture. The executive director must help the new manager adjust to the different culture, focus, pace, and other aspects of your nonprofit. Business managers often feel like visitors in a foreign country as they learn the subtle ways of getting things done within a nonprofit environment. Rob Waldron was a successful for-profit CEO until he took over as CEO of the nonprofit Jumpstart. When speaking to my Stanford social entrepreneurship class he said, "I feel like I have moved from being a general in the army to a member of the Senate. In for-profits I gave a direction and people jumped to it. In the nonprofit I have stakeholders, various interest groups, a whole different culture, and I have to lead through persuasion rather than through authority." On the shop floor of the venture, the manager may have the ability to be more directive. But when working with fellow managers, board members, funders, and others, the manager must adapt to a very different, collaborative approach.

Real Competitive Advantage

Being "the good guy" in the market is not really a competitive advantage. *The customers of your social business won't buy your goods or services because you are a nonprofit, but rather because they believe they are getting the best value—* welcome to the wonderful world of business. Too many nonprofits assume that the "halo factor" will get them customers and continued sales. In study after study of customer behavior, however, the fact that a product or service has a social benefit associated with it is typically a tertiary decision factor, after quality and value. All other things being equal, many will choose the nonprofit option, but, as Carrie Portis, a former general manager of the Rubicon Bakery (a highly successful social business in the San Francisco Bay Area) once said to me, "Our Rubicon Cakes have to be the best cake, not the best nonprofit cake, in the dessert case in order for customers to buy them."

There may be some circumstances where the social purpose of the organization matters, such as governments that create "set aside" contracts for businesses that achieve social outcomes considered a public good. For example, the Javits-Wagner-O'Day Act established the principle that a certain amount of federal contracts would go towards organizations that hire disabled workers otherwise unable to secure employment in "competitive settings." In order to succeed, social businesses must identity such opportunities and lobby to advance policies that create additional ones (tips on lobbying can be found in Chapter Twelve). However, this is a small and limited pie, and the entry of additional nonprofits does little to further the overall social benefit; it merely moves the jobs from one nonprofit to another.

The Right Investor or Customer

Although tough to plan for, finding an "angel" customer or investor at the early stages of activity has made all the difference for many of the most successful social enterprises. Greyston Bakery in Yonkers, New York, has done a marvelous job of creating jobs for hard-to-employ people while generating revenues for its parent nonprofit, Greyston Foundation. Ben Cohen of Ben & Jerry's Ice Cream was key to their early success. By joining them as a significant pilot customer, Ben and Jerry's helped Greyston flourish by keeping up a healthy volume of purchases, by supporting their work in the early years, by remaining flexible on their working relationship, and by making a long-term commitment to continue to purchase from Greyston at a sustainable price. *Who do you know, or could you get to know, that could become your angel?*

But beware. The flip side of the angel is the foundation investor that has a fast growth agenda and pushes a nonprofit too far, too fast. A 20-year-old, highly regarded nonprofit nearly went bankrupt in 2001 when the overly ambitious growth plan it had developed in partnership with a foundation led it to the brink of financial collapse. Two million dollars of foundation and bank debt went into a business plan that had never been adequately tested, all in the interest of proving a theory that the business could rapidly increase in size. When the business crashed and burned, the parent nonprofit shrunk overnight from a budget of $8 million and 150 employees (mostly hard-to-employ workers) to a budget of $2 million with fewer than 30 staff. This rapid collapse provides a cautionary tale for the field, highlighting the intrinsic challenges of business growth in the nonprofit social enterprise arena. On the for-profit side, businesses come and go and it is primarily the capital that is lost. In the nonprofit world, the entire social beneficial organization is at stake.

Social Enterprise Dos and Don'ts

Dos	Don'ts
Examine carefully what your organization does well, and what unique competitive advantage you might have in the marketplace.	Start a business within your organization because a board member thinks it would be easy and lucrative.
Make sure you develop a business plan, raise twice as much money as you need, and prepare your organization for a long-term engagement in a business that may take years to succeed.	Assume that being a nonprofit will get you regular steady customers if you don't have a great product or service.
Hire experienced and passionate people from the industry you are entering to lead the business, not talented nonprofit managers.	Kid yourself with a self-serving business projection—everything can be made to work on an Excel spreadsheet.
Make sure the leader of your business is given the resources, authority, and "protection" she/he needs within your organization.	Forget to "stress test" your budget to understand what happens when you sell less, or more than you expect.
Remember the earned income strategy that makes the most sense is the one that directly advances your mission.	Expect the best nonprofit manager within your organization to become the right manager for the social business you are starting—*industry expertise is essential.*
Make sure the product or service is one that reflects well on the overall brand and mission of your organization.	Expect your current nonprofit/grant cash flow cycles to be the same as for the business you will operate—*make sure you have access to cash or lines of credit* for the long periods between when you buy the ingredients and when your customers pay you for the finished goods.
Make sure you love the business you're entering, because you will be part of it for many years.	Underestimate the need to have strong organizational support from the board and staff for the business to weather the inevitable long periods of difficulty with the business—organizations with limited resources are quick to scapegoat a social business during its down years.

Conclusion

Many nonprofits are looking for additional funding to supplement their limited resources. As a result, a social enterprise that provides a new revenue stream often looks enticing, but it's something that must only be undertaken with the proper consideration and commitment. The strong recommendation of this author is that a realistic analysis of the risks, rewards, true costs, impact on the organization's culture, and competitive advantage are all steps that must be carefully considered for any organization contemplating a social business.

There can be significant benefits for organizations that succeed with a social enterprise when it also advances the mission. *Balancing the mission goals with the business needs is the critical element in any social business success.*

For many this will mean creating jobs for communities that have limited access to traditional employment, which has proven to be the most common form of social business in the United States. Selecting business opportunities that create jobs, promise to be financially viable, and which blend with the organization's goals and "brand" are the keys to success for these kinds of ventures.

Successful social businesses not only advance the mission and generate revenue, they can also have a positive "halo" effect overall on the organization. Funders and communities think highly of organizations that can successfully run competitive businesses to further their mission. It connotes a scrappy, can-do, business savvy approach and lends a positive aura to the organization's mission-based services.

For those social businesses that have succeeded, the next challenge and opportunity is finding ways to grow the impact of the work through business expansion. If there is a strong competitive advantage, a unique business need being met, and the organizational and entrepreneurial desire to build the next generation of social businesses, a huge benefit can ensue. This scaling of social businesses is the next frontier for the field, and it remains the work of organizations such as Rubicon National Social Innovation and New Foundry Ventures to forge social change through growing social businesses.

Rick Aubry, PhD, is the founder and CEO of New Foundry Ventures (formerly Rubicon National Social Innovations) and a faculty member at the Stanford Graduate School of Business, where he is a fellow of Stanford's Center for Social Innovation. His work at Rubicon has had a significant and measured impact on the lives of over 40,000 people confronting homelessness, poverty, and the challenges of living with mental health disabilities. He is a five-time winner of Fast Company Magazine's Social Capitalist Award and is a coauthor of <u>Generating and Sustaining Nonprofit Earned Income</u>.

Social Business Resource Review

New Foundry Ventures (www.newfoundryventures.org/)

A useful website providing information and links about building scalable social enterprises.

John Elkington and Pamela Hartigan. <u>The Power of Unreasonable People</u>. Boston: Harvard Business, 2008.

The definitive book about social entrepreneurs around the world and the work they are doing to change the world.

David Bornstein. <u>How to Change the World</u>. Oxford, Oxford University, 2004.

A great book profiling some of the world's leading changemakers, and telling the story of how they achieved inspiring victories in the world of social entrepreneurship.

Sharon M. Oster, Cynthia W. Massarsky, and Samantha L. Beinhacker. <u>Generating and Sustaining Nonprofit Earned Income: A Guide to Successful Enterprise Strategies</u>. San Francisco: Jossey-Bass, 2004.

A comprehensive review of all the issues involved in developing a social enterprise.

Stanford Social Innovation Review (www.ssireview.org)

The quarterly publication of the Stanford Center for Social Innovation—currently the best place to find the leading thinking on social impact.

REDF (www.redf.org)

A valuable website to learn about the lessons learned from one of the leading funders of social enterprise.

Social Enterprise Alliance (www.SEalliance.org)

The leading U.S. membership organization for social entrepreneurs. A very hands-on organization for nonprofits starting social enterprises. Beware, however, the glut of "consultants" in the field—they have a vested interest in telling you to start a business.

Muhammad Yunus. Building Social Business: The New Kind of Capitalism That Serves Humanity's Most Pressing Needs. New York: Public Affairs, 2010.

The Nobel Peace Prize winner lays out his vision for what a "social business" is and how it can change the world. In Professor Yunus's view, a financially viable business that reinvests all its profits back into the business of helping people is the highest form of social business.

J. Gregory Dees, Jed Emerson, and Peter Economy. Enterprising Nonprofits: A Toolkit for Social Entrepreneurs. New York: Wiley, 2001.

Greg Dees, now professor at Duke University, and Jed Emerson, most recently of Uhuru Capital, are two of the most savvy luminaries in the field of social enterprise, offering great concepts like "blended value theory" and helping readers understand social impact as the goal of all social activities.

Fast Company Magazine. "Social Capitalist of the Year Award" articles from 2004 to 2008.

In partnership with the Monitor Institute, Fast Company Magazine ran one of the country's most rigorous social impact competitions, selecting 25 winners each year. Examples from the winners during this period are still an invaluable tool for people considering how to create impact and achieve scale.

○ ○ ○

All these resources, plus nonprofit management tips of the week and more, can be found at Nonprofits101.org.

Part Six

Marketing and Communications

Strategy and timing are the Himalayas of marketing.
Everything else is the Catskills.

—Al Ries

Earlier, I spoke about the impact of modern technology on how we communicate with an audience. I touched briefly on the new bottom-up paradigm, on viewers pulling information rather than advertisers pushing it, and on the abundance of free tools and resources. Let's dig a bit deeper, especially as these apply to nonprofit marketing efforts in the modern day.

First and foremost, know that marketing is part art, and part science. In fact, the word "advertising" was first coined by William Shakespeare, who invented a full 10% of the words he wrote, including "excitement," "lonely," and "champion." All I mean by this is that *there is no set formula, and finding a unique voice and style for your efforts is crucial if you want to stand apart.*

To find success, learn to appreciate this new environment as a more *affectionate* one. If you'll indulge me, I equate marketing in the past to a long-distance relationship, where marketer and viewer interacted only sporadically via one-way mass media messaging. Nowadays, in the era of Facebook and Twitter, people are used to hearing from just about everyone more frequently (perhaps too frequently). To the marketer, this means the opportunity for more *touch points* with your constituent base. This keeps you top-of-mind, and through the use of technology, it allows you to *develop an increasingly better sense of the individuals that make up your audience over time—* what I call "progressive profiling."

This newfound, now two-way relationship also makes it possible to grow your staff a hundredfold, if not more. Our biggest supporters can now easily get involved with helping to spread the word about our fundraising campaigns, new programs, volunteer requirements, impact, and needs. Those of you with a development background may have heard that *the most effective kind of ask is a peer ask, and modern technology facilitates that through viral marketing* (more on this in Chapters Sixteen, Twenty-Two, and Twenty-Six).

I also spoke earlier of a flatter information hierarchy that's increasingly disintermediated, and of the accelerating speed of change. In a world where the president of the United States is doing a weekly fireside chat via YouTube, where the only way for us to get breaking news about Iran or Burma is through the Internet, and where anything that happened more than an hour ago is considered old news, how is a resource-strapped nonprofit meant to thrive? In this section, we'll get into a wide variety of practical strategies and techniques, and also point you to a host of great resources, many of them free. As an example, Google Grants (www.google.com/grants) offers $10,000 a month of free advertising to nonprofits—how can that kind of support, highlighted in Chapters Twenty-Five and Twenty-Three, benefit your efforts?

For now, suffice it to say that *success in this new environment is a factor of to what degree you keep in communication with the people who matter most,* and to what extent you embrace an open, transparent culture, since anything else is quickly falling out of favor.

Finally, one last piece of advice. Today, *everybody matters, since everyone is in a position to help or hurt your efforts.* Consider Laura Stockman, who started a blog called "25 Days to Make a Difference," which highlighted various nonprofits and causes she wanted to promote. Within a few days, she had over 25,000 readers from around the world and had received major media attention. So what? Well, she was only 10 years old at the time.

Again, everyone counts, everyone matters in today's information economy, so play nice and think twice before ever burning a bridge. On the mass scale, it was the <u>New York Times</u> who said back in 2003 that global public opinion is the world's second superpower—put it to use for your cause.

So how do we move beyond all these ideas and concepts, these "maps," into some practical tips for success?

The following section of this handbook will take you through the broad spectrum of marketing disciplines. We will begin with an overview of nonprofit marketing as a whole, including some tangible dos, don'ts, and how-tos. Then we'll look at the online landscape, including how to leverage the Internet and the Web 2.0 platforms I mentioned earlier to tell your story and increase awareness of your efforts, and at techniques for utilizing newsletters as a platform to optimize the touch points mentioned above. From there, we'll shift back to the real world to look at events, with a focus on considerations for smaller nonprofits, and finally, into PR and maximizing your media outreach.

Once more, let me connect the dots to the comments I made in my introduction to the technology section. As we consider marketing in this 2.0 world, whether you're planning to launch a new website, host a community-driven event, or kick off a new program, the real question is, how are you enlisting your community's support? *How are you putting your constituents to work for you in a collaborative partnership that benefits the two of you, and the community at large?* The organizations that can answer these questions are in a great position to make the most of their marketing efforts, and to increase impact. I encourage you to be one of them.

CHAPTER 25

Nonprofit Marketing

By Jennie Winton, Founding Partner, and Zach Hochstadt,
Founding Partner, Mission Minded

Introduction to Nonprofit Marketing

On January 12, 2010, a 7.0-magnitude earthquake struck 10 miles southwest of the Haitian capital of Port-au-Prince. Doctors Without Borders/Médecins Sans Frontières teams responded immediately by creating makeshift hospitals and triage centers throughout the capital.

For weeks and months following the quake, Doctors Without Borders continued to provide aid, supplying food, medical care, and other tangible assistance.

But that's not all the Nobel Prize–winning agency did. They also published immediately on their website. They posted updates on Twitter and Facebook and uploaded video to YouTube. They met with reporters and shared stories in their newsletter.

In other words, they *immediately* took their story to the public.

Because of this storytelling—this marketing—hundreds of thousands of supporters channeled their grief and shock into financial and in-kind donations for Doctors Without Borders' critically important work.

Of course, we're not all Médecins Sans Frontières; in fact the vast majority of nonprofits are small, resource-starved organizations. But like Doctors Without Borders, most nonprofit professionals recognize that it's not enough to do great work. *Without marketing, without getting the word out, even the greatest program hovers in a vacuum—in fact, to potential donors, volunteers, and journalists, it doesn't "exist" at all.* You have to let people know about your enterprise, and make it relevant and compelling to every constituency.

If your organization is like most of our clients, you know it's essential to continuously engage people in your mission: recruit new volunteers, appeal to new donors, sell tickets to events—and of course invite new program participants. But it takes dedicated resources to tell your organization's story and ask for involvement. That is the essence of marketing in the nonprofit sector. *If people don't understand you—how your organization is different and why you're important—they have no reason to support your work.*

Marketing is about being understood and irresistible.

What Is Marketing?

First and foremost, it's not a dirty word, and it is not just for profit-making enterprises. Marketing is how you reach those who need to know you're out there and will want to support you.

Your nonprofit exists because there's a problem that needs to be solved. Maybe . . .

- A forest needs to be protected.
- A child needs a home.
- A community wants access to world-class theater.
- Parents want to educate their children.
- New legislation is needed to ensure that toxins are kept out of the water system.

Marketing is a process of listening and response. It begins with listening (really listening) to your clients, donors, customers, and volunteers, and then responding.

For the people already inclined to care about your cause, you are fulfilling a need. You give the philanthropist an outlet for her desire to do good in the world. You give the music patron an opportunity to pursue her intellectual curiosity. And you give the volunteer an opportunity to give back to his community.

In truth, good marketing is a public service. If you do it well, if you really listen to what your public wants from your organization and then give it to them, you can provide the most compelling outlet for their need to contribute.

Core Skills and Competencies

To market your organization effectively, you'll need to establish your competitive advantage. Then you'll need to craft a marketing plan, in which you will:

- Analyze your situation

- Establish your marketing goals

- Determine your audiences

- Identify your strategies

- Brainstorm tactics

- Create and prioritize your budget

- Establish metrics for success

Let's explore this process.

Establish Your Competitive Advantage

Every charity is worthy, and every cause has good reason to exist. The nonprofit marketplace is crowded—really crowded. Being noticed, let alone standing out, is not easy.

You must become the go-to organization by standing for something the public values, and that no one else is standing for.

Trouble is, most nonprofits we know think that's what they're doing already. You hear it in claims like, "No one else serves meals to the hungry in our town seven days a week." That may be true . . . but if another organization serves meals <u>five</u> days a week, the average donor may not be paying enough attention to distinguish between the two of you. Or the difference in services may not be sufficient to sway them in your direction.

Establishing a competitive advantage means talking about your organization in a way in which no one else is talking about theirs.

Even if you do similar work to that of other nonprofits, we guarantee that there are ways to make your organization stand for something utterly unique. Think about the difference between two toothpaste brands. Are they really that different? Probably not. But one promises "sex appeal," the other sells "fresh breath." If both brands stuck with the unadorned truth—"Your teeth will be clean so you won't get cavities"—neither would have a competitive advantage. Having an advantage means selling more toothpaste.

The big difference between a nonprofit's marketing message and that of a for-profit company is that the benefits are different; in the case of your nonprofit, you're not selling products and services, you're selling social impact.

Let's look at the competitive advantages of the American Red Cross and The Salvation Army. Both come to the aid of disaster victims after fires, floods, and earthquakes. Both have expertise and have been effectively serving people for more than a century. Both have the color red in their logo, rely on volunteers to provide help, and seem to be run by nice people. So why do some people choose to donate to the Red Cross and some to The Salvation Army? What competitive advantage does each organization have over the other?

Each stands for something valued by a different group of people. People who choose the Red Cross may value the organization's international stature, its commitment to political and religious neutrality, or its overt affiliation with federal government organizations such as Federal Emergency Management Association (FEMA). Those who choose to make a gift to disaster victims through The Salvation Army, on the other hand, may like its commitment to Christian principles, love The Salvation Army's affiliation with Christmas (all those bell-ringing Santas asking for donations into the kettle are Salvation Army volunteers), or value its commitment to the poor.

Marketing may be the one activity in which stereotypes are not only valid, but valuable. Identifying the type of person(s) most likely to care about your organization is the fastest way to understanding *how* to reach your audience. You absolutely must speak "their" language if you want to be heard above the many other appeals they're receiving.

So who is most likely to care about *your* organization?

Here's how to develop your competitive advantage:

1. Make a list of the impacts your mission has on the world, making it as personal as possible. (Hint: "ending hunger" is a very broad stroke. It's easy to tune out when the mission sounds generic. "Feeding the soul," on the other hand, has a powerful and intimate impact.)

2. List all other organizations of which you're aware that aim for similar impact in similar arenas. (Hint: focus on their missions and intended outcomes rather than on *how* they go about getting the work done.)

3. Now describe the supporters who currently care about your mission. These are your "birds in hand." You'll be most efficient—especially with a limited nonprofit marketing budget and staff—if you aim to appeal to more people like them, rather than scouting new kinds of supporters. (Hint: though you may have many individual profiles of people who support you now, 80% are likely to have characteristics in common that will allow you to paint a better picture of them as a single group.)

4. Make a list of why you think these people choose to support you. What do they believe about your organization that makes them give?

5. Now list what these supporters value about you that the competing organizations from #2 either don't or can't offer. (Hint: the answer probably won't be program-related; it will be about mission or inspiration. Service based on the principles of Christianity is how The Salvation Army distinguishes its very similar programs from those of the American Red Cross.)

Create a Marketing Plan That Promotes Your Competitive Advantage

Smart organizations develop a marketing plan, whether they are multimillion-dollar international nonprofits or grassroots groups on a shoestring budget. Why? Because no matter how much money you have to spend on marketing, you could always spend more. Without a plan, you end up prioritizing the wrong efforts. *Wise nonprofits make a plan in order to get the best possible results while spending the least amount of money.*

A marketing plan exists to provide guidance over a set amount of time, about:

- Who you're trying to reach (your audience)

- What you want them to do

- How you expect to reach them

- How and when you'll know whether you were successful

Step 1: Analyze Your Situation

Before moving forward with a marketing plan, you must know where you are now. Assess your current situation:

1. Review any past marketing plans. Also review fundraising plans, which are usually linked to marketing (at least they should be).

2. Review your organization's strategic plan, if you have one. (Hint: even if you don't have a formal strategic plan, you *are* operating from a set of value-driven priorities; list and evaluate those.)

3. Interview other leaders in your organization, including board members, to understand their perspectives and priorities.

4. Audit your current marketing materials, including your website. Ask yourself:

    ○ Are we consistent in what we're saying?

    ○ Are we telling stories or just repeating facts?

- Do we talk about *how* we do our work, or are we focused on promoting *why* we do what we do? (*In marketing, the why is infinitely more important than the how.*)

- Do your pictures tell a story? If so, what do they say about your organization? Do they convey your most powerful messages?

- Is design consistent from piece to piece? If a donor picked up a brochure, could she identify that it came from your organization, even without seeing your name?

5. Research how past marketing efforts have fared. What received a response and what did not?

6. Look at what your competitors are doing and saying. Ask yourself what makes you different.

7. Consider what other factors are at play in your community and nationally that could affect how people perceive you. For example, the recent global financial crisis shifted the way people viewed services for the poor.

Step 2: Establish Your Marketing Goals

Ask yourself: Why does your organization need to invest in marketing? What changes are you trying to bring about?

For example:

1. Revenue: Are your marketing efforts focused on raising more money for the organization? Exactly how much do you need to raise, by when, and exactly what for?

2. Volunteers: Are you asking people to commit time to your cause? How many people do you need, and where do you need them? For what kind of time commitment?

3. Tickets: Are you selling tickets to an event? How many tickets do you need to sell to break even? To make a profit? Can you afford to just break even, if it will mean wider exposure for the organization?

4. Advocacy: Are you trying to pass a law or change a policy? Why? Who are you lobbying?

5. Behavioral: Are you trying to change a behavior, such as getting people to stop littering in a public park? Has this been tried before?

Exercise

Take a moment right now, and write down your marketing goals. These should be high-level objectives for your organization.

Step 3: Determine Your Audiences

Everyone should care about your cause, but not everyone will. It's just a fact of life. *Your job is to identify the people you think are most likely to take action and target your messages to them.*

Let's take our soup kitchen example and start to think about who our audiences are in relation to the first goal: raising $500,000 in general operating support. There are a few ways we could reach this goal, including:

1. Receive a single gift of $500,000

2. Receive 20 gifts of $25,000

3. Receive 100 gifts of $5,000

4. Receive 10,000 donations of $5

Now, most likely your strategy will be to go after a combination of gifts. Your donors will be a mix of major donors who give more than $5,000 and those who give smaller gifts in the $5 to $5,000 range. The challenge is to *recognize that this range of gifts is not all coming from the same people.* We have identified several different giving levels and two different audience types:

- Major donors (people who can give gifts of $5,000 and above)

- Individual donors (people who can make gifts of $5 to $4,999)

We might further refine this list by thinking about *what kinds of people* would be most inclined to give for the prevention of hunger, and *when* they're most likely to give.

- People eating in restaurants

- Grocery store shoppers

- Donors to other food banks

- Communities of faith

Then we might ask ourselves about audiences in regards to the second goal: where are we likely to find people who are willing to contribute food?

- Grocery store shoppers

- Food distribution warehouses

- Schoolchildren

- Religious groups

Finally, let's identify audiences in relation to the third goal: recruiting new volunteers.

- Volunteering organizations

- Religious groups

- Local businesses

Now take a moment to identify your own audiences in relation to your goals. Ask yourself:

1. Who are the people *most* likely to care about my cause?

2. Who are the people with the greatest means or inclination to take action?

3. What are the common characteristics of many of the people in my audience? (Not all; there are always exceptions, but with any group of people there are also some common characteristics.)

4. How would I characterize each audience in terms of age, income, giving level, and geography?

Step 4: Determine Your Strategies

Now that you know whom you're trying to reach and what your goals are, your next step is to *determine the high-level strategies for engaging each audience and urging it to take the action you want it to.*

A few sample strategies might look like this:

1. Encourage new major gifts through one-on-one meetings with existing donors

2. Engage religious groups to make your group the beneficiary of their fundraising

3. Establish a grocery store presence that makes it easy for shoppers to give either gifts of food or money

Brainstorm Tactics

Tactics are the steps we take to reach people. They include everything from a printed T-shirt to an engaging website to a social media tool like Facebook to a sign outside your offices.

There are thousands of tactics for engaging your audiences; *which* tactics you use should be based on the goals, strategies, and the audiences you've already identified. Using Twitter may be a brilliant tactic. . . . but it's probably not the best approach if you're trying to get elementary students to bring canned food to school. That's when a flyer or poster might make more sense.

Looking at our earlier strategies, we might decide to pursue the following tactics (there could be several others).

1. Strategy: Encourage new major gifts through one-on-one meetings with existing donors

    ○ Tactic 1: Pull names of existing major donors and make personal phone calls to each

- Tactic 2: Schedule one-hour meetings with each prospect

- Tactic 3: Create printed leave-behind material

- Tactic 4: Follow up with interested prospects and donors within two weeks

2. Strategy: Engage religious groups to make our group the beneficiary of their fundraising

- Tactic 1: Identify local religious organizations

- Tactic 2: Create a brochure that explains the benefits of supporting our soup kitchen

- Tactic 3: Mail an introductory letter and brochure about the soup kitchen to each organization

- Tactic 4: Schedule and make follow-up phone calls

- Tactic 5: Create introductory packet for organizations who agree to raise money for the soup kitchen

- Tactic 6: Create fundraising templates for religious institutions who agree to appeal for money on your behalf

- Tactic 7: Follow up with all partners monthly

3. Strategy: Establish a grocery store presence that makes it easy for shoppers to give either gifts of food or money

- Tactic 1: Create point-of-purchase display that includes donation canister

- Tactic 2: Place food donation barrels in grocery stores

- Tactic 3 Follow up with all grocery stores quarterly

Exercise

Take a moment to brainstorm your own strategies and tactics. Remember, focus on your audiences, ask yourself where you're likely to reach them, and then create a list of tactics. Don't limit yourself at this point—we'll prioritize tactics later.

activity

Here is an abbreviated list of tactics to get you started:

Direct Marketing

- Direct mail

- Telemarketing

- Email marketing

Online

- Blogs

- Search (organic and paid)

- Online banner advertising

- Social networking

- Websites

- Widgets

- Video

Public Relations

- Newspaper

- TV news

- Speakers bureau

- Chamber of Commerce

- Events and sponsorship

- Internal newsletters

Audio/Visual

- TV Public Service Announcements (PSAs)

- Radio PSAs

- Movie or TV product placement

- Podcasts

activity

Experiential

- ○ Cause-related marketing
- ○ Festivals or fairs
- ○ Events
- ○ Galas

Print

- ○ Annual reports
- ○ Cases for support
- ○ Brochures
- ○ Flyers
- ○ Postcards

Out of Home

- ○ Posters
- ○ Transit advertising
- ○ Coffee cup holders
- ○ Street pole banners

Mobile Devices

- ○ Text messaging
- ○ Game ads

Place-Based Signage

- ○ In-store point-of-purchase displays or collection boxes
- ○ Coasters in bars and clubs
- ○ Garbage barrels on beaches
- ○ Book covers at schools
- ○ Water bottles at health clubs
- ○ Pencils at bowling alleys and golf courses

 One of the cheapest and easiest ways to get *free* advertising is to apply for a Google Grant (www.google.com/grants). When your registered nonprofit receives a grant from Google, you receive up to $10,000 per month in in-kind "AdWords" advertising, so people see your link when they search Google. It's an easy way for you to get more exposure for your cause.

Establish and Prioritize Your Budget

OK. You've brainstormed tactics right down to poodle-collar tags for the local grooming shop. Now for the limitations: you may have created a brilliant list of tactics, but you probably won't have the budget to do all of them. Your budget will determine which tactics you can actually pursue. *Establish your overall marketing budget and then divvy up your tactics budget for each of your strategies.*

Now we come to it: how do you prioritize tactics? The cost-benefit ratio can help you decide. Essentially, *you should pursue tactics that cost the least to implement while providing the greatest benefit*—and by cost, we don't just mean the out-of-pocket expense. Factor in your time, as well as that of your staff and volunteers. How much work and money will it cost you to get the impact you want? Then ask yourself, could you get the same impact with less headache?

To reach your answers efficiently, *conduct a simple cost/benefit analysis, based on your gut sense of costs, labor, and expected benefits*:

1. List your tactics.

2. Rate each tactic on <u>cost</u>, using a scale from 1 to 5 (1 = least expensive).

3. Rate each tactic on <u>labor</u> (1 = least amount of work).

4. Rate each tactic on <u>anticipated benefit</u> (1 = least impact).

5. Add cost to labor and divide by benefit, and rank the results from lowest total to highest.

Table 25.1 offers an example.

Table 25.1: Sample Cost/Benefit Analysis

Tactics	Cost	Labor	Benefit	(Cost + Labor)/ Benefit
Quarterly newsletter	3	3	3	2
Facebook Page	1	3	3	1.3
iPhone app	5	5	2	5
Speakers bureau	2	3	4	1.25

The lowest number represents the least cost for the greatest benefit. Start there.

Establish Your Metrics

By now you've created a great marketing plan. You know who you're trying to reach, what you want them to do, and how you will reach them. You've prioritized your tactics and weeded out the high-cost/low-benefit ideas. The next step is to establish metrics for measuring the impact of your efforts—in other words, *how will you know when a tactic has worked?*

For instance, let's assume that one of your tactics is to invest in paid advertising on a major search engine. You have a gut sense that this will lead traffic to your site. But a gut sense isn't enough. You must *establish a specific goal and then measure against it.* Based on that measurement, you can make informed decisions when it comes time to revise your plan. *Nonprofits should review their marketing plans annually, and update them as needed.*

In the case of your search engine advertisement, for instance, we can measure the number of people who click on the ad and get to our site (known as "click-throughs"). Let's say you've set a goal of 250 people clicking on your paid ad. When you review your actual success versus your goal, were you over or under? Did your ad wildly overperform or underachieve?

You should *continue to invest in the tactics that performed well and eliminate those that had little impact.*

Things you might measure per tactic include:

- Number of donations

- Donation amounts

- Tickets sold

- Click-throughs

- Phone calls received

- Overall awareness (as measured by a survey before and after the marketing effort)

- Number of new fans or followers (Facebook and Twitter)

- Re-tweets (Twitter)

- Supportive actions taken (e.g., people sending letters to an elected official)

Nonprofit Marketing Dos and Don'ts

- DO make a plan. With a smart marketing plan, you can get the results you want—even on a small budget.

- DO focus on specific audiences. You can't afford to reach out to everyone. Focus on the specific groups of people you need to move to action, especially the ones that have already proven responsive.

- DO stay consistent. Remember that *just when you're beginning to tire of using the same words and phrases, your audience is just starting to remember them.*

- DO know what makes you unique. Having a clear brand is a shortcut for your donors, helping them to know and trust you more quickly.

Dos and Don'ts

- DO teach your staff how to talk about your group. Every person in your organization—staff, volunteer, and board member—is a potential first contact. Equip them all to be ambassadors.

- DON'T stick with something that isn't working. "We've always done it that way" is no reason to keep an ineffective marketing tactic in place.

- DON'T use your staff as a test audience. Everyone in your office is an insider. *Look to people outside your inner circle to help you know if what you're saying makes sense.*

- DON'T get focused on internal issues. Sorry, but the public just won't read a description of your board retreat. Use marketing communications to tell stories about the people whose lives are changed by your work.

- DON'T use bad photos. A strong picture is worth a thousand words, so choose images that tell the story of your impact.

Conclusion

Marketing your nonprofit program clearly and consistently is one of the best ways your organization can advance its mission. Clarify what your organization stands for and then build that reputation through repeated application of your message. Use words and visual imagery to stand for something unique and valuable. Enroll everyone in your organization to extend your brand and message.

If you do this, existing and potential donors will respond more quickly to your appeals, you will have greater success urging your audience to action, and your customers (donors, volunteers, patrons, and so on) will remain loyal over the years.

Now, go for it!

Jennie Winton is a founding partner of Mission Minded (www.mission-minded.com) and an expert in nonprofit branding and positioning. Clients include National Equity Project, Levi Strauss Foundation, and San Francisco Opera. She was chief marketing officer of the American Red Cross Bay Area Chapter and account executive at several advertising agencies. She worked with Elizabeth Dole at Red Cross headquarters and Norman Lear at the Declaration of Independence Road Trip, fundraising millions for charity. Jennie graduated from the University of Maryland with a degree in radio, television & film and is an adjunct professor in the Graduate School of Business at University of San Francisco.

Zach Hochstadt is a Mission Minded founding partner and leads the company's creative teams in message development, writing, naming, graphic design, and web design and development. A strategic communications expert, Zach transforms organizational initiatives into creative concepts and communication tools. He's consulted for a range of clients, including Denver Art Museum, Sierra Club, San Francisco AIDS Foundation, and Denver Public Schools Foundation. He lectures frequently, and through Mission Minded's Minute Message Model™, has taught hundreds of nonprofit leaders how to improve their communication. Zach earned his BA in English from the Robert Clark Honors College at the University of Oregon.

Nonprofit Marketing Resource Review

Mission Minded (www.mission-minded.com/resources)

Free, short, practical, and easy-to-read downloadable marketing guides.

Andy Goodman's <u>Why Bad Ads Happen to Good Causes</u>

How to make a successful print advertisement. Goodman also offers *Free Range Thinking*, a monthly newsletter with useful nonprofit marketing advice (www.agoodmanonline.com/newsletter/index.html).

Chip and Dan Heath. <u>Made to Stick: Why Some Ideas Survive and Others Die</u>. New York: Random House, 2007.

A smart guidebook on how to be an effective storyteller.

Sarah Durham's <u>Brandraising: How Nonprofits Raise Visibility and Money Through Smart Communication</u>. San Francisco: Jossey-Bass, 2009.

Fun, clear guidance on how to think big about your organization's brand.

Scott Bedbury and Stephen Fenichell. <u>A Brand New World: Eight Principles for Achieving Brand Leadership in the 21st Century</u>. New York: Penguin, 2008.

How some of the best brands in the world go about it.

Frog Loop (www.frogloop.com)

Good insight into improving your online marketing efforts.

Peleg Top and Jonathan Cleveland. <u>Designing for the Greater Good: The Best in Cause-Related Marketing and Nonprofit Design</u>. New York: CollinsDesign, 2010.

Take a cue from those who know what works.

Katya's Nonprofit Marketing Blog (www.nonprofitmarketingblog.com)

A good beginner's guide to nonprofit marketing.

o o o

All these resources, plus nonprofit management tips of the week and more, can be found at Nonprofits101.org.

CHAPTER 26

Using Web 2.0 Tools to Tell Your Organization's Story: Blogs, Flickr, and YouTube

By Beth Kanter, CEO, Zoetica

Introduction

Storytelling is not a solitary, one-way endeavor. The best stories are participatory, ongoing threads, and the most useful ones for nonprofits are not created by the organizations themselves. This is particularly true of the stories that emerge through "social media," web platforms that rely on user-generated content, i.e., Facebook, craigslist, YouTube, and so forth. *Storytelling 2.0 uses social media tools to convey how your organization's programs have made a difference in the world. Storytelling 2.0 is a new genre of web content—a fusion* of content created both by the organization and by engaged stakeholders, either in its raw conversational form, or as adapted by the organization. The real question is: how do you get your community to tell your story for you, thereby generating even better results than you could have on your own? Unlocking this mystery can be the key to success for your nonprofit.

We know that people are more likely to become interested in your organization's work and donate or volunteer if you can engage them. And telling stories is the most effective way of engaging people, versus dry statistics or institutional jargon. *Storytelling helps build momentum and energize your network.* Using social media to relay your story helps you accelerate the process of connecting with like-minded, passionate people who want to help you. This is the heart and soul of an authentic social media strategy that can have winning results.

In this chapter, I'm going to give you two views, the balcony and the dance floor, which I learned early on in my 30-year nonprofit career. This metaphor is similar to the concept of maps versus picks and shovels, as described in the introduction.

When you are on the balcony, you consider the big picture, the long view, and how all the parts fit together. When rocking the dance floor, you focus on tactics and tools. It's important to do both, because they inform and enhance each other. Especially *if you're working with other people on social media strategies, you'll be more effective if you can see both the balcony and the dance floor.*

Critical Skills and Competencies

First, I'm going to lead you up the stairs, sit you down, and watch how the dancers move from a distance. I'll share a framework for storytelling and engagement that works for social media. Then you can take these principles onto the dance floor and learn the actual steps: the tools. Although there are many different social media tools you can use for storytelling, I'll focus my comments on three popular platforms to help you get started: blogs, Flickr, and YouTube. Finally, I'll share some pointers for getting people in your network and beyond to share your story. Let's begin.

The Balcony: A Few Simple Frameworks

Let's start with a couple of important frameworks that you need to know and leverage in order to be successful with storytelling 2.0. Here are some crucial concepts to keep mind:

Storytelling Must Be Linked to Your Overall Communications Strategy

If you've crafted an overall communications strategy and fundraising plan that includes both traditional tactics and tools (see Chapters Twenty-Five and Eighteen, respectively), your social media storytelling efforts will be hard-wired for success. Though your plan doesn't need to be a formal, written document, *you must be able to articulate your objectives, audience, messaging, and, of course, what channels you are using to connect with your audience.* Channels might include your website, an email newsletter, search engine marketing, print newsletters, flyers, signs, posters, traditional advertising, and so on. In addition, *your strategy should be based on audience research* (rather than internal discussions and navel gazing), such as surveys and focus groups, and should absolutely include the use of social media listening techniques. For a primer and step-by-step, skills-based approach to learning how to listen to your community, see my Social Media Listening Wiki at www.socialmedia-listening.wikispaces.com. Listening in this way helps you understand who your audience is, what they're doing on the Web, and what motivates them to share their story about your organization or cause. As a bonus, your research is sure to lead you to new stakeholders who are already doing just that!

Telling your story via social media won't have as much impact if you lack the clear objectives and accurate identification of your audience(s) that comes with research and strategy formation. The other pitfall that nonprofits fall into is failing to realize that *the use of social media must be part of a multichannel strategy that includes email, a strong website presence, face-to-face events, reaching out to the mainstream media, and Google ads* (which nonprofits can receive for free at www.google.com/grants).

Storytelling 2.0 Is a New Genre of Web Content Creation

A *story* has three parts: a protagonist, a problem or series of challenges to overcome, and an ending that resolves the problem. Whether read from a book, cave drawings, or told to you by your grandmother, all good stories basically follow this three-part structure.

At the heart of good storytelling is a narrative arc, or storyline. A simple narrative arc includes:

Beginning

- Protagonist: The leading character, hero, or heroine in a story. For nonprofits, this person or group (or animal) should represent someone who benefits from your organization's services or is affected by the cause your organization promotes. Let's take a food bank. A protagonist might be a family who is receiving a weekly food donation. You would describe the family, their names, how many children, where they live, and so forth. *The key to a good story is to make it personal, and to fill in the details.*

- Setting: These are the important details that provide context for the protagonist and that describes her or their situation. Again, it's important to keep this interesting by providing details and personalizing the situation—*the goal is for your reader to be able to visualize himself in the storyline*. In the food bank example, this might be describing the program's services and facilities in detail.

Middle

- Antagonist/ Obstacle/Tension: The protagonist encounters a problem. Traditionally this is the guy with the thin moustache, dressed in black, with the evil laugh, but for nonprofit stories, this can be an unexpected event, an act of G-d, or some tension in the protagonist's life. In order to establish the strength of your lead character, *tell the story of how the protagonist tried to solve the problem but was not successful*. In the food bank example, this could be the story of how the family went from living comfortably to needing help after the mother lost her job, followed by months of struggling.

- Emotion: It's really important to incorporate emotion into your story. This can be something funny, scary, sad, or whatever is appropriate. In the food bank example, this might be sharing how the family's children were so hungry during school that they couldn't concentrate, leading to poor performance in school.

End

- Resolution: The organization solves the protagonist's problem in a way that inspires readers to support its efforts to do more of the same. This is where you can widen the lens and bring in overall statistics and trends relating to your program. To conclude our example, the organization helped the family get back on their feet—with the newfound breathing room enjoyed from donated meals, Mom was able to secure a new position and now volunteers at the food bank every Sunday.

If you're looking for additional effective storytelling and narrative arc examples, look no further than the Disney favorite, <u>Cinderella</u>. The various elements described above are insightfully analyzed at www.slideshare.net/ RowanManahan/power-point-20th-anniversary-cinderella?src=embed. Also be sure to check out Chapter Twenty-Nine of this book, where David Fenton relays clear tips for effective story writing.

But that's Storytelling 1.0. Today, with social media, the way stories are being shared is changing dramatically. Storytelling 2.0 incorporates the best of the principles of good storytelling, as modeled by blockbuster Hollywood scripts and fairy tales, but also effectively leverages social media. This enables your story to go "viral," when your audience and others pass it along for you, and integrates valuable user-generated content. Stories are now open-ended conversations, participatory, experimental, and as mentioned earlier, many times not created by the nonprofits themselves. Social media makes creating, remixing (see below), and sharing stories between nonprofits and their stakeholders easy and fluid. It also expedites generation of these stories and augments opportunities for participation, while revealing new opportunities for nonprofits to communicate and connect with new stakeholders.

Once your organization has mastered the art of story and narrative arc, *it is important to both listen and engage on social media outposts to motivate your audience to "remix" your story.* Here's what a sequence of steps looks like:

- Establish a "listening post" that searches social media sites, based on keywords or terms or monitors particular blogs or online communities (see Chapter Twenty-Two for tips on using an RSS feed to accomplish this, or set up Google Alerts)

- Understand which stories resonate with audiences who are using social media

- Know the right conversation starters, or questions that jumpstart conversations with supporters, leading to story creation or co-creation (see Chapter Sixteen for more on this)

- Use feedback from social media conversations (blog comments, Facebook comments, and the like) to fine-tune stories and incorporate the audience's voice

- Repurpose stories shared by supporters into content on your organization's website or other channels

- Develop a deep understanding of what is being said about your organization, cause, or program on the Web and in the community

- Translate stories into "micro" content (new blog posts, Twitter "tweets," YouTube videos, and so on)

Understand the Ladder of Engagement: From Passive to Active Cocreation

Think about all the various ways your organization interacts with different groups of people through your communications and fundraising efforts— through social media or other traditional channels. You will undoubtedly discover that some people engage with you lightly, whereas others dive in more deeply. Face it: your audiences will not have the same level of passion or interest in your program as you do. And that is not a problem—it's just the way it is.

To be successful using social media, you need to use different techniques, tactics, and tools that map to each person's level of interest. You need a portfolio of approaches that meet people where they are at, and that help get them more engaged with your efforts. Let's look at this more closely (Table 26.1):

Table 26.1: The Storytelling 2.0 Ladder of Engagement

Degree of Engagement	Role in Storytelling 2.0 Content Creation	Description
Very Low	Happy Bystander	Reads your content, views your videos, or joins your Facebook Page or network, but only lurks
Low	Conversationalist	Responds to a conversation starter on your blog, Facebook Page, or YouTube Channel by leaving a comment, rating, or "liking" it
Medium	Promoter	Shares your content with other people
High	Evangelist	Actively encourages other people to participate in the conversation and remixes your content
Very High	Instigator	Creates and shares their own story with friends and others

It is important to understand that these roles and levels of involvement are part of an ecosystem—just like the donor pyramid and ladder of engagement you already read about. Only a few people will rise to the Evangelist or Instigator levels due to the required commitment of time and skills, or because they're not yet sufficiently engaged in your work. Nonetheless, these supporters are still important to the ecosystem because they spread your stories and demonstrate clear community interest. *Recognize and appreciate people where they're at*, and don't take it personally if they're not interested in or able to get more engaged as you strive to gently nudge them further down your pipeline.

o o o

Now that you've seen the view from the balcony, let's head down to the dance floor and learn a few steps that can help you get the party started.

The Dance Floor: How to Get Your Groove On(line)

I could write an entire book on "Nonprofit Storytelling 2.0" and cover the many, many tools and platforms that you could use. Because I'm limited to a brief chapter, I'm going to focus on a short list of tools that are most useful to causes looking to get the word out: blogs, Flickr, and YouTube. See Chapters Sixteen and Twenty-Two for information on Facebook and Twitter, two additional Web 2.0 platforms that can also support your fundraising and marketing efforts.

You don't have to, nor should you, use every social media tool to be successful in getting your stories out to the masses. Many nonprofits, particularly small ones, just don't have the manpower to be everywhere on the Web. *Less is more, but wherever you go, go deep.* Test one platform at a time—for several weeks or months, or for as long as you need to fully explore its potential, practicing and mastering one outlet at a time. *Only once you have internalized the skills and techniques of one channel should you consider adding another.* Trust me, taking this sequential, incremental approach will lead to success; otherwise you will spread yourself too thin.

Blogging: The Pen Is Mightier Than the Sword

There are many different ways to use blogs to support your organization's goals, from sharing organizational news as it happens to recruiting volunteers and supporting fundraising. Blogs can be platforms for thought leadership or to show off staff expertise—they offer fertile ground for Storytelling 2.0 content.

Different Uses of Nonprofit Blogs   Blogs (short for "web logs") are similar to online bulletin boards, and are usually focused on a particular topic, organization, or person. They enable visitors to leave comments, providing an interactive forum for dialog, and many are free to set up (via Typepad.com or other websites). There are many uses for nonprofits blogs, but here are a few that particularly lend themselves to storytelling and narrative arcs:

- Field Reports: Blog posts from staff working "in the field" with your clients. These should focus on a particular individual or group of individuals being served by your programs.

- Inside Stories: These posts are used to that tell stories that share insights on how your staff and volunteers actually do their work—think of it as career day for people interested in how you achieve impact.

- Event Coverage: Blogs are a great place to share interviews or tell stories from fundraising and other events.

- Client Posts: Content written by someone who has been served by your organization's programs. To build engagement, this could be an ongoing feature or diary from that person.

- Contests: Blogs are a great place to promote giveaways, storytelling, or idea contests. *Consider challenging your audience to see who can share the most compelling story of your nonprofit's impact*—offer a prize to readers who share the best story about benefiting from one of your programs or services.

Before getting started, you need to *map out the topics you are going to cover on your blog.* In addition, you should do a little research to see if there are other bloggers writing about similar issues, as you will want to link to them in your posts. As you evaluate other bloggers, ask yourself what your unique approach to the topic will be.

Multiple Author Blogging: Many Hands Make Light Work   *Smaller organizations should engage multiple authors to distribute the workload.* Plus, it's more fun when you can bounce ideas off others. Consider assigning "beats" to key staff and volunteers based on the their program area, expertise, and interests. Most important, consider how much time you or your team have to write, since *once you begin a blog it should be updated at least weekly* to "keep the lights on." Beginning bloggers generally require more time for writing, but you do get faster.

Incorporate Good Conversation Starters   Blogging isn't just about writing content for someone to passively read—the goal is to get readers to discuss the topic by making comments, to share their insights and anecdotes, and tell their friends. It's all about engaging your audience in a dialog—with you and with other readers. *Blog posts that are good conversation starters are not comprehensive, leaving gaps for readers to fill in, and many have a question in the title, or at the end* ("What do you think?" works wonders). Posts are generally written in an intimate, informal style, as if you were sitting a café table having a conversation. It certainly isn't the institutional boilerplate, which is a huge conversation stopper.

My best blog posts create threads of conversation—with readers and other bloggers building on the topic. It isn't only about expressing your opinion and ideas, it is about listening and hearing what your audience or stakeholders have to say. This does take some time and practice to master, but the rewards when leveraging this platform for Storytelling 2.0 can be great.

Listen, Listen, Listen   Writing frequent, compelling, and instigative posts is only part of the workflow in Storytelling 2.0. As mentioned, it's also key to listen to your audience, and to incorporate what you hear into future posts. For example, if other bloggers have linked to you in their posts about a particular topic, write a post adding to or explaining what they said. You should also *respond to your blog readers' comments*, turning a post into a conversation. If you are successful at activating a lively discussion, write a follow-up post summarizing the dialogue and linking back to readers. This type of weaving inspires an audience to share their stories and gets them more engaged in future postings.

Flickr: A Picture Is Worth a Thousand Words

Photos and visuals can quickly convey powerful, engaging stories. You can post photos onto your blog and combine them with posts, but you can also use photo-sharing sites like Flickr to share your organization's stories, or to inspire your supporters to share theirs.

Different Uses of Flickr by Nonprofits

- An international organization sends volunteer doctors to developing countries to perform medical services. The physicians document the impact of their work by uploading photos to the organization's private Flickr group. Not only does Flickr help the volunteers exchange photos and related stories, it also creates an image bank from which the nonprofit can select photos for its website and blog.

- An environmental organization that supports organic farmers had thousands of amazing photographs documenting organic farming techniques. The organization uploaded the photos to Flickr, then enlisted volunteers and members to help organize and annotate the photos.

- A museum was mounting a collaborative exhibition with other institutions in five cities around the world. As the group prepared the installation, they used Flickr to share photos with one another, which allowed them to check in on construction efforts before approving the contracting work. This way, they got a visual reference of the exhibition space when selecting picture frames; and see work completed to date. Flickr provided a way for the collaborators to easily upload and share photos, both publicly and privately.

- An executive director wanted to use photos to emphasize her points during a presentation, but disliked clip art and lacked the budget for stock photography. Using Flickr's Creative Commons licensing search feature, she was to find appropriate photos that she could use for free with attribution.

- Volunteers and talented photographers at an animal shelter had taken beautiful photos of the dogs and cats at their facility. The organization uploaded the photos into Flickr and created thank-you cards featuring the pets for their donors.

If you decide to use Flickr, make sure you identify a staff member or volunteer who is passionate about taking photos, and charge them with doing so on a regular basis to keep your page fresh. If you'd like to learn more about the basic principles of taking good photos, visit www.betterphoto.com/exploring/tips.asp.

Every blog post you write should be illustrated with a photo. You can also create a compelling slide show from your Flickr photos using simple cut and paste code. Whenever uploading Flickr photos into a blog post, *make sure you carefully annotate the photo on Flickr and include a link back to the post.* Finally, take the time to add tags or keywords to your photos, since this will increase their "findability" by the broader community.

YouTube: Tell Your Story with Video

Video is a powerful way to share your organization's story, and it has never been easier and cheaper to do! With an inexpensive video camera that comes with an easy editing program and one-click upload to YouTube, nonprofits are sharing their stories in many ways:

- Interviews at events

- Field work

- Insider tours

A compelling video clip is short, uses humor, tells a story, and sparks an emotional response.

With a little bit of training, you can tell your story with video fairly easily—YouTube offers a great nonprofit program (www.youtube.com/nonprofits) that provides valuable seminars, product discounts (e.g., Flip Cams at 50% off), and a number of other benefits. You can easily set up and customize the look and feel of your YouTube channel by adding a logo and editing some basic HTML, the popular coding language that almost all websites are built on. There is a link to Google Check Out, so you can collect donations at no cost. You can use a feature called "annotations" to insert a call to action as text or links into your video. Finally, you'll gain access to "Video Volunteers," where you can find a talented video blogger to create engaging content for your organization.

Getting Others to Tell Your Story

Earlier, I mentioned the potential for your well-told stories to go "viral"—the Holy Grail of Storytelling 2.0 is getting your audience to create or cocreate content on your behalf. But how can nonprofits encourage this great behavior? Here are a few insights I've gleaned during my years in the industry:

Give Permission to Share   Tell your blog, Flickr, YouTube (and so on) audience that you <u>want</u> them to take your content and repurpose, remix, or recreate it. Using a Creative Commons "Share, Share Alike" license makes your intentions explicit.

Be Explicit   Sometimes people are inspired on their own, but it also helps to reward them for sharing or creating your content. *There's nothing better than a contest with a prize.* Give away a mug, a free program membership, a T-shirt, or whatever you think is desirable by the audience—you'd be amazed at what people will do for free tchotchkes.

Stock the Pond You may need to *get staff and other insiders to participate and help jumpstart your effort*—after all, no one likes to be first. But if you have a few examples of how other people have remixed or created content, that only helps to inspire others.

Lift Up Examples *Encourage and publically recognize people who create content for you.* This can be done by highlighting their contribution in a blog post, on your website, or at an event. Or, use their content in your organization's brochure, but be sure to get their permission first.

Storytelling 2.0 Dos and Don'ts

Dos and Don'ts

- DO tell the story of your organization's impact on *one person*.

- DON'T use boring statistics or jargon to share your story.

- DO share your story with words, pictures, and video.

- DO include conversation starters in every story you tell.

- DO use Creative Commons licensing to encourage others to share and remix your story.

- DO as much listening as you can before talking.

- DON'T try to use every tool—start with one and add incrementally.

Conclusion

I've taken you up to the balcony to learn how to tell compelling stories, listen, and engage with your audience so they're inspired to read and share your stories. We also looked at different social media tools that allow you to artfully convey your impact with text, photos, and video. Applying these techniques and leveraging important resources like blogs, Flickr, and YouTube will make your organization's activities more successful, engage and attract more people for your cause, and power your fundraising campaigns. Now that you are equipped with the view from the balcony and have a few dance steps down, you're ready to dance the night away and change the world!

Beth is the author of Beth's Blog (www.bethkanter.org), one of the longest running and most popular blogs for nonprofits, and coauthor of the highly acclaimed book, The Networked Nonprofit. Beth is the CEO of Zoetica, a company that serves nonprofits and socially conscious companies with top-tier, online marketing services. In 2009, she was named by Fast Company magazine as one of the most influential women in technology and one of Business Week's "Voices of Innovation for Social Media." She is currently the Visiting Scholar for Social Media and Nonprofits for the Packard Foundation.

Storytelling 2.0 Resource Review

Web 2.0 Storytelling: Emergence of a New Genre by Alan Levine and Bryan Alexander

(www.educause.edu/EDUCAUSE+Review/EDUCAUSEReview
MagazineVolume43/Web20StorytellingEmergenceofaN/163262)

Provides an easy framework and context for storytelling on the social web, and although geared towards people working in education, provides many useful links and resources.

"7 Things You Should Know about Digital Storytelling," Educause, January 2007 (www.connect.educause.edu/Library/ELI/7ThingsYouShouldKnowAb out/39398)

Explains the concept and key principles of digital storytelling.

Center for Digital Storytelling resource page (www.storycenter.org/resources. html)

An excellent set of resources and how-to pieces on digital storytelling.

How to Blog by Beth Kanter (www.howtoblog.wikispaces.com)

My blogging workshop wiki that provides information about how nonprofits can get started with blogging.

"How Nonprofits Can Get the Most out of Flickr" by Beth Kanter, TechSoup (www.techsoup.org/learningcenter/internet/page8291.cfm)

This is a more detailed piece on how nonprofits can strategically use Flickr as part of their social media strategy.

YouTube Nonprofit Channel (www.youtube.com/nonprofits)

Information on how to set up your own channel, including an excellent collection of how-to resources.

YouTube and Nonprofits by Michael Hoffman (www.see3.net/youtube-for-nonprofits)

Great tips and frameworks for getting your nonprofit's YouTube Channel up-to-speed quickly.

Need Some Inspiration to Video Blog with a Flip Camera? (www.beth.typepad.com/beths_blog/2009/06/on-the-road-in-tanzania-un-world-food-programme-video-blog.html)

An example of a nonprofit using a flip camera to capture stories in the field, plus a roundup of the best how-to resources.

WeAreMedia (www.wearemedia.org)

This is a wiki created by people from nonprofits who are implementing social media strategies. It is filled with information about strategy, tactics, and tools. Particularly relevant to this chapter are:

The Art of Storytelling (www.wearemedia.org/Strategy+Track+Module+4)

Sharing Your Story Social Media Style (www.wearemedia.org/Tactical+Track+Module+3)

Storytelling Webinar with Michael Hoffman, Britt Bravo, and David Neff (www.wearemedia.org/Storytelling)

Blogging, Flickr, Podcasting, and Flickr by Britt Bravo and Nina Simon (www.wearemedia.org/Workshop+Day+2+Sharing+Your+Story)

Andy Goodman's "Why Bad Presentations Happen to Good Causes" (www.agoodmanonline.com/publications/how_bad_presentations_happen/index.htm)

Great overview of how to ensure you get your nonprofit's message across in a compelling, concise, and credible manner. See my blog post where I interview Andy at www.beth.typepad.com/beths_blog/2007/10/story-telling-a.html

"50 Ways to Tell a Story" by Alan Levine (www.cogdogroo.wikispaces.com/StoryTools)

Great resource for those looking for practical storytelling tips.

"Ten Ways Nonprofits Can Use Blogs" by Britt Bravo (www.netsquared.org/blog/britt-bravo/10-ways-nonprofits-can-use-blogs)

Wonderful article on nonprofit blogging by an industry veteran.

○ ○ ○

All these resources, plus nonprofit management tips of the week and more, can be found at Nonprofits101.org.

Crafting an Effective Newsletter Strategy

By Kivi Leroux Miller, President,
NonprofitMarketingGuide.com

Introduction: The Evolution of Nonprofit Newsletters

When I think back to a newsletter I produced for a nonprofit association in 2000, I remember an eight-page print newsletter that we mailed out quarterly. We'd write eight to ten stories per issue, most of which focused on the work the organization had performed in the previous quarter. We highlighted individual staff and board members in personal profiles. We referred to "staff" and "members" in the text. This print newsletter was, with the exception of conference marketing brochures, the only means of communication from the organization to its members. We archived copies of the newsletter as PDF files on our website.

At the time, it was just like what every other nonprofit was sending out. It seemed fine. But if that same newsletter landed on my desk today, I would think, "Yikes. This sucks."

Unfortunately, many nonprofits are sending out newsletters just like that one still today, completely ignoring the profound changes that have occurred in the way that people communicate not only with each other, but with the institutions in their lives, including the nonprofit causes they support.

If I worked for that same nonprofit today, I'd recommend that we drop the print newsletter entirely, and instead produce a monthly email newsletter. Instead of writing 2,000–4,000 words of copy for each edition, we'd write two or three stories totaling 500–1,000 words. Rather than looking back at the last quarter, the stories would look forward to the weeks and months ahead. Instead of featuring the people *doing* the work, we'd profile the people *who benefited from* our programs. We'd refer to staff in the first person as "I" or "We" and we'd refer to the members, our readers, as "You"—it would be personal. The email newsletter would be integrated fully into a broader, multichannel communications strategy that would likely include a blog and a strong Facebook presence.

Don't get me wrong. I'm not telling you that print newsletters are dead and that email and social media is the only way to go. *Decision making about your newsletter strategy should be driven by a few key questions, namely: who is your audience; what kind of content do they want to receive from you and how often; and what do you hope they will do with the information upon receipt.*

Critical Skills and Competencies

Regardless of whether you decide to communicate via print, email, RSS feed (see Chapter Twenty-Two), or some combination, keep in mind these *five critical elements of a successful nonprofit newsletter*:

1. Frequency: Send fewer words, more often

2. Look Forward: Preview more, review less

3. Personality: More of them, less of you

4. Next Steps: More action, less FYI

5. Integration: More planning, less improv

Think of these five elements as sliders on a mixing board, where you can adjust each element up or down, with the sum position of the sliders blending into a newsletter customized for your organization and its supporters. You'll need to find a comfortable balance for your nonprofit, and in this chapter I offer what I believe to be the best direction on these five key components.

Frequency: Send Fewer Words, More Often

The conventional wisdom is that *people need to see or hear a message seven times before they will remember it.* And the reality is that your supporters won't read everything you put in front of them, whether online or off. If a supporter actually reads one in three articles you send in print or via email, and they need to see the message in that article seven times before they respond to it, that means you need to communicate the same message 21 times.

If this is true (or anywhere close), how can we possibly believe that sending a quarterly newsletter is adequate communication to inspire supporters to do anything?

At the same time, cultural changes from fast food and 24-hour news networks to social networking and web browsing on smart phones mean that we want everything in our lives to be convenient, fast, affordable, and easy to digest—including our philanthropy.

Therefore *your newsletters need to grab your readers' attention immediately and get to the point fast.* You need to reach out more frequently, but with newsletters that are bite-sized snacks, not seven-course meals.

Matthew Bregman, author of the <u>Tactical Fundraising</u> blog, describes a strange syndrome that he's seen consume the brains of many nonprofit newsletter writers. "Somehow, perhaps fantasizing that they work for a magazine," says Matthew, "they decide that important topics merit high word counts. The result is that the staff person spends an inordinate amount of time writing the piece, which is guaranteed to be read by almost no one."

Matthew recalls asking a colleague to write a simple, short three-paragraph article on a recycling project. "She spent a week squirreled away in a conference room and then turned in four or five pages," says Matthew. "I doubt anyone but the two of us read it from beginning to end."

Exactly why you produce your newsletter is a decision that everyone on your staff, and everyone contributing to the newsletter, must understand. Some organizations use their newsletters as a way to provide services to members, such as lists of resources, deadlines for upcoming grant applications or event registrations, and reviews of new research. Others use their newsletters as donor stewardship tools, where with each story, you reinforce your donors' decisions to support your cause and you inspire them to do more. *Rarely, if ever, should a nonprofit newsletter be used as a platform for staff to explain everything they know about a topic.*

Until you have good intelligence from the recipients of your newsletter that urges you to do otherwise, *start by communicating with your supporters monthly.* Send an oversized postcard or two-page newsletter. Send a 500-word email. Mix it up and trade off between channels if you feel like experimenting. The most important thing is communicating often enough so you aren't easy to forget, and with enough brevity that your messages can be consumed immediately; if your message is filed away in a "read later" folder, odds are it will never be seen. Of course, you must also consider your organizational capacity to meet a regular publishing schedule.

If you are providing on-target, valuable information each and every time (or darn close), your readers won't feel bugged by frequent mailings. *If you don't have enough content for a short monthly newsletter, you either don't know what your readers want from you, or you aren't thinking creatively about ways to talk about your work.*

Look Forward: Preview More, Review Less

As you select which stories to include in each edition of your newsletter, *think more about the future and less about the past.* While nonprofits have traditionally used newsletters to report back to their supporters about their recent work, if you aren't careful, this approach quickly devolves into lackluster recounts of what was checked off of staff to-do lists.

Take the omnipresent event wrap-up article, for instance. Whether it's a board meeting, a seminar, or a conference, *the events your organization hosts or attends can provide great fodder for newsletter articles—if you highlight the most important points and forget about the rest.* Don't tell us "a good time was had by all."

People who weren't in attendance don't care, and people who were are already in the know.

Instead, turn what would otherwise be boring old news into something interesting or helpful to all. *Pick just a few highlights from the event and summarize them in a more creative format than straight reporting.* Try "Top Ten Insights from the Workshop" or "How to [Insert Task]: Lessons Learned at the Workshop."

Even when you turn the past into lessons for the future, the majority of your newsletter should be about what's happening now and what's coming up next. *Your newsletter should inspire people to take action today and tomorrow, which is difficult to do when you are living in—and writing about—the past.*

Nonprofits that are required to produce quarterly progress reports for government and foundation funders seem to have the most trouble with this element. *Resist the urge to save time by cutting from your last foundation quarterly report and pasting into your newsletter* for individual supporters. They are two different audiences with different motivations for supporting your work, and therefore need different communications with you. Focus on the future in your newsletters.

Personality: More of Them, Less of You

Even though odds are your newsletter readers are caring, generous people, it's sometimes helpful to think of them as egomaniacs. Here's why: if they don't see immediate, personal value in your newsletter, why should they take the time to read it? We know what's in it for you, but *what's in it for them*?

As you write your newsletter articles, *always put yourself in your readers' place* by asking yourself these questions: How will this article make our readers feel? How will it make their lives easier or better? Does this article show our readers how important they are to us? Will this article make them feel like they are making the world a better place *through us*? Will it reassure them that their investment of time or money in our cause was a great decision?

When Rebecca Arnold, director of marketing for Arrowhead Ranch, a treatment facility for troubled youth outside Coal Valley, Illinois, joined the organization, the cover of the print newsletter included a board member profile and the back page (with the mailing panel—the most visible part of a print newsletter) listed the board of directors and management team. In other words, Arrowhead Ranch was using the hottest real estate in the newsletter to talk about itself, not its supporters.

Now, Rebecca always features a success story of a young man or woman whose life was transformed as a result of their time at the residential treatment facility. The back panel space is reserved for photos of children in different activities, artwork they have drawn, poetry they have written, and other items that express their creativity and portray their lives at the facility. "It puts a personal face on what we do, and it reminds readers that our clients—youth-at-risk—are regular kids who need a little extra help," says Rebecca. "I want readers to be 100% sure of the impact we make on the lives of youth-at-risk and the impact we have in our community."

Speak directly to your readers, one on one, through your newsletters. By using the word "You" in headlines, subheads, and first sentences of paragraphs, you signal to your readers that you are talking directly to them. If you aren't talking to me, the reader, why should I care what you have to say? In other words, talk to me or about me, or else I'm easily bored, and moving onto the next email on my screen or piece of paper in my stack.

On the flip side, ensure that your readers know who is writing. Consider ways to *make your newsletter sound as though it is written by one staff person speaking directly to one supporter.* Use bylines and refer to yourself as "I" or "We." Write in a conversational style and friendly tone.

Storytelling is an incredibly powerful tactic for nonprofit communicators, because we remember stories much more easily than facts and figures, which means we can share them more easily with friends and family. Sharing stories in your newsletters will engage your donors in your work, reinforce their giving decisions, inspire them to do more, and encourage more word-of-mouth marketing on your behalf.

Your stories will be much more powerful if they are about the people you serve or who otherwise benefit from your work, rather than about people who work for your organization. These kinds of stories play a dual role: they educate your readers about the work you do, while also providing examples of your successes.

Joan Purcell, executive director of Prison MATCH in Raleigh, North Carolina, which works with incarcerated mothers, knew that including stories about the people her organization serves was important. At the same time, she realized that they lost much of their emotional power when she told their stories in her voice. Instead, she decided to ask the women to write a story about the most memorable visit they had with their children. Joan now has more than fifty stories to choose from when she writes a newsletter, all written in genuine first-person. She also collects drawings from the children. Not only are the stories and drawings more powerful than anything Joan could reproduce in their place, but it's also easier on her as the newsletter editor, because others create the content!

Next Steps: More Action, Less FYI

Once your supporters read your newsletter, what's next? Do you want them donate, volunteer, register, tell a friend, learn more, write an email, make a call, or what? Reader education is a valid goal, but it's usually not enough to justify that time and expense required to produce a newsletter. *What do you want people to physically do once they are educated*?

If, for example, you want your newsletter readers to donate money to your cause, then all of the content in your newsletter should describe what you will be doing with new donations, remind your donors how important they are to your success, and offer clear and simple ways for them to support your work.

If you want to use your newsletter to recruit volunteers, then fill it with articles about how to be a great volunteer and how important volunteers are. Profile current volunteers and their positive experiences so prospective volunteers will think, "I want to do that, too!"

Chip and Dan Heath, authors of <u>Made to Stick: Why Some Ideas Survive and Others Die</u>, say that *"good stories provide both the simulation (knowledge about how to act) and inspiration (motivation to act)."* These stories are the perfect content for your nonprofit newsletter, because they do more than simply educate. They give your readers direction in what to do next.

The TAILS Humane Society in DeKalb, Illinois, has intentionally started to include more stories in all of its communications, including its e-newsletter, and is seeing that decision pay off with more website traffic, donations, and adoptions. Lane Phalen, chair of the board's public relations committee, says *the stories that get the most clicks from the e-newsletter to the website are those that involved happy endings* for pets, especially those who were hard to adopt.

Lane recounts this story as the kind that produces a great response:

> Watson and his brother, Rayden, were rescued from a hoarding of more than 300 dogs and cats in 2007. They're huge bloodhound-husky mixes. Lisa B. worked with Watson when he was caged and, slowly, he began responding to her presence. After two months, Watson was adopted by Lisa, but Rayden was sent to an animal sanctuary in Arizona where female Buddhist monks work with feral dogs. Two years later, Rayden was socialized, but still timid and unsure of being touched by people. He was reunited with Watson and the two, weighing 95-pounds and 105-pounds, reacted like wiggly puppies to see each other. Lisa adopted Rayden immediately.

Why does this kind of story work? It provides *simulation* by showing that it can take awhile, sometimes years, for abused animals to recover, but that patience pays off. At the same time, it demonstrates that this nonprofit is committed to helping animals, no matter how desperate their situations or how long it takes. It also provides *inspiration*, by motivating others to be more like Lisa B. or the monks in the story, and to take a chance on adopting a dog that others would consider a lost cause. The reunion of the two brothers who obviously remembered each other, even after two years apart, closes the story with a visual, emotional reward that any donor to TAILS would love.

Integration: More Planning, Less Improv

Many nonprofits treat their newsletters like random items on the to-do list, failing to integrate them fully into either core programs and services, or into a communications or fundraising strategy. When the time comes to publish the next edition, the office scrambles to create the content, with little purpose or cohesion and no integrated editorial calendar to ensure strategic timing and coordination of messaging (more on this below).

It's the executive director's responsibility to avoid this scenario. Newsletters can be time-consuming to produce, and executive directors need to ensure that time is well spent. *Fully integrating the newsletter into the organization's programmatic or marketing strategies is essential, as is allocating the appropriate levels of staff time and financial resources to produce it.*

If you view your newsletter as a way to provide services, rather than primarily for marketing or fundraising, integrate it into your mission-oriented programs. The Cancer Prevention and Education Society, based in London, has embedded its Health & Environment e-newsletter deep into the organization's overall strategic plan. "We need to present ourselves as science experts, to get environmental health experts in our contacts database, to develop our own knowledge, and to produce regular educational content," says editor Paul Whaley. "Our newsletter helps us do all of these, synergizing with every single one of our major objectives. Running a newsletter as a quality educational and journalistic service to readers creates so many opportunities, it's unreal," says Paul.

If you do not see your newsletter as service per se, but rather as a marketing or fundraising tool, integrate that tool into your overall strategy (see Chapters Twenty-One and Twenty-Two for additional advice on email fundraising). Penelope Burk, author of <u>Donor-Centered Fundraising</u>, advises, "Meaningful information on their gifts at work is the key to donors' repeat and increased giving. Communication is the process by which information is delivered. Fundraising under-performance, therefore, is actually a failure to communicate." In other words, *communicate well through a regular newsletter, and you will see positive fundraising results.*

Whether you are motivated to produce a good newsletter as part of your programmatic or fundraising strategy, one way to improve the integration of your newsletter into those strategies is to use an editorial calendar. Editorial calendars are schedules that let you plan out what you will say, when and where you will say it, and to whom. Rather than creating each edition of your newsletter on the fly, which will produce inconsistent, hit-or-miss results, and possibly lead to multiple, disjointed communications to the same person in a short period, *editorial calendars enable you to think strategically ahead of time about the different categories of content you want to produce.* Then you fill in the editorial calendar by sketching out the specific articles that fall into each category for each edition of the newsletter, along with other appeals and communications. This powerful tool is also useful when strategizing the exact timing for your marketing efforts—for example, research shows that *"open rates" on emails are highest at mid-morning and mid-afternoon on Tuesdays, Wednesdays, and Thursdays*, so send your newsletters out at these times.

As a professional journalist, Gina MacArthur of Spruce Grove, Alberta, thought that volunteering to produce the newsletter for the parents' council at her children's elementary school would be an easy job. After producing it mostly on her own for three years, her advice to new newsletter editors is simple: *Set up an editorial calendar at the beginning of year, including standing items that should appear in each issue.* "The standing items should be things that can be written well in advance, and just plunked in when the newsletter is being laid out," says Gina. "This will save you a lot of time on deadline day." Creating this kind of plan well in advance also lets you ask others for help, because you know what you need well before the deadline.

Email Newsletter Dos and Don'ts

Dos and Don'ts

- DO use an email newsletter service provider. You can't do bulk email from your desktop for a variety of reasons, including the potential you'll be labeled a spammer. When you hire an email newsletter service provider, they not only help you comply with the spam laws, but also help you manage your email list.

- DO let your readers talk back. If someone replies to your email newsletter, make sure it goes to an email box that someone is monitoring, rather than an impersonal and unfriendly "donotreply@" email address.

- DO master the art of subject line writing. *The "From" field and the "Subject" line determine whether your email gets opened or deleted.* Ensure what's in the From field is recognizable and what's in the Subject line is interesting, intriguing, or otherwise compelling to your readers.

- DO master the art of headline writing. Once your email newsletter is opened, your headlines determine whether the newsletter is read. People naturally skim email, starting with the headlines and subheads.

- DON'T send attachments, including PDFs of your print newsletter. Email newsletters should have the content in the body of the email since *fewer people will open and read an attachment versus content actually in a message.* Most email newsletter providers won't let you send attachments, anyway.

- DON'T rent or sell your email list, and let your subscribers know that's the case. One of the primary reasons that people are reluctant to give their email addresses to nonprofits is the fear that their email address will be sold to other organizations and they'll be inundated with spam.

In addition to this chapter, see Chapters Twenty-One and Twenty-Two for more information on email marketing tips and tactics.

Conclusion

Newsletters are a tried-and-true way for nonprofits to both deliver services and stay in touch with participants, donors, and other important supporters. But the quality of nonprofit newsletters varies widely. By deciding how you want to use your newsletter, integrating into a larger strategy, learning what your readers want to receive from you and how often, and tracking their responses to what you publish, you can create a newsletter that helps you achieve your organization's mission.

Kivi Leroux Miller is president of NonprofitMarketingGuide.com and author of The Nonprofit Marketing Guide: High-Impact, Low-Cost Ways to Build Support for Your Good Cause. *Through training, coaching, and consulting, she helps small nonprofits and communications departments of large ones make a big impression with smart, savvy marketing and communications. She teaches a weekly webinar series and writes a leading blog on nonprofit communications. She presents highly rated workshops and keynotes on a variety of nonprofit marketing topics around the country. More than 2,500 nonprofits in 50 states, across Canada, and in more than two-dozen countries have participated in Kivi's webinars.*

Nonprofit Newsletter Resource Review

NonprofitMarketingGuide.com (www.nonprofitmarketingguide.com)

Kivi Leroux Miller and Katya Andresen. <u>The Nonprofit Marketing Guide: High-Impact, Low-Cost Ways to Build Support for Your Good Cause.</u> San Francisco: Jossey-Bass, 2010.

> This website and companion blog and book include specific advice on producing both print and email newsletters.

Aherncomm.com (www.aherncomm.com)

Tom Ahern. <u>The Mercifully Brief, Real World Guide to . . . Raising More Money with Newsletters Than You Ever Thought Possible</u>. Emerson & Church, 2005.

> Tom Ahern explains how to create newsletters and other donor communications that produce results through his website, newsletter, and books.

Fundraising123.org (www.fundraising123.org)

> The learning center of Network for Good offers many free e-books, articles, and training conference calls on producing great nonprofit email newsletters.

<u>The Nonprofit Email Marketing Guide: 7 Steps to Better Email Fundraising & Communications</u> (www.NonprofitMarketingGuide.com).

> This free e-book, written by Kivi Leroux Miller for Network for Good, gives you step-by-step instructions for launching an e-newsletter.

Email newsletter providers

> Numerous companies provide email newsletter services to the nonprofit community, including EmailNow by Network for Good (www1.networkforgood.org/for-nonprofits/fundraising/emailnow), MailChimp (www.mailchimp.com), Vertical Response (www.verticalresponse.com), iContact (www.icontact.com), and Constant Contact (www.constantcontact.com), to name a few. Using one of these—or another provider—is essential.

Newsletters from your colleagues

Subscribe to the newsletters of organizations that compete with you for attention, or that you simply admire. You'll see who is trying what techniques and get many ideas for your own newsletter.

○ ○ ○

All these resources, plus nonprofit management tips of the week and more, can be found at Nonprofits101.org.

CHAPTER 28

Painless and Effective Event Planning: Let's Get This Party Started!

By Marika Holmgren, Founder, Principal, and Lead Event Producer, Organic Events

At some point, every nonprofit says, "We want to have an event." Images of galas, frolicking guests, and loads of money for the organization dance in our heads. And at another not-too-distant point, almost everyone of those same groups say, "I thought events would be easier." Events can be of tremendous benefit to organizations: they can raise your profile, raise critical funds for your work, and engage community, volunteers, and board members in an exciting and rewarding process.

They can also be a big headache.

How do you ensure that your event is fun, productive, profitable, and doesn't drive your staff and board running for the hills? *Events should be approached with the same methodology that you use for a capital campaign or a strategic planning process: with ample time, realistic goals, and a clear sense of the desired outcome.*

Critical Skills and Competencies

In this chapter, I will demystify event planning and break it down into bite-size pieces that you can tackle one at a time. I will address the role of events in your larger organizational vision and mission, and by the end of this chapter, I hope you'll have a clear sense of how events fit in to your organizational development, and of how to begin planning the perfect event.

Once you've decided it's time to plan and produce an event, you will want to step back, take a deep breath, and prepare to dive in. I'll work to make that dive less frightening with some quick and dirty rules and lessons in this chapter.

What It Takes to Make a Great Event Happen

Before you call the caterer or book the hotel, *take a look at how an event fits into your organization's big picture.* Start with a set of questions:

- Why do we want to have an event?

- How do events fit into our larger development strategy?

- What are the desired outcomes?

- Are we planning a one-off or an annual event?

Whether your organization is just starting out or approaching its twenty-fifth anniversary, these questions are all relevant.

Events can serve many purposes, including:

- Raising funds

- Raising your profile

- Launching new programs

- Increasing your membership or donor base

Which of these are important to you? Are they being addressed in other ways? How will your event address these goals?

When you take a look at these factors, you may decide that an event is the right choice (see Chapter Twenty-Five for a great example of how to use a cost-benefit analysis to decide between different tactics). You may also decide that these needs can be met by other means.

Once you've decided that an event is the best choice for your organization, you're ready to begin planning. The good news is that many before you have hosted Bowl-A-Thons, Starry Night Balls, anniversary luncheons, awards ceremonies, and every other event you can imagine. The event wheel has been invented, and the more you learn from anecdotal evidence and examples, the more successful you'll be.

In this chapter, we'll look at *the key components to successful event planning*:

- Setting goals
- Evaluating resources
- Managing expectations
- Creating a budget
- Event committees
- Creating and managing a time line
- Pulling off a great event
- Evaluating what you've done, earned, and learned

Setting Goals

Before you pick out linens and flatware, start by asking some basic questions. This goes back to what I addressed above: goal setting.

Why do we want to have an event?

This is the most critical question of your planning process. The answer will likely include some of the following answers:

- Raise money

- Honor key supporters

- Present awards to those who exemplify our cause

- Raise our profile

- Thank key allies and supporters

- Generate press

- Have a community presence

These are reasonable and achievable goals for an event—but not all at the same time. Although an event should strive to achieve several goals at once, it's a tall order to expect your event to achieve all goals at one time. As you begin planning, *identify the most important goals for your event, and then prioritize.* No one event can equally address every goal, so you need to rank your goals in order of importance. This will help you ground your event in reality and set you up for success.

You might decide that the goal is to honor key supporters, to present awards, and to thank allies. This event may not be a big moneymaker, but it will help you cement your relationships with donors and the community, and raise your organization's profile.

Perhaps the most important goal is to raise money for your organization. If so, *spend ample time mapping out your fundraising goal and identifying the elements that will entice donors to support your event.*

If your goal is press, which is difficult to earn on events, identify what the "news" is. Are you releasing a major report? Recognizing someone notable with an award? Is your keynote speaker a high profile figure the press would like to interview? Bottom line: *if your goal is press, your event needs to be press-worthy.*

Setting goals early with input from key players will help you plan the most appropriate and effective event to get the job done.

Evaluating Resources

You've set your goals and you've decided *why* you want to have an event. Now you need to *identify the how*. This requires evaluating resources. One myth about event planning is that it's easy and fun. Not to say it can't be either or both, but events takes time, money, and a good measure of sweat. *Taking time to evaluate what resources you can allocate toward your event is as critical as setting your goals.*

The resources that are required include a combination of the following:

- Time

- Money

- Volunteer and board support

- Community and business support

Remember the old saying *"Good, cheap, fast: Pick two."* The same can be said about event planning. Events require resources, whether they are paid for, pro-bono, or in-kind. Start by taking stock of what you have to make your event happen.

This phase of planning is even more important if yours is a small or new organization. If you have limited resources, it's important that you evaluate carefully—and realistically—what you allocate to an event. Because nonprofits operate with limited budgets and staffing, this phase of planning is critical.

We'll start with the first resource: time. Anyone who has planned an event knows they are like home renovations—they seem to cost twice as much and take twice as long as you expect. Whether it's a house party for 20 or an awards ceremony for 5,000, *a successful event requires time from your staff, board, and volunteers.* With your development staff and/or your event consultant, creating a timeline and task sheet (outlined later in this chapter) will help map out where your time will be required and where your staff and board will need to pitch in.

Let's talk next about money. Although the ideal scenario is one in which local businesses, caterers, performers, and audiovisual companies are compelled enough by your issue to donate all the elements of a great party, this is not usually the case. *Organizations often erroneously assume that they can throw an entire event based on donated goods and services.* We will dive into budget planning later, but in short, you need to evaluate what funds you can direct toward your event before you begin so there are no surprise bills in the end. Many nonprofits fall into the trap of poor budgeting, investing time and money, only to break even or incurring a loss at the end of the day. *A budget that is realistic, detailed, and carefully managed is one of the best tools in your toolbox.*

Next, review your potential *volunteer and board support.* Some groups have an extensive network of volunteers to stuff envelopes, staff a registration table, or approach local businesses for in-kind donations. Others have little or no volunteer program. Though all nonprofit organizations have boards of directors, they can vary in size, capacity, and engagement level. As a board chair myself, I believe it's critical to engage your board in your event. Your board may have fantastic connections, whether its guests who will purchase tickets or tables, a friend at a winery to donate the wine, or access to a high-profile speaker to deliver the keynote. *Talk with your board members and ask them how they see themselves contributing to a successful event.*

An often underutilized area of resources is *community and business support.* As a nonprofit you give back to the community on a daily basis. It's perfectly appropriate to approach local businesses and members of your community to solicit support for your event—you might be surprised at the amazing resources waiting to be tapped. Perhaps your local restaurant will provide an appetizer station for your reception, or a videographer will produce your opening video, or the neighborhood brewpub can donate beer for your dance party. *If you don't ask, you don't get. Be sure to back up your request with well-produced materials about the event and your organization, along a description of the benefits they'll receive in exchange for their donation.* Your organization has plenty of opportunities that are appealing for businesses and community partners, including:

- Tax deductions

- Advertising in your event materials

- Links on your website

- Recognition or booth opportunities at the event

- Tickets or tables to the event

- The opportunity to address your audience

Managing Expectations

Once you've figured out the why and the how, it's time to plant your feet firmly on the ground and repeat after me: "I will not have unrealistic expectations. I will not have unrealistic expectations."

It's easy to think big when planning an event, and this may generate great ideas and identify your stretch goals. However, *revisit your goals and resources and you are more likely to stay grounded and realistic.* Having a huge benefit concert with Madonna may sound great, but is it doable? A gala dinner for 900 certainly sounds like a party worth having, but if your organization doesn't have an individual donor base yet, it may not be possible.

Plan something that invigorates, instead of exhausts, your staff, board, and volunteers. *Create a plan for an event that is achievable and manageable.* If an event takes you away from your work with foundations, for example, you may hurt your organization rather than help it.

It's not just important to manage your own expectations, but those of your board, event committee, and key players. It's easy for board and committee members (and I'm speaking as one here) to dream and talk big, because after the brainstorming we get to walk away and leave the bulk of the work to the staff and consultant. Brainstorming is a great process and shouldn't be discouraged, but you don't have to say yes to every wild idea that is presented. Set your team up for success by creating realistic and achievable goals.

Creating a Budget

Before you spend a penny on your event, *you must create a budget based in reality, on both the expense and income sides.* If you haven't managed an event before, consult an event professional when creating a budget. I've worked with clients that create budgets overlooking significant costs, whether it's forgetting to include a line item for a venue, neglecting service and tax* on a catering estimate, or leaving off the audio-visual equipment you'll need to present your program. On the income side, I've seen clients create income structures that are not reflective of what their donor base can bear. *Envision all aspects of your event, account for every component that has a cost associated with it, and think through how you're going to raise money and what's realistic.* After this, you'll be ready for the next step: putting numbers down on paper.

Expenses and In-Kind

Here are the items to include in the expense side of your budget. Even if you can secure some of these items pro-bono or in-kind, you still need to include them in your budget.

- Catering (food, beverages, service)

- Venue

- Rentals (chairs, tables, linens, flatware,)

- Design of signage, programs, and other on-site and campaign materials

- Printing (invitations, program, signage)

- Mailing (postage, mail house)

- Audiovisual (sound, projection, screens, recording)

- Insurance

- Permits

- Decor

- Event consultant

- Additional day of staff

- Travel (honorees, special guests)

- Performers

*Some venues and vendors will waive sales tax based on your nonprofit tax status. Always ask, and be ready to supply your 501(c)(3) paperwork.

- Awards

- Video production

- Photographer

Once you've outlined these items, identify what you'd need to spend on each item versus what you can spend. This is when you'll *identify items and services you need to get donated.* An event professional can help you identify where you can save money, and in which areas you'll want to avoid being penny-wise and pound-foolish.

Add a 5–10% contingency line item to cover unexpected costs without breaking your budget. If all goes well, you won't have to use it, but it might come in handy when you realize that the baseball hats you ordered for guests were printed with ".com" instead of ".org" (true story).

Income

Next, *draft your income structure.* Again, stay grounded in reality. When you look at revenue streams, you'll likely include some of the following:

- Ticket sales

- Table sales

- Sponsorship

- Exhibitors

- Ad sales

- Cash donations, fund-a-need

- In-kind donations

- Live auction

- Silent auction

- Raffle or door prize

- Book sales

These are all effective and proven methods of raising money. However, when estimating revenue in each area, it's critical that you *analyze your member and donor base to evaluate its giving potential is in each area.* If your largest donor in 2009 was a $5,000 contributor, how can you justify anticipating selling a $25,000 table for your gala? Conversely, if you raised $36,000 at your auction last year, consider raising this year's goal to $40,000.

If you're a smaller group just getting started, don't worry if these numbers seem big. You may start out with a fundraiser at a friend's house to raise $500. I know organizations that started with backyard barbecues that now raise hundreds of thousands of dollars.

Consider the 2-to-1 ratio. *If you raise $2 for every $1 you spend, that's considered a respectable expense/income ratio.* Even if you're planning a modest fundraiser with the goal of bringing in $500 for your project, you still need to create a realistic budget and time line, just as you would for a large gala.

Often times, as you develop your income structure you'll already know with some certainty who your largest sponsors and donors are going to be—put their names in your budget, right next to the name of the staff or board member who is taking point on securing their support. Do the same with your less likely prospects, and even with your various revenue-generating tactics (e.g., cold calling local businesses). *Ultimately, the key to event-based fundraising success is ensuring that everyone is on the same page regarding who is in charge of what.*

Once you've got your budget developed, reviewed, refined, and approved, don't let it languish ignored and unattended. Be sure to *keep careful track of every expense, no matter how small.* A budget that is regularly reviewed and updated is much more likely to be adhered to.

Risk Management

Next, look at risk management. Making the decision to have an event involves certain risk. Although there's no way to know exactly what might come up, you'll need to consider the possibilities and identify what measures you will take to mitigate risk.

Scenarios that you should consider include:

- Event income or registration does not meet your goals, financial or otherwise

- Natural disasters

- Hotel strikes and boycotts

- A key team member or event planner leaving the project

- A keynote speaker falling through

Review these and other scenarios and identify what you would do in each case and how you can reduce the risk and liability of your organization. In event planning, always seek to expect the unexpected—*always come up with a Plan B and hope you never have to implement it.*

Event Committees

You may have worked with a committee when planning an event, or even served on one. If you've done either, you have an idea of the complexities involved with event committees. Generally speaking, *there are two primary types of committees for events*, both of which are volunteer-based:

- **Event committee:** a group of volunteers involved in the logistics and planning of an event

- **Host committee:** a group of connected supporters and donors who promote the event to their friends and colleagues

Not every event needs both, or even one, of the two committees. Some events benefit by having extensive committee involvement, whereas others move along just fine without any at all.

There are pros and cons to consider when deciding whether or not to recruit committees:

Pros:

- Increased involvement from your supporters and broader circle

- Many hands make light work

- Potential resources, including access to donors, in-kind donations, speakers, bands, and other vendors

- Increased breadth and depth of outreach

Cons:

- Committees, no matter how effective, require management and oversight

- "Too many cooks in the kitchen" potential

- Increased number of stakeholders has the potential to slow decision-making

As you begin to plan, take stock of the benefits and drawbacks before you put out a call to action.

Creating and Managing a Time Line

A well-thought-out, comprehensive time line is an event planner's best friend. Invest time creating this tool and I promise you'll feel much more in control throughout the planning process.

A good time line is detailed, comprehensive, and indicates clear responsibilities, due dates, who is responsible for what, and status updates.

Table 28.1 shows a very quick outline of a simple, but effective time line that you can create in Word or Excel.

Like your budget, *for a time line to be effective you must review, update, and revise it frequently*—a time line is a living document that evolves throughout your

Table 28.1: Sample Event Planning Time Line

What	Who	Due By	Status	Notes
Select venue	Event Planner	April 1	Done	Be sure to consult board for suggestions
Send out sponsorship packets	Development Director	May 1	Already sent 5; 10 more to go	XYZ expressed interest in sponsorship

planning process. This document will also help your successor immensely, and she will revere and thank you!

Pulling off a Great Event

Somewhere on that perfect time line you've created, you'll see the words "Event Day," probably in bold, 18-point font, all CAPS. There's no getting around it—after the goal setting, resource evaluation, budget planning, and time line, it's time to have the event.

This is where the rubber meets the road, and where you see how your meticulous planning and preparation come together to result in a gorgeous, inspiring, and lucrative event.

I believe that *all nonprofit event planners should live by five golden rules*:

Rule #1: No Assumptions

It's critical that everyone involved be crystal clear on how event day will flow, what their role is, and what all the key players will do. If anyone starts a sentence with "Well, I assumed . . ." then you've got a problem. Call it transparency or the right hand knowing what the left hand is doing, but a beautifully executed event is a well-oiled machine where all the parts work independently, but as one.

Rule #2: Start the Day with Nothing Left to Do

When you begin event day, there should be nothing on your list that could have been done the day, week, or month before. Avoid leaving anything to collate, stuff, or compile on event day unless there's no way around it. You're better off splitting up your volunteers and bringing some in on the days before the event to stuff name tags, assemble goody bags, or label auction items. Event day is a strange parallel universe where time accelerates to the speed of light— plan for that and you'll be OK. Further, you need to leave yourself time to address the unexpected (see Rule #5).

Rule #3: The Curtain Rule

I tell all my volunteers and staff participants about the curtain. I like to think there is a curtain between the public side of an event and behind the scenes of the event. When we are out in front of guests, at the registration table, staffing the silent auction cash-out, or even backstage with the master of ceremonies, we are in front of the curtain, where *we must remain professional, composed, and gracious, as though we've been doing this our entire lives.*

When you are behind the curtain—whether it's in the makeshift event office or in a private corner, that's when you can gripe, cry, tear your hair out, or curse the day that someone thought of silent auctions. Remember the old ad campaign, "Never let 'em see you sweat."

Rule #4: Remember That You Are Part of a Team

No matter what size event you're planning, it takes many hands to create a great event that your guests will enjoy and to which they'll want to return next year. From staff participants, to Junior League volunteers, to the team running the audiovisual, a cohesive and comfortable team knows how to communicate to pull off true event magic.

Remember that *all team members need to be briefed, trained, and managed throughout the process.* In order for the team to function seamlessly, each part needs to work independently, but be comfortable with the other key players. Think of your event team like a baseball team. The shortstop doesn't need to know how to pitch, but he needs to be able to work with the pitcher and know what the pitcher's job is.

There's a good chance that you'll want to work with at least some of your teammates again. Once the event is over, or during if appropriate, *be sure to personally thank your team, ideally by publicly recognizing their hard work and contribution.*

Rule #5: Don't Expect Perfection, but Do Expect Perfect Troubleshooting

Events are a live show that you get to perform only once, without a dress rehearsal. *Because of the live, one-time nature of events, you should anticipate glitches.* As much as you've planned, prepped, and prepared, something (with luck, something minor) will not go as you hope or expect. I always tell my clients, don't expect that nothing will go wrong, but *do* expect that when something goes awry, your team will be ready and able to deal with the snafu in the most professional and efficient way possible.

Evaluating What You've Done, Earned, and Learned

Your event is over. The caterers have left, the awards have been presented, the guest have fabulous goodie bags. You've had a huge group high five—after all, there's no better time to congratulate and thank your team than with a glass of champagne at the end of your event. Now what?

You're probably itching to check into a spa for a week (or two), but your work is not done yet. This next task is just as critical as all of the work you did leading up to the event. This is where look back and figure out what worked and what didn't.

Evaluations are best done when information is fresh, so *schedule debriefs within two weeks of the conclusion of the event.* Although it's good for people to take a couple of days after the event to digest what happened, don't take too long or the feedback—good and bad—begins to lose focus and specificity.

Who do you invite to a debrief? You'll want to include the key players involved in the event planning. That might include any combination of:

- Development staff

- Executive director

- Event consultant

- Event chairs

- Event committee

Some organizations invite a larger circle of people to join, such as host committee members and staff that were only peripherally involved. However, *effective debriefs are ones in which those present feel safe, comfortable, and have been involved in the event in a meaningful way.*

A debrief can be a surprisingly challenging. By the time you reach the debrief, your nerves are raw and you have what I call "Post-Event Depression." It's difficult to work on a project for months or even years, only to hear, "Well, it would have been nice if we'd had better name tags." *In order to ensure debriefs are effective and comfortable, and that participants don't get defensive or cast blame, focus on the parts of the event that went well as much as on the parts that need improvement.* Start by highlighting your achievements and successes, and then delve into areas for improvement, making sure to acknowledge those elements and record them for the next year. *Make sure you hear from everyone, and that everyone is heard.*

A sample debrief agenda might look something like this:

1. Welcome and introductions

2. Celebrating our success—We did it!

3. What worked and what needs improvement

    a. Planning process

    b. Committee

        i. Need a larger, more diverse committee in future years

    c. Program

        i. Work to shorten speeches of awardees

    d. Logistics

        i. Set up

        ii. Break down

    e. Food and wine

        i. Need more wine—ran out early

    f. Staffing and volunteers

        i. Ensure that volunteers know where volunteer check-in is

4. Next Steps

After the debrief, *circulate clear and concise minutes* as appropriate. When you begin planning for next year's event, pull out those notes and memorize them as you begin your next planning cycle.

Event Planning Dos and Don'ts

- DO start the planning process early—at least six to eight months out—setting clear and achievable goals.

- DON'T assume that having an event will be easy.

- DO a careful analysis the resources your organization can allocate to the event including time, money, and staffing.

- DON'T assume that hiring an event producer means you won't have work to do.

- DO create a time line and a budget that is grounded in reality as your very first step.

- DON'T forget to thank everyone who has supported your event.

- DO conduct a thorough and inclusive debrief and evaluation within two weeks of your event.

Dos and Don'ts

Conclusion: The Final Word

Events can be an exciting and effective way to showcase your work, your achievements, and to raise critical funds for your organization. When done with thought, attention to detail, a little bit of humor, and a lot of patience, they benefit your organization, your volunteers, your board, and the community at large.

Take time at the beginning to set goals, evaluate resources, and manage expectations. During the process, adhere to your budget and time line, updating and revising as needed. When it comes time to execute your event, ensure that there are no assumptions, don't leave until tomorrow what can be done today, remember the curtain, work as a team, and be ready for anything. And when the party's over, debrief and evaluate so that next year's event is an even bigger success.

And of course, don't forget to have fun. It's your party, after all.

Marika Holmgren is the founder, principal, and lead event producer of Organic Events, a boutique event production firm specializing in sustainable event production for progressive nonprofit organizations. In addition, she produces the annual Goldman Environmental Prize ceremony, the largest environmental prize program in the country. Her clients include The Jane Goodall Institute, the Tides Foundation, Environmental Grantmakers Association, Mother Jones, Global Green, Wikimedia, and many other social change leaders and innovators. She serves as the president of the board of ForestEthics, and leads the Team LUNAChix Bay Area Mountain Bike Team, which raises critical funds for the Breast Cancer Fund.

Event Planning Resource Review

Special Events Galore (www.stevensoninc.com/products.php?cat=7)

This newsletter offers the latest tips from the trade.

Here Comes the Guide (www.herecomestheguide.com)

Developed initially for brides, this site provides info on venues, caterers, photographers, bands, and more.

Grassroots Fundraising Journal (www.grassrootsfundraising.org)

A resource for nonprofit organizations navigating their way through development work.

Terry Axelrod, the <u>Raising More Money</u> book series

A terrific resource for donor cultivation and "ask" events.

Soul of Money (www.soulofmoney.org)

Lynne Twist (see Afterword of this book) is an expert fundraiser, and her work will help demystify "the ask" and believe it or not, get you excited about raising money.

Green Meeting Industry Council (www.greenmeetings.info)

Visit this site if you'd like to venture into green event planning.

Sustainable Communities Network (www.sustainable.org/information/susevent.html)

Additional resources for green event planning.

Google (www.google.com)—need to find a vendor that does photo booths? Someone who rents whiteboards? Google it—there's a pretty good chance that exactly what you need is just a couple of clicks away.

Local sites dedicated to charitable events. In San Francisco, there's www.sfphilanthropist.com—a great spot to see what other nonprofits are doing, what parties and events are hip and hot, and to view a calendar of upcoming events.

Venues Online (www.venuesonline.com)

Ideas, tips, event products, or visit simply to brainstorm about what's possible when planning an event.

o o o

All these resources, plus nonprofit management tips of the week and more, can be found at Nonprofits101.org.

CHAPTER 29

Public Relations for Nonprofits: Getting Ink for Your Cause

By David Fenton, CEO, in conjunction with Lisa Chen, Senior Vice President, Fenton

Introduction

This chapter is subtitled "getting ink for your cause." Ink—how quaint. Nowadays most communications happens without ink—more people get their information from local television news (Lord save us all) and the Internet than from newspapers.

But the basics of getting attention for your cause, the principles of public relations, remain largely the same across platforms, whether broadcast, online, print, or at the water cooler.

How do I know this? I've been doing communications (and advertising) for nonprofit organizations and causes for 40 years, and I'm only 59. I've watched nonprofits evolve to where, finally, communications are an important part of what they do. It wasn't always thus. And even today, many important and heartfelt nonprofit leaders intrinsically believe that the facts alone will set them free. They believe a purely rational argument presented in the best lawyerly or scientific fashion to someone influential will change the world. Empirical research in the cognitive sciences proves this just isn't so.

Core Skills and Competencies

There are principles behind good public relations. In this chapter, I review these principles and offer some practical pointers on how to be an effective communicator.

Eight PR Principles

1. Tell Unforgettable Stories

At the heart of every successful PR strategy is a compelling story. Stories work because we're hardwired to remember them. Opponents of California's "Three Strikes" law, for example, have used the story of a man sentenced to 25 years to life for stealing a slice of pizza to underscore why the draconian law should be repealed.

What makes a story "sticky"? There must be characters—ideally, a clear hero and a clear villain. As mentioned in Chapter Twenty-Six, *there absolutely, positively should be conflict in the story*—in America today, without conflict, there is no story. Put these elements together and you'll have the makings of a story that is emotional, moving, and memorable.

Tell the conclusion of the story first, then the details, or you will lose people's attention. The story must resonate with people's lives. Policy questions cannot be approached as abstractions—they have to be relayed in terms of real impact on real human beings.

Short and compelling is best. What you say or write in your opening statement, paragraph or email subject line will determine whether people keep paying attention. It's the opening of your pitch that will largely determine the outcome. So get really creative with those subject lines!

2. Meet People Where They Are—Then Bring Them Along

Before you can take people where you want them to go on your issue, you first have to find common ground with them. *When you aren't getting traction on your cause, chances are it's because you haven't yet found a way to engage people on a level they can relate to.*

According to linguist George Lakoff, we make sense of the world and our place in it through internal metaphors and narratives. The key is to activate these so-called "frames" by evoking them in your communications. For example, if you frame a discussion of energy in terms of climate disaster, you will lose many conservatives who don't believe in it. But if you make it about jobs and profits from green energy, and national security, it will appeal to conservatives and liberals alike. Lakoff called one of his books, *Don't Think of an Elephant.* Okay, now try not to. As psychologist Drew Westen pointed out, it's ultimately our emotions and not our rational or political brain that drives us to take action. Use the right frame and you'll trigger those emotions.

3. Repeat Yourself

You must design scenarios that repeat the story many times in many different venues. *Without repetition, stories don't stick.* Without repetition, there is little education. Do you remember the Dial soap ads? They used to be long— "Aren't you glad you use Dial? Don't you wish everybody did?" After quite a few years, they dropped the second sentence. Why? Because they had achieved so much repetition it became superfluous—people repeated the second line to themselves. Now that's a marketing breakthrough.

Social change works the same way. *People don't absorb new ideas without repetition.* Paradigms won't change if you say something once or twice. Political pressure also works the same way. Are you happy your story appeared once on local TV? Was it embarrassing to a politician? Bravo to you. But that politician will likely ignore it. If it's reported a few times, however, the politician will be forced to respond. More times, and they will appoint a commission. Enough times, they may resign. It really does work that way.

4. Build Relationships of Trust with Reporters

Most human commerce is greatly influenced by relationships. If you know someone, and they have learned to trust you even a little, you have more access, you stand out, and they pay more attention to what you say. If you don't, you're one of 1,000 emails. *Relationships run the world.* The same holds true for PR. As NBC's Chris Matthews once put it, "It's not who you know. It's who you get to know."

I have learned many times in my career that no matter how fair-minded the journalist, and most are, if you know them, and do a good job, your clients and causes get more attention than if you are not already acquainted in person.

But the world is changing. More and more journalists are losing their jobs. A good part of our communications landscape is shifting to user-created content on "Web 2.0" platforms. Nonprofits now have to make their own media content for distribution online and through social networks. Journalistic mediation is becoming become less important. Users will rate content and what rises to the top will get the most attention.

But there will still be real, live human beings choosing what to feature on Yahoo!, YouTube, Facebook, your local news website, and the rest. So *get to know the decision makers, and help them do their jobs even better.* This applies equally to the increasingly influential role of bloggers.

Journalists and bloggers alike value trusted relationships with communicators. But the stress is on trust. *Bombarding people with emails and press releases for dubious stories that often don't even fit their beat or interests won't win you any friends.* Journalists often complain they are deluged with material that shows the publicists haven't even read their stories or columns, or seen their broadcasts. So know your audience.

Of course, *writing clearly, getting right to the point, and most of all, being factually accurate and reliable are essential to building trust* (later in this chapter, see my Seven Rules for Writing an Effective Press Release). And, of course, one critical way to build a relationship with reporters is to follow what they cover and understand what makes them tick.

5. Simplify Your Issue

Many of the issues we work on can be complicated. It's the communicator's job to break down these complexities into something simple. "Simple" does not mean dumbing down—just the opposite. *Simple is smart because it means more people will understand why your cause is so important and be inspired to act.*

In the mid-1990s, Republicans in Congress put forward a bill they called "regulatory reform." It should have been called "end regulations." The bill would have made it incredibly difficult for executive agencies like the EPA and USDA to do their jobs. It would have tied up proposed new rules in the courts for years, among other things.

The environmental community was deeply concerned that the bill, if passed, could be used to gut all kinds of environmental and health regulations. But how could we get the public and the news media concerned and even roiled up about "regulatory reform?" The very phrase can cause narcolepsy.

My friend and client at the time, the late Phil Clapp, founder of the National Environmental Trust, came up with the solution. One day, he brought a woman into my office whose child had become horribly ill and almost died after eating a fast-food hamburger poisoned with the virulent strain of E. coli that had caused the infamous "Jack in the Box" episode, where four children died and at least 700 people became ill after eating bad meat.

She was articulate and authentic. The organization she founded, Safe Tables Our Priority (STOP) had been leading the fight to get tighter USDA regulation of the meat supply. STOP was composed of parents whose kids had either died or become violently ill after eating bad meat. And they were up in arms about "regulatory reform," because it would stop the USDA from instituting new regulations for many years. Which meant more kids would die.

So Phil discovered how to *turn a snooze of a story into compelling drama—with characters, conflict, pathos, narrative, and with good guys and bad* (concerned parents and irresponsible companies, respectively). The center of the campaign was not "regulatory reform." It was the great American symbol that we could all relate to: the hamburger.

We succeeded in getting the STOP parents a tremendous amount of media attention. One well-known columnist wrote four consecutive columns about it in a row. The STOP parents were featured on "The Phil Donahue Show" and other national outlets.

I knew we had won when Bob Dole took the Senate floor and said, "I have been accused of being a purveyor of tainted beef!" Now that was a frame he could never recover from, kind of like when President Nixon said "I am not a crook." Regulatory reform soon went down in flames because of *the power of the right story, well told.*

6. Harness Influential Messengers

Sometimes the messenger is as important as the message. This was the case for a campaign we developed for SeaWeb, a project of the Pew Charitable Trusts, to save the North Atlantic swordfish, a victim of overfishing, from the brink of extinction.

I thought a consumer boycott would do the job. But I didn't think people would necessarily listen to what an environmental group had to say. So *who would they listen to?*

I recommended we recruit some of the nation's leading chefs to refuse to serve swordfish, and call on the country to stop eating it until the government protected its spawning grounds so it could recover. Nora Pouillon, the fabulous chef of Nora's restaurant in Washington, DC, agreed to recruit celebrity chef contacts of hers.

We announced the campaign in New York with 27 leading chefs. And then, much to our surprise, it went "viral" as they began to recruit their colleagues. More than 750 chefs across the country joined the boycott. Cruise ship lines, hotel chains, restaurant chains, all announced they would stop serving swordfish. It was a spontaneous grassroots uprising.

Soon, the price of swordfish dropped dramatically due to decreased demand. As a result, even the fishing industry started urging the government to protect the spawning grounds. Which they did. And now swordfish in the North Atlantic have recovered significantly.

7. Use Advertising to Make News

Many nonprofits think advertising is not an option because it's too expensive. But it can be cheaper than you think. And *with the right combination of bold strategy and media outreach, it's possible to parlay a modest ad buy into millions in free, "earned media"* (editorial coverage).

Advertising was the linchpin of a campaign we did for the American Medical Association. They had long campaigned against teenage drinking as a tremendous public health problem. For years, they had successfully lobbied to keep advertising for hard liquor off television and radio. Then NBC announced they were changing the policy and accepting ad dollars from Seagram's, which many charged was to be aimed at young people in particular.

The deal was done. NBC was going ahead. The AMA turned to our firm. We counseled them to buy one full-page ad in <u>The New York Times</u> to embarrass NBC out of taking the money. The <u>Times</u> is the media bible—it'd be like picketing the homes of NBC's president and owners to embarrass them in their own communities—plus we knew that a campaign like this was sure to attract attention from journalists, leading to additional coverage.

The ad featured a large photo of a television set, with a Surgeon General-like warning label across the TV screen. "WARNING," it read. "NBC MAY BE HAZARDOUS TO YOUR CHILDREN'S HEALTH." We also created a micro-site where people could send protest e-letters to NBC's president. Less than a month later, NBC caved under the negative press and public outrage.

Advertising can make news. It need not only be used to repeat messages and persuade audiences. It can *be* the story. Consider it part of your arsenal.

8. Don't Let the Opposition Control the Conversation

Hunkering down and hoping that negative publicity will simply "go away" is never a good PR strategy. It makes even less sense in today's information economy. We live in a 24/7 news cycle where information—and *misinformation*—can rapidly spread, as easily and as fast as the time it takes to write a 140-word tweet. *You must be vigilant about positioning your issue and protecting your brand.* Silence works against you.

Some years ago, the Natural Resources Defense Council hired my firm
to help get attention for a report they were planning on the impact of various
pesticides on the diets of infants and children. The evidence was growing clear
that these chemicals were affecting the nervous system of children (and, we
later learned, their hormones). Some were probable human carcinogens.

According to NRDC's peer-reviewed study, children were getting much too
high a dose of the chemical Alar, which was then used to redden and ripen
apples for harvesting. Alar was a strong carcinogen. Several states had banned
it as a result, and the EPA had been sued for delaying action on the chemical.
EPA scientists were very concerned, but industry pressure kept slowing them
down. Going through regulatory channels would likely take months or years,
so we asked ourselves, *"How can we use the power of public pressure to make the
company do the right thing?"*

Kids, who consume a lot of apple juice and applesauce for their size, were
really getting dosed, so the pesticide concentrations were way above what had
been guessed previously would be a "safe" level. That level had been set for
adult consumption (which is still a huge problem today in the regulation of
other pesticides).

Apples. An apple a day. As American as . . . We could see the symbolism of
focusing on apples—and on kids. We took it to a TV news magazine producer
with whom we'd worked in the past and briefed other national reporters after
we were able to *get journalists to agree to cover the story on an "embargoed" basis*
(meaning they agreed not to run stories until the magazine segment aired).
We also filmed a TV commercial with a volunteer celebrity washing fruits and
vegetables, explaining the dangers of pesticides.

Well, there was a media firestorm beyond what anyone could have predicted.
News stories kept appearing for days and days. People stopped buying apples.
The bottom literally fell out of the apple market. So Uniroyal, Alar's
manufacturer, announced they were unilaterally removing it from the market.
Only then did apple sales come back (of course the remaining apple harvest
was dumped on developing countries). The news magazine show we gave the
exclusive to was CBS "60 Minutes" and the celebrity in the TV spot was Meryl
Streep. These helped, but they are not essential to make news. If you've got a
local story, a local news station and a well-known local personality can work.

For more tips on press strategy, see Public Relations Frequently Asked Questions later in this chapter.

Ultimately, Alar was taken off the market not because of a court case, an act of Congress, or the EPA. The public effectively banned Alar by exercising their consumer power. (Months later, the Bush Administration EPA also decreed that there could be "zero" tolerance of Alar, effectively banning it from food, as urged by their expert panel of scientists.)

Meanwhile, the Washington State apple growers sued NRDC, "60 Minutes," and my firm. They claimed we had purposely and maliciously disparaged their apples with no scientific evidence. It was a classic harassment, or "slap" suit, designed to muzzle the anti-pesticide movement and the media from ever doing this again.

NRDC's outside lawyers advised the group to go silent while the case wound its way through the courts. Now that it was in the legal arena, the public relations advisors were put in the background. Many argued against silence, saying that the pesticide and agribusiness companies would certainly not be silent. This would lead, possibly for years, to a situation where one side would be putting out their story while NRDC would remain silent. And *in a vacuum, opposing interests that go on the offensive often succeed in rewriting history.* And that's what happened.

I understand why NRDC's leaders decided to listen to the lawyer's advice. The legal case was serious, and giant interests were up against them. But it's too bad. Because by the time the case was rejected by the U.S. Supreme Court several years later, the other side had successfully convinced reporters, and part of the public, that Alar had been a "scare," unjustified by science. And that's what you may find on Google today. Never mind that EPA's scientists banned it based on the evidence.

Postscript—shortly thereafter, some states, egged on by the chemical industry, passed so-called "veggie hate crime bills," which were clearly unconstitutional infringements on free speech. They made it a crime to say bad things about food. Poor Oprah Winfrey got charged with these laws in Texas after running a show on problems with hamburger meat contamination. Sorry, Oprah, they passed these laws because of the Alar campaign. Luckily, she was found not guilty of falsely defaming hamburgers.

Seven Rules for Writing an Effective Press Release

1. Your writing should be about what's interesting to a journalist and to the public, not what's important to your organization. *The best press releases read like the story you want to see in the newspaper.*

2. Headlines must be short and provocative. Less is more. On emails, subject lines are key.

3. *Lead paragraphs must get right to the point and state the story briefly and compellingly.* Any press release that starts out with "So and so, the head of so and so organization, today commented on the new status of so and so" is not going to be read and should never be sent.

4. *Use the style of an inverted pyramid.* Short conclusions on top. Then some background. Put the details towards the bottom. This is the basic rule of journalistic writing, and it applies to communicators, too.

5. Quotes should only be used when they have something to say— not to satisfy the boss's ego so she can make a bland statement. Envision the sound bite that you want to see repeated in news stories (and be tuned in to what reporters are most likely to use). Make that your quote.

6. Write crisply. Study what you've written and take out many of the words, focusing especially on if, and, but, yours, his, hers, the, and other extraneous verbiage. Usually, I can cut out up to a third of the words in a press release or personal email pitch and it becomes far more clear and digestible. You can too. Less is more—practice finding and editing out words you don't need. *Clarity and brevity communicate intelligence.*

7. Avoid overusing buzz words like "leveraging" and "strategic." It's the equivalent of using "like" twice a sentence when talking.

Public Relations Frequently Asked Questions

When Should I Give Exclusives to Reporters?

In general, exclusives should be used when a story is not a "must cover" for the whole press corps. If it is optional, its visibility can be raised with an exclusive to one news organization. This is always risky, as it can upset the other media. But there are times it helps a good deal. *If you know you are sitting on a strong story that almost everyone will want, do not give an exclusive.* You don't have to, and it will really upset media contacts that you may need in the future.

Should I Hold a Press Conference or Not?

If you are not confident of a significant turnout, don't have one. Speak to reporters individually instead, or consider a telephone press conference so reporters don't have to travel. That way, if a story is marginal, more of them will listen in.

Whenever possible, connect reporters either in person or by phone with your spokespeople prior to announcing a story. These can formal briefings or more informal "meet and greets," where the conversation is more free-wheeling and your goal is to establish your organization as an important, reliable source. *Journalists will almost always cover something more accurately if they have an opportunity to meet you or your spokesperson and hear the background on a story.*

How to Prevent or Handle a Crisis

If you have bad news, deliver it first. Don't let your enemies beat you to it, as they will frame the story before you can. Also, confessing error and taking the blame is always the right thing to do, and to do first, if you are to restore credibility.

If you are attacked, respond immediately. In today's 24-hour cable and internet news circles, you can't afford to wait. An accusation that goes without a response can become set in stone and hard to change.

Media Relations Dos and Don'ts

- DO meet people where they are. The first step to getting people to listen to what you have to say is to find common ground.

- DO translate your issue into a story. The news media is in the business of telling stories. The better you are at packaging a narrative with compelling characters and a juicy conflict, the more likely they'll respond.

- DON'T overcomplicate your issue. Facts and nuance won't move people. *Getting to the emotional core of your story will inspire sympathy or outrage—and ultimately action.*

- DO recruit influencers. Sometimes it's not what you say, but who says it. In the age of Information Overload, people are more likely than ever to tune into people they already trust.

- DON'T assume you can't afford advertising. If one ad is provocative enough and featured at the right place at the right time, you can get a lot of mileage from it by turning it into an earned media story.

- DON'T allow "no comment" to be your rapid response strategy. If you are under attack from the opposition, respond immediately so their point of view doesn't become gospel.

- DO invest in communications as an organization. Educate the rest of your staff about how communications will amplify their program work and help you achieve your organizational goals.

Conclusion

We can't make the world better if we don't communicate thoughtfully, effectively, and frequently. And in general, rightists (you know, conservatives) pay much more attention to communications than leftists (liberals). This is a big part of why their ideas tend to be dominant in the public policy arena. And no wonder. The so-called conservatives largely come from business, where they had to market or die. Liberal nonprofits come largely from law, science, academia, government, and the humble, do-good world.

So to the readers of this book, the future nonprofit public policy, change-the-world leaders of tomorrow, I hope you will *make communications central to what you do.* If you're a policy-oriented nonprofit, if you're not spending at least 25% of your budget on communications, in my view you are not facing contemporary reality.

It's up to us to tell the truth—and to tell it in ways that will inspire sympathy or outrage—and ultimately, *action.* We are in an era, abhorred by reporters and many of the rest of us, where there is less and less acceptance of facts. There are just points of view. There is much conscious manipulation of the media and body politic by forces intentionally spreading misinformation. The truth is really the best weapon, but only if you get it out there. That's where great PR comes in.

David Fenton, named "One of the 100 most influential PR people of the 20th Century" by PR Week magazine, founded Fenton (www.fenton.com), the largest public interest communications firm in the country, in 1982 to create public relations campaigns for the environment, public health, and human rights. Over more than four decades, he has pioneered the use of professional PR and advertising techniques by nonprofits. David cofounded four nonprofits: Environmental Media Services; New Economy Communications; the Death Penalty Information Center; and The American Freedom Campaign. He was formerly director of public relations at Rolling Stone magazine and coproducer of the "No-Nukes" concerts in 1979 with Bruce Springsteen and others.

Lisa is a senior vice president at Fenton, where she focuses on campaign strategy, branding, and messaging for nonprofits. She is a member of Fenton's health, education, and women's practice teams and the coauthor of The She Spot: Why Women Are the Market for Changing the World and How to Reach Them. She is a former reporter for the San Jose Mercury News.

Public Relations Resource Review

Don't Think of an Elephant!: Know Your Values and Frame the Debate—The Essential Guide for Progressives by George Lakoff (Chelsea Green, September 2004)

If you want to learn how the other side thinks, this is book to read. Lakoff, a key advisor to the Democratic Party, explains how conservatives have framed the issues and how to counter their arguments. Also check out Lakoff's Moral Politics: How Liberals and Conservatives Think (University of Chicago Press, May 2002) and The Political Mind: Why You Can't Understand 21st-Century American Politics with an 18th-Century Brain (Viking Adult, May 2008)

The She Spot: Why Women are the Market for Changing the World and How to Reach Them by Lisa Witter and Lisa Chen (Berrett-Koehler, June 2008)

This is a provocative and practical primer for changemakers on how to harness the power of women for change, written by two of Fenton's senior strategists. Their argument: women vote, volunteer, and give more to causes than men do—that makes them the number one "get" for nonprofits. www.shespotter.com

Manufacturing Consent: The Political Economy of the Mass Media by Edward S. Herman and Noam Chomsky (Pantheon, January 2002)

This seminal work on the power of modern-day media and propaganda and the forces that drive it is a must-read for any student or practitioner of communications.

The Tipping Point: How Little Things Can Make a Big Difference by Malcolm Gladwell (Little Brown, 2000)

This book has swiftly become a classic among communicators, with important insights on what it takes to build a movement or change behavior—or what Gladwell calls "social epidemics."

The Political Brain: The Role of Emotion in Deciding the Fate of the Nation by Drew Westen (Public Affairs, 2008)

Psychologist Drew Westen shows how Americans don't vote with their heads, but with their hearts, and how the role of emotions drives our decision making—and the outcome of elections.

The Communicators Network (www.comnetwork.org)

The Communicators Network is a important hub for social change communicators. The Network offers free webinars and other services and holds an annual conference each year.

Fenton (www.fenton.com)

The Fenton website offers a number of guides and tips for nonprofit communicators on both new and traditional media channels.

M & R Strategic Services (www.mrss.com)

Another leader in this field, M&R, does great work. Check out their advice on grassroots mobilization.

The Nieman Journalism Lab (www.niemanlab.org)

Housed at Harvard University, this site bills itself as "an attempt to help journalism figure out its future in an Internet age." A good resource for the latest innovations and trends.

Romenesko (www.poynter.org/column.asp?id=45)

Follow what reporters are following—this blog, popular with journalists, delivers daily news, analysis, and inside industry gossip.

○ ○ ○

All these resources, plus nonprofit management tips of the week and more, can be found at Nonprofits101.org.

Part Seven

Boards and Volunteers

If you want to go fast, go alone. If you want to go far, go together.

—African proverb, as quoted by Al Gore

It would be impossible to put together a truly comprehensive nonprofit management handbook without talking about the volunteers who make all our work possible. As psychologist Amos Tversky pointed out, *human nature leads us to believe that price infers quality*—we value something more if we have to work or pay for it. Volunteers and board members may provide the strongest evidence that this is simply not true. Yes, they donate their time, but if properly leveraged, a board can provide strategic direction, important introductions, and the funding needed to fulfill your mission. At the same time, volunteers have the potential to not only fill the beast of burden roles to which they're traditionally assigned—pouring soup, stuffing envelopes, and so forth—but they can also contribute skills, experience, and more.

The chapters that follow will provide you with concrete tools and tactics for optimizing your board and volunteer efforts. We'll begin with a primer on board governance—the roles and responsibilities associated with this honorable post—then we'll move onto the often vexing topic of how to get your board to actively contribute to your fundraising efforts. From there, we'll dive into strategies for identifying volunteer needs and recruiting quality talent, followed by tips on how to effectively manage your volunteers and keep them engaged in your efforts. But before we transition into the valuable maps, picks and shovels, and nuggets associated with these crucial topics, I'd like to share a few of the most helpful concepts I've come across when thinking about how to best leverage volunteer support.

The Volunteerism Revolution

Know this: *"skills-based" volunteerism will explode in our lifetime.* VolunteerMatch's "Great Expectations: Boomers and the Future of Volunteering" study points to the fact that the very concept of retirement is about to undergo a radical transformation. Baby Boomers aren't interested in sitting in a rocking chair, on the beach, or on the golf course and seeing their grandkids a few times a year. Just as the younger generation is flocking to opportunities to learn about social entrepreneurship and corporate social responsibility, Boomers consistently say they want to help. That said, they aren't as interested in performing mindless tasks that anyone can do—if a woman is an accountant with 30 years' experience, she may prefer to balance your books. If a guy is a master carpenter, ask if he wants to help with construction needs at the office. Then stand back and be amazed at the power of volunteers to help you meet mission and cut costs.

The Spectrum of Engagement

As you've read is the case with donors and the media (see Chapters Twenty-Six and Twenty-Nine, respectively), perhaps the most important concept when working with any kind of volunteer, including board members, is to *meet them where they're at.* Some people get upset at folks who are unwilling to get deeply involved with a cause. Lately, the term "slacktivist" has popped up to describe the "netizens" who sign an online petition or join a Facebook Cause, but leave it at that (see the "Ladder of Engagement" in Chapter Twenty-Six). This line of thinking is counterproductive and takes us completely in the wrong direction—instead, we must *appreciate that we all show up differently for different causes, at different times.* I may want to take a leadership role in one organization, but only be willing to make a small contribution to another, even if they both work on the same cause. Why? Aside from timing, the real determinative factor is a supporter's *connection to the cause and to the organization*, especially as it relates to how she came to know of it. Is my brother pressing me for support, or is it direct mail? If you're interested in learning more about this, check out a video from a panel I spoke on at San Francisco's Commonwealth Club at www.youtube.com/ watch?v=VmKPYBCqziI.

Hence the concept of the *spectrum of engagement*. As someone who works on the Power to the Peaceful festival in San Francisco, an annual free concert for peace and social justice that draws crowds of over 70,000, I often wonder how we can do more than just throw a big party and then watch everyone go home. On one end of the spectrum are the people who we can convince to sign a petition or make a small donation. This may not sound like much, but as they say in Ethiopia, *"When a thousand spiders unite, they can tie down a lion."* Point is, it all helps, and it all adds up. Further down the spectrum are those who actually want to learn more and get involved. They can stop by booths to get engaged, or even come out to an all-day training the next day to learn what they can do to contribute to solutions. For the truly hard core, I envision a five-week, intensive community leadership fellowship where participants can design and implement social justice initiatives. This model is just one example of what a spectrum of engagement can look like in the real world—think about how you can put this concept to work for your organization.

The Power of Intention

I once saw a De La Vega painting in a New York café that said, *"Be mindful, even if your mind is full."* Another important factor in maximizing the value of your board members and volunteers is your organization's ability to be proactive, intentional, and explicit about what kind of support is needed. Though it's always important to be open-minded and opportunistic when resources make themselves available, it's even more important to *know what you're looking for and ask for it.*

At the board level, this frequently takes the form of a "board matrix" or a "board member agreement," both of which you'll read about in Chapter

Thirty. Whether you're putting these powerful tools to work to support board development, or using a "volunteer job description" to fuel your volunteer recruitment and management efforts (as described in Chapters Thirty-Two and Thirty-Three), the key is to be cognizant of your needs and to communicate related opportunities both internally and to the outside world—to be proactive versus reactive as you expand your team. But remember what I said about the power of intention in the introduction to the book, *"Be careful where you point that thing."*

As you'll read in the chapters throughout this section, the key when using any of these tools is to take the time to be as specific as possible, and to *map volunteer contributions directly to impact.* In particular, when working with high-end volunteers and board members, I encourage nonprofits to embrace a management philosophy that I call "low touch, high value."

Low Touch, High Value

Everyone has value they can add to an effort. Think of the sum total of that value as a pyramid, with the time-intensive, easily replaced contributions at the bottom (e.g., filing documents, serving food, holding a sign, and so forth). That is not to say that these functions are not important. On the contrary, they are the focal point of many a nonprofit's efforts. The point, though, is that you have access to some people—ideally including the kind of people you have on your board, or that you're recruiting—that have much more to offer, but they also have limited time. *The best way to optimize your relationships with time-constrained but potentially high-impact volunteers is to focus on the top of the pyramid—on their low-touch, high-value contributions.* Put another way, what are the three things you really want your board's help with, if each member only has a few hours a month to offer? Contacts and introductions? Strategic input on major decisions? Voting on issues that require their approval? <u>These</u> are the contributions that a board should be focusing its time on.

Along these lines, a consent agenda (as discussed in Chapter Thirty) is a powerful tool for making the best use of precious group time at board meetings. Pay special attention to this portion of the chapter—personally, it was *the* most effective tool I ever implemented at my board meetings when serving as executive director of Craigslist Foundation. If you're spending more than 20% of group time giving reports and updates, in monologue versus dialogue, then you're missing a lot of the value that this group can provide.

Leveraging a High-Opportunity Network

Valuing volunteers' time is a crucial element in keeping them properly engaged. Another factor, especially at the board level, is ensuring that they and other VIPs see their relationship with the organization as a two-way street. Certainly, they are there to support the good work being done, and again, *identifying and communicating the impact of their support on your efforts is of paramount importance.* But board members are people, too, and most of them have a lot going on. To the extent you can help them benefit from participating in the high-opportunity network that is the board, perhaps by simply making a choice introduction every now and then, the impact on their engagement can be astounding. Suddenly, they are in *partnership* with you, rather than serving exclusively as a patron. Accordingly, it's important to take the time to get to know your most valuable supporters, and not only to gain an understanding of what they can do for you, but also where you may be able to support them.

Volunteerism on the Rise

Finally, one last bit of good news: volunteerism is on the rise. You'll see some statistics quantifying recent growth in Chapter Thirty-Two, but if we take a longer-term view, the numbers are even more impressive. In 2006, 30% of U.S. citizens volunteered—that represents a 36% increase since 1989 for adults, or growth of almost a third in less than ten years. More impressively, we witnessed a whopping *212% increase in teen volunteerism* over the same period[1]—it more than doubled.

At times, I liken my beloved United States of America to an alcoholic, and perhaps we just needed to hit rock bottom before enough of us woke up and realized, "We have a problem." The good news is that we have indeed woken up and people are looking to be a part of the solution; and they're doing so in record numbers in the nonprofit sector, in business, and in government. Perhaps one other reason why people are helping out: as mentioned in Chapter Thirty-Three, in my home state of California, older adults who volunteered enjoyed an impressive 44% lower mortality rate than their counterparts.[2] So encourage the people you care about to volunteer—they'll live longer. ☺

CHAPTER 30

Board Governance

By Vernetta Walker, Director of Consulting, and
Emily Heard, Senior Staff Consultant, BoardSource

Introduction

Every nonprofit organization in the United States is governed by its own board of directors (sometimes called a board of trustees). This group of volunteers ensures that the organization operates in the public trust, to which every nonprofit organization is accountable. Collectively, the board makes decisions about an organization's strategic direction, ensures financial and other resources, and provides oversight. *Having an effective board can make all the difference in an organization's ability to carry out its mission.*

As a nonprofit professional, the level of interaction you have with your board depends on your position within the organization. The executive director (sometimes also referred to as the chief executive) is the only employee directly supervised by the board, and generally interacts frequently with them. Senior leaders and development professionals at many nonprofits also work with their boards, whereas other staff may have less interaction.

Our experience working with boards at nonprofits of all sizes and mission areas continuously demonstrates that *there is a strong correlation between good governance and effective organizations.* Accordingly, learning about some of the best practices utilized by responsible boards, as well as ways that the staff can best support the board, will serve you throughout your career as a nonprofit professional. If you are considering becoming an executive director, or if you recently assumed that post, pay particular attention to board governance—it will and should take a significant amount of your time, which catches many new EDs by surprise.

Research illustrates that *the effectiveness of a board is important to the longevity of an executive director.* In fact, the "Daring to Lead" report found that executives "who are unhappy with their boards are more than twice as likely to be planning near-term departures than those who have positive perceptions of their boards."[1]

Critical Skills and Competencies

Although a short chapter is not nearly sufficient to cover all important facets of board governance, we will introduce some of the most important fundamentals—including information on board roles and responsibilities, board size and structure, recruiting effective boards, board meetings, and the fundamentals of working well with your board. Let's begin.

Board Roles and Responsibilities

As a collective, a board of directors governs the organization, whereas the staff—led by the executive director—is responsible for the management and operations of the organization. As stated in BoardSource's <u>Ten Basic Responsibilities of Nonprofit Boards</u>, nonprofit boards are entrusted to:

1. Determine mission and purpose

2. Select the executive director

3. Support and evaluate the executive director

4. Ensure effective planning

5. Monitor and strengthen programs and services

6. Ensure adequate financial resources

7. Protect assets and provide financial oversight

8. Build a competent board

9. Ensure legal and ethical integrity

10. Enhance the organization's public standing[2]

In short, *boards exist to establish strategic direction, ensure important resources, and provide oversight.*[3]

In some small organizations with no staff, boards sometimes also carry out staff functions until the organization is able to hire full-time staff; these boards are referred to as "working boards." In these situations, it is imperative that the board does not neglect its governance responsibilities. As the organization matures and hires staff, the board should ensure that it focuses squarely on governance (e.g., establishing strategy, and so on).

Regardless of where an organization is in its life cycle, as individuals, board members are responsible for three key duties:

- Duty of Care: Board members must use their best judgment in all dealings with the organization by, for example, attending board meetings, raising questions, and providing careful oversight.

- Duty of Loyalty: Board members must be faithful—avoiding conflicts of interest when making decisions affecting the organization.

- Duty of Obedience: Board members must stay true to the organization's mission and to applicable laws when making decisions for the organization.

At a glance, it may appear that the role of the board is very straightforward. Indeed, some boards are fabulous—they understand their roles and carry them out effectively. Other boards, however, are less effective. *When boards lack an understanding of their roles and responsibilities, they can delve too deeply into operations*, which can be a source of frustration for the executive director and staff. In order to mitigate against this challenge and ensure board members are clear on roles and responsibilities, we recommend that you put the two following tools in place:

- Board job description: Defines the role of the board as a collective, including items like the ten basic responsibilities mentioned above. The board job description should be shared with the full board.

- Board member agreement: Outlines the duties of individual board members. *Be as specific as possible in this document, and detail the exact expectations of your board,* i.e., attending 90% of all board meetings, serving on at least one committee, facilitating three introductions to possible funders per year, and so forth.

Be certain to *update both documents as the role of the board and expectations of individual board members change,* so that your documents and practices continue to meet your current needs.

Board Size and Structure

Nonprofit boards vary in terms of size and structure. Let's take a look at best practices for both of these key considerations.

Board Size

Wherever your nonprofit is incorporated, *state law defines the minimum size for your board,* which typically ranges between one and three members. Note, however, that minimum size is not synonymous with ideal size—*your board must determine its optimal size and revisit that decision over time.* If you are founding an organization and forming an initial board, or if the board is revising its size, think about whether it has enough members to carry out its work, and enough diversity of skills, backgrounds, perspectives, and contacts to further the organization's mission.

Ideally, *your board should have no fewer than five members* to include these different types of diversity. *Avoid growing your board to over 20 members,* as it takes significant staff resources to support a board of this size, and fully engaging board members in meetings becomes more difficult. If you are wondering, the average board in the United States has 16 members.[4]

Most executive directors sit on the board as a nonvoting, "ex officio" member (meaning to serve by virtue of their position). Not having a vote helps preserve the reporting relationship of the director to the board and prevents conflict within the board if the ED and the board don't see eye-to-eye on an issue. Along these lines, *never appoint any other staff members to the board*, in order to preserve the reporting relationship of staff to the executive director.

Board Officers

The most common officer positions, which are often required by law, include:

- Chair: Provides leadership to the board, leads meetings, and interacts closely with the executive director

- Treasurer: Coordinates financial oversight and chairs the finance committee (discussed in the following section), if appropriate

- Secretary: Keeps records for the board and takes the minutes of board meetings

Committees

Given the extent of the board's responsibilities, many boards use committees to manage their work. *Committees make recommendations to the board, but do not act on behalf of the board unless specifically authorized to do so.* Common committees include:

- Finance: Reviews and makes recommendations regarding the budget before it goes to the full board, reviews financial statements, and addresses fiscal issues

- Audit: Hires the auditor and oversees the audit process, as required for organizations over a certain budget size in most states; some states require separate audit and finance committees (check requirements in your jurisdiction)

- Resource Development/Fundraising: Oversees the board's role in fundraising

- Governance/Board Development: Identifies, recruits, orients, and engages board members

Many organizations with larger boards also have an executive committee. If you have one, it's essential to define its powers (or limitations on power) in your bylaws (the operating rules for the board). *The executive committee is generally the one committee authorized to act on behalf of the board in emergency situations.* This power should be used sparingly, however, so as not to overstep and disengage the rest of the board.

As you think about your board's committees, always remember the following guidelines to ensure that form follows function:

- Be strategic about the board's committee structure—make sure that committees focus on the board's ongoing work (e.g., finance). *Boards should use a task force, which is similar to a committee with a clearly defined start and end date, to conduct time-limited tasks like strategic planning.*

- Unless your board falls into the "working board" category and the organization has no or limited staff, *the board should not establish committees that overlap with staff functions* (e.g., marketing committee).

- *All board members should serve on at least one committee;* this should be specified in the board member agreement.

- *Invite non-board members to join a committee* as a way to add needed expertise in areas, such as the audit. It can also be an effective way to recruit potential board members (recruitment is discussed below).

- Ensure that committees consist of at least three members to provide enough capacity and diversity of thought to complete the tasks assigned.

- In order to ensure that board members aren't stretched too thin, *limit the number of committees that any board member can serve on to two or three,* but be sure to have at least one board member on each committee, if only to serve as a liaison with non-board members and to provide clear direction.

- Clearly define the role of a committee in a written description, so all members are clear about their responsibilities.

- Assign a chair to each committee—use these positions to groom potential board chairs.

Recruiting Effective Boards

If established, it is the responsibility of the governance (or board development) committee to lead the board in identifying the most important skills and qualities the organization needs as it seeks to expand its board, and to engage the existing board in identifying and recruiting candidates. A founder often handles this task at first, but once a board is established, the board itself should assume this responsibility.

Board Matrix

In order to help determine what skills and types of candidates are needed on the board, use a board matrix. *A board matrix is a very powerful tool that helps boards visually chart various characteristics, skills, and talents that currently exist on the board and among prospects, while also identifying gaps.* Typical items found on a matrix might include:

- Demographic information to help ensure diversity—age, gender, race, ethnicity, geographic location, and the like

- Professional expertise—accounting, finance, law, and so on

- Leadership qualities

- Community connections, including various types of potential funders— corporate, foundations, major donor prospects, among others

- Past board experience

- Capacity to give

Table 30.1 offers an example of a *very* simplified board matrix—more detailed examples can be found online, or in the resources listed at the end of the chapter:

Table 30.1: Sample Board Matrix

	Member 1	Member 2	Prospect 1	Prospect 2
Hispanic	X		X	
African American				X
Under 30		X		
Age 30–50				X
Accounting	X			
Legal		X		
Fundraiser			X	X

Using a matrix forces the board—or founders—to be deliberate about the board's composition and avoid the temptation of simply recruiting one's friends to serve on the board. *It is crucial to the success of the mission that the board recruits leaders that stand to significantly advance the work of the organization.*

∘ ∘ ∘

Also, as previously mentioned, diversity at the board table is crucial to the success of any organization. *Diversity helps the organization stay relevant, promotes creativity and innovation, and can help mitigate against "groupthink."*[5] Yet research demonstrates that communities of color and young professionals are underrepresented on boards—as of 2010, 84% of all board members were Caucasian, whereas only 2% of board members were under thirty years old.[6] A board matrix helps you plan for broad representation and advances your efforts to become an inclusive organization.

Recruitment

Once the board's needs and priorities are identified, its next step is pinpointing specific individuals for recruitment. There are various resources that boards or founders can leverage when seeking out candidates that match their criteria, including:

- Personal networks of business and community leaders

- Media articles

- Volunteers and non-board member committee members

- Participants in leadership programs

- Current MBA students

- Online sites that specialize in board matching (e.g., www.boardnetUSA.org) or that list board opportunities (e.g., www.Bridgestar.org)

Every board member should provide board prospect suggestions as part of their role. Also, the executive director and staff will undoubtedly have some suggestions—these should be routed through the ED to the board.

Once the board has specific individuals in mind, the governance committee, possibly in conjunction with a board member that has a preexisting personal relationship, contacts these prospects, begins to cultivate relationships, and gauges interest in serving on the board. The ED should play a role during the recruitment process, sharing the organization's mission, stories, and impact with prospective board members.

When assessing possible candidates, make sure they are:

- Passionate about and committed to supporting the mission of the organization

- Clear about their potential role and the time commitment required—share the board job description and board member agreement and answer questions about the work of the board

- Able to fulfill the expectations you have of them

Let's review a case study that highlights how one organization used a board matrix to support board development:

The Art of Founding an Inclusive Board[7]

In 2007, The Opportunity Agenda (OA)—which works with social justice organizations—began the process of securing its 501(c)(3) status. As part of the process, they began strategizing around board development, but they wanted to be sure that their board would be representative of the diverse community they serve. An insider, Jason Drucker, PhD, director of development and operations, explained the process and reflected on how the principle of diversity was then shaping its nascent board:

> We have learned that *finding, training, and retaining a diverse group of board members requires hard work and a concerted effort.* We started by creating a long list of qualities, experiences, expertise, and backgrounds that we want on our board. Racial and ethnic diversity is very important to us, but we also are interested in finding candidates from the worlds of entertainment, politics, and philanthropy. We want to attract a social justice luminary and people well versed in employment law, communications and advertising, and accounting, because we believe these skills are essential to our organization's health and prosperity. We developed a broad list of candidates and created a matrix to assess their contribution to our diversity goals. After spending a few days researching and brainstorming, we were able to identify nearly 100 candidates from diverse backgrounds—people who, have the skills, time, and potential to become excellent board members for OA.
>
> Our nascent board has been very helpful in identifying, vetting, and growing the list of candidates—members have spent approximately half of their meeting time this past year discussing nominations. Our conversations, which are based on candidate profiles created through prospect research, have been lengthy and fascinating. Do we have too many candidates who are lawyers? Enough people with deep pockets? Someone who would be an inspiring and capable board chair? Someone with expertise in Human Resources, and someone able to oversee a future budget committee? Can we have too *many* African-American candidates?

While *there is always a subjective aspect to how individuals evaluate potential board members*, our board matrix keeps us accountable and honest about the overall board that we are building. At each meeting, we look at our matrix and see the pattern that we are creating. Because we set diversity goals in terms of talent, skills, and background, we can very quickly see what is missing.

Orientation

All new board members should go through orientation to ensure they are properly acclimated to the board, and to the organization's work. The governance committee or board chair should lead the process and ensure it includes:[8]

- An informational overview of the organization (e.g., history, programs, staff, financials, and so on) with the executive director and chief financial officer (or equivalent)

- Background information on the board (e.g., bylaws, board job description, and the like)

- A rundown on board culture

Term Limits

Term limits, which limit the number of years an individual can serve on a board, are a good idea. They help an organization avoid stagnation, ensuring that it's regularly connected to new resources and ideas—plus they offer an effective, graceful way to rotate off ineffective board members. Most boards have two- or three-year terms of service, one- or two-year terms for officer positions, and the opportunity to serve two consecutive terms. *Never implement automatic term renewals*—the board should be reserved for energetic board members who are fulfilling their duties and making a real contribution to the organization, thereby earning their reelection. Also, note that if you fail to officially adopt term limits, many states mandate default terms; if you consciously decide not to pursue this approach, be sure your board formally adopts a resolution.

Of course, this rotation implies that the board must constantly identify and recruit new members, which is why a governance committee is so important. It also means that the board itself is not static. As members rotate, the dynamics on the board will change, hopefully reinvigorating the board on a regular basis.

For more information on recruitment, orientation, and term limits, visit the sites listed in the resource review.

Board Meetings

Making the most of valuable group time is important in any setting, especially when it comes to optimizing board meetings. The board chair and executive director should collaboratively plan board meeting agendas to maximize time and attention on issues that matter most, strategizing how to best leverage the gathering to most significantly advance the organization's mission. The process of setting the agenda should also involve input from committee or task force chairs. Although it is important to quickly relay key updates and action items, *it's crucial to ensure meetings provide time for strategic thinking and discussions, and are not overly focused on reports and updates—that's where a consent agenda can help.*

Don't fall into the trap of talking at versus with your board—the meeting should be a place of conversation (e.g., strategic discussions and voting), not one-way communication (reports and updates, unless incredibly important). *A consent agenda groups items that do not need to be discussed, such as potentially important committee and staff reports or previous board meeting minutes, under one meeting agenda item.* These items are then approved relatively quickly with one vote, thereby saving time to focus on issues of strategic importance. If a board member feels an item merits discussion, you can do so before voting in the consent agenda. To be used successfully, however, all board members should receive the materials far enough in advance so that they have an opportunity to review the contents before the meeting. Even still, don't assume that everyone present has read the materials, and *take five to ten minutes in silence at the beginning of every board meeting for the members to review the docket and then ask any questions before voting it in.* This way, board meetings can be a time for dialogue, not monologue, and make the best use of the board's time together, thereby further engaging current members and advancing your work.[9]

Additional meeting materials should include an agenda with set times allocated to each item, urgent committee, financial, and staff reports not included in the consent agenda, supporting documents for discussion and action items, and the executive director's update. For more information on planning and running effective board meetings, visit the resources listed below.

Fundamentals of Working with the Board

As noted previously, the type of relationship that nonprofit professionals have with the board at their organization depends on their position; it also depends on the size of the board and the size of the staff. Though there are always exceptions, the following discussion is based on the most common practices in the nonprofit sector.

Executive Directors

The relationship between the board and the executive director forms the nexus for effective nonprofit leadership. If you are the ED (or contemplating a future as one), here are a few tips to help ensure a productive and effective relationship with your board:

- Expect to spend a significant amount of time working with your board.

- Establish a strong working relationship with the full board and with the board chair in particular. Set time aside periodically to talk about communication preferences, mutual expectations, and work styles.

- Keep the board informed with timely communications based on the board's preference versus your own, and *ensure that there are never any surprises for your board.*

- Establish clear and agreed-on expectations. *Have a job description in place for your position, the board chair, and for the board* to ensure that everyone knows the line between governance and management, and that everyone is held accountable for fulfilling their roles.

- Work with the board to *establish formal, explicit, and measurable annual goals* (e.g., executing tactics within the strategic plan, growing the organization by a defined amount, ensuring a balanced budget, and so forth), against which the board will assess your performance and conduct your annual performance review (always document this in writing).

Staff

If you are a staff member other than the ED and your position or duties require that you interact with the board, here are a few tips:

- If you are asked for information for a board packet, or to present information at a board meeting, *be clear, concise, and accurate*—the board will be using the information provided to make decisions for the organization. Don't provide the board more detail than is necessary; their time is valuable.

- If you are supporting a committee, be sure to determine expectations— including the type of support the committee needs from staff and a clear delineation of roles—in advance.

- *Remember that board members are volunteers*, so be considerate. They are, after all, dedicating their time to ensure the success of the organization, and they tend to be quite busy. So be respectful of their time and keep routine communications as brief as possible.

Fundraising: A Common Challenge

Executive directors, development directors, and other staff often encounter reluctance on the part of many board members to engage in fundraising. Chapter Thirty-One by Bob Zimmerman provides guidance on how to get your board to fundraise, so we will not spend time on it here, except to say that expectations have to be very clear and that there are a variety of roles available to board members in the fundraising process—*don't expect everyone to make an ask in order to contribute*, although all board members should help in some way, such as making introductions or thanking donors.

Other Essentials

Before we conclude, here is a short list of other items requiring your attention:

- *Every nonprofit should have a conflict-of-interest policy.* Conflicts of interests arise when the personal interests of a board or staff member conflict, or might conflict, with the interests of the organization. Avoiding these situations is an important part of fulfilling the "duty of loyalty" outlined above. Your policy should define what constitutes a conflict, processes for recusing (disabling the ability to vote or weigh in) board members and staff from discussions involving a conflict, and processes for resolving any such conflicts.

- Be sure to *secure Directors and Officers (D&O) insurance*, which protects the board from liability resulting from board action (see Chapter Seven for more on this). Many board candidates will refuse to join an organization without this protection.

- Be aware that most nonprofit organizations need to complete the IRS Form 990 annually—ask the IRS what version of this form your organization needs to complete. Note that the Form 990 asks a number of questions pertaining to governance and should be shared with the board.

- Regular assessments are a great tool for board self-reflection, improvement, and accountability. *Conduct annual board self-assessments, board chair assessments, and individual board member reviews.*

Board Governance Dos and Don'ts

- DO create a board member job description and board member agreement so that board members are aware of their duties as a collective and as individuals.

- DO be strategic about board development. Effective board composition is crucial to advancing the work of the organization.

- DO establish a board orientation that includes information about the organization (e.g., mission, history) and the board (e.g., board meeting minutes, bylaws).

- DO implement a consent agenda in order to focus board meetings on strategic issues and discussions versus reports and updates.

- DON'T overstep! Remember *the board's only direct report is the executive director*. All other staff reports directly or indirectly to the ED and must work through her on board and other matters.

- DON'T stack the board with personal connections that lack the right skills to advance the organization's mission in significant ways.

- DON'T forget that board members are volunteers. Thank them for their service and be respectful of their time.

Conclusion

As a nonprofit professional, equipping yourself early on with knowledge about the role of your board will significantly advance your ability to deliver results. This chapter introduced some fundamentals pertaining to board governance—but by no means is this a comprehensive overview. Implementing the strategies and tactics outlined here will help ensure that your board has the leadership it needs and is well positioned to advance the organization's mission in significant ways, but just as with all relationships, realize that this is an ongoing journey.

Vernetta Walker works with multifaceted organizations and consults on nonprofit compliance issues, effective governance, and developments in the nonprofit sector. Prior to serving as director of consulting at BoardSource, Vernetta served as associate general counsel for the Maryland Association of Nonprofit Organizations and provided technical assistance, counsel, and nonprofit expertise in the areas of board governance, organizational structure, and advocacy. Vernetta practiced law in Florida for several years and served as a grant officer for the Florida Bar Foundation. She received her JD from Washington University in St. Louis and her BA from the University of Maryland.

Emily Heard is a senior staff consultant for BoardSource, where she provides consultative guidance to nonprofit organizations on effective board governance. Prior to BoardSource, Emily served as director of education and professional services for the International Business Ethics Institute, where she designed training, revised codes of conduct, and provided other consulting services to multinational corporations. Emily also worked at the Corporate Executive Board and served as a consultant for various think tanks. Emily holds a BA in history from McGill University (Montreal, Quebec), and an MA in history from Dalhousie University (Halifax, Nova Scotia).

Board Governance Resource Review

BoardSource (www.boardsource.org)

Nonprofit dedicated to advancing the public good by building exceptional nonprofit boards and inspiring board service. Their website features valuable articles, books, and resources on board governance.

Blue Avocado (www.blueavocado.org)

A provocative online magazine for community nonprofits, with a strong focus on board governance and engagement topics.

Board Café (www.compasspoint.org/boardcafe/archives.php)

Offers great articles on board governance.

The Chronicle of Philanthropy (www.philanthropy.com)

Provides news on board governance and other important topics pertaining to the nonprofit sector.

Bridgestar (www.bridgestar.org)

Lists board opportunities and provides resources and insights for nonprofit organizations looking for new board members.

boardNet USA (www.boardnetusa.org/public/home.asp)

Matches nonprofits looking for new board members and individuals looking for board service opportunities.

VolunteerMatch (www.volunteermatch.org)

Connects individuals to opportunities for civic engagement, including board service.

Young Nonprofit Professionals Network (www.ynpn.org)

A nonprofit organization that engages and supports future nonprofit leaders.

The Nonprofit Times (www.nptimes.com)

Contains articles on nonprofit management, including tips on working with your board.

Chait, Richard P., et al. <u>Governance as Leadership: Reframing the Work of Nonprofit Boards</u>. New York: Wiley, 2005.

This book introduces "generative governance." Once you're familiar with governance basics, this is a great resource for staff and board members looking to take board governance to the next level.

○ ○ ○

All these resources, plus nonprofit management tips of the week and more, can be found at Nonprofits101.org.

CHAPTER 31

Getting Your Board to Fundraise

By Bob Zimmerman, President, Zimmerman Lehman

Introduction

It is the rare nonprofit that is blessed with a board of directors that enjoys raising money without prodding. Although some board members acknowledge that raising funds is part of their job, all too many claim that theirs is a "program," "working," or "policy" board, and that fundraising is therefore not part of their job description. Assuming that you're part of the rule and not the exception, you can likely benefit from a quick review of some of the ways that have proven most effective at getting boards to fundraise.

Critical Skills and Competencies

Board members need to be trained in their fundraising responsibilities. In this section, we'll focus on how to get your board members ready to raise money.

Board members have a variety of fundraising responsibilities and they must be apprised of those as soon as they consider the possibility of joining the board (that is, this information should be in the board job description, as overviewed in Chapter Thirty). This chapter includes concepts that board members must understand to be successful fundraisers, plus examples of how board members should be deployed in particular kinds of fundraising campaigns.

Set Expectations and Create a Culture That Favors Fundraising

It is vitally important to understand at the outset that *the board's reluctance to raise money is not the fault of individual board members.* The fault lies with organizational cultures that (1) do not alert new board members to the fact that fundraising is one of their responsibilities; (2) do not train the board in successful fundraising techniques; and (3) do not recruit new board members with an eye toward giving and getting money. Is it therefore any wonder that so many boards fall down on the fundraising job?

Also, board members must understand that fundraising is not "tin-cup begging"; words like "contribution," "donation," and "gift" distract board members from the fact that they should be asking people to *invest* in successful community enterprises. Remember the Bill Cosby story from Darian's introduction to Part Five: *if fundraising is viewed as community investment instead of begging, board members will be proud to solicit money on behalf of their organizations.*

Members of nonprofit boards have four fundraising responsibilities, and prospective board members should be explicitly alerted to these responsibilities when they are considering board membership.

- To make a financial contribution to the nonprofit that constitutes a "capacity" gift

- To solicit friends, relatives, and colleagues for contributions

- To add "ability to give and get money" to the list of considerations when recruiting new board members

- To oversee the nonprofit's fundraising activities

Let's look at each of these in a bit more detail.

To Make a Financial Contribution to the Nonprofit That Constitutes a "Capacity" Gift

Charity begins at home: *the willingness of board members to donate generously to their nonprofit is the key to successful fundraising.* If board members aren't making capacity investments, why should anyone else in the world give? Thus, 100% board giving, meaning that every single board member makes a financial contribution, is critically important in two ways: it represents significant revenue for the nonprofit, and it advertises to prospective donors and grantors that those closest to the organization have "put their money where their mouth is." *Agreeing to make a capacity gift must be part of the written board member agreement.* More and more foundations require 100% board participation in giving before they will consider making grants. The financial capacity of board members varies widely; *each board member's contribution should be one of the three largest that he or she makes to any nonprofit organization in the calendar year.*

To Solicit Friends, Relatives, and Colleagues for Contributions to the Nonprofit

Nonprofits have two "hot lists" of prospective donors: people who have a substantive interest in the work of the organization; and the friends, relatives, and colleagues of those closest to the organization (of course, these lists overlap to some degree). The most important tactical issue in fundraising is *access*: raising money from strangers is much more difficult than raising it from friends, acquaintances, and colleagues. *Board members' willingness to solicit contributions from the folks they know will often spell the difference between fundraising success and failure.* Conduct a half-day fundraising training for the board that concentrates on the importance of asking for contributions from this "low-hanging fruit." Whether the training is led by a staff person or an outside consultant, the focus should be on ensuring that the nonprofit doesn't leave money on the table by failing to ask for gifts from the board's contacts. A good trainer will provide detailed information on how board members can ask for gifts in a variety of ways (e.g., direct mail, events, and major gift campaigns).

Although some board members may not be comfortable with face-to-face solicitation, which must be accepted and honored, they can still play a vitally important fundraising role by appending notes to friends on direct mail appeals, serving as "door-openers" to colleagues who might make contributions, thanking existing donors, and being ambassadors for your nonprofit by speaking at events.

To Add "Ability to Give and Get Money" to the List of Considerations When Recruiting New Board Members

A well-functioning nonprofit board will include people with expertise in finance, program development, and human resources. It is crucial to add "fundraising" to this list. Fundraising is certainly not the only responsibility of a nonprofit board, nor is it necessarily the most important. But it is a responsibility that cannot be shirked. When considering new members, nonprofit boards should include "ability to give and get money" as one of the criteria in their assessment (see "board matrix" in Chapter Thirty).

To Oversee the Nonprofit's Fundraising Activities

Just as the board of directors has oversight of finances and programs, it has a similar responsibility for fundraising. The board should require the staff or a consultant to prepare a written two- or three-year fundraising plan divided into six-month or shorter segments (see Chapter Eighteen for more on this). Each segment includes: the kinds of fundraising to be undertaken in each period (e.g., foundations, corporations, individual donors) with corresponding goals for each; the tasks to be addressed in each fundraising area; and the person(s) responsible for those tasks. The board should then require staff to report at each board meeting on the progress made on realizing plan objectives.

A board that is willing to give money, get money, recruit people to the board who can help with fundraising, and exercise oversight on the organization's fundraising activities will ensure the ability of their nonprofit to compete successfully for grants and donations.

Key Principles of Board Fundraising

The board's successful involvement in fundraising depends on the understanding and application of five key principles:

1. The Biggest Problem in Fundraising Isn't Getting People to *Give*; It's Getting People to *Ask*

Even in difficult economic times, there is a great deal of philanthropic money available to nonprofits: witness the $303.75 billion that was donated privately in 2009 (see Chapter Nineteen), an allegedly catastrophic year for the nonprofit sector. The tragedy in fundraising is not that there isn't any money; the tragedy is *unrealized potential*: the billions of dollars that nonprofits leave on the table every year by not asking for enough money, or not asking for it at all. *The willingness of board, staff, and volunteers to ask is the bedrock of successful fundraising.*

2. Fundraising Must Be Done from the Perspective of the Donor, Not the Applicant

Nonprofits have an unfortunate tendency to assume that the world must be interested in every aspect of what they do. What nonprofits have to "sell" is of far less importance than what donors and grantors want to "buy." Which of your program offerings is of the greatest interest to a particular contributor or prospect? Successful fundraising depends on "active listening": what "spin" will appeal to a particular donor? Fundraising is not done whole cloth; it is done with reference to specific programs or "pitches" that resonate with prospective donors. *Take the time to identify a prospect's hot buttons, either through research or conversation, and then frame your work accordingly.*

3. People Give to Strength, Not Crisis

In difficult economic times, nonprofits all too often throw themselves on the mercy of the prospective donor. "Without your help," they whine, "our little organization is threatened with extinction." *In soliciting donations and grants, board members and staff must understand that they are asking folks to invest in a thriving organization with exciting plans for the future.* Why would anyone invest in a sinking ship? It doesn't make any sense. People want to invest in success, not failure. Remember what Kay Sprinkel Grace said in Chapter Nineteen, "people don't give because you *have* needs; they give because you *meet* needs."

4. People <u>Love</u> to Give Away Money

There is a warm and wonderful feeling that comes over a person when he or she has made a donation to a deserving nonprofit. This is one of those rare "win-wins" in life: the donor feels good having made the gift, and the nonprofit takes the gift and does good things with it. There is no reason for board members to be embarrassed about asking for contributions, or to feel that they are taking advantage of friendships. *If done right, people are honored to be asked and are thrilled to give*, plus they're given a graceful way out if they decline to give.

5. Accentuate the Positive

Rather than whine about another organization having an easier time raising money than their organization, nonprofit board and staff members <u>must</u> focus on the value of their work to the community and the most effective means to make the case for a gift. *In a challenging economy, it is particularly important to make the case in a positive and engaging manner.*

Raising Money Through Grants

Nonprofits raise philanthropic dollars from grants and individual contributions, and board members have roles to play in both areas. Looking first at grants, the universe of grantor possibilities includes foundations, corporations, religious institutions, and government agencies. *Board members are essential to the grant solicitation process, and they can help with their connections, introductions, and presence*:

Connections

Though grantors may try to convince nonprofits otherwise, personal relationships matter as much in grant solicitation as they do in seeking donations from individuals. *Once development staff have identified prospective grantors, it is vitally important for board members to review the names of board and staff members at prospective grantors* to determine whether anyone on the nonprofit board knows anyone at the grantor agency. It is remarkable how often a nonprofit board member, in reviewing the names of contacts at a foundation that the nonprofit plans to pursue, will say: "I knew that person in college. I had no idea she was on a foundation board!"

Introductions

Having identified a personal connection, and <u>following</u> discussions between staff members from both organizations (see Chapter Twenty), the nonprofit board member should send a note or email to her contact at the grantor agency soon after their nonprofit has submitted its letter of intent or full proposal. The note might say: "I hope this note finds you well. It was quite a coincidence to discover that you're on the board of the [name of foundation]. I'm proud to serve on the board of the [name of nonprofit], and our executive director recently sent your foundation a proposal with reference to [short description of the project for which the nonprofit is seeking funding from the foundation]. I hope you have the opportunity to review our proposal. Please give me a call if you'd like to discuss the work of [name of nonprofit]. Thanks so much."

Presence

If a grantor is considering making a grant to the nonprofit, one of their representatives may make a site visit or request that some of your team come to their offices to discuss the proposal. Though the executive director or development director should certainly be present at that meeting, it is also valuable for the board president or another board member to attend. The presence of a board member at the meeting tells the program officer that a volunteer cares enough about the work of the nonprofit that she is willing to take the time from her busy day to meet with the grantor, not to mention that she can add a new perspective and dimension to your pitch.

Corporate Grants

Board involvement, then, is critically important to successful solicitation of grants of all types. The world of corporate philanthropy deserves special mention in this regard. Corporations give to nonprofits for two reasons: first, they want the world to know that they are "good corporate citizens." A corporation loves sponsoring walkathons and other events, because it knows the nonprofit will mount large banners trumpeting the corporation's largesse. Second, corporations are extraordinarily responsive to the philanthropic priorities of their employees. *If someone inside a company makes a pitch on behalf of a particular nonprofit, the opportunity to secure a grant is exponentially greater than if the nonprofit sends that company a cold letter.*

Nonprofit board members should prepare lists of folks they know in local and national companies and be prepared to put in a good word in order to help secure a meeting with their corporate philanthropy or marketing department. They should ask their company contact to talk to the corporate philanthropic officer to communicate his excitement about the work of the nonprofit, and to report back with any feedback he is able to garner from colleagues.

Raising Funds Through Individual Donations

Although grants are important, *individual donations should be the primary goal of virtually every nonprofit's fundraising efforts* for three reasons, as indicated in Chapter Nineteen. First, four out of every five dollars raised from private sources in the United States come from individual contributions, not grants, and this figure hasn't budged for years. Second, most individual gifts represent unrestricted income that the nonprofit can use any way it wants to (unlike, say, foundation grants, which are usually tied to a specific project). If a nonprofit holds an event, solicits gifts on its website, or conducts a direct mail campaign, the resulting revenue can be used for any legal purpose deemed important to the organization.

The third reason that individual gifts deserve pride of place goes to the very heart of the nonprofit philanthropic effort. *If an individual makes a donation to a nonprofit, and if that person is pursued consistently and respectfully, there is every reason to expect more and more money from that person* far into the future. This is simply not the case with grantors. Hence the $25 direct mail contributor in year one may become the $10,000 major donor in year seven and the $5 million planned gift donor in year twenty. Successful individual fundraising depends on bringing a donor into the "system" and continuing to cultivate that person and to ask her for larger and larger gifts.

Though board involvement is important in seeking grants, it is absolutely fundamental in the pursuit of individual donations. It is no exaggeration to state that the success of most campaigns seeking contributions from individuals rests on the active, intelligent involvement of the board of directors. Here are a few examples of how the board can be of critical assistance to a nonprofit's individual fundraising campaigns:

Direct Mail

Board members should assemble address lists of friends, relatives, and colleagues who might contribute and *append personal notes to fundraising letters.* As corny as it might sound, these short written notes atop the letter persuade people to give at substantially higher levels.

Events

Board members must be expected to sell sponsorships and individual tickets. In addition, if the nonprofit is planning a complex event, like a sit-down dinner with a cocktail party beforehand and music and dancing afterward, the event should be managed by an event committee, which will include board members and other volunteers with a passion for the organization and a flair for producing events.

Telephone Solicitations

Even though many nonprofits hold their noses when it comes to telephone fundraising, the statistics are undeniable: it works. What is paramount is that the people making the calls and the people getting the calls care deeply about the nonprofit. Private schools, for example, have been very successful in asking board members and other volunteers to call parents, grandparents, and alumni families. *When there is passion on both sides of the call, money is raised.*

Online and Social Networking Solicitations

More and more people are living their lives online, and this has had an enormous impact on philanthropy. As with direct mail, board members should supply the nonprofit with the names and electronic addresses of friends, relatives, and colleagues, and should stand ready to send personal notes in support of the organization's email, web, and social networking fundraising efforts.

Major Donor Campaigns

Over 80% of the money raised by nonprofits from individuals comes from the 20% of the population that can afford to give the most. The people with the greatest capacity to give should be approached face-to-face: *the most effective way to raise money is to sit across the table from someone who has lots of it and ask for some.* A "major donor" is someone who makes a financial contribution significantly larger than the average individual gift to the nonprofit. For some organizations, this will be $250; for others it will be $250,000. Once the nonprofit comes up with a list of prospective major donors, it is time to initiate a campaign by convening a major donor committee made up of appropriate board members, staff members, and other volunteers with a knack for face-to-face asking. The committee is responsible for determining the overall campaign dollar goal; matching solicitors and prospects; meeting with prospects to solicit gifts; and providing the organization with information on what transpired during the solicitations. *Board members are particularly well situated to ask for major gifts* because prospective donors are impressed that a volunteer board member has taken the time from her busy day to meet with the prospect. This "modeling" is not possible for a staff solicitor, because part of what the staff person is asking for is his salary. Board members are therefore crucially important to the success of major gift solicitation.

case study

The Show Must Go On: A Case Study in Board Member Fundraising

A modern dance company in a city in the western United States had reached an important and troubling crossroads. In existence for just over five years, the company's funding had come from two sources: box office receipts and foundation grants. Box office receipts covered barely half of the company's expenses and, as is often the case, though foundations had been eager to help the company to get off the ground, they were reluctant to provide sustaining funding.

Therefore, it was imperative that the dance company begin to solicit contributions from individuals. The company had a database that included information on folks who had attended performances, but those people had never been approached for donations. In addition, the board was comprised of dancers, choreographers, and friends of the company's artistic director, none of whom had connections to big dollars.

With the assistance of a fundraising consultant, the company's board of directors and artistic director reviewed its database of people who had purchased tickets to performances. The database contained just over 1,500 names, with street addresses or email addresses, or both. The board and artistic director decided to cultivate and pursue these prospective donors in three ways:

- A direct mail campaign aimed at those people whose database information contained only street addresses

- An email/web campaign aimed at people for whom the dance company had email addresses

- An event at the company's performance space to celebrate its fifth anniversary and to alert folks to the company's exciting plans for the next two years

Board members had a number of responsibilities to help ensure the success of these activities:

- Providing names, addresses, and email addresses of friends, relatives, and colleagues for the campaign

- Appending personal notes on direct mail letters to their contacts

- Sending emails encouraging contacts to make contributions (for those prospects who received email solicitations)

- Sponsoring tables at the company's event

- Striking up conversations with event attendees to alert them to the company's exciting plans

Due in large part to the board's enthusiastic involvement in these fundraising activities, the modern dance company secured over $40,000 in contributions. Perhaps more important, the ticket purchaser database of 1,500 names grew to over 1,800 names of donors and ticket purchasers.

Board Member Fundraising Dos and Don'ts

- DO require that every board member make a capacity financial contribution.

- DON'T assume that you've recruited folks to the board only to serve as experts on policy and programs, but make sure they understand their role in both fundraising and governance.

- DO make sure that board members ask friends, relatives, and colleagues for contributions, or at least open the door to those discussions.

- DO make sure that the board makes the ability to give and get money one of its criteria in recruiting new members.

- DON'T let board members "poor-mouth" your efforts to solicit contributions; instead, coach them on singing the praises of your nonprofit and making the prospect understand that she is supporting a successful, valuable enterprise.

- DO give board members specific "fundraising marching orders" so they understand their roles in such areas as grant solicitation, direct mail, and events.

- DO understand that Rome wasn't built in a day—creating an effective fundraising board takes time, but it will happen if everyone understands that fundraising is a top board responsibility.

Conclusion

Nonprofit organizations must forge a "culture of philanthropy" and train and encourage board members to raise money. The success of a nonprofit's fundraising efforts depends primarily on a board of directors that is willing to give money, get money, recruit people to the board who can help with fundraising, and oversee the organization's development work.

Once board members understand their fundraising roles, they must be trained in the importance of "accentuating the positive." Fundraising is not begging; it is alerting prospective donors to the great work of the organization and asking them to invest in advancing the impact of a successful enterprise.

The board is vitally important in the solicitation of grants and individual contributions. Every nonprofit must review the ways that it raises funds, decide whether there are other approaches that make sense for the organization, and ensure that the board is being tapped to help out with every fundraising strategy.

Though people rarely join boards because they like to raise money, they will rise to the occasion once they are coached and educated to understand that their fundraising work will ensure the survival and success of the organizations they love.

Robert M. Zimmerman passed away on December 26, 2010. He was president of Zimmerman Lehman, has over 35 years of experience in nonprofit fundraising. He served as director of development at several nonprofits, including the Youth Law Center and the Westside Center for Independent Living. Bob taught workshops on topics including major donor solicitation, capital campaigns, and overcoming the fear of fundraising. He served on the board of directors of the Golden Gate chapter of the Association of Fundraising Professionals (AFP), and was the coauthor of Boards That Love Fundraising: A How-To Guide for Your Board *and* Board Members Rule: How to Be a Strategic Advocate for Your Nonprofit. *Using his wit and wisdom, Bob dedicated his life to teaching board members to be fearless in the pursuit of resources for their nonprofits. Please keep his philosophy in mind as you continue to do your important and essential work—it's the best way to honor his wonderful legacy.*

Board Fundraising Resource Review

Robert Zimmerman and Ann Lehman. Boards That Love Fundraising: A How-To Guide for Your Board. San Francisco: Jossey-Bass, 2004.

A comprehensive survey of how boards can bring value to all nonprofit fundraising activities. www.zimmerman-lehman.com or www.josseybass.com.

Boardsource (www.boardsource.org)

An excellent online resource on all matters affecting nonprofit boards of directors.

Chronicle of Philanthropy (www.philanthropy.com)

The premier online and print publication in the field of philanthropy.

National Council of Nonprofits (www.councilofnonprofits.org)

A network of state and regional nonprofit associations providing information and resources for small- to mid-sized nonprofits.

The NonProfit Times (www.nptimes.com)

An excellent national publication that will help board members stay up-to-date on developments in the world of philanthropy.

The Partnership for Philanthropic Planning (formerly the National Committee on Planned Giving) (www.pppnet.org)

Excellent resource for those board members interested in getting involved in planned giving.

Bernard Ross, <u>The Influential Fundraiser: Using the Psychology of Persuasion to Achieve Outstanding Results</u>. San Francisco: Jossey-Bass, 2009.

An invaluable resource to teach board members how to ask for contributions successfully. (www.josseybass.com)

Robert Zimmerman and Ann Lehman. <u>Board Members Rule: How to be a Strategic Advocate for Your Nonprofit</u>. San Francisco: Zimmerman Lehman, 2007.

A thorough survey of board responsibilities, with a particular emphasis on the board's advocacy role. (www.zimmerman-lehman.com, www.unlimitedpublishing.com, or download the smartphone application)

o o o

All these resources, plus nonprofit management tips of the week and more, can be found at Nonprofits101.org.

CHAPTER 32

Volunteer Recruitment

By Greg Baldwin, President, VolunteerMatch

Introduction

It may not be easy to change the world, but it has never been easier to *try*—particularly if you can find the right help.

Since 1998, VolunteerMatch has been helping organizations like yours do just that: find the right help. We've seen thousands of new organizations capture the imagination and energy of volunteers to advance their cause. We've seen established organizations engage new supporters and diversify their volunteer and donor bases. And we've seen organizations of all kinds learn how to engage volunteers more successfully.

Volunteering is changing. The willingness, interest, and ability of regular people to make a difference underscores a renaissance of sorts in public participation that has been going on for more than decade. New technologies, new attitudes about involvement, new and more flexible roles, and new ways to discover volunteer opportunities are all contributing to a revival of the ethic of service and volunteering.

533

The timing couldn't be better. In an era when the natural limits of what you can do in a single day are easily reached, finding great volunteers is a critical strategy for meeting your mission, delivering services, telling your story, expanding your financial health, and much more. The question, of course, is how to do it.

That's what this chapter is about. We'd like to help you understand who volunteers, why they do it, and what you can do to make it easy for them to help you.

Purpose Is Priceless

Rule number one of volunteer recruiting is to *avoid underestimating people's willingness to help*. This may be harder to do than it sounds.

According to Stanford business school professor Francis Flynn, we tend to "grossly underestimate how likely others are to agree to requests for assistance." He suggests that *our discomfort asking for help leads us to assume others are more likely to say no to a request than they actually are—by as much as 50%!*

This blind spot not only hampers many would-be social leaders, but it also reinforces the misconception that it's easier to attract volunteers if you don't ask too much of them.

At the same time, some people think volunteers work for free because they're do-gooders who don't care about money. Not true. *Volunteers don't care less about money; they are just less willing to let it get in the way of doing important work.* Volunteering is about meaning—it's about our willingness to forgo payment and profit when we believe we have an opportunity for purpose and progress. Volunteering is not about the importance of doing things for free— it's about the freedom to do something important.

Just ask Alexis de Tocqueville. In the early 1800s the French critic visited this young country and couldn't get over how different things were in Europe. He was particularly interested in our strange aptitude for cooperation, as he wrote: "[I] admired the extreme skill with which the inhabitants of the United States succeed in proposing a common object for the exertions of a great many men and in inducing them voluntarily to pursue it."

It turns out volunteering is one of our most defining and enduring values. And that's where you come in. *Your job as a volunteer recruiter will be to master the art of proposing a common object and inducing others to voluntarily pursue it.* Ready to get started?

Who Actually Volunteers?

Each year the Corporation for National and Community Service, the federal agency chartered with promoting volunteering and service, combs through U.S. Bureau of Labor Statistics and Census figures to report on volunteering habits. Over the last decade, *around one-fourth of Americans volunteered each year*—with a slight rise since 2007. Among the groups that are volunteering more are young people ages 16–24, Baby Boomers (46–64) and older adults (65 and older).

What Do Volunteers Want? The Six Key Motivations

When we've asked volunteers why they choose to give back, we tend to get the same answers again and again. Here are the top six:

1. To help others

   This is the top answer by a wide margin in all our surveys. Most volunteers really do want to be helpful. They want to make a contribution to something they care about and *make a difference* in the lives of others.

2. To be involved in their community

   For many volunteers being helpful also gives them an opportunity to be more connected to the community they live in. The experience of giving back strengthens their *sense of community.*

3. To contribute to a cause

   Sometimes volunteering is organized to advance a cause that has a personal meaning for the volunteer, such as raising money for cancer research or building a new neighborhood playground. In these cases the motivation may not be to directly help others, but to work on a project and *solve a problem.*

4. To develop new skills and have new experiences

   For some busy people, volunteering is a break from the everyday and an opportunity to take on new challenges. For these volunteers, service is a way to *learn new things.*

5. To use their skills in a productive way

   Some talented folks are eager to apply their particular skills for the public good. Lawyers, business consultants, and designers often yearn for the opportunity *to use their skills to help others.*

6. To stay fit

   New research shows that *volunteers tend to be healthier and live longer than nonvolunteers.* Many older adults, in particularly, volunteer in part to stay physically and mentally fit.

Regardless of motivation, most volunteers feel strongly about their volunteering. In our biggest survey, nearly 70% of respondents said that volunteering is either "very important" or "one of the most important things" in their life.

With the right context, and the right plan, any volunteer role can provide what volunteers really want—and keep them coming back for more. The key is to *identify and stay focused on giving supporters a genuine opportunity to be part of something larger than themselves.*

The Barriers to Involvement

You can't eliminate all the barriers that can keep people from helping you out, but you can avoid some of them. A 2009 study from Fidelity® Charitable Gift Fund and VolunteerMatch touched on this. When asked about their volunteer habits, survey respondents said that a *lack of time* (46%) kept many of them from volunteering. No surprise: we lead busy lives. But the study also found that one-third of respondents *want to see immediate results* when they volunteer and nearly one-half (44%) say if an organization only wants menial work, they'll go elsewhere.

What the data tell us is that people don't want to waste their time. *If your opportunities largely revolve around tasks your staff would rather not do, you're going to have a tough time finding interested volunteers.*

The good news is that by aligning the needs of your organization with the interests of volunteers, you can help eliminate barriers that can keep people who care about your cause from volunteering to serve it.

If all this talk of alignment, barriers, and efficiency sounds familiar, it's because it represents one of the most fundamental shifts in the volunteering world today: the recognition of volunteer engagement as a marketplace where some organizations are better than others.

A Market-Centric Approach

Picture a huge market with thousands of stalls. On one side of the hall stand 60 million individuals with time and talent to spare. On the other stand 1.5 million nonprofit organizations pursuing a variety of worthy causes.

It's supply and demand, just like any market. Except that all along the sides of the hall are doors leading *out*, to a world of video games, book, movies, comics, TV, and all manner of other things people can do with their time instead of volunteering.

For your organization to succeed in this marketplace, you need to not only captivate prospective volunteers with inspiring stories and meaningful opportunities, but also to engage and motivate people who are already volunteering with your organization.

Core Skills and Competencies

The tools your nonprofit needs to succeed in the volunteer recruitment marketplace are needs assessment, opportunity design, and outreach. Let's get to work.

Needs Assessment: Determining Your Capacity to Engage Volunteers

You may be thinking about recruiting volunteers, but what if you don't actually need them? Or worse, what if no one at the organization really has the time, skills, or inclination to lead them? *Needs assessment is the process of figuring out not only the potential for volunteers to help your organization, but also your organization's potential to effectively engage volunteers.*

In the following chapter you'll learn all about managing volunteers. Needs assessment is an area where volunteer recruitment and management really need to work together to build a successful volunteer program.

Needs Assessment Questions:

- How is your organization already using volunteers?

- What more could volunteers be doing for your organization?

- What are organizations like yours doing with volunteers?

- What volunteer projects or roles can be developed to reflect those needs?

- What skills or expertise will the volunteers need to have to succeed?

- Who in your organization will manage the new volunteers?

- What skills and expertise will staff need to manage the new volunteers?

- What other resources, policies, or processes will your organization need to effectively support the new volunteers? Do you need a committee?

There are many tools out there to help you conduct a needs assessment, and we've included some resources at the end of this chapter. What they tend to have in common is *a rigorous, process-oriented structure designed to help you collect important information about your organization and identify areas of potential upside or risk.* Whether the leaders of each function at your organization are paid or not, and whether they have any experience managing volunteers, they should all be asked to take part. And whatever the result, they should all be notified of the findings.

Don't shirk this process. A common outcome of needs assessment is the discovery that although volunteers are desperately needed, your organization isn't ready to effectively organize them yet. Since 2009, we've collected more than 3,000 volunteer reviews at VolunteerMatch.org. Most are very positive. Where they are negative, however, they are often <u>very</u> negative. Usually the points raised by those disappointed volunteers relate to organization and leadership.

Designing Great Opportunities

Your needs assessment should have helped you figure out what needs to be done, what kinds of folks will be best at doing it, and who within your staff will oversee them. Now comes the fun part: designing the opportunities. Your goal here is to *take needs developed in your assessment and translate them into discrete opportunities for individuals to get involved.*

There's no formula for doing this right, but there are some best practices. Keeping in mind the "Six Key Motivations" discussed earlier, you can figure out the best way to package your needs in ways that will attract talented and enthusiastic volunteers.

Among the variables you'll want to consider are:

- *Does the opportunity connect clearly to our mission?* If not, it is going to be hard for volunteers to see how their work really makes a difference.

- Is the opportunity a *role* or a *project*? Roles ("web designer") have the advantage of being easiest to understand because they parallel the world of paid work. Projects, on the other hand ("Design banner ads for this year's fundraising campaign"), are more appealing for skilled professionals, or others who want to put tangible items on a résumé or school application. Many volunteers don't want to lock themselves into a long-term role.

- Can the opportunity be done from anywhere, or only at your office? So-called *"virtual" volunteering is an emerging trend for organizations whose opportunities can be performed remotely* using a computer or phone. Most important, virtual opportunities let you recruit from a larger pool of prospects.

- Does the opportunity allow for flexibility? Will the volunteer feel constrained, or does it allow the volunteer exceed expectations?

- For skilled work, what will you do if your volunteer leaves mid-project? However rudimentary, *preparing project plans with time lines, phases, evaluation points, and deliverables helps ensure the organization can pick up where somebody else has left off.*

Just like a job description, *developing a volunteer position description is crucial.* Do this for each opportunity you create, and use it to advertise your opportunities and keep you focused on what you're looking for. Each description should include the following:

- Agency overview: a brief summary of your organization

- Position overview

- Title: an attractive title summarizing the opportunity

- Key responsibilities

- The support the volunteer will get from the organization

- Short-term impact and sustained outcomes of the assignment

- Training provided or needed

- Time commitment and preferred location

- Desired qualifications

- Desired skills

- Benefits to the volunteer

Make sure your website has a section where volunteers can learn about serving your organization, and be sure to post these new opportunities there so they are easy to find, read, and act on.

Time to start recruiting.

Outreach: Choosing Channels to Build Awareness

Where are the volunteers these days? How do they find out about volunteer opportunities or learn about important causes? Which sources of information do they trust the most?

A few years ago, we asked more than 1,000 organizations what they thought were the most useful ways to find volunteers. Not surprising, the most effective strategy for volunteer engagement was good old-fashioned word-of-mouth—let this be a reminder to you that *great recruitment often starts with great management of your existing volunteers.* (More on this later.)

But the study found another interesting thing. *After word-of-mouth, the most useful strategies for volunteer engagement were the organization's own website (45%) and online recruiting services* like VolunteerMatch (37%). These easily outscored traditional media such as newspaper ads (29%), direct mail (8%), and radio/TV (8%). In just a few short years, the Web has eclipsed the more traditional forms of volunteer recruiting to become an essential tool for sourcing support.

When we launched VolunteerMatch.org back in 1998, it was clear that volunteer recruitment hadn't yet caught up to the changes in technology. The revolution didn't take long. Since then, more than 70,000 U.S. nonprofits have used VolunteerMatch.org to recruit new volunteers. Thousands of others have used Idealist.org, especially for overseas opportunities. Still others are using VolunteerSolutions, craigslist.org, 1–800-volunteer.org and a host of other online services.

In combination with word-of-mouth and your own website, these third-party services are probably all you'll ever need to reach new volunteer prospects who've never heard of your organization. They're cheap or free, easy to use, and they get more traffic from prospective volunteers than your own site will probably ever have.

Of course, *the best volunteers are often already part of your organization's network.* You can reach these prospects through both traditional and Web 2.0 media (see Chapters Sixteen, Twenty-One, Twenty-Two, and Twenty-Six). Some other traditional channels include public relations to get your story into mainstream media, buying a booth at industry events or conferences, dropping fliers at job fairs, or partnering with service clubs like the Elks or Rotary. Service clubs continue to be a strong social glue for millions of people.

Definitely *publicize your opportunities in all your online social networks.* If you're not already using Facebook, Twitter, and YouTube, consider this your wake-up call to start building a community of followers on those services to draw attention to your volunteer opportunities. Some nonprofits also use niche sites like Change.org, Ning, and LinkedIn.

Getting Noticed: Putting Your Best Face Forward

You get one chance to make a first impression. Prospective volunteers are making assumptions about your organization and your program based on how you present yourself. They can be energized, motivated, and excited to help based on what they learn about your opportunities, or they may pass right over your organization without a second glance.

No matter where you publish your opportunities, it's important to tailor them for the channel. Facebook, for example, works best with short blurbs that link to your website. Twitter only allows 140 total characters per message. VolunteerMatch, Idealist, and other online volunteer services invite full descriptions, graphics, and other detailed information.

A few years ago, we evaluated VolunteerMatch listings from over 56,000 organizations to figure out which were the most successful. The findings don't apply to every channel, but they can help you get started:

- Titles are <u>really</u> important

  Make your titles compelling, fun, and informative, and above all else, *focus on the impact their service will make possible.* For example, "Unlock the World—Teach a Child to Read" has much more impact than "Volunteers Needed to Teach Reading." A few more terrific examples: "Use Your PR Skills to Share the Story of Our Housing Successes" and "Host A Foreign Student and Open a Heart."

- A picture is worth 1,000 words

  Words don't rival the power of a single well-chosen image of a volunteer making an impact. If you don't have one, make it a priority to find or capture one.

- Get to the point

  Successful listings are short and to the point, but still descriptive. Be succinct. Don't use more than three sentences per paragraph, or more than four paragraphs.

- Keep it simple

  Use terms that your volunteers can relate to, and try saying it out loud first before writing it. Using jargon or acronyms will create more questions than answers in the minds of potential volunteers.

- Describe your tasks accurately

  Just about every single successful listing had a clear description of the volunteer opportunity.

- Spelling counts

  Making silly spelling or grammatical errors is a huge liability, so get a second pair of eyes. The 100 worst performing listings on VolunteerMatch *all* had major spelling or grammatical errors.

- Let opportunities stand alone

  Listings stuffed with many opportunities confuse prospects and diffuse your message—*include only one opportunity per listing.*

As mentioned, it's also important to integrate important parts of the job description, especially details about the impact that volunteers can expect to make, the support they'll have, and what skills and experience they need to have.

Turning Interest into Action—Screening for Ideal Candidates

If you've covered the bases above, chances are good your organization will attract some people interested in volunteering. Now it is time to make sure you've got the right volunteers for your team.

Sorting a pool of interested prospects is one of the most important jobs in volunteer recruitment. The investment of time and resources goes up exponentially when you try to fit a square peg in a round hole. But done well, screening and interviewing creates a solid foundation for success together.

Many organizations use applications to ask for contact information, current and past employment, availability, reasons for volunteering, and so forth. Some even ask for references. *Formal applications are a great idea for roles that require deep involvement, specific skills, or close interaction with children and the elderly.*

You should conduct phone or in-person interviews with all prospective volunteers as part of your recruitment process if at all possible. Interviewing has lots of benefits—not only does it let you ask questions about the person's interest in volunteering with your organization, it also gives her a better sense of your expectations. Not all volunteers work out, and an interview gives you a chance to spot potential problems before they occur, plus they provide everyone a graceful opportunity to move in a different direction.

Remember: this is an opportunity to promote your organization. Be inspiring, but also represent your work candidly. If all goes well, this person will soon become an important part of your team.

Leveraging Word-of-Mouth

Earlier I mentioned our survey of how organizations find volunteers. Though the Web is a very popular tool, it was still outperformed by the oldest medium in the book: word-of-mouth. Four in five organizations say it's still the best way to find volunteers! *The Web can amplify positive word-of-mouth, but it can't replace it.*

Computers don't talk to people—people do. Your volunteers, board, staff, and other supporters are vital links to a slew of people who can also help advance your organization. What they say about you can boost your ability to raise money, create awareness about your issue, and of course, recruit more volunteers. The trick is to *make it easy for them to share* (see Chapter Twenty-Six).

Start by making sure your supporters know what your organization needs, and why. If you have an e-newsletters, use it to detail new openings, showcase great volunteers, or highlight impact. Regularly send your supporters emails as new openings come up, or remind them to the check your website or other online platforms for opportunities. Events are another great way to spread the good word about volunteer needs.

You can also arm supporters with boilerplate snippets (short blurbs about your organization and needs), photos, videos, and any number of digital assets to help volunteers communicate opportunities on their blogs, Facebook, or LinkedIn.

The process of actively listening to how others talk about you may inspire you to look closely at your volunteer program's "brand." *Branding a volunteer program with messaging or visuals helps to differentiate it from other nonprofits.* For example, if you recruit college students to read to at-risk youth, a T-shirt, hat, or button that simply says "I volunteer for kids" doesn't say as much as "I'm a Silver Lake Kids volunteer rock star!" Now you're communicating.

Listen to what volunteers may already be saying about your program by tracking reviews at VolunteerMatch.org or GreatNonprofits.org, and comments on their Facebook profiles and blogs. As you read in Chapter Twenty-Six, you can set up free monitoring with Google Alerts, which can send you an email when your organization's name (plus the word "volunteer") appears anywhere on the Web.

case study

Creating a Well-Oiled Volunteer Recruitment Machine: A Case Study

The Huntington Beach Public Library discovered that *the secret to successful volunteer recruitment is hard work and smart planning*. With a shared commitment to best practices, the five-branch library system has been able to turn its volunteer program into an engine for meeting its mission—all in less than 18 months.

The new focus is most visible in its Volunteer Program Development Team. Composed of the volunteer services coordinator, three librarians, and two literacy coordinators, the committee was formed in early 2009 to explore how volunteers can help and what resources are needed to support them.

The first change they made was in identifying volunteer opportunities. Volunteer roles used to be developed in department silos, but today they're often conceived in collaboration between the committee and department heads. For example, when they heard about an amazing volunteer working in circulation, the tech services division became curious how she might fit with them. Today she is that department's first-ever volunteer—and she has been joined by a second as well. The library has also created an innovative computer coach program, which uses power computer users from the community as IT trainers for the public—a need that was identified by the reference division in coordination with the committee.

The committee also helped the volunteer services coordinator formalize standards for opportunity descriptions and listings. Today all needs are documented and preserved (lessening the impact if a volunteer leaves). When it's time to promote, the coordinator keeps the listings consistent and in the same format. These standards help to reinforce the messaging for both the program and the library as a whole.

To get the word out, the library relies heavily on its own website and VolunteerMatch.org. To save time, the library installed a "widget" that enables its VolunteerMatch listings to automatically show up on its site—which means less data entry for the coordinator.

The library also employs best practices for listing opportunities, including using a title that speaks to the benefits and impact of volunteering. Instead of "Computer coach needed," for example, the headline is "Share your computer skills with novice computer users." The listings are specific and easy to read, and they clearly spell out any technical or personal requirements. The coordinator has also sourced a great photo of volunteering in action.

The committee also fixed a fragmented application process. There used to be a general application for all available roles, plus applications for each department. Today, all prospects fill out a single application, which goes directly to the coordinator, who then contacts the prospects to learn about their objectives.

Their new hands-on approach accomplishes several crucial goals. Volunteers learn about the library and where they might fit in. The coordinator uses her experience to suggest a specific path for each volunteer—one where they have the best chance of succeeding and making an impact, thereby increasing the likelihood that they stay engaged and keep volunteering. And, if a role is currently filled, the coordinator can come up with a plan to keep the prospect involved, so the library doesn't lose them in the meantime.

The outcome? Within a year of implementing the new program, the library generated more than 300 new volunteer referrals from its efforts, including 33 computer coaches—compare that to only 50 volunteers the year prior. There's still plenty of work ahead, but the library is on its way.

Dos and Don'ts

Volunteer Recruitment Dos and Don'ts

- DO try to understand the specific motivations of each volunteer so you can help them find the right fit.

- DON'T recruit volunteers unless you can support them with resources, time and training.

- DO involve the entire organization in your needs assessment process.

- DO create a volunteer job description for every need, and focus on the impact the opportunity will make toward your mission. Make it clear how the volunteer stands to benefit from the opportunity personally, socially, or professionally.

- DO use photos, logos, and multimedia to help communicate the value and benefits of volunteering.

- DON'T include more than one opportunity in a single listing.

- DON'T depend solely on your website to spread the word; use popular online social networking services to publicize your opportunities.

- DO interview all volunteers directly to explain the opportunity and learn more about their interest.

- DO ask all volunteers to complete an application.

Conclusion

A community of individuals is ready and willing to support your organization, but it won't happen by accident—you need to eliminate the barriers that keep people from getting involved. Utilizing tried-and-true methods of needs assessment, opportunity design, outreach, and screening, you can identify meaningful roles and projects, reach out to those who care about your cause, and effectively harness their goodwill and energy to fulfill your mission. And best of all, over time your relationship with your volunteers can deepen and grow in wonderful new ways—and real partnerships can occur.

Greg Baldwin joined VolunteerMatch in 1998 as its Chief Imagination Officer to launch the first website for the popular volunteering network. Today the award-winning VolunteerMatch service is helping tens of thousands of nonprofit organizations unlock the volunteer support of their community. Greg is a lifelong volunteer and regularly speaks at nonprofit events and conferences on the subjects of volunteering, communication, and the Internet. Greg earned his degree in public policy from Brown University.

Volunteer Recruitment Resource Review

Idealist.org (www.idealist.org)

A website from Action Without Borders, Idealist offers a popular posting service for volunteer opportunities (particularly international).

VolunteerMatch (www.volunteermatch.org)

The most popular volunteer network on the Web, VolunteerMatch.org provides tools, trainings, and services to help U.S.-based organizations more effectively recruit from a large audience of individual and employee volunteers.

AL!VE (Association of Leaders in Volunteer Engagement; www.volunteeralive.org)

A national membership organization of leaders and professionals in volunteer engagement, offering tools, resources, professional development, and advocacy programs for volunteer managers.

Council for Certification in Volunteer Administration (www.cvacert.org)

CCVA administers Certified in Volunteer Administration (CVA) certifications, the only international professional certification in the field of volunteer resources management.

Corporation for National and Community Service (www.nationalservice.gov/for_organizations/overview/index.asp)

Federal agency that supports and strengthens the volunteer sector by providing grants, training, and technical assistance to volunteer organizations.

Energize Inc. (www.energizeinc.com)

An international training, consulting, and publishing firm specializing in volunteerism.

JFFixler Group (www.jffixler.com)

Expert consultants who help nonprofit organizations attain excellence in volunteer engagement, strategic planning, and board and organizational assessment and development, with special emphasis on Baby Boomer volunteer engagement.

Points of Light Institute (www.pointsoflight.org)

Innovates, incubates, and activates new ideas for civic engagement and volunteering.

Volunteering in America (www.volunteeringinamerica.gov)

Interactive site from the Corporation for National and Community Service with research and reports on U.S. volunteering trends in local communities.

∘ ∘ ∘

All these resources, plus nonprofit management tips of the week and more, can be found at Nonprofits101.org.

CHAPTER 33

Volunteer Engagement and Management

By Michelle Nunn, CEO, Points of Light Institute, and Cofounder, HandsOn Network

Introduction

Without volunteers, most nonprofits would cease to exist, or would at least suffer a drastic reduction in their capacity to serve communities and achieve their missions. What we don't often think about, though, is that successful volunteer programs are critical to improving civic life, with ramifications well beyond the specific impacts of the service itself. As overviewed in the previous chapter, if volunteers believe their service makes a difference and they are satisfied with the organization they are serving with, they're more likely to keep volunteering—they're also more inclined to donate money and deepen their commitment to the organization and other social causes.[1] This chapter highlights the key pieces of volunteer engagement and management that increase volunteer satisfaction and, thus, increase their commitment to service and civic life.

Think of effective volunteer engagement as building a house. First, you need to create a blueprint of where you want to go, and a plan for getting there. This involves organization-wide support and planning, developing meaningful service opportunities, and agreeing on clear volunteer expectations. Next, you must have the right tools to ensure the house can be built to specifications. Critical tools include effective orientation and training, logistics planning, ongoing communication, and development of volunteer leadership roles. Finally, you need to add the finishing touches that make the house a home— something special. Unique touches, such as providing growth and development opportunities, recognizing volunteers, and clarifying impact will drive loyalty and increase the passion your volunteers have for your cause and organization. Ultimately, your effectiveness at managing the volunteer process by implementing the strategies below (and summarized in the following "Volunteer Management Planning Checklist") will serve both your organization *and* the community.

Critical Skills and Competencies—Building a House of Service

We'll cover all aspects of building our house of service in the context of this chapter, but first let's start out with a snapshot of the ten steps that you should have in mind as you prepare to launch your volunteer engagement efforts.

Volunteer Management Planning Checklist

1	Identify champions	Who is passionate about the potential of volunteers to address priorities? Who has the appropriate position and the skills for leading the effort?
2	Assess landscape	How are departments already using volunteers, formally or informally? Long-term or episodically? What gaps and opportunities exist?
3	Frame priorities	What are the two or three strategic priorities where volunteers can help scale work or deepen impact?

4	Map priority roles within departments	How do the volunteer roles support priorities at the department or program level?
5	Build clear definition of "volunteer"	Who is considered a volunteer (service-learning students, board and task force members, career explorers, etc.)? Work with human resources to make this distinction clear.
6	Clarify purpose	What are clear job descriptions and reporting requirements for all parties involved?
7	Clarify deliverables and measures of success	What does success look like for the volunteer, staff, and organization? How will this be measured?
8	Build support	How will you engage staff, volunteers, and others in the new work of volunteer management?
9	Build adequate training for volunteer managers	How will you ensure that staff has the skills and resources needed to manage volunteers effectively?
10	Create space for citizen input	How can you ensure that community members have a voice in determining which needs volunteers will be addressing?

The Architecture of Volunteer Management: Begin with the End in Mind

Consider the case of Hands On Atlanta, where I was lucky enough to work with Richard Goldsmith, a volunteer who started the Discovery Program. Many years ago, we were looking for a way to support the educational goals of the public school system. Through discussions with principals and administrators about unmet needs (tutoring to improve test scores and opportunities for increased after-school and weekend programs) and a clear understanding of when we were most likely to recruit ongoing volunteers (weekends), Richard developed a Saturday school program where volunteers run a day of educational and social activities for children each week. It was a win-win for all sides—the schools were able to increase educational hours by training and then leveraging volunteers to support the curriculum, Hands On Atlanta was able to meet its goals of engaging more people in meaningful service, the volunteers had a well-organized project with clear goals to step into, and the students had fun and educational activities during a time when they were previously not productively engaged.

To begin crafting an effective volunteer management program, you must approach it from the perspective of the organization, the population served, and the volunteer. By starting with the interests of these constituents and focusing on the overlap of needs, you can create the perfect volunteer position—one that serves you and your constituents, as well as the volunteer.

Organizationally, *the most successful volunteer programs are prioritized as critical to meeting the mission of the organization,* truly breeding a culture of volunteerism. If your organization is not at this level yet, start small and develop relevant volunteer projects that help you achieve your goals without dramatically increasing expenditures. If you build your program slowly, you can develop your organization's infrastructure for maximum effectiveness. As a leader, *your ultimate work is creating the strategy for volunteer efforts and finding staff or other resources to run the program over time.*

Successful Volunteer Programs:

- Are supported and understood organization-wide
- Are planned beyond the near-term
- Have specific, measurable goals that are tracked over time
- Ensure volunteer management is a staff member's job and linked to performance
- Create pathways for deepening volunteer engagement over time

Whether you lean on human resources or professional volunteer managers, ensure that whoever oversees your volunteer efforts understands that they are *not* staff, and why they may need to be managed differently. For small or emerging volunteer management programs, *tapping into your human resources channels provides an existing infrastructure, ensures all policies and procedures are thought through, and provides accountability for the volunteer program until it is strong enough to stand on its own.*

Managing the Scope of Service

If your organization decides to recruit and leverage volunteers as a means to achieving its goals, *you must begin by clarifying the scope of volunteer service* (see Chapter Thirty-Two for more on this). Explore all of the things that your organization wants to do but doesn't have resources to accomplish, and creatively identify ways volunteers can meet mission needs. Can you use a volunteer to conduct a financial audit, or to produce a graphic redesign of your website or logo? Have you always wanted a long-term fundraising plan, but never had the capacity to conduct one? I'm amazed at how *volunteers can transform an organization programmatically and administratively.*

Volunteers can be used to help accomplish almost any mission-related goal you have. Of course, you must be mindful of confidentiality (for example, not allowing access to personnel or client records) and not pushing paid employees out of their jobs. Get to know your volunteers personally and have confidence in their capacity to achieve something you would like to see accomplished, and then invite them to commit to helping you reach your goals. Just be sure that you (1) follow the steps outlined in this and the prior chapter, (2) make sure the role is something your friends and family would be excited about, and (3) know that (just as with employees) there may be missteps along the way.

Although volunteer position descriptions were covered in the last chapter, it is important to go over three key points as they relate to volunteer *management.* The first is that *to engage volunteers to their fullest potential, be sure to give your clients and constituents a voice.* By understanding the challenges they face that might be served by volunteers, you will be able to build meaningful volunteer opportunities that strengthen your program. For example, in one urban community, a partnership formed to make streets safe for children to walk home from school. But when the partnership conducted focus groups, parents said that their priority was finding a safe place to send their children while they were at work. The partnership ultimately shifted its priorities to work with parents on developing after-school childcare. Or you may want a volunteer to help update your Facebook page regularly, yet after discussions with constituents, you find that they'd rather read an insightful blog related to the mission of your organization (see Chapter Twenty-Six).

Secondly, *assess your volunteers.* This means asking questions about what they want out of their experience and what their interests and skills are, and how these intersect with what they want to spend their volunteer time on. This will help you uncover ways that volunteers can help that you had not even considered possible. For example, the Center for Civil and Human Rights in Atlanta found an experienced volunteer manager to run their volunteer program—as a volunteer. She loves the mission, and they enjoy the expertise of someone with two decades of experience running volunteer programs.

Finally, as you develop your project plan and volunteer position descriptions, *keep your targeted impacts in mind and put a plan in place to monitor and evaluate them.* This maximizes the ongoing performance of your volunteers. There are many available resources on impact measures and evaluation, such as the National Service Resource Center and HandsOn Network, which are listed in the Resource Review at the end of the chapter. The key is to *start thinking about measurement from the very beginning, so that you're able to capture the results in a meaningful way.* When volunteers and the organization understand their roles, it allows volunteers to take ownership of their contributions and the organziation to assess the effectiveness of its volunteer program.

Once your blueprint is complete, communicate your plan to volunteers multiple times. Although they are not paid, volunteers are people you need to invest in to accomplish your goals. If you take the role of coach and leader seriously from the beginning, your volunteers will continue to surprise and delight you with what they contribute and accomplish.

Tools of the Trade: Volunteer Management Necessities

Think about Hands On Atlanta's Discovery Program again. The way the effort was designed truly tapped into the power of volunteer leadership. Each school where the project operated had specific volunteer roles: (1) a school captain who oversaw all recruitment, logistics, and relationship management with Hands On Atlanta and the principal. This volunteer leader committed to at least a year of managing the site, showing up every Saturday and doing the necessary work in between to make each weekend a success; (2) grade captains who oversaw the specific efforts of their assigned grade. These volunteer leaders also committed to at least a year, perhaps sharing the role with another volunteer, and provided consistency to the program. They managed the volunteers, ensured that the curriculum was implemented correctly, and handled any challenges that arose; (3) Saturday volunteers who signed up for the specific amount of time they could commit. Whether attending every Saturday, once a month, or less frequently, these volunteers were the stable of power that implemented the program. Although it would be ineffective to have this type of weekly transition in a typical volunteer set-up, with the consistent structure of steady volunteer leadership, each volunteer had a trainer and a manager to ensure that they were meeting goals, and everyone knew their role in the bigger picture.

Once your plan is set, implementation of your program is the meat of your engagement with your volunteers—the building of your house—though it will only be as successful as your plans and organizational support allows. Although you think about the work of your organization on a daily basis, don't forget that volunteers have other competing interests. Regular communication is important, yet out of respect *ask your volunteers how frequently and in what way they'd like to hear from you.* By keeping volunteers abreast of news and staying in touch with them frequently, they'll begin to create an attachment to your efforts even before they arrive.

Orientation and Training

In planning any orientation or training, you must consider the question, *"What do volunteers need to know to feel comfortable and competent in carrying out their tasks?"* The answer to this question should lead you to the design of your training program. Most volunteers attend projects with little to no understanding of the work that is to be done, nor how it's going to be accomplished. *For your volunteers to be effective, they need to understand the goal of the project and its impact on the community.* Volunteer orientation can be conducted prior to a project, or on the first day of service.

Orientation should include a brief history of the issue, current statistics, current events related to the effort, and other related civic engagement opportunities (e.g., advocacy training, future projects). Give a brief outline of the project and what the volunteers will be doing, so that everyone knows what to expect. *By framing the service within a larger context of the agency and overall social issue, you are taking the critical step of connecting the volunteer to the agency, clients, and community.* This makes their work more meaningful, and in turn makes them more likely to engage in future service.

As supporters continue their service with you, possibly committing to a long-term engagement, *work with your volunteers to determine opportunities based on their personal skills and goals.* This kind of dialogue deepens their commitment and enthusiasm, while also providing interesting and unique avenues for engagement that might not otherwise be explored. A friend once volunteered for a help line, committed to the cause, and was ready to assist. Unfortunately, after a week she realized the phone rarely rang. Though the help line volunteer manager knew she had a strong background in nonprofit management and fundraising—and that the organization was struggling to raise funds—she never attempted to engage my friend in other ways, even when my friend offered. After three weeks, 30 service hours, and two calls, my friend left the agency and they lost a valuable (and underutilized) asset.

Logistics Oversight

You prepared your project plan, your organization, and your volunteers. Now your role is to make sure the project flows smoothly and to make <u>certain</u> that their experience is a success for them, the organization, and the community. The three best ways to ensure this are:

- Welcoming volunteers

  Welcome volunteers and make sure they know where to check in as they begin their work. This allows for better management and tracking. Use name tags and get to know your volunteers. Introduce them to staff and other volunteers, and give them a tour of your office to encourage interaction.

- Contingency planning

  Especially with group projects, always think through worst-case scenarios and map out strategies to handle problems. When you plan ahead you can handle problems with minimal disruption and cost.

- Managing time

  Continually monitor progress while volunteers are with you and adjust their work according to the progress being made. *Make sure there is always something for volunteers to do.* Underutilization is one of the biggest threats to retention; if people don't feel needed, they won't come back.

Nurturing Volunteers

Whether you are an extrovert or an introvert, connect with and get to know your volunteers during their time with your organization, especially when they first get started with you. *Make sure volunteers are confident in their roles, have the resources they need, and are comfortable seeking you out for further information and inspiration.* As volunteers transform from "episodic" (someone who volunteers for a specific, limited period of time; for example to paint a recreation center for two hours) into long-term volunteers, look for other ways to nurture them and renew their commitment to the cause, as discussed later in this chapter.

If your project is a group undertaking, understanding volunteers' personalities and interests will help you position them so they have the best chance of success, not to mention compatibility with you and other volunteers. As shown in Table 33.1, the McClelland and Atkinson Motivational Theory [2] identifies three separate motivational needs, affiliation, achievement, and influence, which will help you gain more insight into your volunteers.

Table 33.1: McClelland and Atkinson Motivational Theory

Affiliation	Achievement	Influence
Affiliation-motivated people enjoy:	Achievement-motivated people enjoy:	Influence-motivated people enjoy:
Group projects	Gathering statistics	Challenges
Writing personal notes	Keeping records	Influencing others
Celebrations	Filing	New ideas
Parties	Being alone	Creating
Collaboration	Technology	Teaching
Meeting people	Skill-building tasks	Positions of authority
Position sharing	Checkpoints	Fundraising
Family gatherings	Goals and objectives	Publicity
Social opportunities		The spotlight

Some volunteers want to lead, some want to socialize, some pay attention to details, and others are compassionate and dependable. You may also encounter volunteers who are headstrong, who aren't actively involved, or who complain excessively. Treat every individual with dignity and respect: Talk openly and professionally with your volunteer to get a clear sense of what motivates them and their personality type, and eliminate any problems by being honest about the organization's needs.

○ ○ ○

Volunteer Leadership

As a volunteer program evolves, it is useful to develop specific roles for those interested in taking on more responsibility. In particular, a trained volunteer leader can assist with the planning and implementation of your volunteer program, leaving you to tend to the overall health of your organization. This position also provides an avenue for dedicated volunteers to engage more deeply in the organization and its work. Ultimately, volunteer leadership is the cornerstone to a successful program, as it truly leverages the power of volunteers to support your work and to effect change.

The community is full of potential leaders, and by tapping into their skills, ideas, and passion, an organization can greatly expand the work it does. Volunteer leadership also creates a community of committed leaders who care about and understand your work. Select people with excellent organizational skills, attention to detail, enthusiasm and a penchant for motivating others. Promoting volunteers into leadership roles is a great way to recognize volunteers for their service, increase retention, and leverage one volunteer to engage many.

The Finishing Touches: Reflection, Results, and Recognition

Consider the Discovery Program again. As it evolved, staff and volunteer leaders constantly reviewed feedback from volunteers, students, and school administrators. This helped them improve the program and the experience for all parties. In addition, as results were reviewed, the curriculum improved and schools saw the current and potential impact of the program. The partnership between the schools and Hands On Atlanta was strengthened into a long-term relationship that achieved the goals of each group. Many volunteers who started by contributing a few Saturdays a month became grade captains and then school captains, deepening their commitment to improving education in their city and allowing the program to expand to new schools. Students even grew up in the Discovery Program and decided, as they became of age, to join in as volunteers. Now there are countless stories of volunteer leaders transformed by service—changing careers to join the nonprofit or public sectors and becoming teachers, administrators, and principals to improve the educational system. The ripple effect of one effective program lives on in the impact it had on the lives of countless volunteers and students.

At the point of departure, don't just shake your volunteers' hands and let them leave. *There are three finishing touches that transform a volunteer and her experience into something inspiring and motivating: reflection, results, and recognition.* Let's look at how these three keys encourage volunteers to take additional action as a result of their service.

Reflection

Provide structured time for volunteers to examine what they learned, how it affects them, and where they go from here. This is the primary avenue for connecting service with greater civic involvement. Through the process of reflection, volunteers will have the opportunity to create a larger social construct around the service they are providing, and this can also lead to the identification of additional roles and opportunities. Encourage this introspection in three stages:

- At the beginning of the project

  Begin a conversation. Include information on your mission and the community served. Explain how the work being completed will directly impact that community. *Begin a dialogue to identify the opportunities for engagement that most interest your volunteer.*

- During the project

  Use signage, one-on-one conversations, and interviews to educate volunteers about the impact of the project on the community served. *Ask volunteers for quotes and personal stories about their impact, and audio or videotape these if possible*—capturing these can be useful later to help volunteers remember their contribution, plus these stories can support fundraising and marketing efforts.

- At the end of the project

  Ask volunteers to share their stories about what was accomplished during the project and how it made them feel. If possible, include people from the community served in this discussion, so volunteers can hear other perspectives on their impact. At the conclusion of the discussion, ask your volunteers if they'd like to make a commitment to serve your efforts or those of another organization, and how they envision inspiring others to serve.

Results

Evaluate how effective the project planning and volunteer experience was—the coordination, delivery, implementation, logistics, and management. As discussed, your project plan should effortlessly lead you to gathering the necessary results. Gathering and reviewing this information provides an opportunity to reflect on the overall success of the project. If you never learn what volunteers think, you will never be able to adequately address future needs. To get feedback, *ask those involved to complete a form at the end of the project;* you already have them there, the experience is fresh in their minds, and you can get it from them quickly. If immediate feedback is not an option, mail or email participants a survey within a week of the project. Both evaluation and feedback should be used to continuously improve your program and evaluate your effectiveness.

Recognition

Even the smallest expressions of gratitude or mementoes of appreciation can do wonders to inspire and incent volunteers. In addition to knowing that their service made an impact, *volunteers want to be recognized by the community, by fellow volunteers, and by program staff.* If their contribution doesn't feel valuable or necessary, they won't return, but if they feel appreciated and connected to significant impact, they'll often increase their involvement (e.g., as a volunteer, positive spokesperson, prospective donor, and so on).

Recognition can take many forms, from a simple thank-you card to an award given out at a large annual event. An ideal recognition system makes use of many different procedures. Over the years, we developed a set of rules:

Recognize . . .

. . . **or else.** If volunteers do not get recognition for productive participation, they may stop volunteering with you.

. . . **frequently.** Recognition's effects start to wear off after a few days, and after several weeks of not hearing anything, volunteers start to wonder if they are still appreciated.

. . . **with variety.** One of the implications of the previous rule is that you need a variety of methods of showing appreciation.

. . . **honestly.** Don't give praise unless you mean it.

. . . **the person, not just the work.** If a volunteer organizes a fundraising event and you praise the event without mentioning who organized it, the volunteer will likely feel some resentment. Make sure you connect the volunteer's name to the accomplishment, i.e., "John did a great job of organizing this event," rather than, "This event was well organized."

. . . **in a way appropriate to the achievement.** Small accomplishments should be praised with low-effort methods, large accomplishments more.

. . . **on a timely basis.** Praise for work should come as soon as possible after the achievement. Don't save up your recognition for the annual banquet.

. . . **in an individualized fashion.** Different people like different things. One person might respond favorably to football tickets, while another might find them useless. Some like public recognition; others find it embarrassing.

. . . **for what you want more of.** Too often your staff pays most attention to volunteers who are having difficulty—this may result in ignoring good performers.

A House into a Village: The Volunteer Leadership Ladder

An intense study of HandsOn Network's New York affiliate titled "The Leadership Ladder: Fostering Volunteer Engagement and Leadership at New York Cares" (www.newyorkcares.org/news_events/leadership_ladder.php) offers new perspectives and strategies to improve volunteer engagement. Similar to the study mentioned in the Chapter Thirty-Two, the report details strategies for maximizing volunteer impact by better understanding volunteers' motivations for volunteering and other forms of civic engagement. Most important, it found that *if volunteers believe their service makes a difference and they are satisfied with the organization they are serving with, they're more likely to keep volunteering and deepen their level of commitment to the organization and other social causes.*

Taking it a step further, the resultant New York Cares Volunteer Engagement Scale (VES) categorizes volunteers by commitment level and assesses their evolution from episodic to more engaged participation. The continuum starts with those who are just checking out the cause and proceeds upwards in engagement as follows:

- Shoppers

- Episodic contributors

- Short-term contributors

- Reliable regulars

- Fully engaged volunteers

- Committed leaders

The study does a great job explaining each rung on the ladder, helping you categorize your volunteers, and conveying clear strategies and tactics for increasing volunteer engagement over time. The VES tool also can be used to help assess how successful you have been in encouraging deeper commitment among volunteers through improved communication, better orientation, leadership training, and outreach.

It's imperative to think about how your organization can use volunteers at all levels of the scale, knowing that they can each contribute differently to your volunteer engagement goals. The report also provides evidence that *moving volunteers up the leadership ladder may increase the likelihood that they will be more philanthropic*, in general, and more likely to serve as community leaders.

Volunteer Management and Engagement Dos and Don'ts

- DO remember volunteer management has some related costs (e.g., staff time, training, recognition programs), and include these in your budget.

- DON'T forget to continually "promote" your strongest volunteers. They have the passion, desire, and time to help—use it!

- DO ask the question "How can volunteers help us achieve this goal?" during every strategy discussion your organization holds.

- DON'T review feedback at the project site or in the moment—give yourself some space so you can truly reflect and utilize the messages.

- DO engage volunteer leaders to recruit, train, and manage other volunteers, and to expand your programs and impact.

- DON'T forget to track volunteer accomplishments, from numbers of volunteers and hours served to impacts on the organization and community.

- DO develop reflection activities that provide context for your volunteers' efforts and challenge your volunteers to consider the underlying causes of the issue they are addressing.

Dos and Don'ts

Conclusion

As our volunteer engagement efforts have grown from a few small pilot cities to an international movement, HandsOn Network, the largest volunteer network in the country, continues to dissect what makes a volunteer experience meaningful, and what makes volunteers deepen their contributions to the common good. Clearly people are ready to serve; in the first half of last year we reported a 58% increase in people signing up for new volunteer opportunities. The real question is how to get volunteers engaged with your cause and organization. Remember, *volunteer activities that meet real needs and incorporate reflection get people more deeply involved in solving challenging social issues.* By effectively managing and engaging your volunteers in ever-deepening levels of commitment, you are planting the seeds for their continued involvement. Look at your volunteer program as a way to teach people how they can contribute to public life and participate in solving public problems, and watch as your efforts help build a strong volunteer sector—the key to a healthy democracy.

Michelle began her career as the founding director of Hands On Atlanta. She later became President and CEO of HandsOn Network, and in 2007 took the helm of the combined Points of Light and Hands On Network after their merger. Now the largest volunteer organization in the nation, HandsOn Action Centers engage millions of volunteers every year. Nunn graduated Phi Beta Kappa from the University of Virginia, and has studied at Oxford University and in India. She was a Kellogg National Fellow and has a master's degree in public administration from the Kennedy School of Government at Harvard University.

Volunteer Management Resource
Volunteer Engagement Resource Review

HandsOn Network (www.handsonnetwork.org)

   HandsOn provides resources, tips, and strategies on a variety of volunteer recruitment, engagement, and management issues.

The Leadership Ladder: Fostering Volunteer Engagement and Leadership at New York Cares (www.newyorkcares.org/news_events/leadership_ladder.php), New York Cares, Inc. New York: Baruch College Survey Research Unit, 2009.

This useful study offers new perspectives and strategies to improve volunteer engagement.

Energize, Inc. (www.energizeinc.com)

Energize, Inc. trains, consults, and publishes research and opinion pieces on volunteerism.

e-Volunteerism (www.e-volunteerism.com)

e-Volunteerism offers volunteer managers useful files, printable training materials, electronic "roundtable" discussions, and commentaries.

National Service Resource Center (www.nationalserviceresources.org)

Administered by ETR Associates, National Service Resource Center provides training and technical assistance to organizations that use volunteers.

OurSharedResources.org (www.oursharedresources.org)

This website is a user-generated resource compilation for volunteer managers that provides downloadable forms, manuals, and position descriptions.

Service Leader (www.serviceleader.org)

Service Leader provides a framework to organize your thinking and structure your work with volunteers through their Volunteer Management Program Cycle©.

ServeNet (www.servenet.org)

ServeNet aggregates relevant content for volunteer managers, provides tools to explore issues, and organizes online networking and learning communities.

Idealist Volunteer Management Resource Center (www.idealist.org/en/vmr)

Idealist collates resources and tools, and provides networking opportunities for volunteer managers.

○ ○ ○

All these resources, plus nonprofit management tips of the week and more, can be found at Nonprofits101.org.

CLOSING THOUGHTS

I am of the opinion that my life belongs to the whole community,
and as long as I live it is my privilege to do for it what I can.
I want to be thoroughly used up when I die,
for the harder I work, the more I live.
I rejoice in life for its own sake.
Life is no "brief candle" to me.
It is a sort of splendid torch which I have gotten hold of for a moment,
and I want to make it burn as brightly as possible
before passing it on to future generations.

—George Bernard Shaw

Alas, our time together has drawn to a close. My hope is that in the process of reading through this book and the chapters herein, you gained access to a toolkit of useful strategies, techniques, and resources—may these aid you in your valiant effort to make the world a better place in whatever way you feel called to serve.

As you move forward, may you strike gold. May you remember the importance of collaboration, of going big, painting the picture, and striking the root. May you dream your dreams with open eyes and plan more and react less, filling in the A to the Z while you spend more time reaching out and less time staring inward. And most of all, may you always remember the wisdom of Bill Cosby's grandmother—never forget that you are a pourer, *not* a drinker. Thank you for the nourishment you provide.

We who work in the social sector have seized the opportunity to serve. We are a counterbalance in society, modeling a different value system, where *success is defined as impact*, instead of as profit. Our role in the community is to tackle the problems that would otherwise go unaddressed, to bring about the world we all know is possible.

Remember to always put the cause first, and in so doing to proactively seek out opportunities to support the work of other valuable organizations. For *we truly are all in this together.* Take inventory of the gifts you've been given, and of the resources available to you, as both will prove integral to your ability to maximize impact. And get outside yourself—flip silos, as Kay Sprinkel Grace says, on their side, and turn them into pipelines. When you come across other groups working on similar issues, ask what I've found to be the most powerful question available to nonprofit sector professionals: "How can I help?" Share, support, and encourage—it will come back to you tenfold, as it has to me.

At the same time, remember to take care of yourself. Heed your inner voice and seek a work-life balance, since *you are too talented to be unhappy*, and the sector, the Movement, needs you at full capacity. As you seek to engage volunteers, board members, donors, and others in your efforts, don't forget that we need *you* optimally engaged, too.

In their landmark environmental white paper calling for more cross-sector collaboration, "The Death of Environmentalism," Michael Shellenberger and Ted Nordhaus noted, *"The world's most effective leaders are not issue-identified but rather vision- and value-identified. These leaders distinguish themselves by inspiring hope against fear, love against injustice, and power against powerlessness."*

I trust that in the time you spent with me, and the 50 contributors who helped make this book possible, you have gained a strong sense of some tangible ways that you can step into your leadership potential, and that you now have the tools you need to go about your day-to-day work. As I mentioned earlier, there are plenty of people peddling maps out there, but our focus here is on providing picks and shovels, and hopefully even a few nuggets. Now it is up to you to decide how to best utilize these resources and insights.

So before I hand it over to Lynne Twist for some final words, let me once again say thank you. Thank you for heeding the call to do this work, as opposed to performing just another job. Thank you—not only on behalf of myself, or of the many contributors and partners that brought this handbook to life—but thank you on behalf of the thousands, hundreds of thousands, or even the millions of people, animals, and causes out there that the readers of this book collectively serve. It is truly our honor to serve you as you serve the greater good.

In closing, I'd like to share part of an inspiring poem by activist, author, and founder of The Peace Alliance, Marianne Williamson:

> Our deepest fear is not that we are inadequate. Our deepest fear is that we are powerful beyond measure. It is our light, not our darkness, that most frightens us. We ask ourselves, Who am I to be brilliant, gorgeous, talented, fabulous? Actually, who are you *not* to be? . . . Your playing small doesn't serve the world. There's nothing enlightened about shrinking so that other people won't feel insecure around you. We are all meant to shine, as children do. We were born to make manifest the glory . . . that is within us. It's not just in some of us; it's in everyone. And as we let our own light shine, we unconsciously give other people permission to do the same. As we're liberated from our own fear, our presence automatically liberates others.[1]

AFTERWORD: WE ALL HAVE THE CAPACITY TO BE SOCIAL PROPHETS

By Lynne Twist, Founder and President, Soul of Money Institute, and Cofounder, The Pachamama Alliance*

We are all familiar with using the terms "nonprofit" and "not-for-profit" to describe our sector, but I believe these terms are misleading. Why are we defining ourselves by what we are *not* rather than what we are? Why are we using terms that place us on the sidelines rather in the mainstream? Most major transformations in human history have come from what we are calling the "non" or "not" sector. This is where Gandhi worked, where Martin Luther King Jr. worked, where Mother Teresa worked. It's where Nelson Mandela ran the ANC, and where suffragettes fought for half of humanity—women—to have a voice.

This sector, where real and truly transformational projects take place, is at the center of the action and is full of people working from commitment and vision. I believe that this sector, our sector, is better defined as the "social profit" sector. We are creating a *social profit* not just for ourselves, but for all life.

More important than the sector itself is the people who make it real—the visionary, committed people working in this transformational sector. I believe that these people are *social prophets*, spelled p-r-o-p-h-e-t. *Social prophets are people who stand for a new future and live and work in a way that brings that future forward.* Social prophets are people who are called to this work, who

---

*Drafted by Laila Brenner and based on an interview by Darian Rodriguez Heyman with Lynne Twist.

take a stand. Social prophets don't take a position, because with any position there is always an opposition. When you take a stand, positions melt and you honor, validate, hear, see, and respect all positions. A stand is not a point of view, but a vision. A stand allows you to occupy a place in the universe that sees all views. A great social prophet is a visionary with a stand.

Social prophets aim to do more than merely right a wrong or fix something. Their work goes much deeper than that. It involves making a *transformational* change. It involves rising up and expressing something that's morally powerful to the world. As a social prophet, you are motivated by your heart, mind, and soul, and these lead you to your best self, your best work, and what's really yours to do. You bring the wholeness of who you are to the work that you've chosen to do and that's chosen you—your physical health, your relationships, the ethics of your life and your family, your heart, your soul. To be satisfied, fulfilled, and to make a real difference with your life, you have to bring *everything* to it, meaning that nothing is left on the table, and nothing is left behind. I believe that is what people ultimately want, although they may not know it. And when they follow through and experience the fulfillment of taking a stand and wholly giving themselves to it, it lights them up like a candle. That, I believe, is what life is actually about.

Social prophets have integrity. This means keeping your word and giving your word only when you know you can keep it. Working from a place of integrity, truth, passion, and authenticity will keep you healthy, inspired, and engaged. *Exercise* keeps your integrity intact. There will be times where we are exhausted and sick and take on more than we can possibly deliver. There will be times where we realize that we have taken the wrong path. But getting ourselves back on the right path is an act of integrity. Our integrity is more powerful than all of our doubts, fears, mistakes, and failures combined. For me, *integrity is never, ever giving up when I know that what I'm committed to is true and morally and ethically right.*

Social prophets are inspired to create possibilities. I try to stay in a permanent state of inspiration and consider it my duty, my responsibility, to be inspired. I am not seeking to have someone or something in particular inspire me, but rather to stand and bask in being inspired. Place yourself in a state of being where no matter what you look at you can see *possibility*, and can create possibility for others—no matter how hopeless, daunting, resigned, or completely intractable a situation may be. Social prophets create conversations and interactions that generate possibilities for them and everyone else. This ability comes from being inspired.

Great social prophets of history are a wealth of inspiration and knowledge. Working with Mother Teresa taught me that you should never shy away from suffering. She was so completely engaged with the people she was serving, and she never shied away from their suffering, but instead went towards it. *We can't resolve the pain and suffering in the world unless we're willing to embrace rather than resist it, unless we're willing to know it.* When faced with horrendous, sometimes indescribable situations, I often recall her saying "The unadulterated love of one person can nullify the hatred of millions." Because of the lessons I've learned from social prophets like Mother Teresa, I can embrace and know that the most inhuman acts are a function of a tortured, troubled human being who has lost her way. And this capacity—to embrace rather than reject, to own rather than deny, to include rather than separate myself—has come from working with social prophets like Mother Teresa and His Holiness the Dalai Lama, and from having the opportunity to know Archbishop Desmond Tutu and other great people whose courage and capacity to love goes well beyond anything I ever knew was possible. Their actions are embodiments of what Gandhi, Martin Luther King Jr., and other social prophets actually taught. We must never forget the importance of these lessons.

To be a social prophet, you must *abandon the idea of scarcity.* In today's world, and particularly in our sector, we are constantly confronted with the idea of scarcity. This idea of never having enough, which has become a frame of mind for many, is the enemy of our sector. We cry, "There aren't enough funds, there aren't enough volunteers, there isn't enough time . . ."

When we shift our perspective to sufficiency versus scarcity, we gain the strength, the power, and the wherewithal to marshal the resources that are all around us to get the job done. *If you let go of trying to get more of what you don't really need, it frees up oceans of energy to make a difference with what you already have.* When you pay attention to what you already have, when you nourish and nurture it, when you make a difference with it, what you have expands before your very eyes. If Mahatma Gandhi had complained about not having enough money and not having enough volunteers, India wouldn't ever have become independent.

I believe there are solutions for absolutely every problem we have on this planet. In his new book <u>Our Choice: A Plan to Solve the Climate Crisis</u>, Al Gore says that we are swimming in solutions to the climate crisis. We have enough solutions to solve three climate crises and yet we only have one. I know from working on hunger issues that we have enough to feed everyone on this planet three times over. So, I advocate methodologies like appreciative inquiry and what's called positive deviance, which is working with what you have and growing it, rather than swimming in what you don't have and worrying or fretting about that. Another way of saying this is *"what you appreciate, appreciates."* In our sector, we have the most committed people, the most passionate, visionary leadership. We have contributors and donors and investors who are passionate about these visions. I've never met someone who doesn't want to make a difference with her life when given a pathway or an invitation to do so.

If you feel it is your calling to become a social prophet, but aren't quite sure where to apply your service, I invite you to consider the possibility that you are on this planet at this critical time in human history, and that your presence here at this time is *not* an accident. I invite you to drop all of your "shoulds": "I should be making money," "I should get married," "I should have three kids," "I should have a certain faith."

Drop all of the "shoulds" and *listen to the call of the universe for your service*; it's always there. Look inside and ask yourself, *"What makes my heart sing?"* When you look at your life, at the people and things that inspire you, what do you see, and what are you drawn to? We all have things we are drawn to—whether justice, beauty, love, or something else. And if you look at your life, there's always a pattern where there's something larger than the content—the context, which has called you to your best self as a child, as a teenager, and as a young person. If you open yourself to listen to the universe you will be presented with opportunities to serve that are uniquely suited to you, opportunities that will fulfill your soul and make your heart sing. Successful social prophets are listening to a call that is deeper than their own wants and desires.

The job requirements for a social prophet include taking a stand, having a vision and integrity, giving your whole self to the job, and never, never, never giving up. If you are standing powerfully in the mission, you are an attractor—a field of energy. If you know that you are unstoppable, you can stand in a place where you can see what no one else can, a place where obstacles, doubts, and fears are transformed into lessons to be learned, rather than becoming stopping blocks. Your stand will give you vision and authority. You don't get authority or power from your position, but from the stand you take to get the job done, to fulfill the mission. And that is a power that is unlimited—it is the power of love, rather than the love of power. That is where all of us need to stand in order to get the world to be the kind of world we dream of. *Together, we are a genius.*

When we collaborate, when we cooperate, when we know that each person has their unique contribution, and when we give people the space and the grace to express the best of themselves, every single human being can shine. We all have the capacity to be social prophets.

Lynne Twist—global activist, speaker, and award-winning author of <u>The Soul of Money</u>*, has dedicated her life to global initiatives that create a sustainable future for all, including protecting the world's rainforests and empowering indigenous people. She is the cofounder of The Pachamama Alliance with her husband, Bill Twist, and is cocreator of the global media campaign, Four Years. Go. (www.fouryearsgo.org). Lynne has been responsible for raising hundreds of millions of dollars and has trained thousands of fundraisers. She is the president of the Soul of Money Institute, based in San Francisco, CA (www.soulofmoney.org).*

Book Partners

Nonprofit Management 101 would not have been possible without the support of a wide variety of support organizations, many of which are represented by the fifty contributors that provided the various chapters for this handbook.

These organizations provide crucial support, often low-cost or free, to emerging nonprofit leaders across a diverse array of capacity building needs.

Consider this your nonprofit support yellow pages.

The Nonprofit Leadership Alliance (formerly American Humanics) (www.nonprofitleadershipalliance.org)

The Nonprofit Leadership Alliance (formerly American Humanics) provides work-ready talent for the nonprofit sector. They offer the only national nonprofit management and leadership credential recognized by the nonprofit sector, affirming the knowledge and expertise essential for nonprofit managers and leaders. Through our national certification and workforce development initiatives, they ensure that nonprofit organizations have the talent needed to meet the challenges our world faces.

Nonprofits101.org
(www.Nonprofits101.org)

Nonprofits101.org is the online home of this book. The website contains an online directory featuring all the resources listed in *Nonprofit Management 101* and more, as well as a tip of the week and interviews with nonprofit experts across all fields. Enjoy blogs written by Darian Rodriguez Heyman and other leaders in the field, all with a focus on practical, tactical tips and takeaways.

Alliance for Nonprofit Management
(www.allianceonline.org)

The Alliance for Nonprofit Management is the national association of capacity builders focused on strengthening and supporting the nonprofit sector. Alliance members are consultants, trainers, coaches, researchers, and funders of nonprofit capacity building. The Alliance serves as a national learning community wherein expert practitioners advance the practice of capacity building by sharing and co-developing new models and ways of working with nonprofits and their leaders to increase their impact and sustainability.

Ashoka's Youth Venture
(www.GenV.net)

Ashoka's Youth Venture aims to help an entire generation of young people develop as changemakers, who will improve their communities now and throughout their lives. Youth Venture inspires and supports teams of young people to launch and lead their own civic-minded organizations and businesses. Youth teams access workshops, tools, adult allies, a global network of like-minded young changemakers, and seed funding to establish their own ventures that solve problems around them. Youth Venture operates in 18 countries and was created by Ashoka, the global pioneer of the social entrepreneurship sector and the world's biggest network of changemakers. They believe that the greatest contribution we can make to the world is to increase dramatically the number of changemakers today and in every future generation. This is the key factor for success for every part of society, from a school to a company to an entire country.

BoardSource
(www.boardsource.org)

BoardSource is dedicated to advancing the public good by building exceptional nonprofit boards and inspiring board service. It provides cutting-edge knowledge through training, assessment tools, a website, membership, consulting, publications, and an annual conference that convenes governance experts, board members, chief executives, and staff to discuss the latest thinking and practices in nonprofit governance. BoardSource's Next Generation and Governance project is designed help nonprofit leaders explore the benefits of and strategies for including emerging leaders in nonprofit governance; this project also aims to inspire board service among members of Generations X and Y. BoardSource is a 501(c)(3) organization.

Bridgespan Group
(www.bridgespan.org)

The Bridgespan Group is a nonprofit organization that helps nonprofit and philanthropic leaders make strategic decisions and build organizations that inspire and accelerate social change. Bridgespan offers strategy consulting, executive search, and philanthropy advising to help nonprofit organizations and philanthropists develop and implement strategies with the potential to achieve significant results. Insights developed through research and client engagements are shared through extensive knowledge resources, tools, and articles. Through its Leadership initiative (www.bridgespan.org/leadership) Bridgespan provides a nonprofit job board, content, and tools designed to help nonprofit organizations build strong leadership teams and individuals pursue career paths as nonprofit leaders.

Capaciteria
(www.capaciteria.org)

Capaciteria was designed by Internaut Consulting as a free, peer-rated resource for the nonprofit sector. It consists of capacity-related websites, reports, books, and more, all categorized for easy searching, reference, rating and commenting. The website offers a comprehensive, searchable database directory of categorized administrative resources that help nonprofits leverage their own capacity. It promotes peer review because site members can comment on and rate individual resource links, as well as add useful new links they come across. Like Google, searches return results are weighted based on ratings and popularity assigned to them by nonprofit users. Members can use the "Favorites" feature to personalize their list of easily accessible links.

Care2 (www.Care2.com)

Care2.com is the largest online social action network of "do gooders" seeking to make a difference. With 14 million members, the Care2 audience is highly engaged with strong "green" values and a desire to support social justice, save the environment and live a healthy, sustainable lifestyle. For more than 550 leading nonprofit organizations, Care2 is the preferred source for recruiting new supporters and donors. In 2010 Care2 greatly extended the reach and impact of its nonprofit clients' campaigns via partnerships with dozens of websites that together reach an additional 50 million people.

Center for Lobbying in the Public Interest (www.clpi.org)

Founded in 1998, the Center for Lobbying in the Public Interest (CLPI) promotes, supports, and protects nonprofit advocacy and lobbying in order to advance the missions of charitable organizations and strengthen democracy. A national 501(c)(3) nonprofit, CLPI accomplishes its mission through state-based training and coaching for charities and foundations; research and education; and policy reform to protect, simplify, and strengthen nonprofit advocacy rights. CLPI is committed to making advocacy a core function of the nonprofit sector, thus making the "extraordinary ordinary." Their vision is of a revitalized civic sector, working together to serve as an engine of social and economic progress.

Change.org
(www.change.org)

change.org

Change.org is an online platform for social change that raises awareness about important issues and connects people to opportunities for action. They work with more than 1000 of the world's leading nonprofits and millions of activists to empower anyone to start a social action campaign that makes a difference.

The Chronicle of Philanthropy
(www.philanthropy.com)

THE CHRONICLE OF
PHILANTHROPY

For more than 20 years, The Chronicle of Philanthropy has been connecting nonprofit leaders to news, jobs, and ideas as the number one news source in the nonprofit world. Philanthropy.com offers the most comprehensive news and interactive platform to keep emerging leaders at the forefront with the best information to make decisions that matter. With up-to-the-minute news updates, the latest job postings, archives of grant information, tips, trends, and advice on the most challenging issues, The Chronicle of Philanthropy is the first and only choice for the most active and influential professionals who run the nation's leading charitable groups.

Commongood Careers
(www.cgcareers.org)

Commongood Careers was founded by a group of nonprofit professionals who experienced the challenges of recruiting and hiring in their own organizations and were amazed by the lack of effective solutions in the sector. Today, their mission is to enable innovative nonprofits to build strong organizations through the recruitment and hiring of outstanding talent. Each year, they recruit, screen, and hire for hundreds of positions in all functional areas and at every level of the organizational chart, from assistants through executives. Resulting in a 93% successful hire rate, Commongood Careers has completed over 400 searches with 130 organizations in 26 states.

CompassPoint Nonprofit Services
(www.compasspoint.org)

For over 35 years, CompassPoint has served the nonprofit community through the delivery of high quality capacity building programs for nonprofit organizations and staff, including training, consulting, initiatives, conferences, research, and publications. They believe it is important to the future success of the sector to build a strong, well-prepared pipeline of emerging nonprofit leaders and to sustain and support those currently in leadership. CompassPoint addresses this goal through innovative leadership development programming for executive directors, senior managers, and emerging leaders, including intensive trainings and leadership development initiatives that focus on multidisciplinary management skills and participants' personal development as leaders; executive coaching and content coaching; and facilitated peer networks.

Dorothy A. Johnson Center for Philanthropy
(www.gvsu.edu/jcp)

Established in 1992 as a multidisciplinary, university-wide center at Grand Valley State University, the Johnson Center for Philanthropy serves nonprofits, foundations, and others that seek to transform their communities for the common good. They do this through applied research, professional development, and the advancement of social technologies. Their programs include the Community Research Institute, *The Foundation Review*, Frey Foundation Chair for Family Philanthropy, The Grantmaking School, Nonprofit Services, and the Philanthropy Library and Archives.

Earth Island Institute
(www.earthisland.org)

Over the course of its 27-year history, Earth Island Institute has provided over 120 individual projects with the resources that they need to develop and pursue ideas that promote the conservation, preservation, and restoration of the Earth. In addition to offering fiscal sponsorship and supporting established activists, Earth Island is deeply committed to nurturing the next generation of environmental leaders. It is in this spirit that the New Leaders Initiative was launched in 2000. Since then they have honored 67 young environmental leaders with our annual Brower Youth Awards. These 67 past winners, all now 31 years old and younger are leading the change toward a sustainable future.

Echoing Green
(www.echoinggreen.org)

Echoing Green unleashes next generation talent to solve the world's biggest problems. Since inception almost 25 years ago by the private equity firm General Atlantic, Echoing Green has invested in nearly 500 social entrepreneurs who have launched innovative social change organizations around the world, including Teach For America, City Year, Genocide Intervention Network, The SEED School, Global Fund for Children and hundreds of others. They also build a robust ecosystem of changemaking by supporting young people to select careers in social change; working with donors to approach their philanthropy in an engaged manner; and providing data that builds the field.

Georgia Center for Nonprofits
(www.gcn.org)

For 20 years, The Georgia Center for Nonprofits has served as a cornerstone of support for the Georgia nonprofit and philanthropic community by delivering a wide range of services and support—from training, policy work, and advocacy, to job services, consulting, and networking. Today, GCN offers more ways than ever to help their 1,100 member organizations meet their missions and maximize their impact. As a member, you gain access to the critical tools, resources, services, and expertise you need to build your nonprofit's success.

Global Exchange
(www.globalexchange.org)

Global Exchange is an international human rights organization that addresses issues of social, environmental, and economic justice by building collaborative networks of nonprofit, for-profit, and governmental organizations. With more than 20 years of nonprofit social enterprise under our belts, they understand that saving humanity from itself will require us to switch from a system where money values rule over the life cycle to one where life values rule over the money cycle.

Green Festivals
(www.greenfestivals.org)

Green Festivals are the nation's largest, most successful green consumer event. Noted for their massive attendance, high energy, authenticity, and community focus, Green Festivals bring together hundreds of green enterprises and nonprofits, hundreds of inspiring speakers, organic food and drink, live music, and something for all members of the family. For the last nine years across six cities, the Green Festivals have presented the best environmentally and socially responsible products and services, while educating the public about our need to accelerate the transition to sustainability.

HandsOn
(www.handsonnetwork.org)

HandsOn Network is the largest volunteer network in the nation and mobilizes people through 250 Action Centers in 16 countries.

Humanity in Action
(www.humanityinaction.org)

HUMANITY IN ACTION

Humanity in Action is an international educational organization that educates, inspires, and connects a network of emerging leaders committed to protecting minorities and promoting human rights—in their own communities and around the world.

Idealist
(www.idealist.org)

Idealist.org is a global network of people and organizations that want to change the world. 60,000 organizations in 200 countries use Idealist to promote their mission, connect with supporters, and post job openings, events, and volunteer opportunities. And every day 100,000 people come to the site to find a job, an organization, or a new idea, and to connect with inspiring projects and like-minded people.

Network for Good
(www.networkforgood.org)

Network for Good, an independent nonprofit organization, makes it easy to support any charity, anywhere online by offering simple, affordable, and effective online fundraising services, including donation processing, online events, email outreach, and surveys. To foster continued growth in online fundraising and nonprofit marketing, Network for Good provides free tools and expertise in online giving through the website Fundraising123.org so that small- and medium-sized charities can see bigger returns from their online marketing efforts. Network for Good has processed over $400 million in donations for more than 65,000 nonprofits since its 2001 founding by AOL, Yahoo!, and Cisco.

Net Impact
(www.netimpact.org)

Net Impact is an international nonprofit organization with a mission to inspire, educate, and equip individuals to use the power of business to create a more socially and environmentally sustainable world. Spanning six continents, their membership makes up one of the most influential networks of students and professionals in existence today. Net Impact members are current and emerging leaders in corporate responsibility, social entrepreneurship, nonprofit management, international development, and environmental sustainability who are actively improving the world. The Net Impact network includes more than 260 volunteer-led chapters in cities throughout the world and a central office in San Francisco, CA.

New Sector Alliance (www.newsector.org)

New Sector Alliance is a 501(c)(3) nonprofit consulting and leadership development firm dedicated to accelerating social change by strengthening organizations today while developing leaders for tomorrow. In partnership with leading academic institutions and management consulting firms, New Sector recruits, trains, and supports diverse top talent to deliver consulting services and capacity to clients, helping organizations better serve their constituents. At the same time, they provide transformative professional and personal development experiences to program participants, inspiring lifelong civic engagement.

Nonprofit Central (www.npocentral.net)

Nonprofit Central—where nonprofit leaders can find consultants with references. Nonprofit Central is the home of the NY/NJ Consultants Directory and the Capacity Building Events Calendar.

Nonprofit Coordinating Committee of New York (www.npccny.org)

The Nonprofit Coordinating Committee of New York, Inc., (NPCC) is the voice and information source for New York nonprofits. Established in 1984, NPCC informs and connects nonprofit leaders, saves nonprofits money, and strengthens the nonprofit sector's relations with government. NPCC publishes a monthly newsletter, *New York Nonprofits*; offers workshops and roundtables on management issues, provides cost-saving vendor services; manages a Government Relations Committee that works on sector-wide government and legislative issues; supports emerging nonprofit professionals through a Leadership Lunch program, periodic workshops, and other programs targeting young nonprofit leaders; and maintains a website loaded with information on operating a nonprofit. NPCC has more than 1,700 dues-paying members in the New York City area.

Nonprofit Finance Fund (www.nonprofitfinancefund.org)

Nonprofit Finance Fund (NFF) works to create a strong, well-capitalized, and durable nonprofit sector that connects money to mission effectively, supporting the highest aspirations and most generous impulses of people and communities. They offer an integrated package of financial and advisory services, including loans; asset-building programs; intensive workshops; and strategic financial consulting to help nonprofit management understand the impact on their finances of management and program decisions. Since its inception, NFF has cumulatively lent over $290 million and leveraged $1 billion of capital investment on behalf of its nonprofit clients.

Nonprofit Quarterly (www.NPQmag.org)

We live in a world that needs more of what nonprofits can achieve. We know that our communities hold untapped courage, compassion, and support; and nonprofits are uniquely positioned to build relationships and understanding. The Nonprofit Quarterly, consisting of a print magazine, website, and electronic newsletters, is committed to providing a forum for the critical thinking and exploration needed to help nonprofits stay true to this democratic calling—and to achieve their potential as effective organizations alongside their constituencies.

Nonprofit Roundtable of Greater Washington (www.nonprofitroundtable.org)

The Nonprofit Roundtable works to build the strength, visibility, and influence of the nonprofit community in order to create a more just and caring community in Greater Washington. Their Members include advocacy organizations, direct service providers, grant makers, and corporate partners all working together to solve regional problems in and around our nation's capital.

Nonprofit Technology Network (www.nten.org)

The Nonprofit Technology Network (NTEN) helps nonprofits use technology strategically and confidently to create the change they want to see in the world. By connecting community members—across the full spectrum of nonprofit work and tech comfort—NTEN promotes the sharing of best practices and provides professional development, access to experts, and research on nonprofit technology issues. The NTEN community is transforming technology into social change.

The NonProfit Times (www.nptimes.com)

The NonProfit Times is the leading business publication for nonprofit management. They deliver content to the nonprofit sector through many different formats, which include a print magazine, a useful website, e-newsletters, and Web TV (www.nonprofittimes.tv).

Opportunity Knocks (www.opportunityknocks.org)

Opportunity Knocks is the national online job site, HR resource, and career development destination focused exclusively on the nonprofit community. They are committed to helping nonprofit organizations build successful human resource strategies through hiring services to find employees locally or nationwide, knowledge sharing, training, and research.

The Phoenix Project (www.phoenixproject.org)

The Phoenix Project is a catalyst for social innovation, providing the sparks that turn great people into leaders and promising ideas into groundbreaking solutions. As a not-for-profit corporation, The Phoenix Project models the social entrepreneurship principles it promotes. Their initiatives are designed with transformational impact, scalability, and sustainability in mind. These include their Social Innovation Program, Accelerating Social Entrepreneurship Conferences, the AVAIL service learning platform, and their consulting firm, Social Innovation Professionals. The Phoenix Project proves the viability of their programs in Virginia and then makes them available for replication.

Public Allies (www.publicallies.org)

Public Allies advances new leadership to strengthen communities, nonprofits, and civic participation. They identify young adults from diverse backgrounds who have a passion to make a difference and help them turn that passion into a career working for community and social change. "Allies" serve in paid, full-time apprenticeships in community organizations, where they create, improve, and expand services to address issues such as education, health, poverty, and the environment, and participate in a rigorous weekly leadership development program. Over 3,700 Allies have completed the program in 21 cities and 87% have continued careers in community and public service.

Razoo (www.razoo.com)

Founded in 2006 and based in Washington, DC, Razoo is a trusted and innovative way to give and raise money online. Razoo offers a secure platform, a streamlined donation process, and a suite of free and easy-to-use fundraising tools that inspire individuals and nonprofits to give and fundraise online. To date, more than $25 million has been donated to thousands of charities in the United States and around the world through Razoo. With over 106,000 donor members to date, Razoo is rapidly growing its community and establishing a movement that inspires people to contribute and fundraise more than ever before.

RSF Social Finance (www.rsfsocialfinance.org)

RSF Social Finance is a nonprofit financial services organization dedicated to transforming the way the world works with money. Inspired by the work of Rudolf Steiner, RSF offers investing, lending, and giving services that foster social and spiritual renewal. In partnership with its investors and donors, RSF has made over $200 million in loans and over $90 million in grants since 1984 to for-profit and nonprofit social enterprises working in the areas of Food and Agriculture; Education and the Arts; and Ecological Stewardship. Underlying all of its work is a spirited conversation about the role that money can play in the development of humanity.

Salsa (www.democracyinaction.org)

Salsa Labs is the creator of the popular Salsa platform, an integrated, flexible, and affordable set of tools to organize and energize people. From fundraising to advocacy, CRM, communications, and event management, Salsa empowers thousands of nonprofits and campaigns of all sizes to achieve their online goals. Organizations can create their own unique recipe for organizing by choosing from the dozens of available tools they provide, as well as by plugging in dozens of other applications produced by third parties in the Salsa Market. Part of Salsa's mission is to help its users become expert organizers and they provide a robust training and online community support program through SalsaCommons.org. Salsa's robust set of services are supporting thousands of user groups' relationships with over 40 million supporters, members, donors, activists, and fans all around the world.

Silicon Valley Council of Nonprofits (www.svcn.org)

Silicon Valley Council of Nonprofits (SVCN) champions the interests of health and human service nonprofits in Silicon Valley. SVCN works to ensure the nonprofit sector's voice is heard and that solutions are developed in ways in which everybody wins. They are a collaborative organization that takes positions on issues that impact our sector. To achieve results, SVCN develop extensive groundwork in data collection, understanding government budgets, and developing the nonprofit perspective. They work in partnership with our nonprofit agencies, which are primarily health and human services community-based agencies.

Social Edge (www.skollfoundation.org)

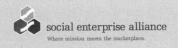

Social Edge, a program of the Skoll Foundation, is the global online community where thousands of social entrepreneurs and other practitioners in the social benefit sector connect to network, learn, inspire, and share best practices. Weekly conversations highlight key issues in the field and spur discussion on critical topics. Blogs offer practical and inspirational information from experts and from fellow social entrepreneurs. The Social Edge community also receives weekly highlights by email and follows @socialedge on Twitter for real-time news in social entrepreneurship, including deadlines for funding and award opportunities.

Social Enterprise Alliance (www.se-alliance.org)

social enterprise alliance
Where mission meets the marketplace.

The Social Enterprise Alliance (SEA) is the leading membership organization in North America for social enterprises, service providers, nonprofit organizations, corporations, and venture capitalists that is actively building the field of social enterprise through networking opportunities, educational forums, strategic partnerships, and impact legislation. SEA seeks to connect the vibrant and growing community of social enterprise by hosting learning and networking opportunities among social enterprises, foundations, lenders, educators, corporations, and service providers in regional hotspots throughout the United States and Canada. With a community of nearly 700 members, they actively connect members with potential clients, sources of capital, marketing opportunities, helpful informational resources, and leaders in the field to build their business and strengthen social impact.

Support Center for Nonprofit Management (www.supportcenteronline.org)

SUPPORT CENTER FOR NONPROFIT MANAGEMENT
CONSULTING ‖ TRANSITION MANAGEMENT ‖ TRAINING
for nonprofit & philanthropic organizations

The Support Center works with organizations and their leaders at all stages in their development to increase their effectiveness and sustainability. They are committed to working with nonprofits of all sizes, especially small- and mid-sized organizations. The Support Center helps nonprofit leaders and managers at all stages of their career develop practical knowledge, build productive relationships, and find the information and resources they need to further their professional development. While their focus is on the Greater New York/New Jersey/Connecticut Tri-State area, their work extends beyond the region, both nationally and internationally.

Taproot Foundation (www.taprootfoundation.org)

Most organizations tackling social problems don't have access to the marketing, design, technology, management, or strategic planning resources they need to succeed. Without this talent, few are able to have their intended impact on critical issues like the environment, health, and education. Taproot is a nonprofit that engages the nation's millions of business professionals in pro bono services, both through its award-winning programs and by partnering with companies to develop their own pro bono programs. One day, they envision all organizations with promising solutions will be equipped to successfully take on urgent social challenges.

TechSoup Global (www.TechSoup.org)

TechSoup Global, a 501(c)(3) nonprofit, was founded in 1987 on the belief that technology is a powerful enabler for social change. Since that day, they've assembled a worldwide network of individuals and organizations that share this conviction. This network includes foundations and corporations, governments and NGOs, social entrepreneurs and volunteers. Together, these unlikely allies have developed sustainable, community-driven technology solutions to meet today's most urgent social challenges. TechSoup Global's website serves more than 300,000 nonprofits and libraries each month with software and other product donations and articles about the best use nonprofits can make of technology to help them achieve their missions.

UniversalGiving™ (www.universalgiving.org)

UniversalGiving™ is a web-based marketplace that helps people give to and volunteer with top-performing, vetted organizations all over the world. All projects are screened through UniversalGiving's trademarked, proprietary Quality Model™ 100% of each donation goes directly to the cause. UniversalGiving Corporate is a customized service for Fortune 500 companies, helping them expand their Corporate Social Responsibility programs globally. UniversalGiving's CEO Pamela Hawley is a Jefferson Award winner, a finalist for Ernst and Young's Entrepreneur of the Year Award, an Expert Blogger on corporate social responsibility for Fast Company, and recently attended the White House's Consortium on Next Generation Leadership and Social Innovation.

Volunteer Consulting Group (www.vcg.org)

Volunteer Consulting Group (VCG), a nonprofit founded in 1969 by the Harvard Business School Club of Greater New York, focuses on strengthening nonprofits by increasing the governing and management capacity of their boards. VCG brings together boards and board candidates across boundaries of skill, ethnicity, age, and geography. VCG provides services: (1) matching board candidates and boards; (2) consulting to make boards more effective; (3) educating current board members and also maintains www. governancematters.org. Their free www.boardnetUSA.org website expands opportunities for nonprofit boards to explore a diverse pool of emerging leaders desiring to serve as board members.

VolunteerMatch (www.volunteermatch.org)

VolunteerMatch is a national nonprofit dedicated to strengthening communities by making it easier for good people and good causes to connect. Its popular online service is the number one search result for "volunteer" on Google, Yahoo!, and Bing. VolunteerMatch provides many of the nation's most recognized businesses and organizations with hosted solutions to facilitate volunteer engagement at local and national levels. The VolunteerMatch network welcomes more than 190,000 visitors each week and has become the preferred volunteer recruiting service for tens of thousands of nonprofits.

WiserEarth (www.wiserearth.org)

WiserEarth helps the global sustainability movement connect, collaborate, and share knowledge. All tools and content are free to use, and the site is commercial-free. Emerging leaders in the nonprofit world will find vast resources, best practices, and discussion forums on WiserEarth to spark their creative energies and connect them to potential collaborators. They can post jobs, events, and resources of their own, and get questions answered. WiserEarth hosts a community of 43,000+ members, over 2,000 community-led groups, close to 9,000 resources, and the world's largest international directory of nonprofits and socially responsible organizations (over 112,000 in 243 countries).

YES!
(www.yesworld.org)

YES! connects, inspires, and collaborates with young and multi-generational changemakers in building thriving, just, and sustainable ways of life for all. The organization offers transformational gatherings for diverse leaders, called "Jams," and has alumni in 65+ nations. Jams help social change leaders to deepen the root system that underlies their work, to sharpen strategic thinking, to build partnerships with diverse allies, and to grow in their personal as well as professional development. YES! also offers facilitation and keynote speaking services, produces books and action guides, and convenes authentic dialogue across historic divides like religion, nationality, race, class, and gender.

Young Nonprofit Professionals
Network
(www.ynpn.org)

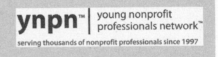

The Young Nonprofit Professionals Network (YNPN) is a robust national network rooted in grassroots energy and leadership whose mission is to promote an efficient, viable, and inclusive nonprofit sector that supports the growth, learning, and development of young professionals. They engage and support future nonprofit and community leaders through professional development, networking, and social opportunities. YNPN offers programming through 30 local chapters around the country serving over 20,000 members, as well as planning and coordination at the national level. In 2009 alone, YNPN chapters provided over 300 high impact professional development events in over 15 states to an estimated 6,000 members.

Youth Leadership Institute
(www.yli.org)

The Youth Leadership Institute has been an innovative leader in the field of youth development for over 20 years—teaching communities to invest in developing youth, and training youth and their adult allies to inspire their communities by being advocates for change. The Youth Leadership Institute believes that cultivating engaged and dynamic young people today will lead to a more equitable and sustainable society tomorrow. Youth Leadership Institute specializes in helping organizations use youth-led research, policy action strategies, and building the capacity of diverse stakeholders to accomplish change and improve systems.

ABOUT THE EDITOR

As executive director of Craigslist Foundation (2004–2008), Darian Rodriguez Heyman worked to educate, inspire, and connect emerging nonprofit leaders and social entrepreneurs. He helped conceive its flagship program, *Nonprofit Boot Camp*, which grew into the largest nonprofit gathering in San Francisco Bay Area history, and launched a website that connected thousands of leaders to helpful resources, and to each other. While there, he started and led several coalitions, including the *Environmental Nonprofit Network* and the *Next Generation Leadership Forum*. At the same time, he was appointed as a Commissioner of the San Francisco Department of the Environment by Mayor Gavin Newsom. He has since moved on to serve the United Nations as a senior adviser to the Global Alliance for ICT & Development, as well as lecturing on "The Economics of Philanthropy" at the Haas School of Business at University of California, Berkeley.

In addition to consulting for a variety of nonprofit organizations on all aspects of nonprofit management and fundraising, Darian currently works as a managing partner at Code Green Agency, an environmental consultancy providing strategy, messaging, stakeholder engagement, facilitation, and fundraising support to nonprofits, businesses, and government agencies. He is a frequent public speaker, keynoting and MCing events around the world, and recently led several civil society consultations for the United Nations Environment Programme. Darian launched Nonprofits101.org in 2010, which provides a tip of the week to emerging nonprofit leaders and social entrepreneurs and offers a directory of all the resources and contributors highlighted in this book.

In his past career as a dot-com entrepreneur, Darian cofounded and later sold the digital advertising agency Beyond Interactive to Grey Global Group, now WPP. He is passionate about supporting young leaders, integrating interactivity into educational environments, and helping noble efforts connect vision to action. He can be reached at darian@darianheyman.com.

Endnotes

Chapter 1

1. Michael O'Neill, <u>Nonprofit Nation</u>. (San Francisco: Jossey-Bass, 2002), 13.

2. Lester M. Salamon, <u>America's Nonprofit Sector: A Primer (2nd ed.)</u>. (New York: The Foundation Center, 1999), 10.

3. National Center for Charitable Statistics, "NCCS Quick Facts About Nonprofits" (Urban Institute Oct. 2009), www.nccs.urban.org/statistics/quickfacts.cfm (retrieved Feb. 2, 2010).

4. The Independent Sector, "Scope of the Nonprofit Sector" www.independentsector.org/scope_of_the_sector (retrieved April 30, 2010).

5. National Center for Charitable Statistics, "NTEE Core Codes Overview" (Urban Institute n.d.), http:/nccs.urban.org/classification/NTEE.cfm (retrieved Feb. 16, 2010).

6. The Foundation Center, "Frequently Asked Questions: How Many People Are Employed in the Nonprofit Sector?" (The Foundation Center, n.d.) www.foundationcenter.org/getstarted/faqs/html/employed.html (retrieved Feb. 16, 2010).

7. Amy Blackwood, Kennard T. Wing, and Thomas H. Pollak, "The Nonprofit Sector in Brief: Facts and Figures from the Nonprofit Almanac 2008." (Washington, DC: The Urban Institute, Center on Nonprofits and Philanthropy, 2008), 4.

8. Amy Blackwood, Kennard T. Wing, and Thomas H. Pollak, "The Nonprofit Sector in Brief: Facts and Figures from the Nonprofit Almanac 2008." (Washington, DC: The Urban Institute, Center on Nonprofits and Philanthropy, 2008).

9. United States Government Accountability Office, <u>Tax-Exempt Sector: Governance, Transparency, and Oversight Are Critical for Maintaining Public Trust</u>, GAO-05–051T (Washington, DC: April 20, 2005), 9.

10. Molly F. Sherlock and Jane G. Gravelle. <u>An Overview of the Nonprofit and Charitable Sector</u>, (Washington, DC: Congressional Research Service, November 17, 2009), 19.

11. Kennard T. Wing, Thomas Pollak, and Amy Blackwood, <u>The Nonprofit Almanac 2008</u>, (Washington, DC: The Urban Institute Press, 2008), 20.

12. Shelly Cryer. "Fact Sheet: Nonprofit Size and Scope" (The Nonprofit Career Guide, 2008), www.nonprofitcareerguide.org/fact_sheet-scope.php (retrieved April 29, 2010). For World Bank data, see www.siteresources .worldbank.org/DATASTATISTICS/Resources/GDP.pdf.

13. Amy Blackwood, Kennard T. Wing, and Thomas H. Pollak, "The Nonprofit Sector in Brief: Facts and Figures from the Nonprofit Almanac 2008." (Washington, DC: The Urban Institute, Center on Nonprofits and Philanthropy, 2008), 1, 6.

14. Peter Dobkin Hall, "A Historical Overview of Philanthropy, Voluntary Associations, and Nonprofit Organizations in the United States, 1600–2000," in <u>The Nonprofit Sector: A Research Handbook, Second Edition</u>. (New Haven: Yale University Press, 2005).

15. Ibid.

16. Ibid.

17. Michael O'Neill, <u>Nonprofit Nation</u>. (San Francisco: Jossey-Bass, 2002).

18. Peter Dobkin Hall, "A Historical Overview of Philanthropy, Voluntary Associations, and Nonprofit Organizations in the United States, 1600–2000."

19. Ibid.

20. Ibid.

21. Ibid.

22. Ibid.

23. Lester M. Salamon, "The Changing Context of American Management," in The Jossey-Bass Handbook of Nonprofit Leadership & Management, 2nd ed. (San Francisco: Jossey-Bass, 2005).

24. Michael O'Neill, Nonprofit Nation. (San Francisco: Jossey-Bass, 2002).

25. Peter Dobkin Hall, "Historical Perspectives on Nonprofit Organizations in the United States," in The Jossey-Bass Handbook of Nonprofit Leadership & Management, 2nd ed. (San Francisco: Jossey-Bass, 2005).

26. Ibid.

27. National Center for Charitable Statistics, "501(c)(3) Public Charities" (Urban Institute n.d.), www.nccsdataweb.urban.org/PubApps.nonprofit -overview-segment.php?t=pc (retrieved Feb. 2, 2009).

28. Lester M. Salamon, "The Changing Context of American Management," in The Jossey-Bass Handbook of Nonprofit Leadership & Management, 2nd ed. (San Francisco: Jossey-Bass, 2005).

29. Lucy Bernholz, Stephanie Linden Seale, and Tony Wang, "Changing the Ecosystem of Change" (report, Blueprint Research & Design, Inc., 2009).

30. "Strains in the Safety Net" (Chronicle of Philanthropy, Dec. 10, 2009), www.philanthropy.com/article/Strains-in-the-Safety-Net/49499 (retrieved Feb. 23, 2010).

31. Paula Wasley. "100,000 Nonprofit Groups Could Collapse in Next Two Years, Expert Predicts" (Chronicle of Philanthropy, Nov. 27, 2008), www.philanthropy.com/article/100000-Nonprofit-Groups-Co/56951 (retrieved Feb. 27, 2010).

32. Heather Gowdy, Alex Hildebrand, David La Piana, and Melissa Mendes Campos, "Convergence: How Five Trends Will Reshape the Social Sector" (report, The James Irvine Foundation, November 2009).

33. Ian Wilhem, "The Future Starts Now: Looking Ahead to the Trends that will Remake the Nonprofit World by 2020" (Chronicle of Philanthropy, Jan. 7, 2010), www.philanthropy.com/article/Trends-That-Will-Remake -the/63586 (retrieved Feb. 23, 2010).

34. Heather Gowdy, Alex Hildebrand, David La Piana, and Melissa Mendes Campos, "Convergence: How Five Trends Will Reshape the Social Sector" (report, The James Irvine Foundation, November 2009).

35. Ian Wilhem, "The Future Starts Now: Looking Ahead to the Trends That Will Remake the Nonprofit World by 2020" (Chronicle of Philanthropy, Jan. 7, 2010), www.philanthropy.com/article/Trends-That-Will-Remake -the/63586 (retrieved Feb. 23, 2010).

36. Heather Gowdy et al., "Convergence: How Five Trends Will Reshape the Social Sector."

37. Howard Adam Levy, "Top Nonprofit Trends to Watch" (The Nonprofit Brand Institute, Nov. 10, 2009) www.npbrandit.com/articles/nonprofit -trends/trends-top-nonprofit-trends/ (retrieved Feb. 23, 2010).

38. Alliance for Children and Families, "Nonprofits: Volunteers" (Alliance for Children and Families, n.d.) www.alliancetrends.org/nonprofits.cfm?id=59 (retrieved Feb. 23, 2010).

39. United States Department of Labor, Bureau of Labor Statistics, "Volunteering in the United States—2009," www.bls.gov/news.release/ volun.nr0.htm (retrieved April 30, 2010).

40. Bryan Barry, "Five Nonprofit Trends and Their Implications for Capacity Builders" (Fieldstone Alliance, 2004), www.fieldstonealliance.org/client/ articles/Article-5_np_trends.cfm (retrieved Feb. 23, 2010).

41. Ian Wilhem, "The Future Starts Now: Looking Ahead to the Trends That Will Remake the Nonprofit World by 2020" (Chronicle of Philanthropy, Jan. 7, 2010), www.philanthropy.com/article/Trends-That-Will-Remake -the/63586 (retrieved Feb. 23, 2010).

42. Heather Gowdy et al., "Convergence: How Five Trends Will Reshape the Social Sector."

43. Lucy Bernholz, Stephanie Linden Seale, and Tony Wang, "Changing the Ecosystem of Change" (report, Blueprint Research & Design, Inc., 2009).

44. Ibid.

45. Susan K. E. Saxon-Harrold and Aaron J. Heffron, "Crossing the Borders: Competition and Collaboration Among Nonprofits, Business and Government" (research brief, Independent Sector, Facts and Findings, Vol. 1 No. 1, n.d.).

46. Ian Wilhem, "The Future Starts Now: Looking Ahead to the Trends that will Remake the Nonprofit World by 2020."

47. Heather Gowdy et al., "Convergence: How Five Trends Will Reshape the Social Sector."

48. Lucy Bernholz, "In a Changing Ecosystem, Whither Nonprofits?" (Stanford Social Innovation Review, Feb. 10, 2010) www.ssireview.org/opinion/entry/in_a_changing_ecosystem_whither_nonprofits (retrieved Feb. 23, 2010).

49. Lucy Bernholz et al., "Changing the Ecosystem of Change"

50. Suzanne Perry, "Public Confidence in Nonprofit Groups Slides Back, New Survey Finds" (Chronicle of Philanthropy, April 3, 2008), www.philanthropy.com/article/Public-Confidence-in-Nonpro/60905/ (retrieved May 10, 2010).

51. Alliance for Children and Families, "Nonprofits: Credibility and Survivability of Nonprofits" (Alliance for Children and Families, n.d.) www.alliancetrends.org/nonprofits.cfm?id=53 (retrieved Feb. 23, 2010).

52. Robert Herman and Associates, <u>The Jossey-Bass Handbook of Nonprofit Leadership & Management</u>, 2nd ed. (San Francisco: Jossey-Bass, 2005).

53. Lucy Bernholz et al., "Changing the Ecosystem of Change."

54. Kim Silver, "The Quiet Conversation about Measuring Social Impact" (Mission Measurement, Feb. 16, 2010), www.missionmeasurement.com/content/thought-capital/thought-scraps/2010/02/16/quiet-conversation-about-measuring-social-impact (retrieved Feb. 25, 2010).

55. Heather Gowdy et al., "Convergence: How Five Trends Will Reshape the Social Sector."

Chapter 2

1. Karen Armstrong, <u>The Great Transformation: The Beginning of Our Religious Traditions</u> (New York: Knopf, 2006), xi–xiv.

2. Ibid., p. xiv.

3. Martin Luther King, Jr., "Beyond Vietnam," address delivered to the Clergy and Laymen Concerned about Vietnam, at Riverside Church, New York City, April 4, 1967.

4. James Carse, <u>Finite and Infinite Games: A Vision of Life as Play and Possibility</u> (New York: Ballantine, 1986).

5. After I had written this passage, I saw a better list from David James Duncan's book <u>G-d Laughs and Plays</u> (Great Barrington, MA: Triad, 2006): "I hold the evangelical truth of the matter to be that contemporary fundamentalists, including first and foremost those aimed at Empire and Armageddon, need us nonfundamentalists, mystics, ecosystem activists, unprogrammable artists, agnostic humanitarians, incorrigible writers, truth-telling musicians, incorruptible scientists, organic gardeners, slow food farmers, gay restaurateurs, wilderness visionaries, pagan preachers of sustainability, compassion-driven entrepreneurs, heart-broken Muslims, grief-stricken children, loving believers, loving disbelievers, peace-marching millions, and the Ones who love us all in such a huge way that it is not going too far to say *they need us for their salvation.*"

6. Duncan, <u>G-d Laughs and Plays</u>, p. 118.

7. Personal communication, Wolfgang Sachs.

8. David Orr, <u>The Last Refuge: Patriotism, Politics, and the Environment in an Age of Terror</u> (Washington DC: Island Press, 2004), 74–77.

9. Mary Oliver, <u>Dream Work</u> (Boston: Atlantic Monthly Press, 1986), p. 38. The last lines read: "But little by little, as you left their voices behind, the stars began to burn / through the sheets of clouds, and there was a new voice / which you slowly / recognized as your own, that kept you company / as you strode deeper and deeper / into the world, / determined to do / the only thing you could do—determined to save / the only life you could save."

10. Harold, <u>Way of the Cell</u>, p. 101.

CHAPTER 4

1. Urban Institute's National Center for Charitable Statistics. www.nccs.urban.org/statistics/quickfacts.cfm. Retrieved 11/30/2010.

2. Jim Collins, <u>Good to Great and the Social Sectors: Why Business Thinking Is Not the Answer</u> (a monograph). New York: Harper Collins, 2005.

CHAPTER 6

1. Adapted in 2009 from David La Piana, <u>The Nonprofit Mergers Workbook</u>. (Saint Paul, MN: Amherst H. Wilder Foundation, 2000), 5–7.

2. Names and other details in this case have been changed.

3. In the vast majority of the 200 mergers that we have facilitated, there is little evidence of significant cost savings from the act of merging itself. Annual audits can be rolled into one, insurance programs can be combined, and of course administrative staffs, executive directors, finance staff, and so on can be consolidated. These savings, however, are likely to be offset by the need for greater management capacity to run a larger and more complex organization.

PART 2

1. "Doing the Most Good" is The Salvation Army's national brand strategy.

CHAPTER 14

1. Resource Guide: 11 Qualities of Successful IT Managers, (CNET networks, 2008) www.downloads.techrepublic.com.com/thankyou.aspx?cname=Business+Functions&tag=content%3BleftCol&docid=382804&view=382804&load=1, (Retrieved January 5, 2010).

2. Chris Bernard, Writer/Editor & Dr. Kimberly Pukstas, Research Consultant, Nonprofit IT Staffing: 2008 IT Staffing & Spending Report, May 2009 www.nten.org/research/it_staffing_2008, (Retrieved January 5, 2010).

3. Robert D. Atkinson and Andrew S. McKay, Digital Prosperity: Understanding the Economic Benefits of the Information Technology Revolution. The Information Technology and Innovation Foundation, 2007.

4. Robert Lemos, CNET News "Counting the Cost of the Slammer." www.news.cnet.com/2100-1001-982955.html January 31, 2003.

5. BBC News, "60,000 devices are left in cabs" www.news.bbc.co.uk/2/hi/7620569.stm.

6. IdealWare, "Selecting Software on a Shoestring Budget" www.idealware.org/articles/selecting_shoestring.php.

CHAPTER 15

1. Anne Keenan, EchoDitto, July 11, 2008. "Be Gentle with Me (I'm Not as Young as I Was)", blog entry. www.echoditto.com/blog/be-gentle-me-i%E2%80%99m-not-young-i-was

2. George Weiner, Huffington Post, December 7, 2009. "Will You Marry Me? What Non-for-Profits Get Wrong on the Web", blog entry. www.huffingtonpost.com/george-weiner/will-you-marry-me-what-no_b_383216.html.

3. These names have been fictionalized.

PART 5

1. Giving USA's 2009 annual report of philanthropic gifts to nonprofits.

CHAPTER 18

1. Giving USA (2009), www.givingusa.org.

2. Barbara R. Levy and R.L. Cherry, Association of Fundraising Professionals. The AFP Fundraising Dictionary: www.afpnet.org//ResourceCenter/ ArticleDetail.cfm?ItemNumber=3380. Page 54. Original edition: The NSFRE Fund Raising Dictionary. San Francisco: Wiley, 1996.

CHAPTER 22

1. Mark Zuckerberg, Facebook, February 4, 2010. "Six Years of Making Connections", blog entry. www.blog.facebook.com/blog.php?post =287542162130.

2. Wikipedia, www.en.wikipedia.org/wiki/RSS. Retrieved December 6, 2010. This page was last modified on 28 November 2010 at 01:23.

3. The CAN-SPAM Act: A Compliance Guide for Business, www.ftc.gov/bcp/ edu/pubs/business/ecommerce/bus61.shtm.

4. About.com, a part of the New York Times Company. © 2010, retrieved December 6, 2010. Definition of "Double Opt-in", www.email.about.com/ library/glossary/bldef_double_opt-in.htm.

5. Timothy Seiler. Roadmap to Fundraising Success, www.philanthropy.iupui .edu/TheFundRaisingSchool/PrecourseReadings/roadmap_to_fundraising _success.aspx. Copyright © 2010 The Center on Philanthropy at Indiana University. The Center is a part of the Indiana University School of Liberal Arts at Indiana University-Purdue University Indianapolis. Retrieved December 6, 2010.

6. The Salvation Army Western Territory is comprised of the 13 western states as well as the Marshall Islands, Guam, and Micronesia. The territory has more than 300 corps community centers (churches) and numerous social service units.

PART 7

1. Corporation for National and Community Service. "Issue Brief: Volunteer Growth in America: A Review of Trends Since 1974." December 2006. www.nationalservice.gov/pdf/06_1203_volunteer_growth_factsheet.pdf.

2. Corporation for National and Community Service, Office of Research and Policy Development. The Health Benefits of Volunteering: A Review of Recent Research, Washington, DC 2007. www.nationalservice.gov/pdf/07_0506_hbr.pdf.

CHAPTER 30

1. Jeanne Bell et al., <u>Daring to Lead 2006: A National Study of Nonprofit Executive Leadership</u>, CompassPoint Nonprofit Services and The Meyer Foundation, 9.

2. Richard T. Ingram, <u>Ten Basic Responsibilities of Nonprofit Boards, 2nd ed.</u>, (Washington, DC: BoardSource, 2009).

3. Lakey, Berit M. <u>Nonprofit Governance: Steering Your Organization with Authority and Accountability</u> (Washington, DC: BoardSource, 2000).

4. BoardSource, <u>Nonprofit Governance Index 2010</u>, 19 (Washington, DC: Boardsource 2007).

5. Vernetta Walker, "Beyond Political Correctness: Building a Diverse Board," <u>Board Member</u> (May/June 2009, Volume 18, Issue 3).

6. BoardSource, <u>Nonprofit Governance Index 2010</u>, 27 (Washington, DC: Boardsource 2010).

7. Adapted excerpt from Jason Drucker, "The Art of Founding an Inclusive Board," <u>Board Member</u> (November/December 2008, Volume 17, Issue 6).

8. Berit M. Lakey, <u>The Board Building Cycle, 2nd ed.: Nine Steps to Finding, Recruiting, and Engaging Nonprofit Board Members</u> (Washington, DC: BoardSource, 2007).

9. For more information, a White Paper on Consent Agendas ("The Consent Agenda: A Tool for Improving Governance") is available from www.boardsource.org.

CHAPTER 33

1. Cynthia Gibson, <u>The Leadership Ladder: Fostering Volunteer Engagement and Leadership at New York Cares</u>, (New York: Baruch College Survey Research Unit, 2009) www.newyorkcares.org/news_events/leadership _ladder.php.

2. David C. McClelland, "Methods of Measuring Human Motivation", in John W. Atkinson, ed., <u>The Achieving Society</u> (Princeton, NJ: Van Nostrand, 1961), 41–43.

CLOSING THOUGHTS

1. Marianne Williamson, <u>A Return to Love: Reflections on the Principles of "A Course in Miracles."</u> (New York: Harper Collins, 1992).

NAME INDEX

A

Adkins, Sue, 386
Ahern, Tom, 456
Aldous, Jay, 373, 385
Alexander, Bryan, 442
Allison, Michael, 65, 74
Amidei, Nancy, 196
Andresen, Katya, 341, 354, 456
Anning, Douglas A., 179
Armstrong, Karen, 22
Arnold, Rebecca, 449–450
Arons, David, 194
Aubry, Rick, 389, 402
Avner, Marcia, 181, 193, 194
Axelrod, Terry, 476

B

Baldwin, Greg, 533
Barton, Clara, 11
Bechard, Richard, 38
Bedbury, Scott, 427
Beinhacker, Samantha L., 402
Bell, Jeanne, 63, 74, 234
Bornstein, David, 402
Bowen, William G., 39
Bravo, Britt, 444

Bregman, Matthew, 447
Brinckerhoff, Peter, 141, 149, 159
Brokaw, Tom, 150
Buddha, 22
Burk, Penelope, 307, 323, 453
Butler, Lawrence, 75

C

Campbell, Peter, 230
Carlson, Mim, 340
Carnegie, Andrew, 12
Carse, James, 24–25
Carson, Emmett D., 29, 38
Carver, John, 215
Carver, Miriam, 215
Chait, Richard P., 518
Chen, Lisa, 479, 491, 492
Chen, Nancy, 181, 193
Chomsky, Noam, 492
Clapp, Phil, 483
Clinton, Bill, 2
Cohen, Ben, 399
Collins, Jim, 50
Confucius, 22
Cortez, Alexander, 91
Cosby, Bill, 287, 520, 569
Costner, Kevin, 347

Covey, Franklin, 60
Covey, Stephen, 38
Cryer, Shelly, 41, 54

D

Dalai Lama, 575
Danaher, Kevin, 2
Darwin, Charles, 2
Davis, Pamela, 93, 104
Dees, J. Gregory, 323, 403
Dole, Elizabeth, 426
Dropkin, Murray, 215
Drucker, Jason, 510
Duncan, David James, 25
Durham, Sarah, 426

E

Earle, Richard, 386
Economy, Peter, 323, 403
Elkington, John, 402
Emerson, Jed, 323, 403

F

Fenichell, Stephen, 427
Fenton, David, 479, 491
Filipczak, Bob, 146
Foster, William, 91
Fox, Jeannie, 181, 193–194

G

Gammal, Denise L., 92
Gandhi, Mahatma, 575, 576
Gates, Bill, 219
Geier, Philip H., Jr., 237
Gladwell, Malcolm, 492

Glavin, Robert, 5, 20
Godin, Seth, 40, 347
Goethe, 57
Goldsmith, Marshall, 38
Goldsmith, Richard, 553
Goodall, Jane, 24
Goodman, Andy, 426, 443
Gore, Al, 495
Grace, Kay Sprinkel, 309, 320, 322, 323, 324, 523
Greco, David, 197
Greenfield, James M., 237
Gross, Virginia C., 165, 178, 179
Grossman, Allen, 395
Gunn, Allen, 254

H

Handy, Charles, 38
Harmon, Elliot, 239, 254
Harold, Franklin, 27
Harrington, Robert, 77, 90
Hart, Ted, 237
Hartigan, Pamela, 402
Hawken, Paul, 21, 28
Heard, Emily, 501, 517
Heath, Chip, 426, 451
Heath, Dan, 426, 451
Heifitz, Ronald A., 39
Hendler, Kimberly, 41, 53
Herman, Edward S., 492
Hernandez, Manny, 268
Hesselbein, Frances, 38
Hicks, Kathy, 159
Hicks, Rick, 159
Higman, Rebecca Ruby, 341, 354–355
Hillel, Rabbi, 22
Hochstadt, Zach, 409, 426
Hodgkinson, Virginia A., 39

Hoffman, Michael, 443
Hollister, Robert M., 39
Holmgren, Marika, 459, 476
Hopkins, Bruce R., 165, 177–178, 178, 179
Horrigan, John B., 141
Hyman, Vincent L., 149, 159

J

Jeremiah, 22, 24
Jibrell, Sandi Brock, 338
Joyaux, S. P., 307

K

Kanter, Beth, 271, 429, 442
Kanter, Rosabeth, 38
Kaufman, Pat, 38
Kaye, Jude, 65, 74
Keller, Helen, 27
Kim, Helen, 145
King, Martin Luther, Jr., 24, 59, 573, 575
Komen, Susan G., 377, 380
Kouzes, James M., 39
Kunreuther, Frances, 145

L

La Piana, David, 63, 75, 77, 89, 90
Lakoff, George, 481, 492
Lancaster, Lynne C., 146
Lao-tzu, 22
Lawrence, T. E., 58
Lear, Norman, 426
Lehman, Ann, 531, 532
Lencioni, Patrick, 38

Levine, Alan, 442, 444
Levine, Allison, 237
Linsky, Marty, 39

M

Maathai, Wangari, 24
MacArthur, Gina, 454
McKibben, Bill, 24
MacLaughlin, Steve, 237
McLaughlin, Thomas A., 90, 214
McManus, Andrea, 291, 307
Mandela, Nelson, 573
Martin, Carolyn, 159
Masaoka, Jan, 74
Massarsky, Cynthia W., 402
Matthews, Chris, 482
Maxwell, John, 157
Meadows, Donella, 24
Mehta, Nayantara, 181, 193
Mencius, 22
Miller, Clara, 215, 216
Miller, Kivi Leroux, 355, 445, 455, 456
Milway, Katie Smith, 91
Mirabella, Roseanne, 55–56
Moses, Susan, 160

N

Nemani, Arun, 3
Noble, Nicci, 357, 370
Nordhaus, Ted, 570
Nunn, Michelle, 551, 566

O

O'Connell, Brian, 39
Oliver, Mary, 27

O'Neal-McElrath, Tori, 325, 339, 340
Oster, Sharon M., 394, 402

P

Pallotta, Dan, 215
Perry, G., 307
Phalen, Lane, 452
Plato, 22
Podolsky, Joni, 238
Porter, Michael, 391
Portis, Carrie, 398
Posner, Barry Z., 39
Pouillon, Nora, 484
Pringle, Hamish, 386
Purcell, Joan, 451

R

Raines, Claire, 146
Ralser, Tom, 323
Ries, Al., 405
Rodriguez, Robby, 145
Ross, Bernard, 532
Ross, Holly, 221, 236, 237
Rosso, Henry A., 287, 323, 361
Ryan, Bill, 218

S

Sage, Margaret Olivia Slocum, 12
Salls, Manda, 160
Scarano, Cassie, 107
Schenkelberg, Thomas J., 179
Schuller, Robert H., 1
Seiler, Timothy, 365
Senge, Peter, 38
Shaw, George Bernard, 569
Shellenberger, Michael, 570

Smucker, Bob, 194
Socrates, 22
Solomon, Joe, 257, 271
Stern, Andy, 163
Stillman, David, 146
Stockman, Laura, 406
Streep, Meryl, 486
Sullivan, Sean, 357, 370
Suzuki, David, 24

T

Tagore, Rabindranath, 161
Teresa, Mother, 573, 575
Thompson, Marjorie, 386
Thoreau, Henry David, 59
Tocqueville, Alexis de, 534
Top, Peleg, 386, 427
Tulgan, Bruce, 159
Tutu, Archbishop Desmond, 306, 575
Twist, Lynne, 290, 476, 570, 573, 577

V

Verclas, Katrin, 237

W

Walden, Gwen, 325
Waldron, Rob, 398
Walker, Vernetta, 501, 516
Ward, Amy Sample, 268
Warnow, Jonathan, 257, 271
Warwick, Mal, 324
Watson, Michael, 127, 145
Watson, Tom, 255
Weinberg, James, 107, 123
Weiner, George, 241
Weiner, Robert, 371

Wendroff, Alan, 320, 323
Westen, Drew, 481, 492
Wetmore, Cindy, 38
Whaley, Paul, 453
Williamson, Marianne, 571
Wilson, Tim, 223, 231
Winfrey, Oprah, 487
Winton, Jennie, 409, 425–426
Witter, Lisa, 492
Wright, Steve, 273

Y

Young, Dennis R., 39
Yunus, Muhammad, 403

Z

Zemke, Ron, 146
Zimmerman, Robert M., 514, 519, 531, 532
Zimmerman, Steve, 74

Page references followed by *fig* indicate an illustrated figure; followed by *e* indicate an exhibit; followed by *t* indicate a table.

A

The AAA Way to Fundraising Success: Maximum Involvement, Maximum Results (Grace), 324

Ability Magazine, 147

About.com's Fundraising Essentials, 308

Accident insurance, 98

Achieving Excellence in Fund Raising (Rosso and Associates), 323

ACRJ's Movement Building Indicators, 196

Advertising, 485

Advocacy: using coalitions for, 185–186; Constituent Relationship Management (CRM) used for, 277–279; differentiating between lobbying and, 187; Hmong Health Collaborative (HHC) case study on, 191–192; media role in, 183*fig*, 186; no partisan rule for nonprofit, 189; nonprofit expertise as benefiting, 182–183; planning for, 190; questions to begin planning, 183–185; resources on, 194–196; rules governing 501(c)(3) organizations and, 186–187; triangle diagram representing nonprofit role ink, 183*fig*. *See also* Lobbying

AFP, 50

Age differences: characteristics of generational and, 140–141; Nonprofit Diversity Analysis Matrix on, 130*t*; nonprofit volunteer analysis by, 133*t*; people with disabilities and, 142; U.S. population by selected age groups, 140*fig*

Ageism, 33

Aging populations: increasing disabilities associated with, 142; social issues related to, 16; U.S. population percentage of, 142*fig*; volunteerism health benefits for, 500, 536

The Agitator blog, 340

Alar campaign, 487

Alliance for Justice (AFJ), 188, 194

Alliance for Nonprofit Management, 54

Alliance of Nonprofits for Insurance, 100, 104

AL!VE (Association of Leaders in Volunteer Engagement), 548

American Association of Grant Professionals (AAGP), 333, 335

American Demographics, 160

American Institute for Managing Diversity, 146

American Medical Association, 485

American nonprofits: diverse needs response by, 8–9; earned revenue of, 8–9; economic impact of, 9–10; 501(c)(3) nonprofits classification of, 2, 7–8, 9t; history of, 10–15; social impact of, 10; statistics on, 7t. *See also* Nonprofit organizations

American Red Cross, 11, 312, 412

Americans with Disabilities Act (1990), 142

Annual giving fundraising strategies, 297e–300e

Antivirus protection, 227

Apple, 241, 242*fig*

Apple pesticides boycott campaign, 486–487

Arrowhead Ranch, 449–450

The Art of Cause Marketing: How to Use Advertising to Change Personal Behavior and Public Policy (Earle), 386

Asian Communities for Reproductive Justice (ACRJ), 196

AspirationTech.org, 237

Association of Fundraising Professionals (AFP), 292, 307, 333

Auto insurance, 98

Axial Age: description and legacy of, 22; Golden Rule and spiritual teachings of, 22–23

B

B to the Y vision, 58, 61

Baby Boomers (Boomer Generation) [1946–1962]: characteristics of, 141; description of, 151; retirement of, 60; work-life balance of, 141–156

Backup devices, 227

Balance Sheet, 205–206

Believe in Zero call-to-action campaign (UNICEF), 378

Ben & Jerry's Ice Cream, 399

Beth's Blog, 371

Beyond Fundraising (Grace), 323

"Beyond Vietnam" (King speech), 24

Big Online USA, 339

Blackbaud/Target Analytics: Donor Centrics Internet Giving Benchmarking Analysis, 356

Blogging: different uses of nonprofit, 436–437; incorporating good conversation starters, 437–438; listening to your audience, 438; multiple author, 437

Blue Avocado, 517

Board committees, 505–506

Board fundraising: capacity investments form of, 521; case study on, 528–529; corporate grants solicitation form of, 525–526; dos and don'ts of, 530; event sponsorships and ticket sales form of, 527; individual donations form of, 526–527; key principles of, 522–524; major donor campaigns role as, 528; online and social networking solicitations form of, 527; by overseeing nonprofit's fundraising activities, 522; personal relationships and connections used for, 524; presence at fundraising meetings form of, 525; providing direct mail lists form of, 527; providing introductions as form of, 525; providing training for, 318–319, 514, 519–520; resources on, 531–532; set expectations/create culture for, 520; soliciting friends, relatives, colleagues as, 521–522; telephone solicitations form of, 527

Board fundraising principles: accentuate the positive, 524; fundraising from perspective donor, 523; getting people to ask, 523; people give to strong nonprofits, 523; people love to give away money, 524

Board governance: dos and don'ts of, 515–516; issues to consider for, 501–502; resources on, 517–518; role of committees in, 505–506; roles and responsibilities of, 502–504

Board matrix, 507–508*t*

Board meetings, 512–513

Board members: ability to give/get money criteria for selecting, 422; annual reviews of, 515; capacity investments by, 521; case study on fundraising by, 528–529; diversity of your, 130*t*, 134–135, 504, 508, 510–511; duty of care, duty of loyalty, and duty of obedience by, 503; executive directors (EDs) as "ex officio," 505; fundraising training for, 318–319, 514; "gold standard" of engaged, 176; orientation of, 511; recruitment of, 508–509; spectrum of engagement by, 496–497; term limits of, 511–512

The Board Member's Book (O'Connell), 39

Board Members Rule: How to be a Strategic Advocate for Your Nonprofit (Zimmerman and Lehman), 532

BoardNet USA, 517

Boards: annual reviews of, 515; CEO relationship with, 34–36; clear strategic planning roles of, 67–68; committees reporting to, 505–506; conflict-of-interest policy for, 515; consent agenda tool for, 498–499, 512; D&O insurance coverage of, 97; diversity of, 130*t*, 134–135, 504, 508, 510–511; enforcing organizational values, 32–33; executive director relationship with, 513–514; legal

compliance issues related to governance by, 175–176; leveraging high-opportunity network of, 499; officers of the, 505; Opportunity Agenda (OA) case study on inclusive, 510–511; power of intention by, 497–498; recruiting effective, 507; risk management role of, 101–103; size of, 504–505; staff relationship with, 514; tools and tactics to optimize your, 495–496. *See also* CEOs (chief executive officers); Leadership

Boards That Love Fundraising: A How-To Guide for Your Board (Zimmerman and Lehman), 531

BoardSource, 179, 502–503, 517

Bona Fide Occupational Qualifications (BFOQ), 112

Boomers, Xers, and Other Strangers: (Hicks and Hicks), 159

BOP (Business Owners Policy), 101

A Brand New World: Eight Principles for Achieving Brand Leadership in the 21st Century (Bedbury and Fenichell), 427

Brand Spirit: How Cause Related Marketing Builds Brands (Pringle and Thompson), 386

Brandraising: How Nonprofits Raise Visibility and Money Through Smart Communication (Durham), 426

Brandraising, 370

Brass Tacks Manager (Kaufman and Wetmore), 38

Bridgespan, 75

Bridgestar, 54, 517

Broadband Adoption and Use in America (Horrigan), 141

Broker (insurance), 100

Buddhism, 22

Budgets: event planning, 465–466; marketing plan for prioritizing your, 422–423*t*. *See also* Costs; Financial management

Building Social Business: (Yunus), 403

Burnout, 51

Business in the Community (UK), 386

Business intelligence, 282

C

California: Proposition 8, 367–368; Proposition 63, 280; "Three Strikes" law opponents in, 480; volunteerism rate in, 500

CAN-SPAM Act, 362–363, 369

Canadian Environmental Assessment Agency (CEAA), 278

Candidate Assessment Form: Program Director, 112*e*

Candidates: attracting and selecting great, 113–114; creating pool of, 115; legal guidelines for screening/hiring, 112–113; numbers to expect in metropolitan area, 118*e*; offer negotiation and hiring, 120; planning the hiring process for, 111–112*e*; reference and background checking, 118; screening for quality, 115–120. *See also* Human capital management; Staff

Capacity investments, 521

Carnegie Corporation of New York, 12

Cascading style sheets (SCC), 248

The Case Flow Management Book for Nonprofits: (Dropkin), 215

Case studies: board fundraising, 528–529; cultural integration in merger, 86–87; East Bay Music Collective (EBMC) web design, 251–252; Enterprise Community Partners, 351–353; Equality California (EQCA), 367–368; Family Service Agency (FSA) use of CRM, 279–281; Girl Scouts outreach for diversity, 143; Hmong Health Collaborative (HHC) advocacy, 191–192; Huntington Beach Public Library volunteer recruitment, 545–546; Hurricane Katrina online fundraising, 366–367; lesson on what not to do when grant seeking, 336–337; No Tankers campaign facilitated by CRM, 277–279; Opportunity Agenda (OA) inclusive board, 510–511

Cause Effective Perspective, 308

Cause Marketing Forum, 385

Cause Related Marketing (Adkins), 386

Cause-related marketing: definition of, 373; dos and don'ts of, 384; five truths about, 377–384; legal compliance of, 381; profitability issue of, 375–376; resources on, 385–387; sustainability of, 377; three forms and evolution of, 374–375

Cause-related marketing truths: both business and nonprofit must benefit, 382; it takes time, 380–381; its about more than money, 377–379; must result in measurable mission impact, 383; success is built on establishing clear objectives, 379–380

Center for Civil and Human Rights (Atlanta), 556

Center for Digital Storytelling, 442

Center for Lobbying in the Public Interest (CLPI), 195

Center on Philanthropy, 361

CEOs (chief executive officers): actions taken to support diversity, 139; cultural integration in merger role of, 86–87; enforcing the organization's values, 31–32; importance of board relationship with, 34–36; legal compliance issues related to governance by, 175–176; listening skills of, 36–37. *See also* Boards; Executive directors (EDs); Leadership

Change: maximization of, 59–60; social entrepreneurship for creating, 17–18; social prophets to bring about, 573–577

Charitable giving: benefits of focusing on individual, 311–324; examining the motivations behind individual, 310–311; major gifts, 300*e*–303*e*, 528; statistics on annual 2009, 291–292, 309–310. *See also* Donors; Fundraising

Chi (energy), 162

Children's Miracle Network, 377

Christianity: hostile takeover by fundamentalists, 25–26; origins of, 22

The Chronicle of Philanthropy, 54, 288, 308, 324, 339, 517, 532

Civil Rights Act (1964), 128

Civil War, 11

Classifications of Revenue: permanently restricted revenue, 202; temporarily restricted revenue, 201–202; unrestricted revenue, 201

Cleveland Foundation, 13

Cleveland, Jonathan, 386, 427

Collaboration: cross-sector partnerships for, 17; leadership as following, 2–3; Partnership Matrix on, 78*fig*–79. *See also* Partnerships; Strategic restructuring

The Collaboration Prize—Nonprofit Collaboration Database (The Lodestar Foundation), 91

Commongood Careers Knowledge Center, 123–124

Communication: of "crisitunity" opportunities, 267; generational differences in preferences, 141; generational techspectations for, 154–155; listening component of, 36–37, 438; listening skills component of, 36–37; newsletter, 445–457; nonprofit financial "story," 210–211; skills and competences for, 49; storytelling, 348–349, 430–444, 480–481, 483–484

Communication technologies: Constituent Relationship Management (CRM), 273–285; dos and don'ts on, 235; individual giving fundraising through, 312–313; marketing role of, 405–407; resources on, 236–238; skills and competences required for, 222–235; trends and impacts of, 17. *See also* Social networks media; Technology; Web design

The Communicators Network, 493

The Community Chest, 13

Compensation: appropriate, 120–121; standard annual salary adjustments, 121<u>t</u>

Competency model: building a, 108–110; for specific staff positions, 110*t*

Competitive advantage: creating marketing plan to promote your, 414–419; description of, 391; marketing to establish your, 411–414; social enterprise, 398–399

Computers: laptops, 225; other hardware in addition to, 226; questions for selecting, 224–225; security-related issues, 226–228. *See also* Software

Conflict-of-interest policy, 515

Confucianism, 22

Connections. *See* Relationships

Consent agenda, 52, 498–499

Constituent Relationship Management (CRM): business intelligence facilitated by, 282; description and benefits of, 273–274; dos and don'ts of using, 282–283; FSA program management case study on using, 279–281; how to use, 274–275; managing contacts and communications using, 275–276; online advocacy and No Tankers campaign case study on, 277–279; outreach campaigns managed using, 276–277; resources on using, 284–285; user adoption of, 281–282

Content management system (CMS), 248–250

Contributed income, 19

Convio: Nonprofit Online Benchmark Study, 356

Corporate grants: board role in getting, 525–526; grant writing for, 333–335; seeking, 325–340

Corporation for National and Community Service, 548

Costs: assessing if surpluses are sufficient to meet, 205; Balance Sheet on, 205–206; event planning, 466–467; items included to calculate "full," 205; operating activities, 204; Statement of Activities on, 199–200t, 203–205; understanding dynamics of, 203–204. *See also* Budgets; Financial management; Revenues

Council for Certification in Volunteer Administration (CCVA), 548

Craigslist Foundation, 290, 499

craigslist.org, 219

"Crisitunity" opportunities, 367

Cross-sector partnerships, 17

Cultural and racial composition. *See* Diversity

Cure-Yoplait partnership, 380

D

D&O (Directors & Officers) insurance, 97, 515

Dashboards: components of, 71, 72t; strategic planning using, 71; technological, 234–235

"The Death of Environmentalism" (Shellenberger and Nordhaus), 570

Delegating, 34

Designing for the Greater Good: (Top and Cleveland), 386, 427

"Digital natives," 141

Direct mail, 527

Disability Statistics, 146

Discovery Program (Hands On Atlanta), 553, 556

Disqualified person, 173

Diversity: actions by CEOs to support, 139; actions emerging leaders can take to support, 139; cultural and racial composition, 16; definition of, 128; definitions related to, 140fig–142fig; dos and don'ts of, 144; of employed staff members, 129–132; ensuring that your nonprofit is serving everyone, 133–134; Girl Scouts outreach to increase membership, 143; historic roots of workplace, 127–128; insights about, 135–137; integrating into your organization, 129–135; keeping up with trends of, 139–140; legal issues related to, 128; Nonprofit Diversity Analysis Matrix, 130t; resources on, 145–147; of volunteers, 132–133t; of your board,

130*t*, 134–135, 504, 508, 510–511. *See also* Ethnicity; Race

Diversity Executive Magazine, 146

Diversity Inc. Magazine, 146

Diversity plan: guide for creating successful, 137–139; making the case for diversity, 136–137

Do More Than Give campaign (Salvation Army), 367

Doctors Without Borders/Médecins Sans Frontišres, 409–410

Dogwood Initiative (DI) case study, 277–279

Donate button, 348

Donor stewardship relationships, 319–320

Donor-Centered Fundraising (Burk), 323, 453

Donors: converting into fundraisers, 363–364; fundraising from perspective of, 523; individual giving by, 309–324, 526–527; stewardship relationships with, 319–320. *See also* Charitable giving; Fundraising; Relationships

Don't Think of an Elephant (Lakoff), 481, 492

DoSomething.org, 241

Duke University, 403

Duty of care, 503

Duty of loyalty, 503

Duty of obedience, 503

E

e-Volunteerism, 567

Earned income: statistics on American nonprofit, 8–9; trends and implications of, 19

East Bay Music Collective (EBMC) web design, 251–252

Economic pressures, 15

Elevator speech, 317

Email fundraising: CAN-SPAM Act governing, 362–363, 369; Google Alerts for, 545; seven golden rules of, 362–363; steps for successful, 350–351

Emerging Practitioners in Philanthropy (ePIP), 56

Employee benefits liability, 99

Employee dishonesty insurance, 99

Energize Inc., 549, 567

Enridge Inc., 278

Enterprise Community Partners case study, 351–353

Enterprising Nonprofits: A Toolkit for Social Entrepreneurs (Dees, Emerson, and Economy), 403

Equality California (EQCA) case study, 367–368

Ethnicity: sample Nonprofit Diversity Analysis Matrix on, 130*t*; U.S. population by, 140*fig*. *See also* Diversity

Event planning: board role in, 527; committees for, 469–470; creating a budget, 465–466; creating and managing a time line, 470*t*–471; dos and don'ts for, 475; evaluating your resources, 463–465; evaluating/debriefing, 473–474; expenses and in-kind, 466–467; golden rules for success, 471–473; income and revenue streams, 467–468; issues to consider for, 459; managing expectations, 465; resources on, 476–477; risk management, 468–469; setting goals, 461–462; what it takes to make a great, 460–461

Event planning rules: the curtain rule, 471–472; don't expect perfection/do expect perfect troubleshooting, 472–473; no assumptions, 471; remember that you are part of a team, 472; start the day with nothing left to do, 471

Excess benefit transaction, 173–174

Executive assistant competency model, 110t

Executive directors (EDs): competency models for, 110t; description of, 35; as "ex officio" board member, 505; "ex officio" position of, 175–176; legal compliance issues related to governance by, 175–176; relationship with board, 513–514. *See also* CEOs (chief executive officers)

F

Facebook, 260t–261, 359, 360, 542

Family Service Agency (FSA) case study, 279–281

Fast Company Magazine, 403

Fax machine, 226

Federal Trade Commission, 362

FEMA (Federal Emergency Management Association), 412

Feng Shui, 161

Fenton website, 493

Fidelity Charitable Gift Fund, 536

Fidelity (or employee dishonesty) insurance, 99

"50 Ways to Tell a Story" (Levine), 444

Financial management: assessing how leveraged the nonprofit is, 208; assessing if agency saving is sufficient, 205–206; Balance Sheet used for, 205–206; communicating your financial story, 210–211; Constituent Relationship Management (CRM) used for, 276–277; debate over nonprofit as a business, 198; distribution of assets, 206, 208; dos and don'ts of, 212; five steps to mastering

nonprofit, 198–199, 203–205; importance of understanding, 197–198; items included to calculate "full cost," 205; liquidity of nonprofits, 208, 209; "Months of Cash" measurement of, 208–209; Net Assets, 205, 208, 209–210t; resources on nonprofit, 214–216; restrictions on use of funds, 201–203; skills and competences for, 49; Statement of Activities used for, 199–200t, 203–205; tips for effective, 212–214. *See also* Budgets; Costs; Managing/management; Revenues

Finite games, 25

Fired-Up Fundraising (Perry), 307

Firewall, 226–227

Fisk University, 11

The Five Temptations of a CEO (Lencioni), 38

501(c)(3) nonprofits: categories of, 9t; joint ventures of, 170–171; legal limits on lobbying at, 187–189; legislative activities/political campaign activities by, 169; no partisan political activities allowed by, 189; organizational test of, 167; public benefit organizations classification of, 2, 7–8; rules governing advocacy and lobbying by, 186–187; subsidiaries belonging to, 170; which insure other nonprofits, 100. *See also* Legal compliance; Nonprofit organizations; Tax-exempt organizations

501(c)(4) nonprofits, 169, 188

501(c)(5) nonprofits, 188

501(c)(6) nonprofits, 169, 188

501(h) expenditure test, 188

Flickr, 438–439

Follow-up interviews, 117–118

Ford Motors, 377

Form 990, 174, 515

Form 990-EZ, 175

Form 990-N, 175

Form 990-PF, 174

Forum of Regional Associations of Grant Makers, 339

The Foundation Center, 50, 339, 386

Foundation Center, 308

Foundations: grant seeking from, 325–340; private, 171

FoundationSearch America, 339

14th Amendment, 127

"Friend raising" online fundraising, 364–365

Frog Loop, 427

The Fund Raising School, 361

Fundraising: board, 318–319, 514, 519–532; dos and don'ts of, 305–306; "go big, or go home" story on, 288–289; Haitian earthquake fundraising (2010), 312; half full or half empty story applied to, 287–288; hindsight perspective of effective, 303–305; Hurricane Katrina case study on online, 366–367; identifying your best strategies for, 296–303e; individual giving, 311–324; online, 341–356, 527; online peer-to-peer, 357–372; resources on, 307–308; six key fundraising principles of, 294–296; skills and competences for, 49. *See also* Charitable giving; Donors

The Fundraising Beat blog, 307

Fundraising Campaign in a Box, 355

Fundraising Dictionary Online, 292

Fundraising strategies: annual giving, 297e–300e; major gifts, 300e–303e

Fundraising When Money Is Tight (Warwick), 324

Fundraising123.org, 456

Future Fundraising Now, 340

Future trends/implications: aging population, 16; communication technologies, 17; contributed income, 19; cross-sector partnerships, 17; cultural and racial composition, 16; earned income issue, 19; economic pressures, 15; focus on results, 18; global concerns, 16; scrutiny and transparency, 18; social entrepreneurship, 17–18

G

GAO (Government Accounting Office), 9–10

Gen@ (GenY or Millenials), 60, 152–153, 155, 156

Generating and Sustaining Nonprofit Earned Income: (Oster, Massarsky, and Beinhacker), 394, 402

Generation X (1963–1980), 60, 152, 156

Generational differences: Boomer Generation (Baby Boomers) [1946–1962], 60, 141, 151, 155–156; Gen@, GenY, Millenials (1981–2002), 60, 152–153, 155, 156; Generation X (1963–1980), 60, 152, 156; Greatest Generation (1901–1924), 150; issues to consider for, 149–150; leadership sensitivity to, 154–155; remember the cultural differences of, 153–155; resources on, 159–160; Silent Generation (1925–1945), 151; work-life balance rules for, 141, 155–157

Generational diversity: characteristics of, 140–141; Nonprofit Diversity Analysis Matrix on, 130t; nonprofit volunteer analysis by, 133t; people with disabilities and, 142; U.S. population by selected age groups, 140fig

Generational leadership: dos and don'ts for, 158; leading across the generational divide of, 157; remember the cultural differences of generations, 153–155; resources on, 159–160; sensitivity to generational differences, 154–155

Generations: The Challenge of a Lifetime for Your Nonprofit, 154

Generations at Work: (Zemke, Raines, and Filipczak), 146

Geneva Conventions, 25

GenY (Millennials), 141

Girl Scouts, 143

Giving USA Foundation, 291, 309

Global concerns, 16

Global social networks, 261–262

Golden Rule, 3, 22–23, 24

Google, 477, 487

Google Alerts, 545

Google Grants, 379, 406, 422

Governance: board, 501–518; legal compliance issues related to, 175–176

The Governance of Financial Management, Revised and Updated (Carver and Carver), 215

Governance as Leadership: Reframing the Work of Nonprofit Boards (Chait), 518

Governing, Leading and Managing Nonprofit Organizations (Young, Hollister, Hodgkinson, and Associates), 39

Government: nonprofit and historic role of, 13–15; variations of HR laws of individual state, 162–163. *See also* Internal Revenue Service (IRS); Legal compliance

Grant Professionals Association, 333, 340

Grant seeking: board role in, 525–526; case study on what not to do, 336–337; clearly stating your case, 329–330; dos and don'ts, 337; evaluating your organization's capacity to deliver, 330–331; highlighting your organization's unique background, 331; identifying foundations aligning with your mission, 326–329; include a theory of change in, 327; issues to consider for, 325–326; Letter of Intent (LOL), 327, 329, 331, 332; relationship as key to successful, 335, 336–337, 338; resources on, 339–340; stick to the basics, 331–332; writing the grant, 333–335

Grant writing: costs of writing services for, 334–335; deciding who will do the, 333; outsourcing the, 333–334

The Grantsmanship Center, 340

Grassroots Fundraising Journal, 340, 476

Great Depression (1930s), 13, 150

"Great Expectations: Boomers and the Future of Volunteering" study, 496

Great Society (1960s), 14

The Great Transformation (Armstrong), 22

Greatest Generation (1901–1924), 150

GreatNonprofits.org, 545

Green Meeting Industry Council, 476

Greyston Foundation, 399

GuideStar, 55, 124

Gulf War, 25

H

Habitat for Humanity-Whirlpool partnership, 380

Haitian earthquake fundraising (2010), 312

Hands On Atlanta, 553–554, 556–557, 561

HandsOn Network, 556, 564, 566

Health insurance, 99

Here Comes the Guide, 476

"Hidden in Plain Sight: Understanding Nonprofit Capital Structure" (Miller), 216

High Impact Philanthropy (Grace and Wendroff), 320, 323

Hinduism, 22

Hiring procedures. See Human capital management

Hmong Health Collaborative (HHC) advocacy, 191–192

"How Nonprofits Can Get the Most out of Flickr" (Kanter), 442

How Nonprofits Can Use Social Media (Beth's Blog), 371

How to Blog (Kanter), 442

How to Change the World (Bornstein), 402

Howard University, 12

HR.com, 124

HTML language, 247, 440

Human capital management: attracting and selecting great people, 113–114; building competency model for hiring, 108–110t; compensating staff, 120–122; dos and don'ts for, 122; ensuring legal compliance, 112–113; generating a candidate pool, 115; planning the hiring process, 111–112e; resources on, 123–125; screening for quality, 115–120. See also Candidates; Staff

Humility, 50

Huntington Beach Public Library case study, 545–546

Hurricane Katrina online fundraising case study, 366–367

I

Idealist Volunteer Management Resource Center, 568

Idealist/Action Without Borders, 55

Idealist.org, 124, 548

Idealist's Tools for Nonprofits, 308

idealware.org, 228, 229, 236

Improper sexual contact insurance, 98

Individual giving: benefits of fundraising focus on, 311–312; board role in, 526–527; building relationships for, 316–317; donor stewardship relationship for, 319–320; dos and don'ts of, 321; fundraising toolkit for, 317–318; motivations behind, 310–312; resources on, 323–324; securing and stewarding recurring, 313–315; social media vehicle of, 312–313; statistics on 2009, 309–310; training board and volunteers for, 318–319, 514

Infinite games, 25

The Influential Fundraiser: (Ross), 532

Information architecture, 245–246

Initial in-person interview, 117

Inside the Boardroom: Governance by Directors and Trustees (Bowen), 39

Insurance: D&O (Directors and Officers), 97, 515; health insurance, 99; importance to nonprofit sustainability, 93; purchasing, 99–101; Worker's Compensation, 99. See also Risk management

Insurance broker, 100

Insurance coverage: accident insurance, 98; BOP (Business Owners Policy), 101; business auto, 98; D&O (Directors and Officers), 97, 515; employee benefits liability, 99; fidelity or employee dishonesty, 99; general liability, 97; improper sexual contact, 98; limits of, 99; non-owned/hired auto liability, 98; periodic review of, 102–103; property, 98; social service professional, 98; types of risks and, 74, 95t–96t; Umbrella, 98; understanding your policy and, 101

Intermediate sanction rules, 173–174

Internal Revenue Service (IRS): filing and disclosure requirements of, 174–175; Forms 990, 990-PF, 990-EZ, 990-N, 174–175, 515; legal definition of nonprofit organizations, 166–167; official website of, 178; on private benefit doctrine, 168–169; on private inurement doctrine, 168; rebuttable presumption of reasonableness shifting burden of proof on, 174; reporting on nonprofit revenues (1998–2008), 14; on UBIT (unrelated business income tax), 169–170. See also Government

Internet Management for Nonprofits: Strategies, Tools, and Trade Secrets (Hart, Greenfield, MacLaughlin, and Geier), 237

Interviews: effective questions for, 119t; follow-up, 117–118; initial in-person, 117; phone, 116–117

Islam, 22

IT (information technology). See Communication technologies; Technology

J

"Jack in the Box" E. coli poisoning, 483

James P. Shannon Leadership Institute, 55

Javits-Wagner-O'Day Act, 398

Jeremiad (recitation of woes), 24

JFFixler Group, 549

Joint venture tax issues, 170–171

Judaism, 22

K

Katya's Nonprofit Marketing Blog, 427

L

La Piana Consulting, 89

Ladder career path, 45–46

Laptops, 225

Lattice career path, 46

Law issues. See Legal compliance

The Leader of the Future (Hesselbein, Goldsmith, and Bechard), 38

Leaders: awareness of racism, sexism, and ageism, 33; delegation by, 34; enforcing organizational values, 31–33; listening skills of, 36–37; understanding the big picture, 4; volunteer, 560–561

Leadership: critical skills and competencies of, 30–37; dos and don'ts of, 37; enforcing organizational values, 31–33; as following collaboration, 2–3; importance for nonprofit success, 29–30; partnerships and roles of, 84–85; resource review on nonprofit, 38–40; sensitivity to generational differences, 154–155; social enterprise and required, 396–398; tips for effective financial management by, 212–214; volunteer, 560–561. See also Boards; CEOs (chief executive officers)

The Leadership Challenge (Kouzes and Posner), 39

Leadership development: for building a sustainable career, 50–51; critical nonprofit career skills/competencies for, 43–45; in the diverse nonprofit sector,

42–43; networking dos and don'ts, 52; nonprofit career paths for, 45–47; personal and professional, 47–49; of "universal" nonprofit sector skills, 49–50

The Leadership Ladder:, 567

Leadership on the Line (Heifitz and Linsky), 39

Leadership skills/competences: CEO-board relationship and success, 34–36; good leaders are good listeners, 36–37; leaders delegate and managers manage, 34; leadership style matching the circumstances, 31; passion motivates people, 34; understanding racism, sexism, and ageism, 33; values guiding your leadership, 31–33

Leadership style, 31

Leading IT Transformation: The Roadmap to Success, 237

Legal compliance: Americans with Disabilities Act (1990), 142; CAN-SPAM Act, 362–363, 369; cause-related marketing, 381; defining nonprofit organizations for, 166–167; dos and don'ts of, 177; ensuring human capital management, 112; equal opportunity statement, 114; filing and disclosure requirements, 174–175; hiring practice guidelines, 113; intermediate sanction rules, 173–174; Javits-Wagner-O'Day Act, 398; joint ventures of nonprofits, 170–171; legislative and political campaign activities, 169; maintenance of tax-exempt status, 167; nonprofit governance and, 175–176; operational test, 168; organizational test, 167; private benefit doctrine, 168–169; private inurement doctrine, 168; resources on, 178–179; subsidiaries of nonprofits, 170; Title VII (Civil Rights Act), 128; UBIT (unrelated business income tax), 169–170; variations of state HR laws for, 162–163. See also 501(c)(3) nonprofits; Government

Legislative activities: legal limitations for, 169; understanding allowed advocacy and lobbying, 182–196, 277–279

Letter of Intent (LOL), 327, 329, 331, 332

Leveraged debt, 208

Liquidity: Months of Cash measurement of, 208–209; ULNA (Unrestricted Liquid Net Assets), 209; understanding your nonprofit, 208; unrestricted "liquid" Net Assets, 209–210t

Listening: blogging and role of, 438; developing skills for, 36–37

Listservs, 260t, 262

LLC (limited liability company), 171

Lobbying: differentiating between advocacy and, 187; 501(h) expenditure test on, 188; legal limits of 501(c)(3) nonprofit, 187–189; resources on, 194–196. See also Advocacy

The Lobbying and Advocacy Handbook for Nonprofit Organizations: (Avner), 194

Lodestar Foundation, 91

"The Looking Glass World of Nonprofit Money" (Miller), 215

M

M+R Strategies/NTEN: eNonprofit Benchmarks Study, 342, 356

M & R Strategic Services, 493

McClelland and Atkinson Motivational Theory, 559–560t

Made to Stick: Why Some Ideas Survive and Others Die (Heath and Heath), 426, 451

Major gifts campaigns: board role in, 528; fundraising strategies for, 300e–303e

Management services organization (MSOs), 79

Managing the Generational Mix: (Martin and Tulgan), 159

Managing Technology to Meet your Mission: A Strategic Guide for Nonprofit Leaders (Ross, Verclas, and Levine), 237

Managing Technology to Meet Your Mission: (Campbell), 230

Managing/management: description of, 34; human capital management, 111–125; risk, 95t–96t, 101–105, 468–469. See also Financial management

Mandel Center for Nonprofit Organizations at Case Western Reverse University, 91

Manufacturing Consent: The Political Economy of the Mass Media (Herman and Chomsky), 492

Marketing: communication technologies role in, 405–407; description and function of, 410–411; Doctors Without Borders/Médecins Sans FrontiŠres, 409–410; dos and don'ts of, 424–425; establishing competitive advantage through, 411–414; Google Grants for free advertising, 422; resources on, 426–427

Marketing plan: analyze your situation to create, 414–415; determine your audiences, 416–418; determine your strategies through brainstorming, 418–421; establish and prioritize your budget, 422–423t; establish your marketing goals, 415–416; establishing your metrics, 423–424; promoting competitive

advantage through, 414–419; sample cost/benefit analysis, 423t. See also Strategic planning

Media: cause-related marketing and role of, 378–379; public relations and, 480–493; seven rules for writing press release, 488. See also Social networks media

The Mercifully Brief, Real World Guide to . . . Raising More Money with Newsletters Than You Ever Thought Possible (Ahern), 456

"The Merger Proposal: Before You Say 'I Do'." (Gammal), 92

Mergers. See Strategic restructuring

"Merging Wisely" (La Piana), 90

Mighty Putty, 241, 242fig

Millenials (GenY), 141

The Minneapolis Foundation, 33

Mission: assessing software critical to, 229; cause-related marketing must result in impact on, 383; choosing online tools to fit with your, 259–260; grant seeking from foundations that align with your, 326–329; importance over technology, 222–223, 235; social enterprise focus on, 390; viewing technology as investment in meeting your, 223. See also Nonprofit organizations

Mission Minded, 426

Mission-Based Management Blog, 124

Mobile Active, 371

Monitor Institute, 403

Monkey bars career path, 46

Monotheistic Judaism, 22

"Months of Cash," 208–209

Moore's Law, 220

Moral Politics: (Lakoff), 492

Motivation: McClelland and Atkinson Motivational Theory, 559–560t; of online

fundraising donors, 346–347; passion as driving, 34; volunteer, 535–536
My Charity Connects Web 2.0 Glossary, 371

N

National Association of State Charity Officials, 179
National Center for Charitable Statistics, 340
National Climatic Data Center, 366
National Committee on Responsive Philanthropy (NCRP), 195
National Council of Nonprofits, 55, 532
National Environmental Trust, 483
National Service Resource Center, 556, 567
National Taxonomy of Exempt Entities (NTEE), 8
Natural Resources Defense Council, 486
The Nature Conservancy, 383
NBC alcohol advertising protest, 485
Needs assessment for volunteers, 537–538
Net Assets: assessing distribution of, 206, 208; composition of, 208; liquidity of, 208–210t; Statement of Activities on, 205; Statement of Financial Position on, 207t; ULNA (Unrestricted Liquid Net Assets), 209
NetSquared, 268–269
Network for Good, 355
Networking: career building through, 45; dos and don'ts of, 52. *See also* Relationships; Social networks media
The New Form 990: Law, Policy and Preparation (Hopkins, Anning, Gross, and Schenkelberg), 179
New Foundry Ventures, 402
The New York Times, 485

Newsletters: dos and don'ts for, 454–455; evolution of, 445–446; five critical elements of a successful, 446–454; focusing on the future, 448–449; focusing on how your readers' feel, 449–451; frequency of, 447–448; infused with more planning and less improv, 452–454; resources on, 456–457; storytelling approach used in, 450–451
The Next Generation of American Giving, 370
The Nieman Journalism Lab, 493
Ning, 260t, 262
"No Tankers" campaign case study, 277–279
"The Nonprofit Boom from the Boomers" (Salls and Moses), 160
The Nonprofit Career Guide: How to Land a Job That Makes a Difference, 55
Nonprofit Counsel (Hopkins), 178, 179
The Nonprofit Dashboard: A Tool for Tracking Progress (Butler), 75
Nonprofit Diversity Analysis Matrix, 130t
The Nonprofit Email Marketing Guide: 7 Steps to Better Email Fundraising & Communications, 355, 456
Nonprofit Finance Fund, 214
Nonprofit Governance: Law, Practices, & Trends (Hopkins and Gross), 178
Nonprofit Guidebook Series, 340
The Nonprofit Lobbying Guide (Smucker), 194–195
"Nonprofit M&A: More Than a Tool for Tough Times" (Cortex, Foster, and Milway), 91
Nonprofit Marketing Blog, 356
The Nonprofit Marketing Guide: (Miller and Andreason), 456
Nonprofit Marketing Guide.com, 356

Nonprofit Mergers and Alliances: A Strategic Planning Guide (McLaughlin), 90

The Nonprofit Mergers Workbook, Part I: (La Piana and Harrington), 90

The Nonprofit Mergers Workbook, Part II: (La Piana Associates), 90

Nonprofit movement: creating a social profit, 573; examining the underlying values of, 23–26; hopefulness for the future of, 27–28; nature of, 26–27; sacredness of all life value of, 24

Nonprofit organizations: creating a social profit, 573; dashboards of, 71–72t; future trends and implications for, 15–19; legal definition of, 166–167; reality check for, 2; serving the greater good, 571; six defining characteristics of, 6; social prophets of, 573–577; staff as the linchpin of, 60–61; strategic restructuring of, 77–92; values served by, 6–7, 23–26, 569–570. See also American nonprofits; 501(c)(3) nonprofits; Mission

The Nonprofit Quarterly, 75, 215, 216

Nonprofit sector career: building a sustainable, 50–51; career paths to develop, 45–47; critical skills and competencies to develop, 43–45; key resources on, 54–56; leadership development for, 42–43; networking dos and don'ts for, 52; personal and professional development, 47–49; "universal" skills for, 49–50

Nonprofit sector professionals: critical skills and competences of, 43–45; executive directors (EDs), 35, 110t, 175–176, 505, 513–514; origins and development of, 12–13; program director, 110t, 112e; taking charge of career, 41–56. See also Staff

Nonprofit Social Network Benchmark Report, 371

The Nonprofit Strategy Revolution: Real-Time Strategic Planning in a Rapid-Response World (La Piana), 75

The Nonprofit Strategy Revolution (La Piana), 63

Nonprofit Sustainability Making Strategic Decisions for Financial Viability (Bell, Masaoka, and Zimmerman), 74

Nonprofit Technology Conference, 237

Nonprofit Technology Network, 222

The Nonprofit Times, 518, 532

Nonprofit Workforce Coalition, 145

NonprofitExpert.com, 91

NonprofitMarketingGuide.com, 456

Nonprofits' Insurance Alliance of California (NIAC), 100, 104, 105

Nonprofits' Insurance Alliance Group, 97, 104–105

Nonprofits101.org, 308, 324, 356, 387, 403, 427, 457, 477, 493, 532, 549

North County Housing Coalition, 86–87

NRDC, 482

NTEN 501 Tech Clubs, 371

Nten.org, 229, 236

O

Offer negotiation/hiring, 120

Online community: best approaches for going viral, 265–266; choosing tools to fit your mission with, 259–260; creating goals for building, 258; dos and don'ts for building, 269–270; global social networks for, 261–262; locating your, 258–259; mobilizing for action, 266–268; NetSquared case study on, 268–269; resources on, 271–272; sample social network analysis for, 260*t*; steps for building an, 263–265; UtDiabetes case study on, 268. *See also* Relationships

The Online Fundraiser's Checklist, 355

Online fundraising: board role in, 527; CAN-SPAM Act compliance for, 362–363; checklist on essentials of, 343–346; donate button for, 348; dos and don'ts of, 353; email used for, 350–351, 362–363, 369, 545; Enterprise Community Partners case study on, 351–353; four questions for motivating, 346–347; key reasons for growing importance of, 342–343; making it easy and quick, 349–350; peer-to-peer, 357–372, 541; resources on, 355–356; storytelling to entice giving, 348–349. *See also* Websites

Online Fundraising Tools Checklist (Weiner), 371

Online gift processing map, 230*fig*

Online peer-to-peer fundraising: as being about relationships, 361; CAN-SPAM Act compliance for, 362–363, 369; converting donors into fundraisers through, 363–364; create an organizational cause and fan bases for, 360; dos and don'ts of, 369; email solicitation, 350–351, 362–363; Equality California (EQCA) case study on, 367–368; establish your online presence for, 359; "friend raising" approach to, 364–365; leverage personal social networks for, 360–361; resources on, 370–372; Salvation Army's Hurricane Katrina campaign, 366–367; same fundraising rules applying to, 361

Online Red Kettle campaign (Salvation Army), 367

OnPhilanthropy.com, 386

OpenSourceCMS, 254

Operational test, 168

Opportunity Agenda (OA) case study, 510–511

Organizational culture: underlying values of nonprofit, 6–7, 23–26, 569–570; values shaping, 31–33

Organizational test, 167

Osocio, 386

Ouellette and Associates Consulting, Inc., 237

OurSharedResources.org, 567

P

Pampers, 380

Pampers-UNICEF partnership, 380, 383

Panel on the Nonprofit Sector, 179

Partnership Matrix, 78*fig*–79

Partnerships: cause-related marketing types of, 373–387; critical skills and competences for, 84–85; dos and don'ts of strategic restructuring, 88; five things to know about, 84–85; management services organization (MSOs) form of, 79; Partnership Matrix on, 78*fig*–79; resources on, 90–92; self-assessing readiness for, 80–83; strategic restructuring case study on cultural integration of, 86–87. *See also* Collaboration

Passion, 34

Passwords (computer), 227

Peabody Fund, 11

The Peace Alliance, 571

Peer-to-peer fundraising. *See* Online peer-to-peer fundraising

People with disabilities: ADA (1990) protection of, 142; issues related to,

141–142; Javits-Wagner-O'Day Act promoting hiring of, 398; Nonprofit Diversity Analysis Matrix on, 130t

Personal development, 47–49

PESI Law and Accounting, 179

Pew Charitable Trusts, 484

Phone interview, 116–117

Physical security measures, 228

"Plant a Billion Trees" campaign, 383

Points of Light Institute, 549

The Political Brain: (Westen), 492

Political campaign activities, 169

The Political Mind: (Lakoff), 492

Political savvy/confidence, 50

Power of intention, 497–498

Power in Policy: (Arons), 194

Power to the Peaceful festival (San Francisco), 497

The Power of Unreasonable People (Elkington and Hartigan), 402

Practices for Good, 145

Praxis Project, 196

Press release writing, 488

"Principles for Good Governance and Ethical Practice" (Panel on the Nonprofit Sector), 179

Printers, 226

Prison MATCH, 451

Private benefit doctrine, 168–169

Private foundations, 171

Private inurement doctrine, 168

The Procrastinator's Guide to Year-end Fundraising, 355

Professionals for Nonprofits, 124

Program director: Candidate Assessment Form for, 112e; competency model for, 110t

Progressive Era, 12

Property insurance, 98

Proposition 8 (California), 367–368

Proposition 63 (California), 280

Public charities: description of, 171; institutions classified as, 172

Public relations: dos and don'ts for, 490; eight principles for, 480–487; frequently asked questions about, 489; resources on, 492–493; seven rules for writing press release, 488

Public relations principles: build relationships of trust with reporters, 482; don't let the opposition control the conversation, 485–487; harness influential messengers, 484; repeat yourself, 481; simplify your issue, 483–484; taking people where you want them to go, 481; tell unforgettable stories, 480–481; use advertising to make news, 485

Publically supported charities, 171–172

R

Rabbinical Judaism, 22

Race: sample Nonprofit Diversity Analysis Matrix on, 130fig; U.S. population by, 140fig. See also Diversity

Race for the Cure, 377

Racism, 33

Raising More Money book series (Axelrod), 476

Reasonableness standard, 168

Rebuttable presumption of reasonableness, 174

Red Cross, 11, 312, 412

REDF, 403

"Regulatory reform" bill (mid-1990s), 483

Relationships: board fundraising through connections and, 524–525; built with reporters, 482; donor stewardship, 319–320; grant seeking and role of, 335, 336–337, 338; as key to individual giving, 316–317; peer-to-peer fundraising is about, 361. *See also* Donors; Networking; Online community; Social networks media

Resources: board fundraising, 531–532; board governance, 517–518; cause-related marketing, 385–387; Constituent Relationship Management (CRM), 284–285; diversity, 145–147; event planning, 476–477; fundraising, 307–308; generational leadership, 159–160; grant seeking, 339–340; Human capital management, 123–125; individual giving, 323–324; lobbying and advocacy, 194–196; marketing, 426–427; newsletter, 456–457; nonprofit career-building, 54–56; nonprofit finance, 214–216; nonprofit law and legal compliance, 178–179; nonprofit leadership, 38–40; online community, 271–272; online fundraising, 355–356; online peer-to-peer fundraising, 370–372; public relations, 492–493; risk management, 104–105; social enterprise, 402–403; storytelling, 442–444; strategic planning, 74–75; technology, 236–238; volunteer engagement and management, 566–568; volunteer recruiting, 548–549; web design, 254–255

Revenues: Balance Sheet on, 205–206; classifications of, 201–202; contributed, 19; diversified or at risk, 203; earned income, 8–9, 19; event planning, 467–468; fluctuations in expenses in line with changes in, 204–205; Statement of Activities on, 199–200t, 203–205;

understanding dynamics of, 203. *See also* Costs; Financial management; Tax issues

Risk management: board's role in, 101–103; dos and don'ts for, 103; event planning, 468–469; monitoring suits, threats of suits, or accidents, 102; periodic review of, 102–103; recommendations for, 95t–96t; resources on, 104–105. *See also* Insurance

"Risk Minus Cash Equals Crisis" (Miller), 215

Risk Retention group (ANI), 100, 104

Risk tolerance, 396

Risks: insurance coverage of, 95t–96t; periodic review of, 102–103; types of, 94, 95t–96t

"Roadmap to Fundraising Success" (Seiler), 365

Rockefeller Foundation, 12

ROI for Nonprofits: The New Key to Sustainability (Ralser), 323

ROI (return on investment) analysis, 234

Romenesko blog, 493

RSS (Really Simple Syndication), 361

Rubicon Bakery, 398

Russell Sage Foundation, 12

S

Sacredness of all life value, 24

Safe Tables Our Priority (STOP), 483–484

Salesforce.com Foundation, 280

The Salvation Army, 364, 366–367, 413

Savings: assessing state of nonprofit, 205–206; leveraged debt versus, 208

Screening candidates: effective interview questions for, 119t; phone interview, 116–117; preparing for process of,

115–116; reference and background checking, 118

Scrutiny demands, 18

Sea Changes Strategies: The Wired Wealthy—Using the Internet to Connect with Your Middle and Major Donors, 372

SeaWeb project, 484

Security: computer-related, 226–228; physical, 228

ServeNet, 567

Service Employees International Union (SEIU), 163

Service Leader, 567

Service providers, 172

"7 Things You Should Know about Digital Storytelling" (Educause), 442

Sexism, 33

sfphilanthropist.com, 477

Share Our Strength, 377

The She Spot: (Witter and Chen), 492

Silent Generation (1925–1945), 151

"Slammer Worm" (2003), 227

So You Want to Make a Difference: (Amidei), 196

Social capital market, 395

Social Capital Partnerships, 385

Social change: maximization of, 59–60; social entrepreneurship for creating, 17–18; social prophets to bring about, 573–577

Social enterprise: dos and don'ts of, 400; finding the right investor or customer for, 399; funding environment for, 394–396; issues to consider for, 389–392; leadership skills required for, 396–398; mission at the center of, 390; organizational environment for, 392–394; real competitive advantage of,

398–399; resources on, 402–403; risk tolerance and, 396

Social Enterprise Alliance, 403

Social entrepreneurship, 17–18

Social networks media: blogging, 436–438; board role in solicitations using, 527–528; building your own, 262; definition of, 357; Facebook, 260t–261, 359, 360, 542; Flickr, 438–439; global, 261–262; Hurricane Katrina fundraising case study on, 366–367; leveraging your personal, 360–361; listservs, 260t, 262; Ning, 260t, 262; online fundraising through, 345; online peer-to-peer fundraising using, 357–372; promoting fundraising events through, 366; recruiting volunteers using, 541; Twitter, 260t, 261, 359; YouTube, 439–440. See also Communication technologies; Media; Networking; Relationships

Social prophets: characteristics of, 574–575; description of, 573–574; examples of, 575; listening to the calling to become a, 576–577; sufficiency perspective of, 575–576

Social service professional insurance, 98

Society for Human Resources Management (SHRM), 124

Software: assessing mission-critical, 229; selecting, 228–229. See also Computers

Soul of Money, 476

The Soul of Money (Twist), 290, 577

Special Events Galore, 476

Spectrum of engagement, 496–497

Spitfire Strategies Smart Chart 3.0, 195

Staff: clear strategic planning roles of, 67–68; compensation of, 120–121; competency models for specific positions, 110t; conflict-of-interest policy for, 515; debriefing following event, 473–474; as the linchpin of nonprofit's work, 60–61; partnership roles and adjustment by, 85; relationship with the board, 514. *See also* Candidates; Human capital management; Nonprofit sector professionals

Stanford Social Innovation Review, 75, 90

Stanford Social Innovation Review, 402

Starting and Managing a Nonprofit Organization (Hopkins), 177, 178

Statement of Activities, 199–200t, 203–205

Steps to Fall & Holiday Fundraising Success, 355

STOP (Safe Tables Our Priority), 483–484

Storytelling: blogging as, 436–438; building momentum and energizing your network, 430; Creative Commons license for sharing, 440; dos and don'ts of, 441; to entice online fundraising, 348–349; Flickr used as, 438–439; getting others to tell your story, 440–441; ladder of engagement process of, 434–436; linked to your overall communications strategies, 431; newsletters using, 450–451; public relations and, 480–481; resources on, 442–444; simplify your issues using, 483–484; web content creation of 2.0, 431–434; YouTube used as, 439–440

Storytelling structure: linking to overall communication strategy, 431; motivating social media audience to "remix," 433–434; narrative arch of beginning, middle, end, 432–433

Strategic alliance: definition of, 79; Partnership Matrix on, 78*fig*–79

Strategic Fund Development: (Joyaux), 307

Strategic planning: core skills and competencies of, 50, 66–71; dashboards used for, 71–72t; description of processes of, 64–65; determining which set of strategies to use, 63–64; dos and don'ts of, 73; resources on, 74–75. *See also* Marketing plan

Strategic planning competencies: clarifying questions to be answered, 68–69; clear staff-run and board-directed roles, 67–68; description of, 50; making the numbers work, 66; planning in real time, 66–67; rigorously consider environment and external input, 69–70; set milestones and benchmarks for success, 70–71

Strategic Planning for Nonprofit Organizations: A Practical Guide and Workbook (Allison and Kaye), 74

Strategic Planning for Nonprofit Organizations (Allison and Kaye), 65

Strategic restructuring: cultural integration in merger, 86–87; dos and don'ts for, 88; Partnership Matrix on, 78*fig*–79; partnerships, 79, 80–85. *See also* Collaboration

Strategic Tools for Social Entrepreneurs (Dees, Emerson, and Economy), 323

Strategies: annual giving, 297*e*–300*e*; definition of, 63; determining how to use, 63–64; major gifts, 300*e*–303*e*

Streetsmart Financial Basics for Nonprofit Managers (McLaughlin), 214

Subsidiary tax issues, 170

Supporting organizations: Type I, II, III functionally integrated, 172–173; Type III distribution requirement, 173; Type III nonfunctionally integrated, 173

Sustainable Communities Network, 477

SWOT analysis, 69

T

Tactical Fundraising blog (Bregman), 447

Tactical Philanthropy, 324

TAILS Humane Society, 451–452

Talent identification, 50

Tax issues: Forms 990, 990-PF, 990-EZ, 990-N, 174–175, 515; intermediate sanctions rules requiring initial tax, 174; LLC (limited liability company), 171; tax-exempt legal basics, 171–173; UBIT (unrelated business income tax), 169–170. *See also* Revenues

Tax-exempt organizations: institutions classified as public charities, 172; intermediate sanction rules on, 173–174; private foundation, 171; public charities, 171, 172; publically supported charities, 171–172; service providers, 172; typical functions of supporting organizations, 172–173. *See also* 501(c)(3) nonprofits

TCC Group, 75

Technology: dos and don'ts for, 235; as investment in meeting your mission, 223; leveraged to put the community work for you, 219; resources on, 236–238; safety and security issues related to, 226–228; skills and competences required for, 222–235; Web 2.0 in context of Web 1.0, 218–219. *See also* Communication technologies; Web design

Technology skills/competencies: assessing your hardware needs, 224–226; build a strong technological foundation, 224; dashboards for, 234–235; importance of mission over technology, 222–223, 235; long-term thinking about, 232; planning for future needs, 231–232; ROI (return on investment) analysis, 234; safety and security issues, 226–228; short-term action/annual technology plans, 232–234; software needs, 228–231

TechRepublic.com, 237

Techsoup Global, 236

techsoup.org, 229

Techspectations, 154–155

Telephones: board solicitations over the, 527; interview using, 116–117

Temple University, 287

Ten Basic Responsibilities of Nonprofit Boards (BoardSource), 502–503

"Ten Ways Nonprofits Can Use Blogs" (Bravo), 444

Thanks: A Guide to Donor-Centered Fundraising (Burk), 307

Theory of Change, 327

"Three Strikes" law storytelling, 480

Through the Looking Glass (Carroll), 341

Times, 485

The Tipping Point (Gladwell), 492

Title VII (Civil Rights Act), 128

Transparency demands, 18

Tribes (Godin), 40

Trust: building relationships with reporters based on, 482; partnerships and need for, 84, 85

TuDiabetes, 268

"25 Days to Make a Difference" blog (Stockman), 406

Twitter, 260t, 261, 359, 360

Type I supporting organizations, 173

Type II supporting organizations, 173

Type III supporting organizations, 173

U

UBIT (unrelated business income tax), 169–170

Uhuru Capital, 403

ULNA (Unrestricted Liquid Net Assets), 209

Umbrella insurance, 98

Uncharitable: How Restraints on Nonprofits Undermine Their Potential (Pallotta), 215

UNICEF, 378

UNICEF-Pampers partnership, 380, 383

Uniroyal, 486

United Way, 13

United Way of King Country, 379

Up Next: Generational Change and the Leadership of Nonprofit Organizations (Kunreuther), 159

Urban Affordable Housing Group, 86–87

Urban Institute, 9

U.S. Census, 160

U.S. Christian Commission, 11

U.S. Equal Employment Opportunity Commission, 113, 125

U.S. Sanitary Commission, 11

U.S. Trust/Bank of America study (2008), 320

USDA regulations, 483

User stories, 245

Using Mobile Phones in Fundraising Campaigns, 371

V

Values: nonprofits and underlying, 6–7, 23–26, 569–570; shaping organizational culture, 31–33

Venues Online, 477

Vietnam War, 24

Vision: B to the Y, 58, 61; "do less" insight about, 60; keeping your sense of connection to community, 59–60; what is and what is not a, 58–59

Volunteer engagement: dos and don'ts of, 565; issues to consider for, 551–552; nurturing volunteers for, 559–560t; resources on, 566–568; Volunteer Engagement Scale (VES) for, 564–565

Volunteer Engagement Scale (VES), 564–565

Volunteer management: architecture of, 553–555; dos and don'ts of, 565; facilitating reflection by volunteers, 561–562; logistics oversight of, 558–559; necessary tools for, 556–557; nurturing volunteers, 559–560t; orientation and training, 557–558; planning checklist for, 552–553; positive results of effective, 562–563; recognition of volunteers, 563–564; resources on, 566–568; of the scope of service, 555–556; volunteer leadership development, 560–561

Volunteer recruiting: barriers to, 536–537; designing great opportunities to encourage, 539–540; don't underestimate people's willingness to help, 534; dos and don'ts of, 547; Huntington Beach Public Library case study on, 545–546; leveraging word-of-mouth for, 544–545; market-centric approach to, 537; needs assessment for, 537–538; outreach to build awareness, 540–541; putting best face forward for, 541–543; resources on, 548–549; screening for ideal candidates, 543–544; understanding volunteer motivations, 535–536

Volunteering in America, 549

Volunteerism: barriers to, 536–537; changes in, 533–534; health benefits of, 500, 536; increasing rate of, 499–500; personal value of, 534–535

Volunteerism revolution, 496

VolunteerMatch, 496, 518, 533, 536, 542, 545, 546, 548

Volunteers: age differences of neighborhood, 133*t*; converting donors into fundraising, 363–364; diversity of, 132–133*t*; fundraising training for, 318–319; health benefits of volunteerism to, 500, 536; increasing number of, 499–500; leveraging high-opportunity network of, 499; orientation and training of, 557–558; personal value of volunteering by, 534–535; recognition of, 563–564; recruiting leaders among, 560–561; reflection by, 561–562; six key motivations of, 535–536; spectrum of engagement by, 496–497; tools and tactics to optimize your, 495–496; value added by, 498–499

W

W3Schools, 255

Wal-Mart, 377

The Way of the Cell (Harold), 27

"Wealth" (Carnegie), 12

WeAreMedia, 443

Web 1.0, 218–219

Web 2.0: in context of Web 1.0, 218–219; storytelling genre of, 348–349, 430–444; user-generated context principle of, 218–220

Web 2.0 Storytelling: Emergence of a New Genre (Levine and Alexander), 442

Web browser, 248

Web content management system (CMS), 248–250

Web design: collaboration or paint-by-number approach to, 251; conceptualizing your website, 245–246;

dos and don'ts of, 253; East Bay Music Collective (EBMC) case study on, 251–252; establishing website's purpose, 240–241, 243; identifying stakeholders, 243–245; importance of your nonprofit, 239–240; information architecture draft for, 245–246; Mighty Putty and Apple examples of, 241, 242*fig*; resources on, 254–255; wireframes used in, 246–247*fig*; working with a designer for, 250; WYSIWYG (what you see is what you get) editor included in, 248. *See also* Communication technologies; Technology

Web jargon, 247–248

Web server, 248

Websites: content management systems for, 247–250; donate button on, 348; East Bay Music Collective (EBMC), 251–252; establishing purpose of, 240–241, 243; fundraising through your, 347–350; Mighty Putty and Apple examples of, 241, 242*fig*; recruiting volunteers using, 541; setting and measuring goals of your, 243; story to entice giving on your, 348–349; user stories on, 245; wireframes for, 246–247*fig*. *See also* Online fundraising

Western Arts Alliance (WAA), 223, 224, 230–234

"What Bad Presentations Happen to Good Causes" (Goodman), 443

When Generations Collide: (Lancaster and Stillman), 146

Whirlpool-Habitat for Humanity partnership, 380

White House Social Innovation Fund, 18

Why Bad Ads Happen to Good Causes (Goodman), 426

Wikipedia, 218–219, 357

Winning Grants, Step by Step (Carlson and O'Neal-McElrath), 340

Wired for Good: Strategic Technology Planning for Nonprofits (Podolsky), 238

Women's Funding Network, 340

Women's suffrage movement, 127, 573

Work-life balance, 141, 155–157, 570

Worker's Compensation, 99

Working Across Generations: Defining the Future of Nonprofit Leadership (Kunreuther, Kim, and Rodriguez), 145

Working Mother Magazine, 146

Worry Free Lobbying for Nonprofits (Alliance for Justice), 188

WYSIWYG (what you see is what you get) editor, 248

Y

YMCAs, 13

Yoplait-Cure partnership, 380

Young Nonprofit Professionals Network (YNPN), 56, 518

YouTube, 439–440

YouTube Nonprofit Channel, 443

YouTube and Nonprofits (Hoffman), 443